TRADE MARK

CORK PORTER
BREWERY
ESTᴰ 1792

BEAMISH & CRAWFORD

The History of an Irish Brewery

Donal Ó Drisceoil

+

Diarmuid Ó Drisceoil

Dedicated to the workers of Beamish & Crawford
1792–2009

'without our brains and muscle not a single wheel can turn'
'Solidarity Forever', 1915

BEAMISH & CRAWFORD

The History of an Irish Brewery

Donal Ó Drisceoil &
Diarmuid Ó Drisceoil

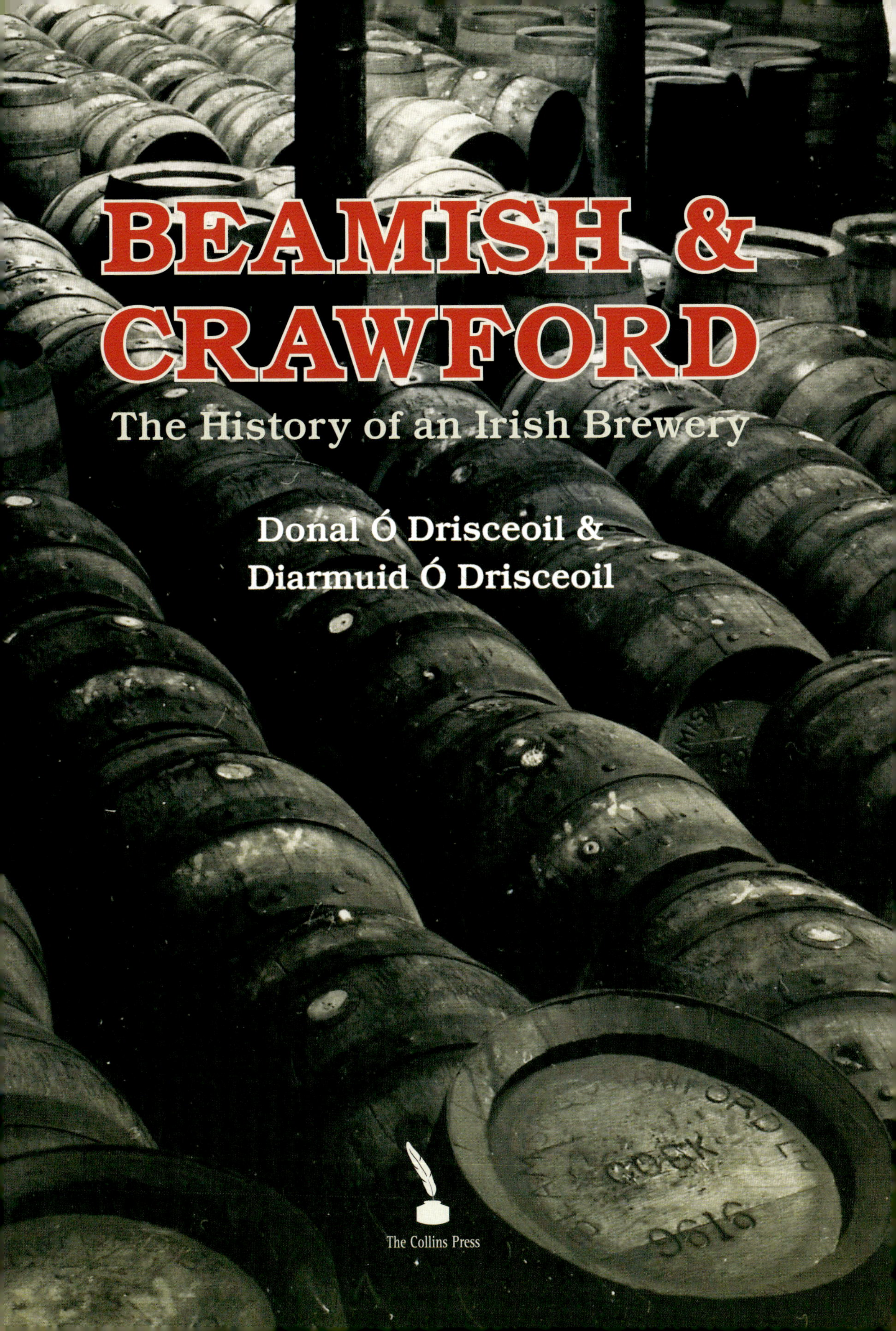

The Collins Press

First published in 2015 by
The Collins Press
West Link Park
Doughcloyne
Wilton
Cork

A CIP record for this book is available from the British Library.

Hardback ISBN: 978-1-84889-258-3

Design and typesetting by edit+ www.stuartcoughlan.com

Typeset in Adobe Garamond Pro

Printed in Italy by Printer Trento

Endpapers: Beamish & Crawford brewery workers, *c.* 1915. (Courtesy Ed Hinchy)

Contents

Preface

Beamish & Crawford brewery closed finally in May 2009, bringing its 217-year history to an end. With the support and co-operation of Heineken, those company records that remained in the brewery were transferred to the Cork City and County Archives. An earlier tranche of company papers had already been deposited there in the early 1970s. This unique collection formed the basis for this book: the most comprehensive history of an Irish brewery ever published in one volume.

In 1791 two successful merchants, William Beamish and William Crawford, entered into a partnership with two Cork brewers, Richard Barrett and Digby O'Brien, and established the Cork Porter Brewery on South Main Street, which began production the following year. It quickly established itself as Ireland's leading brewery, and one of the foremost in these islands. Its early success reflected Cork's heyday as a leading port of the British empire, and its subsequent fortunes also mirrored the history of the city and the country: the economic decline following the end of the Napoleonic Wars in 1815; post-Famine commercialisation and urbanisation; the impact of the First World War and the subsequent war of independence and civil war; the growth of trade unions; the prolonged economic stagnation following independence; the age of the multinationals from the 1960s. International events form the large backdrop: the First World War was the key watershed, after which Beamish & Crawford never regained its former stature, while the consolidating dynamics of the international brewing industry eventually heralded the brewery's demise in the early twenty-first century.

The story of Beamish & Crawford is told in the context of the history of brewing in Britain, Ireland and Cork over four centuries. The book includes accounts of the other breweries that operated in Cork over the years, many long forgotten, especially Lane's Southgate Brewery on South Main Street and Arnott's St Finbarre's Brewery

Beamish & Crawford brewery from Clarke's Bridge, 1959. (Courtesy Mike Hannon)

on Fitton (now Sharman Crawford) Street. These were absorbed by their larger competitors, Beamish & Crawford and James J. Murphy & Co. respectively, at the turn of the twentieth century, showing that consolidation and closures were a fact of brewing life in Cork long before its new owners closed Beamish & Crawford in 2009 and centralised large-scale brewing in the city at Heineken's (formerly Murphy's) Lady's Well Brewery.

This is also the history of two remarkable families – the Beamishes and the Crawfords – who left indelible marks on Cork's physical, political and cultural, as well as its economic, landscape; and of multiple generations of workers whose pride in their work and the firm's products, and their family ties to the brewery, helped to make Beamish & Crawford the cherished institution that it became. Also integral to the story are the managers and directors, the agents, the publicans and their houses, and, of course, the drinkers. The physical development of the brewery is detailed in word and image, and the company's other concerns, such as its stables, malthouses and ancillary businesses like the River Lee Porter Brewery in Cork and Allman and Dowden in Bandon, are all featured. Beamish & Crawford's business fortunes are presented in extensive tables and graphs, as well as forming part of an overall narrative that gives preferential emphasis to its most successful period: the 'long' nineteenth century.

This book would not have been possible without the support, co-operation and assistance of many people and institutions, whom we would like to acknowledge and thank sincerely. First of all, Heineken, who supported the project from the beginning and who wished, through the publication of this book, to have the history of Beamish & Crawford properly recorded; we would like thank, in particular, managing director Maggie Timoney, former managing director David Forde, Padraig

Conway, Declan Farmer, Kathryn D'Arcy, Finbar McCarthy and Barry Cassidy for their support throughout the project. At the Cork City and County Archives Brian McGee, Timmy O'Connor, Michael Higgins and Peter McDonnell were at all times most accommodating and helpful. We also record our thanks to Boole Library Archives Service, UCC, especially Emer Twomey; UCC Boole Special Collections, especially Mary Lombard; all at the Local Studies department of Cork City Library; the Guinness Archives; the National Library of Ireland; the Cork Public Museum, and Examiner Publications Cork.

Many individuals helped us in our work by sharing their knowledge, lending photographs and other material, pointing us in worthwhile directions and by being available for discussion on the myriad of topics that arise from a research project such as this; in no particular order, many thanks to the following: Michael Lenihan, Des O'Driscoll, Ronnie Herlihy, Dan Breen, Tom Spalding, Antóin O'Callaghan, John Borgonovo, Valerie Cooper, Richard Beamish, Michael B. Cosgrave, Norma Ryan, John Crowley, Pat Poland, Denis Lenihan, Fintan Lane, Maurice Hurley, Frank Roche, Adrian Beamish, Steve Murray, Clíona O'Carroll, Niall Kelly, Caen Harris, Colin Rynne, Andy Bielenberg, Emma Nic Cárthaigh and Luke Kirwan.

Former workers whose valuable insights and memories informed the later chapters include: Johnny McCarthy, Martin Lynch, Eamonn O'Sullivan, Dave Creedon, Tim Murphy, Denis Murphy, John O'Regan, Rory Bevan and Jim D'Arcy.

Special thanks to Ed Hinchy, who worked at Beamish & Crawford for almost forty years and was the unofficial custodian of much of the material related to the brewery's history. Ed was unfailingly generous in sharing the fruits of his researches into the brewery's history and kindly provided many of the images that are reproduced in this book.

Thanks to Dori O'Connell and John Sheehan for the original photography; to Mike Hannon, director of *My Beamish Boy* (2009), who generously shared his image bank; to the family of the late Roy Hammond for permission to use a number of his photographs; Mike Murphy for the cartography; Martin Lynch for his DVD compilation of Beamish & Crawford-related material.

A work such as this relies for much of its impact on its design and layout, and we were lucky to have Stuart Coughlan of edit+ as the book's designer. Our thanks also to all at The Collins Press in Cork.

Finally we express our thanks to our respective families, Orla, Kim and Fionn, and Miriam, Méabh and Aonghus – our constant supports.

Donal Ó Drisceoil
Diarmuid Ó Drisceoil

BEAMISH & CRAWFORD
BREWERS, CORK.
LIMITED.
TRADE MARK
Established 1792.
TRADE MARK
Established 1792.
DOUBLE STOUT.

1

Cork, Porter and the Origins of the Modern Irish Brewing Industry

William Beamish, William Crawford, Digby O'Brien and Richard Barrett began brewing at their Cork Porter Brewery on South Main Street in Cork on 17 January 1792. The brewery was to survive for 217 years and it grew out of the overwhelming popularity of porter, a beer that had originated in London in the 1720s and crossed the Irish Sea to become Ireland's drink of choice by 1800. By then William Beamish and William Crawford were the sole partners in the firm and they helped create a brewing tradition that saw porter, or its stronger version, stout, grow to become the iconic Irish beer. However, the advent of porter was only the most recent development in the history of brewing in Ireland in general and in Cork in particular.

Brewing in Cork before porter

As the town of Cork grew and developed from the eleventh century, it took on many of the features of similarly sized towns elsewhere in medieval Ireland and Britain: defensive walls enclosing a network of narrow streets and laneways; open-air marketplaces; stone-built parish churches; and rich and poor all living cheek by jowl in tightly packed dwellings.

In the thirteenth century three monasteries were founded outside Cork's walls: a Dominican foundation to the southwest, a Franciscan friary to the north and an Augustinian friary, the Red Abbey, to the south. An earlier monastery that pre-dated the town of Cork had been in existence from at least the seventh century on the high ground near where St Fin Barre's Cathedral now stands.

Alehouses and taverns were also a key feature of medieval towns, and Cork was no exception. Brewing has long been associated with monastic life and monks have made a significant contribution to the development of that art, which is most celebrated

Left and top right: The industrialisation of brewing (Beamish & Crawford Brewery Collection)
Bottom right: Brewing in the eighteenth century. (Heineken)

today in the famous abbey beers of Belgium. Cork's medieval monasteries would also have brewed ale and the monks of Cork's older monastery would have had a variety of ales available to them, a fact attested to by the twelfth-century Middle Irish wonder tale, *Aislinge Meic Conglinne* (*The Vision of Meic Conglinne*), set in the monastery of Cork.[1] This variety is suggested by the range of Middle Irish terms for these drinks used in the text: *cuirm*, *lind* (later *lionn* and *leann*), *brocoit*, *beoir* and *braichlis*. *Cuirm* and *lind* are usually translated as 'ale'. It is interesting that in the text, *cuirm* is usually said to be new and *lind* is in one instance said to be clear and sweet, indicating that these drinks were probably forms of sweet, unhopped ale, which was commonly consumed in Ireland and Britain prior to the introduction of hops as a bittering agent in the fifteenth century. *Brocoit* describes a drink known in English as 'bragget', made with sweet ale and fermented honey. *Beoir* is clearly 'beer' and *braichlis*, coming from the Irish word *braich*, meaning malt, is probably 'ale wort' or 'mash'.

Taverns, alehouses and brewhouses

The old city of Cork was well served by a number of taverns and alehouses – a survey of the city dating to the mid-seventeenth century lists twenty-three such premises.[2] While the section of the survey relating to the southwest quadrant of the city (where the Beamish & Crawford brewery was later located) has not survived, the extent of brewing-related activity in the rest of the city is indicated by the listing of twenty-five malthouses, twelve 'kill' (kiln) houses and seven grist mills. While some of the malt produced in the city was used in the distillation of spirits, a good proportion would have been used by the many retail brewers, which in that period were far more numerous than their larger commercial counterparts. The survey lists only three brewhouses, which, it is assumed, were examples of bigger commercial concerns.

There are references in extant leases to brewhouses in the area later occupied by the Beamish & Crawford brewery dating to the second half of the seventeenth and the early eighteenth centuries. A bond of 30 August 1667 recites that George Syms purchased a dwelling house, malthouse and brewhouse then occupied by George Gamble in that area.[3] That, or another brewhouse in the same area, is mentioned in two documents dating to 1682 and in a conveyance from 1719.[4] In August 1682 George Rogers transferred the title to 'one house formerly called a brewhouse in Martells lane extending to the City Walls formerly in the possession of Walter Lane as a Sugarhouse' to Robert Phaire. This property came into the possession of Onesipherus Gamble, the son-in-law of Robert Phaire, in 1719. References in later documents dealing with that and other properties in the area indicate that Martell's Lane later became Gamble's Lane and then Cremer's Lane.[5]

Many entries in the *Council Book of the Corporation of the City of Cork* from the seventeenth and eighteenth centuries refer to brewers and brewhouses, and in 1743 the brewers of the city formed a guild for which they received a charter from King George II. The strength of the brewers as a group within the city is suggested by the fact that they defied the corporation in applying directly to the Crown for their

(Beamish & Crawford Brewery Collection)

charter, bypassing the municipal authority, which regarded the brewers' action as an infringement of the privileges granted to the city.[6]

The story of porter

Porter (or stout, its stronger or 'stouter' version) was not created in response to a specific demand; nor was it the end product of a planned development in brewing in the late seventeenth and early eighteenth centuries. Rather, it was a type of beer that grew out of a series of different forces in brewing technology, as well as in fiscal matters and in public taste, that came together in London at that time. As one writer on the topic has put it:

> ... [in the development of porter] it was not so much a specific event as a series of ill-related and sometimes external happenings, not so much a particular invention as an almost imperceptible modification, not so much absolute novelty as the re-ordering of familiar and even superseded elements, which was pertinent.[7]

Ale is the name used for the unhopped, fermented malt liquor widely brewed in Britain and Ireland prior to the introduction of hopped malt liquor, or beer, in the late fifteenth century. This ale was sweet tasting and it was consumed while fresh or 'young'. Prior to the introduction of hops, other additives, such as wild rosemary and bog myrtle, were used during brewing to give the ale a measure of bitterness.[8] It was brewed in small quantities as it neither kept nor travelled well. Alehouses or taverns brewed their own ale and any wider distribution was confined to a very small area, as unhopped ale was not suited to large-scale brewing. The introduction of hopped beer from the Low Countries and elsewhere in northern Europe into Britain and Ireland from the late fifteenth century led to the first major change in brewing in these islands. By the mid-1500s hopped beer dominated in Britain, especially in cities and large towns, and the first growth in commercial or 'common' brewing occurred, as this beer could be produced in larger quantities. The addition of hops lengthened the life of the beer as well as giving it a more bitter taste that better suited the palate. Unhopped ale continued to be produced in rural regions into the seventeenth century, but by 1700 it had been almost totally supplanted by the near universal adoption of hops in all brewing.

While distinctions were sometimes blurred and terms occasionally interchangeable, by the early eighteenth century the terms 'beer' and 'ale' had taken on different meanings: ale was by then a lighter-coloured hopped malt liquor, brewed mostly outside of the larger cities in Britain, while beer became the term for the heavier, darker brews, including the new porter, which dominated in the cities, especially in

London. There were as many variations in the basic products as there were brewers producing them – brown ale, pale ale, brown beer, brown stout and much weaker and cheaper small beer or table beer. The latter was consumed by children and adults alike in the absence of other safe and sterile drinks.

Origins

During the seventeenth century, the use of darker malts became more widespread. These malts were harder and more highly coloured as a result of a higher heat in the drying kiln. As a result of the introduction of taxes on coal in the 1660s and 1670s, wood, being a cheaper fuel, was increasingly used in malt-drying kilns. This gave the malt a smoky flavour that transferred to the beers and cheaper barley could be successfully used in this type of malting. Taxation on malt, introduced in 1697, led brewers to use less malt and to increase the amount of hops used in their brews. As a result, a newer, more bitter brown beer was becoming more common in London by the early eighteenth century and it retailed at 2d per quart. This brown beer, and its variations, was significantly cheaper than pale ale, which was brewed with more expensive hops and pale malts, made with high-quality barley. While 'ordinary' ale continued to be popular, amongst the better-off pale ale was often the malt liquor of choice. It was expensive, retailing at 4d per quart or 2d per pint, which gave rise to the nickname 'two-penny'.

It is likely that the bitter brown beers were a little too acidic for palates used to sweeter ales and were therefore mixed with ale by the tavern-keeper. Mixing ale and beer became common and gave rise to the popularity of these new drinks that moderated the less-favoured attributes of their constituent beers and ales while giving the consumer a 'new' drink. Later, pale ale was also added to the mix, improving the flavour due to the superior quality of the ingredients used in its brewing. One of these mixtures is said to have been known as 'three threads', so called because it was made by mixing ale and beer from three separate casks; it retailed at 3d per quart.

The increasing popularity of the mixed drinks such as 'three threads' created an impetus for brewers to brew a single beer that incorporated all the attractive attributes of the mixtures. By the 1720s they had achieved this 'when the brewers conceived there was a mean to be found preferable to any of these extremes; which was, that beer well brewed, from being kept its proper time, becoming mellow, that is neither new or stale, would recommend itself to the public'.[9] This beer retailed at 3d per quart. It was very popular, especially amongst labourers, and tradition has it that carriers and porters were so taken with the new beer that it acquired the name 'porter' (see the 'Origin legend' below).

While this seems to be a plausible explanation of the name and is not disputed by any writer on beer history, and while 'porter' is used in print from as early as 1726,[10] it may date to an earlier period and have a different origin. Richard W. Unger, in his work on the history of beer in the medieval and Renaissance periods, discusses the different types of beer that developed in the Low Countries and in what is now northern Germany in the fifteenth and sixteenth centuries, many of which were exported to Britain. He writes: 'Names such as convent beer, *mol*, *knol*, *porter*, and *uytset* (that is export) also turned up.'[11] This mention of 'porter' suggests that it was applied up to two centuries before the 1720s to a Flemish or German beer exported to Britain.

Origin legend

The complex nature of the origins of porter have led many to rely on the oft-quoted, and possibly apocryphal, story of Ralph Harwood, a brewer in Shoreditch in London, who is said to have 'invented' porter in 1722. The story goes that Harwood managed to brew a single beer that combined the elements of the 'three threads' (see above). Harwood's new beer was known as 'entire butt' or simply 'entire', as it came 'entirely' from one cask or butt rather than from three or more. This new drink became so popular with the labourers, carriers and porters of London that it soon became known as 'porter'.

One of the difficulties with the Harwood story, though, is that it did not first appear in print until 1802 (quoted below), eighty years after the supposed invention:

> a brewer, of the name of HARWOOD, conceived the idea of making a liquor which should partake of the united flavours of ale, beer, and twopenny [pale ale]. He did so and succeeded ... and as it was a very hearty nourishing liquor, it was very suitable for porters and other working people. Hence it obtained the name of porter.[12]

A short verse praising Harwood's 'invention' was published in 1819:

> Harwood, my townsman, he invented first
> Porter to rival wine, and quench the thirst,
> Porter, which spreads its fame half the world o'er,
> Whose reputation rises more and more.[13]

Earlier accounts of porter brewing do not mention the Harwood story, nor do they rely on a simple 'invention' theory. A work on brewing published in 1736 describes how the different varieties of beer and ale were brewed at the time in London. The word 'porter' is not used, but at least two of the beers described – 'stout butt beer' and 'common butt beer' – are variations of what later became more universally

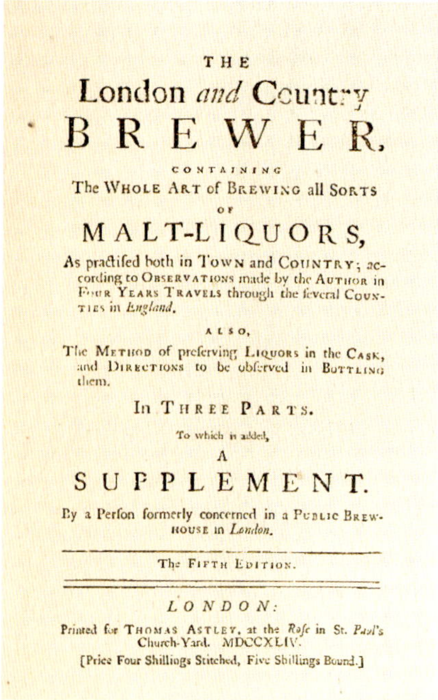
THE
London *and* Country
BREWER.
CONTAINING
The WHOLE ART of BREWING all SORTS
OF
MALT-LIQUORS,
As practiſed both in TOWN and COUNTRY; according to OBSERVATIONS made by the AUTHOR in FOUR YEARS TRAVELS through the ſeveral COUNTIES in *England*.
ALSO,
The METHOD of preſerving LIQUORS in the CASK, and DIRECTIONS to be obſerved in BOTTLING them.
In THREE PARTS.
To which is added,
A
SUPPLEMENT.
By a Perſon formerly concerned in a PUBLIC BREW-HOUSE in *London*.
The FIFTH EDITION.
LONDON:
Printed for THOMAS ASTLEY, at the *Roſe* in St. *Paul's* Church-Yard. MDCCXLIV.
[Price Four Shillings Stitched, Five Shillings Bound.]

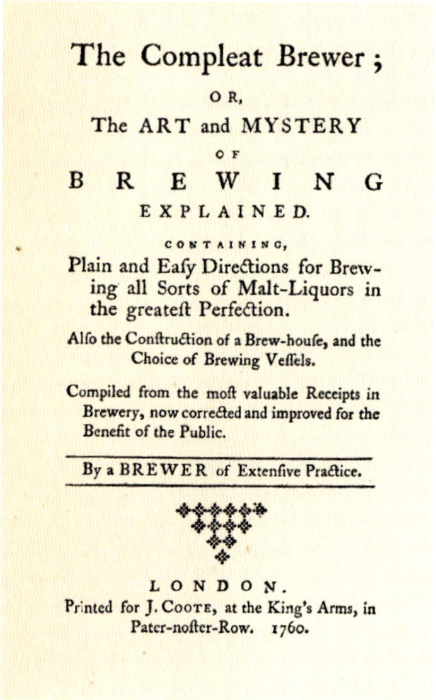
The Compleat Brewer;
OR,
The ART and MYSTERY
OF
BREWING
EXPLAINED.
CONTAINING,
Plain and Eaſy Directions for Brewing all Sorts of Malt-Liquors in the greateſt Perfection.
Alſo the Conſtruction of a Brew-houſe, and the Choice of Brewing Veſſels.
Compiled from the moſt valuable Receipts in Brewery, now corrected and improved for the Benefit of the Public.
By a BREWER of Extenſive Practice.
LONDON.
Printed for J. COOTE, at the King's Arms, in Pater-noſter-Row. 1760.

known as porter. An article from 1760 describes the sometimes complex combination of events that led to the development of porter, including an account of the influence of the taxation of beer and its ingredients on that development. Another work on brewing, first published in the same year, deals in some detail with the malts used in porter brewing as well as giving the 'recipe' for the beer. Again, no reference is made to the Harwood story.[14]

These early writers on porter brewing seem to have appreciated the complexity of the origins of porter, whereas later writers place an over-reliance on the simpler and unlikely Harwood story. Ralph Harwood did play a part in the early history of porter brewing, but not necessarily in the way sometimes described, and although his brewery produced up to 20,000 barrels per year in the later 1750s, it was even then eclipsed by much larger concerns.[15]

The triumph of porter

Eighteenth-century porter was a strong, thick, almost black beer; it had a high hop content, which gave it a greater bitterness than existing ales; and it had a slightly smoky flavour caused by the use of highly dried, slightly scorched malt. It became popular in London from the 1720s, and in the succeeding decades porter became the dominant beer in that city and in the other major cities of Britain and Ireland. Ale and porter brewing continued in parallel in Britain, but the output of porter grew at such a rate that by the late 1700s it was ten times greater than that of ale.[16] This triumph of porter – the rapid growth of a beer style that in the space of a few decades had captured 90 per cent of the beer market in Britain and Ireland – was without precedent. The nearest parallel is the growth of the lager market in Britain and Ireland since the 1960s.

Price was doubtless a factor in porter's growth in popularity. In the 1700s its retail price was 3d per quart, or 1½d per pint, which was 25 per cent cheaper than pale ale. Cheaper malting costs, the opportunity to use barley and hops of a lesser quality without compromising taste or strength, and the cost savings achieved through larger-scale production all contributed to the lower price. Porter was also a more stable product than ale and previous beer styles. This enabled the beer to be distributed over long distances by road, canal and sea and it gave the beer a longer life when it reached its destination. Unlike the ales of the period, age improved the taste of porter, giving it a body and mellowness that no young or fresh beer could achieve. An added advantage was that older, more acidic porter could be returned to the brewery and mixed with immature beer, plus porter could be brewed in summer as well as winter, an advantage not enjoyed by ale due to the more delicate and temperature-sensitive nature of the latter's fermentation.

In the early period of its production, porter was kept at the brewery for five months in casks to mature. By the 1740s it had been discovered that maturing the porter for twelve months improved the product even more, and by that time isinglass (a form of collagen obtained from the dried swim bladders of fish) was being widely used to clarify the porter, which was a further improvement. Longer storage demanded larger storage vessels, so porter brewers began to use large, deep vats for the latter stages of fermentation and storage, which was another factor that enabled mass production.

Geography also played a part in the rapid growth of porter. As mentioned, porter brewing developed and grew first and principally in London. In the 1720s the population of the city was over 500,000 and by the middle decades of the century

Porter vats at the Barclay Perkins brewery in London, 1847. (*Illustrated London News*)

it had risen to over 750,000. This concentrated and easily accessible metropolitan population was porter's first significant market, and its ready acceptance by a large proportion of that city's drinkers was a key element in the beer's establishment and quick ascent to domination. By the end of the seventeenth century, and before the introduction of porter, there was an element of consolidation in London brewing and a small number of breweries were already expanding at an accelerating rate. As Mathias has noted, 'one should not see the changes of the eighteenth century springing simply from the innovation and success of porter.'[17] The great porter breweries grew out of pre-existing breweries and were already moving towards industrialisation and large-scale production when porter was introduced in the 1720s. The growth of porter also coincided with and was helped by other technical innovations: the introduction of the thermometer and saccharometer gave greater control of the brewing process, while greater mechanisation was enabled by the development of steam power.

By the end of the 1700s the great London porter breweries of Whitbread, Truman, Thrale and others dominated what had become a booming industry, brewing well in excess of a million barrels of product annually. Ireland was porter's most significant export market in the eighteenth century, and when Irish porter brewing began to grow in the 1790s the dark beer was already the country's favourite. Within fifty years, Irish porter brewers had grown to rival their earlier London counterparts in scale of production and had established porter and stout, its stronger version, as quintessentially Irish drinks. The domination of porter in Britain began to be eroded early in the 1800s, however, as developments in the control of the fermentation of ale removed one of porter's significant advantages. Public taste in Britain was also changing and by the 1830s ale was gradually replacing porter as the most popular beer.

Irish brewing in the eighteenth century

Before the late eighteenth century Ireland did not have a large-scale, developed brewing industry.[18] Ale was brewed by local tavern or alehouse keepers for sale mostly on their own premises, with minimal local distribution. These retail brewers did not produce a product of consistent quality, taste or strength. In the cities and larger port towns, especially those on the east and south coasts, larger wholesale or 'common' breweries developed, distributing to an accessible local market. These breweries had easier access to imported hops for brewing beers that kept their condition longer and maintained their quality during transportation. Supplying beer to ships as part of victualling contracts was a key element in the modest commercial success of the brewers in places like Cork, Passage West and Kinsale before the development of the large porter breweries in Ireland in the 1790s.

In the early 1700s there were thousands of registered brewers in Ireland; 220 of these were in the south Munster area in 1733. Thirteen of those 220 were larger common or wholesale brewers, nine of which were located in Cork city and two each in the towns of Kinsale and Passage West.[19] The remaining 207 were small retail brewers, most of which brewed on their premises in the smaller towns throughout the region. In addition, there was an unknown number of unregistered brewers who brewed and sold their product in unlicensed outlets known as 'shebeens', from the Irish *síbín*.[20] As the eighteenth century progressed, and with it increasing legislation in the areas of malting, brewing and distilling, the reach of the excise inspectors was extended ever further into all areas of the country. This, along with the growing importation and distribution of London porter and the later development of a native brewing industry, led to the decline of the small retail brewers. By the 1790s the number of registered retail brewers in south Munster had fallen to twenty-four, only one of which was in Cork city. This seems to be a disproportionately small number, considering that there were still 1,800 retail brewers registered for the whole country in 1791.[21] The growth and reach of Cork wholesale brewing by this time, coupled with the distribution of imported porter from the city to outlying towns, goes some way towards explaining the virtual disappearance of the retail brewer from the city.

The produce of the city's wholesale brewers and London porter supplied the demand for ale and beer in Cork and its hinterland throughout most of the eighteenth century. While imports of porter grew spectacularly from the 1740s, Irish brewers consistently brewed about 500,000 barrels of malt liquor annually throughout the century, principally in the cities of Dublin and Cork.[22] This was regular, so called 'strong', ale or beer. These brewers also produced between 150,000 and 200,000 barrels of weaker or 'small' beer annually throughout the century, which was consumed, generally with food, by adults and children alike. In the absence of a clean and hygienic water supply, especially in large towns and cities, weak beer was a safe drink, having been sterilised during the brewing process. However, the consistent production of about half a million barrels per year in Ireland during the eighteenth century is somewhat less impressive when set against population growth in the period. Between 1700 and 1800 the population of Ireland doubled from about 2.5 million to 5 million, suggesting that the Irish brewing 'industry' had essentially lost about half its potential market.

Native Irish ale and beer production was supplemented with imports from Britain, and from the 1740s these imports consisted principally of London porter. In the early 1740s imports averaged about 4,000 barrels per year, growing to over 20,000 by the early 1760s and peaking at over 125,000 in 1793. From then on they fell drastically and had all but ceased by 1810, when Irish porter brewing had grown to such an extent that it dominated the Irish market and was also growing a share in the British market.

British primacy

The unprecedented growth in British brewing during the eighteenth century was not replicated in Ireland, and Irish brewing remained in a relatively underdeveloped state – what David Dickson has called a 'backyard business' – until the end of the century.[23] Irish ale and beer was generally of an inferior quality, and the increasing availability of London porter presented Irish consumers, especially in the port cities in the east and south, with a product of a consistently high quality that outshone native brews. Irish barley and malt were generally below par in comparison to their British counterparts – it was held that two barrels of imported English malt would produce one barrel of beer, whereas three barrels of Irish malt would be needed to brew the same quantity, and even then of a lesser quality.[24] While English malt could be imported into Ireland, it was illegal to import Irish malt into Britain, even if it was of an attractive quality. Irish tillage, including corn growing, was also held back by measures such as an exemption of pastureland from tithes from 1735. However, efforts were made in Ireland to improve agriculture, especially by the Dublin Society (later the Royal Dublin Society), which also tried to encourage the growth of hops. Legislation passed in 1710 required Irish brewers to import only British hops, denying them continental varieties that might have been cheaper and sufficiently different to British varieties to give a distinctiveness to Irish beers.

Rates of excise duty charged on ale and beer were higher in Britain for most of the eighteenth century. British brewers paid between 5s and 8s duty on a barrel of ale or beer (including a duty on hops and malt), while their Irish counterparts paid almost half that, at between 2s 6d and 4s 6d duty per barrel.[25] British brewers exporting to Ireland received a drawback or refund on the duty paid, which partly offset the freight costs to Ireland and a low import duty. In 1741 duty on beer imported into Ireland was increased to 2s 6d. This 'tended to equalise the fiscal burdens', but imports from Britain continued to grow.[26] Irish brewers and their representatives campaigned for changes in the taxation regime that would favour them over their British competitors, but while the government often acceded to their demands, imports of British beer, especially porter, continued to increase. British-produced beer could always be sold in Ireland at a cheaper rate than the native product due to the economies of scale enjoyed by the huge London porter breweries, while the superior quality of the imported product always found favour. Irish brewers needed to improve their product quality and create a competitive advantage over British brewers.

Turnaround

In the Irish Parliament of 1782–1800 Henry Grattan championed the cause of the Irish brewers, and in 1791 the first success was achieved when the excise duty on strong beer produced in Ireland was reduced from 4s 6d to 2s 6d per barrel. Non-

British hops could also now be imported, but with a duty of 1d per lb above that charged on British hops. The system of regulating brewing was also simplified and measures were introduced to counter the excessive consumption of spirits. This factor may well have been more significant in the eyes of legislators than the lobbying of brewers; as Dickson remarks, 'it was not the flood of English imports that was the decisive factor in bringing about fiscal reform but rather upper-class alarm at the escalating consumption of domestic spirits, licit and illicit.'[27]

After its initial success in 1791, the Irish brewing lobby continued its fight to lessen taxes and duties still further while also campaigning for a more punitive regime for distillers. According to Lynch and Vaizey, 'A major argument they [the brewers] advanced was that drunkenness in Ireland was dangerously increasing, and according to them whiskey was the real culprit, the instigator of turbulence, the inspiration of faction fights – and worse.'[28] In 1795 the duty on beer produced in Ireland was lifted and replaced with an increased tax on malt. This greatly favoured Irish brewers over their British counterparts, who had to continue paying beer duties until 1830, while Irish distillers were burdened with increasing levels of taxation and regulation. Conditions were improving on all fronts for Irish brewing.

By the 1790s Irish brewers had managed to improve the quality of their product by the development of improved malting, by bringing experienced brewers from London and by adopting the most up-to-date brewing techniques. Breweries were improved and enlarged and new large-scale porter breweries were established. In Dublin the Guinness brewery, established in 1759, began to grow as porter brewing increased, while other breweries in that city, such as the Phoenix, Anchor and Ardee Street breweries, also prospered on the wave of improved Irish porter brewing. In Cork, William Beamish, William Crawford, Richard Barrett and Digby O'Brien set up the Cork Porter Brewery in 1791, and in 1796 seven businessmen formed a partnership and established the River Lee Porter Brewery.

Britain was at war with France from 1793 to 1815, and from its outbreak shipments of porter to Ireland began to decline. There was some disruption to shipping and war brought higher risks, more expensive insurance and increased freight and other charges, factors that all favoured the Irish brewers. From the late 1790s London porter began to lose its prestige due to a decline in quality. Higher prices for raw materials, increased duties and a fall in demand led to an increase in the adulteration of porter, especially on the part of smaller brewers and publicans, and with a fall in strengths and higher retail prices, the reputation of London porter was undermined – just as the quality, quantity and reputation of Irish porter was increasing. Peter Mathias, historian of British brewing, observes that: 'It is little wonder that the Irish brewers stormed their markets with unnatural speed under cover of this battery of statutes, with the state fighting their domestic battle with the distillers for them, and the French becoming indirectly their ally in the struggle against English rivals.'[29]

By the early years of the nineteenth century, Irish breweries had developed to such an extent that they were reaching the output, quality and economies of scale that had made British brewing such a dominant force in the previous century.

'Best London PORTER three pence per pott'

As the city of Cork grew and expanded throughout the eighteenth century, there was an apparent parallel growth in brewing and related activities. From the middle of the century, for example, the local newspapers carried advertisements for the sale of imported London porter and also for local brewing initiatives. While John Minton at the Gibralter [*sic*] near the Exchange was advertising 'best wines, london porter, and other liquors' in July 1756, Jonas Morris announced in the same day's edition that he had commenced common brewing at the Watercourse, 'where all captains of ships, house keepers, and retailers, may be supplied with beer, ale, and ship-beer'. In September of that year the Blakeney Tavern and Porter-House opened in Boland's Lane, offering 'best London PORTER three pence per pott. A pint of ditto three-half pence. Half a pint one Penny.'[30] In the following decades advertising such as this increased in frequency, reflecting not only economic growth and expansion but also the increasing popularity of porter, both imported and local.

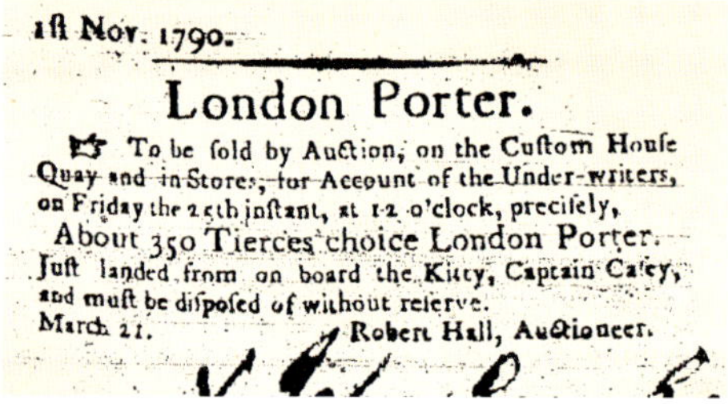

1ſt Nov. 1790.

London Porter.

☞ To be ſold by Auction, on the Cuſtom Houſe Quay and in Stores, for Account of the Under-writers, on Friday the 25th inſtant, at 12 o'clock, preciſely, About 350 Tierces choice London Porter. Juſt landed from on board the Kitty, Captain Caſey, and muſt be diſpoſed of without reſerve.

March 21. Robert Hall, Auctioneer.

Left: From the *Hibernian Chronicle,* 21 March 1791.
Right: Signature and seal of Aylmer Allen who had a porter brewery in Cremer's Square, off South Main Street.
(CCCA/Authors)

In 1772 the brewery of the late John Plaince was advertised for sale. This brewery was located in Cramer's Lane, a site that was to be the nucleus of the Cork Porter Brewery developed by Beamish and Crawford two decades later. Plaince had taken a lease on the brewery in 1735, and it had previously been occupied by Edward Fenn and later Onesiphorus Gamble.[31] Plaince had invested over £3,000 in creating 'the completest and most convenient Brewery in this city'. Aylmer Allen took over the premises, and by 1782, having expanded the facility, he was brewing 'right good Porter'. In an effort to promote locally brewed porter over the imported product, his advertisements state

The premises of the former Copperthwaite's brewery on Wandesford Quay, Cork.
This brewery was later occupied by O'Brien & Barrett. (Authors)

that 'he hopes to do away that prejudice, that none but Thames' Water can make good porter'.[32] In 1787 the Table Beer Brewery at St Finn Barry's in Cork advertised that 'Dan. Lane [proprietor] acquaints his Friends and the Public, that he has for sale BEER of the first Quality', and five years later Luke Shea, a cooper from the Coal Quay, announced that he 'has commenced Brewing Ship and Table Beer, which he hopes from his attention to merit the patronage of the Public in general. He flatters himself its quality will not be found inferior to any Brewed in this City.'[33] The ale breweries of Laurence [elsewhere Lawrence] O'Brien on Marlborough (Marlboro) Street and of Digby O'Brien and Richard Barrett on Clark's Place also advertised their wares in 1791 and 1792.

At this time, London porter was enjoying its final few years of popularity. John Dankert of William Street was advertising 'Whitbread's best PORTER in Bottle'; wholesalers Thomas Moore and Therry & Hopper often promoted London porter in the local press; Robert Hall regularly auctioned cargoes of imported porter; and in September 1791 Edward Haynes had 1,000 casks of fresh London porter on offer.[34] A directory for Cork for the year 1787 lists eighteen brewers or brewing firms in the city. The firms of Aylmer Allen in Cremer's Square, Corker & Cashman in Crosse's Green, Denis McCarthy & Co. of Cross Street, Lawrence O'Brien of Marlborough (Marlboro) Street and O'Brien & Barrett of Clark's Marsh are familiar from other sources, while the other thirteen firms were either smaller concerns or individuals employed as brewers. Of the hundreds of men admitted as Freemen of the city during the eighteenth century, twenty-six are described as brewers, the majority being admitted in the later 1700s, when brewing in Cork was entering its phase of rapid growth. This number is an underestimate, however, as a number of Freemen – Attiwell Hayes, William Beamish and William Crawford, for example – became involved in brewing after they became Freemen.[35]

The dynamics of Cork brewing: a site study

From at least the middle of the eighteenth century, a number of small commercial breweries functioned on the site of the later Southgate Brewery owned by the Lane family on the east side of South Main Street, opposite the Beamish & Crawford brewery. The succession of brewers, partnerships of brewers and breweries on the site throughout the later 1700s and into the early 1800s is illustrative of the nature of the brewing industry in Cork in that formative period. The frequent changes in ownership of the breweries and the forming and re-forming of partnerships were features of the business at that time. (For more detail on Lane's Southgate Brewery, see Chapter 7.)

In 1781 Thomas Fuller and Charles McCarthy were partners in a brewery on this site, while in 1796 George Fuller, the son of Thomas, was in partnership with Walter Fitzsimmons and Jeremiah O'Reilly in running that enterprise.[36] The latter partners took over an adjacent small brewery in that year that had been operated by a partnership of Thomas Fuller and Anthony Hawkesworth, while Hawkesworth had a separate brewery in his own right in the same area. In 1798 Charles McCarthy leased a small nearby brewery that was then in his possession to the George Fuller, Walter Fitzsimmons and Jeremiah O'Reilly partnership. By 1801 O'Reilly had acquired the interest of his other two partners and he formed a new brewing partnership with Thomas Hadigan to operate the business for the next eight years. In 1809 they sold their brewery to Daniel Lane, who sold it back to O'Reilly the following year when O'Reilly formed a partnership with Michael Barry. By 1818 O'Reilly and Barry were bankrupt and their brewery was then bought by the Lane family, who in 1842 acquired another set of buildings at the eastern end of the site, fronting the Grand Parade, that, up to 1800 at least, had functioned as a brewery.

Throughout this period of change and acquisition, there were multiple rebuildings and amalgamations of brewhouses, yards, stores and so on as the various individual enterprises eventually grew into a single entity that came to be known as the Southgate Brewery under the stewardship of the Lanes. This brewery operated until it was bought out and closed by Beamish & Crawford in 1901.

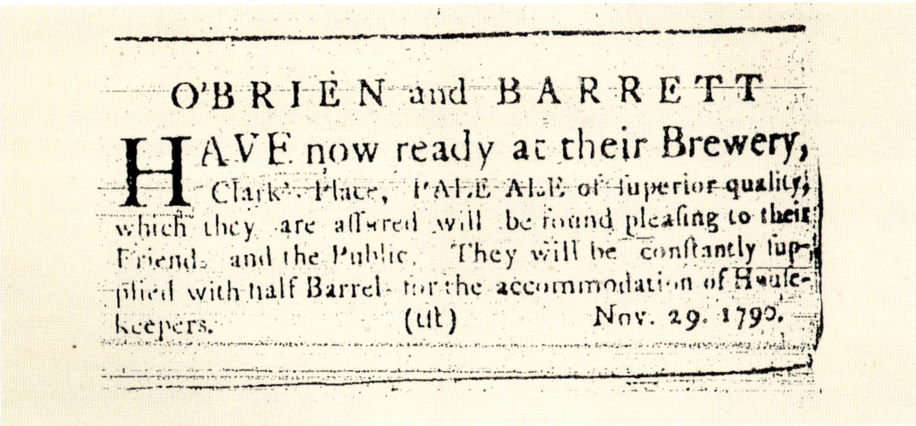

O'BRIEN and BARRETT

HAVE now ready at their Brewery, Clark's Place, PALE ALE of ſuperior quality, which they are aſſured will be found pleaſing to their Friends and the Public. They will be conſtantly ſupplied with half Barrels for the accommodation of Houſe-keepers. (tt) Nov. 29. 1790.

From the *Hibernian Chronicle*, 6 January 1791.

By the early 1790s brewing in Cork was on the cusp of great change. London porter was beginning to lose its reputation and dominance; beer was increasingly seen as a more acceptable alcoholic drink than spirits; the Irish brewing lobby was achieving its goal of a more favourable taxation regime; small and constantly mutating local ale and porter breweries had developed between them a modicum of brewing know-how; and local merchants had accumulated wealth that could be invested in larger capital-hungry porter breweries on the London model. Richard Barrett and Digby O'Brien, partners in an ale brewery in the city, saw an opportunity for a bold new porter brewing enterprise and in 1791 approached two of the city's most prominent merchants, William Beamish and William Crawford, to finance their idea. A partnership was formed and the brewery they developed became one of Cork's leading commercial concerns for over two centuries.

2

Merchants

William Crawford & William Beamish

In 1791 Cork ale brewers Richard Barrett and Digby O'Brien approached two wealthy Cork merchants, William Beamish and William Crawford, with a view to setting up a partnership to brew porter. William Beamish was a descendant of a family that had become established in west Cork in the late sixteenth century, while William Crawford's forbears had acquired lands in County Down, having come from Scotland in the early seventeenth century.[1] The Beamishes and Crawfords followed the classic trajectory of the successful capitalist class in this era of economic transformation: from landowning to merchanting to industry (and land again).

The Beamishes

Following the suppression in Munster of the rebellion of the Earl of Desmond (1579–83), his lands and those of his followers were confiscated by the English Crown and granted to a number of English planters or 'undertakers', so called because they undertook to let these lands to loyal English tenants as part of an effort to dilute and eventually extinguish any further rebellious activity by the native Irish. This became known as the Munster Plantation. One of those planters was Phane Becher of London, who was granted around 14,000 acres west of Bandon. The name Beamish appears in the list of tenants he settled on these lands. The development of the fortified town of Bandon, or Bandonbridge, as it was then known, was a result of the efforts of Becher and his tenants.

Throughout the succeeding decades, the Beamishes extended their holdings and managed to retain possession despite the upheavals of the Nine Years' War (1594–1603), which essentially saw the overthrow of the Munster Plantation, and the 1641 Rebellion and its aftermath. During the 1641 Rebellion a Bandon militia was raised,

Merchants' Quay 1831, viewed from St. Patrick's Bridge. The buildings on the quayside were mostly merchants' warehouses. Beamish, Crawford & Keating, and later Beamish & Crawford, had their base at No. 12 Merchants' Quay.
(G.N. Wright, *Ireland Illustrated, from original drawings, by G. Petrie RHA, W.H. Bartlett, & T.M. Baynes* (London, 1831))

and amongst those to hold commissions were Francis and Thomas Beamish. They were sons of a Catherine Beamish, a widow or daughter-in-law of the original Beamish settler, of the parish of Ballymodan near Bandon, who died in 1642. Two other sons are named in her will: Richard and Thomas. She was the great-great-grandmother of William Beamish, one of the founding partners of the Cork Porter Brewery.

Following the restoration of Charles II to the English throne in 1660, an Act of Settlement was passed by which three of Catherine Beamish's sons retained possession of lands they held to the west of Bandon. Richard and Francis retained lands in Kilmalooda; Francis in his own right retained lands in the parishes of Desertserges, Rossmore and Kilmeen; and Thomas held lands in the Kilmichael parish. Francis died in 1679 and his third son, Richard, acquired further land in the Desertserges parish in 1696 following his marriage the previous year to Mary Townsend of Clonakilty. This Richard Beamish built two mansions on his land, called Willsgrove and Mount Beamish. Richard's third son, William, inherited Willsgrove. He served for a time in the Royal Navy, married Alice Bernard in 1750 and died in 1773. William and Alice had four sons, the third of whom was also called William, who was born on 13 May 1760. This William (the brewery co-founder), like his father, served in the Royal Navy, but then changed to the army and served during the American Wars (1775–83). He returned to Cork and by July 1785 he was in partnership with William Crawford in the merchant trade.

The Crawfords

In 1625 Andrew Crawford took a lease on a mill and land a little to the west of Bangor, County Down. In 1670 William Crawford, a son or grandson of this Andrew, purchased the lands from Lord Clanbrassil and the estate became known as Crawfordsburn. William was succeeded by his son John, who in turn was succeeded by his son James, father of William Crawford (1757–1834), brewery co-founder. Throughout the eighteenth and nineteenth centuries, the Crawfords consolidated their place as a well-positioned landed family. Sons and daughters married other members of the landed gentry, while others made careers in the military, business and politics.

William Crawford, the brewery co-founder, had moved to Cork by 1779, as in that year he became a partner in a merchanting business with John Church. Eighteenth-century Cork was a city of merchants and the quays of the city were lined with their warehouses, stores and offices. A partnership in a merchant house, even a short-term arrangement, could result in relatively quick and substantial profit. It was not uncommon for a younger son of a landed family to spend a short period of years in such a business, first by way of an apprenticeship and later as a partner or independent merchant. The profits made were often subsequently invested in land, with the merchant returning to his more 'natural' habitat as landowner.[2]

Crawford financed his entry into the merchant trade with the help of James Alexander, a wealthy and well-connected relative through marriage. Alexander was born in Derry in 1730 and worked in India with the East India Company, returning to Ireland in 1772 a very wealthy man. He served as MP for Londonderry City between 1775 and 1790 and was appointed High Sheriff of County Tyrone in 1780 and of County Armagh in 1781. In 1776 he purchased the Caledon estate, an extensive holding between counties Tyrone and Armagh, and he bought houses in Dublin and London. He became the first Earl of Caledon in 1800. In 1774 Alexander married a sister of William Crawford, Anne (*c.* 1753–77), who died less than three years later. Two years after that, in 1779, William Crawford approached Alexander for a loan of £2,000 to buy a share in the merchant house of John Church in Cork, based on Merchants' Quay. A one-third share in Church's business was available to Crawford for £2,000 and after a few years he expected to have an equal share.[3] A Mr Bonwell was also a partner in the business; Crawford wrote that Church 'thinks in some few years hence that we will have stock enough to carry on our business independent of Mr Bonwell when he says he shall divide the business with me'. The profits on Church's books for the previous year were in the region of £3,000 and he expected those to rise to £3,700 in 1779. As did many Cork merchants, Church confined his business to low-risk trade on commission, which, as Crawford wrote, 'is always a certain profit'.[4]

Alexander agreed to advance the money, but emphasised that 'it will require both time and pain to raise'. He wondered if it would be possible for Crawford to be a working partner, thus not needing an upfront payment and 'have such a share for your attention to business'. But in the event of the £2,000 being necessary, Alexander was willing to lend it, with Crawford paying interest until he was ready to pay back the principal. The deal went ahead as Crawford had wished. By September 1779, Bonwell had sold his share in the business to Church and the house was then trading

James Alexander's response to William Crawford's request for a loan of £2,000 to enable him buy a share in John Church's merchant house. (CCCA/Authors)

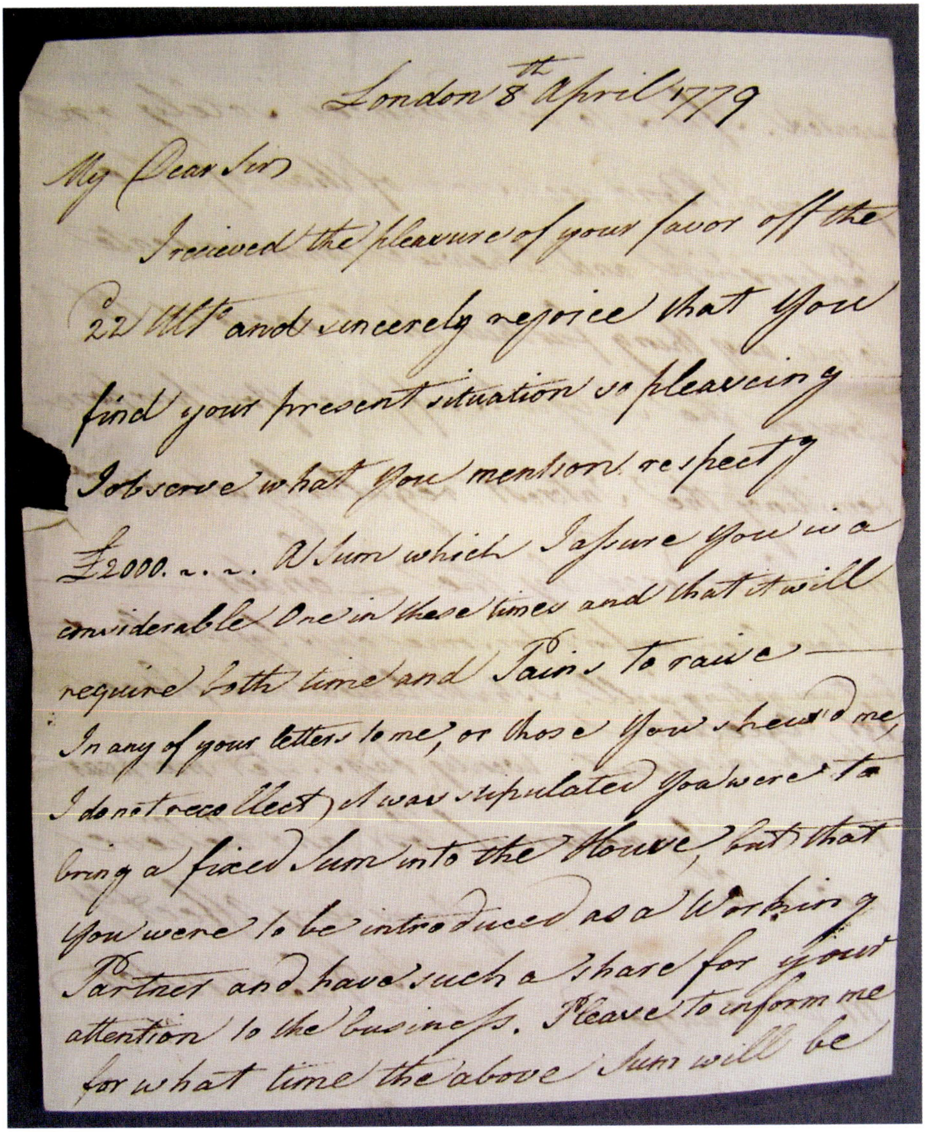
London 8th April 1779

My Dear Sir

I received the pleasure of your favor off the 22 ulto and sincerely rejoice that you find your present situation so pleasing. I observe what you mention respecting £2000.... A Sum which I assure you is a considerable One in these times and that it will require both time and Pain to raise — In any of your letters to me, or those you shew'd me, I do not recollect it was stipulated you were to bring a fixed Sum into the House, but that you were to be introduced as a Working Partner and have such a share for your attention to the business. Please to inform me for what time the above Sum will be

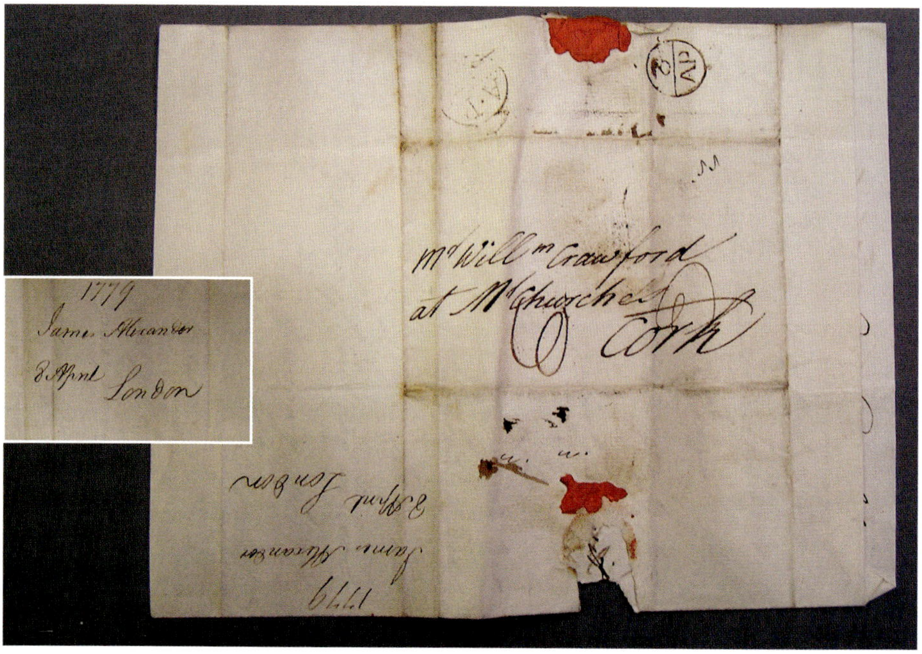

Letter from James Alexander to William Crawford 'at Mr. Churche's', dated 8 April 1779. Inset James Alexander's signature. (CCCA/Authors)

as J. Church & W. Crawford. According to Crawford, Bonwell was aggrieved that Church had taken him as partner, for reasons that are not explained.[5]

A set of accounts of Church & Crawford survives for the years 1780, 1781, 1782 and 1784, which shows the partnership to have been a profitable one. In the year to May 1780, transactions totalled a little over £28,809.1.9, generating a profit of £3,845.18.3, or 13.34 per cent, earning William Crawford £1,281.19.5 as his one-third share, or 64 per cent of his initial investment. In the following year, £31,523.18.1 worth of business was transacted, giving the partners a profit of £5,604.11.5½, or 17.77 per cent, £1,868.3.9½ of which went to Crawford. Transactions in the following year increased to a total of £41,077.19.9, but the profit is not shown. For the year ending June 1784, business in the amount of £32,213.0.1½ was done, but again, profit is not shown. The percentage profits made in 1780 and 1781 suggest that Crawford would have earned something in the region of £2,000 in each of the years 1782 and 1784.[6]

In August 1784 Crawford repaid James Alexander the principal of £2,000 that had been advanced five years previously.[7] The partnership with John Church ended some time between then and the following summer, as by July 1785 William Crawford was in partnership with William Beamish in a merchanting business on Merchants' Quay.[8]

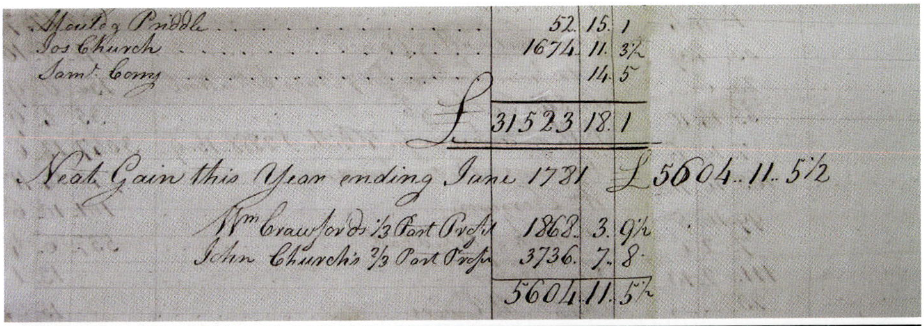

Hould & Priddle	52.15.1
Jos Church	1674.11.3½
Saml. Corry	14.5
	£ 31523.18.1
Neat Gain this Year ending June 1781	£ 5604.11.5½
Wm. Crawford's 1/3 Part Profit	1868.3.9½
John Church's 2/3 Part Profit	3736.7.8
	5604.11.5½

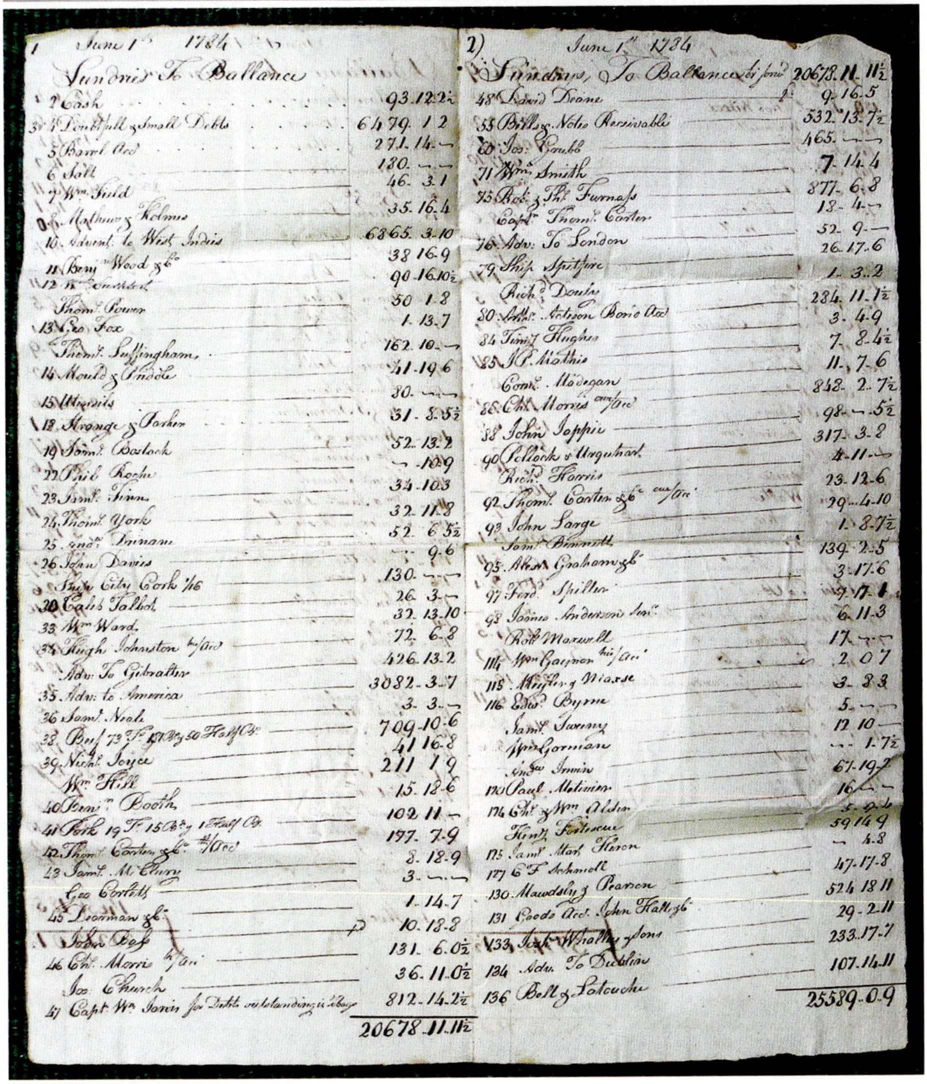

1 June 1st 1784

Sundries To Ballance

2 Cash	93.12.2½
3&4 Doubtfull & Small Debts	6479.1.2
5 Barrel Acct	271.14.–
6 Salt	180.–.–
7 Wm. Field	46.3.1
8 Mathews & Holmes	35.16.4
10 Advent. to West Indies	6865.3.10
11 Benjn. Wood & Co	38.16.9
12 [illegible]	90.16.10½
Thoms. Power	50.1.8
13 Geo Fox	1.13.7
Thoms. Saffingham	162.10.–
14 Hould & Priddle	41.19.6
15 Utensils	80.–.–
18 Strange & Parker	31.8.5½
19 Saml. Baslock	52.13.2
22 Phil Roche	–.10.9
23 Saml. Finn	34.10.3
24 Thoms. York	32.11.8
25 Andw. Drinan	52.6.5½
26 John Davis	–.9.6
Ship City Cork 1/16	130.–.–
30 Caleb Talbot	26.3.–
33 Wm. Ward	37.13.10
34 Hugh Johnston his/acct	72.6.8
Adv. To Gibraltar	426.13.2
35 Adv. to America	3082.3.7
36 Saml. Neale	3.3.–
38 Beef 73 Ts [illegible] & 50 Half Ct	709.10.6
39 Nichl. Joyce	41.16.8
Wm. Hill	211.7.9
40 Benjn. Booth	15.18.6
41 Pork 19 Ts 15 Bs & 1 Half Ct	102.11.–
42 Thoms. Carter & Co his/acct	197.7.9
43 Saml. McClury	8.18.9
Geo Corlett	3.–.–
45 Drorman & Co	1.14.7
John Doe	10.18.8
46 Chs. Morris his/acct	131.6.0½
Jos. Church	36.11.0½
47 Capt. Wm. Jarvis for Debts outstanding in [illegible]	812.14.2½
	20678.11.11½

2) June 1st 1784

Sundries, To Ballance brot. forwd. 20678.11.11½

48 David Deane	9.16.5
55 Bills & Notes Receivable	532.13.7½
60 Jos. Grubb	465.–.–
71 Wm. Smith	7.14.4
73 Robt. & Thos. Furnass	877.6.8
Capt. Thoms. Carter	13.4.–
76 Adv. To London	52.9.–
79 Ship Spitfire	26.17.6
Richd. Doulin	1.3.2
80 Arthr. Arbison Bond Acct	284.11.1½
84 Timy. Hughes	3.4.9
85 W.P. Mathis	7.8.4½
Comr. Modegan	11.7.6
86 Chs. Morris cur/acct	848.2.7½
88 John Joppie	98.–.5½
90 Pollock & Urquhart	317.3.8
Richd. Harris	4.11.–
92 Thoms. Carter & Co cur/acct	23.12.6
93 John Large	29.4.10
Saml. Bennett	1.8.7½
95 Alexr. Graham & Co	139.2.5
97 Ford. Spiller	3.17.6
98 James Anderson Junr.	9.7.4
Robt. Maxwell	6.11.3
114 Wm. Gaynor his/acct	17.–.–
115 Mylers & Mease	2.0.7
116 Edwd. Byrne	3.8.3
Saml. Twomy	5.–.–
Wm. Gorman	12.10.–
Andw. Irwin	–.1.7½
170 Paul Maloney	67.19.2
174 Chs. & Wm. Alden	16.–.–
Henry Fortescue	5.9.4
175 Saml. Mart Heron	59.14.9
177 G F Schmell	–.4.8
130 Mawdsley & Pearson	47.17.8
131 Goods Acct. John Hall & Co	524.18.11
133 Jack Whalley & Sons	29.2.11
134 Adv. To Dublin	233.17.7
136 Bell & Latouche	107.14.11
	25589.0.9

From top: John Church and William Crawford's account showing Crawford's one-third share of the net profit for the year ending June 1781, amounting to £1,868.3.9½. (CCCA/Authors)

Extract from account book of merchant house of John Church and William Crawford for June 1784. (CCCA/Authors)

Beamish, Crawford & Keating[9]

William Beamish and William Crawford were joined in their partnership by James Keating Jr. from 1786 to 1788. Although William Beamish died in April 1828, the mercantile firm of Beamish & Crawford survived until July 1830. Their involvement in the brewing business began in 1791 and ran parallel to, but separately from, their merchanting. A Cork directory for the year 1787 lists 120 'merchants' in the city, though not all of those were necessarily engaged in the import/export business. However, only six of the 120 were located on Merchants' Quay: Beamish, Crawford & Keating; Henry Cuthbert & Co.; James French; Richard Hare Junior; Murphy & McCormack; and Henry Shea.[10] The plot on which Beamish, Crawford & Keating had their premises was originally owned by Richard Hare, a wealthy Cork merchant, who had leased it to another merchant, Henry Shea.[11] Shea had developed the site and William Crawford later acquired it, probably in 1785, Crawford's lease noting that 'he [Shea] had erected said dwelling house with the cellars and other valuable improvements … meared and bounded on the North with the Quay fronting said premises, on the West by the street called North Street, on the South by the holdings of James French and on the east by other holdings of said Richard Hare'.[12]

From left: William Beamish (Courtesy Richard Beamish) and William Crawford (Crawford Art Gallery, Cork)

Keating was based in London and canvassed there for business for the firm. His letters to his partners in Cork detail his work from May 1787 to May 1788, recording the minutiae of his dealings with other merchants, reports of his success or otherwise in obtaining contracts, military and political intelligence, agricultural and general economic information, details of victualling contracts for the army and navy and general business gossip, as well as some personal detail.[13] There are occasional references to Church, William Crawford's former partner, and it is clear that relations with him were not good, suggesting that the parting with Crawford two or three years before that had been somewhat acrimonious and that Church had not let the matter lie. For example, in a letter of 26 June 1787, Keating wrote: 'Mr Church I understand was to leave yesterday evening which I am very glad of, as I am certain [h]is diligence was exerted to do you every prejudice in his power.' On 16 July he wrote: 'J.C. [John Church] has and is still doing an infinity of mischief.'

On 14 September 1787 Keating succeeded in securing a major victualling contract for the firm to supply the garrison at Gibraltar. He was in competition with a Mr Lyons, who had had the contract for the previous two years, but through the intercession 'of my good friend Mr Jackson', Keating got the contract from Thomas

A view of Cork Harbour in 1842 from near Cove (Cóbh), looking southwestwards towards the naval base on Haulbowline Island. Many Cork merchants became wealthy on profits from lucrative victualling contracts for the British army and navy. (J.S. Coyne, *The Scenery and Antiquities of Ireland, Vol. II* (London, 1842))

Everett, who in turn had a contract with the Lords Commissioners of the Treasury. Under the terms of the contract, Beamish, Crawford & Keating were to supply 1,800 tierces [barrels] of beef 'free from Neck, Legs, Skins and Marrowbones' at £4.6.6 per tierce; 700 tierces of pork 'free from Heads, Jowls and Feet' at £4.4.3 per tierce; 1,400 cwt of butter at £2.12.0 per cwt; and 220 tons of oatmeal at £9.10.0 per ton.[14] The order was to be delivered in four stages during the first half of 1788 and loaded onto ships in Cork Harbour provided by Everett. It was a condition of the contract that 'the said provisions shall be such as will keep good for six calender [*sic*] months after the delivery thereof into the Garrison of Gibralter [*sic*]'.[15] In total, the contract was worth £19,513.15.0. It would seem that instead of a fixed commission being paid to Beamish, Crawford & Keating on the value of the contract, it was up to the firm to source the supplies at the best possible price and thus generate its own profit.

Two weeks later, on 28 September 1787, Keating wrote to his partners in Cork suggesting that war with France was imminent, adding: 'As proof of it Mr Everett sent to me today in consequence of an addition he wishes to make to the Gibralter [*sic*] Contract.' This required Beamish, Crawford & Keating to supply an additional 907 tierces of beef, 309 tierces of pork, 375 cwt of butter and 155 tons of oatmeal for a total price of an additional £8,186. The threat of war receded the following month and

Extract from John Keating Junior's letter of 14 September 1787 to Beamish, Crawford & Keating in Cork detailing a large contract he has secured for the British garrison at Gibraltar. (CCCA/Authors)

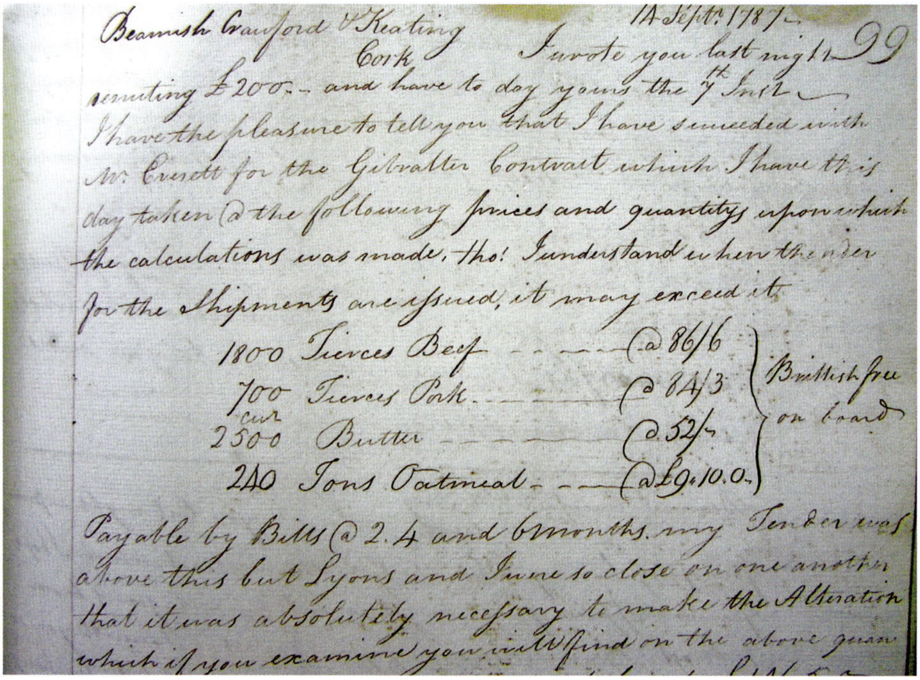
Beamish Crawford & Keating 14 Sept. 1787
Cork I wrote you last night 99
remitting £200.- and have to day yours the 7th Inst.
I have the pleasure to tell you that I have succeeded with
Mr Everett for the Gibralter Contract which I have this
day taken @ the following prices and quantitys upon which
the calculations was made, tho' I understand when the order
for the Shipments are issued, it may exceed it.

1800 Tierces Beef ---- @ 86/6
700 Tierces Pork ---- @ 84/3
2500 cwt Butter ---- @ 52/-
240 Tons Oatmeal ---- @ £9.10.0
British free on board

Payable by Bills @ 2.4 and 6 months. my Tender was
above this but Lyons and Inne so close on one another
that it was absolutely necessary to make the Alteration
which if you examine you will find on the above quan

Keating sent an urgent letter on 30 October to his colleagues in Cork informing them:

> that papers have been signed and interchanged between this court an[d] France, wherein all Hostilities and intentions of them are given up and mutual agreement entered into to disarm ... This news which suppose you will have first in your possession will enable you to act in a most serviciable [*sic*] manner for our interest ...

The following day Keating wrote again, urging Beamish and Crawford to sell their stocks of sugar as the price would drop steeply once the news of the peace agreement became more widely known. Despite the negative effects of peace on some aspects of trade, the firm won another provisions contract from Mr Everett in November 1787, again for the Gibraltar garrison. The contract was worth £8,840.6.6 and was for beef, pork and butter. The goods were to be 'exactly India provisions'. Keating secured another valuable contract the following month with the firm Turnbull & Co. for 7,500 barrels of pork and 2,000 firkins of butter, worth £27,237.10.0.[16] The firm also transacted business on a much smaller scale. Letters frequently deal with the details of shipments of different goods to customers in Cork. Hops, for example, were shipped to Cork brewers such as Corker & Cashman, O'Brien & Barrett, Christopher Allen and Henry Fowks.

William Beamish travelled to England in the autumn of 1787 and remained there until late December to canvass for business in the northwest, mainly in Liverpool and Lancaster. Keating was a little disappointed with Beamish's initial efforts and wrote to him on 5 October at Liverpool:

> ... Park says you are too modest for a Canvasser, and that you should have paid more attention to the Women as well as delayed longer there [Lancaster]. I think so too and I hope you will not be in such a hurry to leave Liverpool for just at the time they are giving orders is when you ought to be on the spot particularly when those letters you desire the House to write come forward. Park is of the opinion from thence that when you are actually coming home to pay Lancaster another visit.

Beamish stayed mostly in Liverpool, and while he apparently succeeded in concluding some business, Keating remained unimpressed. On 18 December, for example, he criticised Beamish over his mishandling of a business negotiation: '... you should therefore study these matters better and I must say be a better judge of Negotiation.' Later in the same letter, Keating expressed satisfaction with his own efforts over the previous year:

> I have most completely succeeded this year here agreable [*sic*] to my wishes and I hope and rely that on your return home you will most actively assist Mr Crawford to see that the whole is so managed that we shall acquire great Reputation.

In February 1788, James Keating was taken ill and William Beamish returned to England to replace him at their London base. Keating's illness continued until 5 May 1788 at least, which is the date of his last letter. His involvement in the partnership may have ended with his resignation or death in that year, as his name does not subsequently appear in any of the surviving documentation relating to the firm. On 13 March 1788, 'J.S.' wrote from London to Mrs Keating, presumably Keating's wife, at Paul Street in Cork regarding the shipping of furniture, carpets, silverware and other household items back to Cork. This may indicate that Keating was clearing his house in London and returning to Cork.

William Beamish was still in London in April 1788 and John Church was continuing to be a thorn in the side of the firm. Beamish wrote to William Crawford on 11 April:

> In a few days I will visit all the Cheesemongers & inform you my Expectations of orders from them next season which I am much affraid [*sic*] will not be so considerable as last year from the infamous letters of J. Church who I assure you has done every thing in his power to injure us.

Exports and imports

The surviving bills of lading in the Beamish & Crawford collection at the Cork City and County Archives show that a number of cargoes were dispatched by William Crawford in his own name in the second half of 1785, even though the title 'Beamish & Crawford Charges Book' suggests that he was in partnership with William Beamish from July of that year in this business.[17] There are thirty-seven bills in the name of Crawford alone, dating from July to December 1785. These may have been contracts that Crawford had entered into before the arrangement with Beamish was formalised. There are seventy-three bills in the name of the firm of Beamish & Crawford dating from December 1785 to July 1786 and from July 1813 to March 1814 and one from July 1816; a number bear the printed logo of the firm. There are seventy-six surviving bills in the name of Beamish, Crawford & Keating, dating from July to December 1786, and they bear the printed logo with the intertwined initials B, C and K.

The bills of lading from the different periods follow the same general format and note the name of the ship on which the goods were to be transported, the name of

View of Grand Parade from the south in 1831. Note the small vessel, or lighter, transporting a passenger and barrels. Large deep-draughted vessels anchored in the lower harbour, and lighters transported cargoes to and from these vessels to and from the city's quays. (G.N. Wright, *Ireland Illustrated, from original drawings, by G. Petrie RHA, W.H. Bartlett, & T.M. Baynes* (London, 1831))

the ship's master, the destination, the nature and quantity of the goods, the brands or marks on the barrels and the freight to be paid. The overwhelming majority of these surviving bills detail exports of butter, chiefly to London. The grade of butter, where it is noted, is 'New Rose' and is described as being carried in casks, firkins or full bound firkins. The size of the cargoes varies greatly, from as few as fifty firkins to as many as 500 in one consignment. Beef and pork were also exported, and where mentioned, the grade is 'Planters', 'Mess' or 'Cargo' beef or pork. 'Planters' and 'Mess' were the same standard and were regarded as being suitable for a gentleman's table. Beef of this grade was cut into 8 lb pieces and did not include neck or shank. Lower qualities of beef were graded as 'best cargo beef' and 'common cargo beef'.[18] Other cargoes mentioned, though infrequently, are ox cheeks, hog cheeks, tongues, palates, hogslard, tallow, barley, wheat and salmon. While the majority of these bills of lading are for cargoes bound for London, the other destinations mentioned include Halifax, Quebec, Lisbon, Trinidad, Jamaica and Barbados.

Further detail on the business of the firm is to be gleaned from the 'Beamish & Crawford Charges Book 11 July 1785–17 July 1830'.[19] The dates in the title of this account book indicate the lifetime of the mercantile firm. William Beamish died in 1828, by which time the business had very much declined in line with the overall shrinkage in the traditional merchant trade in Cork in the 1820s. By the time of the last entry in the book, the level of activity was quite low. The absence of the name of James Keating Jr. in the title of the book suggests that his involvement in the

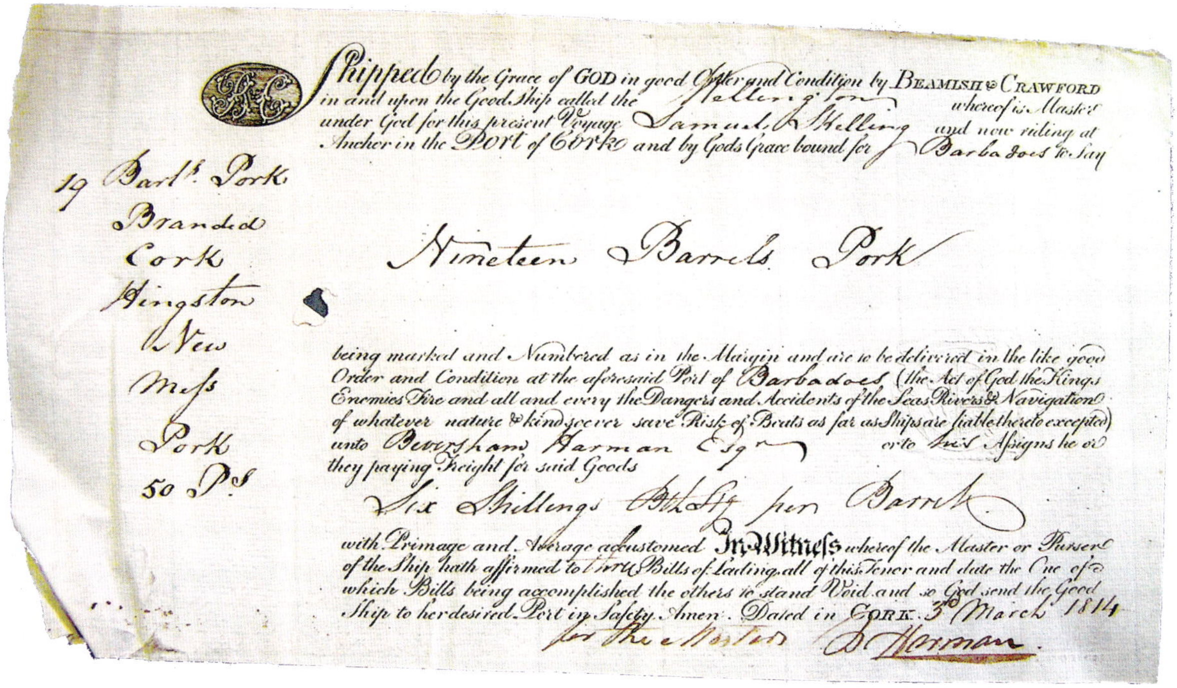

Shipped by the Grace of GOD in good Order and Condition by BEAMISH & CRAWFORD in and upon the Good Ship called the Wellington whereof is Master under God for this present Voyage Samuel Stelling and now riding at Anchor in the Port of Cork and by Gods Grace bound for Barbadoes to Say

19 Barl.s Pork
Branded
Cork
Hingston
New
Mess
Pork
50 P.s

Nineteen Barrels Pork

being marked and Numbered as in the Margin and are to be delivered in the like good Order and Condition at the aforesaid Port of Barbadoes (the Act of God the Kings Enemies Fire and all and every the Dangers and Accidents of the Seas Rivers & Navigation of whatever nature & kind soever save Risk of Boats as far as Ships are liable thereto excepted) unto Beversham Harman Esqr or to his Assigns he or they paying Freight for said Goods

Six Shillings [illegible] per Barrel

with Primage and Average accustomed In Witness whereof the Master or Purser of the Ship hath affirmed to three Bills of Lading all of this Tenor and date the One of which Bills being accomplished the others to stand Void and so God send the Good Ship to her desired Port in Safety Amen. Dated in CORK 3d March 1814

for the Master B Harman

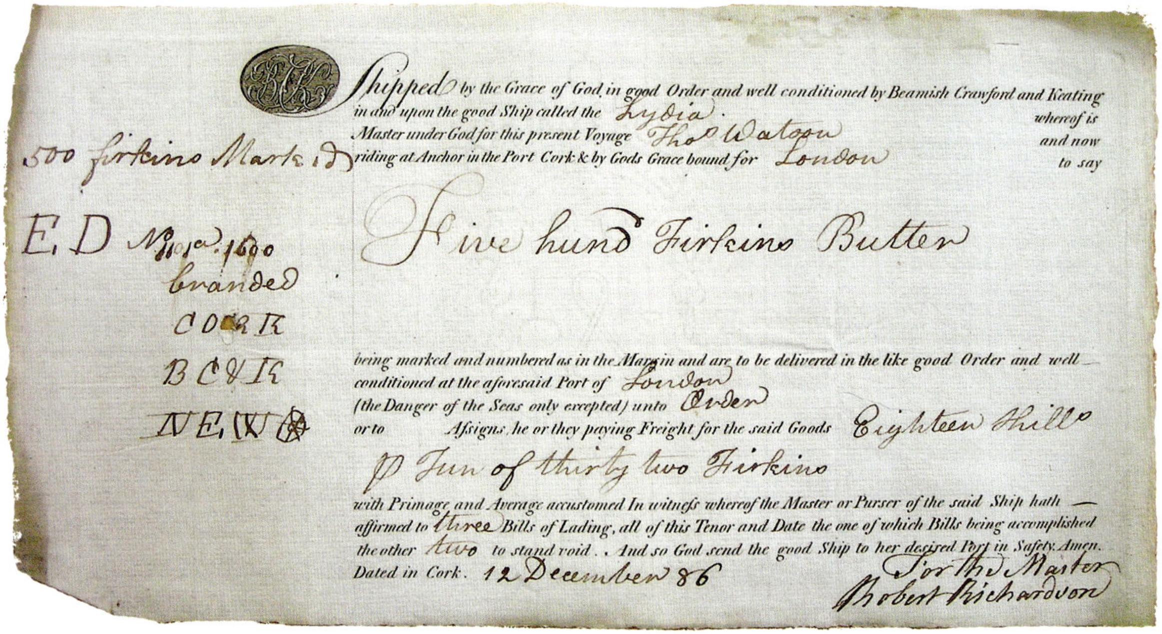

Shipped by the Grace of God in good Order and well conditioned by Beamish Crawford and Keating in and upon the good Ship called the Lydia whereof is Master under God for this present Voyage Thos Watson and now riding at Anchor in the Port Cork & by Gods Grace bound for London to say

500 firkins Mark'd
E.D No 1 to 1500
branded
CORK
BC&K
NEW

Five hund Firkins Butter

being marked and numbered as in the Margin and are to be delivered in the like good Order and well conditioned at the aforesaid Port of London (the Danger of the Seas only excepted) unto Order or to Assigns, he or they paying Freight for the said Goods Eighteen Shills ℘ Tun of thirty two Firkins with Primage and Average accustomed In witness whereof the Master or Purser of the said Ship hath affirmed to three Bills of Lading, all of this Tenor and Date the one of which Bills being accomplished the other two to stand void. And so God send the good Ship to her desired Port in Safety. Amen. Dated in Cork. 12 December 86

For the Master
Robert Richardson

From top: Bill of lading, dated 3 March 1814, for a shipment of nineteen barrels of New Mess Pork from the firm of Beamish & Crawford, bound for Barbados on board the *Wellington*. (CCCA/Authors)

Bill of lading, dated 12 December 1786, for a cargo of 500 firkins of New Rose Butter to be shipped by Beamish, Crawford & Keating to London on board the *Lydia*. (CCCA/Authors) partnership was short-lived. Many of the entries detail payments to 'lightermen', those who operated the smaller, shallower-draughted sailing vessels that transported goods between Cork city's quays and the ships anchored in the deeper waters of the lower harbour. Related payments for freight, porterage, stowage and pilotage are also detailed and there are numerous unspecified payments to ships' masters or captains. Certain goods being imported had other charges attached, such as duty or 'entry' on cargoes of rum. The imported goods mentioned include corn, slate, coal, bark, mahogany, sugar, potash, cotton, herrings, staves, hops, rum, wine, tobacco, cider and treacle, while exports include butter, beef, pork, pigs, barley, wheat, faggots and turf.

Other business concerns

The firm was also apparently involved in corn drying, as there are a number of references to payments for work done on corn kilns and corn lofts, especially in 1785 and 1786. As well as the premises on Merchants' Quay, the firm also rented a number of stores and cellars in the city, the annual rents being noted in this charges book. In the 1790s Falkiner & Co. were paid an annual rent of £34.2.6 for a bacon cellar in Blackpool, Thomas Smith was paid £22.15.0 twice yearly and James Morrogh was paid an annual rent of £70 for other cellars. Thomas Smith also received rent for a butter cellar in Cross Street. Payments to carpenters, masons, painters, smiths, tilers and nailers for the repair and maintenance of stores and

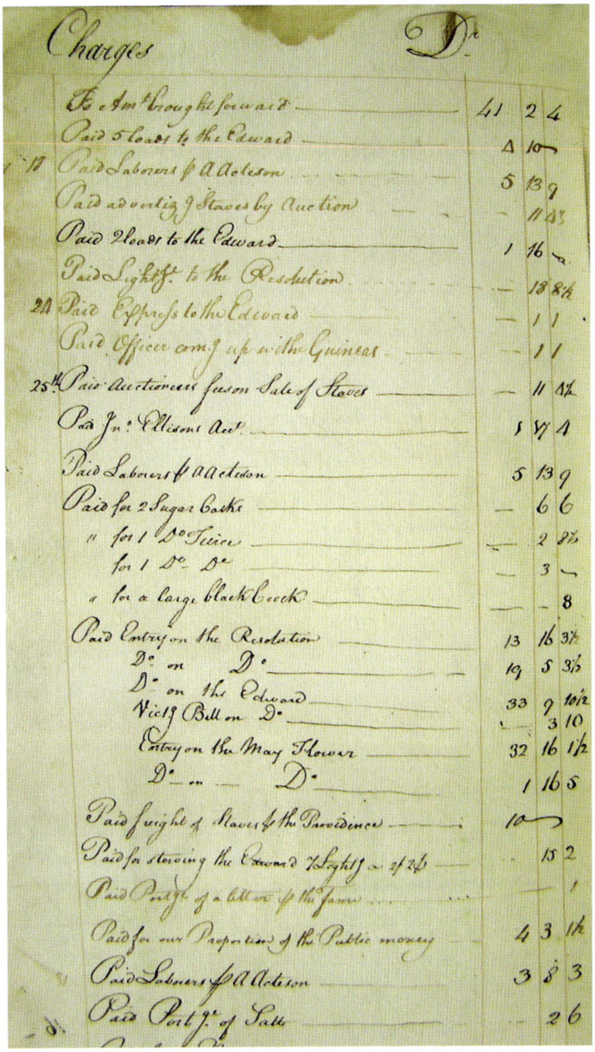
Charges Dr

	To Amt brought forward	41	2	4
	Paid 5 loads to the Edward	4	10	–
17	Paid Laborers pr A Adelson	5	13	9
	Paid advertizg Staves by Auction	–	11	4½
	Paid 2 loads to the Edward	1	16	–
	Paid Lightr to the Resolution	–	18	8½
24	Paid Express to the Edward	–	1	1
	Paid Officer comg up w the Guineas	–	1	1
25th	Paid Auctioneers fees on Sale of Staves	–	11	4½
	Paid Jn: Ellisons Acct	1	17	4
	Paid Laborers pr A Adelson	5	13	9
	Paid for 2 Sugar Casks	–	6	6
	" for 1 Do Tierce	–	2	8½
	for 1 Do Do	–	3	–
	" for a Large black Crock	–	–	8
	Paid Entry on the Resolution	13	16	3½
	Do on Do	19	5	3½
	Do on the Edward	33	9	10½
	Vict Bill on Do	–	3	10
	Entry on the May Flower	32	16	1½
	Do on Do	1	16	5
	Paid freight of Staves pr the Providence	10	–	–
	Paid for stowing the Edward 7 Lights a 2/2½	–	15	2
	Paid Postage of a letter pr the same	–	–	1
	Paid for our Proportion of the Public money	4	3	1½
	Paid Laborers pr A Adelson	3	8	3
	Paid Post of Salt	–	2	6

Extract from Charges Book of the Beamish & Crawford merchant house, dated July 1789. (CCCA/Authors)

cellars are noted, as well as parish rates, lamp money and postage. From the end of 1789, payments for tolls are entered, following the opening of the first St Patrick's Bridge in that year. On 8 November 1785, £3.1.6 was spent on 'Entertaining the Lord Lieutenant'.[20]

The annual totals of expenses noted in this charges book can be used as a measure of the level of business conducted in each year. In the later 1780s these averaged over £4,000, while in the ten-year period from 1794 to 1803 the annual average was just under £3,200. By the 1820s the level of business conducted by the firm had declined greatly; in the five-year period from 1820 to 1824, the annual cost of doing business averaged £830.

The valuation of the concern in April 1798 was £28,235.12.4. William Beamish held £8,666.13.4 in the stock account of the company, while William Crawford held £2,166.13.4. Crawford also had £3,494.1.9½ to his credit in the interest account. The firm had £5,567.19.8 on deposit with the Cotter & Kellet Bank in Cork, while Alice Beamish, William's widowed mother, had £4,882.14.4½ to her credit in the interest account on foot of a promissory note from Messrs. Beamish, Crawford & Keating to her for £4,000, dated 11 August 1787.[21]

Merchants' Quay *c.* 1900, viewed from St Patrick's Quay. The Royal Cork Sailors' Home (the building with the flag on its roof) was the headquarters of the merchant house of Beamish & Crawford until 1830. It was later the home of William Crawford's son, George, who lived there until his death in 1864, after which it became the Sailors' Home. (Courtesy Michael Lenihan)

William Beamish and William Crawford entered into a partnership with two others in 1791 to brew porter, and while this new enterprise grew and prospered and demanded an increasing amount of their time, the merchanting business of Beamish & Crawford continued in parallel. William Beamish died in 1828 and the merchanting business ceased trading in 1830. Following the death of William Crawford in 1834, his second son, George, inherited the premises at 12 Merchants' Quay, where he lived until his death in 1864, after which they were converted for use as the Royal Cork Sailors' Home. In the early 1900s ownership of the building passed to Richard Henrik Beamish and in the early 1930s it became a St Vincent de Paul hostel. No. 12, along with all of the buildings on Merchants' Quay, was demolished in the 1980s to make way for the development of the Merchants' Quay Shopping Centre, which opened in 1989.

3

Beginnings

1791–1800

Digby O'Brien and Richard Barrett were partners in an ale brewery located on Clarke's Marsh off Wandesford's Quay in Cork on the south side of the south channel of the River Lee. It is not known when the brewery or the partnership was founded, but in 1774 Richard Barrett was described as a brewer when he became a Freeman of Cork.[1] Digby O'Brien became a Freeman in 1777, at which time he was a merchant, suggesting, perhaps, that he had yet to form his partnership with Barrett. The partnership was in existence from at least 1787, when the merchanting house of Beamish, Crawford & Keating was regularly sourcing and dispatching cargoes of hops from England to the firm, described as O'Brien & Barrett.[2] A brewery advertised for sale in September 1791 is very likely that of O'Brien & Barrett, as by then they had embarked on the venture to establish the Cork Porter Brewery with William Beamish and William Crawford:

> A well established Brewery and Malt-House, situate in the best part of the City of Cork for Water and every other convenience, to be let for any term of years, and immediate possession given if required. The Brewery is in full business, the Stock and Utensils can be had at Valuation, and time given for payment on Security. The Malt-House is in compleat working order, and is capable of making from nine to ten thousand Barrels yearly, besides sufficient Storage for any quantity of grain, with two large drying Kilns, Malt Stores, &c . . . [3]

O'Brien and Barrett's approach to William Beamish and William Crawford to form a partnership to establish a porter brewery was probably made in the summer of 1791, when the former pair were:

A BREWERY.

A Well eſtabliſhed Brewery and Malt-Houſe, ſituate in the beſt part of the City of Cork for Water and every other convenience, to be let for any term of years, and immediate poſſeſſion given if required. The Brewery is in full buſineſs, the Stock and Utenſils can be had at Valuation, and time given for payment on Security. The Malt-Houſe is in compleat working order, and is capable of making from nine to ten thouſand Barrels yearly, beſides ſufficient Storage for any quantity of grain, with two large drying Kilns, Malt Stores, &c. Any perſon wiſhing to get into profitable home Trade with a moderate Capital, will never meet a better opportunity. Propoſals will be received by Benjamin Hayes, Attorney, and kept ſecret if required. (tſt) Sept. 15.

From the *Hibernian Chronicle*, 19 September 1791.

> desirous to enter into and carry on the Brewing of Porter extensively and not having a capital to embark thereon they or one of them did apply to the said William Beamish and William Crawford (who then were merchants and never had been Brewers or Maltsters) to join with them then to embark and advance a very large and considerable capital in said business ...[4]

Having agreed a partnership arrangement, the four of them took possession of Aylmer Allen's porter brewery. It was ranged around Cremer's (sometimes Cramer's or Creamer's) Square, accessed from the west side of South Main Street by way of Cremer's Lane. The brewery buildings were bounded on the north by Allen's Lane and on the south by Morgan's Lane (sometimes St Laurence's or Lawrence's Lane) and were set some way back from South Main Street, running westwards to the river (see map, p. 37). John Plaince had taken a lease on a brewery on the site in 1735 and had developed and expanded the facilities. When Plaince died in 1772, the premises were advertised for sale:

> To be set for a long term of years (or the interest sold) the Brewery and Malt Houses of the late Mr. J. Plaince, Cramer's-lane, Cork, a large copper furnace, tuns, coolers, &c. are on the premises. They are very convenient to water, and secured by one door. The late Mr. Plaince expended on the premises above £3000 and is allowed to be the completest and most convenient Brewery in this city ...[5]

Allen invested further in the brewery, expanding it and specialising in the brewing of porter. In a series of advertisements in the local *Hibernian Chronicle* in December 1782, he made his case for import substitution and the superior quality of his locally produced product:

> PORTER BREWERY,
> Cramer's Square, CORK.
> Aylmer Allen begs leave to acquaint his Friends and the Public, that he has now a large stock of right good Porter fit for use, hopes to meet that preference from the Friends to this Country that they may think his undertaking merits: such as please to make trial, he hopes to please; they will be careful to attend to the directions on the head of the cask; he hopes to do away that prejudice, that none but Thames' Water can make good Porter. As he has been at great expence in bringing his Porter Brewery to perfection, by erecting large Vats, Stores, &c. and wishing to reduce the price as low as possible, he is determined not to deliver any Porter but for ready money at the following prices:
> Hogshead, at 3l.; 10s. 10d. for each Hhd. Returned.
> Barrels, at 2l.; 7s. 7d. for each Barrel ditto.
> Such Gentlemen as please to send their own empty casks, 8d. h. Per Gallon.
> He has empty Bags to sell.
> N.B. Choice Porter in large bottles, well up, and fine, to be sold at same place, by William Aylmer Allen, at 3s. Per dozen.

Allen's porter brewery prospered until his death in May 1791; his obituary described him as 'an eminent brewer' and 'a Gentleman of amiable manners' who 'dined from home the day before apparently in good health, complained of being heavy in the morning, while in bed, on which a little more rest was recommended; but he was soon after found dead'.[6]

Digby O'Brien, Richard Barrett, William Beamish and William Crawford purchased the Allen family interest in the brewery from Aylmer Allen's son, Edward, and by 29 August 1791 they were placing advertisements seeking barley for their new enterprise, named the Cork Porter Brewery. The details of the purchase and transfer of the various buildings and plots making up the brewery were finalised in January 1792, along with the articles of their partnership agreement. The initial agreements were made on or about the previous 1 August, and the first Monday in August was chosen as the date each year on which the accounts of the new company would be made up and signed off.[7]

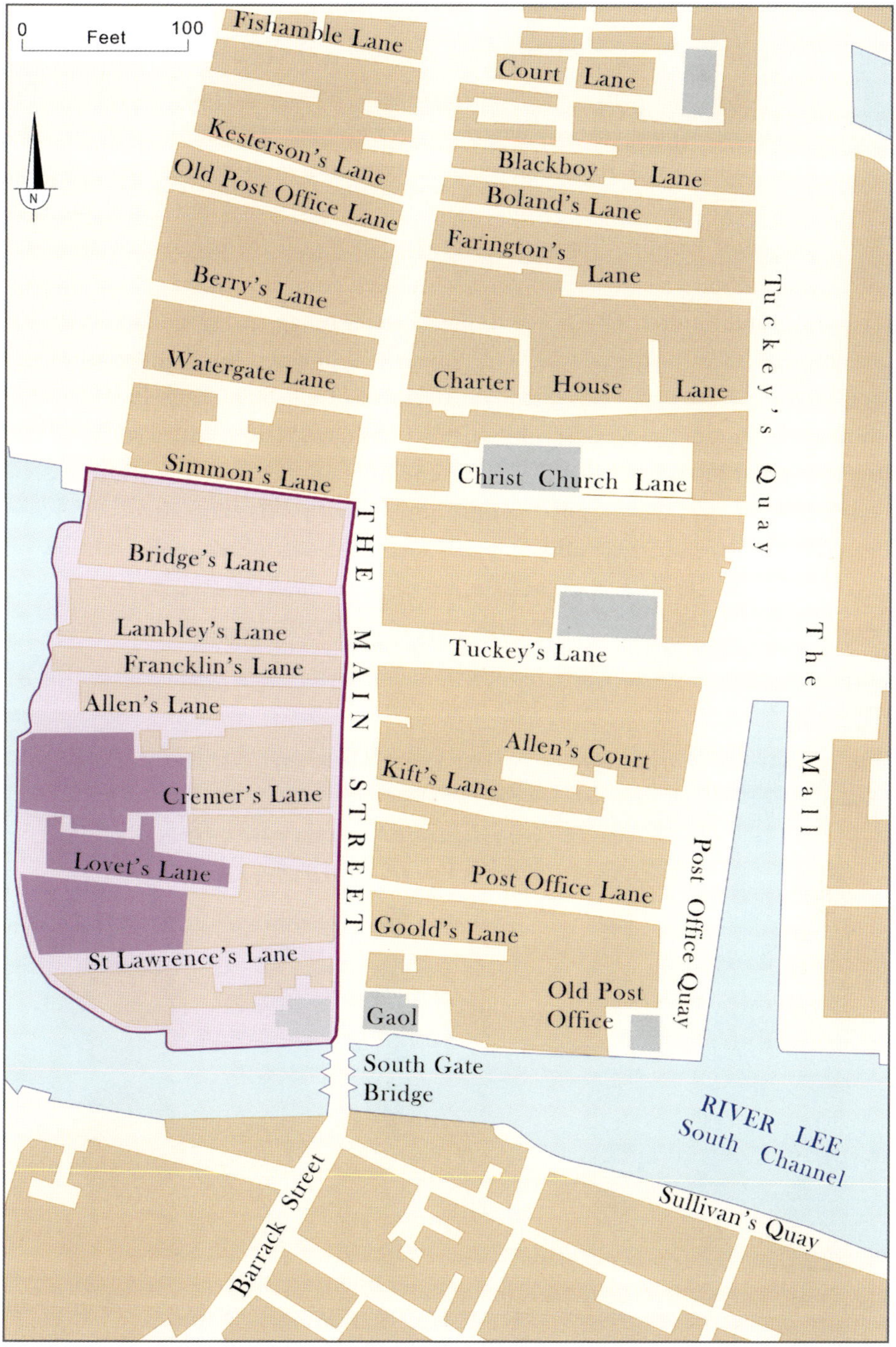

Map based on that of John Rocque (1759) showing the location and extent of the Cork Porter Brewery in 1792 (darker colour), and the eventual extent of the brewery by the end of the twentieth century. (St Lawrence's Lane was also known as Webber's or Morgan's Lane. Lovet's Lane was sometimes rendered as Lavitt's Lane). (Map drawn by Michael Murphy)

The deal

The four partners of the Cork Porter Brewery took possession of the eight lots that had made up Allen's brewery, comprising various buildings and plots of ground. The rents of these lots would cost the new partners £250 per year and in addition they paid Edward Allen £500 'for the purchase of certain utensils and fixtures', listed as 'Two Coppers, One Keeve, One Cooler, One Underback, One Tun, One Sky Cooler, Two Mills, Three Pumps'.[8] The agreement with Allen gave the partners an option to withdraw from the deal after seven years, with Allen returning £350 of the £500 paid for utensils and fixtures if such a withdrawal were to happen. O'Brien and Barrett brought with them to the new brewery 'About 600 or seven hundred empty Porter Hogsheads and Barrels, Five Vatts, Three Horses, One Dray, One large Cistern, About twelve throughs [*sic*] & sundry small articles', which were valued at £300.[9] The partners agreed to work together for thirty-one years, from 1 August 1791, unless, by unanimous consent, they decided to discontinue their partnership after seven years. Beamish and Crawford were initially to advance all monies necessary for carrying on

Facing page: The first of the three pages of the 1792 articles of agreement. (CCCA/Dori O'Connell)

Left: Cover of the articles of agreement, dated 13 January 1792, setting up the partnership of Beamish, Crawford, O'Brien and Barrett. (CCCA/Dori O'Connell)

Right: The signatures and seals of the original four partners in the Cork Porter Brewery (William Beamish, William Crawford, Digby O'Brien and Richard Barrett) on their co-partnership agreement signed 13 January 1792. (CCCA/Dori O'Connell)

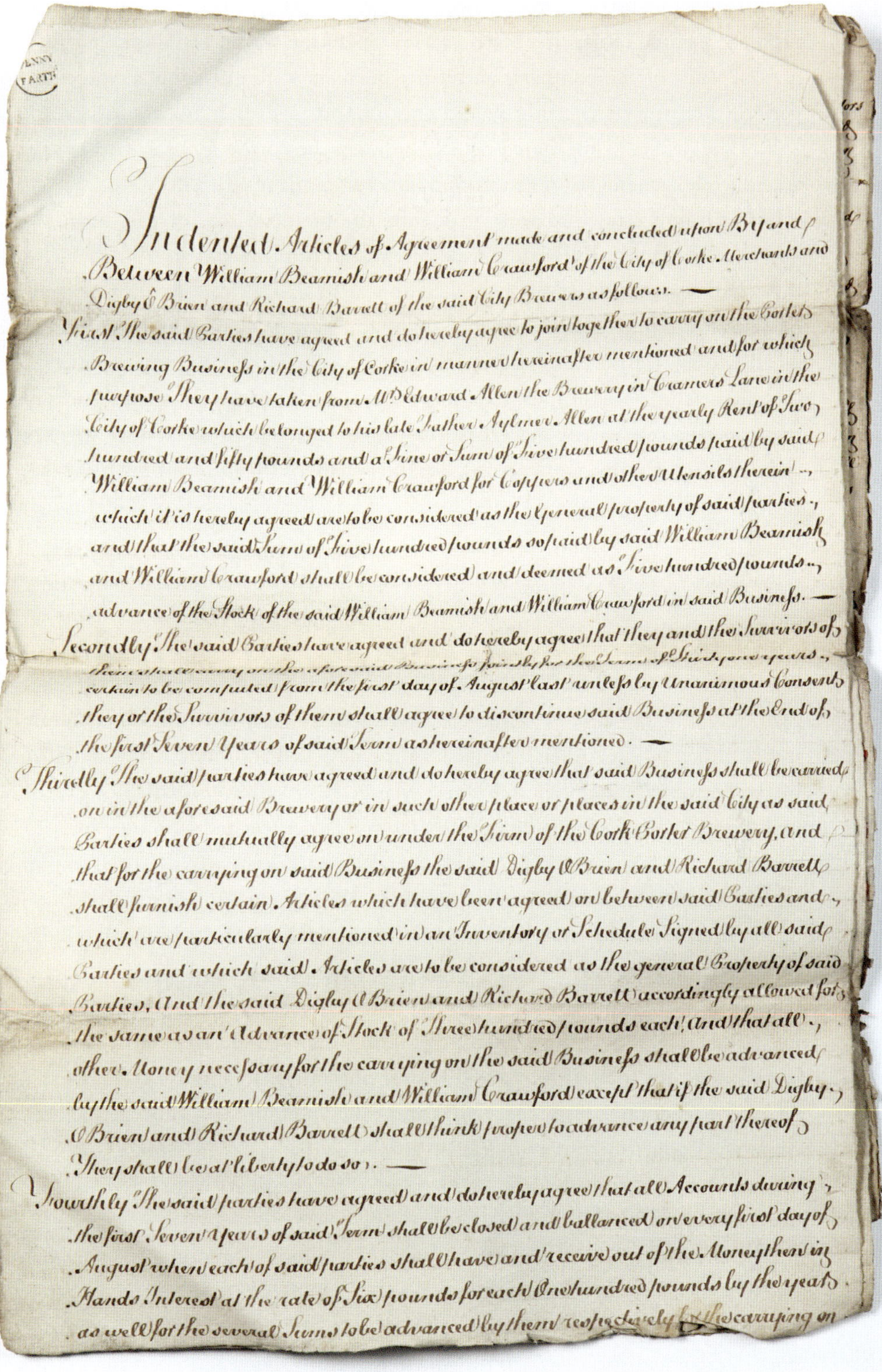

Indented Articles of Agreement made and concluded upon By and Between William Beamish and William Crawford of the City of Corke Merchants and Digby O'Brien and Richard Barrett of the said City Brewers as follows. —

First The said Parties have agreed and do hereby agree to join together to carry on the Porter Brewing Business in the City of Corke in manner hereinafter mentioned and for which purpose They have taken from Mr. Edward Allen the Brewery in Cramers Lane in the City of Corke which belonged to his late Father Aylmer Allen at the yearly Rent of Two hundred and fifty pounds and a Fine or Sum of Five hundred pounds paid by said William Beamish and William Crawford for Coppers and other Utensils therein which it is hereby agreed are to be considered as the General property of said parties, and that the said Sum of Five hundred pounds so paid by said William Beamish and William Crawford shall be considered and deemed as Five hundred pounds advance of the Stock of the said William Beamish and William Crawford in said Business. —

Secondly The said Parties have agreed and do hereby agree that they and the Survivors of them shall carry on the aforesaid Business jointly for the Term of Thirty one years certain to be computed from the first day of August last unless by Unanimous Consent they or the Survivors of them shall agree to discontinue said Business at the End of the first Seven Years of said Term as hereinafter mentioned. —

Thirdly The said parties have agreed and do hereby agree that said Business shall be carried on in the aforesaid Brewery or in such other place or places in the said City as said Parties shall mutually agree on under the Firm of the Cork Porter Brewery, and that for the carrying on said Business the said Digby O'Brien and Richard Barrett shall furnish certain Articles which have been agreed on between said Parties and which are particularly mentioned in an Inventory or Schedule Signed by all said Parties and which said Articles are to be considered as the general Property of said Parties, And the said Digby O'Brien and Richard Barrett accordingly allowed for the same as an Advance of Stock of Three hundred pounds each, And that all other Money necessary for the carrying on the said Business shall be advanced by the said William Beamish and William Crawford except that if the said Digby O'Brien and Richard Barrett shall think proper to advance any part thereof They shall be at liberty to do so. —

Fourthly The said parties have agreed and do hereby agree that all Accounts during the first Seven Years of said Term shall be closed and ballanced on every first day of August when each of said parties shall have and receive out of the Money then in Hands Interest at the rate of Six pounds for each One hundred pounds by the year as well for the several Sums to be advanced by them respectively for the carrying on the business and were to receive interest at 6 per cent per year on those monies. The profits generated in the first seven years of operation would be considered part of the general stock of the company and if the business were profitable at the end of that period, then the partnership would continue for a further twenty-four years, with half of the profits being shared equally between the partners and the other half being added to the general stock of the company to a limit of £12,000.

Beamish and Crawford were to handle the financial side of the business and it was also agreed that O'Brien and Barrett would not 'intermeddle' in that area 'until they shall respectively advance or shall appear to have in the said Business a Capital of Two Thousand Pounds'. At that point they would 'have an equal Management of all Money transactions respecting same'. O'Brien and Barrett's contribution to the partnership in its initial years was to be their brewing knowledge and skill, and they were to oversee all aspects of malting and brewing. They were to receive no remuneration for this work apart from their share of the 'neat profit', and when they each had £2,000 of capital in the firm, William Beamish and/or William Crawford could then, at the request of either O'Brien or Barrett, be required to 'give his or their attendance when necessary at said Brewery in Superintending the Business thereof'.

The Cork Porter Brewery in 1792

The layout of the Cork Porter Brewery is shown in some detail in the annotated plan drawn in January 1792 (p. 41).[10] While it is likely that the layout is largely as it was under Aylmer Allen's ownership, the new owners spent a substantial sum on works between September 1791 and March 1792. Brewery cash books from this early period note weekly payments to masons, carpenters and labourers for a 23-week period from 22 September 1791, averaging £47.13.0 per week, as well as purchases of timber and other building materials.[11] This would suggest a workforce in the region of at least fifty men working on the remodelling of the brewery buildings. In that 23-week period, William Beamish and William Crawford are recorded as having paid in to the firm a net total of £14,474.5.5. As sales of product did not commence until June 1792, that sum covered building materials, wages and salaries, barley, barrels, malting costs, duties and all other outgoings. In August 1792, £1,374.18.3 was spent on copper, lead, oak planks and vats. The following February, almost £300 more was spent on similar materials as well as £39.12.5 for seventy-three bars of copper imported from Bristol. In October 1793, two vats were purchased at a cost of £239.16.0.[12]

The January 1792 plan shows the brewery buildings extending for approximately 200 feet from the river in the west to about halfway to South Main Street, and measuring about 250 feet from the south side of Allen's Lane in the north to the north side of Morgan's Lane to the south. Including yards and open spaces, this gives

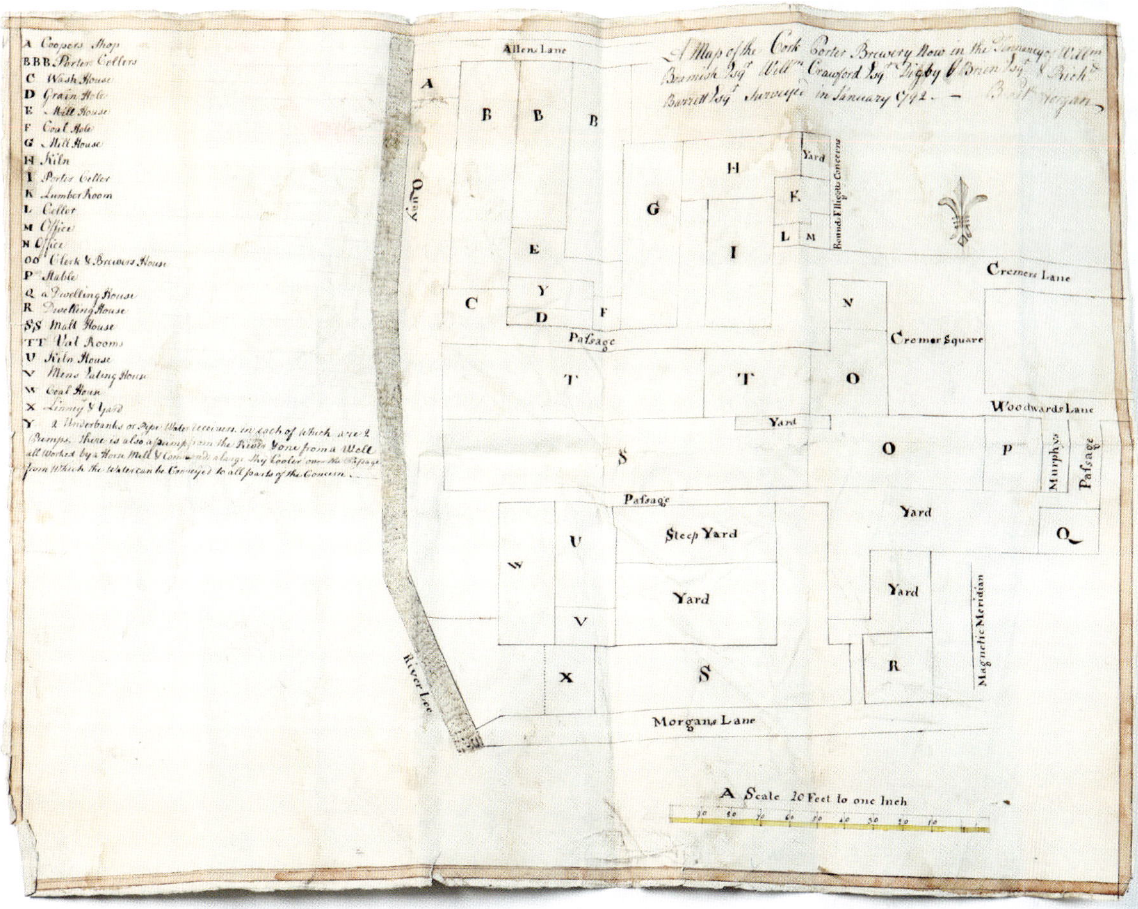

First plan of the Cork Porter Brewery, drawn in January 1792. (CCCA/Dori O'Connell)

the brewery an area of about 5,500 square yards. The main entrance to the brewery was by way of Cremer's Lane, westwards from South Main Street, and this led into Cremer's Square, which was the main yard of the brewery. This laneway is shown on the plan to have been about 10 feet wide. It is unlikely that the brewery would have been visible from South Main Street, as the buildings ranged along the west side of the street would have obscured the view.

The brewery buildings were arranged in three sections, divided from each other by passages running east to west. The northernmost range of buildings comprised four porter cellars, a large and a smaller millhouse, a kiln, a coal hole and lumber stores, a grain hole, an office, a wash house, a small cooperage and two water storage tanks with pumps to drive the water to a large sky cooler that lay above the passage to the river. Water was also pumped from the river and from a well to the storage tanks and

From top:
Detail from fireplace in the Beamish & Crawford boardroom showing the foundation date of 1792. (John Sheehan)
Carved wooden trademark of Beamish & Crawford from the boardroom of the Counting House. (John Sheehan)

all pumps were worked by horse mill. Water could be conveyed from the sky cooler to all parts of the brewery.

The central block of the brewery was made up of two vat rooms, a malthouse, a yard, an office, a stable and the clerk and brewer's house. The narrow passage that ran to the river along the southern side of these buildings is called Gosse's Lane in some documents, after Thomas Gosse, a clothier, who held properties on either side of this passage for some decades from 1702. Woodward's Lane, shown running westwards into Cremer's Square, is called Lavitt's Lane on other maps and may have been another access from South Main Street.[13] The southern range of buildings was bounded to the north by Gosse's Lane and along its southern flank by Morgan's Lane (sometimes also called St Lawrence's Lane, Webber's Lane and D. Goold's Lane).[14] There was a second malt house in this area as well as a large coalhouse, a kiln house, a steep yard, an eating house for employees, an open yard and another yard to the southwest that was partly roofed.

Malt, barley and hops

The Cork Porter Brewery was advertising for barley from 29 August 1791, when the following appeared in the *Hibernian Chronicle*:

> Cork Porter Brewery
> The highest Price will be given for prime Barley, at the Stores of the Cork Porter Brewery, South Main-street, where none but the first Quality can be received, and where ready money will always be paid for every article purchased.

Below:
From the *Hibernian Chronicle*, 15 September 1791.

BARLEY WANTED.

Cork Porter Brewery

WISHING to procure a ſmall immediate ſupply of PRIME Barley to ſet their Malt-Houſes at Work, will pay 30s. per Barrel, until ſuch ſupply is obtained; after which, they will give the higheſt ready Money Market-price for any very PRIME Barley brought to their Stores, South Main-ſtreet, for ſale. (4) Sept. 12.

Variations of this advertisement appeared through the succeeding weeks of that autumn. In the first malting season from the latter months of 1791 to spring 1792, the firm malted barley at the two malthouses on the brewery site and also at a malthouse on Hanover Street. In December 1791, 1,135 barrels of malt were produced;

during the following year, 7,978 barrels were made. In succeeding years the output of malt grew as porter production climbed from 12,003 barrels for the brewery year 1793 to 63,230 barrels in the year 1800.[15]

Quantities of malt were also bought in each year as increasing demand for its porter outstripped the firm's capacity to produce sufficient malt. Malting on the brewery site ceased in June 1796 as production transferred to malthouses elsewhere in the city that the firm had purchased or rented. A malthouse on Morrison's Island was bought in December 1792 and others were acquired on Francis Street in 1799, on Hanover Street in 1808 and on Rutland Street in 1813.[16] Between 1791 and 1798, the Cork Porter Brewery produced malt at fifteen malthouses. While some of these were used for a relatively short period, others, like the Morrison's Island and Hanover Street facilities, continued in use for much longer: Cremer's Square (1791–6), Hanover Street (1791–), Morrison's Island (1792–), Princes Street (1793–), Lapp's Island (1793–4), Ann Street (1794–), Kift's Lane (1794–), Fenn's Quay (1795–), French Church Street (1795–7), Brickfields (1795–6), Mary Street (1796–), Pump Lane (1797), Mardyke (1797–8), St Dominick's (1797–) and Margaret Street (1797–).[17] An indication of the relative capacity of these malthouses can be gauged from the average monthly production (measured in barrels) over their period of use:

Table 3.1

Average monthly production (in barrels) of malthouses used by Cork Porter Brewery

MALTHOUSE	PRODUCTION Average monthly (in barrels)	MALTHOUSE	PRODUCTION Average monthly (in barrels)
Fenn's Quay	472	Mardyke	240
Brickfields	409	Kift's Lane	187
Cremer's Square	389	Ann Street	173
Mary Street	349	Pump Lane	172
Hanover Street	307	St Dominick's	156
Princes Street	294	French Church St	155
Morrison's Island	284	Margaret Street	85
Lapp's Island	255		

In 1810 eight different malthouses are recorded as having been used (Fenn's Quay, Mary Street, Hanover Street, Princes Street, Morrison's Island, Francis Street, Grand Parade and Sand Quay,) but by 1818, malting was concentrated at four sites, all then owned by the Cork Porter Brewery (Fenn's Quay, Hanover Street, Morrison's Island and Rutland Street).[18]

Barley for malting was generally sourced from within County Cork, but occasionally barley was also imported. Between 1792 and 1801, the price of barley bought by the brewery fluctuated greatly, from an average of as low as 10s 2d per barrel in 1798 to almost three times that the following year (see Table 3.2).

Table 3.2

Purchase of barley, 1793–1801

YEAR	BARLEY PURCHASED (Barrels)	TOTAL COST (to nearest £)	AVERAGE COST (per barrel)
1793	22,181	£13,203	11s 11d
1794	20,606	£10,602	10s 4d
1795	18,145	£10,629	11s 8d
1796	40,541	£34,208	16s 10d
1797	40,434	£25,341	12s 6d
1798	45,517	£23,093	10s 2d
1799	24,961	£36,419	29s 2d
1800	46,079	£48,676	21s 2d
1801	24,873	£33,878	27s 3d

All hops used at the Cork Porter Brewery during this period were imported from England and were bought by volume, measured in bags, rather than by weight. Prices varied significantly from year to year and they also often varied greatly within a year. Quality, supply and demand, duties, freight costs and insurance were among the factors influencing costs. Between 1792 and 1800, the brewery paid from as low as an average of £15.10.5 per bag in 1795 to as high as an average of £64.2.8 per bag in 1800.

Table 3.3

Purchase of hops, 1792-1800

YEAR	HOPS PURCHASED (Bags)	TOTAL COST (to nearest £)	AVERAGE COST (per bag)
1793	292	£5,135	£17.11.9
1794	412	£11,063	£26.17.0
1795	592	£9,191	£15.10.5
1796	706	£12,287	£17.8.0
1797	601	£11,127	£18.10.3
1798	834	£16,707	£20.0.7
1799	690	£33,630	£48.14.9
1800	470	£30,143	£64.2.8

Brewing

The first porter was brewed at the Cork Porter Brewery on Tuesday, 17 January 1792. The *Hibernian Chronicle* noted the event and expressed the hope that the local product would replace imported London porter:

> CORK
> Last Tuesday our new Porter brewery commenced brewing that excellent beverage. The goodness of the quality we hope will render importation almost unnecessary.[19]

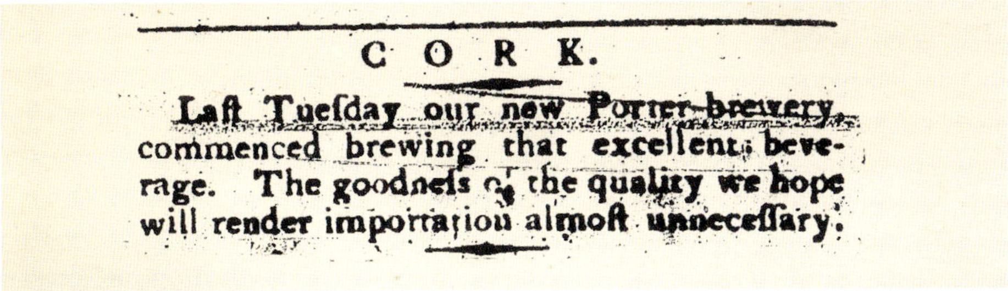

CORK.

Laſt Tueſday our new Porter brewery, commenced brewing that excellent beverage. The goodneſs of the quality we hope will render importation almoſt unneceſſary.

As porter required some time in storage to mature and mellow in flavour, the first sale of porter did not occur until five months later during the week ending 16 June 1792, when 229 barrels were sold to M. Regan for £434.2.11, i.e. at £1.17.11 per barrel. While partners Digby O'Brien and Richard Barrett were to oversee and superintend all brewing, John Topp was employed from 22 September 1791 as head brewer and was then paid £11.7.6 per week, the equivalent of a little over £600 per year. In addition to this, he was also paid a yearly bonus depending on the quantity of porter produced. By 1797 this bonus, at £678.14.9, was greater than his annual salary, and by 1800, when 63,230 barrels of porter were sold, Topp was paid a bonus of £1,007.8.7 in addition to his salary. The average annual income of most clerks and other brewery employees would have been less than £50 at that time.

While a brewer in the 1790s would have had the aid of a thermometer and saccharometer in managing the control of brews, the brewer's experience, instinct and individual skill were the most valuable parts in the process. The success or failure of a brewery essentially depended on the ability of the brewer to produce a palatable, consistent product of high quality. In addition to supervising and controlling the brewing process through all its stages, the head brewer was also responsible for overseeing the quality of barley bought for malting as well as being in charge of all materials, such as coal and barrels. He was also tasked with managing the clerks, superintendents and various labourers and assistants in the brewing department. In 1879 Richard Pigott Beamish, grandson of William Beamish, wrote of John Topp that 'the reputation created by his skilful brewing added to the generally high standing of the firm' and that the Cork Porter Brewery 'had become quite celebrated throughout the South of Ireland' as a result.[20] Topp was head brewer with the firm until 1839.

Porter was brewed throughout all twelve months of the year. During the spring of 1794, for example, over 20,000 gallons per week were being brewed. The following spring this level of production grew to over 30,000 gallons per week, produced in three separate brews. The rate of growth in production is clear from the growth in sales in the brewery's first years. In 1794, 21,688 barrels of porter were sold, growing by almost 22 per cent in 1795 to 26,412 barrels and by 66 per cent in 1796 to 43,911 barrels (see Table 3.3). At this time, porter was the only product brewed.

City customers

In the Cork Porter Brewery's early years, its most significant local customers were George Carr and William McDonnell on North Main Street, John Ryan and Ambrose Mason on South Main Street, James Denison at the Crown Tavern, Thomas Shinkwin at the King's Arms, William Carr on Broad Lane, George Smith on Potato Quay, Patrick McEnery at the Corn Market, Joseph Atkins on Patrick's Street, Michael Shea on Grand Parade and Bartholomew Murphy at the South Gate. Hundreds of customers are listed throughout the city and its environs in the day-to-day porter account books. While most are retailers (alehouse or tavern-keepers), a number are domestic customers in private residences or institutions, such as Cooper Penrose at Woodhill, Benjamin Bousefield at Lakelands, Mrs Coppinger at the Nunnery, the General Hospital on Spike Island and the Catholic bishop of Cork, Dr Francis Moylan, at the North Chapel. Military customers include Colonel Cottrell and Major Clarke of the 46th Regiment at Fermoy, to whom regular shipments were made in 1799 and 1800, the Westmeath regiment and Admiral Kingsmill at Cove. In 1792, 1,200 barrels of porter were supplied 'to the fleet'.[21]

Benjamin Parvin and John Logan were two significant employees at the brewery from the autumn of 1791. In addition to their annual salaries (£90 in 1794, rising to £220 by 1801), they also earned significant sums each year for the 'carriage of porter'. This suggests that they had a partnership to distribute the brewery's product in addition to the other work they were employed to do. As they were the second highest-paid individuals after the head brewer, their work was of some significance and may well have involved managing the day-to-day running of the non-technical aspects of the firm. For the year 1794, they were jointly paid £410.12.2 for the carriage of porter and the following year this rose to £438.6.3; by 1801 it was £1,974.16.6. Parvin's time with the firm seems to have ended in 1824 and by 1822 William Logan had taken over from his father, John, and was with the firm until 1854. He was succeeded in turn by Charles E. Logan (probably the son of William), who worked at the brewery until at least 1878. Other salaried employees noted in the earliest records, whose duties are not specified, are John Maguire, T. Stubbleman, John Philpott, George Callaghan, William Cowen, Samuel C. Austin and James Bell.[22]

Distribution beyond Cork city

As well as sales within the city and its environs, the Cork Porter Brewery also established a strong trade with other parts of County Cork and with towns and cities further afield (see map, p. 66). This trade was key to the growth of the firm. A network of agents and wholesalers was developed throughout the county and further afield who distributed and promoted the firm's product in their respective regions. By 1798, regular shipments were being made to the following in County Cork: Thomas John in Youghal (Joseph Jackson had been the Youghal agent until October 1798), S.H. Coppinger in Midleton, Charles Haines in Mallow, Armiger Sealy in Bandon, William Newman in Kinsale, John Mullanny in Cloyne and Daniel Donovan in Rosscarbery. Outside County Cork, Francis Hannan in Tallow and William Galwey in Dungarvan, both of County Waterford, were the principal agents/wholesalers representing the firm. A brewery ledger covering the years 1798 to 1801 records many shipments made to these agents and shows the significance, even at that early stage, of this aspect of the trade.[23]

In one section of the accounts in this ledger for the year 1799, 'Sundries dr. To Porter', details of the sale of 13,888 of the year's total of 55,103 barrels are recorded. City customers accounted for 6,760 of these sales, while agents and non-city wholesalers accounted for the remaining 7,128 barrels. While only a part of the year's total sales are detailed in this section, the information gives an indication of the spread of the brewery's trade and the means used to service and grow this part of the business. Of the 7,128 barrels shipped to agents and non-city wholesalers, 1,985 barrels (27.8 per cent) went to Youghal, 1,326 (18.6 per cent) to Midleton, 1,152 (16.1 per cent) to Mallow, 864 (12.1 per cent) to Bandon, 570 (8 per cent) to Kinsale, 300 (4.2 per cent) to Rosscarbery, 280 (3.9 per cent) to Tallow and 200 (2.8 per cent) to Dungarvan. The remaining 6.5 per cent was made up of very small shipments to Cloyne, Limerick, Ballydehob, Cove and other locations.

For the following year, 1800, details of the sale of 18,898 of the year's total of 63,230 barrels are recorded in this 'Sundries dr. To Porter' section. Agents and non-city wholesalers accounted for 12,698 of these, a significant increase on the previous year. The figures indicate a growth in sales through agents and wholesalers and a small growth in the spread of distribution. In that same year, Midleton accounted for 22.7 per cent of the shipments, Youghal 21.4 per cent, Kinsale 19 per cent, Mallow 17.7 per cent, Tallow 10 per cent and Bandon 4.7 per cent. Small shipments to Ballydehob, Bantry, Cloyne, Fermoy, Glandore, Rosscarbery and Spike Island in County Cork, Limerick, and Dungarvan, County Waterford, made up the remaining 4.5 per cent.

Shipped by ye Grace of GOD in good Order and Condition, by Beamish Crawford & Barrett in and upon the Good Ship called the Jane of Kinsale whereof is Master under God for this present Voyage Dennis Holden and now riding at Anchor in the River Lee and by God's Grace bound for Kinsale to Say One hundred tierces of Porter

to be delivered at the Yard of Armiger Sealy Esqr in Innishanon

being marked and Numbered as in the Margin, and are to be delivered in the like good Order, and well conditioned at as ye Margin (the Danger of the Seas only Excepted) unto the said Armiger Sealy Esqre or to his Assigns, he or they paying freight for the said Goods, twelve pence ye tierce & port charges in Cork & Kinsale with Primage & Average accustomed. In Witness whereof ye Master or Purser of the Ship hath affirmed to 3 Bills of Lading all of this Tenor and date, the One of which Bills being Accomplished, the Other 2 to stand Void. So God send the Good Ship to her desired Port in safety, Amen. Dated in Cork 13 Feby 179[illegible]

Den. Sholden

Bill of lading, dated 13 February 1798, for a cargo of 100 tierces (barrels) of porter to be shipped from Cork to Kinsale for onward delivery to the yard of Armiger Sealy in Inishannon. Sealy was the Cork Porter Brewery agent in Bandon at that time. (Beamish & Crawford Brewery Collection/Dori O'Connell)

Individual shipments to Mallow tended to be small relative to shipments to other locations, but they were far more numerous. In March 1800, for example, there were twenty-four separate deliveries to the agent in Mallow, averaging just under nine barrels in each delivery – a delivery on nearly every working day in the month. Mallow was serviced by road and the increasing trade through the agency there suggests that a journey of over 20 miles by a swaying and jolting horse-drawn cart or dray did not affect the quality of the porter. At this time the road network from Cork city, while growing and improving, was not developed to an extent that would facilitate the wide distribution of porter throughout the county. There was a serviceable road connection with Mallow and Bandon, for example, but in the case of the latter, transport by sea and river by way of Kinsale seemed, at least in the later 1790s, to be preferable. Most of the other agents and wholesalers outside the city were serviced by sea or river. The size of many of the individual cargoes clearly shows that transport by any other means would not have been possible. There was a well-developed coastal network of vessels trading between the smaller coastal ports and with the city of Cork, which was used to good effect by the Cork Porter Brewery. Shipments to Tallow, an inland town in

County Waterford, went by sea to Youghal and then by way of the River Blackwater northward until its junction with the River Bride, and then by way of that river to a quay near the town. Large shipments for Bandon went by sea to Kinsale, then by way of the Bandon River to Collier's Quay near Inishannon, and from there by road for the last part of the journey.

Tables 3.4 and 3.5 show a breakdown of shipments of porter to agents and wholesalers outside of Cork city for March 1799 and March 1800. The amount of porter being shipped had clearly grown, from 975 barrels in March 1799 to 1,896 barrels a year later. In March 1799, Mallow and Fermoy were the only locations serviced totally by road, while Cloyne would have been serviced by road from Midleton. All the other locations were serviced by sea or by sea and river.

Table 3.4

Shipments to agents/wholesalers, March 1799

AGENT/ WHOLESALER	NO. OF DAYS SHIPMENTS MADE	NUMBER OF BARRELS	LARGEST SHIPMENT	SMALLEST SHIPMENT	AVERAGE BARRELS PER SHIPMENT
Youghal	1	300	300	300	300
Midleton	2	180	100	80	90
Mallow	7	169	39	2	24.1
Bandon	1	150	150	150	150
Rosscarbery	1	100	100	100	100
Dungarvan	1	40	40	40	40
Fermoy	2	16	8	8	8
Cloyne	1	10	10	10	10
Ballydehob	1	10	10	10	10

Table 3.5

Shipments to agents/wholesalers, March 1800

AGENT/ WHOLESALER	NO. OF DAYS SHIPMENTS MADE	NUMBER OF BARRELS	LARGEST SHIPMENT	SMALLEST SHIPMENT	AVERAGE BARRELS PER SHIPMENT
Kinsale	6	617	150	1	102.8
Youghal	2	360	235	125	180
Tallow	2	341	206	135	170.5
Midleton	3	320	120	100	106.7
Mallow	24	212	50	2	8.8
Spike Island	5	36	8	7	7.2
Fermoy	2	8	6	2	4
Bandon	1	2	2	2	2

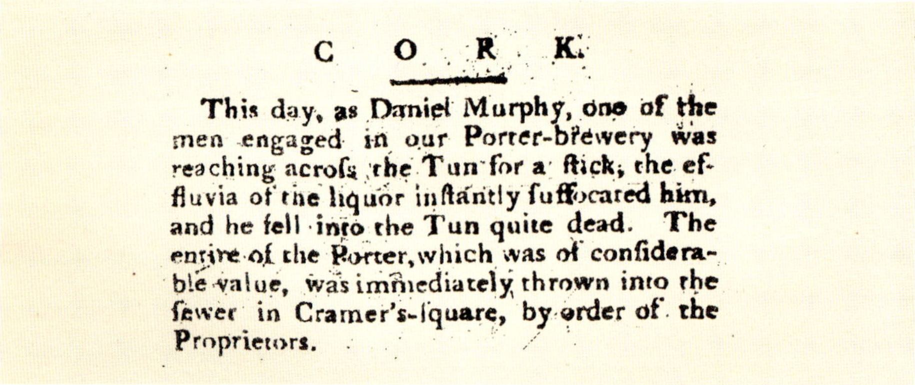

C O R K.

This day, as Daniel Murphy, one of the men engaged in our Porter-brewery was reaching acroſs the Tun for a ſtick, the effluvia of the liquor inſtantly ſuffocated him, and he fell into the Tun quite dead. The entire of the Porter, which was of conſiderable value, was immediately thrown into the ſewer in Cramer's-ſquare, by order of the Proprietors.

Report in the *Hibernian Chronicle* of 19 July 1792 of the death of Daniel Murphy at the brewery.

Accident

In July 1792 the first serious accident at the new Cork Porter Brewery occurred, resulting in the death of an employee. A local newspaper described the incident:

> This day, as Daniel Murphy, one of the men engaged in our Porter-brewery was reaching across the Tun for a stick, the effluvia of the liquor instantly suffocated him, and he fell into the Tun quite dead. The entire of the Porter, which was of considerable value, was immediately thrown into the sewer in Cramer's-square, by order of the Proprieters.[24]

The description of the accident suggests that the unfortunate Daniel Murphy was overcome by carbon dioxide, a gas given off in quantity especially during fermentation, and particularly dangerous in a poorly ventilated location. Accidents such as this were not uncommon in the early years of large-scale commercial brewing and are still not unknown even today.

'Thanks to their Friends and the Public in general'

In October 1792 the partners in the Cork Porter Brewery, clearly satisfied with their first full season's brewing, published an expression of gratitude to 'their Friends and the Public in general' in the local press:

> CORK PORTER BREWERY
> The Proprietors take this method of returning Thanks to their Friends and the Public in general, for the great Encouragement they have received, and are happy to find their PORTER has been found deserving of general Approbation. They beg leave to assure those that may please to favour them

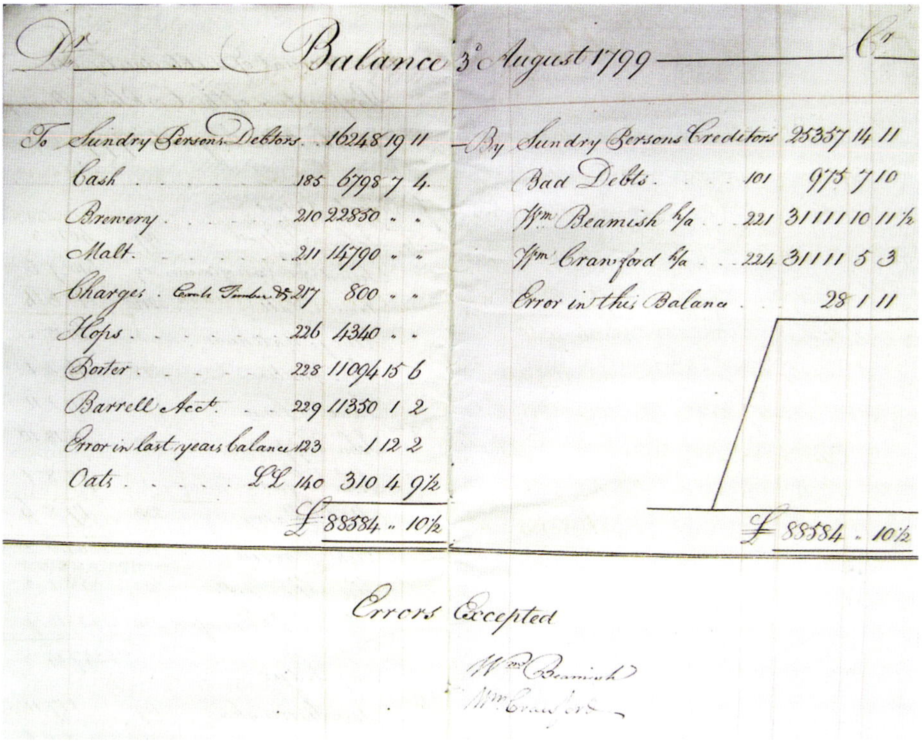

Dr — Balance 3d August 1799 — Cr

	Folio	£	s	d
To Sundry Persons Debtors		16248	19	11
Cash	185	6798	7	4
Brewery	210	22850	.	.
Malt	211	14790	.	.
Charges Corks Timber &c	217	800	.	.
Hops	226	4340	.	.
Porter	228	11094	15	6
Barrell Acct	229	11350	1	2
Error in last years balance	123	1	12	2
Oats	LL 140	310	4	9½
		£ 88584	..	10½

	Folio	£	s	d
By Sundry Persons Creditors		25337	14	11
Bad Debts	101	975	7	10
Wm Beamish ½a	221	31111	10	11½
Wm Crawford ½a	224	31111	5	3
Error in this Balance		28	1	11
		£ 88584	.	10½

Errors Excepted

Wm Beamish

Wm Crawford

Part of the balance sheet of the Cork Porter Brewery for the year ending 3 August 1799. (CCCA/Authors)

with their Custom, that no EXPENCE [*sic*] or TROUBLE has been, or will be spared to render the Quality unexceptionable; and as their demand for BARLEY malt tend [*sic*] in a great degree to promote the Agriculture of this Country, they hope for the Patronage and Support of their Friends in the Country, as well as those in Town, having now a large Supply of PORTER of most EXCELLENT Quality.[25]

And then there were two

An early account book notes a number of payments, amounting to over £5,000, to the executors of Digby O'Brien, one of the brewery's four founding partners, between April 1795 and February 1796.[26] The *Hibernian Chronicle* of 5 February 1795 records his death as follows: 'On the 15th of September last, at Brest, where he had been a prisoner, Digby O'Brien, of this City [Cork] Esq.' This was the period of the so-called Napoleonic Wars (1793–1815), when Britain, and by extension Ireland, was at war with France. Much of the action in this period of over two decades of hostilities happened at sea, where merchant ships sailing to and from the combatant countries were frequently taken as prizes by vessels of the other side. It can be posited that Digby O'Brien, a merchant and brewer of some means, would have made a valuable hostage to be held for ransom if, as seems possible, he was taken prisoner by the French after the capture of a merchant vessel with him on board. In the six months before September 1794, the month of O'Brien's death, three merchant vessels outward bound from Cork are recorded as having been taken by the French: the *Quaker* bound for Barbados, taken by the French vessels *Le Tribune* and *L'Eperion* on 23 March; the *Jeney*, bound for Oporto, taken by *La Fraternité* on 24 March; and the sloop *Freedom*, bound for San Sebastian, taken by *La Bellona* on 27 April.[27] Was Digby O'Brien on board one of these vessels travelling abroad on business? Regardless of the detail of his capture or the reason for his imprisonment, he died of unknown causes in the prison at the French port of Brest in September 1794.

Richard Barrett withdrew from the partnership on 1 August 1799, leaving William Beamish and William Crawford to lead the business from then on. The initial agreement between the four partners allowed for a review after seven years and gave an option to discontinue the arrangement if the business had not proved profitable. However, the Cork Porter Brewery made substantial profits on its trade from its first year: £5,884 in 1793 and £9,124 in 1794, growing steadily to £32,367 in 1798. Although the figure for 1799 fell somewhat, to £23,484, the venture had proved a remarkable success. In September 1798, seven years after first agreeing terms and the purchase of Aylmer Allen's brewery, the three surviving partners had finalised the purchase of the brewery and had agreed to continue in business for a further twenty-four years.[28]

Barrett's departure does not seem to have been acrimonious. The deed drawn up on his departure notes that 'although no disagreement hath arisen between the said copartners the said Richard Barrett hath for some time past been anxious to retire from Business'.[29] His one-third share in the brewery was valued at £21,000 and he was to be paid in instalments of £1,500 on 1 February and 1 August each year until the full amount had been paid. In addition, he would be paid interest at 6 per cent per year on the outstanding balance. This was a substantial return for Barrett on his eight years' involvement with the brewery. It was also a condition of his retirement package that he would not, for twenty-two and a half years in any place in Munster, become involved in any business of brewing or malting.

By 1800 the Cork Porter Brewery had enjoyed eight years of steady growth, reaching sales of over 60,000 barrels of porter in that year. It was the principal supplier of porter in Cork city and it was developing an increasing network of agencies throughout the south of Ireland while also growing an export trade. The firm had also traded very profitably from the start, and by 1800 William Beamish and William Crawford had a surplus of £10,088 shared between them for that year. In accordance with the initial partnership agreement of 1792, all profits were added to the 'general stock' of the firm in the first seven years (see Table 3.6).

Table 3.6
Sales and profits, 1793–1800

BREWERY YEAR	SALES (Barrels)	PROFIT
1793	12,003	£5,884
1794	21,688	£9,124
1795	26,412	£14,007
1796	43,911	£22,160
1797	46,778	£26,406
1798	50,549	£32,367
1799	55,103	£23,484
1800	63,230	£10,088

The firm's success was partially built on the changed system of taxing beer that from 1791 favoured Irish producers over their English rivals, but also on the skill of the brewers at the Cork Porter Brewery – Digby O'Brien, Richard Barrett and head brewer John Topp – who produced a porter that could rival and surpass the best that could be imported from London. The economy of Cork city and the farming areas of the south of Ireland were enjoying a boom from the demand created by Britain's ongoing war with France, and while war created risks for merchants, as evidenced by the imprisonment and death of Digby O'Brien, the potential for profit outweighed that risk. Unrest within Ireland in 1796 with the attempted landing of a French invasion force on the Beara peninsula, subsequent landings in Mayo and the United Irishmen's uprising of 1798 were the political backdrop to the first years of the brewery's trade. The retirement of Richard Barrett and the beginning of William Beamish and William Crawford's dual control of the ongoing fortunes of the Cork Porter Brewery coincided with the passing of the Act of Union in 1800.

4

Ireland's Leading Brewery
1800–1828

From the Act of Union in 1800 to the year of William Beamish's death (1828), the Cork Porter Brewery was Ireland's leading brewery and one of the biggest in the newly created United Kingdom of Great Britain and Ireland. Cork's economy flourished during the Napoleonic Wars, and the brewery's sales soared in the years before the Battle of Waterloo.

Following the retirement of Richard Barrett from the partnership in 1800, Beamish & Crawford was born. The brewery expanded and in 1813 the rival River Lee Porter Brewery was taken over. In 1828 brewery co-founder William Beamish died, and his third son, Francis Bernard, became the acting partner in the firm on behalf of the Beamish family. William Crawford died in 1834 and was succeeded as acting partner by his son, William Crawford (junior).

War and peace

The first half of the period under discussion was a time of general economic well-being and growth, especially in Cork. The population of the city continued to grow, although at a lesser rate than in previous decades, increasing from about 60,000 in 1800 to nearly 75,000 people twenty-five years later. The harbour was thriving from its position as a major provisioning centre for British naval and merchant fleets, and from 1793 to 1815, the period of the Napoleonic Wars between Britain and France, Cork city and its port, its merchants, its butchers, its coopers and the farmers of its hinterland enjoyed a boom. There was an increased demand for agricultural produce from the British domestic market and from the military, and output grew as prices increased with a consequent rise in the wages paid to agricultural labourers. In addition to demand for beef, butter, pork, oatmeal and beer, the hostilities also led to a need for ship repair facilities, sailcloth, rope, textiles and gunpowder, which Cork and its environs was able to supply.

The strategic importance of Cork led to major works of fortification being built

The harbour at Cove, from J.S. Coyne, *The Scenery and Antiquities of Ireland, Vol. II* (London, 1842).

in the later eighteenth and early nineteenth centuries. A large fort was built on Spike Island in the lower harbour; the island of Hawlbowline was developed as a major naval base; the headlands at both sides of the entrance to Cork Harbour were fortified; and a new barracks was built on the north side of Cork city, completed in 1806. The town of Cove (Cobh), which had been a small fishing village up to the 1770s, was transformed into a large and busy port town. Major defensive works were also undertaken on the west Cork islands of Bere and Whiddy, as those islands and Bantry Bay became another important strategic naval base. Works on this scale in the Cork region were a further significant boost to the local economy, as was the frequent presence in the city of over 4,000 soldiers in its two barracks. This boom continued, with minor interruptions, until 1815, when the Battle of Waterloo brought an end to over twenty years of war between Britain and France.

During the years 1799 to 1801, parts of Ireland suffered famine conditions and at least 40,000 people died, with some estimates as much as double this number.[1] This situation is reflected in the price the brewery was paying for barley in the years between 1798 and 1801: the price rose almost threefold from an average of 10s 2d per barrel in 1798 to 29s 2d the following year. It fell to 21s 2d in 1799 and rose again in 1800 to 27s 3d per barrel. Sales of porter fell in 1801 but recovered strongly the following year to continue their upward trajectory. The closure of the Sadleirs' cotton factory in Cork in 1801, which left thousands without work, may have been a contributing factor in the fall in sales that year.

After Waterloo

The year 1815 is regarded as a watershed in Irish economic and social history. The prosperity that had lasted for over two decades came to an end in this year when the Duke of Wellington won his famous victory against the French at Waterloo in June. The Treaty of Paris, signed in November 1815, brought an official end to hostilities and Napoleon was exiled to Saint Helena, where he died six years later. Peace reduced the British demand for provisions for its fleets, which hit Cork severely, as a significant portion of its business was dependent on this wartime demand. Troop numbers in the Cork area were greatly reduced, and while Cork Harbour continued to be a naval base of some importance, the level of activity and investment reached during the war years would not be seen again until the outbreak of the First World War a century later.

The downturn that followed the end of war is reflected in the level of sales from the Cork Porter Brewery. In 1814 sales had reached a peak of 134,039 barrels (a level not surpassed again until 1902), but in the following year they fell by 11.5 per cent to 118,689 barrels. By 1823 sales had fallen from their 1814 peak by over 56 per cent to 58,646 barrels. It is interesting that the fall in sales was under way before the fateful (for Cork merchants as well as for the tens of thousands of military casualties) Battle of Waterloo in June 1815. The Cork Porter Brewery year ended on the first Monday of August each year, and while sales for the year 1814–5 fell by 11.5 per cent, the sales of only six weeks of that year followed the battle, which happened on 18 June. Therefore, the fall in demand had set in some time before Wellington's final victory. This fits the argument that economic decline, such as it was, had already begun before 1815 and that the decline was not as severe as is sometimes claimed.[2]

The provisions trade had been in decline from 1813, but the growing trade to Britain in live cattle compensated for this fall. Butter exports from Cork continued to do well, and as exports of pork declined, a growing trade in processed pork, in the form of bacon and ham, and in live pigs more than made up the difference. The fall in prices for agricultural produce was more significant than any fall in volume, and this also led to a fall in agricultural wages. Ireland's economy continued to grow, albeit at a slower pace, in the post-war years, but the economic impact of the peace was uneven and the Cork region probably suffered disproportionately. The situation was not helped by disastrous cereal and potato harvests in 1816 and 1817 caused by two successive summers of cold, wet weather. The resultant shortages caused the deaths of over 50,000 people in Ireland and contributed to an economic gloom also felt in Britain and Europe. Poor potato harvests led to further mini-famines in the 1820s. The first surge in emigration from Ireland began in this period – it is estimated that 1.5 million people left Ireland in the years between 1815 and the Great Famine of the mid-1840s.[3]

By the mid-1820s the remaining tariffs that had protected Irish manufacturers for the first twenty-five years after the Act of Union were removed and the surviving textile industries in the Cork region suffered under increased British competition, resulting in job losses for many in those industries. Transport between Ireland and Britain was being revolutionised with the increasing use of steam-powered vessels and this also opened Ireland to greater British competition at a time when British industrial productivity was growing. Distilling continued to do well in Ireland and particularly in Cork in the 1820s, but brewing production failed to reach the heights of the pre-1815 period. In the years 1820 to 1828 the Cork Porter Brewery sold an annual average of 66,211 barrels, in contrast to an annual average of 104,645 for the period 1810 to 1818.

It is against this background of war and peace, industrial change, commercial readjustment, economic boom and not quite bust that almost three decades of the Cork Porter Brewery's story, from 1800 to the death of William Beamish in 1828, is set.

Cover of the deed of co-partnership, dated 5 November 1801, between William Beamish and William Crawford. (CCCA/Authors)

The era of Beamish and Crawford begins

Following the retirement of Richard Barrett from the partnership, William Beamish and William Crawford had a new deed of co-partnership drawn up in 1801 and this was to operate for thirty-one years, dating from 1 August 1800.[4] This new agreement is in most respects similar to the original 1792 arrangement, with the added proviso that if either of the two partners were to die during the life of the agreement, his heirs were to get £15,000 in addition to any share in the business. When the deed of co-partnership was signed by the two partners in November 1801, the business was valued at £86,400.[5] On 6 July 1822 this partnership agreement was amended and it was agreed that when either of the two partners died, £80,000 (Irish currency) would be written off the value of the firm as the valuation of capital stock was greatly in excess of the true value.[6]

Rebuilding, remodelling and extending the facilities on the site began as soon as the partners in the Cork Porter Brewery first acquired the premises of Aylmer Allen's brewery in 1791. A number of adjacent properties were acquired and incorporated into the brewery complex. This process continued during the following years, and by 1802 a significant block of properties had been added to the brewery complex, extending from Allen's Lane to Lamley's Lane, as well as a number of smaller lots to the east, which extended the brewery further towards South Main Street. The almost continuous acquisition of small property lots is clear from the detail of the leases of those lots described in a summary account of the firm's title to its properties.[7] A plan drawn in January 1802 (p. 59) shows the detailed layout of the brewery, and when contrasted with the plan of 1792 (p. 41), it shows the extent of building and expansion in the first ten years.[8]

Physical expansion

The 1802 plan notes that the brewery area is 73,000 square feet, or a little over 8,100 square yards, which is approximately 50 per cent more extensive than the brewery had been ten years before. The properties acquired at the northern boundary of the brewery between Allen's Lane and Lamley's Lane and extending from South Main Street westwards to the River Lee are labelled as 'Old Cellar', 'Working Cellar', 'Old House' and 'Yard'. The working cellar is clearly already in use and the remaining buildings have yet to be assigned a function. The porter cellars shown in the northwestern part of the 1792 plan have been replaced by a working cellar, 175 feet long, and a tun room. The tun room is shown to have an area of 1,342 square feet with two tuns, approximately 20 feet each in diameter. The two millhouses shown on the 1792 plan are shown in the same location on the 1802 plan and are now called malt mills. Two mills are shown in one of these buildings, while there appears to be one mill in the other building. The malt for brewing was milled here before being transferred to the adjoining tun room.

The two vat rooms shown in the central area of the 1792 brewery have been converted into one larger vat room over 122 feet in length containing seven vats, each with a diameter of about 15 feet. The 1792 porter cellar labelled 'I' has become

---

Facing page, from top:

Title, and detail, of the plan of the Cork Porter Brewery, drawn in January 1802 by P. Aher. (CCCA/Dori O'Connell)

Later copy of 1802 Aher plan of the Cork Porter Brewery. (CCCA/Dori O'Connell)

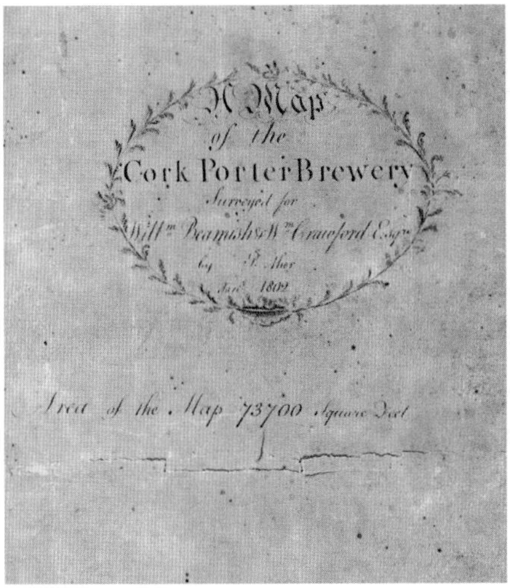
A Map
of the
Cork Porter Brewery
Surveyed for
Area of the Map 73700 Square Feet

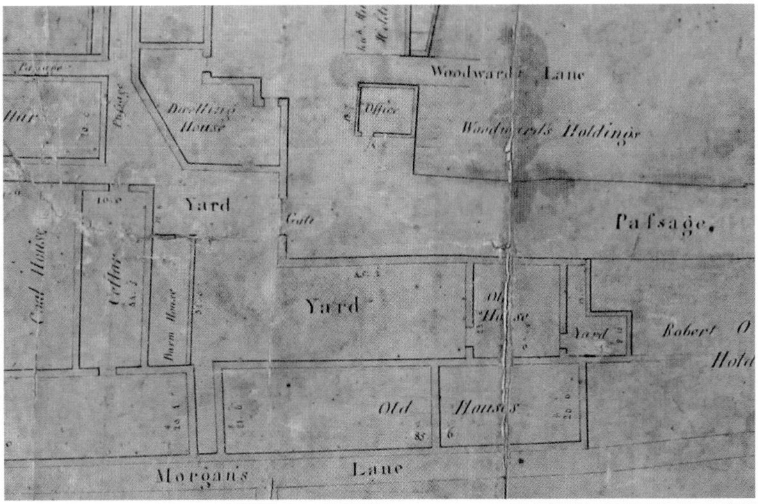
Woodwards Lane
Dwelling House
Office
Woodwards Holdings
Yard
Gate
Pafsage.
Coal House
Cellar
Barm House
Yard
Old House
Yard
Robert O
Old Houses
Morgan's Lane

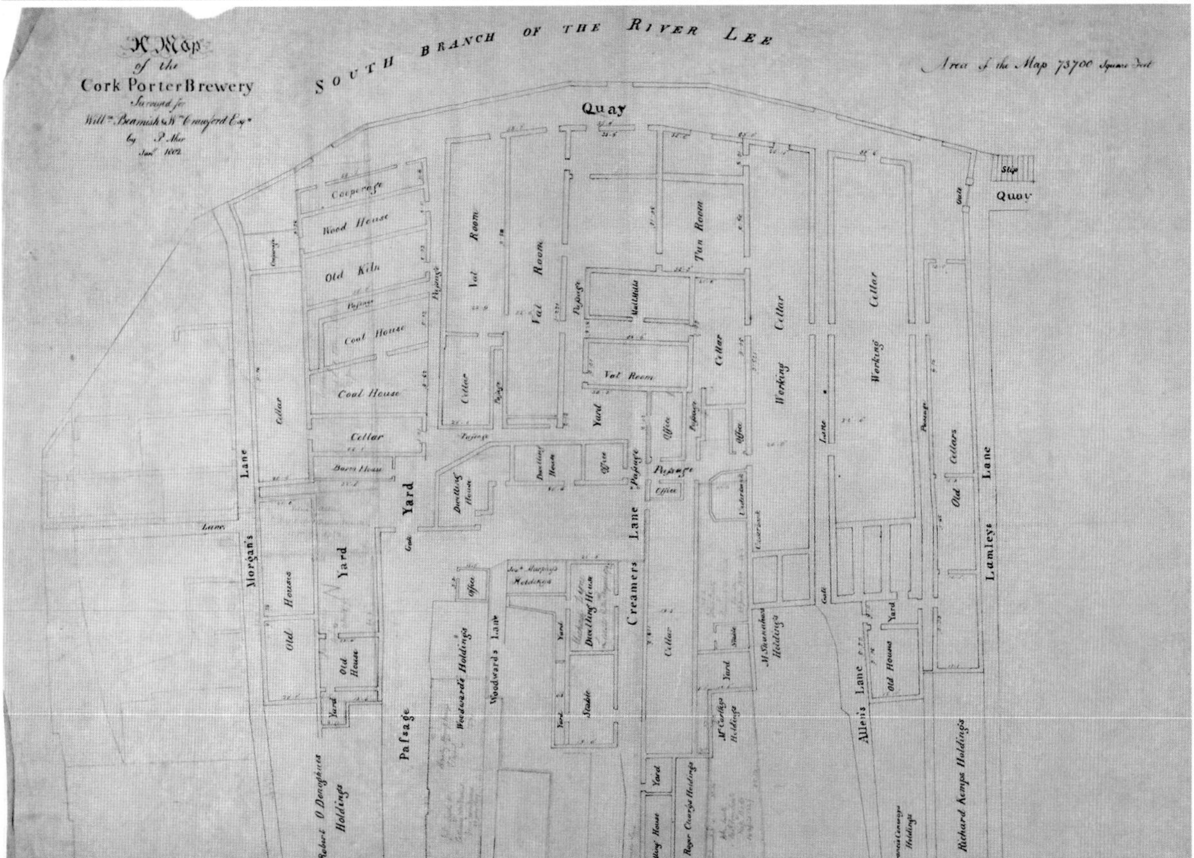
A Map
of the
Cork Porter Brewery
SOUTH BRANCH OF THE RIVER LEE
Area of the Map 73700 Square Feet
Quay
Slip
Quay
Cooperage
Wood House
Old Kiln
Coal House
Coal House
Cellar
Barm House
Vat Room
Vat Room
Tun Room
Vat Room
Cellar
Working Cellar
Working Cellar
Yard
Office
Dwelling House
Old Cellars
Morgan's Lane
Lane
Yard
Old Houses
Old House
Yard
Creamers Lane
Lane
Lamleys Lane
Allen's Lane
Old House
Woodwards Lane
Woodward's Holdings
Dwelling House
Stable
Cellar
Pafsage
Robert O Donoghues Holdings
Dwelling House
Yard
Roger Cleary's Holdings
Richard Kemps Holdings
Gate
South Main Street
Scale of Feet

another vat room with four vats, while the central 1792 malthouse has become a third vat room containing five vats.

The southern range of buildings and yards shown on the 1792 plan has been much altered by 1802. The small cooperage that had occupied a small building in the northwest corner of the brewery in 1792 has been moved to a building and yard in the southwest corner of the 1802 brewery. A large cellar 90 feet in length and a smaller cellar have replaced the old southern malthouse. The old malt kiln is obviously disused and buildings for the storage of coal, wood and barm have been built in the yard and steep yard that adjoined the malthouse. Malting ceased in the two malthouses on the brewery site in 1796.

The acquisition of buildings along the north side of Cremer's Lane, extending eastwards to the west side of South Main Street, allowed for the building of a further large cellar in that area and further properties have been acquired on the southern side of the lane to allow for future expansion. A number of lanes and passages are shown on the 1802 plan as giving access to the brewery complex. Towards the southern end

Left: Date stone on steam-engine house. (Authors)
Below: The engine house and its chimney, *c.* 1920. (Courtesy Mike Hannon)
Right: This building housed the first steam engine installed in the brewery in 1818. (Authors)

of the brewery, a passageway about 20 feet wide is shown running westwards from South Main Street and then turning northwards into an enlarged Cremer's Square. This passageway has a gate on South Main Street. North of this passageway, a narrow lane called Woodward's Lane runs towards Cremer's Square from the street. Cremer's Lane is next, running from the street to Cremer's Square, and north of this Allen's Lane is shown, with a gate where it meets the brewery buildings. The rest of this lane, running westwards to the river, has become a passageway subsumed into the brewery complex. Between Allen's Lane and Lamley's Lane, another very narrow passage or laneway runs from South Main Street westwards to the river. This passage has been walled off where it enters the brewery complex, and as with Allen's Lane, most of its length has been subsumed as a passage between brewery buildings. Elsewhere this is named as Franklin's Lane.[9] The northern boundary of the brewery is formed by Lamley's Lane, which runs from South Main Street westwards to the river, where a slipway and quay are shown.

Work on improving the brewery clearly continued after 1802, but apart from the detail on the brewery plans of the 1820s and 1839 (see Chapter 5), information on building and expansion in the surviving brewery records is sparse. A new lifting engine was purchased for £629.8.0 on 20 April 1805 and two new vats costing £487 were also paid for on that date.[10] A large steam engine was installed, probably in 1818, the date inscribed on the engine house, and this was used for some years in conjunction with horse whims, horse-powered lifting apparatus that had previously provided lifting power.[11] In 1827 a new steam engine was bought from Jonah Davis for £1,010.[12]

Production and sales

The growth and expansion of the brewery buildings ran parallel with a sustained growth in production and sales, at least until 1814. In 1806 the brewery sold over 100,000 barrels of porter for the first time. After a small drop the following year, sales picked up again in 1808 and grew to a peak of over 134,000 barrels in 1814. Production was matching the levels achieved by the famous London porter breweries in the previous century and the Cork Porter Brewery was Ireland's biggest brewer. This level of sales was not achieved again until the early 1900s. Between 1814 and 1828, when William Beamish died, sales declined steadily with some fluctuations and stood at 72,399 barrels in 1828.

John Topp, who had been appointed head brewer in September 1791, continued in that position throughout the period 1800 to 1828, on an average salary of about £1,000 per year. In addition, he continued to receive an annual bonus of 3d for every barrel of porter sold, almost doubling his annual income from the brewery. This annual bonus had fallen from the peaks of over £1,500 in the period 1813 to 1815

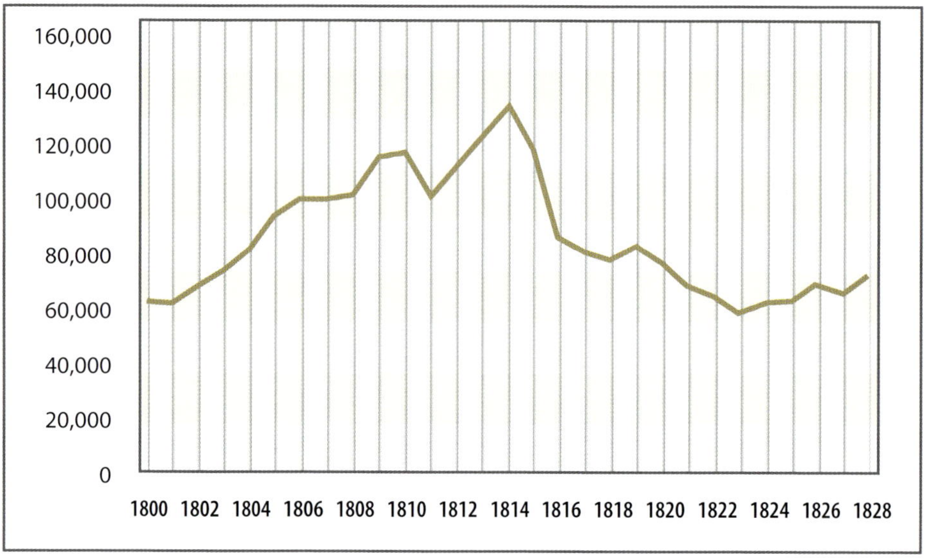

Beamish & Crawford sales (in barrels), 1800–28.

to an average of about half that in the five years to 1828. Topp had overseen the first brewings and had brewed a consistently good product since 1792, which had seen the brewery grow to being Ireland's largest at its peak.

The River Lee Porter Brewery

In 1813 William Beamish and William Crawford completed their first takeover of a rival brewery with the acquisition of the River Lee Porter Brewery. This latter concern was established in 1796 when Charles Henry Leslie, John Moore Travers, Isaac Morgan, Joseph Reeves, Thomas Townsend Somerville, William Bagnell and Henry Persse formed a partnership 'for the purpose of carrying on and exercising the trade of Porter Brewers'.[13] (Charles Henry Leslie and John Moore Travers had, in 1794, established the gunpowder mill at Ballincollig that later became the Royal Gunpowder Mills.) They built their brewery on a plot of land acquired from Atiwell Hayes, a miller and brewer, at the corner of the Mardyke and Prospect Row (a number of the brewery buildings survive and are today occupied by the Tyndall National Institute). The make-up of the partnership changed a number of times during the seventeen-year life of the brewery, and when they sold to Beamish & Crawford in 1813, the surviving four partners were Charles Henry Leslie, John Moore Travers, Joseph Reeves and William Maxwell.

Despite the rapidly growing market for porter in the later 1790s and the level of investment in their enterprise, put at £36,000,[14] the venture failed and Beamish & Crawford bought it for £15,000. No porter was brewed on the site after that, but the Cork Porter Brewery continued to produce malt there and use the buildings for

Above: The buildings of the former River Lee Porter Brewery on Prospect Row, acquired by Beamish & Crawford in 1813, *c.* 1960. (Courtesy Mike Hannon)

Right, from top: Commemorative jug marking the opening of the River Lee Porter Brewery in 1796. (Beamish & Crawford Brewery Collection/Authors) Detail of the jug showing the inscription 'Success to the River Lee Porter Brewery'. (Beamish & Crawford Brewery Collection/Dori O'Connell)

grain storage. A contemporary document explained the failure of the brewery thus:

> Messrs Beamish & Crawford who also traded as Porter Brewers and Maltsters having been previously firmly and so extensively established in the trade that Messrs Leslie and Co. found their concern [the River Lee Porter Brewery] was not as lucrative as they expected.[15]

As part of the transaction, Beamish & Crawford also purchased two malthouses on Rutland Street for £8,000. These had been built around 1792 by Joseph Reeves, who sold them to the River Lee Porter Brewery partnership, of which he was part, in 1796.[16]

Distribution and early ties

A number of brewery journals and ledgers from the early 1800s survive and give a relatively good level of detail on day-to-day sales to city customers, shipments to agents and wholesalers, summaries of annual accounts and balance sheets.[17] While the level of information is not consistent for every year, it is clear that within fifteen years of its foundation, the firm had created a complex but efficient business that had the lion's share of the city trade and had developed a network of agents that supplied customers in large parts of County Cork at a time when transport was still a daily challenge. Porter was also being shipped to ports elsewhere in Ireland and an export trade had been developed.

From the mid-1800s, the larger breweries in Cork were engaged in a race to establish ties with all public houses in their areas of distribution, involving outright purchase, mortgaging and writing off debt in return for an exclusivity for their beers. However, there is clear evidence that the Cork Porter Brewery was establishing a 'tie' with a number of its customers from at least 1799. A fragmentary brewery document from that year shows that £2,351.16.6 was paid out to a number of public houses as an advance towards full or partial payment for their licence.[18] On the surviving part of the document, forty-six names are shown with the amount paid to each, totalling £323, the individual amounts varying between £4.10.11 and £68.5.0, for an average of £7.0.5 each. Most of these houses were in the city, but others were located in Douglas, Passage, Carrigaloe, Cove (Cobh), Midleton, Castletownroche, Fermoy, Mallow and Macroom (shown as Macromp). The total brought forward from the missing section of the document is £2,028.16.6, and if the average payment of £7.0.5 to the forty-six named customers is applied to that sum, then a further 289 separate payments are suggested, for a total of 335 in all. Though this number seems large, given the actual total of public house licences paid for by the brewery in later years, the total sum of £2,351.16.6 paid out by the brewery is a significant expenditure and the return must have been an arrangement for exclusive supply for the year at least.

Between 29 September and 7 November 1804, the brewery paid £5,684.5.0 to 'Wm. Jones, Town Clerk' for 159 public house licences.[19] Each licence cost £35.15.0 and 159 publicans' names are listed, twenty of whom were women. All of the houses are in Cork city and its immediate surrounds. Again, it is to be presumed that in return for paying for the licence, the publican came to an exclusive arrangement with the brewery for at least that year. Between December 1806 and January 1807, the brewery accounts show payments of £42.12.2 to 173 individuals for licences, a total of £7,544.4.10.[20]

Edward Wakefield, who published a statistical and political survey of Ireland in 1812, visited the Cork Porter Brewery in 1808 and 1809 in the course of his work and remarked: 'They purchase no public-houses, but advance money for licences:

30 guineas is the price of a licence in the city.'[21] While there is no year-to-year evidence in the surviving brewery records of ongoing annual payments for licences, it probably continued until more formal tied-house arrangements became the norm. A development of the tie is suggested by a document from September 1814, whereby Cornelius Leary of the Watercourse mortgaged his premises to the brewery because of debt.[22] In addition to paying off his mortgage, Leary undertook to deal exclusively with the brewery. Arrangements such as this became more common in subsequent years. As Lynch and Vaizey remark, 'Indebtedness was the origin of the tie in most instances, and therefore its increase would tend to be associated with the years of extremely bad trade from 1815 onwards.'[23]

Customers in 1804–5

To show the number and spread of brewery customers in this early period, the names and addresses of all customers (excluding non-city agents and wholesalers) appearing in the accounts for two three-month periods, May to July 1804 and January to March 1805, were noted. While most are publicans, it is clear that a proportion are individual domestic customers, such as William Crawford, Merchants' Quay; William Beamish, Beaumont; the Earl of Cork; and the bankers Sir Richard Kellett and George Newenham. It was common for larger houses to provide porter or weaker table beer for their servants and other domestic employees as part of their daily food allowance.

In all, 274 customers are named, most in the city and inner suburbs, but also some in outlying towns and villages (see Appendix C). While not a complete list of Cork's public houses, it shows those with whom the brewery dealt and indicates the density and distribution of public houses in the city in the first decade of the nineteenth century. The list shows fifteen public houses on George's Street (now Oliver Plunkett Street), twelve in Blackpool, eleven on South Main Street, nine each on Blarney Lane and Mallow Lane, seven each on Bandon Road, North Main Street and in Passage and a lesser number on scores of other streets and lanes.

Agents and wholesalers

As production grew the brewery expanded its network of agents and wholesalers outside the city and the volume of porter supplied to them continued to increase throughout the first fifteen years of the nineteenth century. Shipments are recorded as having been made to forty-six agents or wholesalers in the years between 1804 and 1813, but by far the greatest proportion went to Mallow (Charles Haines), Youghal (Thomas John), Midleton (J.W. Coppinger), Cove (Charles Owens), Kilworth (Bartholomew Symmonds/Simmons), Bandon (John Sweete), Kinsale (William Newman, replaced by John Spiller Newman, and George V. Dunn), Inishannon

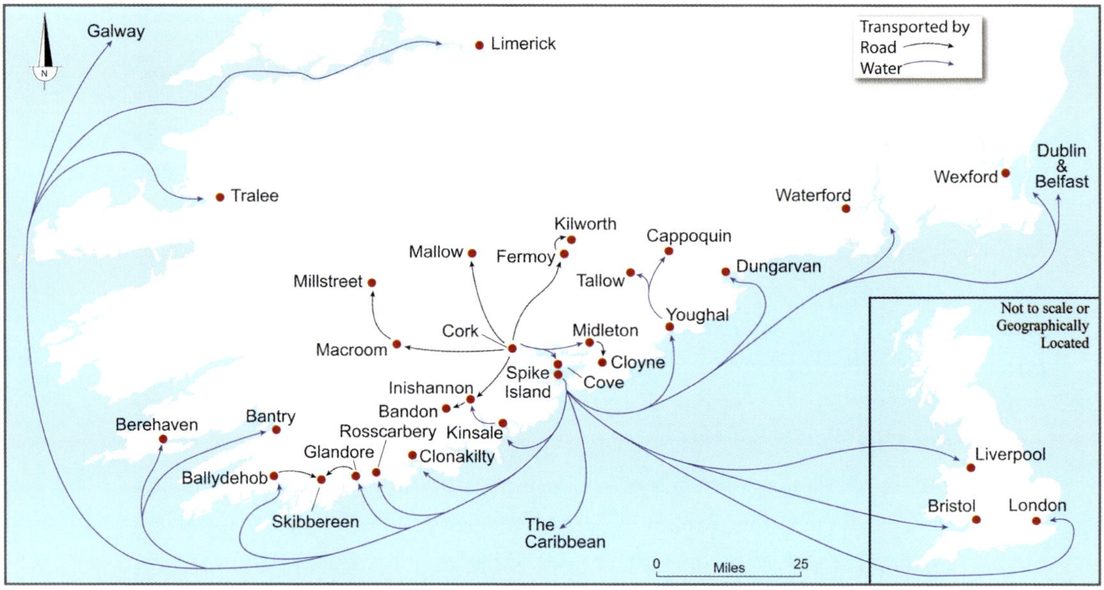

Map showing distribution of Beamish & Crawford products outside of Cork city by road and water transport, 1792–1812. (Map drawn by Michael Murphy)

(William Orr, Jr.) and Macroom (Robert McCarthy, David Barry). (See Appendix D for a complete list of agents and wholesalers supplied from 1804 to 1813.) For the brewery year 1807, for example, 35,751 barrels of porter (of a total 99,889 barrels sold) are recorded as having been shipped to agents and wholesalers outside of Cork city. Table 4.1 shows the quantities and proportions of those 35,751 barrels that went to each location in that year.

Of the twenty-one locations in Ireland to which shipments were made, only those to Mallow, Kilworth, Macroom and Millstreet can definitely be said to have been transported by road. The other shipments were made primarily by sea and river. The road from Cork city to Inishannon and onwards to Bandon and Skibbereen was much improved by the early 1800s and it is likely that some shipments were made by road to Inishannon and Bandon. The number and size of shipments to these two locations by 1811, as shown in Tables 4.2 and 4.3, suggest road transport. However, the return of empty barrels to the brewery was made by river and sea, at least in the earlier years of the period under discussion.[24] The Cork to Mallow road was clearly suitable for transporting porter by cart, as was the Cork to Kilworth road, the first stage of a roadway to Dublin by way of Clonmel. The Macroom road was likewise of a standard to take wheeled carts from 1800 at least. Shipments of porter to Mallow, Kilworth and Macroom were far more frequent than to other locations and the daily quantities transported were much smaller than those shipped by sea to Youghal or Cove, for example.

Table 4.1

Porter supplied to agents/wholesalers, 1807

LOCATION	NUMBER OF BARRELS	PERCENTAGE OF TOTAL
Mallow	5,721	16%
Youghal	4,532	12.7%
Midleton	4,520	12.6%
Cove	3,694	10.3%
Kilworth	3,144	8.8%
Bandon	3,009	8.4%
Kinsale	2,683	7.5%
Limerick	2,096	5.7%
Inishannon	1,347	3.8%
Macroom	1,189	3.3%
Belfast	709	2.0%
Clonakilty	670	1.9%
Galway	634	1.8%
Berehaven	595	1.7%
Bantry	580	1.6%
Coleraine	150	0.4%
Spike Island	132	0.4%
Waterford	130	0.4%
Tralee	100	0.3%
Dublin	78	0.2%
Millstreet	38	0.1%

Tables 4.2 and 4.3 show the detail of shipments of porter to various agents and wholesalers during two months, September 1811 and March 1812. On almost every one of the twenty-five working days of September 1811, porter was transported to Mallow, Kilworth, Macroom and Inishannon and the same was true in March 1812, with the exception of Inishannon, to where shipments were made on seventeen of the possible twenty-six working days.

By the end of the eighteenth century, the old Irish-type cart with solid wooden wheels was giving way to the newer Scotch-type cart that had an iron axle and iron-bound spoked wheels. By the 1810s, carts of this type were most commonly used for the road transport of goods and could carry up to a ton in weight.[25] Four or five 45-gallon barrels of porter would have been the load for one of these carts, suggesting quite a number of daily cart journeys from the brewery to the individual agents serviced by road. The average number of barrels in a shipment transported to locations such as Youghal, Cove and Midleton clearly indicates transport by boat.

Table 4.2
Shipments to agents/wholesalers, September 1811

AGENT/WHOLESALER	NO. OF DAYS SHIPMENTS MADE	NUMBER OF BARRELS	LARGEST SHIPMENT	SMALLEST SHIPMENT	AVERAGE BARRELS PER SHIPMENT
Cove	8	859	120	39	107.37
Mallow	25	781	58	10	31.24
Midleton	8	682	90	57	85.25
Youghal	4	409	140	49	102.25
Kilworth	23	258	33	6	11.21
Macroom	22	224	25	1	10.18
Inishannon	22	220	62	1	10
Bandon	16	134	42	2	8.37
Tallow	2	84	82	2	42
Kinsale	7	74	34	2	10.57
Wexford	1	50	50	50	50

Table 4.3
Shipments to agents/wholesalers, March 1812

AGENT/WHOLESALER	NO. OF DAYS SHIPMENTS MADE	NUMBER OF BARRELS	LARGEST SHIPMENT	SMALLEST SHIPMENT	AVERAGE BARRELS PER SHIPMENT
Cove	8	888	144	24	111
Midleton	8	708	90	84	88.5
Mallow	25	635	51	10	25.4
Youghal	3	440	160	140	146.66
Bandon	15	384	130	2	25.6
Kilworth	26	239	24	2	9.19
Macroom	26	160	20	1	6.15
Kinsale	6	120	104	2	20
Inishannon	17	116	50	1	6.82
Tallow	2	88	80	8	44
Berehaven	1	83	83	83	83
Dungarvan	1	30	30	30	30
Clonakilty	1	2	2	2	2

Exports

The earliest specific reference to the export of porter from the Cork Porter Brewery dates to 1799, when a brewery journal notes the shipping of 100 barrels of porter to the island of Martinique on board the *William*, which sailed from Cork on 9 January of that year. The porter was charged at £1.9.3 per barrel and an extra 16s 3d was charged for each of the barrels.[26] It is likely that porter was being exported before this date – in 1792, for example, 1,200 barrels were supplied to 'the fleet'.[27] Two brewery journals covering the years 1804 to 1808 include detail on quite a number of cargoes exported from Cork, mainly, but not exclusively, to the Caribbean. In 1804 and 1805, cargoes of porter were exported to Liverpool, Swansea, Neith, Lisbon, Dominica, Trinidad, Barbados, New Orleans and New York, amounting to 1,170 barrels. Other shipments are also noted but the destination is not stated, so some of these could have been to Irish ports.[28] In the period 1805 to 1808, a number of export cargoes were also noted and the destinations named were Jamaica, Antigua, Trinidad and Tobago.

The nature of the Cork Porter Brewery's exports, as evidenced by surviving brewery documents, is supported by the remarks of John Carr, who, during a tour of the south and west of Ireland in 1805, wrote of the Cork breweries and noted: 'The Irish are naturally proud of saying that the Cork porter is exported to England; this exportation, however, is very trifling; but the export to the West-Indies and America is considerable … the annual export is nearly two thousand barrels.'[29] While detail is missing from the brewery records on exports to England during the first decades of the nineteenth century, it is likely that there was a trade of some significance. Beamish & Crawford had built a good reputation for its product, it was the biggest brewer of porter in Ireland at the time and sea connections between Cork and English ports, especially Bristol, were good and would have been availed of. A brewery balance sheet for the year 1798 shows William Thomas Locke of Newcastle owing £1,954.10.2 to the firm, presumably for porter delivered. The following year the debt outstanding stood at £1,458.18.3.[30] Brewery records show that Beamish & Crawford had an important agency in Bristol from at least 1842, but other sources show an agency there from 1820 whose trade was twice that of the Guinness agency.[31]

Joseph Coppinger, an Irish native who emigrated to America and wrote a practical guide to brewing in 1815, was aware of the success of the Beamish & Crawford brewery in Cork and used it as an example to American entrepreneurs of how investment in a porter brewery could pay off, citing not only their success in Ireland, but also in the British and Caribbean markets:

> When the mercantile house of Beamish & Crawford, of Cork, erected a porter brewery in that city, about twenty-five years ago, that establishment was the

> first of the kind in that town, and then stood alone, and notwithstanding that many large and rich ones in the same business have since been added, the original company have so progressed in fame and fortune, as to be now considered one of the first-rate breweries in Europe; and by the improved quality of their porter have, in a great degree, excluded the English from the West India market, their porter getting the preference there, as well as in Bristol and Liverpool, to which places large quantities are annually sent by that company.[32]

Prices

The standard cask size used by the brewery was the barrel or tierce, which at that time contained 45 gallons. A larger barrel known as a hogshead was also used, but usually for export orders and for shipping long distances by sea. The hogshead held one and a half times the volume of the barrel. From 1792 until 1812, the price charged to public houses and agents was £1.17.11 per barrel of 45 gallons. By 1804 the price charged to agents had been reduced to £1.13.0, a reduction of just under 13 per cent. These prices were in place until March 1812, when the publicans' price rose by 14.28 per cent to £2.3.4 per barrel and the price charged to agents rose by 16.66 per cent to £1.18.6.

Prices charged to exporters and to wholesalers who were not agents varied, and such customers also had to pay for the barrels in addition to their contents. The brewery's agents did not pay for the barrels, but as part of their contract with the brewery they were obliged to return the empties. On 30 November 1804, for example, a cargo of sixty hogsheads was shipped to Michael O'Brien, a wholesaler in Limerick. He was charged £2.16.10½ per hogshead, the equivalent of £1.17.11 per barrel, the price charged to publicans rather than the lower agents' price. In addition, he had to pay £1.8.0 per hogshead. The porter cost him a total of £187.13.9 but the barrels cost an extra £92.8.0 – almost 50 per cent more. To make an equivalent return on this porter in Limerick, it would have had to be sold at a significantly higher price than in Cork. On 30 March 1805 the same Michael O'Brien was charged £2.9.6 each, a reduction of 7s 4½d per unit, for sixty hogsheads. However, he again had to pay £1.8.0 per barrel. For a shipment of twenty hogsheads to Swansea on 24 November of that year, John Mitchell was charged the lesser price of £2.8.9 per hogshead and a lower price of £1.6.0 per barrel.[33]

Barrels were expensive and a large brewery like the Cork Porter Brewery had a significant amount of capital invested in them. The further barrels travelled to faraway customers, the longer it took for them to be returned, so more barrels had to be purchased to take up the slack. Ensuring the return of empty barrels was a constant priority, not only with distant agents, but also with city customers. At this time the brewery did not manufacture its own barrels, as its needs were being supplied by a number of independent city cooperages. The brewery did have a small cooperage and employed a number of coopers, but their work involved the repair of damaged barrels. The cost of barrels to the brewery is suggested by an entry in a brewery journal for 1 August 1807 when £2,072.10.0 was paid to H. Wigmore for 1,658 new barrels, a cost of £1.5.0 each.[34]

The war between Britain and France that continued until 1815 also impacted on the cost of barrels. Most barrels were made with oak staves imported from America, but due to attacks on American ships and the seizure of their cargoes by both French and British vessels, America introduced the Embargo Act in 1807, which made it illegal to export any goods from America. This resulted in a shortage of barrel staves

Notice, dated 10 December 1808, informing agents of the difficulties caused by the American Embargo Act of 1807, necessitating an increase in the cost of casks. (CCCA/Authors)

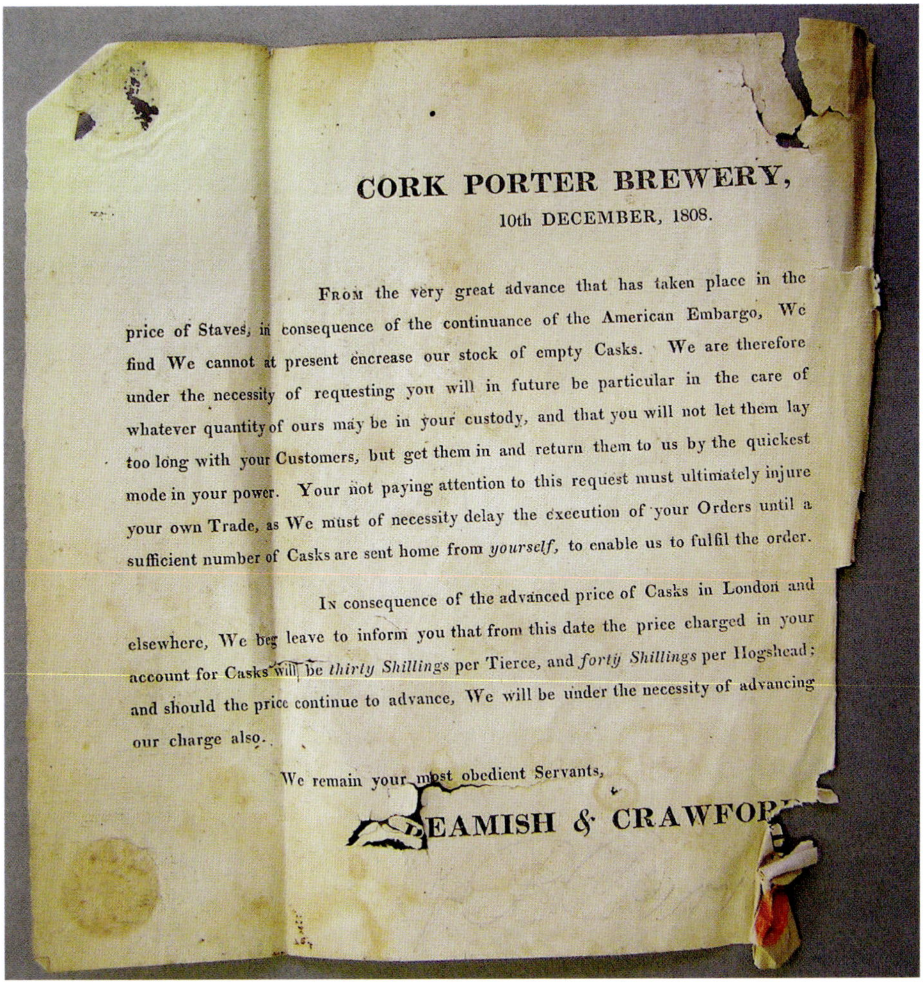

CORK PORTER BREWERY,
10th DECEMBER, 1808.

From the very great advance that has taken place in the price of Staves, in consequence of the continuance of the American Embargo, We find We cannot at present encrease our stock of empty Casks. We are therefore under the necessity of requesting you will in future be particular in the care of whatever quantity of ours may be in your custody, and that you will not let them lay too long with your Customers, but get them in and return them to us by the quickest mode in your power. Your not paying attention to this request must ultimately injure your own Trade, as We must of necessity delay the execution of your Orders until a sufficient number of Casks are sent home from *yourself*, to enable us to fulfil the order.

In consequence of the advanced price of Casks in London and elsewhere, We beg leave to inform you that from this date the price charged in your account for Casks will be *thirty Shillings* per Tierce, and *forty Shillings* per Hogshead; and should the price continue to advance, We will be under the necessity of advancing our charge also.

We remain your most obedient Servants,

BEAMISH & CRAWFORD

and made barrels more expensive to buy and repair. In December 1808, Beamish & Crawford issued a circular to their agents explaining their difficulty:[35]

> CORK PORTER BREWERY,
> 10th DECEMBER, 1808
>
> From the very great advance that has taken place in the price of Staves, in consequence of the continuance of the American Embargo, We find We cannot at present encrease [*sic*] our stock of empty Casks. We are therefore under the nesessity of requesting you will in future be particular in the care of whatever quantity of ours may be in your custody, and that you will not let them lay too long with your Customers, but get them in and return them to us by the quickest mode in your power. Your not paying attention to this request must ultimately injure your own Trade, as We must of necessity delay the execution of your Orders until a sufficient number of Casks are sent home from *yourself*, to enable us to fulfil the order.
>
> In consequence of the advanced price of Casks in London and elsewhere, We beg leave to inform you that from this date the price charged in your account for Casks will be *thirty Shillings* per Tierce, and *forty Shillings* per Hogshead; and should the price continue to advance, We will be under the necessity of advancing our charge also.
>
> We remain your most obedient Servants,
> BEAMISH & CRAWFORD

Barley, malt and hops

The level of detail in the surviving brewery records on barley purchases is quite varied for the period 1800 to 1828. During the 1806 brewery year, when 100,137 barrels of porter were sold, 31,607 barrels of barley were purchased at a cost of £25,139.7.7, an average of 15s 11d per barrel.[36] Seven suppliers are listed as having supplied the barley, and six of them were Beamish & Crawford agents: Richard Hungerford of Glandore, Charles Haines of Mallow, Bartholomew Simmons of Kilworth, Charles Owens of Cove, J.W. Coppinger of Midleton and John Mullanny of Cloyne. The seventh supplier was Samuel McCall. Elsewhere some detail is available from some years in the 1820s and a great variation in price from year to year is apparent. An average of 9s 8d per barrel was paid in 1823 on 56,170 barrels; 17s 1d per barrel in 1824 on 34,291 barrels; 19s 9d per barrel in 1825 on 54,281 barrels; and 30s 2d per barrel in 1828 on 25,881 barrels. The average price per barrel in the following two years fell to 22s 4d.[37] Two ledgers covering the years 1802 to 1822 and 1822 to 1836

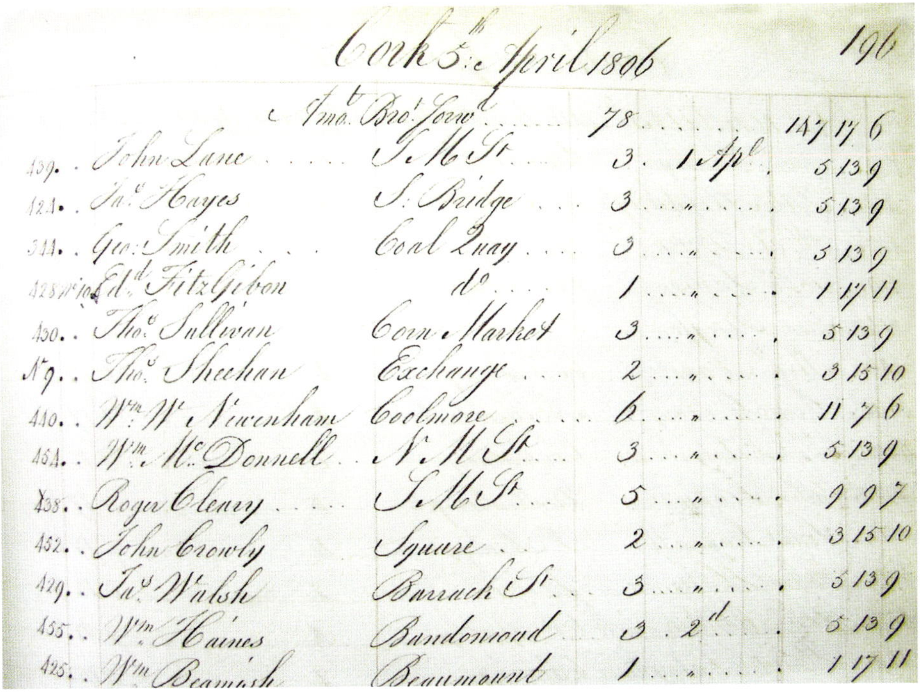

Cork 5th April 1806 — 196

	to Amo. Brot. Forwd.		78		147 17 6
439.	John Lane	S.M.St.	3.	1 Apl.	5 13 9
121.	Jn. Hayes	S. Bridge	3	"	5 13 9
311.	Geo: Smith	Coal Quay	3	"	5 13 9
428 W. 10	Edd. FitzGibbon	do.	1	"	1 17 11
450.	Thos. Sullivan	Corn Market	3	"	5 13 9
No. 9.	Thos. Sheehan	Exchange	2	"	3 15 10
440.	Wm. W. Newenham	Coolmore	6	"	11 7 6
464.	Wm. McDonnell	N.M.St.	3	"	5 13 9
438.	Roger Cleary	S.M.St.	5	"	9 9 7
452.	John Crowly	Square	2	"	3 15 10
429.	Jas. Walsh	Barrack St.	3	"	5 13 9
455.	Wm. Haines	Bandonroad	3	2d.	5 13 9
425.	Wm. Beamish	Beaumount	1	"	1 17 11

Sales entries in ledger for 5 April 1806. (CCCA/Authors)

note a figure for the total cost of malt used in porter production in each of those years.[38] These figures include the cost of barley, malthouse wages, malt duty and so on, but without any breakdown (see Table 4.4).

The rise or fall in malt costs does not always equate to the rise or fall in sales, as the sometimes great variation in costs relates not only to the amount of porter produced, but also to changes in the cost of barley from year to year. The carry-over of surplus barley or malt from one brewery year to the next would also have had an impact on the annual figure, as would costs relating to expenditure on malthouses. In 1806 County Cork accounted for 25 per cent of all malt produced in Ireland and Beamish & Crawford was producing the greatest proportion of this. In 1824, when production of porter was half of what it had been at its height in 1813–14, the Beamish & Crawford malthouses produced 48 per cent of the malt on which duty was paid in County Cork.[39]

These ledgers also note the total spent on hops in each of those years (1802 to 1828), but the quantities are not given. As noted in Chapter 3, the cost of hops varied greatly from year to year and also within a year, and consequently there is not always a correlation between the expenditure on hops and the volume of production. As with barley and malt, there was often a carry-over of hops from one brewery year to the next (see Table 4.4).

Table 4.4

Expenditure on malt and hops, 1802–28

YEAR	SALES (in barrels)	EXPENDITURE ON MALT (to the nearest £)	EXPENDITURE ON HOPS (to the nearest £)
1802	69,239	£80,011	£11,061
1803	74,074	£47,375	£18,547
1804	81,645	£65,197	£17,050
1805	94,142	£78,856	£16,631
1806	100,137	£117,424	£25,141
1807	99,889	£107,213	£19,881
1808	101,305	£95,281	£19,935
1809	115,496	£113,659	£14,162
1810	117,139	£131,577	£15,801
1811	102,473	£115,232	£18,818
1812	112,403	£118,729	£13,250
1813	123,054	£145,592	£30,439
1814	134,039	£184,096	£28,828
1815	118,689	£150,026	£28,259
1816	86,689	£78,220	£20,337
1817	80,884	£70,947	£22,861
1818	78,928	£77,606	£31,760
1819–20 (two years)	83,875 77,971	£203,285	£32,319
1821	69,517	£60,871	£9,535
1822	65,682	£58,735	£12,739
1823	58,646	£31,167	£1,987
1824	63,085	£53,497	£8,123
1825	63,890	£60,209	£14,264
1826	69,695	£56,868	£6,815
1827	66,778	£65,587	£7,678
1828	72,399	£57,485	£7,672

The Lee Mills

In the early 1820s, annual porter sales had fallen to about half of their peak figure in the previous decade. Profits had declined sharply in the years after 1816 and the firm operated at a loss between 1818 and 1820. However, the partners had accumulated a large surplus during the more profitable years and in 1825 they began building the Lee Mills, which were to become the largest flour mills in the Cork region. A mill had been developed on this site, part of the Rough Marshes, on the south side of the

The harbour at Cove, from G. N. Wright, *Ireland Illustrated, from original drawings, by G. Petrie RHA, W.H. Bartlett, & T.M. Baynes* (London, 1831).

north channel of the River Lee in the late 1780s by Atiwell Hayes. From 1813, when Beamish & Crawford purchased the adjacent River Lee Porter Brewery, it began acquiring the remaining lands of the Rough Marshes and by 1825 was in a position to embark on a major building project on the site.[40]

Flour milling had continued to be a profitable business following the economic downturn after 1815, with production and exports growing up to the mid-1820s. Beamish & Crawford clearly saw an opportunity to diversify, and from 1825 to 1831 it invested over £25,000 in building the Lee Mills, a striking complex of six- and seven-storey buildings built of local Old Red Sandstone and limestone. By this time steam power was being increasingly used in milling, but the wheels of the Lee Mills were powered by water.

The returns on these mills did not match the ambition of their construction. In a valuation of the premises in 1862, the valuer remarked that the mills 'were erected on a scale and at a cost more in keeping with the affluence of the Builders, than with

Ground plan of the Lee Mills and Lee Stores (formerly the River Lee Porter Brewery). (CCCA/Dori O'Connell)

GROUND-PLAN
of the
LEE MILLS
AND STORES
THE PROPERTY OF
Messrs Beamish & Crawford
Scale
B
B
B
C
MILL SIX FLOORS IN HEIGHT
OPEN YARD
LEE MILLS
No 3
A
SEVEN FLOORS IN HEIGHT
ARCHWAY UNDER
A
RIVER LEE
BRIDGE
KILN
No 2
MALT-STORE
KILN
BRIDGE
OPEN SPACE
YARD
YARD
KITCHEN
KITCHEN
PARLOR
PARLOR
OFFICE
OPEN YARD
BRIDGE
BRIDGE
ARCHITECT

Above: The Lee Mills, drawn in 1844 by William Roe. (Cork Public Museum)
Below: Detail from profit & loss account 1804–7. (CCCA/Authors)

the capabilities of its power & requirements and uses as a flour mill of the present times'.[41] Beamish & Crawford suspended its use of the mills in 1841, by which time it was calculated that a loss of £3,866 had been made on their working.[42] The detail of the machinery of the Lee Mills is set out in a document drawn up in 1842, when the mills were rented to Samuel Lane.[43]

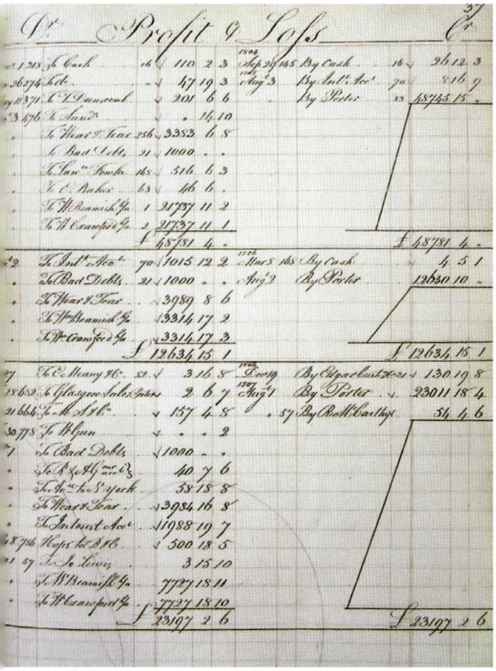

Dr. Profit & Loss Cr.

Profit and loss

The Cork Porter Brewery of Beamish & Crawford recorded substantial profits in most years from 1800 to 1828. The impact of the sharp fall in sales in the years after 1815 is reflected in the losses made in the years 1818 to 1820, following a sharp fall in profits in the previous two years. Between 1820 and 1822 the partners injected £30,478 of capital into the firm. Between 1800, when the partners first drew monies from the business, and 1818, they drew down a total of £549,526 – an average of £14,461 each per year.

From 1813 the eldest sons of the two brewery partners, William Beamish Jr. and William Crawford Jr., were paid an annual sum averaging about £2,000 each, suggesting that they were working for the firm. From the year 1823, only William Crawford Jr. is shown to be paid this salary.[44] Following the death of William

Beamish (senior) in 1828, it was his third son, Francis Bernard, rather than William (junior), who became the acting partner in the firm on behalf of the Beamish family. William Crawford Jr. became the acting partner on behalf of the Crawfords following the death of his father in 1834.

Table 4.5[45]

Profits and amounts credited to partners' accounts, 1800–28

YEAR	PROFIT (before deduction for wear and tear, bad debts, interest and credit to accounts of partners)	AMOUNT CREDITED TO PARTNERS (shared equally)
1800	£10,088	£10,088
1801	£35,183	£30,388
1802	£49,950	£44,024
1803	£54,048	£49,546
1804	£52,009	£47,362
1805	£48,745	£43,474
1806	£12,630	£6,628
1807	£23,011	£15,454
1808	£42,184	£36,194
1809	£42,214	£37,410
1810	£27,413	£21,992
1811	£23,619	£18,290
1812	£59,314	£54,238
1813	£39,234	£32,736
1814	£29,005	£21,594
1815	£27,364	£20,226
1816	£43,883	£34,836
1817	£27,682	£19,586
1818	£3,053	£5,458
1819	£0	£0
1820	£0	£19,350
1821	£32,160	(£24,746)
1822	£15,960	(£5,732)
1823	£31,442	£27,478
1824	£19,594	£14,186
1825	£12,031	£9,936
1826	£20,670	£20,208
1827	£41,738	£41,628
1828	£41,255	£39,586

5

Survival
1828–1863

From the death of William Beamish in 1828 to the accession of Richard Pigott Beamish and William Horatio Crawford, grandsons of the brewery founders, to the position of acting partners, effectively joint CEOs, in 1863, the firm survived rather than prospered. The five sons of William Beamish who inherited his half of the Cork Porter Brewery became engaged in a protracted dispute that hindered the development of the business at a time of challenging economic circumstances when unity of purpose, vision and strategic thinking were needed to guide the firm. By the mid-1830s the firm of Arthur Guinness had overtaken Beamish & Crawford in volume output and had embarked on a programme of expansion and export growth that eventually gave it a dominant position in Irish and world brewing. The second generation of Beamishes and Crawfords did not replicate their fathers' successes and failed to match the momentum of Guinness, thus ceding a dominance that, with appropriate management, could have been held and built upon.

The declining fortunes of the industrial economy of the Cork region from the mid-1820s, following on the severe economic downturn of the immediate post-war period of a decade before, saw sales of Beamish & Crawford porter fall to a low of 32,848 barrels in 1843 – less than a quarter of their peak of 134,039 in 1814. While the Great Famine of 1845 to 1849 did not unduly affect sales, the economic growth of the late 1850s had a very positive impact and brewery output grew again to over 100,000 barrels annually for the years 1858 to 1861. During the three decades up to 1863, the brewery expanded and extended its boundaries and renewed and upgraded some plant and equipment, but no more than was necessary to maintain production at a minimum standard. The old brewery buildings and plant were, as Richard Pigott Beamish later remarked, 'capable … of withstanding the effects of neglect for a considerable time'. [1]

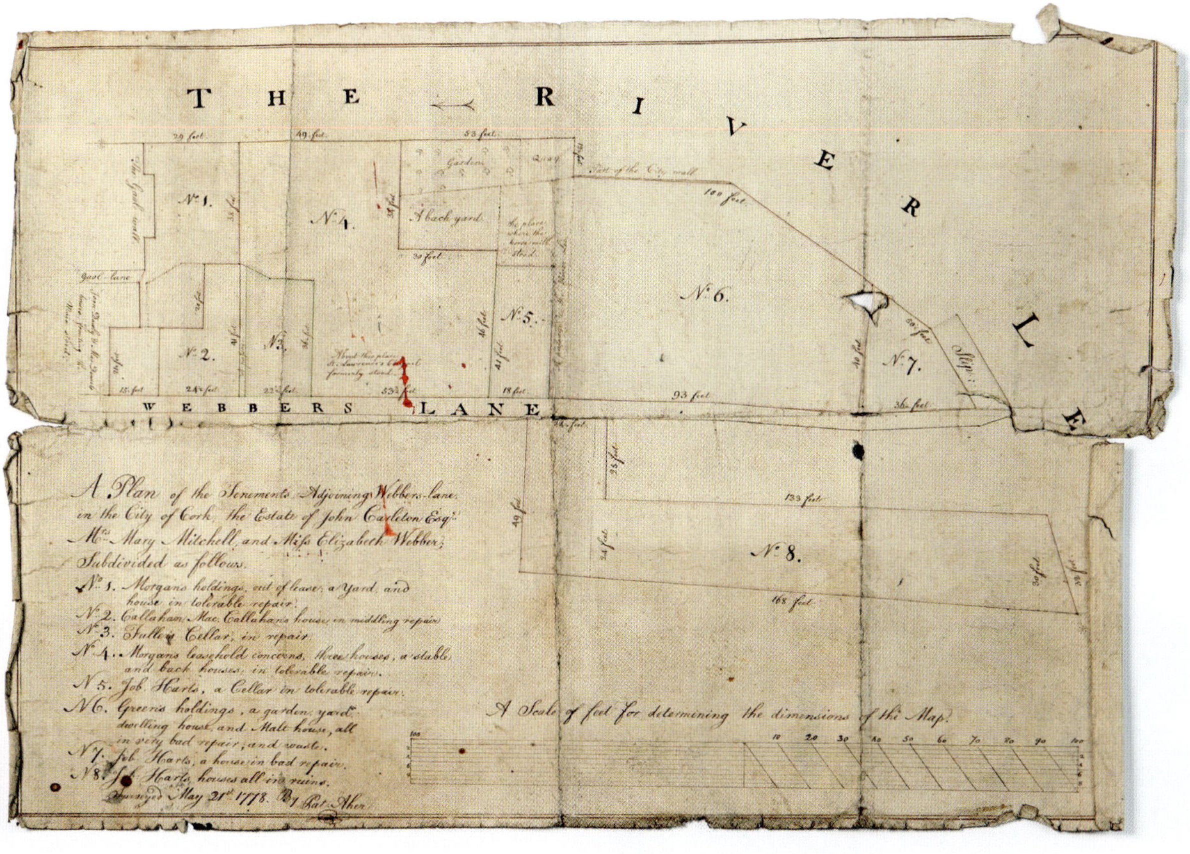

Plan, dated 21 May 1778, of plots of ground between Webber's (also St Lawrence's and Morgan's) Lane and the River Lee. By 1839 the brewery complex had expanded southwards to take in these plots. (CCCA/Dori O'Connell)

Economic context

By late 1820s the population of Ireland had passed 7 million and was to continue growing until the mid-1840s, when it reached an historic peak of 8.5 million, the fastest rate of population growth of any European country in the period. Most of this growth was in rural areas and amongst a population that was increasingly dependent on the potato as a staple food, which, at the outbreak of the Great Famine, accounted for a quarter of Irish agricultural output. There was great income inequality within the working population, with over 1 million agricultural labourers at the lowest level earning an annual income in the region of only £11. The lowest-paid full-time clerical employee in the brewery at the time, about whom some detail survives, was Richard Moore, who took up duty in 1831 on a weekly wage of 15s – the equivalent of £39 per year.[2] Manual workers in the brewery, many of whom would have been employed seasonally, would have earned less than that.

In the twenty-five years before the Famine, many of the industries that had developed in Ireland in the second half of the eighteenth and in the early nineteenth centuries fell into a decline from which some never recovered. The Cork region was particularly affected by this decline. For example, the once vigorous linen and cotton industries that had employed thousands of people in the city and county had all but disappeared by the mid-1800s. Cork was the country's leading centre for shipbuilding up to the 1840s, after which Belfast took the lead by adopting the newer technology of building with steel while the Cork shipbuilders continued to concentrate on wooden vessels. From the 1820s advances were made in steam-powered shipping and the crossings between Ireland and Britain became faster and more numerous. While this facilitated the growing exports of agricultural produce, it also contributed to an increase in the import of manufactured goods from Britain. British industry was enjoying a period of great advance, in contrast to the situation in Ireland, and cheaply made mass-produced goods were easily imported into Ireland. By the mid-1820s the last of the Irish protective tariffs on imports had been removed under the terms of the Act of Union, and this, coupled with improving transport links, gave British manufacturers a great advantage. The entrepreneurship and investment that had been a feature of Irish industrial growth from the middle of the eighteenth century was largely missing in the middle decades of the following century, and while agriculture and some manufacturing industries in certain areas prospered, there was a general decline in Irish industry throughout the nineteenth century.

The Famine of 1845 to 1849 falls in the middle of the period under discussion and is the defining event of nineteenth-century Ireland. The population fell from 8.5 million in 1845 to 6.5 million six years later, over 1 million of whom died, the others having emigrated. The population of Ireland continued to decline, though at a less precipitous rate, until the 1960s. Emigration contributed significantly to this decline – between 1850 and 1914 it is estimated that around 4 million people left the country, mostly travelling to Britain, America and Australia. The human impact of the Famine was incontestably horrific, but its economic impact was somewhat less cataclysmic. The overwhelming majority of the 1 million people who died of hunger and hunger-related diseases were poor, people who lived precariously on the margins, subsisting on potatoes grown on small plots, with rent paid in kind or labour, or with the small amounts of cash it was occasionally possible to earn. The majority of these people were not consumers of manufactured goods, they did not shop in the towns and villages or apparently consume the products of the commercial distilleries and breweries. Indeed, between 1846 and 1848, the worst years of the Famine, sales of Beamish & Crawford porter grew by over 19 per cent.

By the mid-1850s, most of the negative economic impacts of the Great Famine had been overturned and a general rise in wages contributed to an improvement in living standards. Agricultural output grew and average life expectancy improved from less than forty years on the eve of the Famine to about fifty by the 1870s. The number of people living in towns and cities grew as styles of land use changed, with increases in the size of holdings and a greater emphasis on livestock grazing, factors that contributed to the continuing decline in the proportion of the population living in rural areas. Literacy levels advanced with the growing impact of the national schools, and the increase in the circulation of newspapers, as well as the establishment of many new titles, contributed significantly to a growing enlightenment. While the country's roads were improved, the rapid expansion of the railway network from the 1840s was probably more significant in facilitating the rapid movement of passengers and goods – a great boon to brewers, who were then better able to penetrate distant markets. The Guinness brewery was especially successful in using the railways to distribute its product throughout Ireland and Britain as the firm grew to be the dominant Irish brewer in the later nineteenth century. Communication was also improved through the growth of the post office and telegraph network, the latter using the routes of the new railway lines to connect most cities and towns.

The Cork Porter Brewery, like all commercial concerns, was affected by the fortunes of the national and local economies, but it would be wrong to expect the year-to-year changes in sales of porter, for example, to always closely match the ups and downs of the economy, local or national. Other factors also had a bearing on the success or otherwise of the brewery. The disagreements of the second generation of Beamishes from the 1840s to the 1860s took away from their efficient oversight of the business, and an apparent reluctance to make large-scale investment in upgrading the brewery in those years also hindered the firm at a time when Guinness, their principal competitor, was transforming itself into a world leader in brewing.

From 1838 the phenomenal growth of the temperance movement led to a fall in sales of all alcoholic drinks throughout the country. The impact of the moralising crusade had all the weight of an economic downturn in its effects on the brewing and distilling industries.

The temperance movement[3]

Before the temperance crusade of Father Theobald Mathew (1790–1856) began in 1838, the efforts of anti-drink campaigners were largely focused on the consumption of spirits and were concerned with the excesses of the more 'respectable' classes of society. Drinking beer instead of stronger spirits was often encouraged, but by the time of the foundation of Father Mathew's Cork Total Abstinence Society in April 1838, teetotalism had become the aim and the focus had extended to all classes of society. The total abstinence movement was embraced by hundreds of thousands of people throughout Ireland. Father Mathew had a messianic influence and drew huge

Left: Father Theobald Mathew administers the temperance pledge. (Irish Capuchin Archives)
Right: The Total Abstinence Pledge of Thomas Kent, dated 12 April 1838. (Irish Capuchin Archives)

crowds to his public meetings, where his message and passion struck such a chord with his audiences that most of his listeners immediately signed the pledge to abstain from all alcoholic drinks. Within five years of the beginning of his crusade, nearly 3 million people had committed to abstinence.

The zeal of many new abstainers did not survive very long, but there was a perceptible impact on the consumption of alcoholic drinks. Total beer output in Ireland fell from 1,017,000 barrels in 1837 to about 500,000 in 1843.[4] Much of this decline can be attributed to the success of the Father Mathew campaign, which was at its most fervent in those years, although poor harvests, livestock diseases and other factors were also at play.[5] Sales of Beamish & Crawford porter mirrored the national trend, showing a steady decline from 1839 to 1843, when sales fell from 63,031 barrels to 32,848 four years later. Sales would not fall as low as that again until the 1920s.

The Father Mathew campaign lost much of its momentum after 1843, as the initial passion with which reformed drinkers and others took up the cause could not be maintained. This fall in enthusiasm, Father Mathew's abysmal financial management and the virtual hostility of the Catholic Church establishment saw the vigour drain from the movement. The close association of the temperance movement with Daniel O'Connell's campaign for the repeal of the 1800 Act of Union also weakened the former's energy. In the early 1840s, O'Connell and Father Mathew were enjoying celebrity status at the head of their respective campaigns. The two leaders met on a visit to Cork on Easter Monday in 1842 and, with the Lord Mayor, walked at the head of a large procession. O'Connell knelt before Father Mathew and received his blessing to the cheering of the crowd – a symbolic union of the two movements. Temperance bands and groups formed a significant part of Repeal meetings thereafter, and as Father Mathew distanced himself from this political association, the thrust of his campaign dissipated greatly.

From 1843, sales of beer, both nationally and from the Cork Porter Brewery, began to pick up again and quite possibly would have enjoyed a greater growth but for the intervention of the Famine from 1845.

Production, sales and competition

John Topp, who had been taken on as head brewer in 1791, continued in this position until his retirement in 1839 – a career of forty-eight years. In 1823 his sons John W. and Richard W. joined their father as assistant brewers and they succeeded him in 1839 as joint head brewers. In the years from 1828 until his departure, John Topp oversaw production that undulated between a high of 72,399 barrels in 1828 and a low of 52,213 in 1836. The first six years of his sons' tenure in charge of brewing saw sales fall by almost 48 per cent, from 63,031 barrels in 1839 to 32,846 in 1843. While the temperance movement and other factors contributed to this decline, it is possible that a lack of skill on the part of the younger Topps was an additional element. Richard Pigott Beamish, who became an acting partner in the firm in 1863, later wrote: 'The capabilities of these two gentlemen were by no means comparable to those of their father. The absence of all local opposition however, enabled them to hold their own tolerably well.'[6]

However, as outlined above, national output and sales of beer fell by about the same proportion in those years. John W. Topp was paid an annual salary in the region of £1,000, but Richard earned about 25 per cent less, suggesting that his responsibilities were somewhat lighter than his brother's. As was the case previously for their father, the brothers were each paid a bonus of 3d for every barrel of porter sold, giving them an extra annual payment of between £400 and £677 during the 1840s. Sales began to pick up again from their low point in 1843 and rose steadily to 56,233 barrels by 1848, a jump of 71 per cent, before then falling back again following the delayed impact of the worst of the ravages of the Famine.

Immune to famine?

A report on the brewery's business written by North Ludlow Beamish, his family's acting partner, for the two-year period to August 1847 makes no mention of the Famine, then effectively in its third year.[7] Indeed, the report is quite upbeat, reporting increased sales and profits, an expansion of trade in counties Kerry, Limerick and Tipperary and a growing export trade. It predicted that the growth in sales would continue 'from the almost total extinction of the Abstinence System' and 'the extensive employment on Railway and other works in the city and neighbourhood of Cork'. North Ludlow Beamish also reported on improvements in the functioning

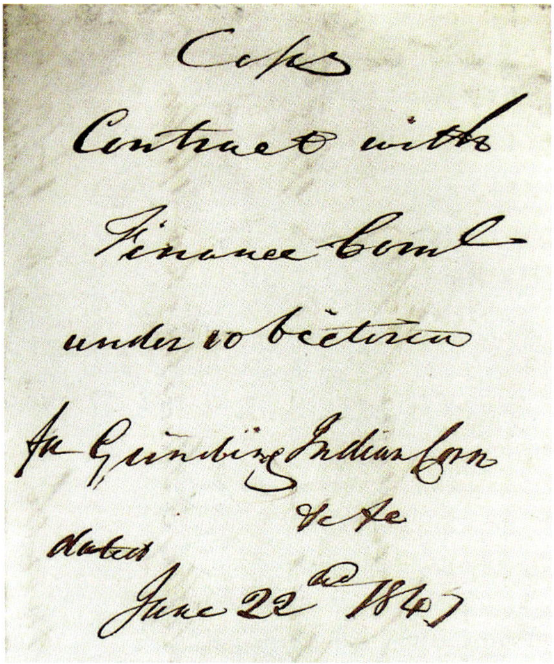

Copy
Contract with
Finance Comt
under 10 Victoria
for Grinding Indian Corn
&c &c
dated
June 22nd 1847

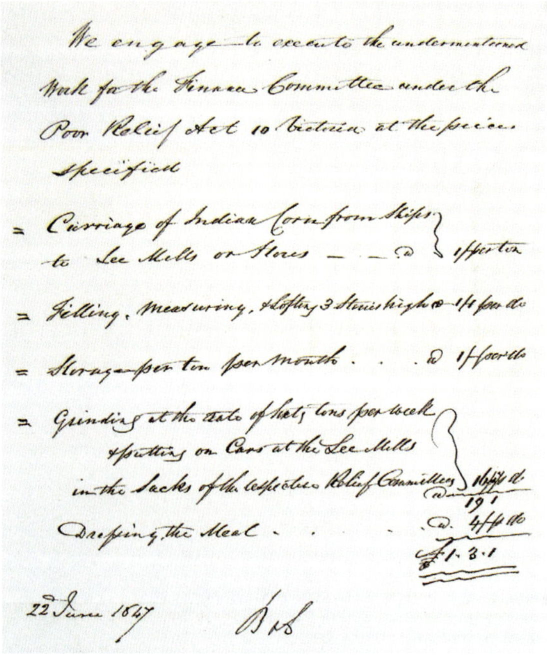

We engage to execute the undermentioned Work for the Finance Committee under the Poor Relief Act 10 Victoria at the prices specified

= Carriage of Indian Corn from Ships to Lee Mills or Stores — — @ 1/- per ton

= Filling, Measuring, & Lofting 3 Stories high @ 1/1 per do

= Storage per ton per month . . . @ 1/- per do

= Grinding at the rate of 60 tons per week & putting on Cars at the Lee Mills in the Sacks of the respective Relief Committees @ 16/- do

19/1

Dressing the Meal . . . @ 4/- do

£1.3.1

22 June 1847 B&C

From top: Cover of contract between the government's Finance Committee and Beamish & Crawford, dated 22 June 1847, for processing Indian corn at the Lee Mills during the Great Famine. (CCCA/Authors)
Detail of the 22 June 1847 contract for the carriage, storage, grinding and packing of corn. (CCCA/Authors)

of the brewing department 'founded on information obtained last year in London'. This involved the erection of a large refrigerator that saved three hours in the cooling of the wort and led to a noticeable improvement in its quality and consistency. The malt screens were converted to steam operation and 'the application of dampers to the steam boiler flues will diminish the consumption of coal'. Beamish also writes that the means of conveying hops to the wort copper, 'at present a clumsy and tedious operation', was also being improved.

This report by the Beamish acting partner also noted the profits made at the Lee Mills directly as a result of the Famine. In the winter of 1846 and spring of 1847, 7,883 bags of wheat and 321 tons of Indian corn (maize) were ground at the mills at a net profit of £639.18.8. On 22 June 1847, Beamish & Crawford signed a contract with the British government's Finance Committee for the preparation of Indian corn for the relief of hunger at a rate of £1.3.1 per ton. This payment was broken down as follows: 1s per ton for carriage 'from Ships to Lee Mills or Stores'; 1s 1d per ton for 'Filling, Measuring & Lofting 3 Stories high'; storage at 1s per ton per month; 16s per ton for 'Grinding at the rate of sixty tons per week & putting on Cars at the Lee Mills in the Sacks of the respective Relief Committees'; 4s per ton for 'Dressing the Meal'. The firm also earned income from the storage of corn in its Morrison's Island malthouse, and in an effort to make further gains from Famine-related government contracts, the River

The Lee Mills in 1932. (Courtesy Michael Lenihan)

Lee Stores (formerly the River Lee Porter Brewery) were refurbished and were, by late 1847, ready to receive corn. The report estimated that £40 per month would be earned from the storage of 3,000 quarters of maize on one floor and the stores had the capacity to take 30,000 quarters in all.

Post-Famine years

Joint head brewer Richard W. Topp's career at the brewery ended in October 1847, either through retirement or death, but his brother John W. continued, assisted by his son, also called John. This latter John had begun in the brewing department in 1846 as an assistant, but when his father became ill, Thomas Adams was appointed brewer in 1850 to assist him. Adams had previously worked in the brewery as a mechanical engineer and his successful superintendence of brewing 'combined with his own natural intelligence eventually enabled him to become Topp's successor'.[8] Adams was head brewer from 1850 until his death in 1860.

In the brewery year 1850 only 43,070 barrels of Beamish & Crawford's porter were sold, but trade began to pick up in the following years and accelerated throughout the following decade to reach a peak of 116,076 barrels in 1861 – a growth of almost 170 per cent. In the 1850s, the market for porter grew throughout the country. Wages were rising, there was an increase in the overall standard of living and growing prosperity in cities and large towns provided concentrated markets that could be exploited by the breweries. Another factor that facilitated the growth of porter in the late 1850s was the rise in the taxation of spirits from 6s 2d to 8s per gallon in 1858 and the reduction in the amount of illicit distilling as the rule of official law spread to even the remotest areas. As the railway network expanded, breweries could more easily and quickly reach markets that had previously been untapped – localities that in the past were accessible only on poor roads or by sea. Beamish & Crawford used the new railways that reached out from Cork city to distribute their porter, but the greater network that radiated from Dublin, as well as the Royal and Grand canals that ran westwards and northwestwards from the capital to the River Shannon, were used by Guinness to extend its market throughout most of the country.

Although the growth in national porter sales benefitted Beamish & Crawford, it was beginning to be left behind by its Dublin rival. Between 1855 and 1860 Guinness's output grew by 230 per cent, but Beamish & Crawford's grew by less than half that.[9] This steep growth by Guinness continued throughout the 1860s, and by 1872 its sales were worth £1 million, £550,000 of which was generated within Ireland, while Beamish & Crawford's income from sales in Ireland was only a little over £140,000 in that year.[10]

Table 5.1 **Irish beer output, 1846–50**[11]

YEAR	IRISH BEER (annual output in barrels)	GUINNESS (annual output in barrels)	BEAMISH & CRAWFORD (annual output in barrels)
1846	732,000	101,000	46,887
1847	617,000	96,000	54,584
1848	640,000	90,000	56,233
1849	602,000	94,000	46,738
1850	582,000	100,000	43,070

Once Guinness started on its steep growth trajectory in the mid-1850s, taking a growing share of the Irish market and expanding aggressively in Britain, the gap between it and Beamish & Crawford grew increasingly wider. The Cork brewery did not have international ambition on the scale of Guinness and focused on holding its share of the porter market, concentrated in Cork and the south of Ireland. Although Beamish & Crawford had agents in Bristol, London and other British cities, exports never grew beyond a small fraction of the firm's business.

The evasion of malt duties

During the early 1830s the evasion of malt duties by some breweries was becoming a significant factor in competition in the market for porter as well as a revenue loss to the Crown. Commissions of inquiry were set up to investigate the matter and submissions were made by maltsters, brewers and others. The malt duty was quite high at over 10s per barrel and its evasion could reduce the cost of producing a barrel of porter by up to 30 per cent. Beamish & Crawford was then Ireland's biggest maltster, and as the firm told the Commissioners of Inquiry in 1833, 'if not the first, we are at all events among the principal maltsters of the United Kingdom'.[12]

Henry K. Feath had been with the firm since 1799 and managed production at its six city malthouses. He gave his evidence on 2 December 1833 and said that the evasion of malt duty had become a particular problem after 1828. Legally produced malt cost at least between 26s and 27s to make, while illicit malt was being offered to brewers and distillers for between 19s and 22s per barrel. Smaller country brewers were using the illicit malt and offering their porter to publicans at between 24s and 28s a barrel, with discounts on large orders, while legally compliant brewers like Beamish & Crawford could not supply theirs for less than 34s to 35s per barrel. Beer made with illicit malt retailed at 3d or 3½d per quart, whereas 'legal' porter could not profitably be sold by publicans at less than 4d. Evading the malt tax was easier in more remote areas and Feath, and others, alleged collusion between illicit maltsters and excise officers. Country brewers were also using a proportion of highly dried barley with malt in their brews, further reducing their costs, and producing a porter of poor taste. Feath commented that 'in country places, where the palates of the people are not so fine as those of the tradesmen, who are drinking it constantly, the name of porter sells it; they cannot be judges or they would not drink it'.[13]

Beamish & Crawford was under such pressure that in the 1834–5 malting season it had worked only three of its six city malthouses and 'next season, I should not be surprised, if they abandoned the trade altogether', Feath wrote to the Commissioners of Inquiry.[14] As Feath and other 'fair traders' saw it, the only solution was the abolition of the malt duty, something that did not happen until 1880 when all duty was imposed on the beer produced rather than on any of its ingredients.

'They threatened serious rivalry': James J. Murphy & Co.

Up to the opening of the Lady's Well Brewery by James J. Murphy & Co. in 1856, Beamish & Crawford dominated the porter trade in Cork and faced only minor competition from the other breweries in the city. The next largest concern was the Southgate Brewery of Daniel Lane & Co., later dismissed by Richard Pigott Beamish as 'having been for years of little or no importance'.[15] The brewery of Samuel Abbott on Fitton Street was relatively small, producing table beer, ale and porter, and in a

From top:
James J. Murphy (1832–97). (Heineken)
A Murphy's Stout bottle. (Heineken)

Below:
Cask label for Beamish & Crawford Extra Stout, 1850s. (Beamish & Crawford Brewery Collection/Dori O'Connell)

very distant third place in Cork's brewery hierarchy. But with the arrival of James J. Murphy & Co. in 1856, the situation became a little more challenging.

The Murphys' brewery was located on Leitrim Street on the north side of Cork city. Having initially brewed porter and ale, the latter was discontinued in 1861 when porter became the sole product. Although 1856 was relatively late for the establishment of a new porter brewery, rising living standards, the growth of towns and cities and an improving economy gave confidence to the new venture. Richard Pigott Beamish, who had begun work at the Cork Porter Brewery in 1852, later wrote that the ongoing differences between the Beamish partners had also opened the way for new competition: '… the private differences and financial difficulties amongst the Beamish partners in the firm having also become matter [*sic*] of public notoriety, the establishment of opposition was naturally to be looked for.'[16] The Murphys were a well-known, highly regarded Catholic family of some influence and stature. The family established the whiskey distillery, James Murphy & Co., in Midleton in 1825; Francis Stack Murphy, a cousin, was MP for Cork from 1841 to 1846 and again from 1851 to 1853 (coincidentally replacing Francis Bernard Beamish in 1841 and being replaced by Beamish in 1853); and their grand-uncle, John Murphy, had been Catholic bishop of Cork and Ross from 1815 to 1847.

The new firm exploited the positive political and religious associations of the Murphy name, an understandable ploy in the post-Catholic Emancipation years of sectarian point scoring, and although the Murphy brewery initially 'threatened serious rivalry',[17] it quickly ran into trouble. North Ludlow, the Beamish acting partner in Beamish & Crawford at the time, wrote in 1857:

> The rival establishment [James J. Murphy & Co.] after the most active exertions and considerable outlay, and with all the advantages of political and religious connections, has only enhanced the reputation of our manufacture, and may be said to have sunk under a heavy pecuniary loss.[18]

Beamish & Crawford's sales rose steeply despite the arrival of new competition, more than doubling from 52,929 barrels in 1855 to 111,113 barrels four years later. The Murphy brewery did not enjoy comparable growth, at least not in its first years, and towards the end of 1857, after less than two years in business, some members of the Murphy family approached Beamish & Crawford with a view to selling their new brewery, but the offer was declined. This rebuff spurred the Murphys to greater efforts:

> Messrs. Murphy, assisted by wealthy relatives, recommenced operations on a much more extended scale. They bought up public houses and licences, expended large sums for the purpose of inducing publicans to quit one Brewery for the other, undersold Beamish & Crawford, and carried on an opposition of such rigour that the whole trade became demoralized.[19]

The efforts of the Murphys paid dividends – sales grew from 22,725 barrels (of 32 gallons) in 1858 to 42,990 barrels by 1861 before falling back to less than 40,000 barrels until 1865.[20] However, the Murphys' aggressive acquisition of tied houses drove Beamish & Crawford to respond in kind and it was forced to spend quite a sum of money in securing its own trade. Publicans in Cork city and county welcomed the competition and played one brewery off against the other to secure the best terms. By early 1861 both breweries had become weary of the struggle and on 14 February that year 'an agreement for mutual non-interference' was signed.[21] As a result of the three years of intense rivalry, Beamish & Crawford had expended a large sum in tying its trade, had an accumulation of bad debts and had lost trade to its new rival. The figure of 116,076 barrels in 1861 for sales of Beamish & Crawford's porter would not be surpassed again until 1901.

Table 5.2 **Comparative sales of Beamish & Crawford and James J. Murphy & Co., 1858–63**

YEAR	BEAMISH & CRAWFORD	JAMES J. MURPHY & CO.
1858	103,826	22,725
1859	111,113	33,937
1860	108,998	41,465
1861	116,076	42,990
1862	94,704	37,429
1863	77,825	39,108

The partners at Beamish & Crawford did not get to enjoy the cessation of inter-brewery hostilities for very long, as in 1861 the old Abbott's brewery on Fitton Street in Cork was purchased by Sir John Arnott and reopened the following year as St Finbarre's Brewery (see Chapter 7). This newcomer also began to acquire tied houses and undersold both Beamish & Crawford and James J. Murphy & Co., the former suffering more as 'the diminished reputation of Beamish & Crawford's manufacture'[22] left it more vulnerable. St Finbarre's Brewery quickly overtook Lane & Co. to become the city's third brewery.

Competition from two new city breweries, falling market share, internal family wrangling and a declining reputation for its porter saw Beamish & Crawford's sales fall from 116,076 barrels in 1861 to 77,825 two years later – a drop of 33 per cent. Factors external to brewing also exacerbated the problem, with harvests in 1860 and the two following years so bad 'as seriously to arrest material progress'.[23] By 1863 Beamish & Crawford sued for peace and a second agreement of 'mutual non-interference' was signed with Arnott's, 'and thereby a further portion of the local Porter Trade passed out of the hands of Beamish & Crawford'.[24]

Guinness in Cork

Patrick Lynch and John Vaizey, historians of the first 120 years of the Guinness brewery, regard the late 1850s and early 1860s as 'a critical time for the conquest of the Irish market'.[25] During these years Beamish & Crawford was at a low ebb, weakened by strong competition from the two new Cork breweries and unable to compete effectively with Guinness as it continued to conquer the Irish porter market. Guinness had earlier used the Irish canal system to spread its reach, and with the growth of the railways from the 1840s they extended this reach ever further, including Cork, where Beamish & Crawford had had no serious rival in its first seventy years.

Beamish & Crawford had used agencies to distribute its product from the beginning, but Guinness used the agency system to a much more successful degree. The Cork Guinness agency grew in importance, especially after 1859, when James Barrett was appointed its agent in the city, replacing an agent called Wigan. Barrett had to pay a security deposit of £3,000 to Guinness, suggesting that its trade there was already quite substantial, and Wigan's move to take on the management of a Bass agency in Cork is another probable indicator of weakness in the Cork brewing industry.[26] By the late 1860s the Cork Guinness agency had a trade of about £20,000 per year, equivalent to about 15 per cent of Beamish & Crawford's total trade at that time.

'Diminished reputation'

Beamish & Crawford Double Stout cask label, 1861. (Beamish & Crawford Collection/Dori O'Connell)

Thomas Adams, who had been appointed head brewer in 1850, died in 1860, leaving John Topp, his assistant and a grandson of the brewery's first head brewer, nominally in charge of brewing. He did not have the confidence of the acting partners and they recruited a new head brewer, William Bowden Weatherman, in July 1860, 'a man of talent and experience but of very dissipated habits'.[27] His tenure was not deemed a success and although the acting partners, encouraged by Richard Pigott Beamish, wanted to dismiss him, they desisted as they felt he would move to Sir John Arnott's new St Finbarre's Brewery, bringing his knowledge of Beamish & Crawford's workings with him. It would have been normal practice at the time to have a clause in the contract of a head brewer preventing him from moving to a rival concern in the same region within an agreed period of years. This was not done in Weatherman's case and

> The acting partners therefore believed themselves powerless to restrain or control their servant [Weatherman], and retained in the entire management of this most important department a man whose reckless conduct entailed heavy loss on the establishment, and reflected disgrace upon the whole concern.[28]

In the spring of 1863, with sales having fallen 33 per cent in two years, the acting partners dismissed Weatherman, despite 'the faulty nature of the agreement made with him'. By then the brewery's porter 'had fallen into a very low estimation' and the Murphy and Arnott breweries were taking significant market share from Beamish & Crawford.

Profits, debts and disarray

The profits generated by the Cork Porter Brewery in this period generally reflect the health or otherwise of sales. In the decade up to 1838 the trading profit averaged a little over £19,000 per year, but following the subsequent downturn in trade, shared by all in the brewing and distilling industries, this fell to an annual average of £9,600 in the following decade. For the five-year period after 1838, the years of the most severe fall in trade, this annual profit averaged a little over £7,000, with a loss of £5,427 in 1840. In the mid-1840s, the years of the Great Famine, profits were quite healthy. Following a dip between 1850 and 1852, profits picked up significantly and remained buoyant until the fall in trade in the difficult years of the early 1860s. In the ten years from 1852, annual trading profits averaged £22,470 per year.

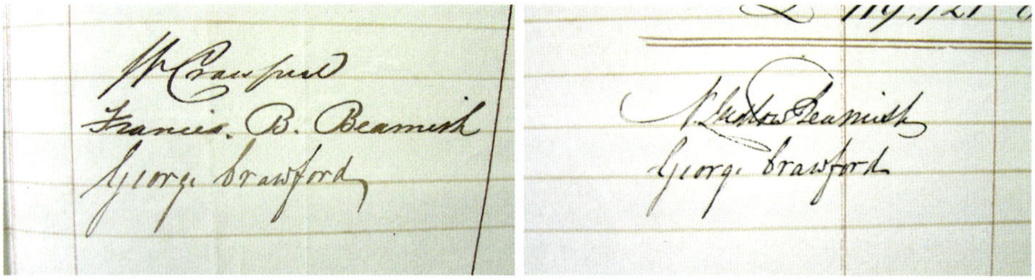

From left:
Signatures of William Crawford Jr., Francis Bernard Beamish and George Crawford, acting partners 1834–40. (CCCA/Authors)
Signatures of North Ludlow Beamish and George Crawford, acting partners 1841–59. (CCCA/Authors)

Following deductions for wear and tear, bad debts and interest payments, the remaining profit was divided equally between the Beamish and Crawford sides of the brewery partnership, and the respective families' acting and sleeping partners were entitled to draw living and house expenses from these sums. The acting partners were also paid an annual salary. The Crawfords were fewer in number and managed their financial affairs quite well, but some of the Beamish partners were less controlled. Francis Bernard, acting Beamish partner from 1828 to 1841, overdrew on his account and was indebted to the brewery for over £10,000 when he was removed as acting partner in 1841. His brother James Caulfield, a sleeping partner, also overdrew and owed almost £5,000 in 1841. These and other Beamish family debts increased, and although Francis Bernard had cleared his debt by 1862 and James Caulfield had cleared his by 1860, the Beamish partners were indebted to the firm in the amount of over £27,000 by August 1863.[29] While these debts were eventually paid, they were the subject of much rancour in the perennial disputes of the Beamish partners up to 1863.

From the death of William Beamish, the brewery co-founder, in 1828 until the installation of his grandson, Richard Pigott Beamish, and William Crawford's grandson, William Horatio Crawford, as acting partners in 1863, the system of keeping accounts and valuing the capital stock of the firm was in frequent disarray. Appropriate deductions for wear and tear, for example, were not applied and the buildings and plant of the firm were grossly overvalued. The book value of the stock of the firm was greatly in excess of the true value, with the consequent overvaluation of the partners' shares causing further difficulty in valuing the estate of a deceased partner or computing the value of the share of a partner wishing to sell.

In 1855 North Ludlow Beamish, acting partner on behalf of his family, wrote a memorandum for his family's sleeping partners as to the valuation of the firm.[30] At that time the nominal capital of the firm stood at £188,739.12.11 in the books, made up of cash in the bank, buildings, plant, land, stock of various kinds, and so on. Beamish felt that the stated value of property at £97,767.15.1 was 'utterly

Table 5.3 **Net profits and amounts credited to Beamish & Crawford partners, 1829–63**

YEAR	PROFIT (before deductions for wear and tear, bad debts, interest and credit to accounts of partners)	AMOUNT CREDITED BEAMISH & CRAWFORD ACTING PARTNERS (shared equally)
1829		
1830	£41,977 (2 years)	£39,586 (2 years)
1831	£16,577	£16,464
1832	£20,892	£16,128
1833		
1834		
1835	£53,238 (3 years)	£43,562 (3 years)
1836	£15,701	£10,678
1837	£14,382	£7,324
1838	£29,741	£22,622
1839	£19,312	£18,442
1840	(£5,427)	(£5,427)
1841	£4,676	£3,238
1842	£4,525	£3,866
1843	£12,735	£12,594
1844	£7,963	£7,764
1845	£9,415	£9,088
1846	£11,069	£10,824
1847	£17,942	£17,652
1848	£13,919	£13,184
1849	£15,035	£14,360
1850	£2,784	£2,348
1851	£3,879	£3,596
1852	£12,884	£12,606
1853	£15,215	£14,808
1854	£16,159	£15,904
1855	£18,039	£17,858
1856	£19,872	£11,988
1857	£14,363	£14,080
1858	£27,768	£26,168
1859	£37,026	£34,938
1860	£35,059	£33,014
1861	£28,307	£27,872
1862	£16,351	£14,936
1863	£8,850	£8,424

preposterous' and should be more correctly given as £11,570. The value of casks shown in the books also needed to be reduced, as no deduction for wear and tear of casks had been made since 1842. North Ludlow Beamish's assessment had validity. In 1862 the Lee Mills, standing in the firm's books at a value of £27,108.9.6, made up of the amount spent on the building and buying out its rents, was valued and given a true value of £5,100. The valuer, John S. Haines, commented that the mills were 'erected on a scale and at a cost more in keeping with the affluence of the Builders [Beamish & Crawford], than with the capabilities of its power & requirements and uses as a flour mill of the present times'.[31] The Lee Stores, the former River Lee Porter Brewery, stood at £8,224.13.11 in the books, but Haines gave their true value as £3,000. The true value of the brewery's casks in 1862 was £7,101.13.1, not the £13,267.13.10 shown in the books.

The problems of the partners' debt, the overvaluation of the firm's capital stock and weak accounting practices were finally tackled and resolved following the change in acting partners and the drawing up of a new co-partnership agreement in 1863.

The physical growth of the brewery

The refurbishment and remodelling of the brewery buildings continued throughout the 1820s and succeeding decades. A series of detailed plans of the brewery complex from this period survives, which show a number of significant changes in the layout and function of different areas of the brewery. These changes involved the acquisition of further property, some demolition and clearance as well as the erection of new buildings, changes in the function of others and the installation of new equipment. Taking the 1802 plan as a starting point, it is possible to set out a narrative of these changes from that year to 1863.[32]

By the 1820s the small central yard shown on the 1802 plan was much enlarged through the demolition of a number of buildings along its western and southern sides. The old houses and yard that lay between Morgan's Lane and the entrance passage from South Main Street were demolished and replaced with a coalhouse, stable and barmhouse. The main entrance from South Main Street has a wider and more convenient access to the larger central yard, with curved corners to ease the movement of horse-drawn vehicles.

In the northwestern corner of the brewery complex, at the western end of Lamley's Lane, a large steam engine and boilers have been installed. This work was done in 1818. The former Franklin's Lane, which lay between Allen's and Lamley's Lanes, has disappeared for most of its length due to the rebuilding and reconfiguration of the large cellars in the northern part of the brewery. (The term 'cellar' on these plans is usually ascribed to a workspace, and not necessarily an underground area.) A little of

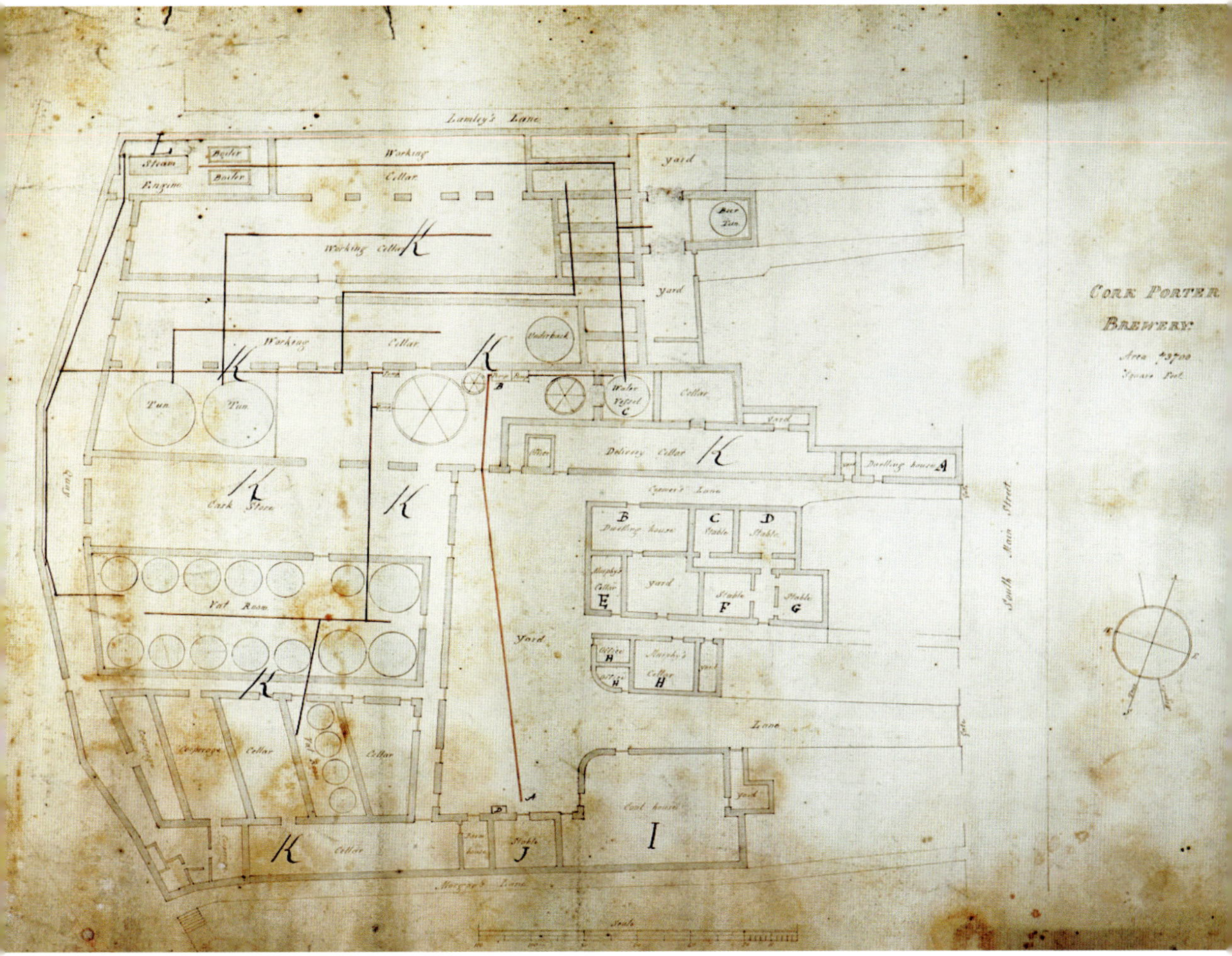

Brewery ground floor plan, late 1820s. (CCCA/Dori O'Connell)

the easternmost part of this laneway survives as a narrow passage from South Main Street into a yard.

The range of buildings that lay between the central yard and the river to the west was also remodelled between 1802 and the 1820s. These buildings are at least two stories high and the various stages in the brewing process took place here, principally on the upper floor. The 'Tun Room' of the 1802 plan has been enlarged and on the 1820s plan, two large tuns are shown in the newly enlarged space with a large third vessel to the east. The large tuns were fermenting vessels where the cooled beer was stored during fermentation and they were clearly of great capacity, rising from the ground through to the upper floor. This area has been extended eastwards and other vessels, pumps and a large water vessel are shown with a network of pipes connecting

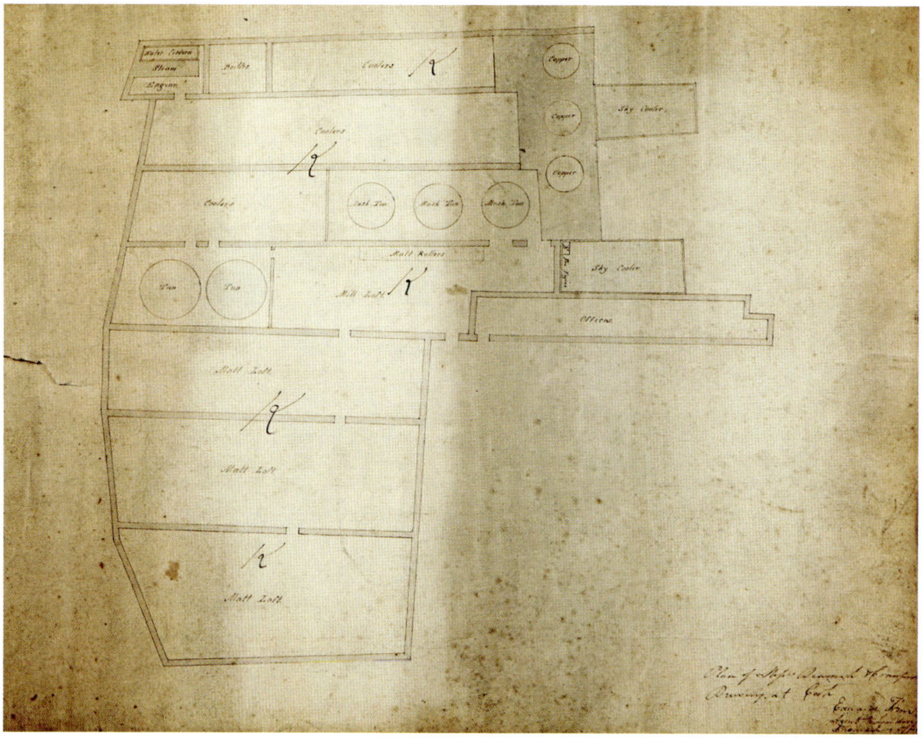

Brewery upper-floor plan, late 1820s. (CCCA/Dori O'Connell)

the different working areas. The 1820s plan of the upper storey of the brewery shows three mash tuns to the northeast, with three coppers to the northeast of these again. Two sky coolers are shown in the eastern part of the upper storey. These elevated containers were located in the highest part of the brewery and water was piped from them to where it was required in the brewing process. The pipes connecting these various vessels are also shown. Three large areas for cooling the newly brewed beer are shown in the northern part of the upper storey.

The southern part of the upper storey had three large malt lofts where malt was stored for brewing. Malt rollers are shown along the northern wall of the mill loft, close to the mash tuns where the milled malt was boiled with water at the first stage of brewing.

The smaller vat rooms shown on the 1802 plan have been enlarged by the 1820s and fourteen vats are shown on the later plan. A smaller vat room with four vats is also shown on the later ground plan, this having previously been a coalhouse. A large cask store is shown north of the large vat room. This cask store, the large vat room and the range of buildings to the south containing the smaller vat room, two cellars and two cooperage areas, occupy the ground floor below the malt lofts.

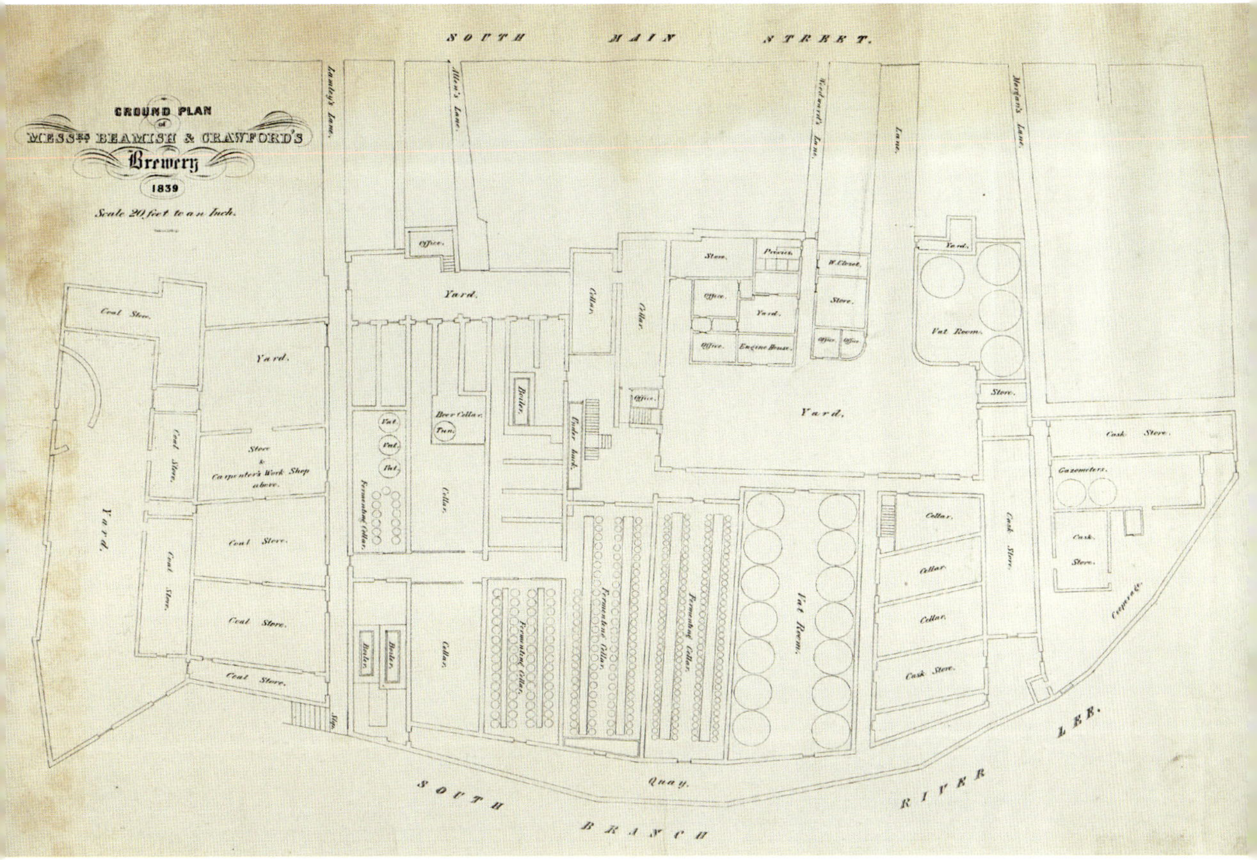

Brewery ground plan, 1839. (CCCA/Dori O'Connell)

The brewery complex in 1839

The 1839 plan of the ground floor area and upper storey of the brewery shows further expansion and change. By this date, the brewery complex has expanded northwards of Lamley's Lane and a range of buildings and a large yard, formerly part of the adjoining Hanover Street glassworks, has been acquired. Six of these buildings are used for the storage of coal and another houses a carpenters' workshop. The brewery has also expanded south of Morgan's Lane towards the river and this area now houses a number of buildings shown on the plan to be a cooperage and cask stores. Two gasometers (gas storage tanks) are also shown in this newly acquired area.

One of the more significant changes in the 1839 ground plan is the large fermentation area shown in the western range of buildings of the brewery. Two large fermentation cellars and a smaller one are shown here to the north of the large vat room, with further fermentation vessels sharing space with storage vats across a passage to the northwest. The large vat room still lies to the south of the fermenting cellars,

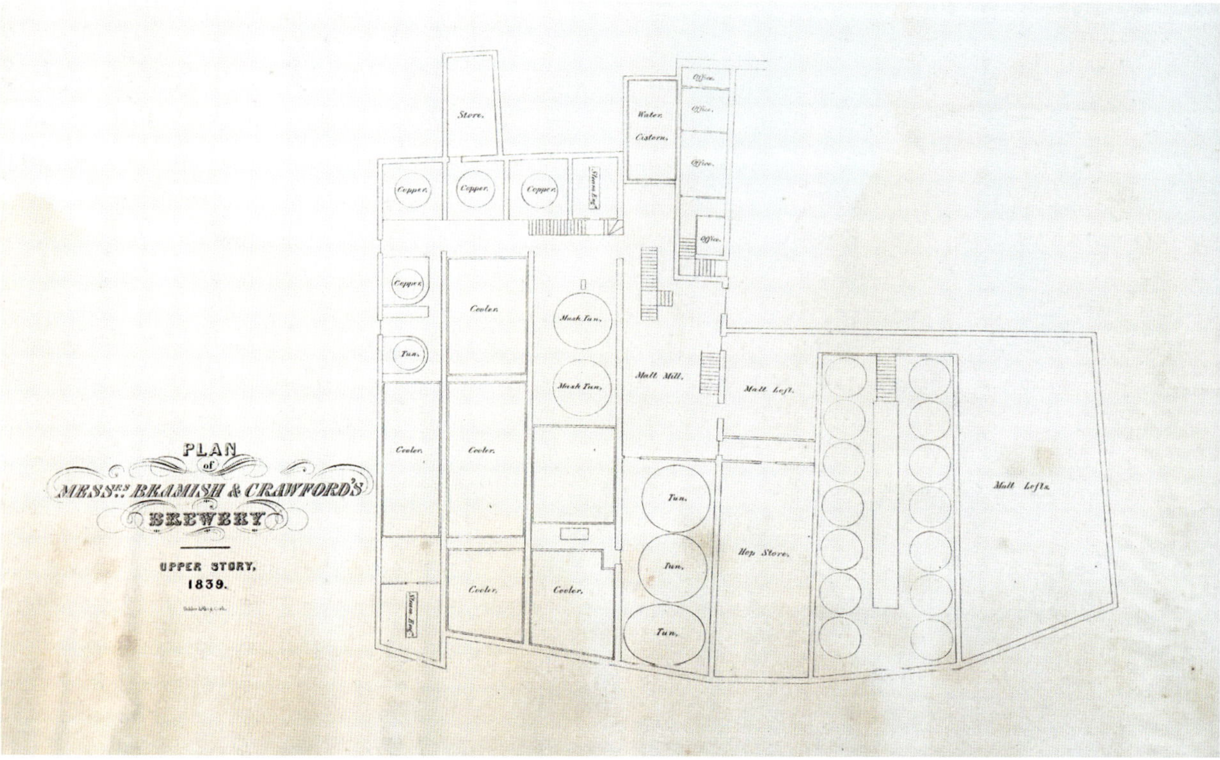

Brewery upper-storey plan 1839. (CCCA/Dori O'Connell)

but on the plan of the upper storey the vats are also shown, indicating that their height rises above the level of the upper floor into what is shown on the 1820s plan as a malt loft. There is a further vat room with four vats located in the southeastern corner of the brewery complex occupying what had been a coalhouse. Motive power has also been improved, with a new engine house on the eastern side of the central yard and another installed in the upper storey of the brewhouse. The earlier steam engine and boilers at the western end of Lamley's Lane are still in position and another large boiler is shown in the northern range of buildings.

The upper storey of the 1839 brewery also shows some changes. While the southernmost malt loft is shown as it was in the earlier plans, the middle malt loft is now the upper part of the vat room, while the third malt loft has been divided by a passage into two spaces, one a hop store, the other a smaller malt loft. The mill loft in the central part of the upper storey has been reduced in size to allow for the installation of a third large fermenting vat. The three mash tuns of the 1820s plan have been replaced with two larger mash tuns and the three coppers are still in the same position, with the addition of a fourth copper to the west. The coolers are shown in the same position but with some subdivision of the larger spaces.

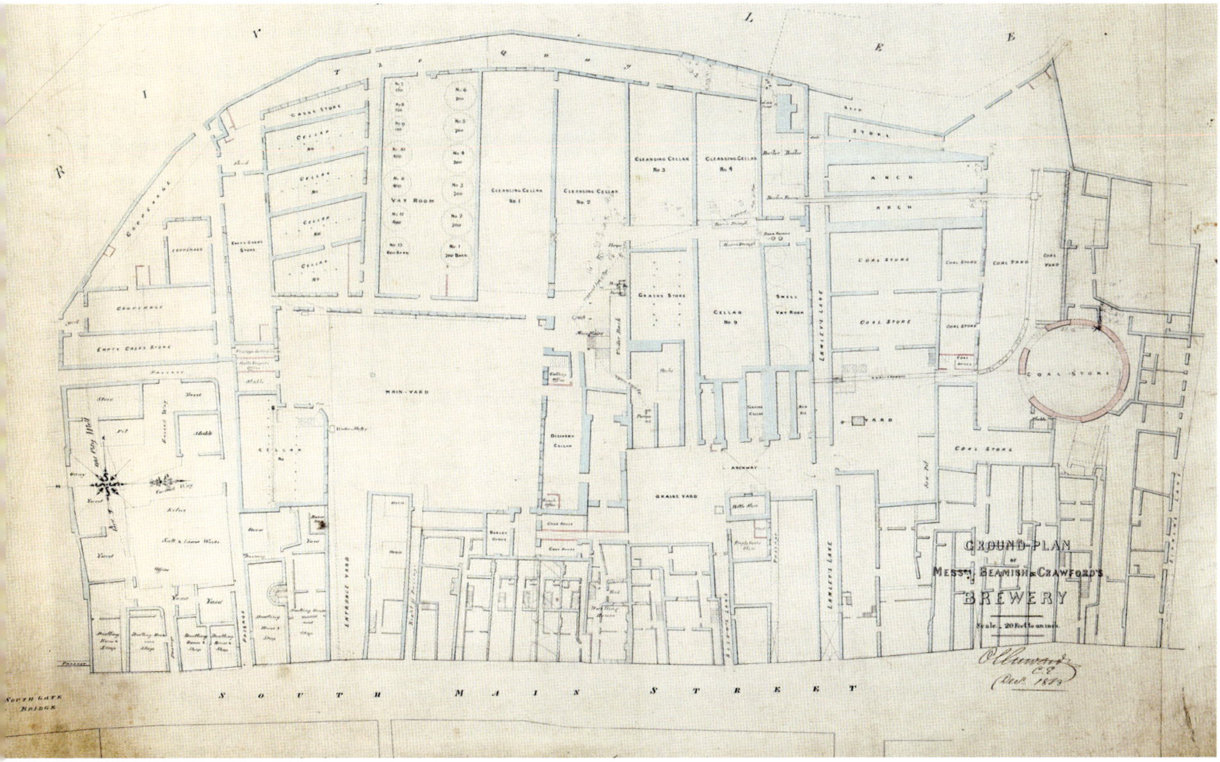

Brewery ground-floor plan 1863. (CCCA/Dori O'Connell)

The brewery complex in 1863

In August 1863, Richard Pigott Beamish and William Horatio Crawford, grandsons of the brewery founders, took over as acting partners in the firm and initiated a period of reorganisation and improvement that was in sharp contrast to the poor standards of business practice that had been allowed to develop under the stewardship of the previous generation. Richard Pigott Beamish was harsh in his assessment of the management of the physical state of the brewery pre-1863:

> … up to the time of the change of management in 1863, no outlay of any value was made upon the buildings and plant. For about 40 years everything was patched and repaired until further patching was useless. The result was, that in 1863 the condition of the buildings and plant had become such as daily threatened a stoppage of trade. Roofs, floors, tuns, vats, coolers, rounds, refrigerators, machinery, shafting, store houses etc. were all in such a state of decay as to have become, in some places, even dangerous to human life.[33]

However, the enlargement of the brewery complex, the changes in layout and

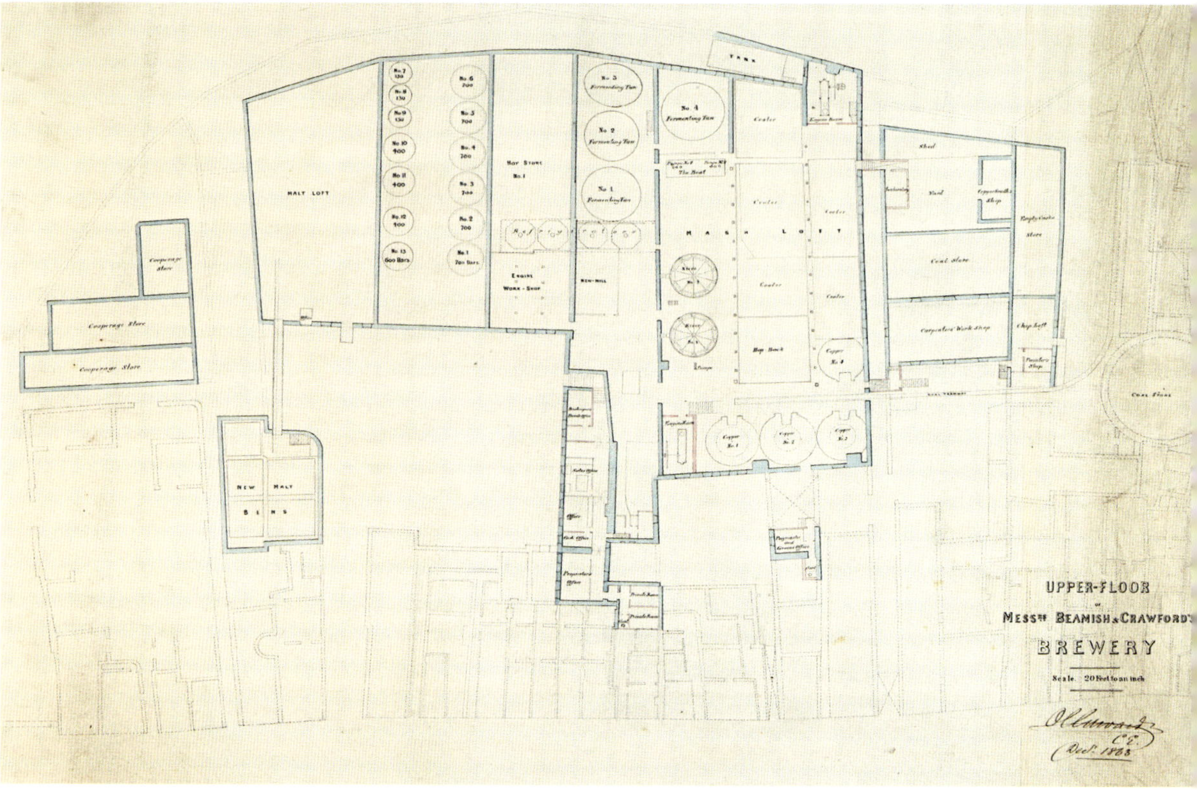

Brewery upper-storey plan, 1863. (CCCA/Dori O'Connell)

function of many parts of the brewery buildings and the installation of new plant and equipment as shown on the various plans suggests that a modicum of investment was maintained to keep the brewery functioning at something like a satisfactory level. In the late 1850s sales rose rapidly, from 52,929 barrels in 1855 to 111,113 four years later. The ability of the brewery to double its output in such a short space of time suggests that Richard Pigott Beamish may have been exaggerating the poor state of affairs at the time.

The 1863 plans of the ground and upper floors of the brewery, drawn in December of that year, show quite a level of enlargement, expansion and improvement in the years between 1839 and 1863, before improvements under the direction of the new acting partners were initiated. At the northern end of the brewery, further acquisitions were made in the area of the former Hanover Street glassworks. This extended the brewery property northwards to the southern side of Simmon's Lane. The buildings and yards in this area north of Lamley's Lane were primarily used for storing coal. Included in these properties was the 80-foot-high brick-built glassworks cone, which was a feature of the Cork city skyline until its demolition in 1915. This cone, in which glass blowers once worked, was used by the brewery as a coal store. The 1863 plans also show that tramway rails extending from these coal storage areas to the boilers in the brewery proper were installed some time after 1839. These rails had a gauge of 2 feet and 9 inches and a design drawing from the brewery archive shows a four-wheeled wagon 5 feet long and 3½ feet wide, with a container with a V-shaped cross-section that pivoted on a bar for ease of emptying (see p. 128).[34]

South of Lamley's Lane, some other changes are also apparent. A new boiler room was added to the east of the steam engine and boilers at the western end of that lane. East of that, the 'Small Vat Room' now occupied the space formerly shared by vats and fermenting rounds. The three large fermenting cellars shown on the 1839 plans are labelled 'Cleansing Cellars' on the 1863 plans and a fourth one has been added. The fermentation and cleansing stages of the brewing process happened together in the vessels in these areas. The yard accessed by way of Allen's Lane from South Main Street has been enlarged, as has another yard north of Lamley's Lane. Both yard expansions were made possible by the acquisition of further property lots between the older brewery buildings and South Main Street.

The large vat room shown on the 1839 plans was refitted by 1863. The new vat room shows thirteen vats of varying capacity where porter was stored after fermentation and cleansing before it was racked, or filled into barrels. The total capacity of these vats is 6,300 barrels. Detailed architectural drawings of this vat room survive and show a building 113 feet long by 50 feet wide. The loft is nearly 23 feet above the floor level and the thirteen vats project over 3 feet above the loft floor into the upper storey, which is over 12 feet high. The larger vats, capable of holding 700 barrels, are shown to have a diameter at their base of over 16 feet, tapering a little towards the top, where the diameter is a little over 14 feet. The vats sit on stands over 3 feet high and the upper floor is shown to be supported by a series of cast iron columns. The small vat room to the north would have had a total capacity of at least 2,000 barrels more.

The vat room off the southeastern corner of the large central yard is now labelled 'cellar' and the 1863 plan suggests that an upper storey has been added to the building since 1839. The plan shows a stairway to an upper level and two rows of columns supporting this second storey. The plan of the upper floor shows a series of malt bins in this space, with access westwards by way of an elevated passage to the malt loft on the upper floor of the main brewery building.

The main central brewery yard has been enlarged through the demolition of a number of buildings on its eastern side. South of the main yard, more property has been acquired south of Morgan's Lane (labelled 'Passage'). The southwest corner of the brewery has also been reconfigured since 1839. The cooperage has been enlarged, occupying a space along the southwestern wall with a lean-to roof, as well as two further buildings in this area, formerly housing gasometers and a cask store. These two buildings, along with a cask store, have had an upper floor added, housing three cooperage stores.

The 1863 upper floor plan shows a new mill in the central mill loft. Two mash tuns are shown in the mash loft, with four coppers to the east and north, as on the 1839 plan. Between the coppers and the coolers a hop-back is shown, a vessel through which the unfermented wort passed on its journey from the coppers to the fermentation area. In the hop-back the wort was filtered to remove the trub (hop debris) after the boiling in the coppers. The upper floor also has an engine workshop occupying a former malt loft and a number of offices.

Some of the buildings north of Lamley's Lane are shown on the 1863 upper floor plan to have an upper level that was not shown to have been used on the 1839 plan. This upper floor has a small laboratory, a coppersmith's shop, a painter's shop, an empty cask store, a chip loft, a coal store and a yard that occupied an area that lay over two arched spaces.

In 1863 the brewery buildings were still set some way back from South Main Street and would have been largely obscured from view by the buildings on the west side of that street.

Beamish family values

Following the death of William Beamish on 17 April 1828, the nature of the partnership controlling the Cork Porter Brewery changed. In his will William Beamish left his share of the brewery equally to his five younger sons, North Ludlow, Richard, Charles, Francis Bernard and James Caulfield. The heads of a new agreement were drawn up in that year and an attempt was made to set out the terms and conditions of a new partnership.[35] It would seem that the details of this proposal were not agreed upon, as it was not until 1831 that an agreement was reached to regularise the partnership following the death of William Beamish.[36] Under the 1831 agreement, William Beamish's five younger sons would hold $^{10}/_{20}$ of the firm, William Crawford would have $^{9}/_{20}$ and his son George would have $^{1}/_{20}$. Francis Bernard was to be the acting partner on behalf of the Beamish family, joining William Crawford in managing the brewery. Francis Bernard's four brothers, the Beamish sleeping partners, had no part in the day-to-day running of the brewery, but they had the right to inspect the books of the firm.

When William Beamish died in 1828, the value of the capital stock of the firm in its books stood at £256,938.6.10. In keeping with a condition in an agreement of 1822 between William Beamish and William Crawford, £73,844.3.0 (£80,000 in Irish currency) was written off that sum, reducing it to £183,092.3.10 to better reflect the true value of the firm, although a notional figure of £180,000 is shown in this new agreement for the value of the capital stock. It was also agreed that the premises of the merchant house of Beamish & Crawford on Merchants' Quay would become the sole property of William Crawford and would no longer be part of a co-partnership arrangement. The 1831 agreement was to run for seven years, computed to have begun in August 1828, thus ending in August 1835.

William Crawford died on 29 November 1834 and in his will he left his share in the brewery to his sons George and William Jr., bringing their individual shares to 5⁄20 each. A new deed of co-partnership was agreed on 8 July 1836 and it was to remain in force until August 1849.[37] The acting partners were now William Crawford Jr., his brother George and Francis Bernard Beamish. The sleeping partners were again North Ludlow, Richard, Charles and James Caulfield Beamish. It was a condition of this agreement that a majority in value of the Beamish and Crawford partners, both acting and sleeping, could, at the end of a three-year period computed from 1 August 1835 or at the end of any succeeding term of three years, remove a Beamish or a Crawford acting partner. All partners, both sleeping and acting, were entitled to draw house and living expenses from the firm's accounts following the balancing of the books on the first Monday in August each year.

The death of William Beamish in 1828 and the accession of his son Francis Bernard to the position of acting partner, effectively joint CEO with William Crawford, began a period of family squabbling, mutual distrust and dissatisfaction within the Beamish side of the partnership that was not resolved until 1863. The Crawford succession, on the other hand, was to prove quite trouble-free, with William Crawford's sons, George and William Jr., succeeding their father as acting partners after his death in 1834. George continued as acting partner on behalf of the Crawfords until his resignation in August 1863. William Crawford Jr. died in April 1840 and his share in the firm was inherited by his sons, Arthur and William Horatio. However, Arthur died only two years later and his estate, and his share in the brewery, went to his only brother, William Horatio. William Horatio Crawford was a sleeping partner until the resignation of his uncle George in 1863, following which he became acting partner on behalf of the Crawford family.

Francis Bernard Beamish, who served his first term as a Liberal MP for Cork city from 1837 to 1841, began to overdraw on his Beamish & Crawford account when he became acting partner and allowed his

George Crawford (1792–1864). (Crawford Art Gallery, Cork)

brother James Caulfield to do the same. By 1841, Francis Bernard was indebted to the Beamish partners by £10,354 and James Caulfield by £4,827. (James Caulfield had fully cleared his debt by 1860, and while Francis still owed the firm over £3,500, increased profits in these years allowed him to clear his debt by 1862.) In October 1841, Richard, Charles and North Ludlow combined with George Crawford, under Article 36 of the 1836 co-partnership agreement, to remove Francis Bernard as acting partner on the basis of his debt and general mismanagement. They replaced him with North Ludlow for an initial three years, which was extended in 1844 and again in 1849, and he remained the Beamish acting partner until 1863. William Horatio Crawford had become a sleeping partner following the death of his father, William Jr., in April 1840, and his uncle George became the sole Crawford acting partner. North Ludlow had no interest in becoming acting partner, having little business experience and many other, mainly scholarly, interests, but he took the position and retained it for over two decades, 'contrary to his own taste and wishes'.[38] He was essentially a compromise candidate. The Crawfords were not disposed to Charles, who comes across as an awkward character, and North Ludlow was the better of the two evils for Charles, given his animosity towards his other brother, Richard, who in any case had even less interest in the position than North Ludlow did.

Table 5.4 **Partnership arrangement: Cork Porter Brewery/Beamish & Crawford, 1792–1863**

YEARS	ACTING PARTNERS	SLEEPING PARTNERS
1792–4	William Beamish William Crawford Richard Barrett Digby O'Brien (d. 1794)	
1794–1800	William Beamish William Crawford Richard Barrett (retired 1800)	
1800–28	William Beamish (d. 1828) William Crawford	
1828–31	Francis Bernard Beamish William Crawford	North Ludlow Beamish Charles Beamish Richard Beamish James Caulfield Beamish
1831–4	Francis Bernard Beamish William Crawford (d. 1834)	North Ludlow Beamish Charles Beamish Richard Beamish James Caulfield Beamish George Crawford

YEARS	ACTING PARTNERS	SLEEPING PARTNERS
1834–40	Francis Bernard Beamish George Crawford William Crawford Jr. (d. 1840)	North Ludlow Beamish Charles Beamish Richard Beamish James Caulfield Beamish
1840–1	Francis Bernard Beamish (removed 1841) George Crawford	North Ludlow Beamish Charles Beamish Richard Beamish James Caulfield Beamish Arthur Crawford William Horatio Crawford
1841–2	North Ludlow Beamish George Crawford	Francis Bernard Beamish Charles Beamish Richard Beamish James Caulfield Beamish Arthur Crawford (d. 1842) William Horatio Crawford
1842–56	North Ludlow Beamish George Crawford	Francis Bernard Beamish Charles Beamish Richard Beamish (retired 1856) James Caulfield Beamish William Horatio Crawford
1856–62	North Ludlow Beamish George Crawford (retired 1859, nominally replaced by William Horatio Crawford)	Francis Bernard Beamish Charles Beamish James Caulfield Beamish (d. 1862) Richard Pigott Beamish William Horatio Crawford
1862–3	North Ludlow Beamish George Crawford/William Horatio Crawford	Francis Bernard Beamish Charles Beamish Richard Pigott Beamish William Horatio Crawford

'A history of the differences between the partners'

The feuding amongst the Beamish brothers continued throughout the 1840s, with acting partner North Ludlow supported by Richard on one side, and Francis Bernard (now a sleeping partner), James Caulfield and Charles on the other. In the late 1840s the latter three considered withdrawing from the firm against a background of declining profits and share values, leading North Ludlow to attempt, and then abandon, a remodelling of the partnership to strengthen the powers of the acting partners as against those of the sleeping partners. Charles had taken successful legal action to gain access to the firm's accounts for the sleeping partners and threatened further legal action if the proposed remodelling went ahead.[39]

The existing co-partnership was renewed in 1849 for a period of fourteen years, with nominal changes, but the fraternal strife continued.[40] A central bone of contention was the question of the true value of the firm and, by extension, the worth of their respective shares, complicated by the indebtedness of Francis Bernard and James Caulfield. North Ludlow had made no attempt to compel them to reduce their debts and they were only charged on the interest; indeed, the debts had increased – by August 1853, Francis owed £10,629 and Caulfield owed £6,862. No accurate valuation of the company had been carried out since 1792. Accounts were kept differently at various stages and annual valuations sometimes exaggerated and at other times underestimated the company's worth. The valuation of property was also consistently overestimated. North Ludlow claimed in 1855 that the true value of the property assets, given in the books at over £97,000, was closer to £11,000. As early as 1822 the founding partners, William Beamish and William Crawford, had executed a deed stating that the valuation of capital stock in the books was greatly in excess of its true value and agreed that when one of them died, £80,000 in Irish currency (£73,844.3.0) would be written off to correct this, which was duly done following the death of William Beamish in 1828.[41]

'A history of the differences between the partners upon this subject' (of valuation), Richard's son Richard Pigott wrote later, 'the arbitrations, threatened chancery suits, correspondences, and personal altercations, would fill a goodly volume.'[42] Charles continued his offensive against North Ludlow, the Beamish acting partner, claiming that the attempted remodelling of 1849 was based on 'hostile and malignant feelings of hatred' for him on the part of North Ludlow, who, he claimed, had falsely claimed the support of acting partner George Crawford for a scheme that was calculated to 'materially injure' the interests of the Beamish sleeping partners. Following a letter from Richard Beamish in 1852, North Ludlow began actively to seek debt repayment from Francis Bernard and James Caulfield, which Charles read as a deliberate attempt to force them to sell their shares. In August 1853, he attempted unsuccessfully to have North Ludlow fined and removed as acting partner on the basis of the charges above, together with claims that he was deliberately undervaluing the firm as part of his scheme to buy out Francis Bernard and James Caulfield at a bargain price, as well as his 'general bad conduct, want of capacity and neglect of his duty'.[43]

Richard Pigott Beamish enters the fray

Richard Pigott Beamish's situation added fuel to the fraternal fire in the early 1850s. It was agreed by North Ludlow and Richard that the latter's twenty-year-old son would enter the business in 1852, despite opposition from their three brothers. North Ludlow's own sons were all too young, and in any event he had no wish for them to become involved in the brewery. As Richard had given Richard Pigott 'neither a collegiate, a professional nor a mercantile education', a position in the brewery was 'the least expensive and troublesome' way of providing for him. North Ludlow's health was not good, and if he was forced to vacate the role of acting partner, the appointment of one of the opposing three – probably Francis Bernard – was certain. Thus, there was a need to establish Richard Piggot's position, in his own words, 'as quickly and firmly as possible'. In 1853, when he turned twenty-one, he was assigned one-quarter part of Richard's one-tenth share. The opposing three, led by Charles, objected, insisting on only five Beamish partners, and after much correspondence and threats of legal action, Richard was legally advised that the best way to establish his son's position in the brewery was to transfer the whole of his share to him, making him a partner in place of Richard. Realistically, this was his only option. If Francis Bernard replaced North Ludlow as Beamish acting partner, he would have prevented Richard's son from becoming a partner 'or even', as Richard Pigott himself noted, 'a clerk'.[44] Under the existing 1836 deed of partnership, Richard had no power to bequeath his share to his son upon his death; the value of the share would have to have been paid out. So the choice was between making the transfer now, while he was alive and North Ludlow was acting partner, or risk his son being excluded entirely by the other three. The full transfer eventually occurred in 1856, following the conclusion of a period of independent arbitration.

In the meantime, young Richard Pigott displayed the ambition and drive that would serve the firm well in subsequent decades. He admitted that he was 'a learner' in his first two years at the brewery, but quickly realised that it was 'an establishment conducted without system, knowledge or principle'. In late 1853, he proposed to his uncle North Ludlow that he would buy his share and replace him in the 'irksome position at the head of our firm'. He offered him what he believed were generous terms, as well as the prospect of being rid of the 'disagreeable tasks of whipping up clerks, securing barley, etc.', not to mention his troublesome siblings. North Ludlow described the idea as 'utterly insane', given Richard Pigott's 'youth and inexperience', but proceeded to use him as an intermediary in his own and Richard's efforts to buy out Francis Bernard and James Caulfield. Richard Pigott assured a suspicious Francis Bernard that he was acting on his own and was merely seeking to devise some mutually acceptable arrangement 'which shall put an end to the present divided and therefore weakened state of our partnership'. Francis Bernard held out until late 1854, when he agreed (on his own and James Caulfield's behalf) to sell, despite Charles's strong opposition. A generous offer, which included an element of effective debt write-off, was funded by North Ludlow and Richard 'for the sake of peace and harmony'. Francis Bernard then pulled out, on the basis that James Caulfield would not agree to the terms, and proceeded to offer to buy out North Ludlow, Richard and Richard Pigott's shares on the same terms as they had offered him. This was rejected, with Richard Piggot explaining to his 'Uncle Frank' that their offer to him was 'merely intended to procure an amiable settlement of the differences produced by your [Francis Bernard and James Caulfield] anomalous position as Partners in a firm from which you had indirectly withdrawn the greatest part of your capital'. This left arbitration as the only course, and in 1856 the arbitrators effectively backed North Ludlow as a 'fit acting partner' (while criticising certain of his actions and ruefully noting their 'conviction that investigations by strangers to the family like the present are highly injurious to the concern and should if possible be avoided').[45]

With the dust temporarily settled following arbitration, the transfer from father to son finally took place in March 1856. Richard assigned to Richard Pigott his one-tenth share in the capital stock of the Cork Porter Brewery and his one-fifth share of the net credit of the five Beamish partners in the firm of Beamish & Crawford. In return, Richard Pigott agreed to pay his father an annuity of £1,200 for life (the average annual return on profits for each partner at that stage) and to pay the whole of the debts then due by him to various persons. Following the transfer, Richard Pigott entered the firm as a full partner with the assent of the two acting partners, the arrangement having been given the go-ahead by the independent arbitrators. He had been serving as a subaltern officer with the West Cork Artillery Militia and in July 1856 received his commission as a captain, just two days before the militia was disbanded. He now began to give his full attention to brewery affairs, becoming, in his own words, 'a servant of the establishment' under the watch of North Ludlow, whom he thanked in a letter of September 1856: 'Step by step you have assisted me along, until I am now about to be placed in a really independent and responsible position.' He also moved into Lota Park with North Ludlow and his wife Aline.

His main work, he told his father, was a continuation of his efforts since 1853 – 'searching out and rectifying of errors, mistakes and oversights in those superior to me in age and position'. With North Ludlow's support, he explored ways of becoming a second Beamish acting partner, but this was blocked by the necessity of every partner supporting the move, which was not very likely. His lawyers were exploring the possibility of having him replace North Ludlow as acting partner before the expiration of the latter's term in 1863, but in the meantime he had to carry on 'at an occupation and amongst a people not the most congenial'. His mood was not lightened by his father's spending and his own impending eviction from Lota Park in the spring of 1857 to make room for a schoolroom and private tutor for North Ludlow's five children. 'Back again therefore to a little lodging in Cork', he wrote to his father in Cheltenham:

> the work at the Brewery; no amusement, no change. I don't think that my

> health will stand this constant town life, without something which will give a breath of fresh air. I am not given to those coarse amusements, in which young men are generally supposed to indulge, and shall therefore feel this the more. And all this time I have the knowledge that a famous income, which would afford the means of healthy relaxation, is being expended, without perceptible result, in another country!

His anger with his father's spending was a constant source of friction. He was continually inviting friends to stay at his house, and Richard Pigott complained to his mother that

> the children of the family [are] reduced to the smallest amount of cash, in order to provide entertainment for the friends! … after the total expenditure of a comfortable fortune, after a constant change of residence from place to place during the last 25 years, and the constant exercise of hospitality, that now, at the time when we might naturally look for some fruits to atone for all this loss – we look in vain for even a respectable class of society into which to introduce my brother and sisters.

He pleaded with her to get Richard to exercise some prudence while he attempted to pay off his father's multiple debts and put his affairs on a 'reputable footing'. In return for his efforts, he was dismissed by his father as a 'senseless grumbler' and admonished by his mother for smoking in the house and staying up late during a visit to Cheltenham.[46]

The profligate Richard continued to demand more money. He was already receiving £100 per annum above the agreed annuity of £1,200, and in mid-1857 this was increased to £1,400, made possible by the firm's healthy profit returns in these years. (Net profits rose from just under £12,000 in 1856 to over £26,000 in 1858 and almost £34,000 in 1859.) The sale of the Inchiglass estate jointly by Richard Pigott and his parents in early 1858 for £4,500 allowed Richard Pigott to pay off his father's outstanding debts of £3,200 and use the remaining £900 (after £400 in costs were deducted) to buy and furnish his new house, Harmony Lodge, near Carrigtwohill (he later moved to Ashbourne House, Glounthane), where he planned to live with his Swedish wife, Huldine, whom he married in May 1858. Richard continued to demand more money and challenged his son's own expenditure, including the £100 set aside annually (as agreed before his marriage) to fund Huldine's annual holiday in Sweden. In response, Richard Pigott set down their respective outlays, which amounted to £1,400 per annum for Richard and £900 for himself. Richard continued to complain that he did not have 'a farthing'. The 'natural generosity' of 'dear old

Paps', sighed Richard Pigott to his sister, continued to be 'too great for our purse'.[47]

In early 1859, William Horatio Crawford replaced his ailing uncle George as the Crawford acting partner. The agreed arrangement, however, was that Richard Pigott would act for him in the management of the business and that he would only pay occasional visits to the brewery, 'as his feelings are averse to a close attendance upon business'. Legal advice was sought on whether this violated the partnership agreement; the fear was that Charles Beamish, who had backed off since the arbitration decision of 1856, would 'take any opportunity which may offer itself for litigation and annoyance'. James Caulfield died in March 1862, and when the existing partnership agreement expired in August of the following year, Richard Pigott Beamish's time would finally come.

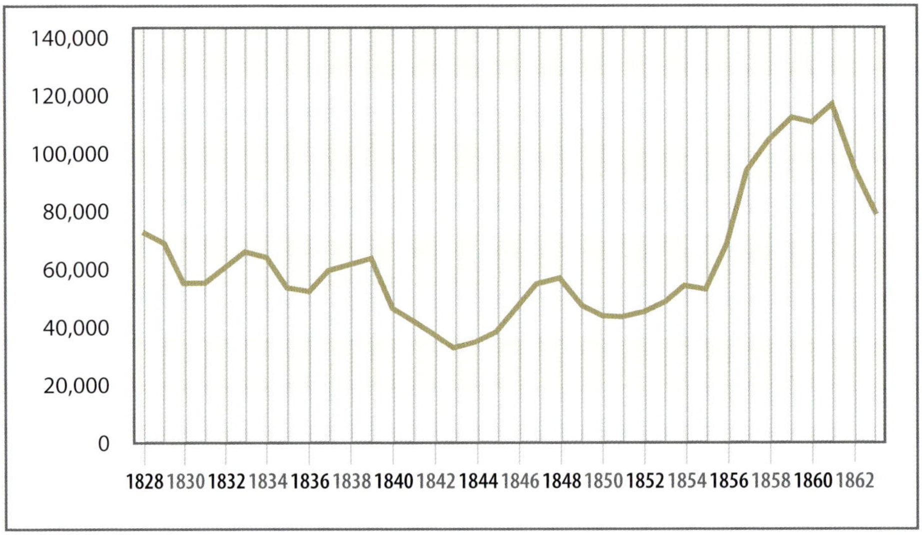

Beamish & Crawford sales (in barrels), 1828–63.

Table 5.5 (facing page)

Sales, sales income, expenditure on malt, malt duty paid and expenditure on hops, 1829–63

Table 5.5

YEAR	SALES (in barrels)	SALES INCOME (to nearest £)	EXPENDITURE ON MALT incl. duty (to nearest £)	MALT DUTY PAID (to nearest £)	EXPENDITURE ON HOPS (to nearest £)
1829	68,318	£112,014			
1830	55,316	?	£111,262 (2 years)	£39,606 (2 years)	£11,360 (2 years)
1831	54,972	£89,772	£46,184	£16,872	£6,046
1832	60,048	£97,805	£48,406	£22,173	£6,760
1833	65,585				
1834	63,394	£210,412 (2 years)			
1835	53,388	?	£151,678 (3 years)	£52,704 (3 years)	£22,681 (3 years)
1836	52,213	£85,457	£43,061	£16,893	£7,317
1837	58,429	£95,782	£48,966	£17,912	£6,744
1838	61,143	£100,975	£36,569	£18,830	£6,694
1839	63,031	£104,312	£47,811	£15,848	£6,105
1840	45,417	£77,066	£47,350	£6,617	£6,294
1841	41,925	£71,977	£38,384	£13,970	£8,400
1842	36,865	£62,227	£33,769	£10,972	£9,821
1843	32,848	£55,045	£22,529	£16,407	£4,718
1844	33,945	£55,826	£19,149	£7,950	£4,180
1845	38,339	£62,844	£26,069	£4,883	£9,430
1846	46,887	£76,505	£32,449	£11,041	£10,354
1847	54,584	£89,408	£46,129	£20,989	£8,254
1848	56,233	£92,044	£50,733	£12,447	£9,145
1849	46,738	£77,050	£42,994	£14,499	£5,710
1850	43,070	£71,576	£43,876	£16,309	£12,106
1851	43,316	£72,211	£44,481	£17,822	£8,675
1852	44,221	£73,539	£36,069	£13,600	£10,348
1853	47,875	£76,762	£35,537	£14,082	£9,173
1854	53,487	£90,595	£43,570	£20,872	£13,613
1855	52,929	£101,230	£51,023	£26,395	£17,853
1856	68,041	£127,758	£78,194	£23,998	£10,236
1857	93,276	£153,425	£100,698	£17,509	£10,598
1858	103,826	£169,161	£104,742	£20,986	£10,445
1859	111,113	£179,295	£104,555	£16,057	£11,852
1860	108,998	£175,158	£99,141	£32,032	£11,447
1861	116,076	£186,584	£111,134	£21,738	£18,819
1862	94,704	£152,717	£90,999	£17,985	£16,719
1863	77,825	£124,883	£71,871	£8,369	£10,521

Cooper stout and the Johnson agency, London, 1862–3[48]

In early 1862, Henry H. Johnson was in communication with Beamish & Crawford in Cork with a view to becoming an agent for the firm in London. At that time Johnson was in partnership with Henry Cremer, trading as Henry Johnson & Co., beer wholesalers, with offices at 33 Mark Lane and stores at Circular Vaults, St Paul's Churchyard, London. Following on his letters, Johnson travelled to Cork in March 1862 and an agreement was reached with the brewery that Johnson's firm would become the exclusive dealer for Beamish & Crawford porter and stout in England and Wales, excluding Liverpool and Barnstaple, where the firm already had established agents. An arrangement was made whereby the brewery would ship stout to London in bulk, where Henry Johnson & Co. would bottle and market it and also sell it wholesale in barrels. Richard Pigott Beamish, who had been working at the brewery since 1852, conducted the negotiations with Johnson.

The young Beamish's acumen is evident in the sophisticated plan designed with Johnson for marketing the Cork stout in London. The stout would be sold under the brand Cooper and new labels were designed for the bottles. A competitive pricing strategy was designed to 'entirely revolutionise the trade' by selling this bottled Irish stout at draught prices. Cooper would be supplied at 2s 6d for a dozen pint bottles, as against 5s or 7s for established brands. The plan was to undermine what was perceived as a monopoly:

> For more than half a century the manufacture and sale of this truly national beverage has been confined to a very narrow circle, the names of the members of which have naturally become 'familiar as household words'. But the consequence has been that what might be termed a 'fancy price' has been maintained – far beyond the fair manufacturing profit which the trader has a right to expect.[49]

Beamish & Crawford and H. Johnson & Co. produced a leaflet for the trade explaining

Letterhead of Beamish & Crawford and Henry Johnson & Co. of London. The partnership marketed Beamish & Crawford stout under the Cooper brand 1862–3. (CCCA/Authors)

the advantages that Cooper had over other bottled stouts and setting out the rationale for their campaign. Cooper was a mix of year-old vatted Extra Treble Stout, for a longer life, and Single Stout, bottled only at Johnson's stores and sealed with corks branded with the Castle trademark 'to prevent bottles being refilled by unprincipled traders with an inferior article'. The leaflet also highlighted the perennial problem of the adulteration of porter by retailers through the addition of sometimes dangerous additives as well as by watering it down. It was claimed that this would be impossible with bottled Cooper stout.

> Families are thus guaranteed a thoroughly sound and perfectly pure beer … [and] the poorer classes will have the opportunity of drinking *at* home instead of *away* from home a pure and wholesome beverage of superior quality.

A touch of originality was added to the Cooper campaign with the composition of a song, 'Where Do You Get Your Cooper?', to promote the product. A printed copy of the song in the Beamish & Crawford archive has an added handwritten note 'as sung by Collins and others at Dr. Johnson's, The Oxford, The Frampton and all other Concert Halls in London'.[50] The last verse reads:

> As it's made in Cork it's strong and light, not a headache in a puncheon;

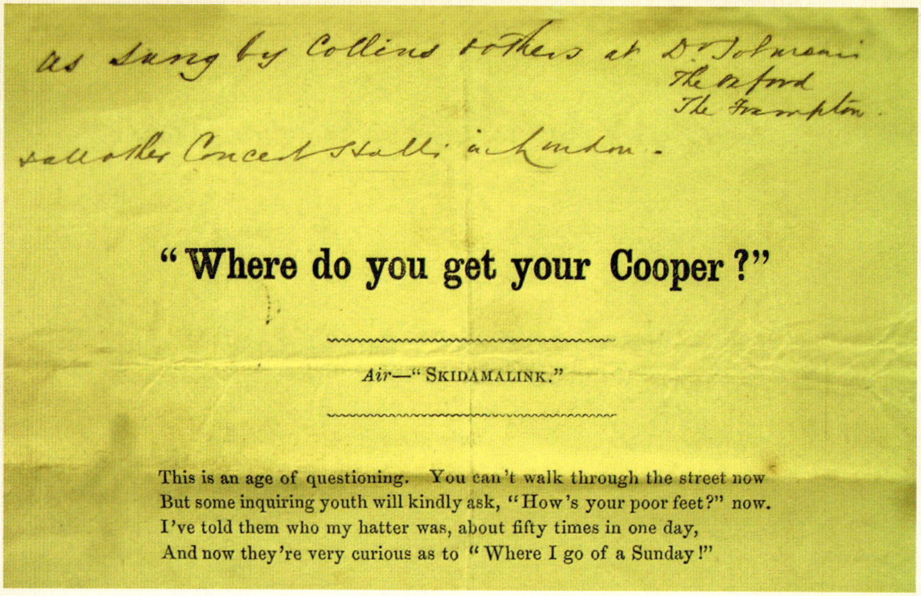

as sung by Collins & others at Dr Johnson's
The Oxford
The Frampton.
& all other Concert Halls in London.

"Where do you get your Cooper?"

Air—"SKIDAMALINK."

This is an age of questioning. You can't walk through the street now
But some inquiring youth will kindly ask, "How's your poor feet?" now.
I've told them who my hatter was, about fifty times in one day,
And now they're very curious as to "Where I go of a Sunday!"

Title and first verse of the song 'Where do you get your Cooper?', composed to promote Cooper stout in London. (CCCA/Authors)

> A pint or two won't hurt each day, before and after luncheon;
> It's the stuff to make you strong, and cause a genuine sensation –
> BEAMISH & CRAWFORD'S Cooper's safe to 'Lick out all creation!'

When the initial agreement was made in March 1862, Johnson had assured Beamish & Crawford that he would sell between 200 and 300 barrels in April and increase this amount month by month. When this level of sales was not achieved, Richard Pigott Beamish became anxious. In response to a letter from Beamish, Johnson replied in September 1862 that he was selling 1,000 dozen pint bottles of Cooper per week and 'before two months are out I shall sell 1,000 dozen per day'. In addition to bottled Cooper, Johnson was also selling barrels of draught stout but at a level far below the agreed targets.

Beamish travelled to London in November to examine the situation at first hand. In the seven months from April 1862, when the venture was launched, Johnson had taken a net total of 834 barrels against a projected target of over 2,000 barrels for the period, or 300 per month. Beamish & Crawford in Cork was left with over 2,000 barrels of Extra Treble Stout that had been brewed specifically for the Cooper venture in Britain, and by November 1862 it was 'almost unfit for use', resulting in a significant financial loss.

After his visit to London, Richard Pigott Beamish received an anonymous letter,

Right: Bottle label for Cooper stout, 1862–3. (CCCA/Authors)

postmarked 5 December 1862, most likely from an employee of Johnson's. The letter set out a number of fraudulent practices by Johnson: empty Beamish & Crawford casks were regularly brought to the London Brewery Co., filled with a poorer-quality porter and labelled by Johnson as Beamish & Crawford's; and he had seen Beamish & Crawford hogsheads (the large 54-gallon casks used for the export trade) topped up with water. The writer continued:

> I have to inform you that your porter has been dealt with in a very unfair manner. There has not been a single drop of ullage [waste beer] belonging to Findlater of Dublin or the City of London Brewery Co. that has not been drawn and filled in your hds [hogsheads].

On 10 January 1863, Beamish wrote to Johnson to inform him that Beamish & Crawford would be terminating their arrangement with him at the end of April. Despite the nefarious behaviour of Johnson, Beamish held out the possibility of entering into a new arrangement after that.

A London acquaintance of Beamish wrote to him on 28 April 1863 to inform him that Johnson had been declared bankrupt a few days before. Beamish & Crawford had a notice printed in the London papers, dated 11 May 1863, stating that Johnson had ceased to be in any way connected with the sale of its porter from 10 May.

The venture had had great prospects and the innovative marketing plan, with its competitive pricing strategy and campaign of raising brand awareness, was very much ahead of its time. Perhaps Richard Pigott Beamish, eager to impress his superiors in the brewery, did not exercise due diligence in entering into business with Johnson. Johnson had previously been in business as a hop merchant, but the venture had failed in 1861. His partner in the beer wholesaling firm had left the partnership in August 1862 at a time when it would have been becoming clear that Johnson was not a man to live up to his promises. Beamish & Crawford's Cooper stout had barely survived a year when it was withdrawn in May 1863.

6

Renewal
1863–1899

> It is evident that at the period of the change of management, nothing short of the entire re-construction of the Brewery, and the re-organization of every department of the business, could have sufficed to save the concern from the collapse which threatened it.[1]

So wrote Richard Pigott Beamish on the state of the firm of Beamish & Crawford in 1863 when he became joint acting partner following the signing of a new co-partnership agreement in August of that year. Although William Horatio Crawford was officially his joint acting partner, Beamish was effectively the sole chief executive and he led the firm for the next thirty years, saving it from 'the collapse which threatened it' and driving a programme of development, costing in excess of £100,000, that enabled the brewery to prosper, albeit in second place from 1878 to its great Cork rival, James J. Murphy & Co. Sales of Beamish & Crawford products grew to 100,000 barrels in the later 1870s but had fallen to nearly half that a decade later before a renewed growth brought sales past the 100,000 mark again in 1899, the year Richard Pigott Beamish died.

The market in Ireland for porter, and its stronger version, stout, grew strongly throughout the later decades of the nineteenth century. In the south of the country, especially in the city and county of Cork, this market was dominated by Beamish & Crawford and James J. Murphy & Co., with two other city brewers and a small number of country brewers having significantly smaller market shares. Guinness was increasing its share in the south at this time, but the estates of tied houses controlled by the Cork brewers, numbering almost 500 in the city alone, protected their trade while Guinness achieved almost complete dominance of the porter and stout trade

Beamish & Crawford brewery, late 1880s, viewed from the southwest. Note the upper portion of the cone of the Hanover Street glassworks (demolished in 1915) to the left of the complex and the small river steamer with a cargo of barrels in the left foreground. This image formed the centerpiece of mirrors produced in the early 1900s for display in Beamish & Crawford public houses. (Beamish & Crawford Brewery Collection/Dori O'Connell)

in the rest of Ireland. Between 1865 and 1900, the annual output of breweries in Ireland grew from 1.2 million to 2.6 million barrels, while the number of breweries in the country fell from ninety to thirty-six in the same period. Between 1865 and 1900, Beamish & Crawford's annual production varied from as low as 55,000 barrels in 1888 to a high of 104,000 in 1900, but in the same period Guinness production grew steadily and steeply from around 300,000 barrels in 1865 to over 1.8 million by 1900, making it the world's biggest brewer.

The general standard of living of most of the Irish population rose in the second half of the nineteenth century. Agriculture and the processing of agricultural produce continued to be the mainstay of the economy, and innovation, improved methods and specialisation saw advances in dairying, beef production and grain growing. Poor harvests still had an impact and the crop failures of the early 1860s, for example, were severe and caused widespread distress, but a repeat of the famine conditions of less than twenty years before was avoided. A fall in Beamish & Crawford's sales by over

30 per cent in the two years from 1861 to 1863 was partly the result of this distress. The years 1879 to 1881 saw another crisis in agriculture caused by bad weather, poor harvests and low prices, and again brewery sales fell, from 101,658 barrels in 1877 to 69,758 in 1881. This was also the period of the Land War (1879–82), when tenant farmers fought for lowers rents, fixed tenure and the right to sell their interest in their land. While some of their demands were met, the question of land reform was to feature prominently in politics into the twentieth century along with the issue of Home Rule.

Between 1863 and 1900, the Beamish & Crawford brewery was renewed, physically and in its spirit, under the stewardship of Richard Pigott Beamish, but the earlier decline in trade during the 1830s and 1840s, the internecine struggles of the Beamish partners, their lack of attention to business and the arrival of serious competition from James J. Murphy & Co. had weakened the position of the firm significantly. A renewal was achieved, but the early nineteenth-century primacy of Beamish & Crawford in Irish brewing was not repeated.

New partnerships

1863

A new co-partnership agreement was drawn up to come into effect from 3 August 1863.[2] The partners in the firm, which was to trade as Beamish & Crawford, were George Crawford (son of William Crawford), William Horatio Crawford (son of William Crawford Jr.), North Ludlow Beamish, Charles Beamish and Francis Bernard Beamish (sons of William Beamish) and Richard Pigott Beamish (son of Richard Beamish and grandson of William Beamish). The Crawford and Beamish partners together each held a 50 per cent share in the brewery. According to the terms of this deed of co-partnership, North Ludlow Beamish and George Crawford retired as the acting partners and William Horatio Crawford and Richard Pigott Beamish replaced them in that position. The others were to be sleeping partners. Any of the co-partners, acting or sleeping, could sell or transfer their share, or part of their share, to any of the other co-partners or to a male descendent of William Crawford I or William Beamish.

On 11 January 1864, George Crawford transferred his 25 per cent share in the firm to his nephew William Horatio Crawford, who then held 50 per cent of the company. In return, William Horatio undertook to pay George £15,000 and the net profits earned by that 25 per cent share for as long as George should live, but George did not live to benefit from the arrangement as he died later that year. Two days after George Crawford completed the transfer of his interest to his nephew, North Ludlow Beamish transferred his share to his son North Ludlow Axel Beamish, the latter becoming a sleeping partner while his father withdrew completely. North

Ludlow Axel committed to paying his father an annuity of £1,200, which he received until his death on 27 April 1872.

Charles Beamish died on 18 January 1867 without having bequeathed his share in the firm to a male lineal descendant of William Beamish, as was required under the terms of the co-partnership agreement of 1863. A legal action was instituted on behalf of his son, also called Charles, to enable him to inherit his father's share in the brewery. This son was only seven years old when his father died and the efforts on his behalf eventually failed, leaving Charles Beamish's share to be divided equally between the other surviving Beamish partners, Francis Bernard, North Ludlow Axel and Richard Pigott.[3]

Francis Bernard Beamish, the last of the sons of William Beamish still involved in the partnership, died on 1 February 1868. His share was inherited by his son, Francis Bernard Servington Beamish, who then became a sleeping partner. The third generation, grandsons of the brewery founders, was now fully in control of the firm. On 22 August 1870, William Horatio Crawford transferred a 1/16 share in the brewery from his holding to William Henry Sharman Crawford, his first cousin and a grandson of William Crawford I, making him a sleeping partner.

From left: Richard Pigott Beamish's signature with those of his acting partner William Horatio Crawford, 1863–88, William Henry Sharman Crawford, 1888–90, and Arthur Frederick Sharman Crawford, 1890-5. (all CCCA/Authors)

1879

The Beamish & Crawford co-partnership agreement was renewed in August 1879 for a further sixteen years. Richard Pigott Beamish (8/48 share) and William Horatio Crawford (21/48 share) continued as the acting partners, and William Henry Sharman Crawford (3/48 share), North Ludlow Axel Beamish (8/48 share) and Francis Bernard Servington Beamish (8/48 share) were the sleeping partners. A schedule was attached to the co-partnership deed showing the capital stock and property of the firm, which was given a valuation of £210,080.6.11.

William Horatio Crawford died unmarried and without children on 18 October 1888 and, as provided for in the 1879 agreement, his cousin William Henry Sharman Crawford became an acting partner. William Henry's younger brother, Arthur Frederick, inherited part of William Horatio's holding and became a sleeping partner. When William Henry died in 1890, Arthur Frederick became the Crawford acting partner. At this time another brother, Robert Gordon Sharman Crawford, also became a sleeping partner. The two Sharman Crawford brothers held the Crawford family half-share in the brewery. Francis Bernard Servington Beamish retired some time between 1891 and 1895 and his $^{8}/_{48}$ share was transferred to his son, Francis Edward de Courcy Beamish.

Table 6.1

Partnership arrangement: Beamish & Crawford, 1863–95

YEARS	ACTING PARTNERS	SLEEPING PARTNERS
1863–4	Richard Pigott Beamish William Horatio Crawford	North Ludlow Beamish (retired 1864) Francis Bernard Beamish Charles Beamish George Crawford (d. 1864)
1864–7	Richard Pigott Beamish William Horatio Crawford	North Ludlow Axel Beamish Francis Bernard Beamish Charles Beamish (d. 1867)
1867–8	Richard Pigott Beamish William Horatio Crawford	North Ludlow Axel Beamish Francis Bernard Beamish (d. 1868)
1868–70	Richard Pigott Beamish William Horatio Crawford	North Ludlow Axel Beamish Francis Bernard Servington Beamish
1870–88	Richard Pigott Beamish William Horatio Crawford (d. 1888)	North Ludlow Axel Beamish Francis Bernard Servington Beamish William Henry Sharman Crawford
1888–90	Richard Pigott Beamish William H. Sharman Crawford (d. 1890)	North Ludlow Axel Beamish Francis Bernard Servington Beamish Arthur F. Sharman Crawford
1890–5	Richard Pigott Beamish Arthur F. Sharman Crawford	North Ludlow Axel Beamish Francis Ed. de Courcy Beamish (replaced his father, Francis Bernard, during this period) Robert G. Sharman Crawford

1895

When the 1879 co-partnership agreement expired in 1895, the partners in the firm of Beamish & Crawford were Arthur Frederick Sharman Crawford, Robert Gordon Sharman Crawford, Richard Pigott Beamish, North Ludlow Axel Beamish and Francis Edward de Courcy Beamish. As had become the practice for many family businesses in the later 1800s, Beamish & Crawford became incorporated in 1895 as Beamish & Crawford Ltd. The nominal capital of the new entity was £186,400, made up of 17,280 preference shares of £5 each and 20,000 ordinary shares of £5

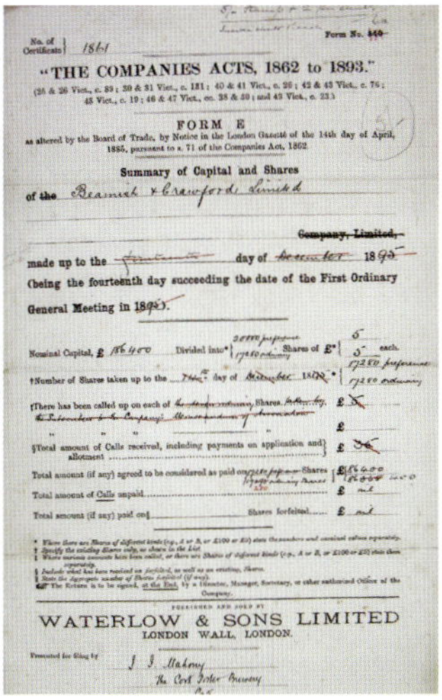

From left: Seal of Beamish & Crawford Ltd, adopted in 1895 on the incorporation of the company. (CCCA/Authors)
Beamish & Crawford Ltd, register of shareholders, 1895. (CCCA/Authors)
Cover of summary of capital and shares of Beamish & Crawford Ltd, incorporated 1895. (CCCA/Authors)

---

each, 17,280 of which were initially allocated. The respective holdings of the Beamish and Crawford families following the incorporation of the firm are set out below.

Table 6.2
Shareholders of Beamish & Crawford Ltd following incorporation in 1895

NAME	PREFERENCE SHARES	ORDINARY SHARES
Richard Pigott Beamish	2,880	2,840
North Ludlow Axel Beamish	2,880	2,880
Francis Ed. de Courcy Beamish	2,880	2,880
Richard Henrik Beamish	0	20
Gustav William Beamish	0	20
Arthur F. Sharman Crawford	4,860	4860
Robert G. Sharman Crawford	3,780	3,780
Total	17,280	17,280

Richard Henrik and Gustav William Beamish were sons of Richard Pigott Beamish and great-grandsons of William Beamish, while the Sharman Crawford brothers were grandsons of William Crawford.

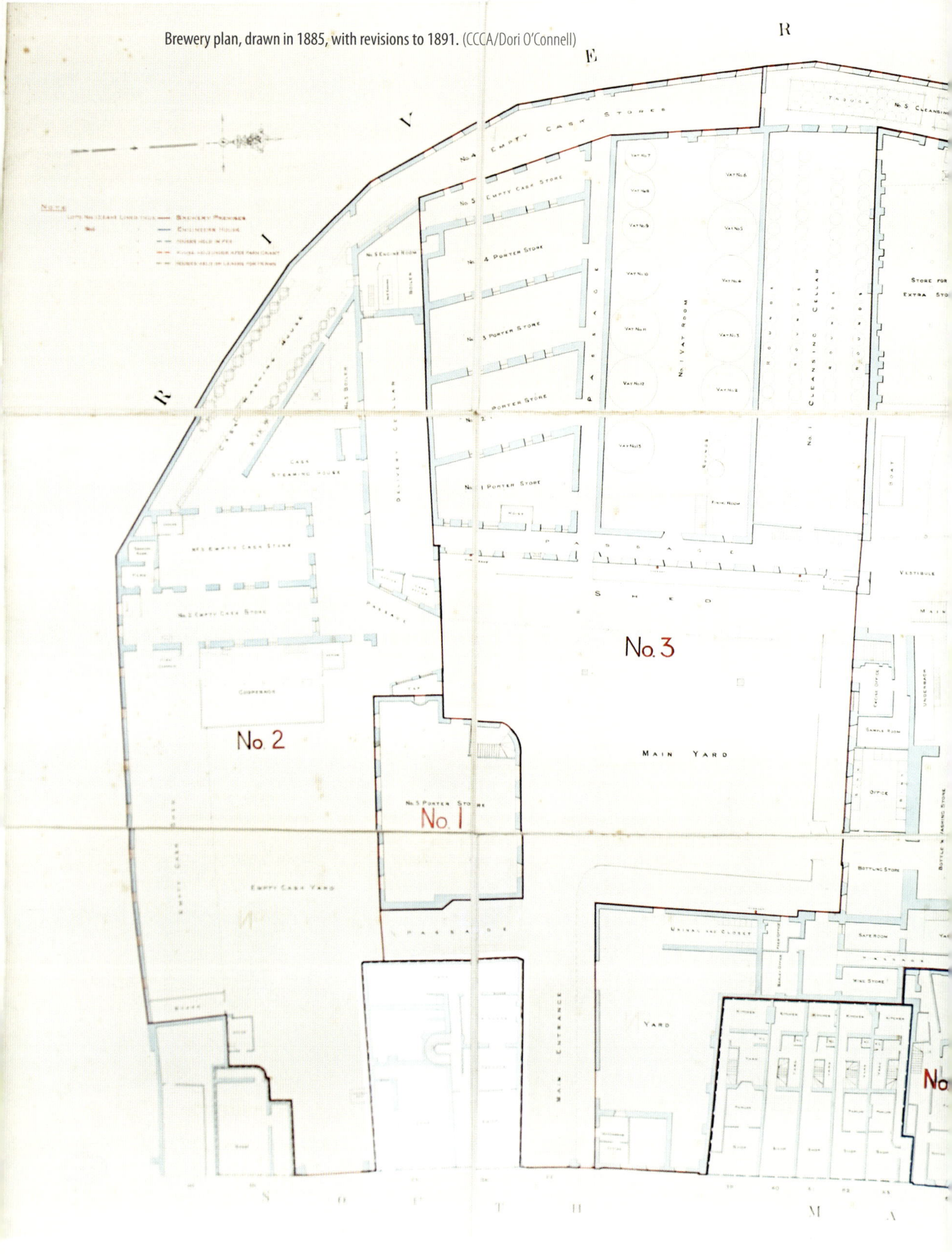

Brewery plan, drawn in 1885, with revisions to 1891. (CCCA/Dori O'Connell)

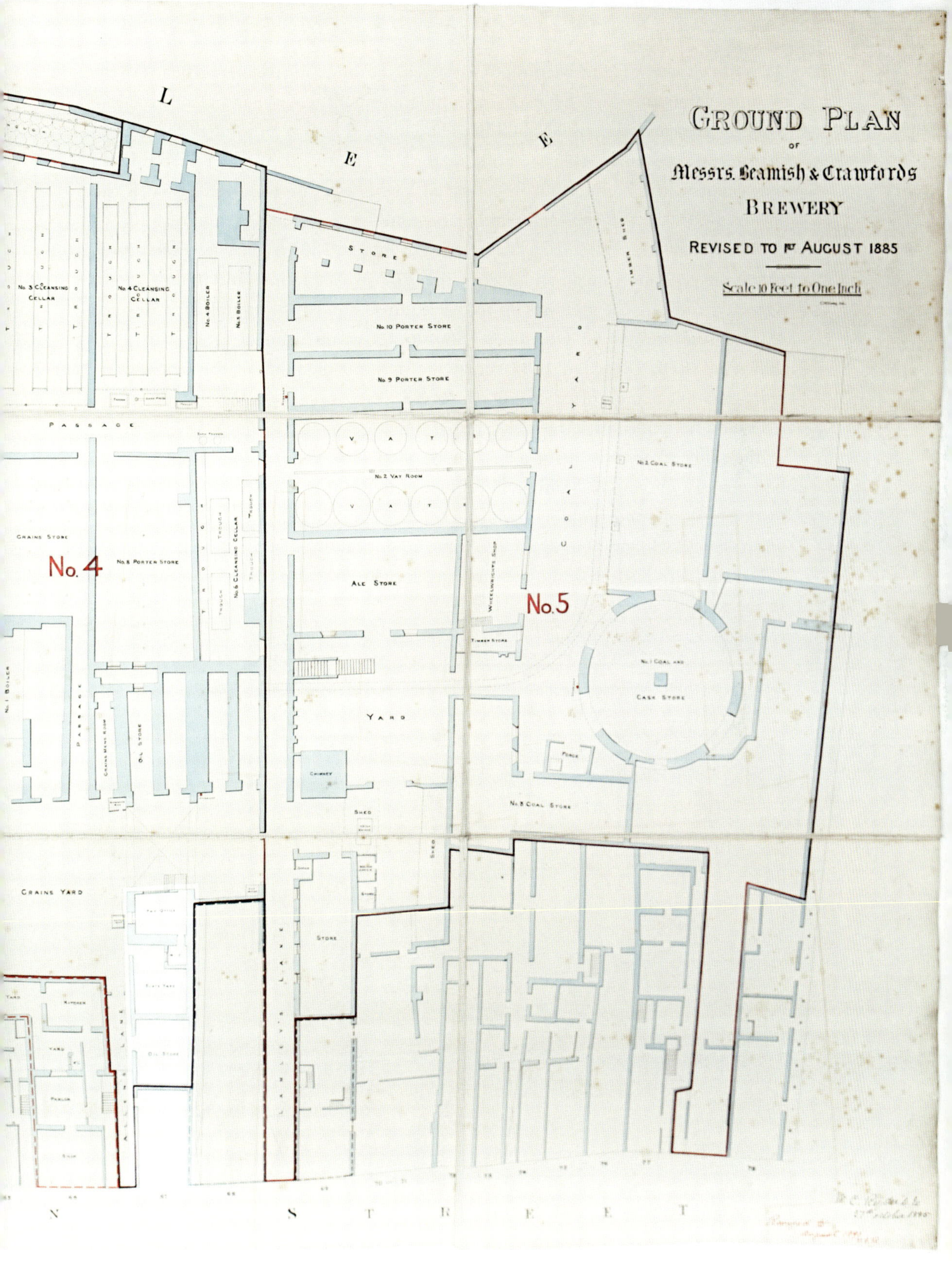

GROUND PLAN
OF
Messrs. Beamish & Crawfords
BREWERY
REVISED TO 1st AUGUST 1885
Scale 10 Feet to One Inch
L
E
E
No. 3 Cleansing Cellar
No. 4 Cleansing Cellar
No. 4 Boiler
No. 5 Boiler
Store
No. 10 Porter Store
No. 9 Porter Store
Timber Shed
Yard
Passage
V A T S
No. 2 Vat Room
V A T S
Coal
No. 2 Coal Store
Grains Store
No. 4
No. 8 Porter Store
No. 6 Cleansing Cellar
Trough
Ale Store
Wheelwrights Shop
No. 5
Timber Store
No. 1 Coal and Cask Store
No. 1 Boiler
Passage
Oil Store
Yard
Chimney
Forge
No. 3 Coal Store
Shed
Grains Yard
Store
Lane
Yard
Kitchen
Parlor
Shop
Lawley's Lane
Oil Store
N
S T R E E T

Brewery renewal

As soon as Richard Pigott Beamish took the reins as the acting partner on behalf of the Beamish family in 1863, he instigated a programme of renewal and reconstruction. This involved investing in new buildings and plant as well as a thorough overhaul of management systems within the firm. Beamish felt that by the time of the change in management, the brewery was in danger of having to cease manufacture, such was the decayed state of its buildings and plant, some 'even dangerous to human life'. A civil engineer, O.C. Edwards, was employed in August 1863 to do a complete survey of the brewery and to plan and oversee the extensive alterations and improvements necessary to bring the premises up to the required standard. Edwards drew detailed plans of the brewery in December 1863, and a comparison of these with plans drawn in 1878, 1885 and 1897 shows the progress of much of the renewal and reorganisation that occurred during the period.

The southern portion of the brewery premises was extended through the acquisition of the salt and lime works shown on the 1863 ground plan and other premises between that and South Main Street. A new entrance from the street was made here by demolishing some buildings, which gave access to a new empty cask yard created when the old salt and lime works and some other buildings were removed.

This southern portion of the brewery stretching from South Main Street westwards to the river became the area devoted to the return, cleaning, repair and storage of casks. By the 1880s the old Morgan's Lane that led from South Main Street had

Detail from the Goad fire insurance plan of 1897 showing Beamish & Crawford Brewery. (Cork City Library)

completely disappeared, its western portion forming part of the new entrance to the empty cask yard. A large cask-washing house replaced the pre-1863 cooperage that bordered the river and a new cooperage was built at the western end of the empty cask yard. This cooperage was used principally for the repair of damaged casks. Prior to 1896, Beamish & Crawford bought their casks from independent cooperages and manufactured only a small number of their own. By 1885, a cask steaming house was added to the east side of the cask-washing house and a large boiler was installed to supply the steam. A new engine room and boilers were installed at the western end of the delivery cellar and the tall chimney from this boiler is clearly shown in the centre foreground of the panoramic view of the brewery drawn in the late 1880s. The large empty cask yard with its large gates leading on to South Main Street is also clearly shown in that view. By 1896, the empty cask shed that lay to the south of the empty cask yard had been converted to a large cooperage, with windows facing on to the river.

The central part of the brewery complex, ranged along the west and north sides of the main yard, housed the buildings of porter brewing: the mash loft, fermenting and cleansing cellars, vat rooms, porter stores, malt and hop stores, malt-milling tower, engine and boiler houses and all plant associated with the production process. The main yard was accessed by way of a gateway and passage from South Main

Brewery plan of 1878. (CCCA/Authors)

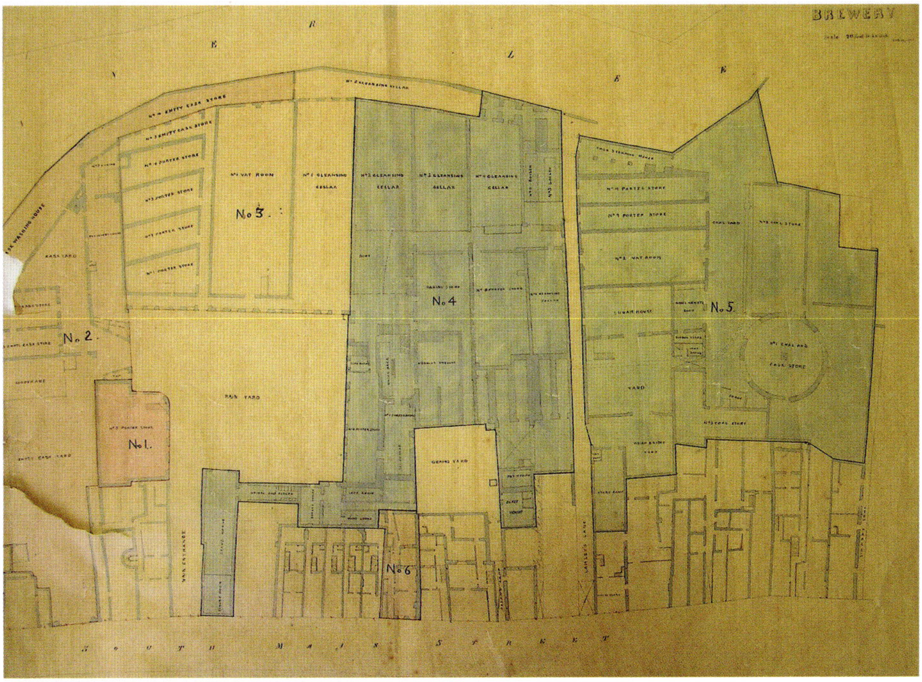

Above: The main yard, or quadrangle, of the brewery. (Courtesy Ed Hinchy)
This photograph was the basis for the drawing (left) published in A. Barnard, *Noted Breweries of Great Britain and Ireland Vol. 2* (London 1889)

Street. The general layout of the brewing department remained broadly unchanged throughout the latter decades of the nineteenth century, but old plant and equipment was regularly replaced and updated and some areas were assigned new functions.

On the ground floor of the principal building on the north side of the main yard were fourteen malt bins capable of holding 21,000 barrels of malt. The malt was conveyed from these up to the top floor of the malt-milling tower by means of an Archimedean screw. Alfred Barnard, who visited the brewery in the late 1880s, described the workings of this area:

> we ascended to the mill-room, a splendid chamber erected entirely of brick and iron, and said to be fire-proof. It is very lofty, and is lighted on all sides by 'slip windows'; here we were shown three sets of powerful steel rollers for crushing the malt, raised some 5 feet from the ground, with iron steps leading up to them for the maltmen to attend to the mills. In the centre of the floor, and reached by an iron ladder, is a raised platform on a level with the top of the receptacles which feed the rollers. Here are the revolving screens for taking

> out the dust and combings from the malt on its downward course to the rollers below; and we should add that these cleaning machines, which were supplied by Messrs. Stopes & Co., of London, are fitted with patent magnetic screens for arresting any metallic substance and preventing it from passing through them.[4]

The tall malt-milling tower is the building to the rear left in the photograph opposite. The mash loft occupied the floor below, 'a noble and lofty hall of cruciform shape, nearly 200 feet long', and there were three mash tuns in this area, one more than in 1863, 'two of which are of iron, covered with timber and brass bound, holding nearly 300 barrels of malt each; and a smaller one entirely of oak, holding 130 barrels'. The milled malt, known as grist, was fed into three hoppers, which were positioned above the mash tuns, then mixed with hot water in the mashing machines before being transferred to the mash tuns. After mashing, the spent grains were separated from the wort in the underback and the wort was pumped to the coppers. There were four coppers, which stood on a raised platform:

> They are handsome domed copper vessels, enclosed in red bricks; three of them have pans over them, which hold 150 barrels each. The contents of all the coppers are 1,560 barrels, and they were manufactured by Llewellin & James, of Bristol, and Murphy, of Dublin; as a matter-of-fact, each of these vessels cost £2,000.[5]

Left: Mashing loft, 1880s. (Courtesy Mike Hannon)
Right: Coppers on the mezzanine floor at the eastern end of the mashing loft. (Courtesy Ed Hinchy)

Left: The refrigerators on the upper floor of Cleansing Cellar No. 3. (Courtesy Mike Hannon) Right: The racking room, late 1880s. Note the two sets of rails for moving the casks to and from the racking area. (Courtesy Mike Hannon)

The hops were boiled with the wort in these copper vessels, then the wort passed through the hopback, where the hop residue was removed, before the wort was pumped to the coolers above. These were large, open tanks with a capacity of 460 barrels each and were housed in a loft area kept cool with a specially constructed ventilated roof.

The next stage in the production process was fermenting and cleansing. A number of fermentation tuns or vats were located on an upper floor above cleansing cellar No. 3, as shown on the 1863, 1878 and 1885 ground plans. The wort ran from the coolers through three large refrigerators into the fermenting vats, where the yeast was added. During fermentation the sugars in the liquor, as the wort is called after the addition of yeast, convert to alcohol. After the initial fermentation, lasting about three days, the liquor was transferred to the cleansing cellars shown on the various plans. On the 1863 plan, four cleansing cellars are shown at the western end of the central part of the brewery complex. By 1878, two more had been added: No. 5 in an area on the riverbank to the west and No. 6 on the south side of Lamley's Lane. On the 1885 plan No. 2 is labelled as a store for extra stout, but on the Goad fire insurance plan of 1897 it is again shown as a cleansing cellar. In the vessels in the cleansing cellars, the porter underwent further fermentation, maturation and settling. Here also the barm, the foamy by-product of fermentation, was skimmed from the surface of the vessels and pressed to squeeze the liquid from the yeast. The cakes of barm were sold with the spent grains as animal feed or sometimes used by bakers.

Following cleansing the porter was pumped to the vats, where it was held for further maturation and conditioning before being racked or filled into barrels for sale and distribution. The 1863 plan shows a large vat room, accessed from the western side of the main yard, and a smaller vat room on the south side of Lamley's Lane. On the 1878 plan the smaller vat room is located on the north side of Lamley's Lane, as it is on the 1885 plan and on the Goad fire insurance plan of 1897. Barnard described the larger vat room following his visit in the late 1880s:

> It is a lofty and cool place 140 feet long and 50 feet wide, while the walls are as white as paint can make them. The building contains nine large and three small store vats; each of the former contains 650 barrels, and the three latter 150 barrels each. In the roof of the vat house is the summer settling tank, the largest single vessel of slate ever manufactured by the firm who put it up.[6]

The second smaller vat room had an arched brick roof and housed twelve vats with a capacity of 160 barrels each. Porter was stored here for about a year for blending purposes. To the south of the large vat room, the four cellars shown on the 1863 plan are labelled as porter stores on the later plans and further porter stores or cellars are shown elsewhere in the brewery. The upper floors above the porter stores and cleansing cellars on the western side of the brewery complex were used for storing malt and hops.

Towards the western end of the range of buildings north of Lamley's Lane, the 1878, 1885 and 1897 plans show porter stores Nos. 9 and 10. On the southern end of the upper floors of the building housing these stores was a small ale brewery, described by Barnard:

> we made our way to through the mashing department, to visit the little compact and model ale brewery exactly adjoining, but in no way connected with the porter and stout department. It is a four-storeyed building, and contains two mash-tuns capable of mashing forty barrels, with the usual copper refrigerators and fermenting vessels, which it is needless here to describe; a five horse-power horizontal non-condensing engine, supplied with steam from main boilers, is used for driving the mashing and other machinery.[7]

A correspondent of the *Wine Merchant and Grocers' Review* in 1889 also described this ale brewery:

> One of the most unique things in connection with Beamish & Crawford's Brewery is the fact that there is a Small Brewery, with entirely separate and independent plant and staff, within and upon the premises of the larger

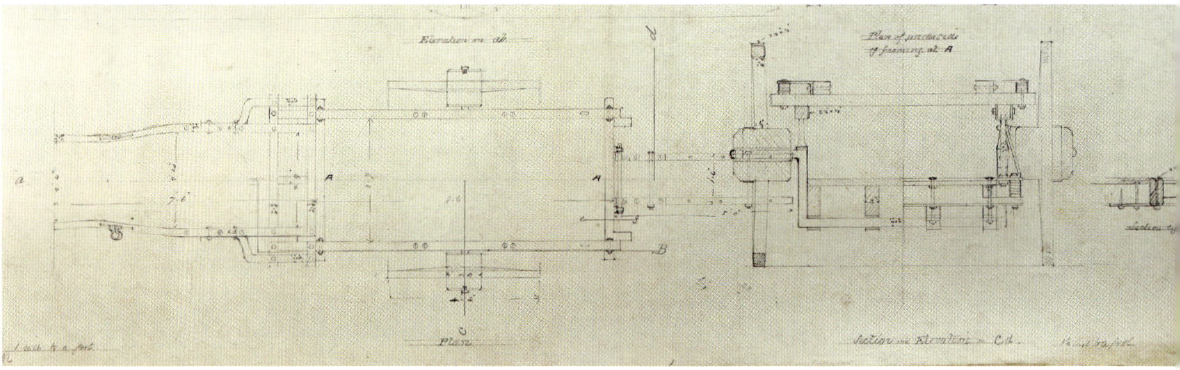

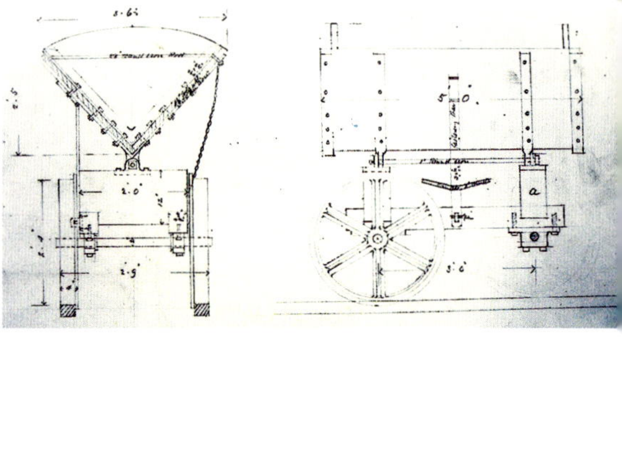

From top: Brewery engineering workshop, *c.* 1900. The figure standing fourth from left, holding a book, is Timothy McCarthy. His son (also Timothy), grandson Harry and great-grandsons Johnny and Len all worked at Beamish & Crawford. (Courtesy Mike Hannon)

Drawing, dated 1871, of a Beamish & Crawford brewery dray. (CCCA/Dori O'Connell)

Drawings, dated 1872, for proposed coal wagons to be used on the brewery's railway for transporting coal from the stores to the various boilers. (CCCA/Dori O'Connell)

> Brewery. In this small brewery is a famous Well which supplies the water for Beamish and Crawford's well-known East India and other Ales. This smaller Brewery is devoted to the manufacturing of Ales and Extra Stouts exclusively, the porter being manufactured in the large Brewery.[8]

The northern range of buildings, situated north of Lamley's Lane, housed the workshops of the engineers, fitters, carpenters, blacksmiths, coppersmiths, painters and wheelwrights whose skills were necessary for the daily functioning of the brewery. The brewery wheelwrights made and repaired the brewery's drays, carts and coal wagons. In this area also were the extensive coal yards and coal stores of the brewery. The old glassworks cone was still in use for the storage of coal and casks and would survive until its demolition in 1915.

The panoramic view of the brewery drawn in the late 1880s shows nine tall chimneys in different parts of the brewery. These were the chimneys of the steam boilers that created the power for driving the brewery machinery and heating the brews in the mash tuns and coppers. Steam power drove the pumps, elevators, malt mills, revolving malt screens, stirring and sparging equipment, hop presses, lathes and cooling fans, while large quantities of hot water and steam were used to clean the returned casks in the cask-washing sheds.

Between 1863 and 1878, over £89,000 was spent on improvements in the brewery, including the purchase of some additional premises and the head rents of others

Drawing of Beamish & Crawford brewery first published in A. Barnard, *Noted Breweries of Great Britain and Ireland Vol. 2* (London 1889)

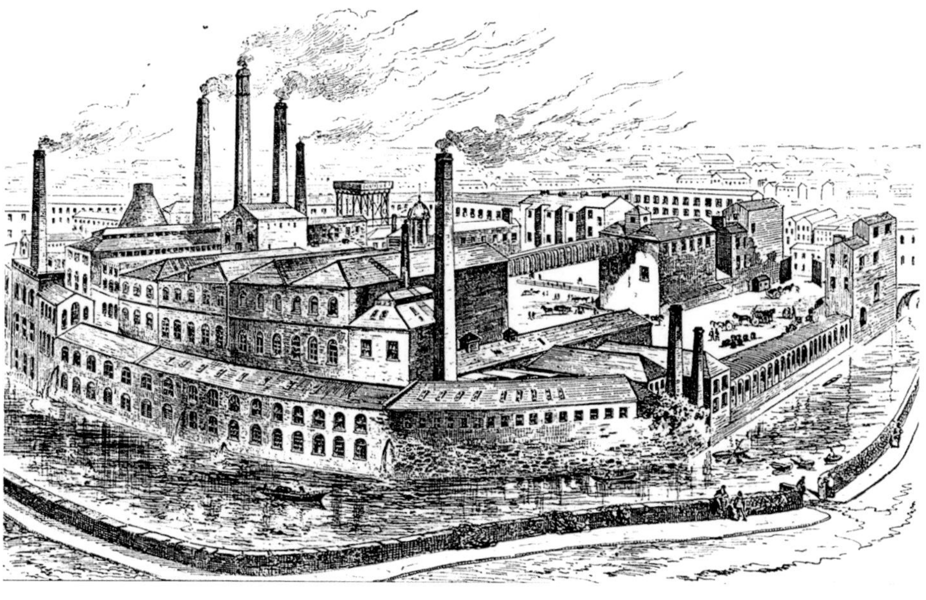

Brewery and city rooftops, viewed from Elizabeth Fort to the south.
- (*Irish Examiner*)

already part of the brewery complex.[9] A further £33,000 was spent on new casks, bottles and equipment. In 1898 the Beamish & Crawford malthouse on Morrison's Island at the eastern end of the South Mall in Cork was sold to coal merchants, George Abraham and Abraham Edward Sutton, for £5,000. A portion of the premises had been rented by the Suttons since 1846.

'Confusion, contradiction and mystery': management changes

George Mazon had taken up employment with Beamish & Crawford in 1823 as a clerk and had risen to become the firm's business manager, a position he had held for a number of years prior to his death in 1863. Richard Pigott Beamish, installed in August 1863 with William Horatio Crawford as acting partner, was withering in his assessment of Mazon's abilities. He blamed him for much of brewery's decline and disorganisation, highlighting his inability to delegate as being particularly harmful: 'In consequence of Mr. Mazon's singular jealousy of interference, there was no one else connected with the establishment who was in any way prepared to fill his position.'[10] After Mazon had died,

> It was then found that the mode in which the accounts of the firm were kept was so voluminous, ill-arranged, and at the same time so incomplete that it was almost impossible to obtain any information as to the working of any department of the concern. No check existed over the stocks of Barley, Malt, Hops, Coals, Casks etc. Indeed in the case of Barley, Coal and Casks, nothing that can be called accounts appear ever to have existed.[11]

The annual accounts were usually five or six months late in being made up, clerks who handled money were not properly supervised and Beamish found that two of them were 'defaulters to a considerable extent'. He added that 'in consequence of the want of system and the secrecy that pervaded the management of the business, a large amount of error, of robbery, and confusion had long existed'.

The legal papers held in the brewery had also fallen into disarray. Given the expansion of the brewery complex, the purchase and leasing of adjoining premises and lots, the number or malthouses and mills owned by the firm, the many public houses mortgaged to the brewery and the increasingly complicated partnership agreements governing the business, the volume of these legal papers had become unwieldy. No system had been put in place for their management and 'they were not even nominally placed under the charge of anyone in particular. They were thrown, unassorted, into large canvass [*sic*] bags, and placed in an iron cupboard which was neither fire nor thief proof'.[12] Many deeds were missing, the renewal dates for leases were not monitored and the legal department of the firm 'was in a state of confusion,

Leases, letting agreements and other legal documents from the Beamish & Crawford archive. (CCCA/Dori O'Connell)

contradiction and mystery, which was the source of error and difficulty'.

Once the new acting partners took over the management of the brewery in August 1863, Richard Pigott Beamish, assisted by the head clerk, Richard McNamara, set about putting new systems in place in all departments of the brewery.[13] The extent of the improvement is evidenced by the great increase in the volume of material relating to the firm's accounts, use of raw materials, production figures, dealings with agents and publicans, and legal matters dating from the years after 1863 in the brewery archive. All clerks who handled cash had to pay a security bond, new agreements were drawn up with the brewery's agents and the level of outstanding and bad debts was greatly reduced. The legal department was put on a proper footing under the management of a confidential clerk, and a new solicitor, P.W. Bass, was appointed to act on behalf of the brewery. Proper statements of title were completed for all portions of the brewery property, expiring leases were renewed, often under better terms, and dealings with tied publicans were formalised with formal legal agreements. As Beamish noted:

> … the firm have now become the masters in place of being the servants of the local publicans, almost all of whom that are Beamish & Crawford customers, being now either monthly tenants or bound by written agreements which secure their dealings.[14]

The matter of the declining quality of Beamish & Crawford's porter in the early 1860s had been partially addressed through the dismissal of the head brewer, William Bowden Wetherman, in 1863. He was replaced by William Gray, who remained as head brewer until his retirement in 1892. While Gray's skills as a brewer seem to have given satisfaction, his mismanagement of his personal finances saw him frequently in trouble with the acting partners (see 'William Gray, head brewer, 1863–92', pp. 157–9). Gray was replaced as head brewer by Frank Thurston in 1892 on an initial annual salary of £650, rising to £850 by 1899. Thurston remained with Beamish & Crawford until 1902. His son, Ernest Temple, married Cork woman Katherine Madden in 1901. Writing as Katherine Thurston, she enjoyed international success as a writer of short stories and novels but died at the height of her fame in 1911 at the age of thirty-six.

As part of the review and reorganisation of all departments in the brewery following the change in management in 1863, the acting partners wrote reports on the different areas of the firm with a view to improving oversight and also to inform the sleeping partners of the detailed workings of the firm. The reports on brewing, management of customers and barley have survived and give relatively detailed accounts of the workings of those departments and the duties and responsibilities of the various employees.

'Workings of Brewing Dept.'

Richard Pigott Beamish and the new head brewer, William Gray, wrote a report on the organisation and working of the brewing department, setting out the duties of employees at each stage of the brewing process.[15] The head brewer was assisted by two assistant brewers and had charge of all raw materials, barley, malt and hops as well as coal and casks. The head brewer was required to be aware of the market prices for the various raw materials and to ensure that the best quality was purchased for the most competitive price. He was also responsible for the supervision of all clerks, superintendents, assistants and labourers in the department.

The first operation in the brewing process was weighing and screening the malt. This was supervised by the malt clerk, who oversaw a weighmaster, twelve men and one boy. Next, the malt was milled or ground and the malt loft gang, consisting of a foreman and two men, had responsibility for this stage. The level of their work depended on the number of brews. In summer five brews per week was the average, falling to a weekly average of three in winter. It was estimated that 100 barrels of malt could be milled in two hours. This gang maintained all the milling machinery in the mill loft and on the morning of a brew transferred the milled malt or grist to the mash tuns. Their hours of work were 6.00am to 6.00pm, Monday to Saturday, but they were often required to work after 6.00pm if brewing was not finished. From 1863 to 1867, Edward Lee, the malt clerk, was earning £100 per year.

The mashing loft lay on a level below the mill loft and is where the mashing of the wort in the mash tuns and the boiling with hops in the coppers took place. The mashing loft gang had a foreman in charge, eleven mashers, four firemen to tend to the boilers and two boys. One of the firemen worked 6.00pm to 6.00am, but all the others on this floor worked from 6.00am to 6.00pm, six days a week. There were also five cleaners who washed and cleaned all of the equipment. This group also saw to the transfer of the wort to the cooling tanks on a floor above the mashing loft.

Fermentation was under the direct supervision of the head brewer and his two assistants. The barm, or foam, that formed on the surface of the fermenting liquor in the cleansing cellars was removed by the cleansing cellar gang, made up of one foreman and nine men, who also worked a twelve-hour, six-day week, but who had to work longer when required. In 1868 the cleansing cellar foreman was John Bolster, who earned £52 per year. This had risen to £71.10.0 by 1872, when he died. He was succeeded by Michael Beale, who was paid £65 per annum initially. One of the gang was in charge of the barm press, where the barm was pressed into cakes to be sold to distilleries and bakers.

From the cleansing cellars the liquor was pumped to the vat room, where one cooper and a gang of thirteen men worked, overseen by the vat-room clerk. In the mid-1860s this was Richard Moore, who earned £130 per annum. The vat-room cooper in 1867 was Henry Carroll, who earned an annual salary of £88.8.0, rising to £130 by 1872. In 1887 his son James took over as vat-room cooper on £93.12.0 per annum while Henry returned to the cooperage on a weekly wage of £2.10.0, where he continued to work until 1896. This gang had the same working hours as

Cask-washing shed, 1880s. (Courtesy Mike Hannon)

the others in the brewing department and had responsibility 'for all Porter from its being finished until actually sold'. In the vat room, finings were added to the porter to clarify it. Traditionally isinglass, a substance made from the swim bladders of the sturgeon or other fish, was used, and when added to the porter it hastened the settling of sediments and impurities that were then more easily removed. When the porter in the vats was judged to be in the appropriate condition, it was racked, or filled, into barrels or casks in which it was sold and distributed. The vat room gang had to ensure that all barrels were properly cleaned before filling them, as the porter would otherwise soon spoil, and when racked they brought the barrels to the storage cellars.

The cask-washing sheds were also considered part of the brewing department, and here a gang of eleven men under the supervision of a cooper received the barrels returned from the trade, examined them for damage and then cleaned and scoured them with hot water and steam. From 1852 until 1883, the cooper in charge of the cask-washing area was Noble Johnson, who started on an annual salary of £67.12.0 in 1852, rising to £117 by 1870. He retired in 1883 and was granted a pension of £1.10.0 per week. When he died in 1885 his widow was given a weekly payment of 10s.

Damaged casks were sent to the cooperage for repair. A foreman cooper was in charge of the cooperage, and up to the early 1890s he led a team of nine coopers, five

A group of brewery workers, *c.* 1890. (Courtesy Mike Hannon)

labourers and a spile maker (spiles were little plugs of wood that were used to seal small leaks and cracks in the wooden barrels or casks). In 1866 the foreman cooper was John Sullivan, who earned £96.4.0 per year at the time, rising to £117 by 1877. He retired in 1887 and was paid a pension of £1.2.6 per week.

The coal yard, which was located at the northern end of the brewery complex, was supervised by a clerk and a weighmaster. William Crowley, the clerk, was paid £70 per annum in 1863 and £100 by 1869.

The final group of workers in the brewing department was the delivery cellar gang, made up of a foreman and seven men. They worked from 8.00am to 8.00pm, Monday to Saturday. Customers could call to the brewery up to 8.00pm in the evenings to collect barrels of stout and porter.

In all, ninety-nine people were employed in the brewing department, the majority of whom worked a twelve-hour, six-day week. They had no entitlement to annual holidays and apart from Sundays, they only had days off on Christmas Day, and Whit and August Monday.

Customers' department

The customers' department dealt with publicans, received their orders, communicated with agents and wholesalers and managed all the accounts connected with those dealings. The managing clerk of this department was required to know the names, addresses, character, family and connections of every agent and customer of the firm and was also expected to keep himself informed of any news from the Munster area that could have an impact on trade. The managing clerk oversaw the work of another twenty-three men in this department.

Five clerks manned the Outside Office, which was open from 7.00am until 8.00pm. They kept account of all barrels delivered to and returned by agents and wholesalers, received money at the counter, issued receipts, made entries in sales books and in customers' pass books, made up the balances in accounts, kept the agents' and customers' ledgers up to date and managed the firm's dealings with the city's railway companies. Richard Herrick worked in this office and was on an annual salary of £75. He was dismissed in 1867 for making false entries in the accounts. Timothy Murray was another clerk in the office and he was dismissed in 1862, aged sixty-five, for drunkenness. He had been on an annual salary of £40. William Philpott began work in this section in 1850 on a yearly salary of £50. By the mid-1860s he was earning £145 and from 1865 he was paid an annual bonus of £50 in addition to his salary.

Three clerks worked in the Delivery Office and dealt with the city customers, whose orders were generally delivered by the brewery drays. They kept the Delivery Book, entering the details of every order, including the numbers of the casks making up the order and the name of the drayman making the delivery, as well as the Return Book, where they entered the details and numbers of returned casks. These clerks worked from 7.00am to 8.00pm in summer and on Saturdays they had to remain on duty until the later time of 11.30pm to facilitate publicans who could call to the brewery for stock up to that time. In winter they had the ease of not starting work until 8.00am, but the late Saturday opening continued.

The yardmen made up another work gang within the customers' department. There were eight men in the group and they loaded the casks onto the drays, checking the cask numbers against the order details. They also unloaded the returned casks and attended to shipments on board the brewery's barge, the *Beamish & Crawford*, and a small steamer that delivered from the city to Queenstown and the lower harbour area. In addition, the yardmen checked and handled malt deliveries.

A further group of six men, known as the Receipt of Empties Gang, took the returned casks once they had been unloaded and checked by the yardmen. They stacked and stored them and moved them to the cask cleaning sheds and cooperage. A man called Cronin had the task of maintaining an 'outside watch' in the mid-1860s. He kept a general watch on brewery shipments to and from the railway stations and city's quaysides. He also 'makes private enquiries connected with Town and Country Customers'.

Barley department

The acting partners' review of all aspects of the brewery's functioning also included an analysis of how barley was purchased, transported to the city and handled and stored by the brewery before it was malted.[16] In the mid-1860s, and in the decades before and after, nearly all of the brewery's barley was bought at the Cork Corn Exchange, and in Cloyne, Midleton, Carrigtwohill, Mallow and Rathcormac. The barley purchased in Cloyne and Midleton was shipped to the city's quays by boat, while the rest was transported by road. The brewery's agents in Midleton, Cloyne, Rathcormac and Mallow also acted as agents for the purchase of barley. Coppinger of Midleton was paid 1s commission on each barrel he purchased for the firm, while the others were paid 5 per cent on the cost of their purchases. As well as paying for the carriage of the barley to the city, the brewery was also liable for tolls, collected by the city corporation, on the barley brought into the city. Barley arriving by boat was liable for a toll of 1½d per barrel, while that arriving by road was tolled ½d per barrel. Loaders, usually ten in number, were employed seasonally to unload the barley from boats, load it onto carts and unload it again at the barley stores. They were paid 1d per stone delivered to the stores.

Beamish & Crawford had four stores in the city for barley with a combined capacity of 28,300 barrels: Morrison's Island (7,300 barrels), Rutland Street (4,000

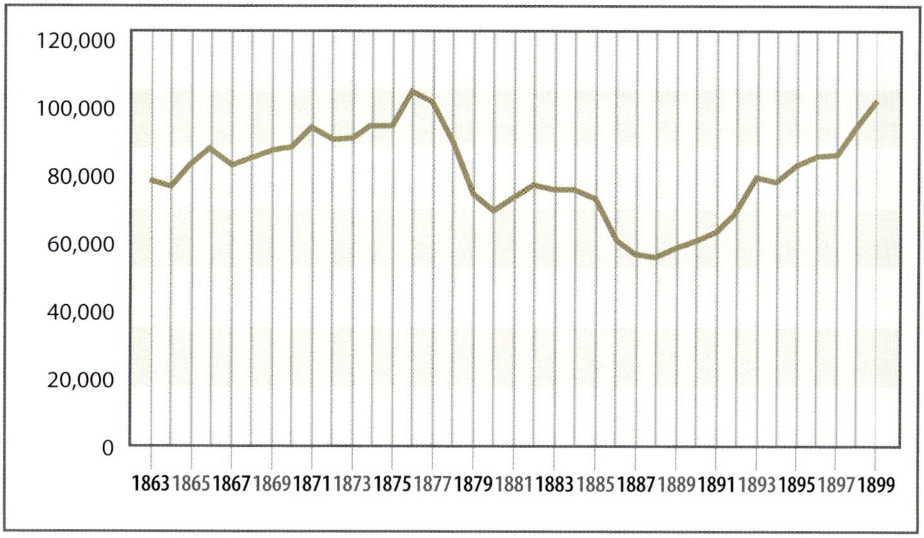

Beamish & Crawford sales (in barrels), 1863–99.

barrels), Hanover Street (5,000 barrels) and the Lee Stores, formerly the River Lee Porter Brewery (12,000 barrels). When the barley arrived at the stores, it was first weighed. This work was done by twelve weighmen, overseen by two weighmasters. The weighmasters were permanent employees and earned 12s 6d and 10s 6d per week. The weighmen were employed seasonally and averaged twenty-nine weeks work through the barley season, which ran from harvest time in August to February or March. They were paid 9s per week.

After being weighed, the barley was screened using screens that were cylindrical in shape and made of wire mesh built around an inner wooden cylindrical core. The screens had meshes of four different widths: the smallest held the dust, the second mesh was a little wider and held the '2nd Quality' grains, the third mesh held the '1st Quality' middle-sized grains, while the fourth and widest mesh caught the full-sized barley grains for malting. Only the latter-quality grain was kept for malting; the two inferior grades were brought to the Lee Stores, where they were sold off. The screens at that time were turned by a long handle operated by two men and were fed by a shoot fed from a hopper placed above it. A long screw within the screen moved the grain along its length as it was turned. Eight men were employed at the Lee Stores to operate the screens, four men each at Hanover Street and Morrison's Island and three at Rutland Street. The screeners worked an average of twenty-six weeks each year, generally from harvest time in late August to February or March the following year. They were paid 9s per week.

While the barley was in storage prior to malting it had to be turned regularly, so the weighmen also worked as turners, turning the grain with wide malt shovels to prevent it spoiling. It was expected that each turner would manage to turn 800 barrels of barley three times a week – the equivalent of shovelling 2,400 barrels of barley per week. Turning also paid 9s weekly.

Four or five boys were also employed seasonally and they assisted as needed. They were essentially apprentices who learned the workings of the different sections of the barley department. They were paid between 6s and 8s each per week. Three clerks (permanent employees) were responsible for the administration of the barley department and a number of cashiers kept the accounts. Thirteen different ledgers and account books were used in the administration of the department.

Connectivity

An indication, perhaps, of Richard Pigott Beamish's drive for efficiency and his willingness to adopt the most up-to-date means of achieving that was the installation of one of the earliest telephone lines in Cork, connecting the brewery with his home at Ashbourne House.[17] Agreement was reached with the Telephone Company of Ireland in November 1888 for the installation of the private line 'with one extension bell at each end unconnected with any other wire or instrument' at a cost of £19.10.0 per year. The first telephone exchange had been opened in Ireland in 1880, and by 1888 the number of lines in the country was still measured in hundreds, the majority of which were in Dublin, Belfast and the intervening towns, the two cities having been connected by a trunk line in 1884.[18]

Porter, stout and ale

Porter is the only product mentioned in the brewery records before the 1860s, but a surviving cask label from the 1850s for Extra Stout and one from 1861 for Double Stout indicate that these products were being brewed also. Between 1862 and 1863 Beamish & Crawford marketed a special stout in England, branded Cooper, made with a mix of Single Stout and year-old vatted Extra Treble Stout, brewed in Cork (see 'Cooper stout and the Johnson Agency, London, 1862–3', pp. 112–15). This Extra Treble Stout is not mentioned in any other surviving records, but from 1893 a Treble or XXX Stout was brewed and sold in small quantities. Through the 1860s Single Stout (also called porter), Double Stout and Extra Stout were produced, and these stouts continued to be the brewery's principal products into the twentieth century. From 1873, ale was also brewed in a separate small brewery within the Beamish & Crawford complex, but in minimal quantities, averaging only in the region of 125 barrels per year between 1873 and 1882.

Single Stout accounted for the greatest proportion of the stouts produced, amounting to about 90 per cent of production in the ten years from 1865. The two stronger stouts, Double and Extra, accounted for the other 10 per cent. From 1873 to 1879, an Extra Stout for Mixing was brewed in significant quantities in addition to Extra Stout, averaging just under 12 per cent of total stout production in those years. It was used, as the name suggests, for mixing with weaker brews to elevate strength. The two Extra Stouts were brewed in the small ale brewery and could be kept for long periods due to their high alcohol content. In the twelve years between 1869 and 1880, the average annual production ratio of Single Stout: Double Stout: Extra Stout, measured in barrels or tierces, was 76,055 : 4,546 : 2,159.

A ledger from the brewing department[19] records the quantities of ingredients used in the brewing of the various products between 1864 and 1890, and Table 6.3 shows that detail for the stouts brewed in October 1868 and the ales brewed in February 1875 as examples. These quantities varied a little from brew to brew depending on the quality of the ingredients.

Table 6.3 **Ingredients per barrel used in brewing stouts (October 1868) and ales (February 1875)**

TYPE OF BEER	PALE MALT	PATENT MALT	BROWN MALT	HOPS	SUGAR	ACID BEER
Single Stout	65.89 lb	3.49 lb	0	2.35 lb	4.59 lb	1.17 gallons
Double Stout	71.34 lb	3.74 lb	0	2.66 lb	5.05 lb	0.11 gallons
Extra Stout	88.73 lb	4.66 lb	8.4 lb	4.16 lb	0	0
Pale Bitter Ale	64.61 lb	0	0	5.02 lb	12.92 lb	0
Stock Ale	127.61 lb	0	0	4.89 lb	6.46 lb	0

Pale malt was essentially a base malt making up the bulk of the malt used in a brew for stout or ale, and during mashing this malt provided the enzymes essential for converting the starch in the grain to sugars that could be fermented in a later stage in the brewing process. Patent malt, also known as black malt, was a malt that had been dried at a very high temperature and virtually carbonised. This malt gave the dark colour and some of the characteristic flavours to the stout. Brown malt served a similar purpose to patent malt but was dried at a lower temperature than patent malt to produce its intermediate colouring. No patent or brown malt was used in brewing ale, hence its lighter colour. The darker, more bitter and stronger nature of Extra Stout is indicated by the quantity of malts used – 101.79 lb in total per barrel as against 75.08 lb and 69.38 lb respectively for Double and Single Stout – as well as the much higher hop content. Sugar was increasingly used in brewing at Beamish & Crawford from 1867 as an adjunct or source of extra fermentable material. The annual spend on sugar rose from £4,463 in 1867 to a high of over £22,000 ten years later and its use declined steadily in the succeeding decades. Acid beer was beer that had aged to become stale and unpalatable. It was used as an additive to balance the flavour of the stout.

By 1893, XXX or Treble Stout was also being brewed, and with the introduction of bottled stout a specific brew for bottled Single Stout was produced between 1893 and 1900. A brewing department notebook from 1893 lists the ingredients used in brewing the various products averaged over the years 1890 to 1893 (see Table 6.4).[20]

Table 6.4 **Principal ingredients per barrel used in brewing stouts, averaged for the years 1890–3**

STOUT	PALE MALT	PATENT MALT	HOPS	SUGAR	ACID BEER
Single Stout	74.05 lb	3.98 lb	2.35 lb	0.91 lb	1 gallon
Single Stout (bottling)	77.76 lb	4.07 lb	2.94 lb	0.80 lb	0
Double Stout	78.26 lb	3.91 lb	2.71 lb	2.52 lb	0.5 gallon
Extra Stout	82.59 lb	3.99 lb	2.91 lb	3.39 lb	0.5 gallon
XXX Stout	97.30 lb	4.05 lb	4.31 lb	3.27 lb	0.5 gallon

Some differences in ingredients and their quantities are apparent in a comparison of the detail for stouts in 1868 (Table 6.3) and 1890–3 (Table 6.4). No brown malt was used in the later brews, and while more malt by weight was used in Single and Double Stout in 1890–3, the quantity of sugar was much reduced, probably resulting in a similar alcohol content in the finished product. The hopping rate was broadly similar in the earlier and later brews of those two stouts. The Extra Stout of 1890–3 was probably weaker in alcohol content and flavour compared to that of 1868 – the quantity of malt used was nearly 20 per cent less, but while the earlier stout had no sugar added, the later product had 3.39 lb per barrel. The hopping rate was also quite different, falling from 4.16 lb per barrel to 2.91 lb. The XXX Stout brewed from 1893 was probably close in strength and flavour to the Extra Stout of 1868, having a similar quantity of malt and hops used in the brew (see Appendix E).

Although up to five stouts of different strengths and ale were produced throughout the 1890s, Single Stout continued to account for the greatest proportion of beer sold by far, averaging about 93 per cent of total sales in each year (see Table 6.5). Ale continued to be insignificant. In the later nineteenth century, and indeed up to the reductions in strength imposed on breweries during the First World War, Irish beers were far stronger than their equivalents today. Single Stout had an original gravity of about 1,060° and an alcohol content (ABV) of over 6 per cent, while Double, Extra and XXX Stout had higher original gravities of between 1,066° and 1,079°, with a correspondingly higher ABV of 7 per cent to 9 per cent.

Table 6.5

Products and quantities sold (barrels), 1891–1900 (except 1893)

YEAR	SINGLE STOUT	SINGLE STOUT (bottling)	DOUBLE STOUT	EXTRA STOUT	XXX STOUT	ALE
1891	59,768		2,049	2,063		281
1892	66,599		1,338	1,801		188
1893[21]						
1894	73,272	1,549	1,193	1,917	93	363
1895	78,144	1,473	1,447	1,864	108	401
1896	80,306	1,564	1,701	1,820	90	435
1897	80,752	1,408	2,412	1,924	62	367
1898	87,306	1,227	3,357	2,386	81	445
1899	93,663	1,109	4,305	2,829	128	537
1900	94,673	1,135	5,614	2,878	156	435

Reports on Beamish & Crawford's bottled stouts and ale

In the spring of 1883 and 1884, William Ladd, a clerk employed in the brewery, visited a number of public houses in Cork city to promote the sale of Beamish & Crawford's ale and bottled stout and wrote a report for the acting partners following each year's visits.[22] As well as dealing with the specifics of the sale of the beers, Ladd's reports give some insight into the difficulties of producing consistent beers, the growing power of the Guinness brands, and class and gender differences in the habits of drinkers.

In March 1883, the bottled Double Stout supplied to its own tied houses by the brewery had recovered from the difficulties it had been having due to 'unevenness of condition' to be 'everything that it ought to be'. However, publicans preferred to take their supplies from the commercial bottlers, who also bottled and distributed the stout, rather than directly from the brewery, as the bottlers called daily to the public houses with supplies, whereas orders from the brewery entailed making a visit there with each order. In addition, many publicans 'because of owing to the bottlers a number of bottles and perhaps cash cannot refuse to take their stout …'

In April 1884, Ladd reported that bottled Double Stout was continuing to present difficulties, having 'an almost indescribable want of flavour and briskness which makes it most unsuccessful with the public'. It was enjoying a small measure of success 'where the customers are not particular about what they drink so long as it is mad up or nearly bursting the cask or bottle', due to ongoing secondary fermentation. The Beamish & Crawford tied houses would find it easier to sell other stouts if they were allowed.

From top: Beamish & Crawford XXX Stout cask label, 1880s.
Beamish & Crawford Double Stout cask label, 1880s.
Beamish & Crawford stout bottle, 1890s.
(Beamish & Crawford Brewery Collection /Dori O'Connell)

In March 1883, Ladd reported that it was too early to report on the success or otherwise of bottled Extra Stout, suggesting that the bottling of the product was a recent phenomenon. Extra Stout had been brewed by Beamish & Crawford from at least the early 1850s and was likely to have been sold on draught by publicans, or used by them to mix with Single or Double Stout. By April 1884, bottled Extra Stout was not selling. An attempt had been made 'to run it against Guinness's Double Stout when that was advanced in price but it did not work well'. When Guinness lowered its price again, the Beamish & Crawford bottled product was abandoned by drinkers. Extra Stout on draught was proving to be a success, however, selling at 2d per pint. Ladd observed that several public houses on the north side of the city were trying it but that it was only men who drank it. In the several public houses near the city's markets, where women were the principal customers, it was impossible to sell Extra Stout on draught. Ladd wrote: 'Though several tried it they had to mix it with the well up Single to get it off their hands'.

Beamish & Crawford ale was, according to Ladd, 'superior to anything in the market' and following the Cork Industrial Exhibition of 1883, where the ale was featured, 'the public … are asking for B&C's ale and prefer it to most of the English and Scotch ales sold here now'. But with at least twelve different agents and wholesalers in Cork promoting imported ales, competition was tough and the agents allowed a number of publicans to run up debts for ale, thus 'tying' the publican to the agent for future dealing.

William Ladd also commented on the class differences in beer drinking:

> But houses such as most of yours which sell any quantity of draught porter are not the places where a large sale of ale is likely to take place, as it is used by a very different class of customers who usually avoid the other. One house in Patrick St. district would sell more ale than 10 in Barrack St., while the exact contrary is the case with draught porter.

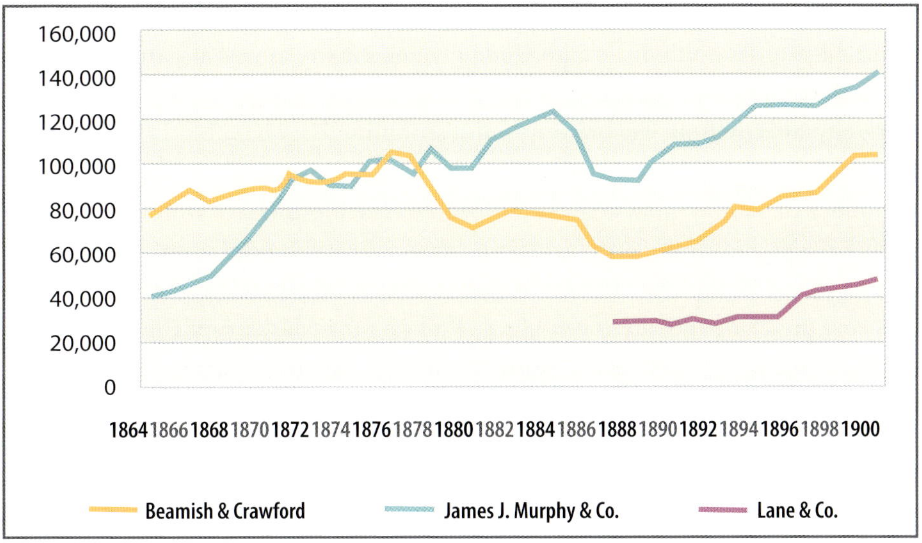

Beamish & Crawford, James J. Murphy & Co. and Lane & Co.: comparative sales (in barrels), 1864–1900.

Sales and distribution

As the second half of the nineteenth century progressed, the Beamish & Crawford share of the Irish market for porter and stout fell considerably. The output of Irish breweries grew from 1.2 million barrels in 1865 to 2.6 million by the late 1890s, the greatest proportion of this produced by Guinness. Beamish & Crawford's production fluctuated between 55,851 and 104,457 barrels in the same period. The phenomenal growth of Guinness's output and the extension of its home market throughout all regions of the country impacted on all Irish brewers, but Beamish & Crawford had the added difficulty of serious competition from its Cork rivals, Lane's Southgate Brewery, Arnott's and James J. Murphy & Co. By the late 1870s, Murphy's brewery had overtaken Beamish & Crawford in output volume and in its share of the local market (see Chapter 7). The Murphy lead over Beamish & Crawford continued to grow throughout the 1880s and 1890s, and by 1900 Murphy sales were 40 per cent greater. Sales figures are available for Lane & Co. Ltd from 1887 to 1900 and show annual sales growing in that period from 27,442 barrels to a high of 46,267 in 1900, the year before the company was taken over by Beamish & Crawford. Detailed sales figures for Arnott's St Finbarre's Brewery do not survive, but during the 1880s sales averaged in the region of 50,000 barrels per year, falling to an average of 27,000 barrels in the 1890s. In 1900 the four Cork city breweries produced a combined total of a little over 317,000 barrels of porter, stout and ale, which was 12 per cent of the country's total beer output of 2.6 million barrels.

During this period, the market for Beamish & Crawford products continued to be principally in the south of Ireland: Cork city and county as well as parts of counties Kerry, Limerick, Tipperary and Waterford. The brewery supplied its customers in Cork city directly from the brewery and distribution elsewhere was in the hands of independent agents, depots controlled by the firm and wholesalers. From the 1840s, a number of railway lines were developed connecting the city with the principal county towns and with places further afield, which were crucial to the building and supply of the Beamish & Crawford market: the Cork, Bandon and South Coast Railway; the Cork and Macroom Direct Railway; the Muskerry Light Railway; the Great Southern and Western Railway; the Cork, Youghal and Queenstown Railway; and the Cork, Blackrock and Passage Railway. The brewery acquired a barge and a small steam vessel to supply the lower harbour towns of Passage, Monkstown and Queenstown as well as Midleton, while the improving road network eased the ordeal of transport to other towns and villages.

The Coppinger family in Midleton had been agents for Beamish & Crawford since 1792 and a century later they were distributing the largest volume of any of the agents. The agency in Mallow also continued to be quite significant, and by the late 1890s these two agencies accounted for 40 per cent of all sales through agents. Other towns still had the brewery agencies that had been set up in the early 1790s, but ownership had in most cases changed. Dungarvan, Youghal, Queenstown (Cobh), Bandon, Kinsale, Macroom and Fermoy continued to have agencies and new agencies were established in Skibbereen, Tralee, Limerick, Kanturk, Mitchelstown, Rathcormac, Tallow and Lismore. The brewery also had agencies in Britain, but their trade was not particularly active in the period under discussion. A breakdown of sales figures for the years from 1891 to 1900 shows that sales through agents accounted for an annual average of just below 60 per cent of all sales.

A document from 1866 in the brewery archive gives a breakdown of the tied public houses in the Bandon district, excluding the town, and in the town of Clonakilty.[23] In the Bandon district, forty-eight of fifty-three houses were tied to one of six breweries, while in the town of Clonakilty all forty-nine houses were tied to one of four breweries. There were two breweries in Bandon in the period, the Clancoole Brewery of J. Hurley & Co. and the Watergate Brewery of Cornwall & Co. The latter brewery was purchased by Allman, Dowden & Co. in 1875. The Deasy Brewery in Clonakilty was founded in 1768 and was first located on Astna Street, moving later to a site off Emmet Square in 1837.

Beamish & Crawford also had a number of depots outside of the city, run directly by the brewery and managed by a paid clerk, to supply towns and villages without an agency. Some customers in country districts were supplied directly by rail from the city. These sales to non-city customers not handled by agents were classified as

Table 6.6 **Tied public houses in Bandon district (excluding the town) and Clonakilty, 1866**

BREWERY	BANDON DISTRICT	CLONAKILTY
Beamish & Crawford	12	4
J.J. Murphy & Co.	3	1
Lane & Co.	3	0
Arnott & Co.	1	0
Hurley & Co.	19	0
Cornwall & Co.	10	4
Deasy & Co.	0	40

Table 6.7 **Breakdown of sales for year ending 5 August 1899 by district/agency**

DISTRICT/AGENCY	NUMBER OF PUBLIC HOUSES	SALES (barrels)	AVERAGE NUMBER OF BARRELS PER PUBLIC HOUSE
City	113	27,370	242.2
Country	88	14,389	163.5
Midleton	85	12,487	146.9
Mallow	150	11,422	76.1
Fermoy	47	5,532	117.7
Mitchelstown	58	4,622	79.6
Lismore	29	4,276	147.4
Youghal	35	4,121	117.7
Kinsale	18	3,755	208.6
Queenstown	18	3,019	167.7
Rathcormac	22	2,354	107.0
Tallow	17	1,607	94.5
Skibbereen	28	1,480	52.8
Macroom	20	1,457	72.85
Kanturk	29	1,380	47.4
Millstreet	8	184	23.0
TOTAL	765	99,455	130
Plymouth	Export	2,539	

'Country Sales' and made up an annual average of 14 per cent of total sales. Exports were quite low as a proportion of total sales in the 1890s but grew to a high of 2,625 barrels in 1900. In the nine years of the decade to 1900 for which figures survive, exports are recorded in eight of those years, amounting to a total of 15,888 barrels or an annual average of 1,980 barrels – a little over 2 per cent of total sales.

The breakdown of sales for nine of the years from 1891 to 1900 has sales in Cork city making up an annual average of just under 24 per cent of total sales, but the proportion grew steadily throughout the decade from 21.5 per cent in 1891 to 27.9 per cent in 1900. The growth in the share of city sales in the period somewhat masks the actual growth in sales in the same years, from 13,856 barrels in 1891 to 29,352 barrels in 1900.

An analysis of all sales for the brewery year ending 5 August 1899 details the number of public houses in the city, country and in each agent's district through which these sales were made, giving the average annual sale through each public house and showing the relative importance of the fourteen agencies then operating.[24] (See Table 6.7.)

Exports

Precise figures for Beamish & Crawford exports have not survived, but the brewery had a foreign trade of some consequence in its first two decades or so, chiefly with the islands of the Caribbean and Britain. It had an agency in Bristol from as early as the 1820s, in Liverpool from 1844, in Glasgow from 1865 and in Plymouth from the early 1890s. When Henry H. Johnson of London became an agent for the brewery in 1862, he was given exclusive rights to deal in Beamish & Crawford's porter and stout in all of England and Wales, excluding Liverpool and Barnstaple, as the brewery already had established agents in those two locations.

The surviving records do not suggest that the trade through these agents was very substantial. Between October 1868 and October 1869, for example, a total of 1,138 barrels of Single and Extra Stout were exported to the Bristol agent, Elias G. Hall, but the trade made a loss of £82.2.10 to the brewery. In the year to October 1872, the agency sold 359 barrels of Extra Stout and fifty-two barrels of Single, but again at a loss. While some agencies survived for a number of decades, others seem to have been short-lived. Exports of small quantities of stout to wholesalers and dealers in a variety of locations in Britain are occasionally recorded, but the total amounts were small. A document detailing the number of casks with foreign dealers in 1862 shows the range of locations the firm was exporting to at that time: London, Plymouth, Swansea, Pembroke, Barnstaple, Haverford West, Bristol, Liverpool, Cardiff and New York.[25] These foreign agents or dealers were holding a total of 159 hogsheads, 592 barrels and 1,521 kilderkins – the equivalent capacity of 1,590 barrels or tierces – an indication that the export trade was not very large. An agent, J.R. Wilson, was appointed in Plymouth in 1891 or 1892 and he seems to have generated a substantial trade. The surviving figures for exports in the 1890s suggest that Wilson accounted for virtually all of this trade. In 1895 Beamish & Crawford recorded exports of 2,271 barrels in total, of which 2,180 barrels were handled by Wilson, while in 1898 he handled

2,107 barrels of the 2,158 total exported. These exports grew to a peak of 2,625 in 1900 and fell steadily in succeeding years to less than 400 barrels by 1913.[26]

A document from the end of the 1890s survives with detailed costings and estimates of potential profits on exports of a bottled stout, called Export Stout, to South Africa, Australia and America.[27] Twenty-seven cases with seventy-two pint bottles in each and twenty-seven cases with forty-eight quart bottles in each made up the first trial shipment to South Africa. The stout was shipped to Southampton and then onwards to its final destination. Potential profit was estimated at between 27.1 per cent and 29.1 per cent of the outlay. The success or otherwise of the experiment is not noted. The projections for shipping to Adelaide in Australia suggested that a profit could not be made. Projections were also made for exporting the stout to the United States of America and it was estimated that significant profits could be made there. The document notes that bottled Guinness was selling in the USA at the time (1900) at 20c per bottle and that the Beamish & Crawford product could sell at 25c 'as B&C can guarantee a thoroughly digestible stout, free from all germs and perfectly fit for all invalids and will keep for 10 years in bottle'. It is not noted if this long-life and health-giving product made it to the bars of the USA.

Profits

Richard Pigott Beamish wrote a review of his first fifteen years stewardship of the brewery in 1879 in which he was keen to highlight the increased annual profits after the 1863 change in management.[28] In the ten years to 1863, the average annual net profit was just over £20,500, which was divided equally between the Crawford and Beamish sides of the partnership. In the ten years to 1878, this average annual net profit had risen to £37,500, an increase of over 80 per cent. Higher sales contributed to the increased profits but the better overall management of the firm, improved standards in the brewing department and increased efficiencies and controls in all areas of activity were key to increasing profitability. These efficiencies are illustrated by the increased net profit per barrel, rising from an annual average of 4s 8¼d in the ten years to 1863 to over 8s in the decade to 1878. The rise in net profits is even more significant when factors like increased wages, higher malt costs and proper deductions being made in the annual accounts for wear and tear are taken into account. (See Appendix F and Appendix G.)

These profit levels were not maintained, however, and bad harvests, severe winter weather and a fall in prices for Irish agricultural exports to Britain in the later 1870s were blamed for the decline in sales and profits. Beamish wrote: 'This has been more severely felt amongst all classes in the South of Ireland than anything which has taken place since the year of famine in 1847.'[29] The restrictions placed on the opening hours of public houses on Sundays, introduced in October 1878, also contributed to the difficulties in this period, as all public houses had to stay closed, except those in the cities of Dublin, Belfast, Cork, Waterford and Limerick, where they were permitted to open between 2.00pm and 7.00pm.

Annual sales reached a peak of 104,223 barrels in 1876, but then began a decline that continued throughout most of the 1880s until they hit a low of 55,851 in 1888. Figures for neither gross nor net profits are available from 1884 to 1891, but gross profits in the years 1879 to 1883 averaged £21,282 annually – a fall of almost 50 per cent on the five-year average up to 1878. Figures for gross profits only are available from 1891 to 1900, and while they show a rise from £15,657 in 1891 to £34,205 in 1900, with an annual average of £25,686, they are significantly lower than the levels achieved in the 1870s. In the 1890s annual sales enjoyed another period of steady growth, rising from 61,527 barrels in 1890 to 104,457 in 1900.

Richard Pigott Beamish was chairman and managing director of Beamish & Crawford Ltd from the firm's incorporation in 1895 until his death on 7 June 1899. His eldest son, Richard Henrik (1861–1938), inherited 2,260 of his father's 2,840 ordinary shares and 2,560 of his 2,880 preference shares and became chairman and managing director of the firm in July 1899. His fellow directors were Arthur Frederick Sharman Crawford and North Ludlow Axel Beamish. Richard Henrik also inherited his father's interest in Ashbourne House, where he lived with his first wife, Violet Campbell, from 1903.

Casks

'Cask' is the general term for hogsheads, barrels or tierces, kilderkins and firkins. A hogshead had a capacity of 54 gallons, a tierce or barrel held 36 gallons, a kilderkin held 18 gallons and a firkin held nine. Hogsheads were generally used for shipments to bottlers or wholesalers, who then distributed the product in smaller quantities, while the lesser capacity casks were used to optimise the distribution from the brewery to customers, the objective being to have the cask away from the brewery for as short a time as possible. The bigger the throughput of beer in a public house, the bigger the cask used.

Until after the Second World War, all casks were made of wooden staves, usually oak, bound with iron hoops. They were a significant cost to a brewery, as they were expensive to make or buy and needed frequent repair. The quicker a cask was returned to the brewery, the lower the number of casks that were required to service the trade. Delay in the return of casks was an ongoing problem for all breweries and added significantly to costs, as more casks were needed to make up the shortfalls. The

The brewery cooperage in 1932. (Courtesy Michael Lenihan)

effective life of a cask was about ten years and the greater the number of usages of a cask in any year, the better the return on the investment in that cask. The number of usages of a cask depended on how far it had to travel to a customer or agent and how long it remained with the customer or agent before being returned. Distant export customers were charged the full value of the casks on orders, at least in the early years of the brewery's history. In 1799 a cargo of 100 barrels of porter was shipped to Martinique at a cost of £1.9.3 per barrel for the porter and an additional 16s 3d for each barrel;[30] in 1804, £1.2.9 was charged for each hogshead exported in addition to the cost of the contents when a consignment of fifty hogsheads of porter was shipped to Dominica.[31] Details of individual export shipments for the later decades of the nineteenth century do not survive, but the brewery's agents in Britain did not pay for casks because they were returned to Cork.

Beamish & Crawford purchased most of their casks from independent cooperages in Cork until 1896, after which they manufactured them on site in their expanded cooperage. Up to 1896, the brewery cooperage, which moved location a number of times within the brewery complex, was used principally for the repair of casks, though a small number were also made.

In August 1862, the brewery had a stock of 19,577 casks of different capacities: 414 hogsheads, 160 of which were in use with the trade; 8,220 tierces or barrels, of which 4,912 were with the trade; and 10,943 kilderkins, of which 8,251 were with the trade.[32] As no figures are recorded for firkins, it is likely that they were not in use until later. The first specific mention of firkins in the brewery records is in June 1869.[33] Since the first casks were purchased in 1791 the firm had spent a total of £93,059 on casks, and in 1862 the brewery's stock of casks in was given a value of £7,101,13.0.

Detail of purchases of casks survives for the period 1867 to 1877 and it shows that the brewery dealt with three named cooperages: the firms of J. O'Shea, A. O'Leary and E. O'Neill. The price paid for hogsheads was 18s, while barrels or tierces varied between 15s 6d each paid for 500 in June 1867 and 19s each paid for lots of 500 and 200 at different times in the 1870s. Kilderkins cost from 8s 6d to 9s 6d and firkins cost between 6s 4d and 6s 6d. Between June 1867 and July 1877, the years for which specific detail survives, a total of 1,200 hogsheads, 7,225 barrels, 7,418 kilderkins and 1,504 firkins were purchased from the three cooperages. A net total of £11,089 was spent on casks in the period, taking account of some income from casks sold.[34]

William Gray, head brewer
1863–92[35]

William Gray was born in 1826 on board a ship, the *General Palmer*, when his parents were en route from India to London. Gray's father worked with the East India Company in Madras and returned there with his wife in 1829, leaving the young William in England, presumably with relatives. He married *c.* 1853 and moved to Cork in 1862. William and his wife Anne had eleven children in all and lived for a time at Springville on the Blackrock Road in the city.

In March 1863, William Gray, giving his address as 27 Sullivan's Quay in Cork, wrote to Beamish & Crawford applying for a position as head brewer. At that time he was working with Lane & Co. and had twenty years' previous experience with

William Gray (1826–98), head brewer at Beamish & Crawford 1863–92. (Courtesy Ed Hinchy)

breweries in Edinburgh, London and Burton-on-Trent. Beamish & Crawford politely rejected his application as 'we scarcely consider that it would be consistent with due courtesy to Messrs. Lane & Co. to entertain any proposition from a Brewer in their establishment'. It was customary for breweries not to poach brewers from nearby firms and brewers' contracts usually had a clause preventing them from taking up a position with a rival firm within a given region for a set number of years. Beamish & Crawford added that they had no intention of replacing their head brewer, William Bowden Weatherman, although Richard Pigott Beamish later wrote that he was 'a man whose reckless conduct entailed heavy loss on the establishment, and reflected disgrace upon the whole concern' at that time.[36] Gray replied that he had given notice to Lane & Co. in January and that he was 'at perfect liberty to apply to you'.

Gray was interviewed and Beamish & Crawford sought references from a number of his previous employers, all of which were positive, although R. Hanley of an unnamed brewery in Spitalfields in London, probably Truman's Black Eagle Brewery, wrote that: 'He was only here for 12 months. I therefore cannot speak of his abilities as a Brewer. His conduct was unexceptional.'

William Gray began work at Beamish & Crawford in August 1863, on an annual salary of £500, following the dismissal of William Bowden Weatherman. His work gave great satisfaction, and by operating the new systems put in place by the acting partners from 1863, waste was greatly reduced and the quality of the firm's porter improved. According to Richard Pigott Beamish, it 'is now admitted to be quite the best in the local trade'.[37]

Within two years of taking up duty, Gray was in some financial difficulty and succeeded in getting loans of £120 and £30 from the firm in March and October of 1865. He made regular repayments on these loans and the firm gifted him £40 and raised his annual salary to £550 in early 1866 to enable him to pay off the debt completely. In March 1866 he again applied to the firm for a loan, this time for £300, as he had 'lost a sum in speculation'. He undertook to repay the loan at the rate of £5.18.6 per month, promised not to allow his spending to exceed his income and to move to a smaller house to reduce expenses. Two years later, in April 1868, Gray's annual salary was increased by £100 to £650 and the following month he approached the firm for a loan of £100 to fund house improvements involving the erection of gates and the installation of a water closet. He was anxious to have the work done as his wife was expecting another child. This was refused.

By March 1870, the acting partners had become quite anxious about Gray's financial travails and he was called before them and asked to produce a detailed statement of his position. It transpired that Gray had previously hidden other debts and loans from the partners and that his total indebtedness stood at £880.17.4. The firm lent Gray £900 without interest to clear his debts. In addition to making regular repayments, he undertook to leave £30 of his annual salary of £650 undrawn as a security against the loan and to assign to the firm two policies of assurance, worth £500 each, as further security. Gray also had to submit a quarterly statement of his financial position.

Despite the leniency and apparent generosity shown to him by the acting partners, Gray's profligacy continued and by 1873 he owed £800 over and above his debts to the firm. By then his annual salary had risen to £750. The acting partners gave him a further loan to clear this debt and accepted new assurances from Gray that he would reform. His wife had often been left without money for household expenses and Gray promised to hand over £20.10.0 to her every month for such expenses and to give her £25 per year for her dressmaker.

Gray occasionally clashed with Richard Pigott Beamish on matters relating to brewing. In 1873 Beamish, a man not averse to imposing his will on any and all of the brewery's various department heads, was attempting to make changes in the brewing department, but was resisted by Gray. Beamish wrote to him on 27 September:

> I have always found that the commencement of any improvement at the Brewery has been interfered with by the idea held by the old hands that their services were indispensible to the firm, and that therefore they might give as much trouble as they pleased.

While these differences were resolved, they resurfaced in 1880 when Beamish was endeavouring again to impose change on Gray's department. Beamish threatened him with dismissal, writing: 'It is therefore essential to your retention of the position of Head Brewer that you still thoroughly acquiesce in these requirements.' Gray was objecting to Beamish's approaches to others in the brewing department for information, demanding that all such requests be made to him. Gray was temporarily removed from his position as head brewer in July 1880 but was reinstated following his agreement with Beamish's demands.

William Gray retired from the firm in 1892 and was granted a pension of £400 per year, with £100 to be paid to his wife if she outlived him. He had never managed to control his overspending and on his retirement he was indebted to the firm in the amount of £2,214.19.7. He assigned two insurance policies to Beamish & Crawford in lieu of this debt, which sold them for £1,473.5.10, leaving it with a loss of £741.13.9. William Gray left Cork and returned to England. He spent his final years in Puckeridge, Hertfordshire, where he died in 1898.

Coopers at work in the brewery cooperage, *c*. 1900. (Courtesy Mike Hannon)

Frank Thurston & the Coopers' Society[38]

Frank J. Thurston replaced William Gray as head brewer at Beamish & Crawford in 1892. By 1895 he was in conflict with the Cork Coopers' Society, the powerful trade union of the city's coopers, as he sought to have changes made in the specifications of the barrels used by the brewery. At this time, most of the brewery's barrels were made by independent cooperages. The brewery did not start making its own barrels on a large scale until February 1896, probably as a result of Thurston's dispute with the Coopers' Society.

In November 1895, Thurston ordered a consignment of barrels from an independent cooperage, McCarthy Bros., General Cooperage, 30 John Street, Cork, giving details of the specifications he required – essentially barrels of a heavier, stronger construction. The coopers refused to make the barrels although Thurston claimed they would be 'similar in substance and dimensions to those made for us on the last occasion'. M.J. O'Connell, secretary of the Coopers' Society, wrote to Thurston and explained that his group had determined a specific gauge for brewers' casks that

> has been in use in Cork from time immemorial, until within the past few years for obvious reasons the firm of Beamish & Crawford began to demand heavy casks, substance increasing year after year, until eventually they became of such a substance that human nature could not endure it longer.

He added that the coopers' existing specifications were 'as strong as are required by Breweries in the United Kingdom and quite sufficient for purpose intended'.

On 17 December 1895, Michael McCarthy of McCarthy Bros. wrote to Thurston informing him that his coopers had been ordered out of his workshop by the society. No coopers were being allowed to work to Thurston's specifications. Thurston persisted in his quest, defying the Coopers' Society, and in January he asked J. Cronin's cooperage on Great Britain Street (Great William O'Brien Street) if his order for 200 barrels and 500 kilderkins could be filled. Cronin would be happy to supply the casks to Thurston's specifications 'provided the Coopers' Society will allow their members to do so'. E. O'Neill & Son were also approached, but replied that their coopers would not make the casks to the required specification. O'Neill's letter suggests that Thurston required the staves of the casks to be curved by steaming, a practice the

From left: Tom, John and Thomas Marrett. Three generations of the Marrett family photographed in September 1936 at the brewery cooperage. (*Irish Examiner*)

coopers objected to, preferring to cut the staves to shape. O'Neill added that he had supplied the brewery for over twenty years without ever receiving a complaint about a cask leaking or bursting.

The surviving communications between Frank Thurston and the Coopers' Society suggest that in addition to the heavier cask, Thurston also required that the bending of the staves be done by steaming, a quicker and less costly method than the traditional shaping. On 20 January, the Coopers' Society again informed Thurston that its members would not be allowed to work to the new specifications or methods and that his demands were being made 'to cut down considerably the earnings of our men as compared with former times'. The letter also told Thurston that the Society had received information that Mr. J.J. O'Neill, Master Cooper, had tendered for making casks for the brewery and

> We are desirous of impressing on you that this gentleman does not employ Society coopers and to avoid any unpleasantness between the firm of Messrs. Beamish & Crawford and the Coopers' Society you are thus notified.

Negotiations between Thurston and the Coopers' Society continued and at the end of January 1896 a compromise was reached whereby the coopers agreed to make casks

The coat of arms of the Cork Coopers' Society. (CCCA/Authors)

of the heavier gauge but to be paid on a time basis for this work, as opposed to being paid for casks produced, as was customary for 'traditional' casks. On 1 February, Thurston requested the Society to send two or three coopers to the brewery for an experiment 'to test the time actually necessary to make new casks of the gauge we require, with the aid of the additional facility afforded by bending the staves by steam'.

Thurston wrote a detailed report of the experiment, which was conducted over five days, measuring the cost of all materials and labour needed to produce ten casks from the preparation of materials through to the finished product. The materials used consisted of 170 staves costing £4.5.0, thirty staves for the heads (top and bottom of cask) costing £1.2.6 and iron hoops and rivets at £1.1.8, giving a total of £6.9.2. The cost of sorting, measuring and sawing the staves was put at 8s 10d. Two coopers expended the equivalent of nine days' labour on the task of making the casks at 6s per day, amounting to £2.14.0, while the cost of steam was put at 1s 3d. The total cost of the ten casks was £9.13.3, or 19s 4d each. Thurston wrote:

> Possibly when the men get more accustomed to the work the cost per barrel might be reduced to 18s 10d. By making our own casks we ensure the high quality of the materials and the exact thickness of timber required.

Two weeks later, on 4 March 1896, Thurston observed an improvement in costs when he measured the cost of making thirty-one casks at the brewery at £29.0.9½, or 18s 8¾d each. One month later, Thurston was still closely monitoring costs at the cooperage and efficiency was improving, with the cost per cask falling to 16s 5½d. It is from this period that the brewery made its own casks in quantity, having built a large cooperage on the southern extremity of the brewery complex overlooking the river.

7

Competitors: Lane's, Murphy's & Arnott's

Besides Guinness, the giant of Irish brewing, the three main competitors faced by Beamish & Crawford were the Cork city concerns of Lane's, Murphy's and Arnott's: the Southgate Brewery, Lady's Well Brewery and St Finbarre's Brewery, respectively. Lane's was never a serious threat and was taken over and closed down by Beamish & Crawford in 1901, while Arnott's was a brief irritant before being sold to Murphy's in 1901 and closed down. Murphy's proved to be the most durable challenger.

LANE'S: THE SOUTHGATE BREWERY

Until the establishment of Murphy's Lady's Well Brewery in 1856, Lane's across South Main Street from the Cork Porter Brewery provided the main competition to Beamish & Crawford in the city. The site on which Daniel Lane & Co. commenced business in July 1819 had almost certainly been used for brewing from an early period; the earliest clear evidence in the surviving records of the brewery dates to the later 1700s and suggests the presence of at least four breweries.

This carved stone was set in the wall at the entrance to the brewery. However, the foundation date of 1758 has no sound historical basis. Note that the foundation date on the company's cask label is 1759. (John Sheehan)

Before Lane's

In 1781 Daniel Satterford leased a plot of ground on the site to brewing partners Thomas Fuller and Charles McCarthy. The following year they acquired further adjoining plots, making up a small complex of buildings and yards set back from South Main Street and accessed by way Morrough's (sometimes Morrogh's) or Sugar House Lane, which was eventually subsumed into the complex of buildings of the later Lane's brewery.[1] A 1798 outline plan of the Fuller & McCarthy brewery shows that it consisted of a small 'beer house', 72 feet long and nearly 21 feet wide, a coal

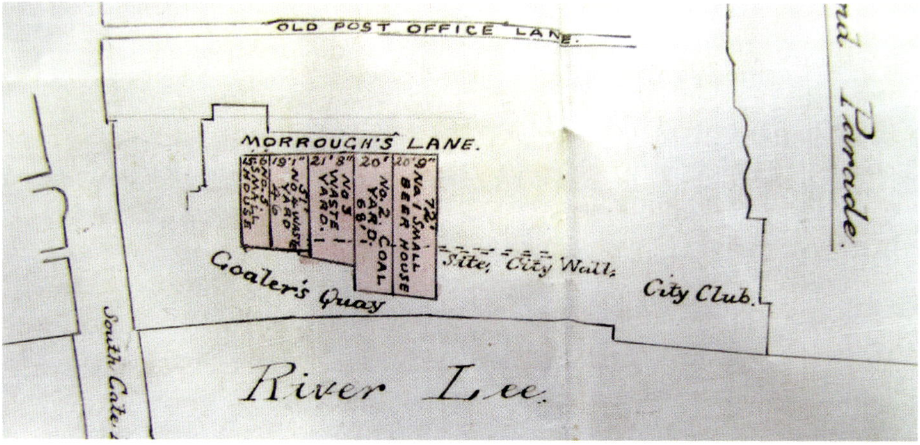

Outline plan, 1798, of the Fuller & McCarthy brewery off Morrough's or Sugar House Lane. (CCCA/Authors)

yard, two further yards and another building labelled 'small house'[2] (see above). In May 1798, Thomas Fuller assigned his share in the brewery to McCarthy, leaving him the sole owner.

Prior to 1796, Thomas Fuller and Anthony Hawkesworth were partners in a brewery that lay to the east of the Fuller and McCarthy holdings, also accessed from South Main Street by way of Morrough's or Old Sugar House Lane. A lease of 1796 describes Fuller and Hawkesworth's holding as 'the Brewery and Malt House with several cellars, linneys, out offices and yard ... in Sugar House Lane'. The southern boundary of their holding abutted the bank of the River Lee and they had a quay there for 'shipping and landing goods and merchantises'.[3] A note added to this lease shows that Anthony Hawkesworth had another brewery in the immediate vicinity in his own name: 'Note that the Small Brewery lately in the possession of Anth. Hawkesworth is a separate concern & not part of this within concern ...'. A fourth brewery lay to the east of the three concerns mentioned above, accessed from the west end of Tuckey's Quay, later part of the Grand Parade. This brewery is mentioned in a lease of 1800:

> ... the dwelling house, still house, Brewing house, Front and back Yards, cellars, sugar house, Mill house, stables and front cellar then formerly in the possession of Nathaniel Lavitt Esquire and lately in the possession of James Mahon Esquire situate on the West side near the tower end of Tuckey's Quay.[4]

These breweries could best be described as small common or wholesale breweries. They were seeking to take advantage of the more benign taxation regime that prevailed from 1791 and the growing local market for home-produced beers.

By 1796, Thomas Fuller was the sole owner of the Fuller & Hawkesworth brewery and in that year his interest was acquired by a partnership of Walter Fitzsimmons, Jeremiah O'Reilly and George Fuller (son of Thomas), described as 'Common Brewers and Maltsters'.[5] This new partnership expanded the brewery, acquiring the holdings of Charles McCarthy in 1798.[6] In 1799 Walter Fitzsimmons sold his one-third share in the business to Jeremiah O'Reilly and in 1801, following the death of George Fuller, O'Reilly bought the remaining one-third share from George's brother, Thomas Gray Fuller, for £1,200.[7] Jeremiah O'Reilly subsequently entered into a partnership with Thomas Hadigan and they traded for a number of years as brewers under the style of O'Reilly & Hadigan. John Carr, an American writer who toured the south of Ireland in 1805, wrote that O'Reilly & Hadigan had one of the two principal ale breweries in the city, the other being Cashman & Sons at Crosse's Green. [8]

In 1809 O'Reilly and Hadigan sold their brewery to Daniel Lane for £1,700. In the sale agreement the partners set out the improvements to the brewery undertaken by them, which they valued at £2,197.15.6, and from this amount they deducted an 'abatement' of £497.15.6, leaving the purchase price of £1,700. The list of improvements includes detailed outlays for building works, but also a number of items specifically connected to brewing: £40 for a sky cooler, £400 for two coppers, £40 for two tuns, £200 for two vats, £15 for an underback, £120 for a kiln and various other amounts for troughs, water and wort pumps, a mill, a dray, carts and tackling. Three old horses valued at £40 were also included, as was a 'new horse' called

Copy of 1815 lease plan showing unnamed laneway, labelled 'Passage from South Main Street to River Lee', connecting the street and Gaoler's Quay. (CCCA/Authors)

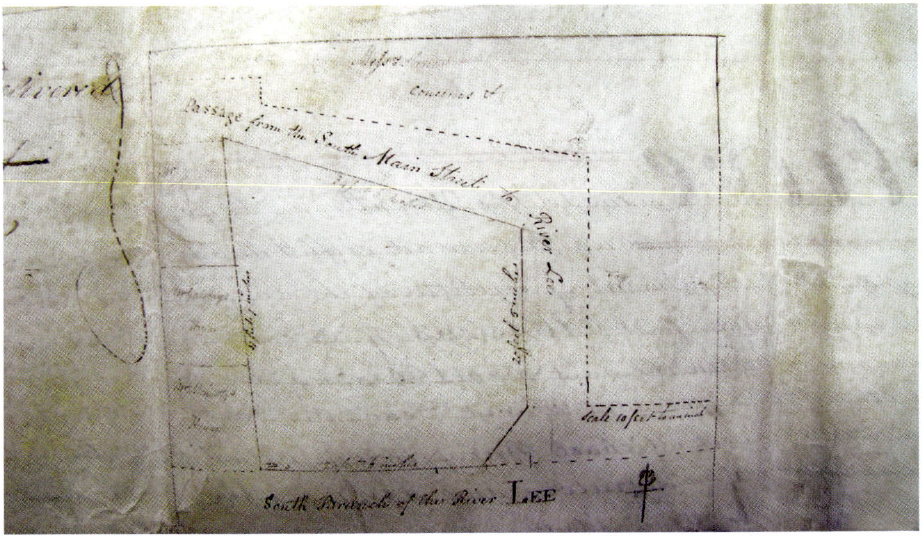

Batty, valued at £40. They agreed to hand over the premises on 1 September 1809.[9]

Eleven months later, in August 1810, Jeremiah O'Reilly bought back the brewery from Daniel Lane for £2,300.[10] No explanation is given for this series of transactions, but O'Reilly was soon in a new partnership with Michael Barry and they continued the expansion of the brewery holdings, northwards to Old Post Office Lane, as well as acquiring lots to the south towards the river. In 1814 they built a range of buildings over Morrough's Lane, which led into the brewery complex from South Main Street, and in 1815 they acquired a yard in the southwestern corner of the site that gave extra river frontage along Gaoler's Quay, which ran eastwards from South Gate Bridge. The plan of this plot attached to the lease shows an unnamed laneway (labelled 'Passage from South Main Street to River Lee') running southeastwards from South Main Street and turning sharply southwards to Gaoler's Quay.

Daniel Lane & Co.

By the end of 1817, porter brewers O'Reilly & Barry were in difficulty, falling victim to the downturn in trade that followed the end of the Napoleonic Wars in 1815 and competition from the increasingly dominant Cork Porter Brewery located across the street. They were declared bankrupt and in March 1818 Daniel Lane, with his sons James and Richard, returned to the fray and bought the brewery for £3,000. In July 1819 a co-partnership agreement was drawn up between Daniel Lane, his sons Samuel, James and Richard, and Abraham Lane, a merchant based in Dublin, either a brother or son of Daniel. The firm was to be known as Daniel Lane & Co. and it had a capital stock of £14,000, half of which was contributed by Daniel and Samuel and the other half by James, Richard and Abraham. Any expenditure on improvements and expansion would be funded equally by the two halves of the partnership.

In 1821 Daniel Lane & Co. acquired the brewery of Andrew Drinan, the buildings of which were located in Drinan Street, off Sullivan's Quay, and in Cove Street.[11] The buildings are listed as a malthouse, yard and office in Cove Street and a brewhouse, two offices, cellars, lofts and yards in Drinan Street.[12] Alfred Barnard, who published a four-volume study of the breweries of Britain and Ireland between 1889 and 1891, visited the old Drinan's Brewery as part of his visit to the Lane's brewery. He remarked that Drinan's was famous for its ale 'more than a century ago' and described the six-storey malthouse, stables and stores as well the former brewhouse, which had been converted to a cooperage.[13] Daniel Lane & Co. used the malthouses for malting, but concentrated their brewing at the South Main Street premises. The Drinan's Brewery buildings were eventually acquired by Beamish & Crawford Ltd as part of their takeover of Lane & Co. Ltd in 1901.

In 1826 Abraham assigned his share in the business to James and Richard, and the co-partnership between the four was continued until the death of Daniel in 1828.

Left: View from the south of Lane's Southgate Brewery, 1866. This image was published in G.S. Measom, *Official Guide to the Great Southern & Western Railway* (London, 1866)
Right: Advertisement for Lane's Double Stout. This advertisement dates to before 1877 when the company was incorporated as Lane & Co. Ltd. (Beamish & Crawford Brewery Collection/Authors)

The nature of the surviving partners' share in the business changed again – Samuel now had a half share and James and Richard had a quarter share each. Richard died in 1834 and his share went to James, making Samuel and James equal partners in the firm. They drew up a new agreement and agreed to continue under the style of Daniel Lane & Co. until 1838. In 1838 James sold his share in the firm to Samuel, making him the sole owner. Samuel continued to run the business until his death in 1847.

Samuel lived at Frankfield House near Cork and was prominent in the business, political and philanthropic life of the city. He served as a town councillor, a grand juror, a sheriff, a justice of the peace and a poor law guardian. In 1838 he paid for the building of Frankfield Church, engaging Sir Thomas Deane as the architect for the project, 'and with a munificence which has but few parallels in the present day, is also engaged in erecting a parsonage in the Elizabethan style for the curate'.[14] During the Great Famine he was prominent in efforts for the relief of distress in Cork. He died on 25 May 1847 'of water on the chest' and was described as 'an eminently humane and charitable man; and his mercantile character in its unsullied integrity held its place amongst the most honourable in Ireland'.[15] The brewery business was left to William, a brother of Samuel's, who lived at Vernon Mount.

In 1867 William sold a 50 per cent share in the brewery to William Shaw. Shaw, born in 1823 in County Tyrone, had been trained as an independent Protestant clergyman and was posted to Cork in 1846. Having married in 1850, he resigned his ministry and devoted himself to a career in business and politics. He lived at Beaumont House, the former Beamish home. He was an independent Liberal/ Home Rule MP for Bandon (1868–74) and County Cork (1874–85) and was a founder and chairman of the Munster Bank. William Lane's diligence to his duty was somewhat lacking and by 1867 he was in debt to Shaw for £9,000. An arrangement was made whereby Shaw would acquire a 50 per cent share in the firm by paying Lane £6,000, the brewery and its business having been valued at £30,000.[16] As part of this agreement, William Lane made over his share in the firm to his son, William Junior. Three years later it transpired that William Senior's debt to Shaw was £2,918 greater than had been assessed in 1867 and the amount had to be made good by William Junior.[17]

Lane & Co. Ltd

The firm became a limited company – Lane & Co. Ltd – in July 1877, with William Lane Jr. and William Shaw as principals.[18] The oft-mentioned foundation date of 1758 for the Southgate Brewery cannot be substantiated, even though the name and date were inscribed on a stone over the brewery entrance. As set out above, there had been a number of brewing enterprises on the site and it is plausible that one of these earlier small breweries or brewing partnerships, mentioned in documents no longer extant in the firm's archive, had a foundation date of 1758. This date was then later inscribed on the keystone of a new arched entrance to the brewery in an effort to give the firm the credentials of greater antiquity and possibly to pre-date the Guinness brewery, founded in 1759, which had grown to be the dominant brewery in Ireland by the later 1800s.

By the later 1870s there were three other breweries of significance operating in Cork – Beamish & Crawford, James J. Murphy & Co. and Sir John Arnott & Co. – and the acquisition of tied houses was seen as key to securing and maintaining market share. Lane & Co. Ltd joined in this race and embarked on a vigorous programme of establishing ties with public houses in the city and county. A document detailing the properties of the company drawn up prior to the takeover by Beamish & Crawford in 1901 includes their estate of tied houses, and in the case of ninety-nine public houses it was possible to establish the date of the first tie. Table 7.1 displays this information and shows the period of greatest acquisition as the 1880s and 1890s, the decades following the firm's incorporation.

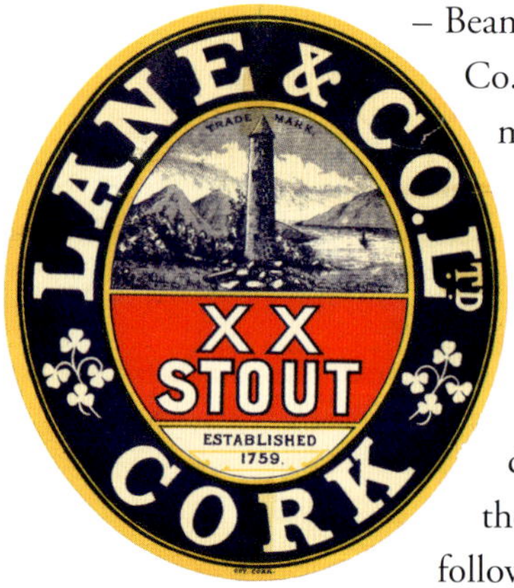

Lane & Co. Ltd. XX Stout cask label. This dates to after 1877, the year in which the company was incorporated.
(Beamish & Crawford Brewery Collection/Dori O'Connell)

Table 7.1
Lane & Co., ties established, 1830s–1900

DECADE	1830s	1840s	1850s	1860s	1870s	1880s	1890s	1900s
Number of ties established	0	0	3	3	9	35	41	8

By 1900, Lane's had 36 tied houses in the city, compared to Arnott's 85, Beamish & Crawford's 120 and James J. Murphy's 223. In County Cork in 1900, excluding the city, Lane's had 232 customers (not necessarily tied), Arnott's had 130, James J. Murphy's had 524 and Beamish & Crawford had 642. (See Appendix D.)

Main image: Plan of Lane's Southgate Brewery, 1880, and its title, bottom left. (CCCA/Dori O'Connell)
Right: Signatures of William Shaw and William Lane Jr. (CCCA/Authors)

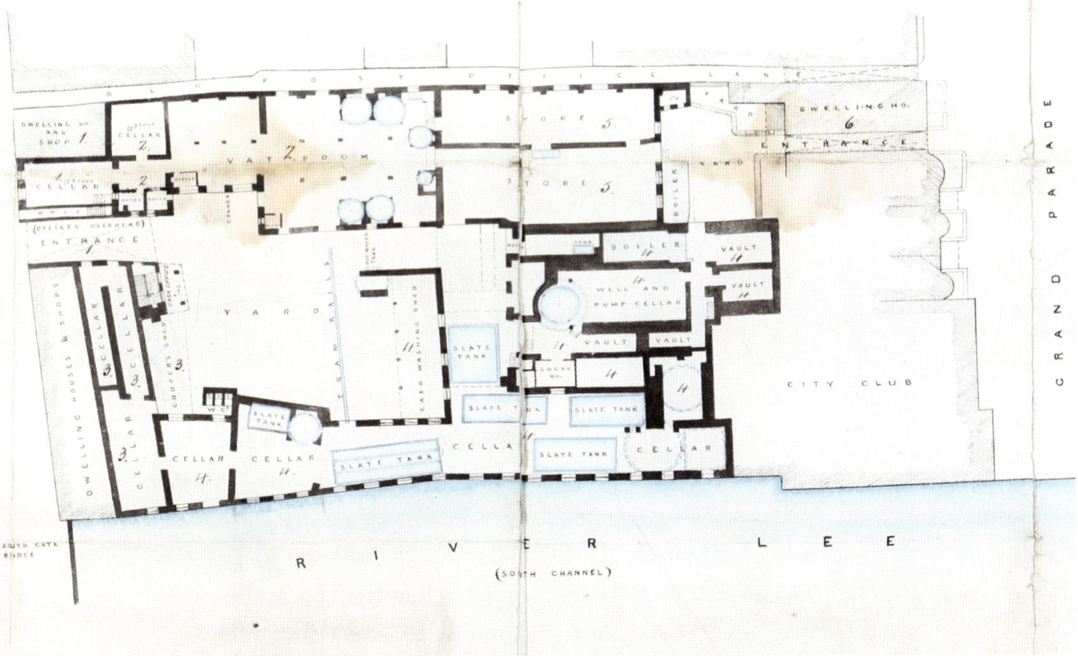

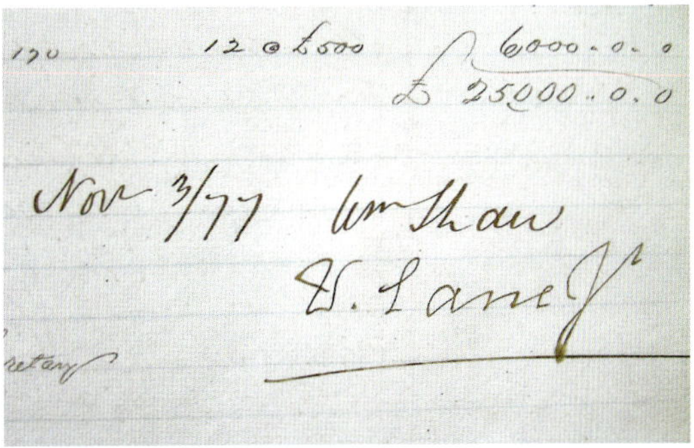

Rogue banker almost sinks Lane's

The Lanes' association with William Shaw was to have near-fatal consequences for the firm. By 1884, Lane & Co. Ltd had became indebted to the Munster Bank for £57,000. This bank had grown rapidly from its foundation in 1864, had forty-three branch offices and had aggressively grown its business. William Shaw was chairman of the board and, along with some of the other directors, behaved quite imprudently. The bank was mismanaged, had fatal levels of bad debt, its liquidity levels were inadequate and Shaw and some of the directors had received large unsecured loans from the bank. Shaw resigned from the bank in 1884 and it collapsed a year later in July 1885. William Shaw was declared bankrupt, owing the liquidators of the bank £130,000 against securities of £41,000. Some of the money Shaw owed was on behalf of Lane & Co. Ltd. In August 1886, the firm reached an agreement with the three liquidators of the bank, one of whom was Cork brewer and former director of the bank, James J. Murphy, and the £57,000 debt of Lane & Co. Ltd was cleared by February 1888 for payments amounting to £30,000.[19]

Trade

The brewery produced a range of products: West India Stout, Extra Stout, Double Stout, Bottling Stout, Mixing Stout, Single Stout, porter and ale. During the years 1893 to 1898, five varieties of ale are named: M (mild?), B (bitter?), X, XX and XB (extra bitter?). After 1898, only the generic term 'ale' is used.[20] Barnard singled out one product for particular mention: 'The brewery is noted for its export stout, which is shipped to various parts of the world, and commands the highest price in some markets.'[21] Sales and other figures survive only from 1887 and show a steady annual trade of between £45,000 and £51,000 in sales in the years up to 1895. For the brewery year ending on 30 September 1896, sales jumped over 24 per cent in value to over £64,000. This jump was due to the firm's success in securing a contract to supply all the military canteens in the Cork district. Up to 1896, each regiment had made its own arrangements with different brewers, but in that year the officer commanding the district invited tenders for the supply of all regiments under his command at a uniform price. Lane's won the contract for the year to the end of March 1897, but at low prices.[22] The military contract was renewed each year up to the takeover of the brewery by Beamish & Crawford in 1901 and made a worthwhile contribution to sales and profits, although the discounts demanded by the military and fluctuations in the prices of raw materials sometimes resulted in a profit fall. In the three-year period 1888 to 1890, the annual average profit was £5,109 on average annual sales of £47,096. A decade later, the impact of the military contracts can be seen in an average annual profit of £11,909 on average annual sales of £74,423 in the three years 1898 to 1900 (see Table 7.2).

The directors of Lane & Co. Ltd feared that the Boer War (1899–1902) would have a detrimental effect on its sales to military canteens due to an anticipated reduction in the number of soldiers based in Cork for the duration of the conflict. This did not transpire, however, and the company achieved record sales in the brewery year 1899 to 1900. The minutes of the annual general meeting of the company for that year note: 'The Military Canteen Contract we still retained and we are pleased to say that the War in South Africa has not interfered with this branch of our business, as was apprehended.'[23]

Table 7.2

Lane & Co. sales and profits, 1886–1900[24]

BREWERY YEAR (to 30 September)	VALUE OF SALES (to nearest £)	NET PROFIT (to the nearest £, after interest, extraord. charges etc. but before payment of dividend)
1886–7	£45,898	£7,229
1887–8	£47,266	£6,612
1888–9	£48,122	£4,870
1889–90	£45,901	£3,845
1890–1	£48,301	£1,721
1891–2	£47,312	£4,004
1892–3	£50,669	£4,420
1893–4	£50,040	£6,214
1894–5	£51,510	£8,211
1895–6	64,024	£10,678
1896–7	£69,968	£10,579
1897–8	£72,165	£9,837
1898–9	£73,722	£13,237
1899–1900	£77,382	£12,653

Above: Cover of the Minute Book of Lane & Co. Ltd. (CCCA/Authors)

Left: Ceramic bottle – Lane's West India Stout. (The Mutton Lane Inn/Authors)

'Amalgamation' with Beamish & Crawford

In the spring of 1901, Richard Henrik Beamish, on behalf of Beamish & Crawford Ltd, and Daniel Henry Lane, on behalf of Lane & Co. Ltd, great-grandsons of the respective brewery founders, successfully concluded negotiations for a so-called 'amalgamation' of the two companies – essentially a takeover of Lane's by Beamish & Crawford.[25] At the same time, James J. Murphy & Co. Ltd was in the process of purchasing Arnott & Co. Brewers Ltd, based on Fitton Street, a sale concluded in April 1901. This left Beamish & Crawford and James J. Murphy & Co. as the only breweries to survive in Cork city.

The premises, plant and goodwill of Lane & Co. Ltd were valued at £37,946.19.10 and included the Southgate Brewery; the premises of the former Drinan's Brewery on Drinan Street; a corn store, kiln, premises, stores and yards on Travers Street; and premises on Mary Street. The 'houses and licences' were given a value of £29,382.19.8 and included 123 public houses, owned by or legally bound to Lane's through tied-house agreements, and a number of other properties in Cork city and county.[26] Barrels were valued at just over £4,500, bottles at £194, horses at £200, drays at £182, hops at £5,365 and barley at £3,268. Other smaller items, cash on hand and the amount owed by debtors brought the total value of Lane & Co. Ltd to £98,353.1.6. The shareholders of Lane & Co. were allocated 16,600 £5 preference shares in the new amalgamated firm at 5 per cent annual interest (out of a total of 56,000 preference and 40,000 ordinary shares) and £84,000 debenture stock, paying 4 per cent annual interest, as payment.

A 'new' Beamish & Crawford Ltd was incorporated on 22 October 1901 to take over the assets of the two previous entities and the directors of the new company, Richard Henrik Beamish, Arthur Frederick Sharman Crawford and North Ludlow Axel Beamish, met for the first time on 26 October. Richard H. Beamish was paid £6,814.18.6 for his work in negotiating the deal, while Daniel H. Lane was paid £1,835.16.0. There was no representative of the former shareholders of Lane & Co. Ltd on the board of the new Beamish & Crawford. John Jerome Mahony was appointed company secretary and manager at this meeting, having already served in that capacity in the previous incarnation of Beamish &

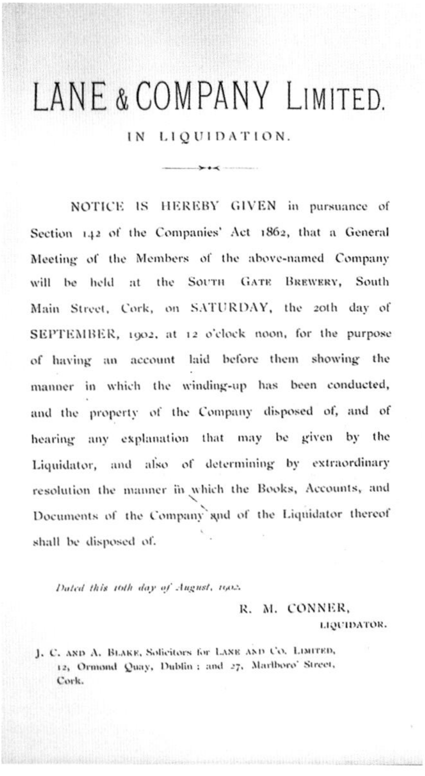
LANE & COMPANY LIMITED.

IN LIQUIDATION.

NOTICE IS HEREBY GIVEN in pursuance of Section 142 of the Companies' Act 1862, that a General Meeting of the Members of the above-named Company will be held at the SOUTH GATE BREWERY, South Main Street, Cork, on SATURDAY, the 20th day of SEPTEMBER, 1902, at 12 o'clock noon, for the purpose of having an account laid before them showing the manner in which the winding-up has been conducted, and the property of the Company disposed of, and of hearing any explanation that may be given by the Liquidator, and also of determining by extraordinary resolution the manner in which the Books, Accounts, and Documents of the Company and of the Liquidator thereof shall be disposed of.

Dated this 16th day of August, 1902.

R. M. CONNER,
LIQUIDATOR.

J. C. AND A. BLAKE, Solicitors for LANE AND CO. LIMITED, 12, Ormond Quay, Dublin; and 27, Marlboro' Street, Cork.

Notice of meeting on 20 September 1902 to formally wind up Lane & Co. Ltd following its sale to Beamish & Crawford. (CCCA/Authors)

Crawford incorporated for the first time in 1895. It was also passed that the round tower superimposed on the shamrock, encircled with the words 'Beamish & Crawford Ltd.', would again be the seal of the company.

Prior to the agreement with Lane & Co. Ltd, Beamish & Crawford had estimated that it could increase its trade by about 40,000 barrels annually following a purchase of that company, with a consequent boost of over £12,000 in their annual profits.[27] Production continued at the Southgate Brewery until the end of August 1901, after which no Lane & Co. Ltd branded products were produced. In the year ended August 1900 Beamish & Crawford sold 104,457 barrels and the following year that figure grew to a little over 120,000, 10,446 barrels of which were Lane's products. By 1902, the first full year after the takeover, sales had grown to over 141,000 barrels. Sales peaked the following year at 151,734, a growth not too far off that estimated in early 1901. However, sales began a period of steady decline after that.

Beamish & Crawford inherited Lane's contracts for supplying military canteens and this proved to be an important part of the company's trade, especially after the outbreak of war in 1914. In 1901 this segment of sales amounted to 2,702 barrels, but in the following first full year after the takeover this grew to 5,466 barrels.[28]

The end of the Southgate Brewery

Lane & Co. Ltd was formally wound up at a meeting on 20 September 1902. Beamish & Crawford used the former Southgate Brewery for storage for some years after that and converted many of the buildings for use as workshops for fitters, wheelwrights, plumbers and other brewery maintenance tradesmen. A brewery workers' club was established in the upper floors of Nos. 40, 40a, 41 and 41a South Main Street, buildings on the corner of that street and Old Post Office Lane. In December 1960 this space was rented to James N. Healy and Declan Flynn for use as a theatre club.[29] By the mid-1930s the site was largely vacant and throughout the following years the buildings of the old brewery were demolished. By the late 1950s all the brewery buildings had disappeared and the vacant site was used for car parking. Attempts had been made to sell the site in the 1930s, but it was 1957 before it was sold for £12,000. Since then it has been used as a commercial car park.[30]

MURPHY'S: LADY'S WELL BREWERY[31]

Five young brothers from one of Cork's wealthy 'merchant prince' families established Murphy's Lady's Well Brewery in 1856 on the north side of Cork city. The arrival of Cork's first major Catholic-owned brewery posed a serious threat to Beamish & Crawford and after 1901 was its sole local competitor. More than 150 years after its foundation, the brewery is the 'last man standing' of the four major Cork breweries, still on its original site on Leitrim Street.

Merchant princes

The Murphy family had grown prosperous through a variety of commercial and industrial ventures and their wealth translated into political, social and cultural power. Having initially prospered in tanning, the family branched out into shipping and international trading from its base at Morrison's Island. The ships brought luxury exotic goods such as sugar, rum, spices, coffee and tea into Cork from the Americas and the Far East. In 1825 James Murphy (1769–1855) of Ringmahon House and three of his brothers established the James Murphy and Co. distillery in Midleton, which amalgamated with four city firms in 1867 to become the Cork Distilleries Company. Another brother, John, was Catholic bishop of Cork from 1815 to 1847. Their nephew, Francis Stack Murphy, was MP for Cork from 1841 to 1846 and again from 1851 to 1853 (replacing Francis Bernard Beamish in 1841 and being replaced by Beamish in 1853), while another cousin, John Nicholas Murphy, was Lord Mayor and High Sheriff of the city in the 1850s. The Murphys were major benefactors of the Catholic Church in the city, helping to build SS Peter and Paul and to secure the lease on the old Mansion House, which in 1857 became the Mercy Hospital, the first hospital in Cork to be placed in the charge of a religious order.

From left: Brothers James J., William, Jerome and Francis Murphy, the four founding partners of James J. Murphy & Co. (Heineken)

James J. Murphy & Co.

James J. Murphy (1825–97) and his brothers William, Jerome, Francis and Nicholas (who was bought out in 1865) bought the premises of Cork's Foundling Hospital on Leitrim Street in 1854, and in 1856 James J. Murphy & Co. opened Lady's Well Brewery, named after the holy well situated across the street. The business started poorly and after less than two years some of the Murphy family offered to sell the concern to Beamish & Crawford. Their offer was refused and Murphy's then went on the offensive, buying licences and public houses, underselling Beamish and inducing many of the latter's customers to switch allegiance. After four years of bitter competition, 'an agreement for mutual non-interference' was signed between the two companies in 1861.[32]

Above: Murphy's brewery in 1906. (Heineken)
Right: An early poster for J.J. Murphy & Co's Famous Stout. (Heineken)

Murphy's began by brewing Lady's Well Ale and Murphy's Porter, but from 1862 concentrated on porter alone. Stout was added in 1889. James J. Murphy & Co. quickly established itself as the city's second largest brewery, surpassing Arnott's and Lane's and becoming a serious competitor to Beamish & Crawford. County trade was supplied through the newly established railway network that radiated out from the city, while city trade was based on its tied houses. By the beginning of the twentieth century, the Murphy tied estate numbered almost 200 houses.

Cork's leading brewery

By the late 1880s, when James J. Murphy & Co. became a limited company, it had become Cork's leading producer, brewing just under half of the city's total porter output. In the early 1890s the brewery was remodelled, upgraded and expanded. (The new malthouse built at this time was converted into the main offices of Murphy Brewery Ireland Ltd in the early 1990s.) Exports to Britain and the colonies also began at this time. In 1896 a subsidiary, the West Cork Bottling Company, was established in Bandon and in 1901 the company took over and closed down Arnott's St Finbarre's Brewery in Fitton Street and its ale brewery at Riverstown. Murphy's success in these years was aided by the profile of the Murphy family and its Catholic philanthropy as well as by the rescue of the Munster Bank in 1885 led by James J. Murphy, which saved many businesses and individuals in the city from ruin. He was also a patron of the nascent GAA, whose Cork County Board adjourned its meeting as a mark of respect on the day of his death in 1897. The level of wealth that accrued to the brothers from the brewery's success at this time can be gauged from the fact that the individual annual incomes of the two senior partners (over £11,000 each) were almost double the total annual wage bill at a time when the brewery employed up to 200 workers.

The entrance to Murphy's brewery, 1902. (Heineken)

Slow decline

Francis Murphy became chairman after the death of his brother, followed by James J.'s three sons in succession: Charles Eustace, Albert St John and Fitzjames. They presided over a period of slow decline that began with the disruption caused by the First World War. As well as the immediate problems caused by the war, the lowering of the strength of beer, the tax-related price increases and the restriction on opening hours that were introduced at this time remained a permanent feature. The fact that Cork county, the heart of the Murphy's trade, was the most violent region during the war of independence and civil war also meant continued disruption (four Murphy's pubs were destroyed in the burning of Cork city in December 1920, for example). Another significant event in this period was a five-week strike by the city's brewery workers in February to March 1920, which seriously curtailed production and gave Guinness a foothold in the city that it never subsequently relinquished. (See Chapter 11.)

Stagnation best describes the brewery's fortunes during the early decades of independence. It celebrated its centenary in 1956 against the backdrop of Irish economic and social crisis. In 1958 the last Murphy to head the company, 'The Colonel', John Fitzjames, a grandson of James J., took the helm. He oversaw a rare successful initiative as the company responded to changes in the city in the late 1950s and early 1960s by closing down old pubs in the depopulating city centre and opening new premises in the expanding suburbs – houses such as the Outpost in Bishopstown, the Tory Top in Ballyphehane and the Orchard in Ballinlough. Another major shift was the switch from the old wooden barrel to the new metal casks in the early 1960s, which marked the end of the line for the coopers, craftsmen that had been associated with the brewery since its inception. By 1964 all the remaining breweries in the rest of the country had either been closed down or taken over by Guinness, which was beaten in the race to buy Beamish & Crawford by Canadian Breweries in 1962. Murphy's rebuffed a Guinness offer but was forced to take action to keep pace with its competitors in the rapidly changing industry and diversifying market.

Takeovers and survival

In 1965 Murphy's entered a partnership with the British brewing giant Watney Mann, which acquired a majority shareholding in 1967. Its Red Barrel ale was a failure on the Irish market and in 1971 Murphy's was placed on the brink of liquidation when the British brewers pulled out. It was rescued by the state, and an interim board kept the company afloat until it was taken over by a group of vintners in 1974. Despite initial success, including the introduction of new brands – most significantly, Heineken in 1975 – the company was in trouble again, and in 1982 it went into receivership. Beamish & Crawford, then owned by Carling-O'Keefe of Canada, came close to buying the brewery, but it was eventually acquired by Dutch brewing giant Heineken in 1983, which created Murphy Brewery Ireland Ltd and began a new era in the history of this Cork institution. In 2001 the company was renamed Heineken Ireland Limited. In October 2008 Heineken Ireland took over Beamish & Crawford following the international takeover of Beamish's parent company, Scottish & Newcastle, by Heineken and Carlsberg. In May 2009, following the closure of the Beamish & Crawford brewery, the brewing of Beamish stout was transferred to Lady's Well.

ARNOTT'S: ST FINBARRE'S BREWERY

A new competitor to Beamish & Crawford, coming soon after the disastrous (for Beamish) entry of Murphy's onto the Cork brewing scene, arrived in 1862. The previous year the prominent Cork-based Scottish businessman and politician Sir John Arnott bought Abbott's Ale and Porter Brewery on Fitton (now Sharman Crawford) Street, near St Fin Barre's Cathedral, located a short distance from the Cork Porter Brewery. It was an ideal location for a brewery, as it was close to a river channel and adjacent to the Cork and Muskerry Railway terminus. Abbott's had been in operation since 1805, initially specialising in a sweet table beer and subsequently brewing ales

Arnott's St Finbarre's Brewery, *c.* 1890. (Courtesy Michael Lenihan/Niall Kelly)

and porter on a small scale. The owner, Samuel Abbott, was declared bankrupt in 1856 and in 1858 the brewery was purchased in trust for George Waters, a former distiller. Waters died early in 1859 and in 1860 the concern was offered for sale. It was bought by Arnott, then Lord Mayor of Cork and MP for Kinsale, in 1861. The following year it reopened as Sir John Arnott & Co.'s St Finbarre's Brewery, better known simply as Arnott's.

Speculator and benefactor

Arnott also operated a 'monster bakery' on the site from 1862 until 1864, established to supply bread at close to cost price to the city's poor in defiance of the city's master bakers, whose high prices at a time of poor harvests, he claimed, were preventing the working class from accessing this staple. He established four other bakeries in the city with the same aim, and according to one sympathetic account, Arnott 'was the means of preventing a famine in Cork' in the early 1860s.[33] While one master baker accused Sir John of being 'a private speculator' portraying himself as a 'public benefactor', Arnott apparently lost £5,000 of his own money on the battle, which he eventually won, forcing down bread prices, following which he gifted the bakeries to those who had helped in their establishment.[34]

The new brewery was advantaged not only by its location, then, but by Arnott's fame and popularity. His 'extensive charities', according to the *Illustrated London News*, 'rendered him a general favourite', while the *Cork Examiner* described him as 'one of the greatest, if not actually the foremost, of [the city's] commercial and philanthropic citizens'.[35] He was Lord Mayor of Cork three times (1859, 1860, 1861) and an independent MP for Kinsale (1859–61); his business interests included, amongst others, the Cork Park Racecourse, linen manufacture, drapery and department stores, and *The Irish Times* newspaper.

His new brewery immediately went on the offensive, underselling both Beamish and Murphy's and beginning the acquisition of what would become a substantial tied-house estate. It quickly surpassed Lane's to become Cork's third brewery. The low level of Beamish's reputation at this juncture is illustrated by Arnott's choice of Murphy's as his first target in a move in which Arnott's dual role as 'private speculator' and 'public benefactor' was clearly evident. In September 1862 the local newspapers carried a £100 challenge from Arnott's to Murphy's: the principal dealers of the city were invited to compare the porter produced by both breweries, with the loser handing over £50 worth of bread, coal and blankets to the workmen of the city's four breweries, and £50 worth of same to the Catholic and Protestant clergy 'for distribution among the Poor'. Arnott's ate into Beamish's local trade as Murphy's had done previously, and just as with its first serious competitor, Beamish & Crawford was forced to sign an agreement of 'mutual non-interference' with Arnott's in 1863,

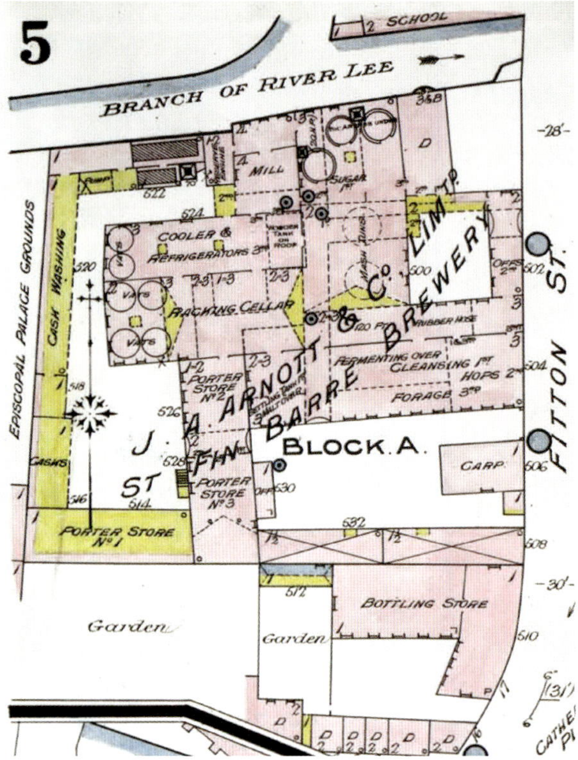

Goad fire insurance plan of 1897 showing Arnott's brewery. (Cork City Library)

Painted advertisement for Arnott's Prize Medal Porter, Shandon Street, Cork. (Authors)

cutting its losses but relinquishing a good portion of its local porter trade.[36]

The brewery and its trade

The old brewery was overhauled and remodelled in 1863 and again in 1870 to such a level that the only part of the original plant that survived was a single fermenting tun. The 7-acre site contained state-of-the-art brewing plant, offices, a malthouse and a bottling plant and store; the brewery's cooperage and cask stores were located on the opposite side of Fitton Street. Among its novelties was the first steam engine in Cork, a beam engine made especially for Arnott's, and an on-site bottling department, the first in any brewery in the city. Porter, stout and ale from the other breweries was either bottled by specialist bottlers or by publicans themselves. 'Boys' (young teenagers) were employed in the bottling department and were transferred to other brewery jobs as they grew older. Porter and stout were bottled for both the export trade and for the local market.[37] Arnott's clashed with the local vintners in 1874 when they objected to the brewery supplying bottled stout to private customers. He agreed to stick to a minimum supply of four dozen bottles; in discussions with the vintners, Arnott declared that his bottling operation was 'the cause of a great deal of trouble and nuisance for the brewery' because it was so time consuming, but he had to do it for his export trade. A report from William Ladd in 1883 stated that all the city's bottlers agreed that 'Arnott spoiled the bottling trade in Cork by cutting down the price of stout to 1s 4d per dozen'.[38]

The export trade became a significant part of the brewery's business. From 3,790 barrels in 1867, exports rose to 18,784 in 1872; the total output of the brewery in the latter year was in the region of 40,000 barrels. Arnott's exported to all the main British cities and had branch houses in Barbados, Demerara and St Thomas. It also supplied the British army in the Mediterranean and had a healthy trade with the military canteens in the south of Ireland. Local trade was centred on the brewery's tied-house network. Arnott's company already had two public houses before he took over the brewery; six more were added in 1862 and the brewery's tied houses numbered approximately thirty by the mid-1870s. In the following two decades the estate grew to between eighty and ninety in the city alone, with another dozen or so houses outside the city.[39]

Sir John Arnott & Co. of Cork Brewers (Limited)

Sir John Arnott & Co. became a limited liability company – Sir John Arnott & Co. of Cork Brewers (Limited) – in April 1876. Share capital of £66,000 was offered in 11,000 shares (8,000 for directors and 3,000 for the public) at £6 each. A further £20,000 was offered in 6 per cent debentures. The prospectus stated that notwithstanding heavy expenditure, the company had average returns of over 10 per cent per annum; its trade was 50,000 barrels of stout and porter a year and net profit for the previous year was £7,500. The company directors were Sir John himself and

Sir John Arnott being celebrated in Cork in 1862 following his three years as the city's Lord Mayor. (*Illustrated London News*)

his son, John Alexander Arnott, together with Edward Lane (appointed managing director in 1878) and his son, Thomas R. Lane, who had overseen the brewery operation since its establishment, together with Thomas and Francis Lyons. The first directors' report of the new limited company in April 1878 recorded a profit of over £10,000 and confirmed the predicted dividend of 10 per cent.[40] In 1883 Arnott's bought the small ale brewery that had been owned by the renowned Cork cultural, political and business figure Denny Lane in Glyntown, Glanmire. Porter from St Finbarre's and ale from Arnott's new Riverstown Ale Brewery featured prominently at the Cork Exhibition of 1883, where Arnott's products won medals.[41]

By the end of the decade, however, clouds were appearing on the horizon. Sales were declining and there are indications that Arnott was involved in under-reporting what was being sold to avoid excise.[42] Sir John was replaced by his son as chairman in 1894. Average annual sales in the second half of the 1890s were 27,311 barrels[43] (nearly half of its output when it was in its prime) and the company was in serious decline at the time of the founder's death in 1898.

Decline and fall

In 1900 John Alexander Arnott led the creation of a new company with a reduced capital called Arnott & Co. Brewers, Limited, and in early 1901 the company decided

Entrance to Arnott's brewery from Fitton Street, *c.* 1895. (Courtesy Michael Lenihan)

to wind up, appoint liquidators and reach an agreement with James J. Murphy & Co. for the sale of the two breweries – St Finbarre's and the Riverstown Ale Brewery – and the tied-house estate. The purchase price of £98,000 was eventually reduced to a net sum of £80,750, and Murphy's issued £50,000 worth of debentures to help defray the cost. The company was bought in April 1901 and the new owners promptly closed down the St Finbarre's and Riverstown breweries; Arnott's tied houses, which then numbered approximately seventy, were taken over and run as Murphy's houses.[44]

The Fitton Street site remained vacant for a number of years until it was bought by the Beamish & Crawford director and philanthropist Arthur Frederick Sharman Crawford, chairman of the Cork Technical Instruction Committee, who donated it for the building of an expanded new home for the Crawford Municipal Technical Institute that had been operating from wholly inadequate and overcrowded premises in the School of Art on Emmet Place. The expansive new 'tech' opened in October 1911, Fitton Street having been renamed Sharman Crawford Street by the corporation as a tribute to the donor in that year.[45] The School of Art transferred from what is now the Crawford Art Gallery (named after William Horatio Crawford) to the old Arnott's site in 1979, becoming the Crawford School of Art and later the Crawford College of Art and Design.

The Crawford College of Art and Design now occupies the site of Arnott's St Finbarre's Brewery. (Authors)

8

Drinking, Pubs and Temperance

Cork at the Turn of the Twentieth Century

The great popular embrace of temperance during the heyday of the campaign led by Father Mathew in the late 1830s and 1840s slackened in the following decades. In post-Famine Ireland the Catholic Church was enjoying a growing power and influence, but remained suspicious of the temperance movement. As Elizabeth Malcolm has written:

> The link between temperance and Protestantism was too strong and the memory of Father Mathew's controversial views too recent to allow the church in the 1850s and 1860s to embrace the anti-drink cause wholeheartedly. Lacking the support of the majority church, the temperance movement had little choice but to pin its hopes on parliament if any substantial change was to be effected.[1]

A measure of success was achieved by temperance campaigners with the passing of the Irish Sunday Closing Act in 1878. Under this Act, public houses had to remain closed to the general public on Sundays but were allowed to serve 'bona fide travellers' – people who had travelled in excess of three miles. Public houses in the cities of Dublin, Belfast, Cork, Waterford and Limerick were exempted and could open on Sundays from 2.00pm to 7.00pm. The campaign for Sunday closing had hoped for a complete closure on Sundays, but popular opposition and the lobbying of the drinks industry led to a measure of dilution. The leading role taken by Ulster Protestants and Unionists in the demand for Sunday closing had given the campaign a sectarian character that did not appeal to ordinary Catholics or to their clergy and bishops.

In the 1880s and 1890s the more pressing concerns of land reform and Home Rule took precedence in parliament and the issue of temperance and greater restrictions on the sale of alcohol reverted to being the concern principally of passionate individuals and temperance groups. The League of the Cross, a Catholic organisation founded in London in 1873, had total abstinence from alcohol as its aim. It had branches in Ireland and was particularly strong in Cork. In 1898 the Pioneer Total Abstinence Association, the most successful of all the abstinence groups, was founded by Father James Cullen, a Jesuit and an extremely competent organiser. His group achieved the sustained success denied to Father Mathew fifty years earlier. The aims of temperance and moderation were by now replaced by that of total abstinence and the movement was unashamedly Catholic in nature, with close associations to the Gaelic revival movement of the time:

> Gaelic sports, music and dancing, to say nothing of language classes, provided exactly the sort of sober, uplifting recreation that the temperance movement had been promoting for decades ... Cullen succeeded where Mathew had failed: he established an enduring total abstinence movement allied to the two most powerful forces in Irish society, Catholicism and nationalism.[2]

'A malignant evil, eating into the very vitals of the nation'

In 1898 the Royal Commission on Liquor Licensing Laws held a series of hearings in Ireland to take evidence in relation to possible amendments to the existing licensing laws. A number of witnesses from Cork gave evidence, and their testimony gives a graphic insight into the issues causing concern to the advocates of abstinence and their opponents, as well as the nature of the public house trade in Cork city and county.[3]

Father Patrick O'Leary, a curate in the Lough parish in Cork city, was interviewed by the commissioners on 4 May 1898. He was an advocate of temperance and president of the local branch of the Society for the Prevention of Cruelty to Children.[4] He told the commissioners that in the previous year, 175 cases of neglect and cruelty had come to the attention of the society involving over 500 children and that all bar one of those cases was the result of 'gross intemperance on the part of the parents'. He was particularly concerned with drunkenness amongst married women and felt that 'the woman who should regulate the home and be the angel of the home' had her status completely undermined 'there being no respect for her authority or guidance once the family know she is intemperate'.

Father O'Leary was not advocating prohibition of alcohol, but was very much in favour of the existing laws being properly enforced and further legislative controls being introduced. He told the commissioners that many publicans were acting irresponsibly by selling drink during prohibited hours and serving people who were clearly inebriated. 'I say that a very large proportion of them break the law without

St Fin Barre's Cathedral viewed from the upper floor of the brewhouse. (John Sheehan)

scruple … a very large proportion are anxious to break the law, and they actually do so when they can,' O'Leary added. At that time Cork city had 542 public houses, one for every 139 people of the city's population, and the pressure for trade forced many publicans to act illegally in order to survive. Many publicans, he said, went into the business as respectable men but 'I do believe that the trade demoralizes them'. O'Leary felt that the city had twice as many public houses as it needed. He also highlighted the continuing practice of casual labourers having their wages paid in pubs and of publicans often acting as agents for the employers of those labourers. The result was that '[t]hese unfortunate men believed they would have no chance of employment unless they became habitual customers of these public-houses'.

Father O'Leary called for the Sunday trading hours of public houses in Cork and in the other cities where they were allowed to open to be reduced to three hours at most, but he would of course prefer that they remained closed for the entire day. He highlighted the contrast between the habits of the female habituées of pubs and their more 'respectable' fellow-citizens on Sundays:

> I have seen on Sundays … numbers of women with their little children in their arms in public-houses, ranged along before the bars under the influence of drink; young girls too going out into the streets under the influence of drink, while a very sad and strange contrast was presented by respectable people going to their place of worship with their little children looking on at this, the young people scandalized, and possibly some of them might get demoralized by the sights they see.

He concluded his evidence by saying that 'the abuses are very general, so general that they have grown to be a malignant evil, eating into the very vitals of the nation'.

Father Maurice Ahern, a priest based in Ladysbridge in East Cork, also gave evidence before the commission and presented a similar case to that of Father O'Leary, but from a rural perspective. He opened his remarks by pointing out that East Cork had a public house for every seventy-one people of the total population – three or four times more than was necessary or desirable. 'The villages and small towns are overcrowded with public-houses,' he said, and gave the example of the village of Ballymacoda, with a pub for every twenty-one people of the population, and Mogeely, with a pub for every fifteen inhabitants. The proliferation of pubs in towns and villages made it difficult for those with a fondness for drink to avoid temptation. Father Ahern told the commissioners:

> I have been told by a person fond of drink, that the very fact of seeing a public-house open is a temptation to him to go in and have a drink, and one person told me that in order to avoid entering a public-house when he had taken the pledge, he had to run across the door to avoid yielding to the temptation.

Most of the pubs shared premises with another business, usually a grocery, and this particularly concerned Ahern, as 'this gives women, of course, a plea for entering such houses, and it protects them from public opinion', while the difficulty of getting alternative refreshments meant that women 'very often take porter there for their lunch or dinner'. He felt that pubs should be compelled to supply tea, coffee and 'especially milk', as well as temperance drinks, although most of the temperance drinks he had sampled were 'of a very inferior quality and very unpalatable'. Boys who had taken a pledge at their Confirmation to abstain from all alcoholic drinks unknowingly broke that pledge in the premises of unscrupulous publicans when they were served claret having asked for temperance wine. 'I believe it is often done,' said Ahern, 'and in order to deceive the people all the more completely they call this claret "League of the Cross wine".'

As O'Leary had pointed out for the city, Ahern also said that the 'over population' of pubs forced publicans in rural areas to act illegally in order to keep their businesses going. Many broke the Sunday closing law by abusing the bona fide traveller rules and the common pub/grocery shop combination made it easier to serve alcohol on a Sunday, as the grocery was legally allowed to function. In his evidence Father O'Leary had spoken about the abuse of Sunday closing in rural areas: 'I know that in certain towns people give themselves up to drunken orgies on Sundays when the public-houses are supposed to be closed, simply because they get the drink in these combined shops.' Both priests felt that the police were lax in enforcing the licensing laws and that the magistrates were too easy on offenders who were brought before them. Father Ahern produced photographs to the commissioners of pubs, illegally open on a Sunday,

(Beamish & Crawford Brewery Collection/Dori O'Connell)

Beamish & Crawford labels. (Courtesy Ed Hinchy)

with a man on watch for the police at the door. He told the commission that when cases came before a magistrate, the word of the publican was usually taken over that of the police. He went on: 'What I blame them [magistrates] for is attaching as much importance to the evidence given by the corner boys of the town, as to the evidence of the most respectable members of the constabulary force.'

He also accused magistrates of possibly accepting money from the agents of a city brewer, ostensibly for travel expenses, to travel to hearings on licence applications and to support such applications. Richard Pigott Beamish appeared before the commissioners ten days later, on 21 May 1898, and expressed outrage at Ahern's allegations of bribery. Beamish was speaking on behalf of the four city brewers and had been assured by them that no such practices were engaged in. Ahern could not produce proof of his allegation but said that a brewer's agent, a relative of his, had approached him asking for assistance in canvassing the support of magistrates for a licence application.

Father Ahern also accused publicans and brewers of joining forces to sponsor horse races and athletic sports meetings to increase sales of drink:

> The funds are subscribed to principally by the local publicans and the brewers, but the stakes are so small, and the class of horses that run there are so very inferior, that I believe they serve no other purpose whatsoever but to bring the country people there for the purpose of drinking.

He proposed an earlier closing time for pubs on Saturday nights, a strict enforcement of the Sunday closing laws and a drastic reduction in the number of pubs in East Cork. He demanded that a new means be devised to choose magistrates for the bench, as those then serving were too favourable to the drinks trade, approving licence applications too easily and not being harsh enough on offending publicans. Father Ahern believed that it was the police and clergy, not magistrates, who were best suited to decide on licence applications.

Beamish & Crawford malt gang at the Lee Maltings (formerly the Lee Mills), photographed *c.* 1913. (Courtesy Ed Hinchy)

'The working classes in Cork are as sober a body as you can get in Ireland'

Other witnesses from Cork gave less extreme evidence, and while contradicting much of what the two priests had said, they agreed on some issues, especially the excessive number of pubs in Cork city and county. Neither Richard Pigott Beamish nor Denis Donovan, secretary of the Cork Licensed Vintners' Trade Protection Association, felt that the magistrates on the bench were as objective as they might have been because there were strong advocates of total abstinence on the bench, while those with links to the liquor trade were excluded from adjudicating on licence applications. Beamish and Donovan spoke against the proposal that Sunday closing should also apply to the cities then exempted and against the proposed earlier closing time on Saturday nights. Joseph O'Brien, secretary of the United Trades and Labour Council in Cork and an employee of the Beamish & Crawford brewery, claimed to speak on behalf of about 4,000 workers in the city and also opposed the mooted changes to opening times. He believed that Sunday closing of pubs in Cork 'would mean the demoralization of the homes of the working classes', as people who wished to drink on a Sunday would bring liquor home on a Saturday night, bringing the evils of drunkenness into their houses, 'where it is not introduced at present'.

O'Brien also commented on the position of the clergy, whom he felt had become distracted by political issues following on from the rifts caused by the divorce of Charles Stewart Parnell:

> I believe it was the unfortunate crisis in the late parliamentary party of Ireland that allowed the temperance movement to be so far forgotten; and if the Catholic clergymen – and I am a Catholic myself – would apply themselves to again trying to enrol the flocks in the League of the Cross, or resuscitate it, and not bother themselves so much about politics I think we could go along better by moral persuasion to bring about temperance in Ireland.

Following on the testimony of Fathers O'Leary and Ahern regarding drunkenness amongst women, the issue was raised with Donovan and O'Brien. When Donovan was asked if he could 'account for so large a quantity of the women in your city being tipplers and drinkers', he replied that he could not, but that the poor conditions in which many families were forced to live was a factor. He continued:

> I think that [female drunkenness] more or less applies to a particular section of the women. It applies to some of the women who do some hawking and marketing in the markets. As a rule I think the women are very sober.

Joseph O'Brien also rejected the notion that the women of Cork drank to excess, adding: 'I think it most unfair to the women of Cork to hold them up as terrible drunkards.' But O'Brien did mention the case of Mary Short, a woman who had been before the magistrates in Cork for drunkenness on at least 300 occasions. O'Brien explained that Short 'and people of her class' were a minority 'and if she is to be held up as any model of the other women of Cork I think it is most unfair'. O'Brien was also very firm in his contradiction of the evidence of those who portrayed the people of Cork as being addicted to drink, 'because the working classes in Cork are as sober a body as you can get in Ireland'.

The Royal Commission published its report in 1899, but many advocates of reform remained dissatisfied. In a paper read in 1902 a barrister, William Lawson, stated the case for further reform, more than was likely to be introduced on the recommendations of the Commission. The oversupply of public houses was a continuing problem and new licences were being needlessly granted in some areas. He referred to Tralee, County Kerry, where there were 117 pubs for a population of 5,367 people. A local police officer had reported:

> In some cases, if a man was blindfolded, and put standing in the centre of the street, and spun round a couple of times and started off in no particular direction, I don't suppose he could go 20 yards without striking against a public house.[5]

Rooskey, County Roscommon, had nine pubs for 174 inhabitants and applications for two further licences were granted on the grounds of increased tourism. However, the local police sergeant said that he had seen only two tourists in the village the previous summer. In the same county in 1900 the village of Ballinlough, with a population of 200, had eight pubs. The following year there were nine new applications for licences, all of which were granted, giving a ratio of one pub for every 11.7 people, 'one of the most glaring travesties of justice'. Such abuses of the licensing system were addressed in 1902 in the Licensing (Ireland) Act. Lawson also bemoaned the fact that the Intoxicating Liquors (Sale to Children) Act of 1901 did not set the minimum age for the purchase of alcohol at sixteen, opting instead for the lower limit of fourteen years of age. He hoped that the pace of legislative change following from the report of the Royal Commission would be speeded up and that restrictive measures applying in England would also be introduced in Ireland. 'Drink,' wrote Lawson, 'is the parent of crime; not only is it fatal to material prosperity, it saps the morals and the health of those who give way to it.'

The breweries and public houses of Cork city and county in 1900

The statistics published by the Royal Commission on Liquor Licensing Laws in 1898 show that there were 2,379 pubs in the city and county of Cork, 536 of which were in the city.[6] Cork city had almost double the density of pubs for its population compared to the Dublin metropolitan area, and the city and county's pubs made up 13 per cent of the country's total, while having only 9.3 per cent of the total population. Temperance advocates and brewers agreed, for different reasons, that Cork would be better served by reducing the density of pubs. Fewer pubs would result in a greater volume of trade in those pubs, giving a better return to the publican and brewer and improving the quality of the premises, while the temptation to break the licensing laws would be lessened by the improved business. For those on the anti-drink side, fewer pubs meant less temptation, and better-run pubs reduced the likelihood of unscrupulous publicans trading illegally and preying on the weaknesses of problem drinkers. The first serious effort at reducing the number of pubs in Ireland came with the passing of the Intoxicating Liquor Act of 1927.

Between 1898 and 1900 a representative of the Beamish & Crawford brewery visited every pub in County Cork, excluding the city, and some in the western part of County Waterford. He interviewed every publican and noted the size of his or her trade, the brewery with which the publican dealt and wrote a brief assessment of each town or district, with particular reference to markets, fairs, agriculture, commercial fishing, industry, the proximity of military barracks and other factors that had a significant impact on the drinks trade. Many of the pubs visited were the property of a brewery and let to a tenant who had to deal exclusively with that brewery or were tied to a brewery for a period of time through mortgage or debt. In some cases publicans chose to deal exclusively with only one brewery without a formal tie, citing good treatment by the brewery or financial assistance in the past as reasons for this. In one case the representative noted:

> When they were commencing business everyone said to them that they need not hope to succeed if they did not sell Messrs. B & C's porter, and when J. J. Murphy & Co. came to hear this they offered them special terms to deal with them and these terms are in existence to this day, but she declined to state them.[7]

In the Midleton district, the Beamish & Crawford agency run by T.S. & R. Coppinger 'advanced money to their Traders in order to secure their dealing'.

The representative visited a total of 1,893 premises, virtually all of which were within County Cork, but a small number were located in the western part of County Waterford in the districts of Tallow and Lismore, whose distribution areas included parts of both counties. The four city breweries of Beamish & Crawford, J.J. Murphy & Co., Arnott & Co. and Lane & Co. supplied 1,528 (80 per cent) of the publicans; the firms Deasy & Co. of Clonakilty and Allman, Dowden & Co. of Bandon supplied 200 (10.5 per cent) more; and the remainder were divided between Guinness, Murphy & Co. of Clonmel, County Tipperary, the Phoenix Brewery of Dublin, the St Brigid's Well Brewery of Dungarvan, County Waterford, and others.

Beamish & Crawford had the most significant market share of business in the eastern and northern parts of the county. The towns and districts of Rathcormac, Fermoy, Mallow, Newmarket, Mitchelstown, Youghal and Midleton had 821 of the county's pubs and Beamish & Crawford had exclusivity in 437 of those. Its nearest rival, J.J. Murphy & Co., dealt with 204 pubs in the region. Beamish & Crawford had a relatively weak presence in the western parts of County Cork, with only fifty-eight customers out of the 654 pubs there. J.J. Murphy & Co. was strongest here, with 215 customers, and the other city firms of Arnott & Co. and Lane & Co. had forty-five and 102 customers, respectively. The West Cork towns of Bandon and Clonakilty had their own breweries, which had a strong trade in their local districts. Allman, Dowden & Co. in Bandon had ninety customers, fifty-two of whom were in the town and vicinity of Bandon. In the late 1890s they brewed in the region of 7,000 barrels per year, almost all of which was sold in the local area.[8] The Deasy & Co. brewery was located in Clonakilty and had 110 customers in the West Cork area, forty-three of which were in that town and district. The Beamish & Crawford representative commented on the Deasy trade and the quality of its porter:

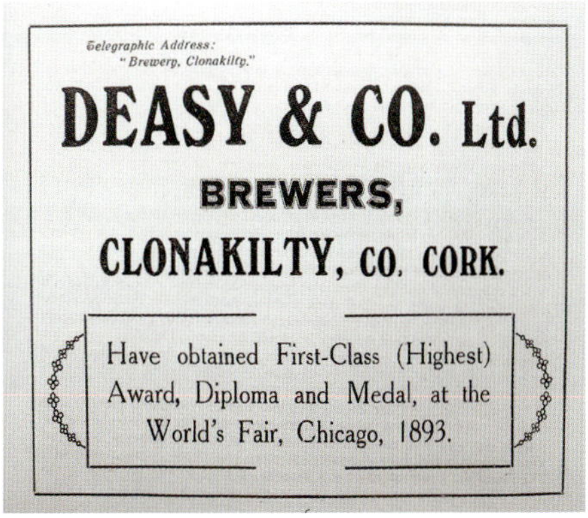

Left: No. 2 copper on the mezzanine floor at the eastern end of the mashing loft. (John Sheehan)
Right: Advertisement for Deasy & Co. Ltd brewery, Clonakilty. Deasy & Co. had 110 customers in the west Cork area in 1900, 43 of which were in the town of Clonakilty. (*Guy's City and County Cork Almanac and Directory for 1897*)

> Deasy & Co.'s Porter is what is almost exclusively sold by the Licensed traders in this town and District, and the house & Licence in most cases belong to that firm of Brewers. The porter is of poor quality but immediately when tapped the flavour is not very bad. The residents in the town and neighbourhood do not dislike it, their tastes are now so tuned to it.

In 1900 Beamish & Crawford sold 58,474 barrels of stout and ale through its agents, the majority of whom were in County Cork, and 14,005 barrels under the heading of 'Country', again mostly in County Cork but also including a little trade elsewhere in Ireland. This combined total of 72,479 barrels was largely accounted for by the 642 brewery customers listed in the representative's report, giving an average sale of 112.9 barrels for each customer (see also Table 6.7). (The pubs in Cork city in 1900 averaged a sale of more than double that, at 244.6 barrels each.) If the average non-city sale of 112.9 barrels per Beamish & Crawford pub is applied to all 1,893 pubs in the representative's lists, a suggested total of 213,719 barrels for the county of Cork is the result. County Cork had a population in the region of 325,000 at the time, giving an estimated annual per capita consumption of 189 pints or 107 litres – approximately 10 per cent higher than it is today.

In Cork city in 1900 there were in the region of 520 pubs, 477 of which were tied to a brewery for exclusive dealing.[9] The number of tied houses varied a little from year to year as formerly independent houses became tied and some tied premises became independent again. The total number of public houses of all kinds also fluctuated a little as a small number closed, either temporarily or permanently, while others opened. Of the 1900 total of 477 tied houses in the city, Beamish & Crawford had 120, J.J. Murphy & Co. had 223, Lane & Co. thirty-six, Arnott & Co. eighty-five and

B&C Own Houses Coloured
B&C Mortgaged Houses Hatched
B&C Customers Houses with
City of Cork
Lane & Co Coloured
Allman & Co Coloured
Guinness & Co Coloured
Nile Street
Court House
Great George's Street West
Great George's Street East
Christ Church
Hive Iron Works
Wandesford's Quay
Timber Yard
Cork Porter Brewery
Southgate Brewery
Cross's Green Mills
Female Orphanage
House of Mercy
Cross's Green Brewery
St. Marie's of the Isle Convent
Tannery
St. Dominick's Flour Mills
French's Quay
Bishop Street
St. Finbar's Cathedral
Grave Yard
Dean Street
Elizabeth Fort
Fort Street
Fruit Market
Potato Market
Old Barrack

Map of Cork city centre showing the locations of public houses, colour-coded for the brewery each traded with. Beamish & Crawford brewery kept a set of such maps for Cork city that were regularly updated. (CCCA/Dori O'Connell)

Public houses on Cornmarket Street, Cork, 1890s. (Courtesy Michael Lenihan)

'Dublin' (Guinness) thirteen. Within the city, eighty-six of the Beamish & Crawford tied houses were in the city centre and on the south side of the River Lee, while Beamish & Crawford had only thirty-six houses on the north side of the city. Murphy tied houses were far more numerous on the city's north side, at one 116 (see Appendix H). The streets with the most tied houses in 1900 were Barrack Street with twenty-four, followed by George's Street (Oliver Plunkett Street) and Shandon Street with twenty-three each, North Main Street with eighteen, South Main Street and Blarney Street with fifteen each, Lower Glanmire Road and Douglas Street with fourteen each and Old Youghal Road with thirteen.

Out of a total of 104,456 barrels of product sold in 1900 by Beamish & Crawford, 29,352 barrels were sold in the city – an average of 244.6 barrels per tied house. If that annual sales figure is applied to all 520 pubs in the city, a total city sale of 127,192 barrels is suggested, the greatest proportion of which was porter and stout. In addition to that, which would have been mostly draught, a quantity of bottled beers, especially imported British ale, was distributed within the city by a number of wholesalers and agents. With a Cork city population of 76,000 in 1900, the 127,192 barrels of suggested consumption gives an estimated per capita annual consumption of 482 pints (a standard barrel held 36 gallons or 288 pints) or 274 litres. This is two and a half times the average per capita consumption suggested by the non-city figures. Annual per capita beer consumption in Ireland today is about 158 pints or 90 litres. The contrast between the 1900 city's estimated consumption and today's is even more startling when it is considered that the average strength of the stout and porter produced at the beginning of the twentieth century was approximately 50 per cent higher than today's average. However, the extrapolated figures for city and county consumption are only estimates.

Cork city sales (by brewery), 1900.

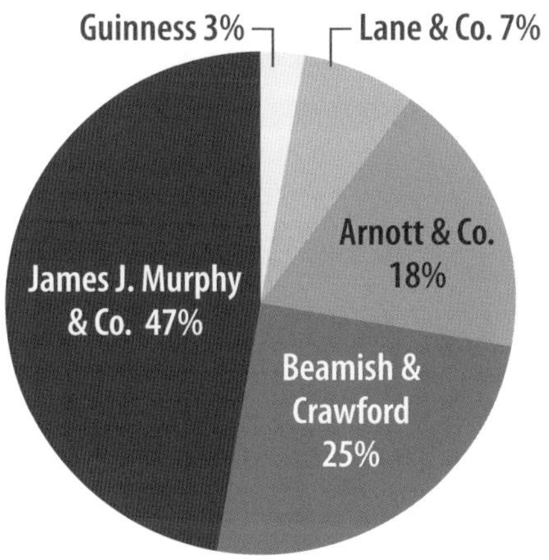

Drinking culture at the beginning of the twentieth century was very different from what became the norm later in the century. A far greater proportion of the population was engaged in daily physical labour and porter and stout were consumed as normal everyday refreshments. Drinking was not purely a leisure activity confined to the night hours and weekends, although those times were significant. Many pubs opened early in the morning and had a steady trade throughout the day with dockers, carters, carriers, labourers and other workers quenching their thirst at intervals during their working day. While drunkenness was not necessarily readily tolerated, attitudes to drink were different from today and were more tolerant of workday drinking.

9

Beamishes and Crawfords

WILLIAM BEAMISH (1760–1828)

William Beamish, the brewery co-founder, was the third son of William Beamish and Alice Bernard, born in May 1760 at Willsgrove near Enniskeane in West Cork. While still in his teens he enlisted in the Royal Navy, but he later transferred to the army and served during the American Wars (1775–83). After his time in the army he returned to Cork and by 1785 was in business with William Crawford and John Keating, trading as merchants from a base on Merchants' Quay. In 1789 Beamish married Anne Jane Margaret, daughter of Robert De la Cour of Mallow, and built one of Cork's finest residences at Beaumont, near Ballintemple to the southeast of Cork city. The house was described as 'a noble mansion consisting of a centre and two wings, with two conservatories, situated in tastefully arranged grounds'. The site of the house is now occupied by the buildings of the boys' and girls' Beaumont primary schools. They had thirteen children in all, with seven sons surviving into adulthood, William, Robert Delacour, North Ludlow, Richard, Charles, Francis Bernard and James Caulfield, and one daughter, Dorcas.

Wealth and health

From 1791 William Beamish was a partner in the Cork Porter Brewery, which grew to be Ireland's biggest brewery within twenty years of its foundation. Porter made Beamish a wealthy man and this was supplemented by his earnings from work as a merchant with William Crawford and from the lands and properties he acquired. He was known for his liberal views and was one of the principal contributors to the building of St Michael's Catholic church in Blackrock, opened in 1822, although he himself was a Protestant. In June 1819 he was invited to lay the foundation stone of the new church along with his business partner, William Crawford, another Protestant who also contributed towards the building.

Left: William Beamish. (Courtesy Richard Beamish) **Right: Beaumont House, built *c.* 1790, the residence of William Beamish and his family.** (Courtesy Norma Ryan and Scoil Barra Buachaillí, Beaumont)

In the spring of 1828 William Beamish became ill and his brother Charles, residing in Paris, wrote a number of letters to him expressing his love and affection with suggestions as to how William might ease his discomforts. Charles was kept informed of his brother's condition by William's son, Robert. On 31 March 1828 Charles wrote from Paris expressing his concern for the health of his brother: 'I would prefer being ill, if by my own sufferings I could relieve yours, calm the irritations of your nerves and by tracing [*sic*] them, remove you to peace and tranquillity of mind.' He felt that William had spent 'too active a life in search of money which produced feverish anxieties' and took a toll on his health. He referred to William's frequent trips to Cheltenham:

> For years past you have drank too much of the Cheltenham waters. They act with so marked a promplitude they purge so quickly and so violently at times that a body as delicately organized as yours, whose nerves are so sensible and so easily irritated, became gradually undermined and enfeebled.

He finished with: 'I implore I entreat you to make up your mind to leave Beaumont the end of May and come to Paris.'[1]

Less than a week later, on 5 April, he wrote again, praising William's son Robert for keeping him informed: 'What shall I say of my excellent, my kind Robert – this – that if he was near me, I would embrace, press him to my heart, and even kiss his black beard – more, his lips – how feeling to write me three letters in 17 days.'[2]

In his next letter, written on 12 April, he again invited William to come to Paris:

> You must get out of the air of the United Kingdoms and fix yourself for some months on the banks of the Seine … I shall accompany you and attend to you with the affectionate and serviceable anxieties of a son. Consider me your son, your brother and your friend … let us live and die together. That can only be effected by your getting out from Beaumont the end of May … Come, Come, Come.[3]

The letter (below) was received in Cork on 17 April, the day William Beamish died at his home.

Left: Letter from Charles Beamish in Paris to his brother William at Beaumont House, posted in Paris 14 April 1828 and received in Cork 17 April, the day William Beamish died.
Right: Reverse of the letter, showing date stamp of 17 April 1828. (CCCA/Authors)

Death and burial

The *Cork Constitution* of 19 April carried a notice of William's death and three days later gave an account of his funeral:

> Yesterday, the mortal remains of this excellent and truly benevolent gentleman were conveyed from his seat, Beaumont House, to the family vault, in the parish of Desert, in this County. The mournful cavalcade was expected to arrive at an early hour, and the streets were in consequence crowded with all ranks and classes, to evince their attachment and respect for the virtues of the venerable deceased. About half-past-eight o'clock it approached by Parliament Bridge, South-Mall, and Grand Parade, to Great George's-street, towards the Western-road, at which time thousands had assembled. The procession was led by hundreds of tradesmen and labourers, with scarfs who had been employed in the firm, and from their respectful demeanour and decent appearance it

> was evident to perceive that they had lost both a benefactor and friend. The next that followed were two mourning coaches, with the female domestics in deep mourning.

The account lists the members of the family, clergymen, gentlemen and other public figures who followed the hearse in their coaches. The account continues:

> The number of horsemen and pedestrians – all wearing scarfs and hatbands – was almost innumerable. The procession extended nearly two miles, and was upwards of an hour passing through the City, during which the bells of the Cathedral, and other Churches tolled. On the whole it is not too much to say that it was the greatest funeral procession that ever left this City, and the venerable deceased was in every respect worthy of the honours paid to his remains.

He was buried in the Beamish family vault in Desertserges churchyard, near Enniskeane, County Cork. In 1844 the sculptor John Hogan carved a memorial to William Beamish, which was erected inside St Michael's Church in Blackrock, Cork. In his will, William Beamish left his share in the brewery, valued at £93,750.10.7, equally between his five younger sons, North Ludlow, Richard, Charles, Francis Bernard and James Caulfield.

Left: Memorial to William Beamish by John Hogan (1800–58) in St Michael's Church, Blackrock, Cork and (right) its inscription. (Authors) Below right: Burial place of William Beamish in Desertserges churchyard. (Frank Roche)

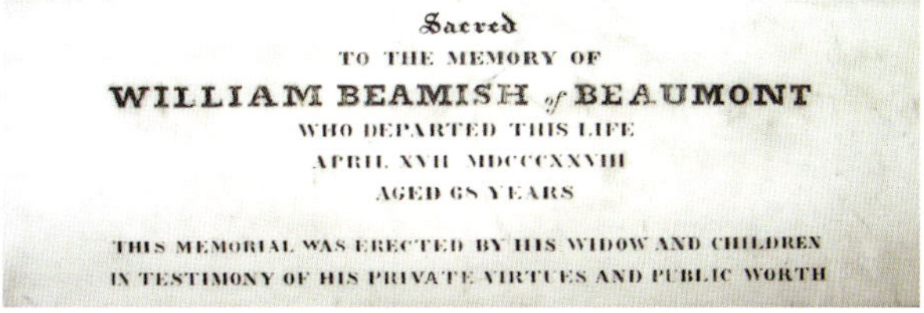

BEAMISH FAMILY TREE (featuring only those who had a direct involvement in the brewery)

- **William Beamish** (1760–1828)
  - **North Ludlow Beamish** (1796–1872)
    - **North Ludlow Axel Beamish** (1842–1923)
  - **Richard Beamish** (1798–1873)
    - **Richard Pigott Beamish** (1832–99)
      - **Richard Henrik Beamish** (1861–1938)
        - **Richard P. Beamish** (1909–93)
  - **Charles Beamish** (1829–67)
  - **Francis Bernard Beamish** (1802–68)
    - **Francis Bernard Servington Beamish** (1839–99)
      - **Francis Edward de Courcy Beamish** (1866–?)
  - **James Caulfield Beamish** (1803–62)

RICHARD BEAMISH (1798–1873)

Richard was the fourth son of William Beamish and Anne Jane Margaret De la Cour and was educated in England, finishing at the Royal Military College. His father bought him a commission in the Coldstream Guards, the oldest regiment in continuous service with the British Army, and he served for a year in Belgium and France following the Battle of Waterloo in 1815. He returned to England, and according to one obituary: 'Being endowed with courtly manners, strong health, high courage, and an ardent nature, he allowed himself to be drawn into the vortex of pleasure open to a young guardsman in the extravagant and licentious times of the Regency.'[4]

He apparently grew bored with that life and in 1818 was to travel to Southeast Asia as aide-de-camp to Sir Stamford Raffles, who had been appointed governor-general of Bencoolen in Sumatra. His parents objected and instead he returned to Ireland, 'entering into the social duties and enjoyments expected of a country gentleman', before settling down to study with the object of becoming a civil engineer. He moved to London in 1826 and in August of that year he took up a position as assistant to Isambard Kingdom Brunel (1806–59), who was working with his father, Marc Isambard Brunel (1769–1849), the chief engineer on the first tunnel to be built under the Thames. These works were abandoned in July 1828 following an accident, but he continued his association with the Brunels, working on various railway and bridge projects. He came back to Cork again and worked for a time on public road and bridge building works. He worked again on the recommenced Thames Tunnel between 1834 and 1836, when he held the position of resident engineer. In 1845–6, at the request of Isambard Kingdom Brunel, he prepared plans for a proposed Cork to Waterford railway line and later worked, again with Brunel, on the Gloucester and Dean Forest railway, completed in 1850. This was the end of Richard Beamish's engineering career – after a two-year stay in Hanover, Germany, he returned to England and settled in Cheltenham.

He wrote a biography of Marc Isambard Brunel, published in 1862,[5] and also had papers published on phrenology, mathematics and on the town and parish of Cheltenham. Richard Beamish married a German, Theodosia Mary Heise, in 1831 and they had four children: Richard Pigott (1832–99), who became the acting Beamish partner of Beamish & Crawford in 1863, Anne Theodosia (1835–1905), Emily Isabella (1838–1933) and Alten Augustus William (1841–1902). In his retirement Richard continued the profligate habits that had become his norm; he was frequently in debt and regularly appealed to his son Richard Pigott for help. He died in 1873 in Southampton.

NORTH LUDLOW BEAMISH (1796–1872)

North Ludlow was the third son of William Beamish and Anne Jane Margaret De la Cour to survive into adulthood. He attended the Royal Military College at Sandhurst, and afterwards had a captaincy in the 4th Royal Irish Dragoon Guards and was promoted to major in 1826. He spent over twenty years with the military in Germany and on his retirement in 1839 the officers of the King's German Legion in Hanover presented Beamish with an ornate silver centrepiece in recognition of his achievement in writing the two-volume work *History of the King's German Legion*, published between 1832 and 1837. This centrepiece is now in the National Army Museum in London. He also translated works on cavalry warfare by Karl Wilhelm Ferdinand von Bismark (1771–1845) into English, published work on the Norse discovery of America and wrote a novel, *Peace Campaigns of a Cornet*, published in 1829.

North Ludlow Beamish became a sleeping partner in Beamish & Crawford following the death of his father in 1828, and apart from enjoying a share in the profits took little part in brewery affairs. His uncle Charles, brother of William Beamish and a clergyman living in Paris, wrote to North Ludlow's brother Robert in the October following William's death and expressed disappointment that North Ludlow had no interest in a direct involvement in the brewery: 'he has gone to Hanover and turned his back on the brewery' and 'he has declined all active cooperation in the first establishment in Ireland – very few more profitable and respectable in England'. Charles wrote, however, that 'it is some consolation that North (he is an able man)

North Ludlow Beamish. (Courtesy Ed Hinchy)

has avowed that he will give it his sleeping support'.[6] By 1841 North Ludlow was back in Ireland and with his brothers Richard and Charles voted to remove their brother Francis Bernard from his position as acting partner on behalf of the Beamish family. North Ludlow became the acting partner on behalf of his family in his place and held the position until 1863, when he was succeeded by his nephew, Richard Pigott Beamish.

After his return to Ireland in 1839 North Ludlow joined the Munster Provincial College Committee under the chairmanship of Cork banker James Roche. This committee campaigned and lobbied to have a university established in Cork and was instrumental in the foundation of Queen's College Cork, officially inaugurated on 7 November 1849. At the inauguration ceremony, Beamish, as vice-chairman of the committee, said: 'We have sown the seed; we have watched its development; we have awaited the growth of the plant, and now we triumph in the fullness of its produce. It is for Ireland's youthful sons to reap the mental harvest.'[7]

On that day the Farm Committee was formed to work towards the establishment of a model farm and garden to complement the work of the new university college. North Ludlow Beamish became a very active member of this committee and its vision was achieved with the opening of the Munster Institute in 1853. This institute laid the foundation for the scientific study of agriculture, especially dairying, and led to the development of the Department of Dairy Science at the university.

North Ludlow married Aline Marie Forsstrom in May 1841 and they had five children: North Ludlow Axel, William Adolph, George Horace Townsend, Aline Matilda and Alice. They lived at Lota Park near Cork and later at Annemount, Glounthane, County Cork. North Ludlow Beamish died on 28 April 1872.

FRANCIS BERNARD BEAMISH (1802–68)

Francis Bernard Beamish. (Courtesy Ed Hinchy)

Francis Bernard Beamish was the last child but one of William Beamish and Anne Jane Margaret De la Cour. He was educated at Rugby School and following his father's death in 1828 he became an acting partner, effectively joint CEO, of the Beamish & Crawford brewery, a position he held until he was removed by a vote of the other partners in 1841. He overdrew on his brewery account and allowed his brother James Caulfield to do likewise. By 1841 Francis Bernard was indebted to the other Beamish partners, his four brothers, North Ludlow, Charles, Richard and James Caulfield, for over £10,000. Due to that and his mismanagement of the brewery, he was removed as acting partner and became a sleeping partner in the firm. He did not clear his debts until 1862.

Being a liberal, Francis Bernard was a strong supporter of Daniel O'Connell and the successful campaign for Catholic emancipation (achieved in 1829), though as a unionist, he was naturally less enthusiastic about the campaign for the repeal of the union. However, he supported the formation, and became a member and later president, of the Repeal-supporting Cork Trades Association (CTA) in 1832 (William Crawford Jr. was also a member). In 1833, following the election of CTA-supported candidates in the general election of 1832, he was presented with a formal address by the association, thanking him for his services. As a wealthy brewer and member of a prominent Protestant family, Beamish 'added respectability to the association'. In turn, the CTA provided the ambitious Francis Bernard with a political base from which to run for parliament in 1837.[8] (In an incident that revealed much about the nature of politics in this period, a delegation of Liberals from the Cork Chamber of Commerce had approached Francis Bernard's brother Charles to ask him to run for parliament in 1829. Beamish asked them if they intended to bribe voters; when they said no, Charles responded, 'Well then, you will lose the election' and declined their offer. Their eventual candidate did indeed lose.)[9]

Francis Bernard was elected Liberal MP for Cork city in 1837 and he sat until 1841, but did not go forward in that year's general election. His absences in London to attend parliament in that period were partly responsible for his removal from the position of acting partner in the brewery in 1841. The passage of the Municipal Corporations (Ireland) Act in 1840 led to local elections with an extended franchise in 1841, and in Cork city Beamish topped the poll and was entitled to be the city's first mayor under the reformed system for 1842. But in recognition of the ending of the era of unrepresentative, corrupt and sectarian local government, the preserve of Protestants for over 150 years, he let the Catholic merchant Thomas Lyons have that honour, making him the first Catholic mayor of the city since 1688; Beamish became mayor the following year. He was elected MP for the city again in 1853 and he held the seat until 1865.

Francis Bernard Beamish married Catherine Savery de Lisle de Courcy in 1837 and they had one child, Francis Bernard Servington, born in 1839. He remained a sleeping partner in the brewery until his death in 1868 in Totnes, England, where he had moved due to ill health.

RICHARD PIGOTT BEAMISH (1832–99)

Richard Pigott Beamish was the eldest son of Richard Beamish and Theodosia Mary Heise, and a grandson of brewery founder William Beamish. He joined the firm in 1852 at the age of twenty, as his father had given him 'neither a collegiate, a professional nor mercantile education'.[10] He had a military career of sorts, but only in a temporary and reserve capacity, serving in a regiment of the Cork Militia, a reserve force for the army. In 1855, at the outbreak of war in the Crimea, he was assigned to a newly formed militia regiment, the West Cork Artillery Regiment, and received his commission as captain on 26 July 1856, two days before the regiment was 'disembodied'. After that Beamish was required to attend annual training camps, but never saw action. That did not, however, prevent him from using the title 'Captain' throughout his life.

Once he started work at the brewery in 1852, Richard Pigott was very much 'a young man in a hurry' and by 1853 was attempting to persuade his uncle, North Ludlow, to assign him his share in the brewery so that he, Richard Pigott, could become the acting partner on behalf of the Beamish family. North Ludlow strongly rejected the idea, calling it 'utterly insane', adding that the 21-year-old's inexperience would 'play the deuce with the concern'.[11] By 1856 he had persuaded his father to assign him his share in the brewery, thus enabling him to become a partner in the firm, though still a sleeping partner. His father also agreed to will him the lands he owned at Coolyduff and Inchinglass to the west of Cork city in return for an annuity of £1,200 per year. For the remaining sixteen years of his life, Richard was frequently in debt, overspending his annuity and regularly seeking extra payments from his son.

North Ludlow Beamish was acting Beamish partner from 1841 to 1863, and although he was taken aback by Richard Pigott's youthful ambitions he was his mentor and sometimes ally as the other Beamish partners, Charles, Francis Bernard and James Caulfield, strongly resisted Richard Pigott's efforts to take over more of the brewery's management and become the Beamish acting partner. The co-partnership agreement of 1849, under which the firm of Beamish & Crawford functioned, was to expire in 1863, and by the time of the negotiations on the new agreement, James Caulfield Beamish had died and Richard Pigott had negotiated the support of the other two Beamish partners, Charles and Francis Bernard. When William Horatio Crawford replaced his uncle, George Crawford, as the Crawfords' acting partner in 1859, it was arranged that Richard Pigott would act for him in the management of the brewery 'as his feelings are averse to a close attendance upon business'.[12] When the new co-partnership agreement was signed in 1863, Richard Pigott became the Beamish acting partner, effectively the CEO of the firm. He was to lead a period of renewal and regeneration for the next three decades as he officially took on the role he had groomed himself for since 1852.

Richard Pigott Beamish. (CCCA/Authors)

In 1894 Joseph Pike, chairman of the Cork Steam Packet Company, a justice of the peace and a well-known and respected member of the city's business community, sued Richard Pigott Beamish for libel, slander and conspiracy to defame and sought £5,000 in damages. Both were members and trustees of the Cork and County Club, and a report had been made to Beamish in 1893 by another club member that Pike had regularly cheated at cards. Beamish decided to investigate and Pike was called before the club committee to answer the charge of cheating. Pike took umbrage at the accusation of cheating, which he vehemently denied, and sued Beamish. The case was heard before a jury in May 1894 and the outcome was in the manner of a draw, the verdict being that the plaintiff, Pike, did not cheat, and that Beamish was within his rights as a committee member to investigate the charges.

Richard Pigott Beamish married Hulda Elizabeth Mosander in May 1858 and they lived at Harmony Lodge near Carrigtwohill and later at Ashbourne House, Glounthane, County Cork. Hulda was from Sweden and was the daughter of Charles Gustavus Mosander, a Swedish aristocrat and Knight of the North Star of Sweden. North Ludlow Beamish had married Hulda's aunt, Aline Marie Forsstrom, a sister of Mosander's wife, in 1841. Richard Pigott and Hulda had two sons, Richard Henrik and Gustav William, and one daughter, Huldine. Richard Pigott died in London in 1899 having fallen ill while on a cruise in the Mediterranean.

CARIN GOERING (1888–1931)

Carin was the granddaughter of Richard Pigott Beamish and the great-great-granddaughter of William Beamish. She was married to Hermann Goering from 1923 until her death in 1931.

Richard Pigott's wife, Hulda, was the daughter of a Swedish aristocrat and made regular visits to her native Sweden with her children. Their eldest daughter, Huldine, married Baron Carl Alexander Fock in Stockholm in 1880 and they had five children; the fourth, Carin (sometimes Karin), was born in 1888. The Focks moved in aristocratic and military circles in Sweden and in 1910 Carin married a Swedish army officer, Niels Gustav von Kantzow. They had one child, Thomas, who was born in 1913, but they separated shortly afterwards. She first met Herman Goering, then a commercial pilot, in 1920 and their relationship was a cause of much scandal in Stockholm society, as she was still officially married and had a child. She divorced her husband in 1922 and married Goering in January 1923.

They settled in Munich in Germany, where Carin became a member of the Nazi Party. In November 1923 Adolf Hitler led a failed coup attempt in Munich, later known as the Beer Hall Putsch, during which Goering was wounded. Carin helped him escape to Austria and later Italy, nursing him back to health and creating the romantic framework for their story, which was later written by Carin's sister, Fanny Wilamowitz-Moellendorf (1882–1958), and published as Carin Göring in 1934 in Berlin.

Carin travelled to Stockholm in September 1931 when her mother, Huldine, died. While there, she took ill and died on 17 October. Carin had been suffering from tuberculosis for some years. Herman Goering called his country house, on a hunting estate northeast of Berlin, Karinhalle in her memory. Carin was buried in Sweden, but Goering had her remains exhumed and brought to Karinhalle, where she was reinterred in a lavish funeral attended by Adolf Hitler. Goering remarried in 1935, but Karinhalle retained its name and continued as a memorial to his first wife. When the Soviet Red Army was advancing on Berlin in April 1945, Goering had Karinhalle demolished and reburied Carin's remains elsewhere on the estate. Five years later the remains were removed, cremated and brought to Sweden, where they were buried in October 1951.

In 1937 Carin's first cousin, Richard P. Beamish (son of Richard Henrik and grandson of Richard Pigott), then a director of Beamish & Crawford Ltd, visited Berlin with his wife and met with Herman Goering. In a newspaper interview in 1976 he explained that he had written to Goering to explain his connection to him through his Swedish cousin. Goering replied and invited Richard and his wife, Ernestine, to come to Berlin to visit. They were put up at the Hotel Kaiserhof, Berlin's best hotel, and also spent two days at Goering's country house, Karinhalle. While in

Berlin they were Goering's guests at a luncheon party at the air ministry attended by senior government officials, and while there Richard Beamish had his only sighting of Adolf Hitler, who appeared in the doorway of the dining room during the meal. 'Quite obviously he looked like a figure of fun, with his moustache and that quiff of hair, yet he held us spellbound,' remembered Beamish, his memory perhaps somewhat influenced by subsequent clichéd portrayals of Hitler.[13]

RICHARD HENRIK BEAMISH (1861–1938)

Born in 1861 at Ashbourne House, Richard Henrik Beamish was the second child of Richard Pigott Beamish and Hulda Elizabeth Mosander and a great-grandson of William Beamish. He was educated at Haileybury College in Hertfordshire, England, and afterwards travelled to Sweden, his mother's native country, where he lived and studied agriculture from 1881 to 1887. His special area of interest was dairying, and while based in Sweden he often travelled to Denmark to study its successful methods of milk production. He wrote a detailed scientific study, *An Improved Method of Feeding Milch Cows*, published in 1889, which led to improvements in milk production amongst progressive dairy farmers in Sweden. He also wrote a study of butter.

He returned to Ireland in the early 1890s and succeeded his father as chairman and managing director of Beamish & Crawford in 1899. He led the firm until his retirement in 1930. He succeeded his father at the brewery as sales reached the highest levels in the firm's history, peaking at 151,734 barrels in 1903, and remaining in excess of 100,000 barrels until 1917. In the years after the First World War, however, he presided over the firm's most precipitous decline in sales as annual sales fell to a low of 25,917 barrels in 1926.

Public man

Richard Henrik had a prominent place in Cork business circles and in public life. He was elected High Sheriff for Cork by the corporation in 1906. After the 1908 municipal elections, the Municipal Association, of which he was chairman, became a new force in the corporation. There were rowdy scenes as opponents from the Irish Parliamentary Party (IPP) accused the mayor and other councillors of being courted by Beamish with free drink and of 'allowing Beamish's people control this Corporation on the tied house system'.[14] In 1911 he was elected to Cork Corporation as an alderman for the South Centre Ward representing the Cork Ratepayers' Association and he was again elected High Sheriff for the city in that year. A popular ditty of the time went:

If I were the new High Sheriff,
I would, I would,
I'd make the Berwick Fountain spout
With Beamish and Crawford's Double Stout,
I would, I would.[15]

An article in the *Southern Star* newspaper described Beamish as

> just the type of citizen one would always desire to find in occupation of the office. Highly cultured, of a respected family, possessing that charm of manner in which urbanity, courteousness, and refinement are the transparent features, with a business acumen derived from study and a thorough course of training in commercial life, possessed of an integrity and candour that throw his other attributes into relief, Mr Beamish has, indeed, all the qualifications requisite to a dignified and successful discharge of the duties of his high office.[16]

He was unionist but liberal in his political views, and in January 1912 the All-for-Ireland League, the nationalist party led by William O'Brien MP, which had broken away from the IPP in 1910, asked Beamish to stand for election as Lord Mayor, 'subject to his giving a public expression in favour of Home Rule'. Some objected to the move and 'strongly protested against their being asked to support a candidate whose political feelings were known to be altogether opposed to those of the great majority of Irishmen.'[17]

The Lord Mayor for 1911 had been James Simcox, the nominee of the All-for-Ireland League, but as he had decided not to go forward again, his supporters thought that Beamish's popularity, coupled with his strong record in local business, would make him an ideal Lord Mayor. On the night of the election, however, Simcox was again elected, the objectors to Beamish within the All-for-Ireland League having held sway.[18]

Richard Henrik Beamish was chosen to chair the Public Works Committee of the corporation and drove the initiative that saw over £30,000 being spent on the improvement and paving of many of the city's principal streets. Beamish had a deep interest in horticulture and maintained a garden of international repute at his home, Ashbourne House. This interest informed his efforts as chair of the Public Works Committee and he oversaw the planting of trees on South Mall and Grand Parade as well as the creation of the gardens at Fitzgerald's Park, which the corporation developed following the Cork International Exhibitions of 1902 and 1903.

Beamish was elected again in the 1914 local elections, but because he failed to top the poll in his ward he was no longer an alderman. The newly elected councillors, the majority of whom were members of the IPP, excluded Beamish from his chairmanship of the Public Works Committee, an act that annoyed many for its pettiness, with one councillor calling it 'the most scandalous act that the Council had perpetrated for many a day'. He was reported in the press as saying that Beamish

> was one of the largest ratepayers in the city, and he differed from the majority of them both religiously and politically. He was the founder of the scheme which brought clean and healthy streets to the city … and now the Corporation had prevented him from executing the remainder of that huge undertaking … They were speaking of toleration and here was one of the few Protestants in the Corporation and they would not give him a seat upon the committee, notwithstanding the fact that he was paying more rates than the whole Corporation, outside him, put together.[19]

Richard Henrik Beamish had been a founding member of the Cork Ratepayers' Association, a group of prominent business owners in the city who campaigned against rate increases by the city's corporation as they felt that ratepayers, especially those with businesses, were carrying an unfair burden and that much of the money raised was being misspent and wasted. After eighteen months as a councillor, Beamish resigned from the association and also withdrew the support of Beamish & Crawford Ltd, much to the anger of his former colleagues. He was, however, praised by the IPP-supporting *Cork Examiner* in an editorial in April 1913 for his change of heart.

> It is very satisfactory to find that a gentleman not holding the views of majority of the people, who entered Corporate life impregnated with prejudices which were due to insufficient information, has, since he discovered the facts for himself, openly declared … that there were no grounds for the erroneous opinions he formerly entertained. Such conduct is rare and refreshing in public life.[20]

He served on the corporation throughout the First World War, switching to the Carnegie Library Committee following his ejection from his beloved Public Works. In the landmark municipal elections of January 1920, Richard Henrik stood as a 'Commercial' candidate and was elected as an alderman. He was an infrequent participant in the new, republican council that elected Tomás MacCurtain as Lord Mayor, pledged its allegiance to the revolutionary Dáil Éireann and flew the tricolour over the city hall. Ever the pragmatist, Beamish was happy to work with the new regime for the good of the city and declared the new council an improvement on the old one run by the IPP. He was re-elected to his old position as chair of the Public

Richard Henrik Beamish.
(W.T. Pike, *Contemporary Biographies* (Brighton, 1911))

Works Committee, but could achieve little as the war of independence raged.

In August 1920 Beamish led a delegation of Cork businessmen to meet the British prime minister, Lloyd George, and put forward proposals for Dominion home rule for Ireland. In the general election held on 16 June 1922, fought principally on the 1921 Treaty question, Richard Henrik Beamish stood as an independent pro-Treaty candidate, backed by the Cork city business community. He received 11.5 per cent of the first preference votes but failed to get elected.

In 1923 the Cork Progressive Association (CPA) was formed by a group of Cork businesspeople to promote the cause of business and to have measures taken to reform Cork Corporation. Beamish was a prominent member of the association and in the general election of 27 August 1923 he was elected along with the other CPA candidate, businessman Andrew O'Shaughnessy, to Dáil Éireann on a joint ticket with the pro-Treaty party, Cumann na nGaedheal. He took the Cumann na nGaedheal whip in 1924 and served on the Committee on Wireless Broadcasting. He spoke rarely, with the exception of the 1924 and 1927 debates on intoxicating liquor licensing legislation and occasional contributions on agriculture.

Beamish had always spoken trenchantly on the need to reform Cork Corporation. A public inquiry into the matter was conducted in August 1924 at which Beamish gave evidence, but his position was undermined when it was pointed out that he had not attended a meeting of the corporation in the previous two years and that he attended only four of twenty-eight meetings in 1921. Following on the inquiry, Cork Corporation was dissolved in October 1924 and the city was run by a commissioner, Philip Monahan, until 1929. In the local elections of 1930 Beamish stood again and topped the poll in his ward. He did not attend any meetings after 1931, by which time he had retired from the business. He moved to England in 1932.

Divorce scandal

In June 1914 Richard Henrik Beamish petitioned for a divorce from his wife of eleven years before a justice and special jury at a hearing in Dublin.[21] The case was widely reported, as the evidence included lurid tales of serial adultery and possible domestic cruelty as the 53-year-old Beamish sought a divorce from his wife, who was twenty-three years his junior, and custody of their three children.

On 14 October 1903 Richard Henrik Beamish married Violet Edith Campbell, the only child of Lieutenant-General Sir William Pitcairn Campbell. They had first met when Violet, aged nineteen, accompanied her father and mother to Cork in 1902 when he was in command of the 60th Rifles. Beamish was a regular guest at their home, and though Violet 'was at that time surrounded by a great number of admirers', principally men of her own age, she accepted Beamish's marriage proposal in June 1903 when he was 42, and they were married in October of that year. 'All promised well for such a union. The husband brought his wife a good position in the southern county, a home wanting no luxury, all her wants were well provided for, and she had an assured position in genial society in a pleasant country.'

Her early married life was 'one round of gaiety' as she attended race meetings, travelled to the Dublin Horse Show and went to London for the 'season'. However, 'Mr. Beamish made complaints from time to time of her love of dress and display, and her habit of frequenting the society of giddy young men, with whom she loved to be surrounded.'

Their children, Huldine, Noreen and Richard, were born in 1904, 1906 and 1909, respectively, and Beamish alleged in evidence that his wife 'had misconducted herself with several military officers' from 1909 to 1912. A collection of love letters from two army officers to Violet was introduced in evidence and extracts were read to the jury. Beamish had come upon them 'accidentally' when he opened a safe in her room, with a view to putting it in order for her while she was away. Violet admitted to having had affairs with two named officers, but 'she alleged that all such acts were condoned by the petitioner' [Beamish] and she denied that there had been any other 'acts of misconduct'. She accused Beamish of cruelty and neglect. Beamish admitted tolerating her earlier affairs but 'pleaded that if there had been any condonation subsequent acts of misconduct were committed by the respondent [Violet]'. Beamish admitted that due to the age difference between them 'he might not have been able to attend her in all her smaller amusements', and in remarks that may explain Violet's quest for young male company, he added: 'I asked her to follow the fashions of those among whom she lived, and not to dress gaudily and foolishly, and I totally disagreed about her painting her eyes and her face, as she was quite good-looking enough without any additions.'

Violet had promised to mend her ways, but the affairs continued and in November

1913 Beamish asked his wife to leave their home. The children remained with Beamish. The petition was successful and the couple were divorced. Following his retirement from the brewery in 1930, Richard Henrik Beamish moved first to London and later to Weybridge in Surrey, where he died in 1938.

NORTH LUDLOW AXEL BEAMISH (1842–1923)

North Ludlow Axel Beamish was the eldest child of North Ludlow Beamish and Aline Marie Forsstrom and a grandchild of brewery founder William Beamish. He studied at Trinity College, Dublin, and graduated with a BA degree. He later became a justice of the peace for County Cork and served for many years as chairman of the Cork Carnegie Library Committee. While he was still at university, Richard Pigott Beamish communicated with him and with his parents about North Ludlow Axel's future career options at the brewery. In a letter to North Ludlow Axel in 1863, Richard Pigott wrote that 'the result of such attention as you have hitherto bestowed upon business matters at the C.P.B. [Cork Porter Brewery] has not been altogether satisfactory', showing none of the energy and interest he gave to his other interests, especially hunting and yachting. Richard Pigott suggested that he get over his 'listlessness and indifference' and decide if he is to become 'a real working man of business or not'.[22] Richard Pigott was writing very much as the 'gung-ho' businessman, impatient with the fecklessness, as he saw it, of a gentleman's son at university, and he exhorted North Ludlow to transfer his share in the brewery to his son to enable him to become properly involved in the firm. North Ludlow Axel eventually agreed to join the firm and his father arranged the transfer of his brewery share to his son. North Ludlow Axel's mother was 'violently opposed to the whole scheme', called it 'a disgrace and degradation' and said that Richard Pigott was effectively degrading her son from his position as a gentleman.[23]

In 1864 his father transferred his share in the Beamish & Crawford partnership to him and in return North Ludlow Axel paid him an annuity of £1,200 per year. North Ludlow Axel continued as a sleeping partner in the brewery partnership until the 1895 incorporation, after which he became a director of Beamish & Crawford Ltd and had one-sixth of the total Beamish family shareholding. North Ludlow Axel inherited his father's interest in agricultural improvement and cattle breeding and regularly exhibited his prize cattle at agricultural shows and at the RDS show in Dublin. He was also a long-time treasurer of the Munster Agricultural Society.

In 1869 North Ludlow Axel married Edith Anne Thompson, a daughter of his first cousin, Anne Jane Margaret Beamish (daughter of William Beamish Jr. and Mary de Courcy) and her husband, Rev. William Hamilton Thompson. They had four children and lived at Ashgrove near Queenstown (Cobh). North Ludlow Beamish died in 1923 while on a visit to Dublin.

From left: North Ludlow Axel Beamish and Ashgrove, his home on Great Island.
(W.T. Pike, *Contemporary Biographies* (Brighton, 1911))

WILLIAM CRAWFORD (1757–1834)

William Crawford was born in Crawfordsburn in County Down, the son of James Crawford and Mabel Johnston. The Crawfords were a prominent and well-connected landowning family. By 1779 William was in Cork organising a partnership with John Church, a merchant of some standing, which he financed with a loan from his brother-in-law, James Alexander, later the first Earl of Caledon. With the £2,000 loaned by Alexander, Crawford was able to buy a one-third share in the business, which traded as J. Church & W. Crawford. The partnership proved to be very successful and Crawford's share of the annual profits grew from almost £1,300 in his first year to nearly £2,000 by 1784. William Crawford repaid his loan to James Alexander in 1784 and shortly thereafter entered into a new merchanting partnership with William Beamish and John Keating. They acquired a premises on Merchants' Quay and exported beef, pork, butter, oats, barley and wheat, while imports included sugar, tea, mahogany, wine, rum, tobacco and herrings. Victualling contracts with the army and navy formed a lucrative part of their business and partner John Keating was based mostly in London, where he lobbied for business. Keating left the partnership in the later 1780s and Crawford continued with William Beamish until the latter's death in 1828. The business ceased trading in 1830.

In 1791 William Crawford and William Beamish went into partnership with Digby O'Brien and Richard Barrett to brew porter at the Cork Porter Brewery on South Main Street. This venture proved to be quite successful and profitable within a short time, and following the death of Digby O'Brien in 1794 and Richard Barrett's retirement in 1800, William Crawford and William Beamish continued as partners

CRAWFORD FAMILY TREE (featuring only those who had a direct involvement in the brewery)

William Crawford
(1757–1834)

William Crawford (1788–1840)
- **William Horatio Crawford** (1812–88)

George Crawford (1818–64)

Louisa Alicia Crawford (1818–87)
- **Arthur Frederick Sharman Crawford** (1862–1943)
- **William Henry Sharman Crawford** (1847–90)
- **Robert Gordon Sharman Crawford** (1853–1934)

in brewing. Their rewards were substantial, as the brewery grew to become Ireland's biggest and most profitable by the first decade of the nineteenth century.

William Crawford married Mary Bordman[24] in 1781 and they had twelve children: James (11 February 1782), John (28 January 1783), Arthur (11 March 1784), Jane (18 February 1786), Ann (17 June 1787), William (22 June 1788), Charles (21 August 1789), Maria (17 August 1790), George (8 April 1792), Bell (3 April 1793), Mary Anne (2 September 1794) and Mabel (or Maybella) (6 February 1796). According to William Crawford's son, William, his father's first wife died 'in the latter end of the year 1797'.

William Crawford married his second wife, Mary Uniacke, in 1798 and they had fourteen children: James Thomas (23 December 1799), Elizabeth (1 January 1801), Mary (29 March 1802), Robert (31 March 1803), James (7 September 1804), John (5 March 1806), Louisa (25 August 1807), Catherine (6 November 1809), Frances (10 January 1812), Emily (24 March 1814), Henry (1 April 1816), Louisa Alicia (31 January 1818), Charlotte (21 January 1820) and James (10 December 1821). Ten of the twenty-six children survived into adulthood: Ann, Mabel (or Maybella), Jane, William, George, Elizabeth, Mary, Robert, Henry and Louisa Alicia.

William Crawford and his family lived first on Merchants' Quay in the city centre and in 1805 moved to Lakelands, a substantial house on extensive grounds at the eastern end of the Mahon peninsula near Blackrock. The house had previously been the residence of Benjamin Bousefield. William Crawford died on 29 November 1834. The *Cork Constitution* newspaper of 2 December carried the short notice of his death: 'On Saturday, the 29th ult., William Crawford Esq., of Lakelands, aged 77.' Elsewhere in the same edition he was described as 'a man who for over fifty years occupied the esteem and respect of the citizens, he was ever foremost in every good work, and his purse was ever open in the cause of charity'.

In his will William Crawford directed that £200 be paid to his wife Mary on the day after his death and that she receive a payment of £200 per annum for the remainder of her life.[25] In addition she was to receive 'all her rings, jewels, ornaments of her person, wearing apparel and paraphernalia of every description. Also my coach and jaunting car with the horses and harness thereunto belonging. Also half of the wine that may be at Lakelands at the time of my decease.' His sons William and George inherited his share in the brewery. In addition, George got the premises on Merchants' Quay and £8,000, while William was to get the £20,000 arranged on his marriage to Dulcibella Morris. William also received 'all my sideboard plate and half of whichever wines may be in my cellar at Lakeland [sic] and Merchants' Quay', the lands at Blackrock that were held from Sir William Chatterton, forming part of the Lakelands demesne, and the house, held from the Bousefield family, was to be William's widow's for one year, after which time their interest in it was to be sold. He left £4,000 each to his daughters Ann, Maybella, Elizabeth and Louisa Alicia, £100 to his daughter Jane, 'for her having already on her marriage with her present husband James Morris esq. amply provided for her'. His daughter Mary had also been provided for on her marriage to Robert Gordon of Florida, County Down.

WILLIAM CRAWFORD (1788–1840)

William (hereafter William Jr.) was the son of William Crawford and his first wife, Mary Bordman. Nothing is known of his early life or education, but by 1809 he was living at Ferney, a substantial house and farm on the Mahon peninsula north of his father's house at Lakelands. He married Ducibella Morris, daughter of Abraham and Thomazin Morris of Dunkathel House, in 1813 and they lived first at Ferney and later at Lakelands, having bought the family's interest in the house and lands after the death of his father.

Patron of the arts

William Jr. had a lifelong interest in the arts and was one of a group of Cork men of business, wealth and learning who in the early 1800s supported the Cork Society for the Promotion of the Fine Arts, a society that organised a number of exhibitions in the city between 1815 and 1833. Crawford, like his father and his father's business partner, William Beamish, was also a supporter of the Royal Cork Institution, founded in 1803, which had an extensive library and promoted adult education in the city through short courses and lectures. The rooms of the Royal Cork Institution were first located on South Mall, but after the building of a new Custom House on Lapp's Island, the old Custom House building on Emmet Place became its new headquarters. In 1850 the building became the Cork School of Design, and after the building of a large extension and new galleries in 1884, funded by William Horatio Crawford, a son of William Jr., it became known as the Crawford School of Art. The patronage of men like William Crawford Jr. enabled the arts scene in Cork to thrive,

From left: William Crawford Jr. (Crawford Art Gallery, Cork); William Crawford Jr., seated, and his son William Horatio, at Lakelands, 1838, by Augustin Edouart. (Crawford Art Gallery, Cork)

and artists like John Hogan, Ireland's greatest neoclassical sculptor, owed much of their success to the support of enlightened men of wealth like him.

Domestic details

William Crawford Jr. kept detailed accounts of many aspects of his life at his home, Ferney, near Blackrock.[26] Under the title 'Pictures' he lists twenty-three works, including 'Head of an Old Woman' by Rembrandt, 'Spanish General Officer' by Velasquez, 'Magdalen & Skull' by M.A. Caravaggio, 'A Smith's Forge' by Roos and two pictures by Albert Cuyp. He also listed the books in his library in 1821, divided into categories such as Greek & Latin, Belles Lettres, History, Antiquities etc., Law & Politics, Poetry, Theology & Morals and many more, all suggesting a man of wide and cultured taste. He also lists all his silver plate, cutlery and bedding.

In his accounts he named all the servants he had employed between his marriage in 1813 and 1838, giving the period of their employment, earnings and titles. These included valets, butlers, grooms, footmen, gardeners, cooks, governesses, nurses, nursing maids, dry nurses, wet nurses, children's maids, kitchen maids and housemaids. In 1817, for example, Crawford had ten servants employed at Ferney at a total cost for the year of £460, including wages, food and other costs. On 10 July 1818, while in Paris, Crawford recruited Louis Duteil as a valet and he began work at Ferney in October of that year. Edmund Murphy, a gardener who worked for Crawford from 1814 to 1834, was paid £25 per year. A groom and footman earned

£15.18.6 per year, while cook Mary Bates, employed between 1814 and 1823, earned £13.13.0 per year, rising to £15.18.6 from 1818. A dry nurse and child's maid earned £13.13.0 per year, but Catherine Callaghan, employed as a kitchen maid in 1818, was paid £5.13.9 per year. Miss Cotter, a governess who began at Ferney in 1819, earned £30 annually.

Crawford did a detailed analysis of the costs of running Ferney for the year 1818. He calculated that the cost of keeping a servant was at least 1s 6d per day, made up of 2d for a quart of milk, 7d for 1 lb of meat, 3d for a quart of porter, 4d worth of bread and 2d worth of butter. This added up to almost £28 per year. The cost of keeping his horses, including feed, stabling, etc., came to £30 per year per horse – £2 more than for a servant.

Crawford also calculated the exact cost of baking a loaf of bread, the rate of growth of a cow, the cost of growing an acre of potatoes and the cost of growing grapes in his hothouse. He categorised all living expenses for 1818 as follows:

> *House and maintenance*: Rent £180; Taxes £60 Rates £6; Tythe £6; Murphy (gardener) £25; Fitzgerald (labourer) £20; Sundries £23, a total of £320.
> *House expenses*: Marketting [*sic*] £150; Groceries, Tea £90; Flour £50; Porter £50; Wine, Spirits etc. £40; Coals @ 90 brls. p.a. @5s 5d per brl. £25; Washing @ 10s per week £26; Oats £20; Hay £14; Sundries £50; Milk, Butter £50, a total of £565.
> *Wages*: Groom's Wages £5.15.8, livery £6.16.6 = £22.15.0; Valet £6.16.6, livery £6.16.6 = £13.13.0; Cook £13.13.0; Kitchen Maid £5.13.9; House Maid £8; Dry Nurse £13.13.0; Dry Nurse £11.7.6; Wet Nurse £13.13.0, Tea £5.7.0 = £19; Boy, clothes £7.17.9, a total of £115.

These costs totalled £1,000. He calculated his income in that year at £1,578, made up of bank interest of £258, income from the brewery of £1,200 and income from hay, milk, cream, butter, fattening cows, sheep and so on at £120.

Death and burial

William and Dulcibella Crawford had four children: William Horatio, Arthur, Thomazin and Janett. William Crawford Jr. died on 6 April 1840 while in Bristol on business. The *Cork Constitution* of 9 April reported that:

> Mr Crawford's death was unexpected. He left this city on Friday week by the *Queen* steamer for Bristol. He was not quite well, we believe, when starting, but the indisposition was so slight that he hoped the trip would shake it off. In Bristol, however, it increased, and medical advice became requisite. For

> two days after that, he was able to be out on business, but an illness at first so trifling as to excite neither apprehension nor anxiety gained ground, and, eventuating in fever, deprived us, on Monday last, of one of the most useful, most popular, and respected of our citizens.

His remains came back to Cork on 12 April and he was interred in the family vault in Brooklodge churchyard two days later. In a strange irony, a temperance procession due to take place in the city on the day of the funeral was cancelled 'in consequence of the lamented death of Mr. Crawford'.[27]

In his will William Crawford Jr. left his share in the brewery between his sons William Horatio and Arthur, and bequeathed them £19,230.15.0 and £10,615.7.6, respectively. To his daughters, Thomazin and Janett, he left £6,461.10.7 each.[28]

William Crawford Jr., sculpted by John Hogan. (Crawford Art Gallery, Cork/Authors)

Crawford's statue

In 1842 the sculptor John Hogan was commissioned to create a sculpture of William Crawford Jr. and he undertook the task in Rome. In a letter published in the *Cork Examiner* of 21 March 1842, Hogan wrote of the work:

> I am still modelling Mr. Crawford's statue, the marble of which is said to be the most splendid and most transparent block that ever entered the Eternal City – being excavated from the first quarry at Carrara … It is more than eleven feet long and measures more than 260 cubic palms – hereby acknowledged the largest block recollected to be removed from that celebrated cave, as such pure marble runs chiefly in small pieces, and is generally used for busts and cabinet figures – always bearing an exorbitant price, even at Carrara.

The finished sculpture was shipped to Cork and erected in the main hall of the Cork Savings

Bank. It was transferred to the Crawford Art Gallery in 1957, where it is now displayed. The inscription reads:

HE WAS ONE OF IRELAND'S WORTHIEST SONS
FROM HIS YOUTH UPWARDS
HIS HEART THROBBED FOR HER PROSPERITY
HE WAS A GENUINE CHRISTIAN HIS PRINCIPLES EMBRACED
LIBERTY OF CONSCIENCE
HIS FIRST VIRTUE CHARITY AS LOVE FOR ALL
WITHOUT REFERENCE TO CREED OR PARTY
THE GREAT CHARACTERISTIC OF HIS BENEVOLENCE
WAS ITS UNIVERSALITY
HE WAS A GOOD CITIZEN AND A
SINGLE HEARTED PHILANTHROPIST
THE ENERGIES OF A CULTIVATED AND ENLIGHTENED MIND
WERE DIRECTED TO THE PUBLIC GOOD
HE DIED IN THE PRIME OF LIFE AMIDST THE REGRETS
OF THE WHOLE COMMUNITY
AND MEN OF ALL PARTRIES FORGETTING THEIR
POLITICAL DIFFERENCES
UNITED IN THUS PERPETUATING THE MEMORY
OF SO MUCH WORTH AND EXCELLENCE

WILLIAM HORATIO CRAWFORD (1812–88)

William Horatio was the eldest child of William Crawford Jr. and Dulcibella Morris. All sources give the year of his birth as 1812, although his parents did not marry until 1813. He studied at Trinity College, Dublin, and graduated with a BA in 1837, after which he studied law at the King's Inns in Dublin. He never practised law but lived the quiet life of a reclusive wealthy gentleman. Following his father's death in 1840, William Horatio inherited nearly £20,000 in cash, as well as securities and bonds, and half of his father's quarter share in the Beamish & Crawford brewery and in its annual net profits. Two years later, Arthur, William Horatio's only brother, died and he inherited his share in the brewery, bringing his holding to a full quarter share, as well as an estate worth over £23,000.[29] He lived at Lakelands near Blackrock and his acquired wealth and ongoing substantial income enabled him to pursue his interests in horticulture, art, bibliophilia and philanthropy.

Commemorative plaque at the entrance to the Crawford Art Gallery, Cork. (Authors)

Reluctant man of business

When he became a sleeping partner in Beamish & Crawford in 1840, William Horatio was quite happy to leave all matters of business, as they related to the Crawford partners, in the hands of his uncle George, the Crawford acting partner. While the Beamish family brothers feuded throughout the 1840s and 1850s, he avoided all conflict by having minimal contact with the brewery. In 1859 William Horatio had to replace his uncle George as the Crawford acting partner, but it was arranged that Richard Pigott Beamish would act on his behalf on an interim basis in the management of the brewery, William Horatio being 'averse to a close attendance on business'. In 1863 a new partnership agreement for the brewery was negotiated, and as George Crawford, the previous Crawford acting partner, was by then quite ill and frail, William Horatio was the sole remaining Crawford partner and would have to become an acting partner. But as he 'in consequence of not having been brought up to the business has stated his unwillingness to assume the entire responsibility', legal opinion was sought. The legal opinion was that a sub-agent or manager could be nominated to act on his behalf 'so that Mr. W.H. Crawford might feel very easy as to the burdens of the office and might make it as light as he thought fit'.[30] Richard Pigott Beamish acted in this capacity, with occasional consultations with William Horatio.

After the death of George Crawford in 1864, William Horatio held the full Crawford 50 per cent share in the brewery, increasing both his wealth and annual income yet again. In 1870 he transferred one-eighth of his share in the business to William Henry Sharman Crawford, his first cousin and a grandson of William Crawford, the brewery co-founder.

Internationally renowned gardener

At his home at Lakelands, William Horatio created a garden that gained an international reputation, most particularly as the place where the Himalayan native tree, *Magnolia campbellii*, flowered for the first time in Britain or Ireland in 1844. Keith Lamb and Patrick Bowe describe the gardens:

> Lakelands was a remarkable garden, the grounds planted with trees and shrubs from the Himalayas and the southern hemisphere. These included a rare and tender *Araucaria angustifolia*, a Brazilian monkey-puzzle, more than twelve feet high and well shaped, the pendulous-branched Huon pine (*Lagarostrobus franklinii*) from Tasmania and the plum-fruited yew of Chile (*Prumnopitys andinus*), the latter about 50 feet high. Firs and spruces included *Abies venusta*, *A. Grandis* and the tiger-tailed spruce (*Picea polita*) of Japan. On the house itself grew vigorous plants of *Berberidopsis corallina*, which must have been a

> splendid sight in autumn, as they were unusually high – up to 20 feet – and carried the long red flowers abundantly. The outdoor rhododendrons included *Rhododendron thomsonii*, *R. Falconeri* and the delicate *R. Dalhousiae*, the latter flowering freely. Glasshouses contained a rich collection of orchids and rare Himalayan Rhododendron.[31]

William Horatio Crawford specialised in growing *Brownea*, a genus of tropical trees and shrubs, and some specimens grew so tall in his glasshouses that rather than pruning the plants, he had the glasshouses heightened. A hybrid of the genus raised by Crawford at Lakelands carries his name, *Brownea x crawfordii*.

The house and gardens at Lakelands have gone, their site now largely occupied by the Mahon Point Shopping Centre, apartment blocks and housing. A tall and distinctively shaped monkey-puzzle tree still stands tall near the ring road that crosses the former gardens, the only vestige of the once great garden.

The Crawford Art Gallery, Cork. (Authors)

Philanthropist

William Kirby Sullivan was president of Queen's College Cork, later University College Cork, from 1873 to 1890 and became friendly with William Horatio Crawford, who admired Sullivan's efforts to expand and improve the college. Crawford became the college's great benefactor: he donated over 2,000 volumes to

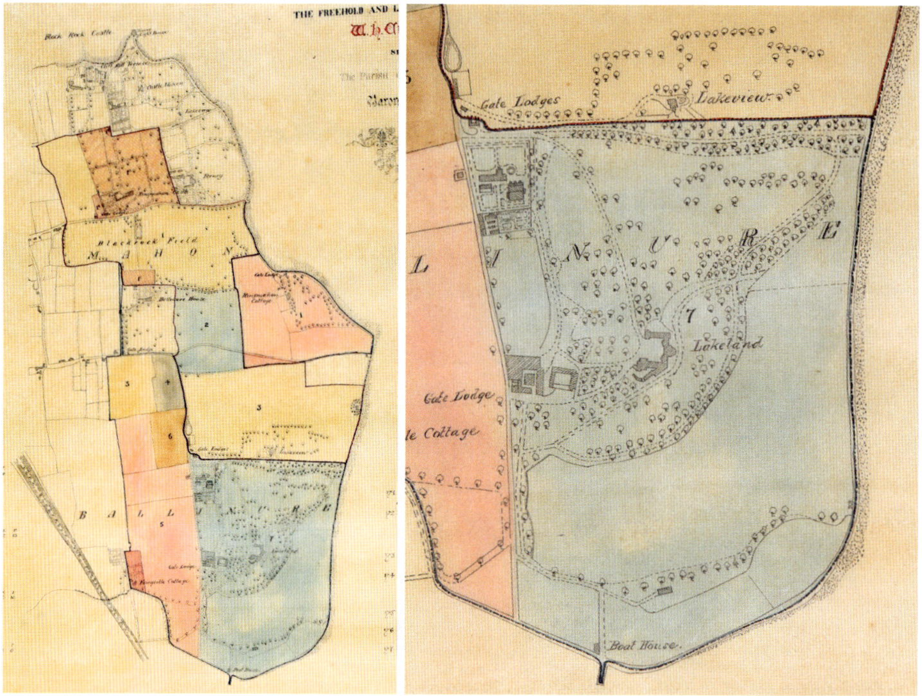

Map of the lands held by William Horatio Crawford at the eastern end of the Mahon peninsula at the time of his death in 1888. Lakelands, its demesne and gardens, lie at the southern end of the map (left), with a detail (right) showing Lakelands and its surrounding demesne and gardens. (CCCA/Dori O'Connell)

the university library in the 1870s; he gave £2,750 towards laying out a botanic garden and the erection of tropical plant houses on newly acquired land to the east of the college quadrangle; he donated many rare plants for the botanic garden; he gave £1,000 to fund the purchase of equipment for the astronomical observatory later named in his honour; he gave £6,000 for the building of Berkeley Hall, a students' residence; and later gave a further £2,000 to clear a debt on the building.

In 1884 William Horatio Crawford gave £20,000 to fund the building of a large extension to the old Custom House on Emmet Place. The building had been the home of the Royal Cork Institution and later the Cork School of Design. The newly extended building had a range of new galleries, a lecture room and large classrooms for the teaching of art, and Crawford also donated a range of art works for display and for the instruction of students. The new School of Art later became the Crawford School of Art in honour of its patron. The newly extended building was officially opened by the Prince of Wales in April 1885, but William Horatio Crawford, ever modest, chose not to attend the celebrations.

Following his death in October 1888, the *Cork Constitution* detailed more of Crawford's acts of generosity.[32] In 1868, following the disestablishment of the

Church of Ireland, he gave £4,000 to the diocesan fund to partly make up for the loss of tithes. In 1875 he donated £10,000 towards the erection of the spires on the western end of St Fin Barre's Cathedral in Cork and he later gave a further £8,300 to pay for the sculptures and carvings on the western face of the building. The account said that 'his private acts of generosity were countless' and that 'he always preferred that whatever he did was not made the subject of public comment', and concluded: 'While his personal expenditure was small, he lavished immense sums in carrying out works for the permanent benefit of his native city.'

Death and burial

William Horatio Crawford did not marry and had no children. He died on 18 October 1888 and the quiet manner of his passing was in keeping with the humble and unassuming nature of his life. He had visited his club in the city and on his return home 'he dined as usual, and then sat in his chair, where his servants saw him reading before retiring to rest. On yesterday morning he was found in his chair dead.'[33]

His funeral was on the following Thursday, 25 October. The *Cork Constitution* of the following day described the event:

> At an early hour yesterday morning, the remains of this much respected and highly esteemed charitable citizen was [*sic*] removed from his residence, Lakelands, Blackrock, and interred in the family burying ground at Brooklodge, Lower Glanmire. Owing to the inclemency of the weather and also to the very great distance of Lakelands from the city, but few people accompanied the funeral from the start, but as it approached the city it was met by great numbers, including nearly 300 *employés* of Beamish and Crawford's Brewery. The number of carriages in attendance was very large, and in consequence of the downpour of rain as the *cortege* passed through the city the majority of them were occupied. In accordance with arrangement, when the funeral reached the Fisheries, most of the citizens as well as the workmen returned to the city and the journey was continued at a quick pace. The coffin was beautifully decorated with wreaths sent by friends of the deceased gentleman. One wreath of white flowers, sent by the ladies of the High School, Sydney Place was particularly noticeable ... The Burial Service was read by Canon Smith, Blackrock, and the Rev. T.B. Herrick.
>
> Canon Smith said he did not intend to deliver any address. He had the honour and privilege of being the minister to the late Mr. Crawford, but knowing his retiring disposition he believed that it would be his wish that no words would be spoken on the solemn occasion. Therefore, regarding and honouring what he believed to be the wish of their departed and beloved

From top:
The churchyard at Brooklodge, burial place of William Horatio Crawford. (Authors)

The catalogue for the auction of William Horatio Crawford's books and manuscripts in March 1891. The sale made over £21,000. (CCCA/Authors)

> friend, he would not say anything, and he felt thankful to Almighty God that due testimony had been borne in other places, not only by the Lord Bishop, but by all the public men of the city of Cork, as they very well knew.[34]

Today Brooklodge churchyard is quite overgrown, many headstones are fallen and the once imposing vaults of wealthy families are slowly falling to decay, the thickening arms of the enclosing ivy pushing the structures apart. The Crawford family vault, last resting place of William Horatio, one of Cork's greatest benefactors, is not recognisable.

In March 1891 William Horatio Crawford's valuable library of books was sold at auction in London at the salesrooms of Sotheby, Wilkinson & Hodge. The sale took twelve days and the books made a total of £21,255.19.6.[35]

ARTHUR FREDERICK SHARMAN CRAWFORD (1862–1943)

Arthur Frederick Sharman Crawford was born in Crawfordsburn, County Down, and was the youngest of three sons of Arthur Johnston Sharman Crawford (1811–91) and Louisa Alicia Crawford (1818–87), a daughter of William Crawford, the brewery co-founder. Arthur Frederick's paternal grandmother was Mabel Crawford, a first cousin of William Crawford, who had married William Sharman (1781–1861) in 1805. Following the death of Mabel's only sibling, her unmarried brother Arthur Johnston Crawford, in 1826, her husband, William Sharman, took on the added surname of Crawford to preserve the name and thus created the unhyphenated surname of Sharman Crawford. Arthur Frederick Sharman Crawford was a first cousin of William Horatio Crawford through his mother and was also William Horatio's third cousin, as his grandmother was a first cousin of William Crawford's, William Horatio's grandfather.

From left: Arthur Frederick Sharman Crawford, and his home, Lota Lodge, Glanmire, Cork. This building is now the Vienna Woods Hotel. (W.T. Pike, *Contemporary Biographies* (Brighton, 1911))

Arthur Frederick was educated at Eastbourne College in England and he came to Cork following the death of his brother, William Henry, in 1890. William Henry had become a sleeping partner in Beamish & Crawford on behalf of the Crawford family in 1870 when William Horatio Crawford gave him one-eighth of his half share in the firm. William Henry lived for a time at Lakelands with William Horatio and married in 1874, after which he lived at Lota Lodge near Glanmire. On William Henry's death, Arthur Frederick and his brother, Robert Gordon, inherited his interest in the brewery, and from 1890 Arthur Frederick was the Crawford acting partner. Following the incorporation of Beamish & Crawford Ltd in 1895, Arthur Frederick and his brother equally shared the Crawford half share of the new company. After the takeover of Lane & Co. Ltd in 1901, a 'new' Beamish & Crawford Ltd was formed, and in this new company the Sharman Crawford brothers had half of the new company's ordinary shares and 17,822 of its 40,000 preference shares. Arthur Frederick was a director of the firm, along with North Ludlow Axel Beamish, under the chairmanship of Richard Henrik Beamish. Arthur Frederick continued as a director (with a brief hiatus in the late 1920s) until his death.

Philanthropist

Arthur Frederick Sharman Crawford took a keen interest in technical education and was a leading member of the Cork Technical Instruction Committee for many years. This group sought the establishment in Cork of a technical institute that would give training in technology, engineering and mechanics to provide a skilled workforce for the region's industries. In 1901 Beamish & Crawford's rival brewery, J.J. Murphy & Co. Ltd, took over the Arnott's brewery on Fitton Street and closed it down. The buildings of the brewery were partly demolished and the site was left derelict. In

Fitton Street was renamed Sharman Crawford Street in recognition of the generosity of the Sharman Crawford family in donating the site of the former Arnott's brewery for the building of the Municipal Technical Institute. (Authors)

1909 Arthur Frederick bought the site and donated it to the city for the building of a technical institute. A grant was received from the Department of Agriculture and Technical Instruction, and between 1909 and 1911 what became known as the Sharman Crawford Municipal Technical Institute was built. Arthur Frederick contributed to the cost of equipping the college and provided annual scholarships for students there and at the city's School of Art. It was officially opened in January 1912, and for over sixty years the Crawford Tech, as it was affectionately known in Cork, provided a technical education and training to many who found employment in car manufacturing, shipbuilding, construction and other industries in the Cork. Arthur Frederick was a member of the management committee of the institute until 1926. In 1911 Fitton Street was renamed Sharman Crawford Street in recognition of Arthur Frederick's contribution. In 1922 he was put forward by the Cork Chamber of Commerce as a nominee for the Free State Senate; in that same year he was founding

Left: Commemorative plaque at the entrance to the Crawford College of Art and Design. (Authors)
Right: The Sharman Crawford Municipal Technical Institute in 1919.

Arthur Frederick Sharman Crawford, holding trophy, photographed in 1937. (Courtesy Ed Hinchy)

chairman of the Cork Town Planning Association, which in 1926 published a major civic survey of Cork city.

Arthur Frederick also had an interest in agriculture and was a governor of the Cork Dairy Institute. He was a keen huntsman, was a founder member of the Cork Golf Club and served as its president. He also sailed and was a lifelong member of the Royal Cork Yacht Club. His yacht, the *Ierne*, was built in 1914 and is regarded as a classic boat in yachting circles. It was discovered in a derelict state in Portugal and was completely refurbished in the early 2000s.

Arthur Frederick married Ida Florence Perry (1868–1941) in 1890 and the couple moved to Cork, taking up residence at Lota Lodge, the former home of his brother, William Henry. They had two children: Gerald Arthur (1891–1945) and Aileen (1897–1964). Arthur Frederick Sharman Crawford died in 1943 and is buried in St Lappan's churchyard in Little Island, Cork, with his wife and daughter.

10

Before the War

1901–1913

The beginning of the twentieth century saw the consolidation of the brewing industry in Cork. In 1901 James J. Murphy & Co. purchased Arnott's St Finbarres's Brewery on Fitton Street and closed it down, while in the same year Beamish & Crawford took over Lane's Southgate Brewery across the South Main Street and did the same. The acquisition of Lane's was technically an amalgamation of the two companies, and a newly constituted Beamish & Crawford limited company, with Richard Henrik Beamish, Arthur Frederick Sharman Crawford and North Ludlow Axel Beamish as directors, was incorporated in October 1901.

Annual sales had passed 100,000 barrels as Beamish & Crawford entered the new century and continued to rise. From 1900 to 1903 sales rose by 50 per cent to just over 150,000 barrels – the highest annual sale in the brewery's history. The takeover of Lane's led to an increase of thirty-seven in its estate of tied houses in the city, bringing the number to 157, as well as an increase of eighty-six in the number of country tied houses. It was estimated at the time that Beamish & Crawford would increase sales by up to 40,000 barrels because of the takeover. They increased by over 20,000 barrels in the first year and by 10,000 the following year, but with overall sales decreasing a little in subsequent years it is not possible to gauge the exact proportion of trade that is attributable to the acquisition of Lane & Co. (see also Chapter 7).

Although annual sales fell from their 1903 peak of over 150,000 barrels, they still averaged over 127,000 yearly until 1914. Net profits grew in line with sales and averaged just under £42,000 each year in the period, netting the shareholders significant dividends and building a sizeable reserve. In the period 1902 to 1905, a total of £65,429 was spent on capital projects, principally the new stables, improvements at the brewery and a renovation of the Lee Mills. This expenditure was totally funded from cash reserves.

A view of the Beamish & Crawford Brewery and the rooftops of Cork from Elizabeth Fort. The top of the glassworks cone is visible to the left of the group of three chimneys. This cone was demolished in 1915. (*Irish Examiner*)

Table 10.1 **Sales, gross profit and net profit, 1901–13**[1]

YEAR	SALES (in barrels)	GROSS PROFIT (to nearest £)	NET PROFIT (to nearest £)
1901	120,073	£80,318	£38,878
1902	141,290	£96,405	£45,336
1903	151,734	£114,695	£58,714
1904	145,741	£114,985	£60,148
1905	144,926	£105,117	£49,847
1906	125,897	£87,254	£40,060
1907	122,181	£99,276	£41,300
1908	121,126	£91,306	£35,119
1909	123,992		£35,669
1910	126,857		£37,040
1911	126,987		£35,805
1912	121,331		£37,261
1913	117,378		£30,312

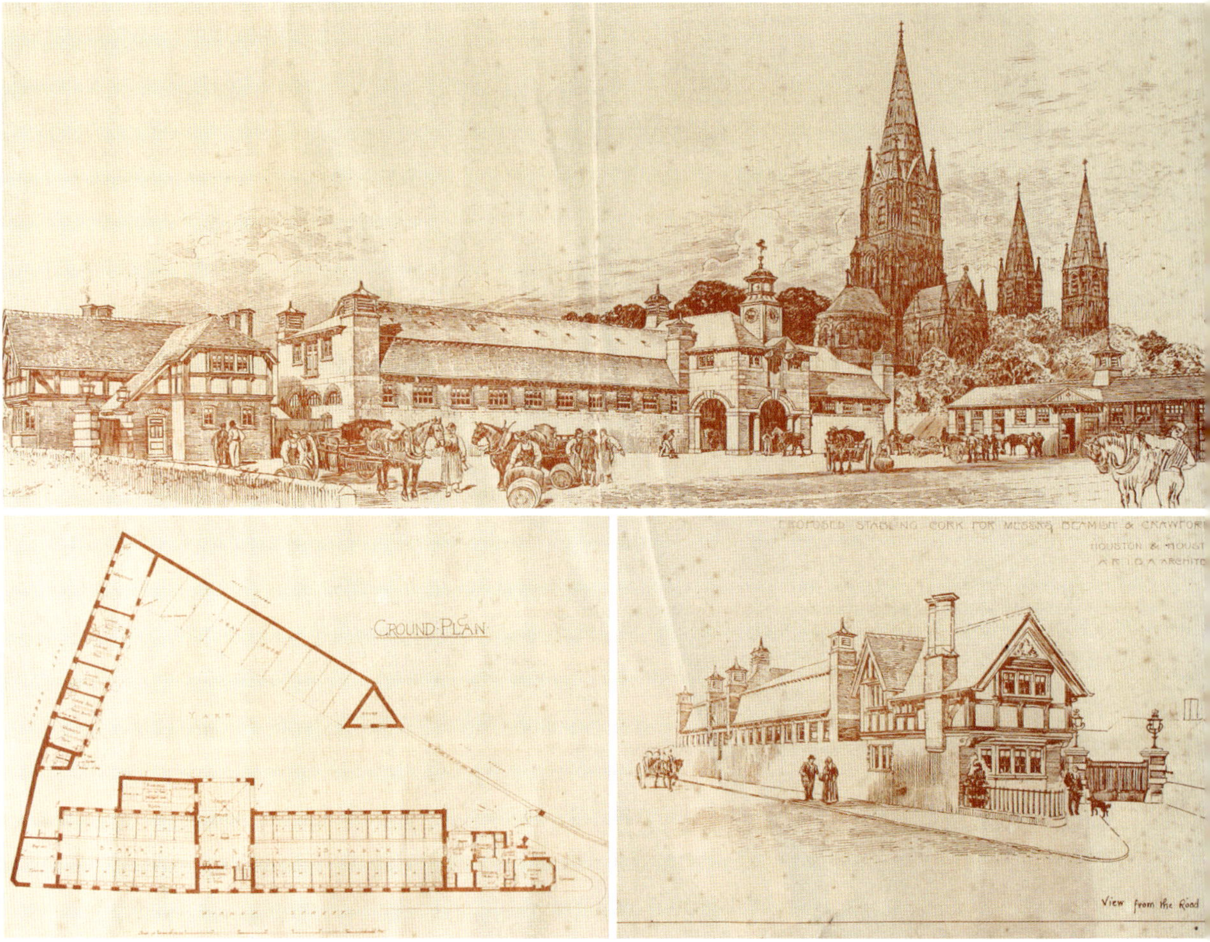

Plan and drawings of the Beamish & Crawford stables, completed in 1902.
(Beamish & Crawford Brewery Collection/Dori O'Connell)

Bishop Street Stables, 1902

Beamish & Crawford had small stables within the brewery complex that were used for stabling the horses of staff members, but the stabling and stores for brewery horses and drays were located off Cove Street, a short distance from the brewery. When Alfred Barnard visited in the late 1880s the brewery had twenty horses, twenty-two drays and other vehicles.[2] By the end of the 1890s, with production and sales steadily rising, a decision was made to build new stables. In 1879 the brewery had purchased a plot of ground on Bishop Street, close to St Fin Barre's Cathedral, as a site for new stables for £1,750. Coincidentally, part of the site had been occupied in the 1750s by a brewer named Robert Dorman, who had a brewery and malthouse there.[3] The plans for the new stables were drawn up by the London firm of Houston & Houston

From left: Stable yard, looking westwards. (Courtesy Ed Hinchy) Entrance in the southern range of stable buildings. The adoption of motor lorries from the 1920s for the distribution of brewery products rendered the stables redundant. (Courtesy Ed Hinchy) The stable buildings today. (Authors)

and the superior design and appearance of the building, reputed to be one of the finest examples of Edwardian architecture in the city, seemed to be at odds with their humble use as stabling for horses. The stables were completed in 1902, the first year of the Cork International Exhibition, and may have influenced aspects of the design of the exhibition's Industrial Hall, particularly the flared 'bell-cast' roofs on the chimney stacks of the stables and on the towers of the Industrial Hall, which gave both buildings a certain Oriental appearance.[4] Beamish & Crawford were exhibitors at the exhibition in 1902 and again in 1903.

The stables were in use until the late 1930s, by which time motorised lorries had taken over the task of distribution and had made the horses, drays and their stables redundant. Between 1939 and 1944 the buildings were leased by the Tropical Fruit Co., following which they were leased by the Southern Shoe Co. In 1947 Ideal Weatherproofs, later Ideal Menswear, a clothing manufacturer, took over the premises and in the 1980s the buildings were converted for use as a complex of small business units.

Products

Up to 1904 the brewery brewed Single Stout (sometimes called porter), Double Stout, Extra Stout and XXX Stout, and after the takeover of Lane & Co. in 1901, ale became more significant in the brewery's portfolio. Up to 1901 annual ale production rarely exceeded 500 barrels, but following the Lane's takeover ale brewing jumped to an annual average of 2,600 barrels. Much of this was supplied to the military canteens in the Cork district with which Lane's had had a significant trade since 1896.

In 1902, for example, Single Stout made up over 87 per cent of sales, followed by Double Stout at 6 per cent, Extra Stout at 3.4 per cent, ale at 1.7 per cent and XXX Stout at 0.15 per cent. From 1902 a beer called Special Bottling Stout was also brewed, with 1.46 per cent of sales; this was probably a substitution for Bottling Single, which was discontinued after 1900.

Left: Beamish & Crawford imported and distributed bottled Bass ale. Sales increased after 1901 when the company took over the military contracts previously held by Lane & Co. Ltd. (Beamish & Crawford Brewery Collection/Dori O'Connell)
Right: Beamish & Crawford's bottling store, early 1900s. (Courtesy Ed Hinchy)

In 1904 it was decided to discontinue the production of Single Stout and from September of that year Double Stout became the standard stout and the brewery's biggest seller. In 1906 Double Stout accounted for 94.1 per cent of sales, Extra Stout 2.6 per cent, XXX Stout 0.5 per cent, Special Bottling Stout 1 per cent and ale 1.8 per cent. As well as brewing its own bitter and mild ales, Beamish & Crawford also distributed imported bottled ales: Bass, Younger's, Simond's and Allsopp's. Bass ales made up the greatest proportion of these.

In December 1904 the brewery entered into a two-year exclusive agreement with Cade & Sons Ltd of Cork to bottle Beamish & Crawford Double and XXX Stouts, the brewery having decided to discontinue bottling. It was agreed that Cades could also bottle Guinness, but no other porter. From the middle of 1905 Cades were also to bottle Beamish & Crawford ales. Problems arose within a short time as to the ownership of bottles, with Cades claiming ownership of the brewery's bottles. At the time a bottle exchange operated in Cork whereby bottlers could retrieve their own bottles, and as Cades were retrieving and using Beamish & Crawford bottles without permission and without payment, a legal action was initiated by the brewery. This resulted in the agreement not being renewed after the end of 1906.[5] The brewery then recommenced bottling at the brewery as well as utilising the services of Cork bottling companies such as John Daly & Co. In 1912 the bottling department at the brewery was in the charge of a foreman who supervised a van man and boy for city deliveries, a country van man, three labellers, four bottlers and five others whose duties are not specified.[6]

Agencies and military canteens

The sale and distribution of Beamish & Crawford products through agents continued to be a significant proportion of total sales. While some agencies were independently owned, others were distribution depots run by clerks directly employed by the brewery. During the period 1906 to 1912 (for which some detail has survived), the brewery employed clerks to run its depots at Rathcormac, Fermoy, Mitchelstown, Tallow, Lismore, Dungarvan, Queenstown, Kinsale and Skibbereen, while the independent agencies were Midleton (T.S.R. Coppinger), Youghal (M. Neville), Aghada (P.F. Martin), Mallow (E. Priestly), Kanturk (P.F. Johnson), Bantry (J. Lyons), Bandon (J. Walsh) and Plymouth (J.R. Wilson).

After the takeover of Lane & Co. in 1901, military canteens became a new segment of brewery trade, which grew to be especially important during the years of the First World War. In the period 1906 to 1912, British army canteens in the following locations were supplied: Cork Barracks; Ballincollig Barracks; two on Bere Island; Moore Park and Old Barracks, Fermoy; Kilworth Camp; Ballynovane Camp, Buttevant; Spike Island; Fort Camden; Fort Carlisle; Royal Navy, Hawlbowline; Sergeants' Mess and Charles Fort, Kinsale; Bandon; Youghal; Limerick and New Barracks, Limerick; Tipperary. Some canteens were supplied with Beamish & Crawford products through wholesalers designated by the military: Canteen & Mess Society Ltd; Dobbin, Ogilvie & Co.; R. Dickerson & Co.; and Lipton & Co.[7]

The continuing importance of the agents in the distribution and sale of brewery products is evident in the proportion of annual sales handled by them. In 1900 a total of 104,457 barrels of Beamish & Crawford product was sold and agents accounted for 56 per cent of this. City sales made up 28.1 per cent, country (distributed directly from the brewery) 13.4 per cent and exports 2.51 per cent. With the addition of sales through military canteens after 1901, the proportions of each segment for the 125,897 barrels sold in 1906 were canteens 5 per cent, city 22.6 per cent, country 17.8 per cent, agents 53.6 per cent and exports 1 per cent. With the outbreak of war in 1914 and an increased level of military activity and the mobilisation of reservists and new recruits in the country, the proportion of sales accounted for by canteens grew significantly: in 1915 it was 13.1 per cent, in 1916 it was 12.7 per cent and in 1917 it was 12.6 per cent. Exports made up a declining proportion of sales in the years after 1901, averaging just under 1,600 barrels annually in the eight years up to 1908.

Beamish & Crawford trade

(in barrels)

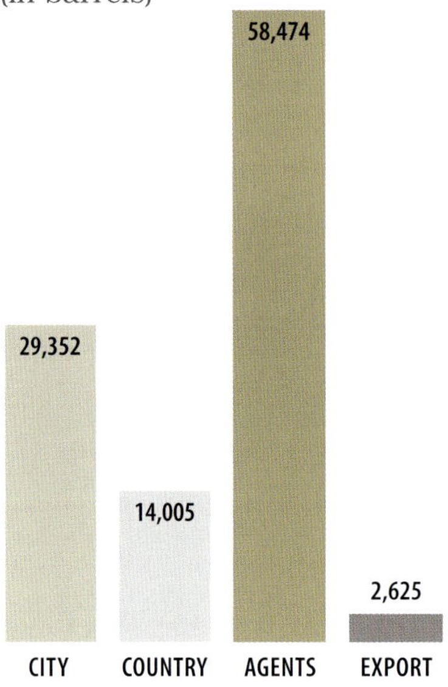

1900

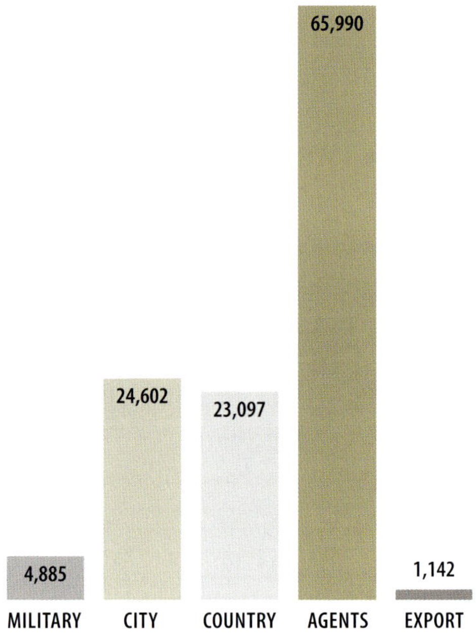

1908

Beamish & Crawford trade (in barrels)**, 1900.** Direct city sales are almost double those in the country. Sales to non-city customers not handled by agents were classified as 'Country Sales'. Sales through agents account for over half of all trade in the late nineteenth and early twentieth centuries. Exports reached their highest level to date in 1900, accounting for 2.5 per cent of sales. By 1908, this was down to 0.9 per cent.

Beamish & Crawford trade (in barrels)**, 1908.** Direct country sales are now almost as large as city sales, partly due to the acquisition of Lane & Co.'s tied houses and customer base in 1901. The new military canteen trade is a direct result of the Lane takeover.

Beamish & Crawford trade (in barrels)**, 1915.** Note the huge increase in the military canteen trade since the onset of war, and the almost total collapse of exports. The wartime boom in the agricultural economy led to direct country sales outstripping those in the city for the first time.

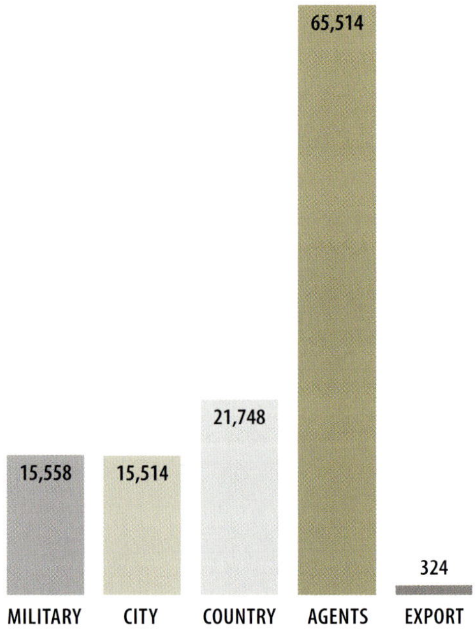

1915

Allman, Dowden & Co., Bandon

In 1913 Beamish & Crawford Ltd took over and closed the Allman, Dowden & Co. brewery in Bandon, County Cork. The brewery, also known as the Watergate Brewery, was located immediately to the east of the town of Bandon on the northern bank of the River Bandon and was founded in 1785 by the Cornwall family, successive generations of which ran the brewery until it was sold to Allman, Dowden & Co. in the 1870s.

The brewery built up a tied estate of about seventy public houses in Bandon and the surrounding areas and also had a number of independent customers. A brewery ledger covering the period 1901 to 1914 lists the tied and free houses that were supplied by the brewery each year, with the names and addresses of between sixty-four and seventy-five tied customers and up to 196 customers in independent public houses.[8] Annual sales, sales income and profit figures survive from 1887 to the brewery's closure in 1914. During this period, sales varied from a low of 6,128 barrels in 1894 to a high of 11,792 barrels for 1903, averaging 8,294 barrels annually. Net profits in this period averaged £1,332 annually, but varied greatly from a loss of £391 in 1892 to the highest recorded net profit of £3,147 in 1888.[9]

The Beamish & Crawford Bottling Co. Ltd occupied the buildings of the former Allman, Dowden & Co. Watergate Brewery. (CCCA/Dori O'Connell)

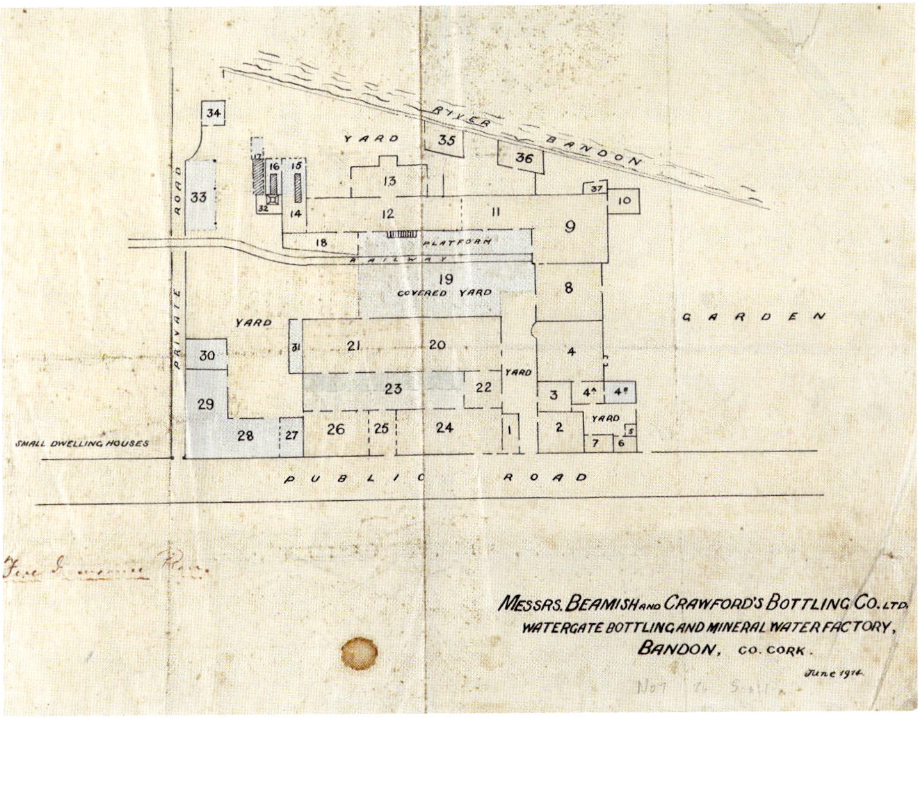

The brewery did not have a large workforce. A brewer was paid an average annual salary of £300 between 1900 and 1912, while the total annual wage bill for the rest of the employees averaged £486 in those years – less than £10 per week, suggesting a workforce of ten or fewer. In 1906 the company began manufacturing and distributing mineral waters and also opened a small bottling plant. Though volumes were small, the sale of mineral waters proved to be quite profitable. The bottling plant bottled the firm's products and Guinness stout.

Table 10.2 **Allman, Dowden & Co.**
Sales, sales income and net profits, 1887–1913

YEAR	SALES (in barrels)	GROSS PROFIT (to nearest £)	NET PROFIT (to nearest £)
1887	8,252	£13,342	£1,980
1888	9,433	£14,251	£3,147
1889	8,967	£14,498	£2,199
1890	8,875	£14,349	£2,501
1891	8,549	£13,821	£791
1892	7,851	£12,694	(£391)
1893	7,124	£11,208	£654
1894	6,128	£9,944	£141
1895	6,367	£10,302	£504
1896	6,743	£10,903	£1,548
1897	6,813	£11,016	£1,340
1898	6,993	£11,415	£1,451
1899	7,052	£11,402	£499
1900	7,338	£11,021	£1,402
1901	7,643	£11,337	£843
1902	9,631	£14,291	£1,179
1903	11,792	£17,531	£1,072
1904	11,406	£16,919	£1,278
1905	10,406	£15,395	£975
1906	8,805	£13,017	£965
1907	8,388	£12,401	£1,445
1908	8,267	£12,228	£776
1909	8,627	£12,761	£1,043
1910	8,698	£12,867	£1,631
1911	8,348	£13,297	£2,039
1912	7,796	£12,409	£2,103
1913	7,652	£12,180	£2,463

From left: James C. Allman, James A. Allman. (W.T. Pike, *Contemporary Biographies* (Brighton, 1911)) and account ledger of Allman, Dowden & Co., Bandon. In 1913 Beamish & Crawford purchased and closed the Allman, Dowden & Co. Brewery. (CCCA/Authors)

The brewery was jointly owned by Richard Lane Allman and James Clugston Allman. Richard died in 1904, aged ninety, and his share was inherited by his wife, Frances, and their son James. By 1911 James Clugston Allman's share was held by his nephew, George A. Armstrong, and the brewery was offered for sale less than two years later. In October 1913 Richard Henrik Beamish, chairman of Beamish & Crawford Ltd, wrote to his cousin William de Courcy Beamish informing him of the decision to purchase Allman, Dowden & Co.:

> The purchase will consolidate our Western trade greatly and will be the means of weakening our competitors ... The Murphys [J.J. Murphy & Co.] are very depressed at the knowledge that we have obtained this Brewery at Bandon and would have jumped at the offer, but the Allmans preferred to sell to us as they place more reliance upon our business.[10]

Beamish & Crawford estimated that the acquisition of the brewery, its estate of tied houses and tied and independent customers would potentially increase its profits by at least £3,000 per annum. The agreed price was £30,000, to be paid by a transfer of 6,000 £5 preference shares in Beamish & Crawford Ltd that would yield 5 per cent per annum, or £1,500.[11] Although the final conveyance to Beamish & Crawford Ltd was not signed until January 1914, the business had been transferred on 30 June 1913.

Brewing continued at the brewery into the autumn of 1913, but news of the sale to Beamish & Crawford was causing concern in Bandon. The editor of the *Cork County Eagle* expressed regret that the brewery had been sold and added that 'it is feared that as far as the brewing of porter is concerned, it will be closed down'. He hoped that the

mineral water plant, at least, would be kept going. Any blame for job losses was going to be put on Beamish & Crawford: 'Of course no blame can be attached to Messrs. Allman, Dowden & Co. for disposing of the Brewery: we feel sure they regret having to dispose with their employees.'[12]

A meeting of the Bandon Town Commissioners in October 1913 discussed the rumours that the sale of the Bandon brewery was going to result in closure and job losses. The meeting decided to write to Beamish & Crawford,

> directing their attention to the widespread rumour that it is their intention, having acquired the Bandon Brewery, to close it up, thus throwing out of employment a large number of men and seriously and irredeemably injuring the prosperity of the town, and asking them not to close the Bandon Brewery while it remains their property.[13]

At the following month's meeting the reply of Beamish & Crawford was read, stating that they must keep their shareholders' interests to the fore and that they would act with the least injury to employment in Bandon.[14] But the local pleas were to no avail and the brewery was closed down.

In 1925 Richard Henrik Beamish told the Intoxicating Liquor Commission that following the approach of the town commissioners, he 'at once turned round to Mr. Walsh who had a large wine and spirit store. I suggested we should join together, and thus by joining together we could re-build the whole of Allman's brewery in respect of the bottling establishment – an up-to-date bottling establishment'.[15] John P. Walsh was an All-for-Ireland League (AFIL) MP (1910–18) for South Cork (the AFIL was a breakaway from the Irish Parliamentary Party, led by William O'Brien MP), a member of Cork County Council and chairman of Bandon Rural District Council. He was also a wine and spirits wholesaler who had previously had an agency for distributing Beamish & Crawford products in the Bandon district and later opened a mineral water manufacturing facility on New Road in the town. In 1914 Walsh entered into a joint venture with Beamish & Crawford and a new company was created to distribute Beamish & Crawford's stout, to manufacture and bottle mineral waters and to distribute wines and spirits. The new company was called Beamish & Crawford Bottling Co. Ltd and it was based at the former Watergate Brewery of Allman, Dowden & Co. with John Walsh as its managing director.[16]

In its first two years the company continued to bottle Guinness stout, a carry-over of the arrangement Allman & Dowden had had since 1906, but this was discontinued in 1916. It proved to be a successful venture, increasing its output from 14,000 dozen

Casks being loaded on to horse-drawn drays in the Beamish & Crawford main yard. (Courtesy Ed Hinchy)

bottles in its first year to 70,000 dozen in 1916.[17] It went from strength to strength and lasted in Bandon until 1967, when production was switched to Beamish & Crawford in Cork. Its most successful product was the Little Norah range of soft drinks and mixers, featuring an image on the bottle labels of the eponymous young woman wearing a red hooded cloak and carrying a tray of drinks.

The clouds of war

The years 1900 to 1913 were, in many ways, the last glory days of the Beamish & Crawford brewery. It had taken over two other breweries, Lane's of Cork and Allman, Dowden & Co. of Bandon, and acquired their tied-house estates in the city and county. A new bottling company was established in Bandon and the crucial military canteen trade of Lane's was a major boon. Sales were at an all-time high, and the opening of the impressive stables at Bishop Street in 1902 was a sign of confidence in the future. Edwardian Cork in general was exuding a similar confidence, hosting the impressive International Exhibition in 1902 and 1903. The Beamishes and the Crawfords were prominent in civic life, sitting on public boards and education and library committees. Richard Henrik Beamish took up the political reins from his late

Event in the mashing loft in the early 1900s, possibly a new year's celebration. Note the Union Jack hanging on the left and the words 'Céad Míle Fáilte' on the banner. The bearded man sitting to the right of the table is North Ludlow Axel Beamish. (Courtesy Ed Hinchy)

grand-uncle, Francis Bernard, and was appointed to the ceremonial post of High Sheriff of Cork in 1906 and again in 1911. He was the main driver of the civic-reformist Municipal Association that performed well in the 1908 municipal elections and was elected to the corporation himself for the Cork Ratepayers' Association in 1911. In his role as chairman of the Public Works Committee, he worked to improve the city's appearance and oversaw the development of the gardens in Fitzgerald's Park (see also Chapter 9).

Behind the pacific façade of genteel improvement, however, lay the reality of mass poverty, inequality and exploitation. Like Guinness and other 'paternalistic' employers, Beamish & Crawford generally managed to maintain cordial working relations with its workforce, many of whom had long family ties to the firm. 'Gentlemen's agreements' on pay and conditions were worked out with the old skilled-trades guilds, such as the Cork Coopers' Society, and strikes and discord were rare. However, the pre-war years saw a shift towards a new kind of trade unionism, as Jim Larkin and his Irish Transport & General Workers' Union (ITGWU, f. 1909) led the way in organising unskilled and general workers and aggressively taking on the employers. There were strikes and lockouts across the country. Cork's employers organised in an Employers' Federation in 1909 to fight back collectively against the unions and succeeded in hobbling the advance of the ITGWU in the city with a lockout of thousands of workers in 1909, presaging the famous 1913 Lockout in Dublin.

Beamish & Crawford managed to avoid large-scale confrontation in 1909 and again in 1911, when the city was hit by a wave of strikes and industrial conflict, but the disruption caused by the disputes in 1909 and 1911 hit trade (although the prolonged closure of the railways in Cork in 1911 disrupted the supply of Guinness to the city, to the advantage of the local breweries). A major strike at Beamish & Crawford had been narrowly averted in November 1907 when over 100 of the brewery's general workers threatened a full withdrawal of labour over the dismissal of ten workers during the slack season. The workers claimed the firm had broken the 'unwritten law' of 'last in, first out'. Only emergency arbitration by local clerics, the Cork United Trades Council and Augustine Roche MP averted a strike that would have shut down production and soured relations between workers and management.[18] The firm was hit by occasional strikes, however, such as that by twenty-five maltsters in 1905 over a demand for double pay on Sundays.[19]

Cork's brewery workers first organised themselves in 1889 as the Cork Breweries Workingmen's Trade Union & Benefit Society. In 1908 it merged with the London-based National Union of Gas Workers & General Labourers, from which it later separated and reformed as an independent body known as the Cork Brewery Workmen's Society (CBWS), which was in turn absorbed by the ITGWU in late 1920.[20] Unlike Guinness, Beamish & Crawford recognised trade unions and negotiated with them. The Irish labour movement recovered from the defeat of the Dublin strike and lockout of 1913–14 and thrived in the circumstances of the First World War after 1916, the year in which the divided trade union movement in Cork also reunited. Compulsory arbitration ensured major gains for workers in pay and conditions, but in 1920 a five-week strike by the CBWS would shut the brewery, with fateful consequences. By then, all had changed utterly in Irish politics, and the key factor in the coming transformation of Ireland was the war that broke out in August 1914. That war would also mark the end of an era in brewing and the beginning a new phase in the history of Beamish & Crawford.

Beamish & Crawford tug-o-war team, c. 1913. (Courtesy Ed Hinchy)

11

In Time of War
1914–1921

The years of the 'Great War', 1914–18, heralded important long-term changes in Irish politics. It was also a period of fundamental change for the drinks trade and the brewing industry. Restrictions on public-house opening times survived the conflict, while wartime reductions in the gravity, or strength, of beer signalled the beginning of the end for the old staple of porter. The war intensified the general trend towards lower consumption of beer in Britain and Ireland and prices rose sharply as taxation became the dominant portion of the price of a pint for the first time. As one historian puts it baldly, 'Drinkers had less time in which to consume weaker, dearer liquor.'[1] Richard Henrik Beamish and his fellow Irish brewers were engaged in constant lobbying to minimise the impact of restrictions on their business, with some success.

The mobilisation of troops, meanwhile, meant an increased demand for beer that Beamish & Crawford and the other breweries were happy to meet, and the military canteen trade became hotly contested between the brewery and its competitors. Some Beamish employees joined the British forces and at least one was killed, while those who remained demanded, and won, increased wages to keep pace with galloping wartime inflation. Despite all the additional problems created by the wartime emergency, in common with most UK brewers, Beamish & Crawford's profits rose during the war. Net profit on the eve of war in 1913 was £30,312; in 1918, the final year of the war, it was £59,688. The compulsory shift to a weaker product lowered unit costs and demand remained relatively steady, despite price rises. A key factor here was the rise in agricultural incomes due to the war.

The world war ended in November 1918 and in the December general election the separatist Sinn Féin party won a majority of seats and established Dáil Éireann as an independent Irish parliament in January 1919. A war of independence ensued and Beamish & Crawford, like the rest of Irish society, was caught in the crossfire.

Military funeral on St. Patrick's Street, c. 1914. This photograph was taken before the opening of the recruiting office in the former Russell premises adjoining the Beamish & Crawford public house. (*Irish Examiner*)

Stout defence

The demands of total war impacted on brewing in three main ways: severe tax increases on drink; the reduction of beer strength to save on cereal use and divert it to foodstuffs (for animals and humans); and restrictions on consumption in the interests of minimising drunkenness in both the military forces and war industries, especially munitions. The temperance advocate Lloyd George was a prominent figure in the dynamics of state intervention in the brewing industry; he was Chancellor of the Exchequer at the outbreak of war, Minister for Munitions from May 1915 and Prime Minister from December 1916. In his war budget speech of November 1914, his desire for increased revenue for the war effort led him to declare, against type, that 'Every half-pint that a man drinks, he will be contributing to the carrying on of the war', which was seized on by the trade for self-serving patriotic advertising. However, within a year, in his new position as Minister for Munitions, he was making his famous statement: 'We are fighting Germany, Austria and Drink; and as far as I can see the greatest of these three deadly foes is Drink.'[2] Some historians have pointed out that Lloyd George was exaggerating the impact of drunkenness on war production and suggest that he was partly using the war to pursue his temperance agenda.[3]

By 1916 the question of reducing barley consumption by breweries became the dominant consideration and led to a series of reductions in output and subsequently in the gravity of beers. While the level of state interference was unprecedented, it could have been even more interventionist: both outright prohibition and nationalisation of the drinks industry were on the table at different stages, but neither came to pass.[4] In November 1914 beer duty was increased from 7s 9d to 23s (£1.15) per standard barrel. This was raised to £1.25 per barrel in 1917 and £2.50 in 1918. Tax increases continued after the end of the war in November 1918: in April 1919 duty per barrel was raised to £3.50 and it reached £5.00 in 1920. Duty paid by Beamish & Crawford rose from £43,217 in 1913 to £151,941 in 1919. These increases were generally passed on to the consumer in the form of price rises, although Beamish & Crawford prices did not increase as much as those of its competitors. The old 2d pint of Cork porter was raised to 3d in December 1914. Murphy's extra stout was raised to 3½d per pint and Beamish to 3d; Guinness was a penny dearer. Murphy's subsequently followed Guinness when it raised the price of a pint of extra stout to 4d in April 1916, but Beamish & Crawford did not increase its prices. By April 1917 Beamish and Murphy's porter was selling at 5d a pint, as was Beamish Extra Stout. Its XXX Stout sold at 6d, the same price as Guinness and Murphy's extra stout.[5]

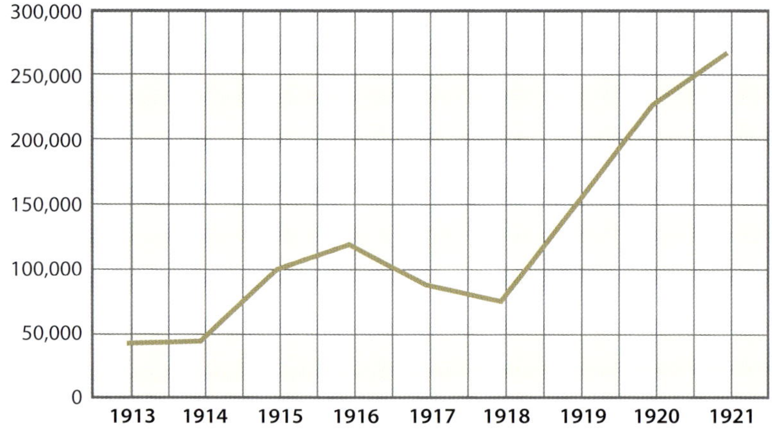

Beer duty (in £s) paid by Beamish & Crawford, 1913–21.

When it came to the question of reducing beer strength, as we shall see, lobbying by Irish brewers, with the aid of Irish nationalist politicians at Westminster, secured special consideration for Irish stout because it had a higher gravity than British beers. In relation to tax, in 1915 they successfully blocked a move to impose a surtax on stronger beers, which would have disproportionately affected Irish producers and customers. Duty on the heaviest beers would have been raised from 7s 9d per barrel to 60s per barrel. As Henry Carter has pointed out, this would have meant the effective prohibition of strong beers, including Irish stout. Irish Parliamentary

Party leader John Redmond told the House of Commons that 'the distinctiveness of Irish stout' was based on its strength; Irish brewers could not brew lighter beers without destroying their product, and in any event, Irish barley was unsuitable for that purpose. The proposed super tax, he warned, would wipe out the Irish brewing industry, with huge economic and social consequences. Redmond, who had been well briefed by an Irish Brewers' Association delegation that included Richard H. Beamish, explained that a large proportion of Irish stout – mainly that brewed by Guinness – was exported to Britain and that this tax increase would cripple that trade. He stressed that he was not speaking just for the Irish brewing industry, but for Ireland in general.[6] The nationalist MP for Cork, William O'Brien (of the All-For-Ireland League) had already put forward similar arguments, with an added Cork twist and a dash of hyperbole:

William O'Brien (1852–1928), by William Orpen. (Hugh Lane Gallery)

> far from Guinness's stout or Cork stout having any pernicious influence upon the health or morals of the people in the same way as absinthe, I have yet to meet any experienced Irish doctor who will not tell you there is no more wholesome, healthy, or fortifying medicine that can be prescribed for delicate people or hard workers, and it is that reputation of Irish stout that has been earned by those very qualities of strength which the Chancellor to-night proposes to penalise in order to satisfy a lot of self-righteous prohibitionists opposite, without daring to deprive the English working men of the particular class of beer of a lighter quality which conforms with their tastes and habits.

As well as the huge unemployment that would result from the impact on the Irish brewing industry, O'Brien highlighted the impact on County Cork's extensive barley-growing regions, which would be reduced to 'a wilderness'. With reference to Beamish and Murphy's (as well as the Midleton Distillery), he concluded his appeal: 'I am not exaggerating when I say that if the Chancellor of the Exchequer, by his surtax, succeeds in annihilating those two great manufactures in Cork, the result will be as appalling as if that city were bombarded and sacked by the Germans.'[7] Protest meetings were held across Ireland in May 1915 and the demonstration in Cork was addressed by Arthur Frederick Sharman Crawford, who warned of the danger posed to the Irish drinks industry, which in Cork alone employed some 5,000 people.[8]

A view of Clarke's Bridge and part of the Beamish & Crawford brewery complex that incorporated the former Hanover Street glassworks cone, drawn in 1844 by William Roe. The glassworks cone was demolished in 1915. (Cork Public Museum)

'Tho' grumblers would be heard': reduced output and strength

The next challenge for Irish brewers and their political champions came with the government's decision to reduce the output of breweries and the strength of beer. These moves were prompted by the success of the German U-boat campaign against British shipping and the need to reduce dependence on imported raw materials, as well as redirecting cereal consumption towards food needs. A new act in 1916 restricted output to 85 per cent of that of the previous year; in April 1917 breweries were required to reduce output even further to one-third of the 1915–16 levels (or 28 per cent of the pre-war level). These restrictions on output placed pressure on Beamish & Crawford to keep its customers supplied, especially given the strong demand in a countryside experiencing a surge in incomes due to the impetus of the war and the strong military canteen trade in the highly militarised county of Cork.

Lobbying for exemptions began immediately. Richard H. Beamish was back and forth to London negotiating improved conditions with civil servants and politicians. One such trip was on Monday, 24 April 1916, the day the Easter Rising began in Dublin; a diary entry noted that 'Mr R H Beamish left for London – 12.45 – Held up at Maryborough [Portlaoise] (owing to Rebellion in Dublin which broke out today) – proceeded to Waterford next morning & got steamer to Fishguard'.[9] Maurice Healy, MP for Cork, and John Redmond were amongst those making representations on behalf of Beamish and the Irish brewing industry. Richard met with such high-level figures as Walter Runciman, president of the Board of Trade, and Ernest G. Pretyman, the board's parliamentary secretary. The primary concern was to change the benchmark date for the calculation of reductions and Beamish was initially successful in this, securing permission to brew an extra 8,800 standard barrels specifically for the military canteens as a result. His attempt to have this exemption rolled on the following year was resisted by the Board of Trade, but the issue became less pressing when the severe restrictions introduced in April 1917 were eased in the second half of the year to allow an output of two-thirds of the 1915–16 figure.[10] The shortage of beer was believed to have contributed to industrial unrest in Britain in the summer of 1917, leading the government to change tack and focus on the reduction in gravities instead as a way to limit cereal consumption by brewers while increasing the availability of beer to customers.[11]

This new restriction raised the particular problem of the higher gravities of Irish stout and porter compared to British beers. In a joint letter to the Food Controller in July 1917, Beamish and Murphy's explained that the strength of Irish stouts had always been higher than that of British ales, 'partly owing to the fact that the Irish consumers, especially the working classes, are accustomed to supplement their sustenance by means of Stout'.[12] The average gravity of medium-strength Irish stout was 1066°, extra strong stout was 1075° and the weaker porter was 1050°, close to the average of 1052° for British beers. When the government announced that all breweries had to reduce their average gravity to 1036°, there was uproar from the Irish industry. Beamish & Crawford joined Murphy's, Guinness and the other two dozen or so smaller breweries in Ireland in demanding modifications for Ireland because the reductions were disproportionate.[13] Beamish & Crawford and Murphy's felt that a transition to 1050° could be accomplished 'without causing too much friction throughout the country ... At the present moment there undoubtedly exists a dangerous feeling here, that our Irish commodity is to be sacrificed to the English Brewing Trade'. In response to the intensive lobbying the rate was raised to 1042° for all, but in March 1918 a drastic reduction to 1030° was announced. Beamish argued that the lowest possible gravity that could be contemplated by them was 1047°: 'If this standard, tho' perilously low, was fixed and the present output maintained,' he wrote to the authorities, '... you need not anticipate any serious disturbance; tho' grumblers would be heard as regards weakness of gravity.'[14]

A higher permitted gravity of 1045° for Irish brewers and beer destined for military canteens was as far as the government would go. In order to maintain stout at some level of acceptable strength, Irish brewers weakened porter so that extra stout now stood at 1049°, compared to 1066° before the war, and porter at 1036°, down from 1050° (gravity reductions were averaged across a brewery's total output). Extra stout was now weaker than porter had been before 1917.

Output control was lifted in July 1919, but an average permitted gravity, at a slightly higher level, remained in force: 1044° for Great Britain and 1051° for Ireland. When restrictions in gravity were eventually lifted in 1921, the huge increase in tax meant that there was no return to the old gravities, as it would have been uneconomical; and at any rate, by this stage customers had become accustomed to the weaker product.

'A loyal and charitable firm'

Cork's position as one of the most important harbours in the British empire, its high concentration of troops and its role as a staging post meant that the city was immediately drawn into the war declared by Britain on 4 August 1914. Within forty-eight hours, the first detachments of army reservists were boarding trains at Glanmire railway station, off to join their units. Victoria Barracks on the city's north side was the headquarters of the British army garrison, the administrative centre of the army recruitment drive, and a temporary base for the tens of thousands of soldiers from across Ireland who would pass through Cork en route to war. Between 1914 and 1918 almost 12,000 men from County Cork joined the British army (one-sixth of whom perished), over half from the city and environs. This meant that at least one in every seven families in the city had a member fighting in the war. Economic factors, especially the dependants' allowance pay or Separation Allowance, encouraged a large number of the recruits, men from the impoverished working-class districts, to join. Middle- and upper-class ladies, Protestant and Catholic, played their part by organising a plethora of committees, appeals and collections in support of the war effort. Belgian refugees were welcomed to Cork in the early months of the war, while convalescing soldiers were visited and entertained. The Soldiers and Sailors Refreshment Committee ran a buffet at Glanmire Station that catered to the many combatants who passed through in both directions in the war years.

Beamish & Crawford, like the rest of Cork, was immediately involved in the 'total war'. The company, along with its directors in an individual capacity, was a major subscriber to the war-related funds and charities, such as the Prince of Wales' National Relief Fund, the Committee for Belgian Refugee Women and Children, the Soldiers and Sailors Refreshment Committee, the Red Cross Fund and the Milk Fund. The company also subscribed to the pro-war Irish National Volunteers, including its rifle fund. Enlistment of employees was encouraged and facilitated. Along with other Cork employers, Beamish & Crawford, 'recognising that our very existence as a free people depends upon our success in this War', publicly undertook, 'as far as is possible', to 'reinstate at its conclusion those men in our employment who volunteer for service at the front'. Lieutenant General Sir Lawrence Parsons, a veteran British army officer who had previously commanded the 6th Division in Cork, came out of retirement at the outbreak of war to command the newly created 16th Irish Division. He spoke to employees at the brewery in November 1914 as part of the recruitment drive for the new Irish Division.[15] There are no surviving statistics of the numbers of employees who enlisted, just occasional references to individuals, with notes regarding 'looking after his wife'. At least one Cork Porter Brewery employee was killed in action with the British Army: Lance Corporal Michael Punch of the Munster Fusiliers, who had joined in September 1914 and was killed in January 1916. Private J.J. Murphy of the South Irish Horse, another former employee, was listed as a prisoner of war in Germany in March 1918.[16]

In the last year of the war Beamish & Crawford agreed to take on eight ex-soldiers at the request of the Military Labour Exchange.[17] However, it was their refusal to reappoint a former employee who had joined the army that attracted public attention, not least because of the man's religion. It seems Mathew Buckley was the only member of the Cork Porter Brewery office staff who joined up – he also happened to be one of the only Catholics employed in that section. According to his father, there were several Protestants of military age in the office who preferred to mind 'their fat jobs'. Buckley was wounded in 1916 and again in 1917 and was militarily discharged. When he applied for his old position at the brewery, he was refused, prompting a public exchange in the *Cork Examiner* between his father and the firm in 1918, during which D.P. Buckley accused Beamish & Crawford of deliberately holding on to young (Protestant) men of military age while dispensing with the services of older staff. The firm claimed that Buckley's work was unsatisfactory before his departure, which was why they refused to re-employ him; it also pointed out, in the context of

Left: British army recruiting rally on St Patrick's Street, 1914. The recruiting office was located next to the Beamish & Crawford public house. (*Irish Examiner*). Right: Former Beamish & Crawford employee Michael Punch, who was killed serving with the British army, 9 January 1916.

the sectarian insinuations of Buckley senior, that a Catholic clerk had been employed to replace his son. Having the final word, D.P. Buckley asked why his son had never been reprimanded during his five years with the firm and no complaints made about him:

> would it be too much to expect from such a loyal and charitable firm that they would say to this young man on his return to civil life, after fighting and bleeding for his King and country, and for the protection of firms like Messrs. Beamish and Crawford Ltd …: 'Young man, you were careless in your work before you joined the army. We recognise what you have done. Go back to your work, and for the future if we have any fault to find, out you go.' Why, even the most contemptible Hun would even do more justice than this.

He pointed out that his son's replacement was a Catholic already in the employment of the firm and that the next vacancy filled was by a non-Catholic from another firm. He concluded by asking Beamish & Crawford to state how many Catholic clerks they employed 'who are better paid than their draymen?'. No answer was forthcoming.[18] The firm not only felt compelled to answer Buckley's charges in the press, but also wrote to both the Recruiting Office in Dublin and the section of the War Office in London responsible for Irish recruitment on the matter, while Richard H. Beamish called to the latter on a trip to London to lay the 'true facts' of the matter before its director, Colonel McLean.[19]

'Suppliers of Stout to His Majesty's Forces': military canteens and restrictions on trade

The brewery's strong trade with the military canteens was another direct link to the conflict. Beamish supplied over thirty canteens in the following barracks and camps in County Cork: two in Cork Barracks; two in Ballincollig; Kilworth Camp; two in Moorepark near Fermoy; the Old and New Barracks in Fermoy; Spike Island; Crosshaven; Fort Camden and Fort Templebreedy near Crosshaven; Fort Carlisle; two in Kinsale and another in Charles Fort; Aghada; two in Queenstown (Cobh); Youghal; two in Bandon; two in Ballyvonare (Buttevant); Mallow; Ballyhooly; Haulbowline, and three in Bere Island. The brewery also supplied military canteens in Limerick, Tralee and two in Tipperary.[20] There was fierce competition between the breweries for this lucrative trade. Murphy's campaigned relentlessly for a portion of the stout trade in canteens supplied by Beamish & Crawford; the canteen at Victoria Barracks was a particular target. The 4th Munsters in Fermoy

Double Stout label, used 1914–21. (Courtesy Ed Hinchy)

Trade directory advertisement, 1919. (*Cork Chamber of Commerce, Cork Commercial Handbook* (Cork, 1919))

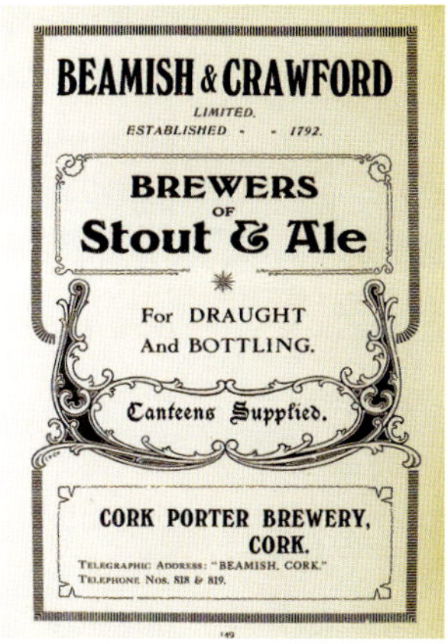

agreed to take Murphy's stout in October 1915, and in February 1916 an agreement was struck for joint supply to Buttevant between Beamish & Crawford and Murphy's. The following month Murphy's gained their main prize when Victoria Barracks agreed to a joint supply from the two Cork breweries, thus breaking the long-standing Beamish & Crawford monopoly.[21] When restrictions on output were introduced in 1917, surveillance increased and the brewery had to supply the Army Canteens Committee with detailed breakdowns of its supplies to the military. The significance of the canteen trade can be seen in Table 11.1.

Table 11.1 **Beamish & Crawford total sales (in barrels), 1913–18**

YEAR	CANTEEN	TOWN	COUNTRY	AGENTS	EXPORTS	TOTAL
1913–14	2,804	17,419	24,645	74,210	442	119,520
1914–15	15,558	15,514	21,748	65,514	324	118,658
1915–16	13,728	14,803	20,198	59,648	139	108,516
1916–17	10,183	12,470	14,504	43,377	78	80,612
1917–18 (46 weeks)	12,490	5,871	8,126	22,587	0	49,074

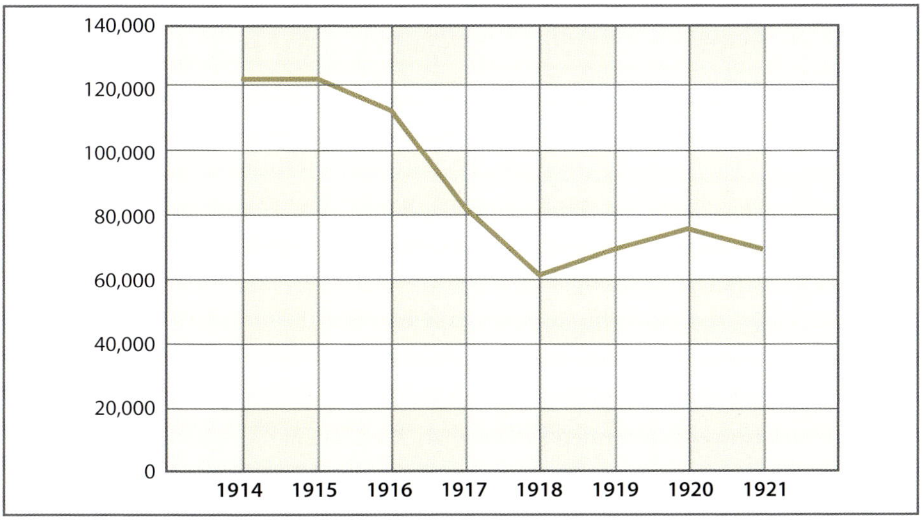

Beamish & Crawford, total output (in barrels), 1914–21.

The importance of canteens was not related to the increased number of soldier-customers alone. The Intoxicating Liquor (Temporary Restrictions) Act 1914 allowed magistrates, on application of the police, to restrict the opening hours of licensed premises. Added to this were emergency powers given to the military authorities under the Defence of the Realm Act, which led to a general reduction of trading hours for public houses in districts with a military presence and special extra restrictions relating to military personnel. In Cork city in October 1914, the police had applied to the courts for an order to close pubs at 8.00pm instead of 11.00pm owing to the large number of soldiers in the city as well as soldiers' wives, who were now in receipt of the separation allowance 'and are open to temptation, and in that way brought disaster to their families while their husbands were away'. There was a noticeable increase in public drunkenness by soldiers, according to the police.

The city magistrates felt there was no need at that time to impose early closing. Magistrates in Passage, Blarney and Ballincollig also refused. The military authorities, however, issued their own warning in the autumn of 1914 to publicans not to serve soldiers or those suspected of acquiring drink for them; publicans were also warned against permitting soldiers' wives to remain 'for an unreasonable time' on their premises. A year later the issue remained live, and Cork magistrates requested the police to warn publicans when soldiers' wives were found drinking on their premises and asked publicans to discourage these women staying 'for hours at a time'. The magistrates also called for the military authorities to extend their ban on serving soldiers to theatres and 'other places of amusement'. In September 1916 the military authorities in Cork negotiated with the publicans to ease their ban and allow soldiers to frequent pubs at specified times under strict conditions.[22]

In various towns in the Beamish & Crawford catchment area, closing orders were issued by the courts and the military. Pubs in Fermoy had to close at 8.00pm and could not serve soldiers; in Buttevant, the initial closing time of 9.00pm was brought back to 8.00pm in November 1914, while no soldier could be served before 5.00pm; in Mallow in December 1914, the military ordered the closure of all pubs at 8.00pm on weekdays and all day on Sundays; pubs in Kinsale, like Cork, were prevented from serving soldiers at all.[23] A major gripe of the licensed trade was that on the one hand, these restrictions led to illicit drinking by soldiers in shebeens and other private premises, and on the other, the military canteens remained open and subject to far less control. The latter fact was a boon to Beamish & Crawford, which supplied many of these canteens, and this trade helped offset the losses in public house custom. In 1913–14, the canteens accounted for less than 2.5 per cent of sales; in 1914–15 they accounted for almost 12.5 per cent.

'Everyone must suffer during the War': workers and wages

The Irish labour movement underwent a transformation from 1916. The state's need for industrial peace led to a new industrial relations context: mandatory arbitration was introduced, forcing employers to negotiate with workers rather than locking them out or holding the line against threatened strikes. This provided added momentum to a trade union movement whose bargaining power was reinforced by wartime manpower shortages. The membership and militancy of all unions increased rapidly. By the war's end, the main Irish union, the Irish Transport & General Workers' Union (ITGWU), had increased its membership twentyfold – from *c.* 5,000 in 1916 to over 100,000 in 1919. The Irish Trade Union Congress more than doubled in strength during the war years, emerging a quarter of a million strong. Workers in the Cork Porter Brewery and the city's other brewing concern at Lady's Well Brewery, as well as in their respective maltings, joined in the country- and city-wide drive for improved wages to keep pace with spiralling inflation, especially in the price of basic foodstuffs. Consumer prices more than doubled during the war, and in mid-1916 the Cork Coopers' Society was declaring that its members were finding it difficult 'to keep our homes together'. The police reported a year later that the 'abnormal prices of foodstuffs make it difficult for workers and their families to maintain themselves on their wages'.[24]

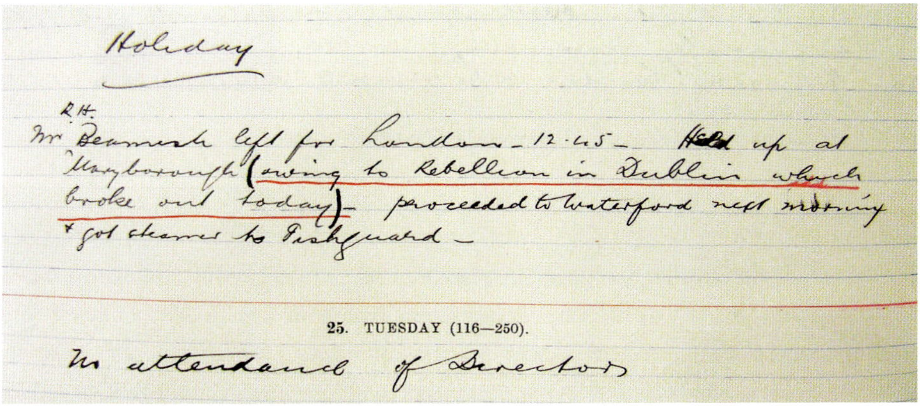
Holiday

R.H.
Mr Beamish left for London - 12.45 - ~~Held~~ up at Maryborough (owing to Rebellion in Dublin which broke out today) - proceeded to Waterford next morning & got steamer to Fishguard -

25. TUESDAY (116—250).

No attendance of Directors

Note in directors' minute book for Monday, 24 April 1916. Richard Henrik Beamish was forced to change his travel plans 'owing to Rebellion in Dublin which broke out today'. (CCCA/Authors)

Beamish & Crawford initially resisted its workers' demands. When the coopers applied for a 6s increase on their weekly wages of 39s in July 1916, the brewery informed them rather grandly, 'Everyone must suffer during the War – Employees have no doubt to contend with the increased cost of living, but Employers have to bear enormously increased taxation of all sorts and curtailment of trade.' While there was clearly no equivalence between what hard-pressed workers and well-off employers had to 'suffer', prospects seemed particularly grim for brewers in 1916, with a reasonable expectation that they would disimprove. The duty paid by Beamish & Crawford had risen from £45,170 in 1914 to £100,334 in 1915 and £120,329 in 1916. Net profits, which had increased from £35,611 in 1914 to £48,699 the following year, dropped alarmingly to £39,816 in 1916. Severe output restrictions were imminent, while barley prices rose due to farmers holding back awaiting higher prices, a situation exacerbated by the entry of British maltsters into the Irish market. Coal prices were also up.[25]

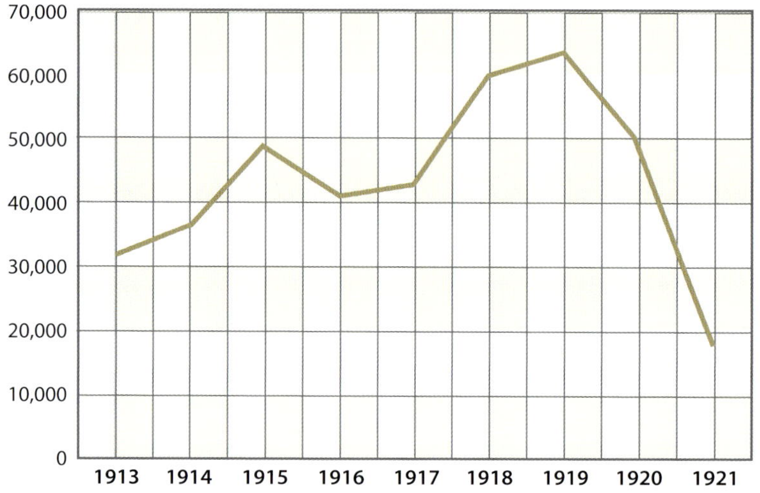

Beamish & Crawford, net profits (in £s), 1913–21 (before dividend and interest payments).

The general brewery workers, who were organised in the Cork Brewery Workmen's Society, had already been refused a wage increase in 1916, but following Cork Corporation's decision to increase its labourers' pay from 21s to 22s per week, the brewery followed suit in May, increasing that of boys by 6d to 10s per week. In June this pay rise (or 'war bonus') was granted to all employees, with the exception of tradesmen (carpenters, masons, plasterers and painters). In August the coopers were granted a 3s per week increase (half of their demand) on the understanding that it was an exceptional war bonus that would terminate with the war; as inflation continued to rise, however, these increasing bonuses were incorporated into basic wage rates. In September 1916 a bonus of 10 per cent was given to those who had not had their wages increased. Pressure from the unions remained constant, and Beamish & Crawford and Murphy's continued to yield reluctantly in most cases. In October labourers, watchmen and carmen received a further 3s per week and maltsters also received an increase; the downside was that allowances, mainly in the form of free beer, were discontinued. The following month the coopers won another 2s per week. In August 1917 all workers received a further 2s weekly bonus. In March 1918 the city's two breweries granted the coopers a further 5s increase (they had demanded 15s), bringing their weekly rate to 52s, and they won increased pay for their apprentices the following month. In June 1918 Beamish & Crawford, along

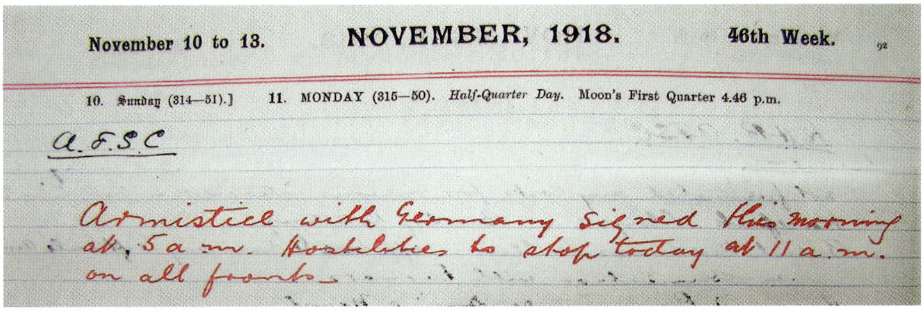
November 10 to 13. NOVEMBER, 1918. 46th Week.

10. Sunday (314—51).] 11. MONDAY (315—50). *Half-Quarter Day.* Moon's First Quarter 4.46 p.m.

A.F.S.C

Armistice with Germany signed this morning at 5 a.m. Hostilities to stop today at 11 a.m. on all fronts.

The cessation of hostilities, marking the end of the 'Great War', following the signing of the armistice on 11 November 1918 is noted in the directors' minute book. (CCCA/Authors)

with the other employers in the city, gave a 12½ per cent increase to engineers, and in July the two breweries agreed to a further 5s to their general workforces, bringing labourers' weekly pay to £2 (double the pre-war rate) and that of coopers to £3. By August maltsters were receiving 50s, double their wages in mid-1915.

The war ended in November 1918, but the unions maintained pressure for better pay and conditions, culminating in a disastrous five-week strike in 1920. As mentioned above, duty continued to rise and the old gravities were not restored. The shift to lower consumption levels continued, and while the industry in Britain at least returned to some form of post-war normality, Ireland was on the brink of its own home-grown wars.

Elections and strikes

In April 1918 the British government made the fateful decision to extend conscription to Ireland, provoking unprecedented opposition in nationalist Ireland. A combination of the old nationalist Irish Party, the newly emergent Sinn Féin and the increasingly powerful labour movement, with the crucial support of the Catholic Church, defeated the measure. The workers at Beamish & Crawford were amongst those who took part in the general strike of 24 April 1918, joining the tens of thousands of workers who took to the streets and signed the anti-conscription pledge. At a meeting of the Cork Technical Education Committee, Sharman Crawford sounded a dissonant note when he praised the bravery of Corkmen in the British army and believed 'their men at the front' should be supported; fellow committee member Canon A.J. Nicholson went further in explicitly supporting conscription. Their stance was met with widespread anger, with the Cork Trades Council calling on the corporation to expel them (along with two Cork Harbour Commissioners – together, the only four dissenters on the conscription issue on public bodies in the city) from all public boards. The councillors eventually demurred, with one declaring that they did not want to be 'as intolerant and as big bigots as they were in Belfast'.[26]

The leading role of Sinn Féin in the campaign against conscription helped to accelerate its growing popularity in the lead-up to the December 1918 general election. Prior to the election, on 2 November, Richard Henrik Beamish, North Ludlow Axel Beamish, Arthur Frederick Sharman Crawford and hundreds of other commercially minded 'Citizens, Merchants and Traders of the City of Cork' published 'Some Suggestions for Ireland's Future Settlement' in the *Cork Examiner*. This reiterated the mild home rule approach of the 'Irish Convention' of 1917–18 (an attempted British solution to the Irish problem, boycotted by Sinn Féin and hard-line unionists) and suggested the granting of a financial package from Britain for Irish development purposes. Such 'moderate' proposals found few takers, and in the election the following month it was hard-line unionists and the Irish Party that lined up against Sinn Féin's candidates J.J. Walsh and Liam de Róiste, standing on a ticket of complete separation from Britain. Sinn Féin comfortably won the two city seats and swept the boards across Ireland with the exception of the northeast, winning seventy-three of the 105 seats in a 'first-past-the-post' electoral system. Sinn Féin, as promised in its manifesto, established an Irish parliament, Dáil Éireann, in Dublin in January 1919 and declared Irish independence to the world. Attempts to secure international recognition for the Irish Republic fell on deaf ears and the British government refused to recognise the Irish right to self-determination. The Dáil was outlawed, as were most other manifestations of advanced Irish nationalism. 'The Republic' went underground, the Irish Volunteers became the Irish Republican Army (IRA) and a war of independence ensued, developing in earnest from the summer of 1920.

In January 1920 municipal elections were held under a system of proportional representation in the hope that the Sinn Féin sweep of 1918 would not be repeated. This was partly successful, but the republican party, in alliance with the ITGWU in many areas, including Cork city, still emerged as the largest party. Richard Henrik Beamish, who had sat on Cork Corporation since 1911, stood in the January 1920 election as a 'Commercial' candidate and topped the poll in the centre ward. He was re-elected to the chair of the Public Works Committee in the new republican corporation where the majority of seats were held by Sinn Féin/ITGWU aldermen and councillors, but the proportional representation system had ensured a variety of voices and perspectives. Sinn Féin's Tomás MacCurtain was elected Lord Mayor at the corporation's first meeting on 30 January. Only one other name was put forward – that of Richard Henrik Beamish; he was proposed without his prior knowledge by the veteran unionist councillor Sir John Scott in a less than serious gesture. Beamish, according to press reports, 'responded indignant that he had not his permission, and if Sir John kept order, the Council would be thankful to him'.

Beamish was a pragmatist who knew a new political order had emerged and he was going to work with it as best he could. When the corporation decided not to appoint a High Sheriff because 'it was a position created by an alien Government' that no 'self-respecting Irishman' could fill, Beamish recorded his disagreement, stating that while he had to bow to 'the will of the majority', he would express his opinion. He said that they were all 'animated with love for their country and anxious for the advancement of the city', and while he was opposed to the decision not to appoint a sheriff, 'the majority were entitled to do as their party decided'. (Sir John Scott was appointed sheriff in April by the lord lieutenant, Lord French.) Beamish said he was 'with' Sinn Féin, however, 'on all matters to develop the city and to secure economic administration'.[27]

Despite disagreeing politically with the republicans, he believed the new corporation, with its emphasis on reform and transparency in municipal affairs, was an improvement on its predecessors, dominated by the Irish Party and its adjunct, the Ancient Order of Hibernians, with their record of jobbery. As an alderman in previous corporations, he said he had always spoken out against 'party politics', believing that the corporation 'should work simply and solely for the city and citizens' and not any party interests.[28] Less than two months later, MacCurtain was murdered in his home by a police death squad. Beamish was the honorary treasurer of the memorial fund established for him; both he and Sharman Crawford attended the funeral, along with many of the brewery's workforce. This was one of a number of occasions when the brewery closed in this period; others included the general strike for the release of hunger strikers on 14 April 1920 and the day of mourning for MacCurtain's successor, Terence MacSwiney, on 29 October 1920.

British troops corral a crowd on King (MacCurtain) Street, July 1920. The Beamish & Crawford public house in the background was on the corner of King Street and Bridge Street. (*Irish Examiner*)

Beamish's position as an employer caused him to be targeted, albeit rather harmlessly, by the labour republicans in the corporation in February and March 1920 when a five-week strike occurred that closed down production at both the Cork breweries of Murphy's and Beamish & Crawford. The Cork Brewery Workmen's Society (CBWS), absorbed by the expanding ITGWU later in 1920, had successfully represented the general brewery workers in the city throughout the war period. Now that the war, and with it compulsory arbitration, was over, the possibility of strikes loomed as the cost of living continued to rise and the labour movement nationally was growing in strength and confidence. Wage increases were won in February and March 1919, though the breweries held out on an ongoing demand for a reduction in the working week from fifty to forty-seven hours.[29] The labourers' pre-war wages of 20s now stood at 50s (£2 10s) and in November 1919 they demanded a further £1 per week, a week's paid annual holiday and a reduction in the working week to forty-seven hours, in line with that gained by a number of the trades. Beamish and Murphy's joined forces in resisting the demands. Eventually, in early February 1920, the union threatened an all-out strike. In an open letter to the CBWS, Richard H. Beamish and his equivalent at Murphy's, Charles E. Murphy, claimed that while the cost of living had risen by 125 per cent since the beginning of the war, wages had increased by 150 per cent across that period. Arbitration efforts by a local cleric failed and on 11 February, 300 workers in both breweries went on strike and stopped production.[30] The strikers were supported by the other workers in the breweries and in the wider labour movement. The Cork Trades Council, a representative body of all unions in the city, made a failed attempt to organise arbitration (as did the vintners) and initiated a strike fund that helped the workers to maintain the strike for five weeks.[31]

The second meeting of the new corporation was held two days after the strike began, and when Beamish was nominated for his old position on the Public Works Committee, Alderman Tadhg Barry and fellow labour republicans objected as he was 'at war with his employees, trying to starve them into submission'. However, as nobody was put forward in his stead, Beamish was declared elected. As the strike dragged on into March, Barry again brought the issue into the corporation when he opposed Beamish's election as chair of the Public Works Committee. 'If Alderman Beamish acted as well towards his own employees,' said Barry, 'as towards the streets, and as his services to this city, there would be none of this trouble. He should show the same public spirit towards them.' Barry eventually withdrew his objection under protest and Beamish was unanimously elected chair.[32] A week earlier, two labour representatives on the Technical Instruction Committee objected to the nomination of Arthur Frederick Sharman Crawford to the vice-chairmanship because of the strike. Sharman Crawford offered to withdraw, but he was overruled and elected unanimously following a complimentary speech by Lord Mayor MacCurtain and the eventual withdrawal of the labour protest.[33] In both cases, the labour representatives were indulging in what were effectively gesture politics; in the final reckoning, Sinn Féin held sway, and that party was committed to class harmony and the minimisation of class conflict. On 15 March, the strike ended when the breweries' offer of a 12s 6d increase (the workers had demanded 20s), 6s for 'boys', plus a 47½-hour week (a half hour above the workers' demand) was accepted. Murphy's had convinced Beamish & Crawford of the need to end the strike.[34] Towards the end of the year an annual paid holiday for men employed for over a year was agreed with the ITGWU, which now represented the brewery workers.

The strike had a major impact on the brewery, and not just because it halted production for five weeks. When the local press reported that 'the requirements of the city publicans are being met by the importation of extra quantities from outside sources', it seemed innocuous enough.[35] But the principal 'outside source' was Guinness, which gained a foothold in the city and county it never subsequently relinquished. Guinness was not only sold in free houses, but in tied houses too, as the alternative for the breweries would have been the demise of many of them. When the strike ended and local brewery supplies were restored, many customers, who had developed a serious taste for the Dublin stout, abandoned the tied houses in favour of the pubs that sold Guinness. [36]

Troubles and strife

These problems were exacerbated by the worsening military situation, as Black and Tans and Auxiliaries arrived in the city in the spring and summer of 1920 and the IRA campaign intensified. Curfews were imposed, civilians were harassed and attacked by Crown forces and the general disruption of economic and social life, such as the cessation of fairs and markets in country towns and the difficulty in travelling, hit the trade, as well as placing impossible strain on Richard Beamish and his Public Works Committee. In the second half of 1920 a number of towns in the brewery's catchment area, such as Mallow and Bandon, were subjected to crippling attacks by the British forces, and in December 1920 a large part of Cork city centre was burned by the Crown forces, including a Beamish & Crawford tied house on George's Street. In 1923 the company received £1,176 in compensation for various properties damaged during the troubles.[37]

On 2 August 1920 prominent Cork businessmen and professionals, including Arthur Frederick Sharman Crawford and Richard Henrik Beamish, assembled in the Imperial Hotel. Under the chairmanship of Beamish, who declared the Irish demand for self-government as unwavering, the meeting denounced the recent Government of Ireland Act, under which the British proposed to partition Ireland into two home rule states, and called for dominion status and financial autonomy for a united Ireland within the British empire. The former unionist Beamish had not suddenly become a Home Ruler, having been, along with Sharman Crawford, on the pragmatic wing of Cork unionism, which was willing to countenance some form of self-government during the Home Rule debates before the war and had made similar arguments at the Irish Convention in June 1917.[38] Beamish now optimistically suggested that many Protestants in Ulster were coming around to his way of thinking and asserted that he and his co-religionists in the south had never felt any fear of the Catholic majority. Sharman Crawford backed him up politically, saying 'the time has come when the moderate feeling of Ireland must speak'. He also agreed on the sectarianism issue, saying that in thirty years of living and working in Cork he had experienced 'nothing but courtesy from all creeds and classes of the community'. Both men were selected to take part in a delegation to bring their proposals to the British government. They travelled to London the following day, where they met a high-powered delegation led by Prime Minister Lloyd George, who welcomed the 'moderate' voices but pointed to stumbling blocks – similar to those that arose the following year during the Treaty negotiations – such as Ulster and Irish responsibility for war debt.[39] Days later, the Lord Mayor of Cork, Terence MacSwiney, was arrested at the city hall and sentenced to two years in Brixton prison. He commenced a hunger strike that ended in his death in October. Positions were hardening on both sides and the 'moderate' voices were silenced again.

As the war heated up, Beamish & Crawford was caught in the crossfire, sometimes literally. On the night of 4 August 1920, while Richard Beamish and Sharman Crawford were in London having discussions with Lloyd George, Daniel MacSweeney from Rosscarbery was aboard a Beamish & Crawford 'lighter' barge that was berthed at Albert Quay in the city. He went on deck to slacken the rope before he went to bed when two shots were fired on the other side of the river. One of the bullets ricocheted and hit him just below the heart. In what the *Cork Examiner* rightly described as 'a marvellous escape', the bullet hit two pennies in the breast pocket of MacSweeney's waistcoat (see opposite). The fortunate boatman, who escaped with a bruise, told a journalist that he taken the two pennies from his trousers pocket that morning to buy a newspaper on Patrick's Street but could not get the newsboy's attention, so hurried on, slipping the pennies into his waistcoat, saving his life in the process. According to the newspaper, the depth of the indentations in both pennies meant that if only one coin, not to mention none, had been present, MacSweeney would almost certainly have lost his life.[40]

On Thursday, 20 January 1921, following the shooting of two policemen by the IRA on Washington Street not far from the brewery the previous Saturday and shooting incidents afterwards, the British military cordoned off a large part of the western side of the city, including Beamish & Crawford. Buildings were raided and

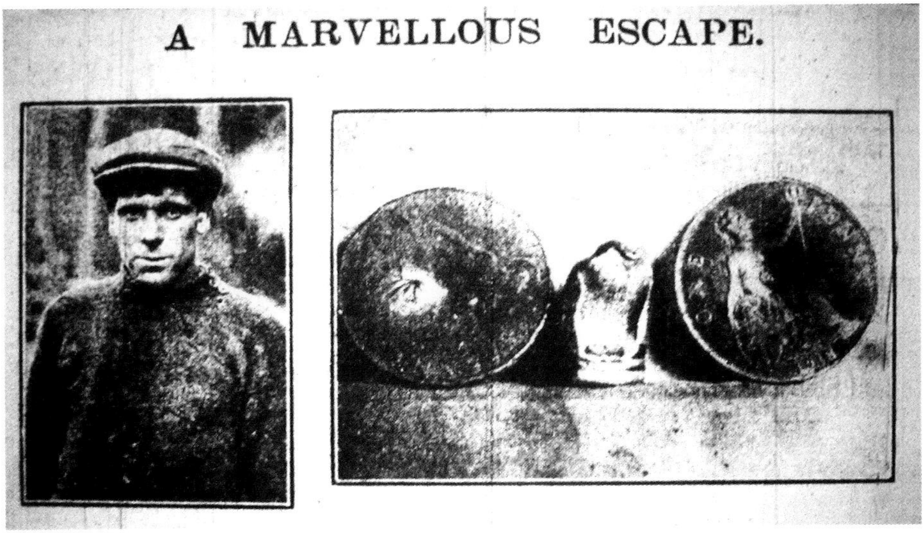

Cork Examiner, 5 August 1920. Beamish & Crawford boatman Daniel MacSweeney and the pennies that saved his life. (*Irish Examiner*)

several houses were deliberately blown up in 'official reprisals'. In a search of the brewery the military claimed they found arms and ammunition, leading to the arrest of Arthur Frederick Sharman Crawford, the brewery foreman, Mansfield, and its secretary, Frederick Le Flufy. Sharman Crawford was released the same night but Le Flufy was detained and charged before a court-martial with having an automatic pistol and thirteen rounds of ammunition in the company safe. He admitted the charge, saying he had the gun for the protection of himself and his family, was convicted, fined £10 and released. Mansfield was charged with storing two disused grenades he had got from his son in the company safe.[41] In Bandon at the end of March 1921 the Beamish & Crawford plant was closed by the military as part of a general shutdown of the town. Early in 1922 that plant was closed by a long strike, and Murphy's moved quickly to supply Beamish & Crawford customers in the area with the aim of keeping Guinness out.[42] Beamish & Crawford products were kept out of another west Cork town, Dunmanway, for a year and a half from November 1921 following the company's sacking of a local employee, who happened to be the branch secretary of the ITGWU. The boycott continued until April 1923, when, following the intervention of local publicans, the company agreed to pay the man compensation.[43]

The disruption caused by the military conflict, together with the long-term impact of the 1920 strike and the ensuing drift to Guinness, had a major impact on profits. Net profit spiked to £63,692 in the post-war 'boom' of 1919 but fell to £48,028 in 1920 and collapsed to £16,139 in 1921. A truce was agreed between the British and the IRA/Dáil in July 1921, and in October of that year the tenants of the two Cork breweries came together to form the Cork Tied House & Retail Vintners Association (CTHRVA) to rally local support for local stout over Guinness, but also to campaign for lower rents, fixity of tenure and, ultimately, the abolition of the tied-house system, which it decried as 'the last remnants of real old landlord tyranny'.[44]

The trade had been in crisis since the strike of February–March 1920 and Murphy's tied tenant, William O'Connell, emerged as a radical and articulate advocate, and a thorny customer for the breweries, which up to that point had had a cosy relationship with the local, pliant Vintners' Association. In September 1921 a Kinsale tied tenant of Beamish & Crawford's was jailed for two months for contempt of court having ignored a court order compelling him to sell only Beamish stout and porter. Following his release, he was introduced grandiosely to a public meeting in Cork as 'a hero of our trade' who went to jail 'for our cause'. O'Connell later complained that there was no mention of the 'hero' in newspaper reports of the meeting because 'it might have insulted the high and mighty brewer that landed him in prison – a gentleman who now has the cheek of asking people to return him as a Parliamentary representative'.[45]

The 'high and mighty brewer', Richard Henrik Beamish, was about to enter the national political fray. The Treaty signed in London in December 1921 was endorsed by a small majority of Sinn Féin TDs in January 1922, leading to a split in the republican movement, both politically and militarily. The result of the general election of June 1922, in which Richard Henrik Beamish had been a candidate, was interpreted by pro-Treatyites as a popular endorsement of the Treaty and opened the way for the start of the civil war.

The Counting House, 1928. (Courtesy Ed Hinchy)

The Counting House, 1919

Brewery sales in 1918, the last year of the war, were 59,326 barrels – less than half the figure for 1914, when war broke out. Despite the declining sales, however, annual net profits averaged £45,236 during the war years as against an annual average of £34,617 in the five years prior to war. Trade had halved and duties had soared, but increased profits were still made. A period of optimism, albeit short-lived, followed the end of the war and brewery management undertook a number of initiatives to bolster trade and improve the image and reputation of the firm.

In 1918 the architectural firm of Chillingworth & Levie in Cork was engaged to draw up designs for two of the firm's public houses, on Albert Street and South Main Street. These were to be managed houses rather than tied houses let to tenants. The brewery planned to employ managers to run each of the new pubs, directly

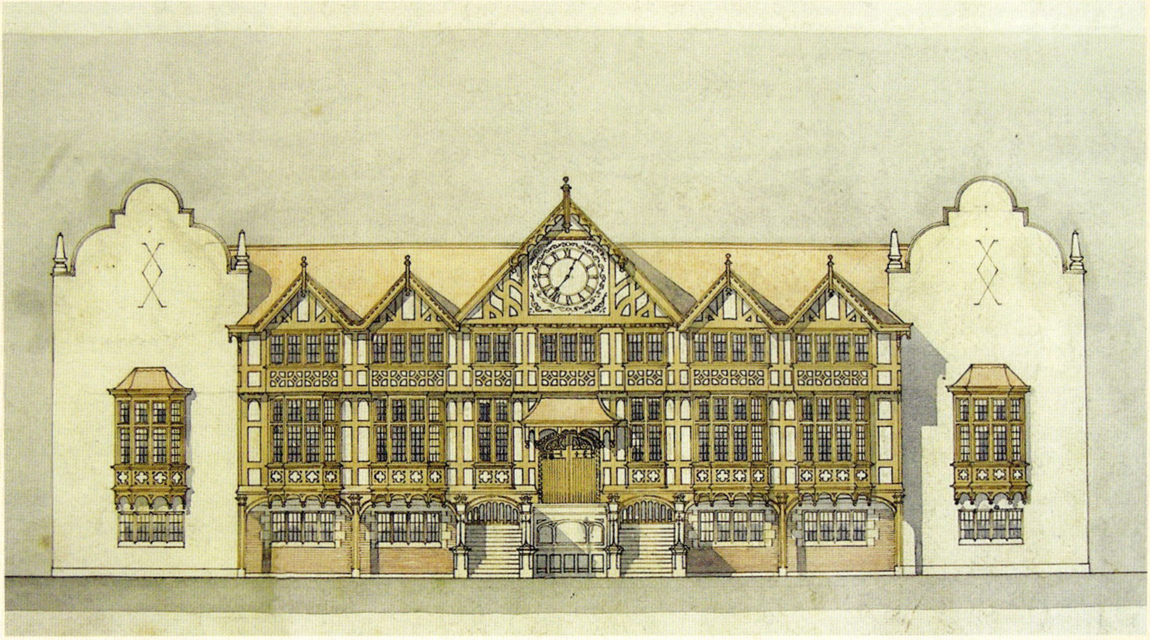

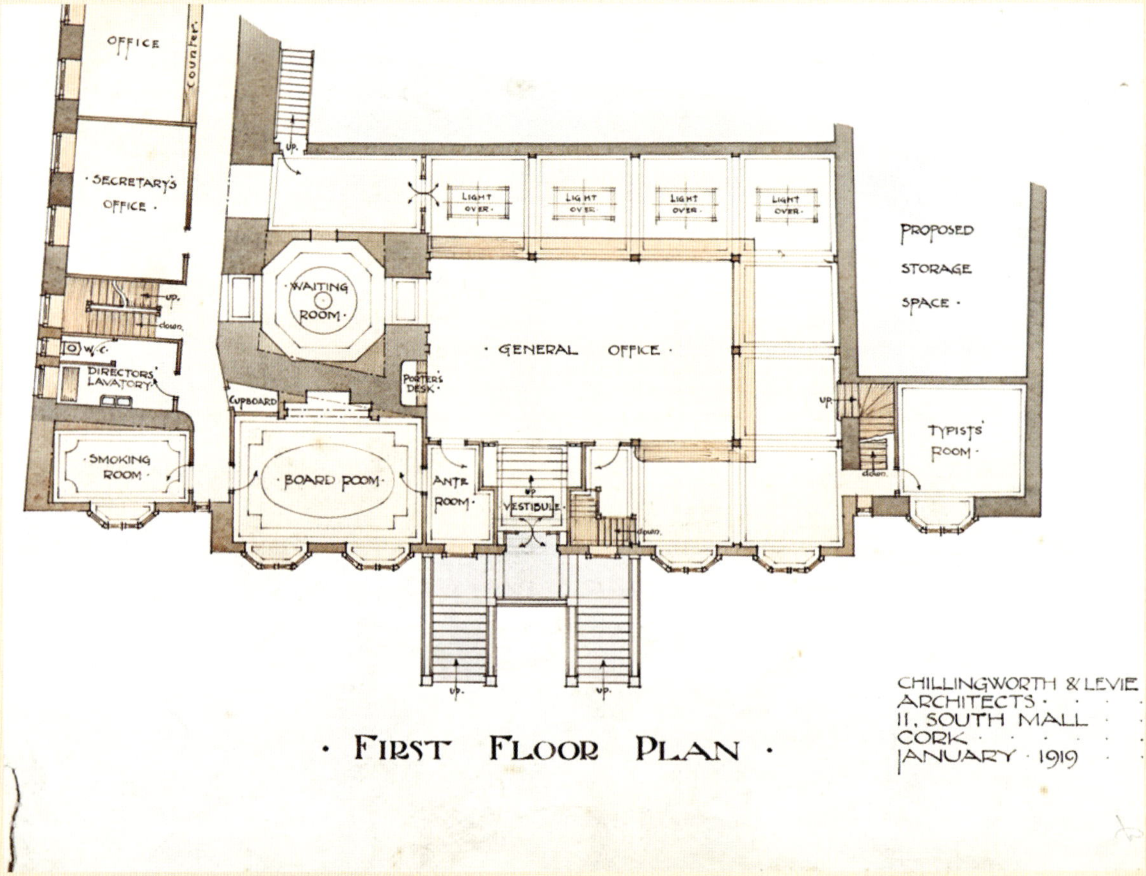
OFFICE
Counter
SECRETARY'S OFFICE
up
down
W.C.
DIRECTORS' LAVATORY
CUPBOARD
SMOKING ROOM
WAITING ROOM
PORTER'S DESK
BOARD ROOM
ANTE ROOM
VESTIBULE
down
LIGHT OVER
LIGHT OVER
LIGHT OVER
LIGHT OVER
GENERAL OFFICE
PROPOSED STORAGE SPACE
up
down
TYPISTS' ROOM
up
up
· FIRST FLOOR PLAN ·
CHILLINGWORTH & LEVIE
ARCHITECTS
11, SOUTH MALL
CORK
JANUARY 1919

answerable to brewery management, in an effort to present the firm's products to consumers in the best condition and in comfortable surroundings. At that time Chillingworth & Levie was the most prestigious architectural firm in the city and had grown its reputation since its foundation in 1911. The result of the initiative was the Oval Bar on South Main Street, opposite the brewery, and No. 1 Albert Street, now The Sextant. Architecture historian Louise Harrington describes the Oval Bar:

> Again preserving a historic style used in the Edwardian era, the Scots Baronial-style of the elevation may be seen in the uneven roofline, crow-stepped chimney gable, corner turret and tripartite windows with block surrounds – probable references to Daniel Levie's Scottish origins.[46]

Today, nearly a century after it was built, the Oval Bar is still regarded as one of the most attractive public houses in Cork. No. 1 Albert Street was also lavished with Chillingworth & Levie creativity, but many of the original 1918 features of the building have not survived.

Given the success of the public house designs, Chillingworth & Levie was also engaged in 1919 to draw up plans for a new brewery office building. Up to that time much of the brewery was hidden from view from South Main Street, but the acquisition and demolition of a series of three-storied premises opened the less-than-attractive industrial buildings to view. The design of the new office buildings was to be of a scale to hide the unattractive appearance of the brewery buildings behind it and to present to the street and the city an attractive façade that spoke of the heritage and solidity of the firm. The provision of a public foyer, boardroom and offices fit for a twentieth-century company intent on success was, of course, also a priority.

Such is the visual impact of the Counting House, as the building was called, that to many it *is* the brewery, the viewer being virtually unaware of the range of other buildings on the brewery complex. One writer observes, 'The unapologetically revivalist design of the brewery … could be a merchants' meeting hall in a medieval English town, such is its use of Tudor detail in the main façade that is flanked by Flemish-style staggered gables.'[47] Louise Harrington writes:

> With a nod to the Edwardian era ended by World War I, the 1919 design features attractive half-timbering, jettied first and second floors in the Tudor Revival style, flanked by crow-stepped gables with Tudor-style windows and hood mouldings … While arguably a façade in its extent, the Counting House

---

Facing page, from top: Proposed layout for the first floor of the Counting House, 1919. (CCCA/Dori O'Connell)
Preliminary drawings by Chillingworth & Levie for the Beamish & Crawford Counting House, 1919. (CCCA/Dori O'Connell)

From top: The foyer of the Counting House shortly after its completion, 1921. (Courtesy Mike Hannon)
The boardroom in the Counting House, 1921. (Courtesy Mike Hannon)

Left: The boardroom in the Counting House, Christmas 2008. (John Sheehan)
Right: The boardroom fireplace. Note the decorated 'marriage stone', dated 1602, used as a lintel. (John Sheehan)

> nonetheless forms an important part of the architectural legacy of the Beamish & Crawford families to the city ...[48]

As noted by Harrington, the Counting House, while impressive in size and appearance, is quite a shallow building. The large public foyer inside the main doors is a two-storeyed space lit by roof lights, with a first-floor balcony giving access to a gallery of offices. The boardroom and other interiors have dark timber-panelled walls, and the style of the façade is also carried through to the design of the boardroom fireplace, stairway and other interior details.

The surviving Chillingworth drawings of the Counting House façade were working drawings and differ somewhat form the finished building. In the drawings, the gables at either end of the façade are rounded rather than stepped and the windows of the gables are very different to those in the finished building. The drawings also show two pointed pediments above the windows on either side of the large central triangular pediment, which are missing from the finished building.

12

The Beamish & Crawford Tied-House Estate

A tied house is a public house that is obliged to trade exclusively with one brewery. The custom has been common in Britain for nearly two centuries, where breweries and other companies have built up large estates of tied public houses. In Ireland the custom was less common but became a distinct feature of the licensed trade in the city and county of Cork, especially from the mid-1800s, and by the early 1900s over 90 per cent of public houses in the region were tied to a brewery for exclusive trading. The practice survived until the 1970s, when the two remaining Cork breweries of Beamish & Crawford Ltd and James J. Murphy & Co. Ltd began selling off their tied houses. The last sales were completed in the early 1980s.

A public house became tied for a variety of reasons: the house was built or owned by the brewery and let to a tenant; a publican in an independent public house became indebted to a brewery and in return for a write-down, or other reasonable terms for clearing the debt, agreed to trade exclusively with the brewery; a publican mortgaged his or her public house to a brewery to clear a large debt or to refurbish the premises; or a publican agreed to an exclusive trading deal in return for other financial assistance, such as the payment of the annual licence or competitive terms for a long period. There was also some variation in the conditions of individual ties, varying from a totally exclusive tie for all drinks to a tie for stout and porter only: 'shall deal exclusively with the Lessor … for all Porter, Stout, Ale, beer or other malt liquors, wines, spirits, and mineral waters' (the latter three products were added to tied agreements after the establishment of the Beamish & Crawford Bottling Co. in Bandon in 1914); 'shall deal with the Lessor … for all Porter and Stout in wood and bottle'; 'shall deal exclusively with the Company … for all Porter, Stout, Ale or beer in wood'; 'shall deal for all Porter and Stout', and so on.

Early ties

Soon after the establishment of the Cork Porter Brewery in 1792, Beamish & Crawford began to establish ties with public houses, initially by paying for the publicans' licences. In 1799 the brewery paid out £2,351.16.6 for licences for customers and in 1804, the next year for which there is detail, £5,684.5.0 was paid for 159 licences. All of these houses were in Cork city and its environs. In 1806–7, £7,544.1.10 was paid to 173 individuals for licences. Edward Wakefield, in *An Account of Ireland, Statistical and Political*, published in 1812, commented on the Beamish & Crawford practice of advancing money for licences instead of purchasing public houses.[1] Although it is not stated in the documents, it is to be presumed that in return for the payment for the annual licence, the publican agreed to deal exclusively with the brewery for at least that year.

In September 1814 Cornelius Leary, a publican of the Watercourse in Cork, mortgaged his public house to the brewery as a result of debt and was obliged to trade only with Beamish & Crawford until the mortgage was repaid.[2] In some cases the brewery acquired ownership of the premises when the publican was unable to meet his repayments, following which the publican continued as a tied tenant. Arrangements such as this became increasingly common as the century progressed. A brewery ledger records details of 109 tied houses that became tied to the brewery between the 1840s and 1890s and in all cases the initial tie was initiated as a result of the premises being mortgaged to the brewery, presumably due to debt.[3]

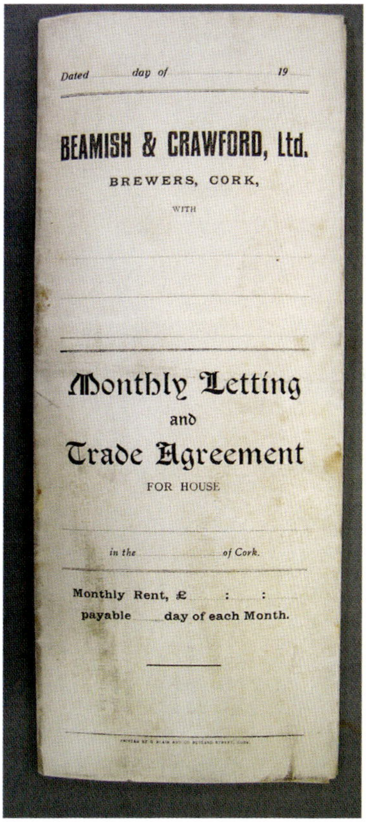
Dated ____ day of ____ 19__

BEAMISH & CRAWFORD, Ltd.

BREWERS, CORK,

WITH

Monthly Letting

and

Trade Agreement

FOR HOUSE

in the ____ of Cork.

Monthly Rent, £ : :

payable ____ day of each Month.

From top:

Gable of Bull McCabes Bar, Kinsale Road, Cork. (Authors)

Letting agreement for a Beamish & Crawford tied house. (CCCA/Authors)

All tied up

Soon after the establishment of the Lady's Well Brewery by James J. Murphy & Co. in Cork in 1856, the acquisition of tied houses became a feature of the competition between the breweries in Cork. Murphy's brewery faltered in its first years, and following a failed attempt to sell the new brewery to Beamish & Crawford, the Murphy family partners embarked on an energetic and well-funded campaign to build up an estate of tied houses to secure a market for their products. They bought public houses and licences and 'expended large sums for the purpose of inducing publicans to quit one brewery for the other', offering very competitive terms for long-term trading agreements.[4] Beamish & Crawford was forced to respond in kind and spent large sums on securing its tied trade, offering loans and inducements to publicans, before a 'truce' was agreed in 1861. The peace did not last, as Arnott's St Finbarre's Brewery began operations later that year, and in addition to acquiring tied houses it undersold both Murphy's and Beamish & Crawford. Lane & Co.'s Southgate Brewery also entered the fray, and by 1900 over 90 per cent of the city's public houses were tied to a brewery. The breweries also established exclusive ties with the majority of the county's public houses – 1,893 of them were tied in some way by 1900. The smaller breweries of Allman, Dowden & Co. in Bandon and Deasy & Co. in Clonakilty, both in County Cork, had tied estates of ninety and 109 licensed houses, respectively.

From the 1860s, the agreements with publicans became more formalised and the terms and conditions attached to the arrangements were set out in legal documents that grew in volume as ties and tenancies were renewed or changed. When Richard Pigott Beamish became an acting partner in Beamish & Crawford in 1863, the race for tied houses was already under way and he found the firm's legal department, such as it was, overwhelmed and disorganised. A new solicitor was appointed to represent the firm, a 'confidential clerk' was put in charge of the legal department and the firm became 'the masters in place of being the servants of the local publicans, almost all of whom that are B&C customers being now either monthly tenants or bound by written agreements which secure their dealings'.[5] By far the greatest proportion of surviving documents in the Beamish & Crawford archive held at the Cork City and County Archives is made up of letting agreements and other items connected to the legal minutiae of the tied-house trade.

In 1900 Beamish & Crawford had a tied estate of 120 houses in the city, compared to 223 for Murphy's, eighty-five for Arnott's, thirty-six for Lane's and thirteen with ties to Dublin breweries. Only forty or so public houses were independent or free traders. While Beamish & Crawford had exclusive dealing agreements with 642 customers in the county area and in parts of west Waterford, it is not possible to establish how many of those were formally or legally tied to the brewery, although a

Clockwise from top: Elevation of proposed Beamish & Crawford premises at Anglesea Street, Cork, 1873. This premises is now The Hub. (CCCA/Authors)

Fitzgerald's premises in Carrigaline, renovated in 1877 by Beamish & Crawford. (CCCA/Dori O'Connell)

The Tower Bar and Gardens, Tower Street, Cork, 1878. (CCCA/Authors)

Phair's premises on the corner of Bandon Road and Lough Road, 1878. (CCCA/Authors)

A legal document relating to a tied-house case. (CCCA/Dori O'Connell) proportion were. A letter from John Linehan, Bloomfield, Ballyhooly, County Cork, to Beamish & Crawford in 1924 shows how less formal ties were established with many rural publicans:

> In consideration of Messrs. Beamish & Crawford Limited, Brewers, Cork agreeing to give or allow to me at the end of Twelve years from this date the sum of One Hundred Pounds Sterling, I hereby undertake to deal exclusively with them for all Draught Porter, Stout & Ale, which may be sold or consumed in or through my licensed premises for a period of Twelve years from this date. The prices to be charged for such goods to be those current in the district. I understand that if I violate any of the conditions of this document I forfeit all right to the said sum of one hundred pounds. [6]

'The man may sin, but the house cannot'

In May 1898 Richard Pigott Beamish gave evidence before the Royal Commission on Liquor Licensing Laws and was questioned at length on the tied-house system as it operated in Cork.[7] Beamish explained that it was difficult for a brewery to generate profit from a tied house, as the brewery was liable for paying the head rent on the property, rates, taxes, maintenance and decoration costs. He also dealt at some length with the legal difficulties that arose in relation to the licences of tied houses, especially in the common cases where a brewery acquired a premises with its licence, often for a considerable sum, let it to the former owner and later ran into difficulties when the licensee refused to transfer the licence to a new tenant, claiming the licence as his property. Beamish explained that there were differing opinions as to the ownership of such licences and he felt, unsurprisingly, that the licence should be attached to the house and not the publican, thus easing the situation for the brewery as owner of the tied house. Any breaches of the licensing laws should penalise the licensee and not the house, or as Beamish put it, 'the man may sin, but the house cannot'. He was in favour of the licensing laws being changed to reflect that, part of his argument being that it would be in the interests of a brewery, as owner of a tied house, to ensure that the house was run in a proper fashion and that the brewery would remove a tenant guilty of any breaches of the law or of running a disreputable house. Beamish, speaking on behalf of the Cork brewers, acknowledged that there were far too many public houses in Cork city and that publicans in smaller houses were forced to break the law in order to keep their businesses going.

Twenty-seven years later, in 1925, Richard Pigott Beamish's son, Richard Henrik, then chairman and managing director of Beamish & Crawford Ltd and a TD in the new Free State Dáil, gave evidence before the Intoxicating Liquor Commission, which was charged with establishing if there were too many public houses in the country.

Beamish submitted that Cork, at least, was grossly oversupplied with public houses and that their number should be reduced by over 50 per cent. He told the commission that there were 467 pubs in the city, of which 191 were free or independent houses, 186 were tied to J.J. Murphy & Co. and ninety were tied to Beamish & Crawford. These figures show that one change that followed the events of the period 1914 to 1923 – economic, political, social, legislative, martial and otherwise – was a small reduction in the number of pubs in the city, from 520 to 467, but a proportionately much greater fall in the number of tied houses, from 477 to 276. Beamish suggested to the commission that 210 public houses would satisfactorily serve the needs of Cork city, divided between eighty-six free houses, eighty-four Murphy's houses and forty Beamish & Crawford houses.[8]

The principal recommendation of the Intoxicating Liquor Commission was that a scheme should be introduced to facilitate a reduction in the number of licensed premises in areas of excessive supply. The Intoxicating Liquor Act of 1927 introduced just such a scheme and 299 licences were abolished in its first year of operation, with £50,000 being paid nationally in compensation to those who lost licences.[9] Both Beamish & Crawford and Murphy's lost a small number of houses under the scheme – houses with a very small trade that in any case were nearing closure in the straitened circumstances of the time.

Beamish also defended the tied-house system on the grounds that ownership by a brewery gave a level of oversight that free houses did not have. He added that free houses, which sold beers from different breweries, were quite likely to mix beers of different quality and strength and to pass off the beer of one brewery as that of another. He also spoke in defence of the combined bar and grocery, a common feature of the rural trade, and rejected the notion that it was an unnecessary temptation to those who might enter such a premises solely for the purchase of groceries or other provisions. He added that the 'country drinker' could not afford excessive drinking due to low agricultural wages and the higher price of drink due to excessive taxation. He continued: 'He finishes his modest drink as sober as when he commenced it, sighs for more, and leaves the shop dissatisfied that his money does not suffice for more.'

Straining the tie: brewery tenants who erred

Where legal agreements had been entered into with tenants or with other tied customers, the penalties for a breach of the tie by selling or stocking the products of another brewery, for example, were quite punitive. Offenders were often pursued in the courts, where the brewery endeavoured to force the payment of penalties of up to £25 for each individual breach by an offending publican.

In 1901 Beamish & Crawford took over Lane & Co.'s Southgate Brewery and James J. Murphy & Co. took over Arnott's brewery, leaving the city with two breweries and their expanded tied estates. Beamish & Crawford then had 157 tied public houses in the city and Murphy's had 308. Apart from each other, the two breweries were under the most competitive pressure from Guinness, so they agreed a non-aggression pact of sorts to protect their tied trade: 'It is in the interest of both companies to secure the consumption of the porter, stout & ales manufactured by them in preference to those manufactured by other than Cork Breweries.'[10]

It was decided that all agreements with tied tenants and customers would be amended to include the provision that both draught and bottled stout, porter and ale were all to be sourced from their respective breweries and that if either brewery became aware of any breach of the tie on the part of a tied house of the opposing brewery, they would pass the information to the competitor.

By the later 1800s Guinness had become the dominant brewer in Ireland, and the quality and taste of its bottled stout were held in high esteem by many stout drinkers. Customers of tied houses in Cork increasingly demanded the Dublin stout and publicans sought to supply that demand secretly, in breach of their tie. Verbal agreements were made with some tenants allowing them to sell bottled Guinness to those who asked for it, but this 'turning a blind eye' arrangement ended once Guinness secured a major foothold following the brewery workers' strike of February–March 1920.[11] Even so, in the first decade of the twentieth century, actions against tenants who supplied Guinness became common.[12] Trusted brewery employees visited suspected publicans and sought to purchase Guinness, and when they were successful the brewery took action.

In 1904 Beamish & Crawford instigated proceedings against Denis J. Murphy, a tied tenant, for dealing with another brewery, claiming a £25 penalty for every such dealing. The brewery also sought an injunction to stop him dealing with the competitor and sought damages and costs.[13] In November 1907 John Canty, who was a brewery tenant at 35 Princes Street, had to have an apology published in the three Cork newspapers:

> I, John Canty, of Prince's Street, in the City of Cork, Publican, do hereby tender my sincere apology to Beamish & Crawford Limited, for having sold as 'Special Extra Stout', manufactured by the Company, their Stout known as 'Double Stout'. I hereby undertake never to so transgress again, and to pay all costs incurred by the said Company in connection with the proceedings instituted by the said Company against me. I also agree to the publication by the said Company of this my apology in the Public Press, or in such other manner as the said Company may think right.
>
> Dated this 9th day of November, 1907.
>
> JOHN CANTY.

Patrick Cagney (or Tagney) had become a tied tenant of Beamish & Crawford at 4 Union Quay in 1908 and the following year the brewery brought an action against him for selling the products of another brewery (Guinness). They sought damages, costs, the profits he had earned from the sale of the offending products and an injunction restraining him from 'buying, receiving, selling or disposing of either directly or indirectly or permitting to be bought, received or sold any porter, stout or ale either in wood or bottle' other than products supplied by them.[14] Such was the vigour of the defence that a compromise was agreed whereby the publican was allowed to sell small quantities of bottled Guinness.

'Control houses'

As well as often attempting to sell the products of a competing brewery, tied-house tenants, and other publicans, sometimes succumbed to the temptation to adulterate their beers in the pursuit of profit. This involved watering down beer, mixing waste or spilled beer with good beer, passing off a weaker beer as something stronger, putting false labels on bottled beers or selling a draught beer as the product of a different brewery. Such was Beamish & Crawford's concern with the damaging effects of these practices on the reputation of their products that they sought opinion on the legality of opening 'control houses' – public houses directly controlled by the brewery but run by a trusted nominee by way of a secret bogus letting so that the customer would not know of the brewery's direct and full involvement.[15] No rent would be paid by the 'mythical tenant' and the details of the trade or tie agreement would not be observed and 'would only be a device to clothe the firm's dummy with an assumed status in law ... the only object of such an arrangement would be to deceive the court as to the real character of the licensed person'. The brewery wished to do this to present their porter, stout and ale to their customers in the best condition, without improper mixing or adulteration of any kind and in a well-run and respectable establishment. The opinion of the solicitor, Cecil Atkinson, was that it would be wrong in law and unworkable.

In a probable effort to exercise a greater measure of control in a legal fashion, the brewery appointed a manager to run the former Lane & Co. tied house on the corner of Albert Quay and Albert Street (today called the Sextant) in 1909. In 1918 the famous Cork architectural firm of Chillingworth & Levie was engaged to draw up plans to rebuild the premises as a showcase Beamish & Crawford house. The Oval Bar, a Beamish & Crawford tied house on the corner of South Main Street and Tuckey Street, was also built to a design of Chillingworth & Levie at that time.

The brewery was making expensive and creative efforts to improve the quality of the appearance and management of at least some of its houses in an attempt to set a standard that would be followed by more of its tenants. The idea of managed houses

The Oval Bar, South Main Street, Cork. (Authors)

was expanded in the late 1920s and early 1930s, and three public houses in Dublin, one each in the cities of Limerick and Belfast, one in Fermoy and six in Cork were run on that basis until the 1950s at least.[16]

Adjusting the tie

Many businesses, including breweries and public houses, suffered a decline due to the depressed economic conditions that followed the First World War, which was worsened by the impact of the four years of the war of independence and civil war from 1919 to 1923. By the mid-1920s Beamish & Crawford sales were at 21 per cent of their 1914 level, the brewery's tied-house estate required continuing costly maintenance and tied-house tenants were becoming increasingly weary of the restrictions the tie placed on them and essentially wanted to sell Guinness, by then the national brand leader in stout. Tenants believed that a loosening of the ties the breweries placed on them would benefit their businesses. In October 1921 the tenants of the two Cork breweries came together to form the Cork Tied House & Retail Vintners Association (CTHRVA) to rally local support for local stout over Guinness, but also to campaign for lower rents, fixity of tenure and, ultimately, the abolition of the tied-house system. At a meeting of town tenants held in Skibbereen in March 1922, one speaker, Mr Courtney, said:

> nothing was bad enough for those Cork brewers Murphy & Co. and Beamish & Crawford. Slavery in its worst form was not half as bad as the tied house system, as the people insist on getting Guinness. No man tied can compete with the untied man.[17]

The CTHRVA campaign died out following the refusal of the Intoxicating Liquor Commission to recommend ending the tied-house system.

In 1925 Beamish & Crawford attempted to address the issue of falling sales and declining reputation by tightening control over its tied tenants. The brewery was concerned about adulteration because 'a custom prevails whereby mixtures from Lemonade, Ginger Beer, Soda Water, Ale etc. have been collected off the counter by means of drainage and … surreptitiously added' to stout, as a result of which 'the working classes must naturally suffer in not receiving the full value of the article for which they have paid a heavy price'.[18] The brewery drew up a new trading agreement and sought to have all its tenants sign up to the new terms. The brewery was 'desirous of standardizing the licensed premises and the liquor sold therein' and stated in the new agreement that its XXX Stout, by then its standard stout, 'will be guaranteed by the Company to be equal in strength to any Dublin stout sold in Cork' – an attempt to stem the growing Guinness tide.[19] A sweetener to the deal would be a discount of £1 per barrel on the price charged to those in the same town or district who did not sign the new agreement. The tenant would commit to keeping the premises to a standard of cleanliness set by the brewery and sell Beamish & Crawford XXX Stout 'in its purity direct from cask or bottle without any drainage waste or other substance added thereto'. The tenant was forbidden to bottle any stout on the premises and could only sell bottled stout supplied by Beamish & Crawford.

While some tenants signed, many objected and the CTHRVA argued that no Beamish & Crawford tenant should sign the new agreement. The tenants had a particular objection to the discount offered to compliant tenants, as the older trading agreements guaranteed that tenants in a specific town or district would all be entitled to the same discounts and allowances. In a court case taken by the CTHRVA in 1926 the judgement was in favour of the brewery, but the issue dragged on until the 1930s, when the brewery eventually relented.[20] It was in this decade that a drive to modernise and improve the

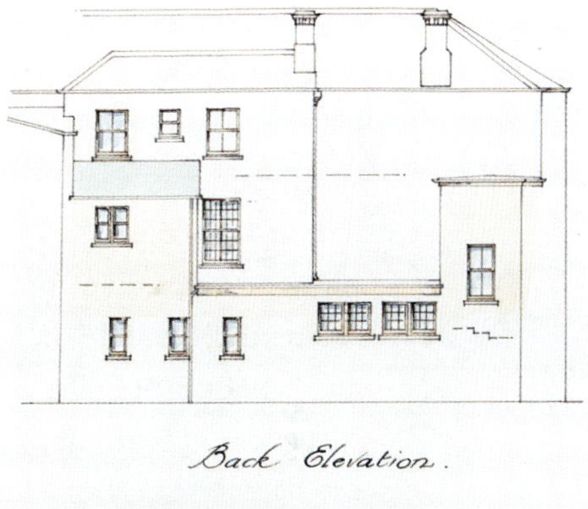

From top:
Drawings of elevations of No. 1 Albert Street premises by Chillingworth & Levie, 1919. (CCCA/Dori O'Connell)

The Sextant, Albert Street, Cork. (Authors)

appearance of key houses in the city took place under the leadership of the last of the Beamishes on the board, Richard P., son of Richard Henrik. Distinctive names such as the Cork Arms, the Golden Lion and the Swan and Cygnet were given to these showpiece houses. Beamish & Crawford, noted a Dublin journalist, could teach the taverners of the capital a great deal'.[21]

Loosening the ties

Throughout the middle decades of the 1900s, the number of Beamish & Crawford tied houses declined as unprofitable houses were closed and others were sold or freed from their tie. In 1948 the brewery still had ties with 266 public houses in Cork city and county and this had fallen to 256 by the following year.[22] By 1967 the brewery's tied estate numbered 195, sixty-eight of which were in Cork city. Such was the popularity of Guinness by that time that the tied houses of Beamish & Crawford and Murphy's in Cork accounted for only a small fraction of the stout sold in the city and county, and to prevent an almost total loss of trade to independent houses, a growing number of them were serving Guinness in breach of their trading agreements. The brewery tried to prevent this trend by taking out injunctions against offending publicans, but by the end of 1969 the pressure proved to be too strong and Beamish & Crawford's tied tenants were allowed to sell Guinness. The previous June an agreement had been reached with Murphy's whereby the two Cork breweries allowed each other's products to be sold through their respective tied houses (see Chapters 14 and 15). The ties had been loosened and by 1970 Guinness accounted for 75 per cent of sales in Beamish & Crawford public houses.

The idea of a tied house was no longer sustainable. The power and lure of Guinness had become too strong and tied tenants were no longer willing to depend exclusively on their local independent brewery for what had become a minority taste – a change driven by the demands of their customers. A decision was taken to sell off the Beamish & Crawford tied estate and the process began in 1972 when thirty-one of the remaining 153 tied houses were sold. The process continued through the following years, and by 1981 all the tied houses had been sold, mostly to the sitting tenants. Murphy's brewery also disposed of its tied houses in the later 1970s.

The legacy of the tied-house system, a peculiarity of the Cork trade, was that it ensured the survival of two breweries in Cork, which continued to brew their own distinctive stouts, while all others in the country succumbed to the inexorable dominance of Guinness.

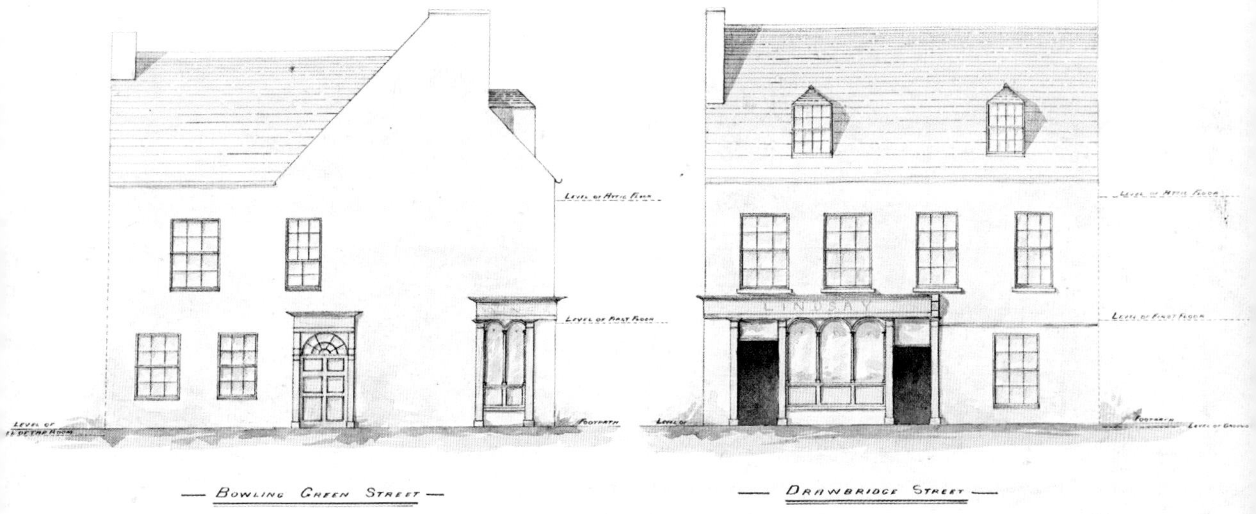

No. 14 Drawbridge Street
The story of a tied house

In 1779 Catherine Mathias, a widow, demised the premises on the northwestern corner of Bowling Green and Drawbridge Streets, then consisting of a house, coach house and stable, to Samuel Williams, who later sold his interest to Robert Evory. Evory died intestate in 1834, but by 1835 his widow, Rebecca, was in a position to sell to Jervis Pye, a publican and vintner. Pye entered into an agreement with Beamish & Crawford and sold only their stout and porter until his death in May 1867. His widow, Anne Millicent, married Thomas Marks six months later, on 10 November, and they continued the agreement with Beamish & Crawford but became indebted to them for £58.8.1. In May 1868 they entered into a mortgage agreement with the brewery by which they were lent a further £50 and

> the said Thomas Marks and Anne Millicent Marks, his wife, have proposed to secure the repayment as well of said sum of fifty pounds as also £58.8.1 so due and owing to them as aforesaid by a mortgage of the said Dwelling House and Licensed Premises … and to enter into the usual trade agreement with the said firm …[23]

Above: Drawing of No. 14 Drawbridge Street before reconstruction in 1877. (CCCA/Dori O'Connell)

No.14 Drawbridge Street after reconstruction in 1877. (CCCA/Dori O'Connell)

The Markses agreed to pay off the mortgage by January 1869 and to pay the £25 annual rent on the premises and annual licence renewal costs. They appear to have not redeemed the mortgage and Beamish & Crawford acquired their interest in the premises, which they subsequently let to a Mr Lindsay. While Lindsay was in possession of the premises as a tenant, Beamish & Crawford did a complete refurbishment of the building in 1877. The plans of the old and new premises survive in the Beamish & Crawford archive, showing that the older two-storeyed building with attic rooms was raised to become a fully three-storeyed building.[24]

The original bar was quite small, with a doorway from both Drawbridge and Bowling Green Streets. There were two snugs or stalls in the main bar area and a tap room to the rear, essentially an area more open than a snug where customers could sit and enjoy their drinks. The 1877 refurbishment gave the building a completely new exterior appearance and changed the interior layout, with the bar area much enlarged and having three snugs or stalls. A WC (water closet, or toilet) was installed off the yard to the back with access from the bar and the tap room. No WC is shown on the earlier plan.

Lindsay was succeeded by Patrick Daniel O'Brien, who left in May 1893 when Mathew Buckley of 11 Copely Place in Cork took possession at a monthly rent of £4.6.8. The brewery was liable for rates and taxes and Buckley agreed to deal exclusively in Beamish & Crawford products, entering into a bond for £150 as security.

The brewery workmen's strike that shut the brewery for five weeks in early 1920 saw the city 'flooded' with Guinness. In 1921, in an attempt to win back lost trade, the brewery began to enforce its tied agreements, even with tenants, like Buckley, with whom it had a long-standing verbal agreement allowing the limited sale of bottled Guinness. A representative of Beamish & Crawford had visited Buckley's premises incognito on 26 January:

> I asked for a pint of Guinness Stout. Mrs. Buckley said she had Guinness in bottle. I then asked for a bottle of Guinness which I got and drank. There was no label on the bottle. I again asked for two bottles of Guinness Stout, which I got and brought away.

These samples were subsequently tested by Philip Baylis, who wrote:

> I certify that the sample of Stout bought of Mr. Buckley, Drawbridge St., and handed to me ... on January 26th and analysed by me on that date, was not of Messrs. Beamish & Crawford's manufacture.

The punishment for breaking the tie was quite severe – a fine of £25 for each breach of the agreement was usual, with liability for any costs incurred by the brewery.

On 29 October 1932 Beamish & Crawford gave notice to Mathew Buckley that it was terminating its agreement with him as and from 1 December. The brewery did not succeed in getting possession of the premises until September 1933, at which time it entered into a new monthly letting and trade agreement with Edwin Stevens of South Main Street at a monthly rent of £5.8.6.[25] Stevens agreed to deal exclusively with the brewery for all stout, porter, ale and other beers. There is no further detail in the file on the letting history after that, but according to *Guy's Cork Almanac and County and City Directory*, a Mrs Martin was the tenant in 1930 and she was still in possession in 1945. In its later years the house was called the Grand Circle, in recognition of its long association with the nearby Opera House. It was demolished in 2007 to make way for the Opera Lane development.

13

'Bad Times and Good Taste'
1922–1959

'Bad times and good taste', according to a Beamish & Crawford advertisement from the late 1920s, 'can both be met by drinking Beamish's Stout on draught.' If only it were true. The 'good taste' of Guinness appealed to increasing numbers of Cork drinkers in the 1920s, while the 'bad times' of higher drink prices together with lower profits, trade and wages continued unabated for the brewery, its tenants and customers. The company had stumbled off the ropes after the blows of the First World War, the war of independence and the 1920 brewery workers' strike. Taxes were up, sales and profits were down and Guinness had come into Cork through the front and back doors. Hopes of an end to the 'troubles' were dashed with the outbreak of civil war in 1922, which lengthened the disruption to trade and, in terms of the effect on transport, was even worse than the period during the war of independence. The coming of peace and independence brought little of the prosperity that was hoped for, and Beamish & Crawford limped along the rocky road until a new era in the 1960s, holding its own at a low level, making occasional attempts at expansion and development, but never regaining the status or success of the pre-First World War years.

Following a brief boost during and immediately after the Second World War, sales went into freefall throughout the 1950s as the Irish economy stagnated and emigration and unemployment reached crisis proportions. Beamish & Crawford, to some extent, followed the people, increasing exports and acquiring a number of breweries in England. In the late 1950s the Irish economy was opened up after decades of protectionism and Beamish & Crawford would become one of the first major Irish companies to come under multinational ownership in the early 1960s.

The Counting House, *c.* 1930. (Courtesy Ed Hinchy)

'A Free State ... why not a free trade?'

The assertive tied tenants' association, CTHRVA, continued to agitate in early 1922, sending a delegation to argue for the abolition of the tied-house system to the Provisional Government's Minister for Home Affairs, Kevin O'Higgins, and gaining the support of Finance Minister and Chairman of the Provisional Government, Michael Collins, in March 1922; the latter reportedly told a delegation that the tied-house system was 'altogether wrong in principle, and would be one of the first problems to receive the consideration of the Irish Government'. William O'Connell told a meeting of the CTHRVA in early June that as they were told 'they had a Free State ... why not a free trade?'.[1]

Collins, the leading pro-Treaty Sinn Féiner, and Éamon de Valera, the political leader of the anti-Treaty wing, signed an electoral pact on 18 May 1922 committing both sides to run on a panel basis in the forthcoming general election on 16 June and to establishing a 'coalition' after the election. The pact was designed to forestall a definitive split and civil war, but was effectively broken when the pro-Treaty side claimed the result as an endorsement of the Treaty because pro-Treaty Sinn Féiners and other pro-Treaty parties won a majority. Twelve days later, the civil war began.

Like almost all businessmen, former southern unionists and home rulers, Richard Henrik Beamish was pro-Treaty. He decided to run in the June 1922 election but also

Loading delivery lorries in the main yard, April 1929. (*Irish Examiner*)

approached one of his 'opponents', Liam de Róiste, a pro-Treaty Sinn Féin candidate in Cork city, in advance of the election to ask him if he considered £500 'an adequate contribution' from Beamish & Crawford to that wing of the party's funds – 'not as a bribe old chap', Beamish added for clarification. De Róiste indicated that someone would come to collect the money at a later stage, given the awkwardness of accepting a donation from an electoral opponent.[2] The CTHRVA announced that the Sinn Féin and Labour candidates had supported the abolition of tied houses and a reduction in beer duty. Anti-Treaty candidate Mary MacSwiney warned voters, meanwhile, against voting for an ex-unionist like Beamish and sending out the wrong message to Britain at this time of crisis – even if Beamish 'had changed his coat', it was 'rather late'.[3] Beamish was beaten for the last of the city's four seats by MacSwiney; the poll was topped by Labour's Robert Day, followed by the two pro-Treatyites, Alfred O'Rahilly and J.J. Walsh. The civil war began on 28 June and Cork remained in control of the anti-Treaty IRA until early August, when it was taken by the National Army. The IRA retreated west, engaging in an orgy of destruction, including the bombing of dozens of bridges. The civil war carried on until May 1923 and seriously disrupted trade through hijackings, the closure of roads and the disruption of railway traffic.

The Irish Free State came into official existence in December 1922, and in August 1923 a general election was held for the new Free State Dáil against a background of widespread industrial unrest in Cork. The Cork Employers' Federation, of which Richard Beamish and A. F. Sharman Crawford were leading members, had demanded wage reductions across the board from the city's workers. The result was a generalised strike and lockout that began in the week before the election and carried on for months. In the election on 27 August, anti-Treaty Sinn Féin stood on an abstentionist platform, while the pro-Treaty wing had constituted itself as Cumann na nGaedheal. The employers had formed the Progressive Association and put forward two candidates on what was essentially a joint ticket with Cumann na nGaedheal – woollen-mill owner Andrew O'Shaughnessy and Richard Henrik Beamish. Their campaign posters advertised them as 'In Harmony with Cumann na nGaedheal' and their 'manifesto' was a vague list promising such delights as 'Peace, Progress and Prosperity'.[4] Labour overconfidently put forward three candidates and poor transfers saw them lose out, while the pro-Treatyites transferred successfully between each other to ensure that the two Cumann na nGaedheal-ers plus both Beamish and O'Shaughnessy were elected, together with MacSwiney of Sinn Féin.

A government-brokered settlement saw the employers achieve a watered-down version of the pay cuts they had been demanding by October 1922, including a cut of 11s 5d per week for the coopers in Beamish & Crawford.[5] The Coopers' Society had been involved in initiating a labour campaign in Cork 'against the consumption of Guinness as being against labour and so much money going to Dublin against the interest of the city'. From August to October, against the background of the local general strike, there were pickets placed on the Guinness offices and interference with deliveries by members of various unions, but this short-term boon to the local breweries made little difference to the overall trend of increased Guinness sales in the city and county.[6]

Public men and public houses

A.F. Sharman Crawford might also have ended up on the national political stage; he was one of the nominees of Cork Corporation, having been put forward by the Cork Chamber of Commerce, for the Irish Free State Senate in 1922. In that same year he was founding chairman of the Cork Town Planning Association, which in 1926 published a major civic survey to influence the future development of the city. The survey recommended slum clearances as well as traffic decongestion and the provision of additional public spaces. He also remained a leading member of the Technical Education Committee. Meanwhile, Richard Henrik Beamish and his fellow Cork Progressive Association TD, Andrew O'Shaughnessy, took the Cumann na nGaedheal whip in April 1924, effectively becoming government party TDs.[7]

As well as being a government TD thinly disguised as an independent, Beamish was a brewer with vested interests thinly disguised as a champion of the poor. In what Minister for Justice Kevin O'Higgins described as 'a rollicking speech', one of the only such speeches he gave in his four years in parliament, Beamish spoke at length against a Seanad proposal to include the closure of pubs on St Patrick's Day in the 1924 Intoxicating Liquor Act. This had long been a demand of the temperance lobby, which was now wielding more influence in an increasingly Catholicised Free State, as well as the Gaelic League. The wealthy brewer denounced the senators who supported the amendment, 'with their cellars full of wines and spirits and plenty of soda water. The ordinary workman, farmer or labourer with very little money in his pocket cannot afford to order in the drink which is probably enjoyed in Senatorial houses.' He rejected the idea that pubs opening on St Patrick's Day led to drunkenness 'owing to the difficulty of procuring drink at a reasonable price'. The government, he declared, had 'practically done away with drunkenness in Ireland by the high taxation which they have imposed'. He referred to the increasing incidence of serving stout in glasses rather than pint pots, 'so that the unfortunate imbiber of a glass of stout can watch it gradually fading away before his thirst is satisfied. Intoxication is not going to result from the opening of the houses on St. Patrick's Day, but a little natural thirst is going to be pleasantly assuaged.' In general, 'the labouring man' could not afford to get drunk: 'In former days, when porter was sold at 2d. a pint, he could order a gallon of it and walk home on his head, but at present he does not even stagger home on his feet.'[8]

Limited St Patrick's Day opening was permitted, but was added to Christmas Day and Good Friday on the total closure list in a subsequent act of 1927. The 1924 act primarily confined itself to limits on opening hours and the control of illegal outlets (shebeens). The minister, Kevin O'Higgins, wanted to tackle the excessive number of public houses in the state but held off due to a lack of funds (needed for compensation) and a lack of data. In 1925 he established an Intoxicating Liquor Commission under the chairmanship of Cork solicitor and coroner J.J. Horgan to investigate the trade, with special reference to general issues such as the excess number of houses and opening hours, and particular local issues such as the tied-house question in Cork. There were 13,000 licences in the Free State – approximately one pub for every 230 people, in comparison to one for every 400 in England and one for every 695 in Scotland. Cork city had approximately one pub for every 180. In Dowra, County Cavan, thirteen of the village's thirty-five houses were licensed, while in Ballaghdareen, County Roscommon, there was one pub for every eighteen inhabitants. Such statistics, said O'Higgins, were 'startling' and the issue needed to be addressed.[9]

Amongst those who gave evidence to the commission were representatives of the vintners and tied-house tenants in Cork as well as Richard Henrik Beamish. According to Beamish & Crawford tied tenant and vice-chairman of the Cork and Munster Licensed Traders Protection Association, Matthew Buckley, who ran a pub on 14 Drawbridge Street (see pp. 285–7), Guinness had got into 'every nook and cranny' in Cork since the 1920 strike and had brought his business to its knees. Since he had taken over the house over thirty years before, he had had a verbal agreement with Beamish, which he said was replicated in the tied trade generally of both breweries, that he could sell Guinness in bottles to those who asked for it. In 1921, however, the brewery had insisted on the tied houses selling its stout only in an attempt to regain sales, but this backfired, as customers abandoned the tied houses in droves. He pointed out that groups would come to his premises and one or two might want Guinness in a bottle, while the rest would drink Beamish; now that Guinness was banned, the whole group switched to houses with Guinness. His location near the Cork Opera House exacerbated the problem, as many of his passing customers were from travelling theatre companies who sought out the familiar Guinness.

William O'Connell of the tied-house tenants' association, CTHRVA, made similar points and explained that the Dublin stout had 'a wonderful difference in taste ... there is something in Guinness which makes it more palatable'. The Cork public had been won over during the 1920 strike, and the tied tenants wanted an end to the restrictions of the tie so that they could compete with the independent houses. When asked if he wanted the city's breweries to die as a result, Buckley replied that it was preferable to the breweries *and* their tenants both being killed off, as was the clear and present danger if nothing changed.[10] All parties agreed that the number of licensed premises in Cork needed to be reduced; the only question was how the issue of compensation would be dealt with.

The CTHRVA made a charge at the commission hearings in June 1925 that Richard Henrik Beamish had abused his political position the previous week in telling a meeting of his tenants that he could assure them that the commission would not recommend a break-up of the tied-house system. This was in the context of a new trading agreement that Beamish was asking tenants to sign up to, whereby in return for a discount on a barrel of stout, they would give guarantees on cleanliness and adulteration and would submit to brewery inspection of their premises and practices. Beamish vehemently denied that he gave any indication of 'inside' knowledge of the commission's workings, and this was confirmed by the commission itself.[11]

In his evidence to the commission, Beamish and his lawyer made an interesting observation on the apparent consensus about the 1920 strike heralding the advent of Guinness in Cork. They argued, rather, that it was the development of the 'medium' (colloquially pronounced 'meejum') measure of stout in Cork before the First World War that had given the Dublin brew its foothold. Guinness sold at 2½d a pint and Beamish and Murphy's at 2d. Customers began to ask for, and were given, 2d worth of Guinness, and this 'non-imperial', unofficial measure became known as a medium. Beamish raised the issue with the Inland Revenue in 1909, asking for action against sales in non-authorised measures (legally, beer could only be served in pint or half-pint amounts). No action was taken, and according to Beamish, publicans promoted Guinness because they could increase profits by serving less than four-fifths of a pint for 2d.[12]

The commission report concluded that no case had been convincingly made to justify the cancellation of tied agreements that had been 'freely entered into' by tenants 'with full knowledge of the obligations imposed'. The resultant 1927 Intoxicating Liquor Act duly ignored the specific tied-house issue in its imposition of a scheme for reducing the number of licensed premises, with the amount of compensation for houses chosen to be closed set by a compensation authority (a circuit court judge) and funded jointly by the state and a levy on the local pubs that gained by the closure of competitors. That scheme operated for a year, during which 299 licences were abolished and £50,000 was paid in compensation.[13] It was soon found that the cost of operating the scheme relative to the value of the licences abolished, which were in many cases worthless, made the scheme as initially established unworkable. Compensation continued to be paid until 1960, but the decline in trade in subsequent decades and 'natural wastage' in the number of houses, including the Beamish & Crawford tied estate, achieved close to the desired result. The most enduring aspect of the 1927 act was the introduction of the 'holy hour'– the closure of pubs in cities between 2.30pm and 3.30pm – designed, according to O'Higgins, to send the drinker 'away to get a meal or to attend to his affairs'. In many cases it sent him away instead to the 'country', or more accurately, to suburban areas, where 'bona fide travellers' could drink both during what Myles na Gopaleen called the 'solemn hiatus' and after 10pm closing on a weeknight and 9.30pm on Sundays. The distances people had to travel to qualify as 'bona fide' were increased because, in the words of O'Higgins, 'the bicycle and the Ford car have revolutionised the conditions with which we are endeavouring to deal'.[14]

'Good For Your Health and For Your Pocket'

The punitive duties on beer and spirits imposed during the First World War were reduced in the UK in the early 1920s, but remained in place in the Irish Free State. The Irish drinks industry consistently campaigned, without success, for a reduction. Duty on a barrel had risen from 7s 9d before the war to £5 (100s). According to the chairman of the Munster Licensed Vintners' Association, Liam Clancy, 'it was a tax put on in order that the war with the Germans could be fought, and it was hardly fair to keep it on when it had been removed in other countries.'[15]

The CTHRVA, meanwhile, continued its agitation against the tied-house system, despite its campaign having been effectively nullified by the Intoxicating Liquor Commission report and recommendations. It encouraged Beamish tenants not to sign up to the new trading agreement devised by the brewery in 1925 in an attempt to improve standards and increase sales, which were reaching crisis point. The scale of the crisis is revealed in the annual sales figures, which show a drop from 74,977 barrels in 1920 to 26,393 in 1925; in the same period, Beamish & Crawford's annual net profits fell from £48,028 to £2,660. The company needed to act boldly. In return for agreeing to a set of terms (including a commitment to keep the premises clean, to sell only stout bottled at the brewery and to sell Beamish XXX Stout, which was now the standard variety, 'in its purity direct from cask or bottle without any drainage waste or other substance added thereto'), tenants received a £1 discount per barrel. The CTHRVA took a test case against the brewery in March 1926 to have the discount declared illegal, but the court found in the brewery's favour. A further aspect of the agreement was the commitment to sell Beamish XXX at 8d, a penny less than its competitors, which would further encourage custom in participating houses. This amounted to a 20s loss per barrel (288 pints) for the brewery and a 4s loss to the publican; the latter gained in the £1 (20s) discount, while a massive spike in sales – an increase of 92 per cent in city sales between 1924–5 and 1928–9 – more than compensated the brewery.[16]

In this period, country sales dropped as city sales rose, replicating the trade pattern of other breweries. The agricultural 'boom years' of the First World War and immediate post-war years had given way to recession and falling incomes in the countryside, a situation that would be worsened in the 1930s during the trade war with Britain. This had a knock-on effect on Cork city, where many were employed in the handling, processing and transport of agricultural goods.

The success of the newly 'guaranteed pure' Beamish stout at discount prices encouraged the company to launch a nationwide sales offensive, accompanied by extensive advertising in the local and national press. A prize at the Brewers' International Exhibition in London in 1928 was a boon to its claims of quality. The advertisements pushed the idea of a quality product at reduced prices. One in particular revealed the confidence underlying the campaign. Under the heading 'Why We Advertise', the text declared: 'Only a product of quality and value can withstand the pitiless glare of publicity. Therefore we seek publicity – as much as we can get – secure in the knowledge that our stout cannot be bettered … There is not a headache nor a touch of indigestion in a barrel of it.' The lack of sediment, wastage or any adulteration was stressed, along with the strength of 'Treble X' and its lower price.

The Beamish campaign was mirrored by a similar advertising blitz by Murphy's in this period, with the rivals' advertisements often appearing together in the local press. In the 1930s Beamish's version of the trademark Murphy's strongman, Eugen Sandow, was West Cork's Danno (O'Mahony), world wrestling champion, who 'does it on Beamish'.[17] (See p. 312)

'Managed' houses were secured in Dublin, Limerick and Belfast, and pubs in working-class areas in particular were targeted for the sale of this 'workingman's pint'. Its success in Dublin led Guinness to drop its prices in mid-1928, and that company

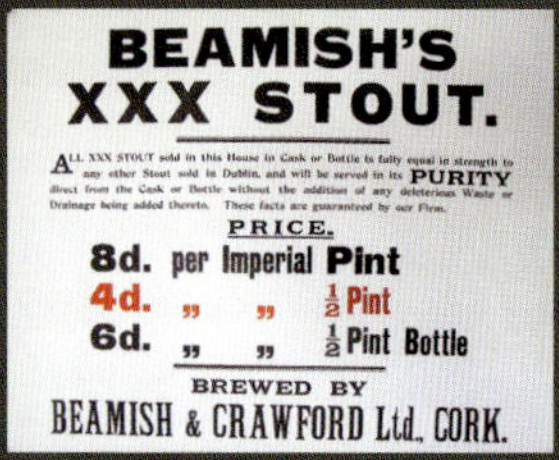

From top:
Label created for exports of bottled stout to Egypt. (Courtesy Ed Hinchy)

Poster displayed in public houses in Dublin where Beamish XXX Stout was sold, 1928–30. (CCCA/Authors)

(Courtesy Michael Lenihan)

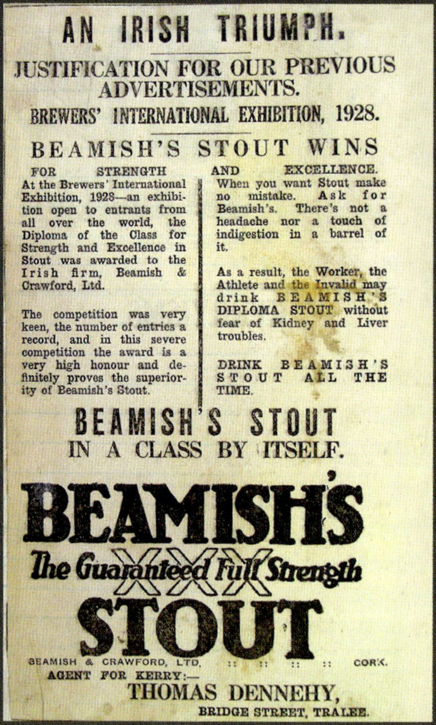

AN IRISH TRIUMPH.

JUSTIFICATION FOR OUR PREVIOUS ADVERTISEMENTS.

BREWERS' INTERNATIONAL EXHIBITION, 1928.

BEAMISH'S STOUT WINS

FOR STRENGTH AND EXCELLENCE.

At the Brewers' International Exhibition, 1928—an exhibition open to entrants from all over the world, the Diploma of the Class for Strength and Excellence in Stout was awarded to the Irish firm, Beamish & Crawford, Ltd.

The competition was very keen, the number of entries a record, and in this severe competition the award is a very high honour and definitely proves the superiority of Beamish's Stout.

When you want Stout make no mistake. Ask for Beamish's. There's not a headache nor a touch of indigestion in a barrel of it.

As a result, the Worker, the Athlete and the Invalid may drink BEAMISH'S DIPLOMA STOUT without fear of Kidney and Liver troubles.

DRINK BEAMISH'S STOUT ALL THE TIME.

BEAMISH'S STOUT IN A CLASS BY ITSELF.

BEAMISH'S
The Guaranteed XXX Full Strength
STOUT

BEAMISH & CRAWFORD, LTD., :: :: :: :: CORK.
AGENT FOR KERRY:—
THOMAS DENNEHY,
BRIDGE STREET, TRALEE.

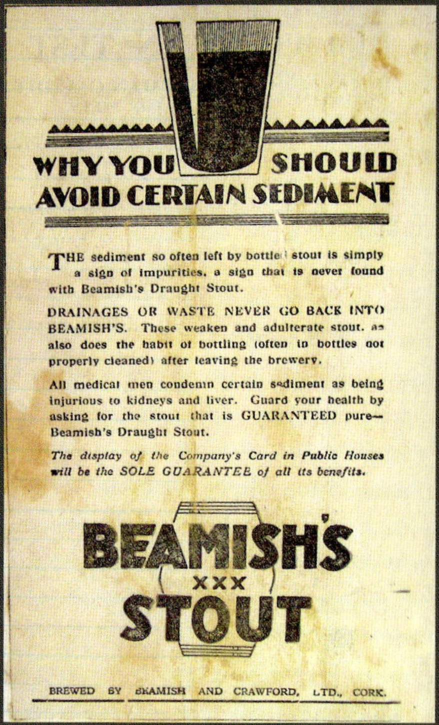

WHY YOU SHOULD AVOID CERTAIN SEDIMENT

THE sediment so often left by bottled stout is simply a sign of impurities, a sign that is never found with Beamish's Draught Stout.

DRAINAGES OR WASTE NEVER GO BACK INTO BEAMISH'S. These weaken and adulterate stout, as also does the habit of bottling (often in bottles not properly cleaned) after leaving the brewery.

All medical men condemn certain sediment as being injurious to kidneys and liver. Guard your health by asking for the stout that is GUARANTEED pure—Beamish's Draught Stout.

The display of the Company's Card in Public Houses will be the SOLE GUARANTEE of all its benefits.

BEAMISH'S
XXX
STOUT

BREWED BY BEAMISH AND CRAWFORD, LTD., CORK.

From the Brewery to you with no chance of adulteration–

as a special gift

Straight from the cask, just as pure and sound as when it left the brewery, comes Beamish's Draught Stout.

Not bottled in doubtfully clean bottles, NOT ADULTERATED BY ADDING DRAINAGE OR WASTE, not leaving sediment in the glass, but just as fresh and strong and health-giving as it is possible for Stout to be.

If you would be sure of purity and strength, see your Stout comes direct from the wood, and see that it is Beamish's Draught Stout.

BEAMISH'S
XXX
STOUT

BREWED BY BEAMISH AND CRAWFORD, LTD., CORK.

The display of the Company's Card in Public Houses will be the SOLE GUARANTEE of all its benefits.

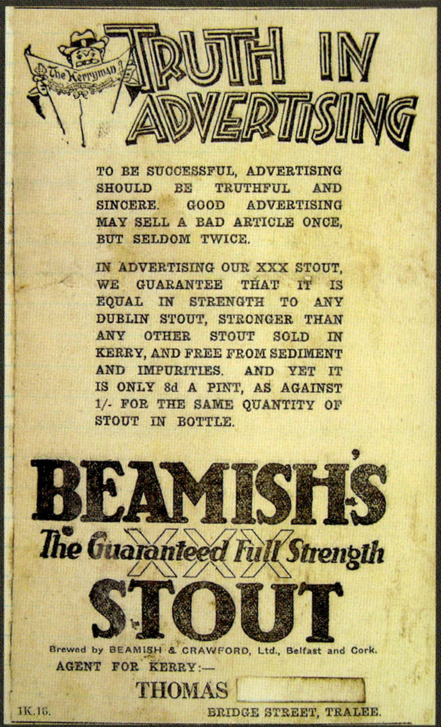

The Kerryman

TRUTH IN ADVERTISING

TO BE SUCCESSFUL, ADVERTISING SHOULD BE TRUTHFUL AND SINCERE. GOOD ADVERTISING MAY SELL A BAD ARTICLE ONCE, BUT SELDOM TWICE.

IN ADVERTISING OUR XXX STOUT, WE GUARANTEE THAT IT IS EQUAL IN STRENGTH TO ANY DUBLIN STOUT, STRONGER THAN ANY OTHER STOUT SOLD IN KERRY, AND FREE FROM SEDIMENT AND IMPURITIES. AND YET IT IS ONLY 8d A PINT, AS AGAINST 1/- FOR THE SAME QUANTITY OF STOUT IN BOTTLE.

BEAMISH'S
The Guaranteed XXX Full Strength
STOUT

Brewed by BEAMISH & CRAWFORD, Ltd., Belfast and Cork.
AGENT FOR KERRY:—
THOMAS
1K.16. BRIDGE STREET, TRALEE.

Above: Newspaper advertisements from 1928–9.

instructed its agents across the country to monitor the progress of Beamish sales and to fight back where it made inroads. Whereas Guinness did not have tied houses, its trading arrangement with publicans effectively 'tied' them to the brewery without any expenditure on its part. Guinness 'awarded' its trademark label and show cards to those who agreed to sell its stout exclusively. As publicans across the country were persuaded by Beamish & Crawford agents to try its product (perhaps in conjunction with Guinness), Guinness was next in the door, cancelling their contracts until they ceased to take the 'Cork stout', thus preventing Beamish from establishing a transitional foothold from which it could expand in areas where it had never been available before. A Guinness agent had reported in August 1927: 'It is evidently the intention of the Cork brewers to open one account for the present in every large town and village.' The one account opened in Naas, County Kildare, in that month did not seem to worry the town's Guinness customers, who felt that 'this Cork house will only attract the less desirable class of customer'.[18] In the year to August 1928, 6,390 barrels were sold in Dublin, 2,269 in Belfast and 4,795 across the country outside Cork, where 24,636 were sold in the same period. A year later, however, Dublin sales were down 41.6 per cent, Belfast was down 48 per cent and sales in the rest of the country had dropped from 4,795 to 3,065.

The short-lived boom seemed to be over and was followed in 1930 by a terrible harvest, increased unemployment and a further drop in local sales. A temporary boost to city trade occurred in 1929 and early 1930 when the Henry Ford & Son's factory in the city had over 6,000 workers employed in the production of tractors. However, the tractor market collapsed in the second half of 1930, leading to the lay-offs of thousands of workers whose wages were vital to the depressed city economy. A three-month builders' strike also hit local trade in 1930. In 1932 Ford tractor production was transferred to England and many Cork employees went to work at the plant in Dagenham. Cork reverted to car assembly, but the earlier peak employment levels were never again achieved.

Another acknowledged factor in the decline in drink sales in the 1920s and 1930s, besides high prices, unemployment and low wages, was the increasing counter-attraction of cinema, dancehalls and other pursuits, such as the Irish Hospitals Sweepstakes, which began in 1930 and absorbed disposable income that might otherwise have been spent on drink. The role of alternative leisure pursuits in diminishing alcohol consumption was noted approvingly by the Intoxicating Liquor Commission, but less enthusiastically by brewers; the directors of Murphy's Brewery doubtlessly spoke also for their fellow Cork brewers when they noted in 1933 that an 'unsavoury talkie picture or a joy-ride on a motor-cycle [was] more to the taste of the younger generation than a pint of stout or porter'.[19]

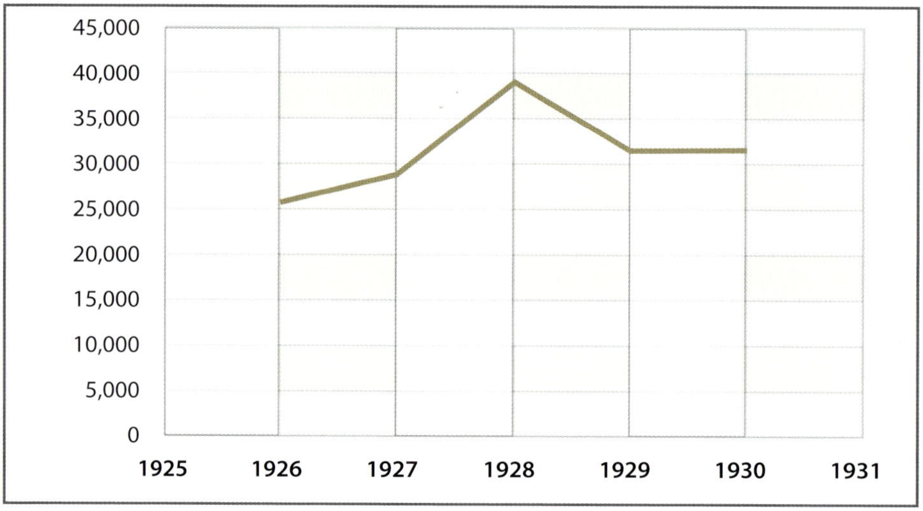

Beamish & Crawford, sales (in barrels), 1926–30.

The departure of Richard Henrik Beamish

Richard Henrik Beamish decided not to run in the 1927 general election. The voluntary ending of his less-than-glittering parliamentary career was followed by the involuntary end to his involvement in the family firm in 1930. The background to his departure was laid out in a statement by his successor as managing director, Lieutenant Colonel James Stafford Cummins, who joined the board and became general manager in 1928.[20] Cummins made this statement as part of the company's legal defence in a court case brought by Richard Henrik against the firm in relation to his pension entitlements. According to Cummins, when he and Major Matthew Croose Parry, former head brewer, joined the board in 1928 (A.F. Sharman Crawford left the board temporarily at the same time), they were uncomfortable with how the company's finances were being run. He claimed that the directors had 'for some years' been paying preference dividends in full on preference shares, though such dividends had not been fully earned. This resulted in a considerable debit on the profit/loss account of the brewery and an overdraft at the bank of £43,500, secured by the guarantees of the four senior directors: Richard Henrik Beamish, Colonel R.G. Sharman Crawford, A.F. Sharman Crawford and Major H.D. Beamish. The four senior directors owned between them all the ordinary shares, a majority of the preference shares and half of the debentures. Although Cummins and Parry, on legal advice, had the other directors sign a letter of indemnity absolving them of any liability, they remained uneasy and made Richard Henrik aware of their concerns, which were backed up by the company's auditors, who urged a change of policy regarding the 'dangerous' position of the company's finances. The company lawyers also indicated that the practice of paying unearned dividends was against company law. Beamish was dismissive, and when the poor harvest of 1930 hit sales and profits still further, he still insisted on unearned dividends being paid on preference shares.

Beamish devised a scheme to buy twenty or more pubs in Dublin, financed through the sale of properties in Cork and a bank loan. The company's bank, Provincial, did not support the scheme and said the directors' guarantee needed to be backed up by first-class securities. Beamish believed that the two Sharman Crawfords should put up security for £44,500 – the amount of the existing guarantees – plus an additional £7,000. This would allow interim preference dividends to be paid and convince the bank to finance the scheme. According to Cummins, Richard Henrik had told him that when A.F. Sharman Crawford was still joint managing director he had given a 'very pessimistic account' of the firm's finances to the local manager of the Provincial Bank, which was then communicated to head office and back to Beamish. This is what led Beamish to suggest the directors' guarantee to the bank, in order to 'break the Crawfords'. He also told Cummins that the brewery's finances were in 'one hell of a mess'. At this stage, according to Cummins, Beamish was acting like 'an absolute dictator' to fellow directors and staff.

Prior to a board meeting in early November 1930, Cummins and Parry called to A.F. Sharman Crawford to discuss the issue with him. His brother, Colonel R.G. Sharman Crawford, was on his way back from the US and Arthur Frederick wrote a long letter to him, which Cummins brought to Liverpool so that he could read it before he returned to Cork. The Sharman Crawfords then met with Richard Henrik before the board meeting on 4 November, at which Beamish announced his resignation as chairman, managing director and member of the board. They agreed that he would be paid a pension of £2,000 per annum, and Cummins and Parry took over as joint managing directors.

Richard Henrik had been elected to the reconstituted Cork Corporation in June 1930, but left Cork for England in August 1932. In 1935 he settled for an undisclosed sum following an action against the company whereby he claimed that the £2,000 per annum pension the firm had agreed to pay him was under a binding contract and not merely gratuitous. The company claimed the agreement was not binding but subject to the provisions of the articles of association of the company. He died in February 1938, leaving an estate worth £674. Major Parry died suddenly in early 1931, leaving Cummins, who, like Parry, had served in France with the British army during the First World War, as managing director and chairman until his retirement in 1950. A.F. Sharman Crawford rejoined the board following Richard Henrik's departure. Cummins's son Bryan later became a member of the board, while Richard Henrik's son Richard P. also became a director and took over as managing director following Cummins's retirement in 1950.

Clockwise from top: Bottling stout at the Beamish & Crawford Bottling Co. Ltd plant in Bandon, 1931. (*Irish Examiner*) Beamish Bandon bottles. (Beamish & Crawford Collection/Dori O'Connell) The Beamish & Crawford Bottling Co. Ltd in Bandon had a railway siding connected to the main line at Bandon railway station. This photograph was taken in 1931. (*Irish Examiner*)

Beamish & Crawford Bottling Company, Bandon

As well as cinema, dancing and motor cars, the increasing popularity of soft drinks or 'minerals' amongst the young was a concern for brewers in the 1920s and 1930s, but not so much for Beamish, which had its own mineral range from its bottling company in Bandon, which was extensively advertised in the late 1920s and 1930s. The company made great play of its own artesian well on its premises at Watergate Street, which from a depth of 250 feet supplied water of 'high purity' – the famed 'Bandon water'. It produced ginger ale, orange squash, lemonade, soda water and

Clockwise from top:

Beamish & Crawford Bottling Co. Ltd calendar for 1940. (Beamish & Crawford Brewery Collection/Dori O'Connell)

Little Norah Quinine Tonic Water, an Orange Squash label and newspaper advertisements from 1926–7.

syphons. Its most famous product was Little Norah lemonade, which it began to make in the early 1930s and which remained on the market until 1971 (being made in Cork for its last four years).

In 1930 healthy sales led to the installation of a state-of-the-art Triplex machine at the Bandon plant, the first of its kind in the country, which could produce 100 dozen bottles per hour. It was described in the press as 'an entire plant in itself', as it combined soaking, brushing, rinsing, syringing, filling, crowning and labelling bottles. While its chief trade was in Cork city and county, Beamish minerals were available across the country. The plant also bottled Beamish XXX for the firm's west Cork market, Bass, Perry's Rathdowney Ale, Devonshire cider, wines, spirits, liqueurs and cordials.

The Bandon Bottling Company was one of the last major firms to use horse transport into the 1930s and it had its own extensive stables. Horse transport was supplemented by lorries and rail, and the factory had it own railway siding where wagons were loaded for conveyance to the Great Southern railway station in Bandon.[21] The plant employed an average of thirty people, including many, as was the case with Beamish & Crawford in Cork city, with long family associations. The 'leading' family was the Walsh family: the son and grandson of John Walsh, whose bottling business formed the basis of the Beamish company established in 1914, both later served as managers of the plant.

'When you drink Beamish Stout, you support the Irish Farmer'

While Richard Henrik's audacious plans for a massive expansion into Dublin did not come to fruition, a number of premises were bought there by the company in 1931. Beamish's strategy in Dublin was to provide a stout equal in strength to Guinness Extra at a price closer to what was charged for its weaker Single Stout. According to Beamish & Crawford documents from the period, there was no other stout *publicly* available in the capital's market. Dublin publicans were selling stouts from other small breweries as 'Guinness' from concealed casks. Beamish, on the other hand, was served openly, from unconcealed casks, 'and this known factor', according to the company, 'is gradually appreciated to the benefit of the Beamish consumption'.[22] In September 1931 Beamish & Crawford was granted licence transfers on seven premises: two on Parnell Street and one each on Richmond Road in Drumcondra, the North Wall, Lower Sheriff Street, Wexford Street and Townsend Street. Objections had been made to the transfer in two of these cases the previous year by one of the Dublin vintners' associations, which was concerned about 'syndicated' licences.[23]

The year 1932 brought bad news economically, with the start of the so-called 'economic war' with Britain after Fianna Fáil came to power. Firms like Guinness, which had large exports to the UK and also imported barley, were more directly affected than essentially local firms like Beamish & Crawford, which had limited exports and depended on Irish, mainly Cork, barley. Indirectly, the trade dispute did affect business, mainly through its impact on agricultural incomes, with the knock-on effect on money circulation and general consumer spending. Economic nationalism was the order of the day and firms like Beamish & Crawford joined in, advertising: 'When you drink Beamish Stout, you support the Irish Farmer, since none but Irish barley is used in its manufacture.'[24] Beamish & Crawford's 'support for the Irish farmer' went further, given the Beamish family's long association with cattle breeding and dairying, and it was a key sponsor of dairy herd and breeding competitions in 1920s and 1930s. It was also a prominent supporter of 'country sports' like greyhound and horse racing, coursing, drag hunting and shooting.

The coming to power of Fianna Fáil was welcomed by small farmers and the landless, but was viewed with apprehension by strong farmers and large landowners, who had been the bedrock of Cumann na nGaedheal support and took the new government's radical rhetoric about land redistribution seriously. Many large farmers joined the fascistic Blueshirts in opposition to Fianna Fáil policies, while a number of large landowners left the country, especially following the outbreak of the economic war in the summer of 1932. It was in this context that the *Southern Star* announced in August 1932 that Richard Henrik Beamish was 'the latest large landowner who has decided to leave this country and take up residence in Great Britain'.[25]

The year 1932 also brought some good news, with Beamish Stout in draught and bottle winning bronze medals at the prestigious international Brewers'

Workers repair a brewery chimney, 1935. (*Irish Examiner*)

Left: Comedian Jimmy O'Dea (second from left) visits the brewery in February 1934. (*Irish Examiner*)
Right: Pupils from Blackpool national school in Cork are shown around the brewery by Philip Baylis, second brewer, 1935. (*Irish Examiner*)

From top:

Knuckleduster bottled stout was produced between 1933 and 1942. (Courtesy Ed Hinchy)

Label created for exports of bottled stout to the Far East in the late 1930s. (Courtesy Ed Hinchy)

Exhibition in London; this was heralded in newspaper advertisements claiming Beamish to be 'Ireland's Best – The World's Best'. The following year the company established a subsidiary in Liverpool called Messrs Beamish & Crawford (Liverpool) Ltd with a capital of £1,000 in £1 shares. It was set up to handle the export trade to Britain and beyond. Beamish products were sent in bulk to Liverpool, where they were bottled and distributed. The following year Beamish & Crawford began to export its new 'super stout', with the dubious name of Knuckleduster (named after a racehorse owned by one of the extended Beamish family), to Britain through its Liverpool subsidiary. This bottled strong stout, which lasted until 1942, was primarily produced for the British market, but was also sold in Ireland in the mid-1930s, where it was advertised in colourful terms: 'Now is the winter of our discontent, Made glorious summer by this "Sun" of Cork – KNUCKLEDUSTER – Cork's Super Stout – Makes a dull day bright – Worth a sovereign a sip, only six pence a nip.'[26] The lifting of Prohibition in the US in 1933 opened the way for limited exports there, and a special Foreign Extra Stout was developed for this and other markets. In November 1934 the Cunard vessel *Britannic* took a consignment of Beamish export stout on board, described in the press as 'the first consignment of its kind to be shipped to America by liner from Cove'.[27]

Because of the curtailment of exports to Ireland's dominant trading partner, the government established a Central Export Office to encourage and facilitate exports elsewhere in the world. Between 1936 and 1939, via its office in London, Beamish & Crawford sent small quantities of stout, together with advertising material, to such locations as Calcutta, Belgian Congo, Rangoon, Samari in the South Sea Islands, Singapore, Baghdad, Colombo, Mombasa, Hong Kong, Sudan, Cairo, Sydney, Sudan, Palestine, Nassau, Trinidad, Reunion, Cairo, Jamaica and Kuala Lumpur.[28]

Meanwhile, back in Cork, Richard Henrik's son, Richard P. Beamish, took responsibility for the firm's managed and tied houses in the 1930s. Following on the improvements in cleanliness resulting from the new trading agreement of 1925, Beamish began a process of modernising and refurbishing the principal Beamish & Crawford houses across the city and giving them distinctive names (previously, most tied houses had simply carried the name of the brewery), such as the Black Lion, Bridge House, the Centre Forward, the Pelican, Tom's Tavern, the Cork Arms, the Mail Coach, the Golden Lion and, in 1939, the jewel in the crown, the Swan and Cygnet at 125 Patrick's Street, first acquired in 1861. 'Patrick's Bridge and Brian Boru Bridge can be seen from the house,' ran the promotional piece on its reopening in December 1939, 'as can the coming and going of cross-Channel steamers; the music of Shandon's Bells drifts with dreamy melody in through the open windows; and half the buses of Cork stop outside the doors.' The architects Chillingworth & Levie oversaw the refurbishment, and four watercolours by rising Cork artist Patric Stevenson adorned the walls of the stylish interior, which is still remembered fondly in Cork.[29] 'Quidnunc' from *The Irish Times* of Dublin visited Cork in 1952 and noted that Beamish & Crawford had paved the way in the 'civilising of Irish pubs' and that Richard P. had set out to improve the houses in the 1930s 'on the premise that the pub is the poor man's club … My only regret is that Beamish's have not more establishments of their own in Dublin – they could teach the taverners of the capital a great deal.'[30]

Other innovations in the mid-1930s included a 'quick one' stout dispenser, a new method of serving draught in high condition; a special new line from Bandon, Beamish's Grape Fruit Crush – 'the latest modern drink';[31] and a light beer called Red Tower Lager, which was produced in small quantities from 1936 to 1942. The

Racking or filling casks, 1953. (Courtesy Ed Hinchy)

market for lager would not develop in earnest until the 1960s, when Beamish & Crawford was well placed, having been taken over by Canadian Breweries, the makers of Carling Black Label, in 1962. Since its foundation Beamish & Crawford had always employed top-quality brewers, and in 1937 J.L. Shimwell, who had been head brewer since 1932, was awarded a doctorate by the University of Birmingham for his internationally renowned work on the bacteriology of fermentation, carried out at the brewery on South Main Street.[32]

The economic war had eased in 1935 and ended in April 1938 to general relief. Beamish & Crawford sales (helped by the early success of Knuckleduster) had held relatively steady at around 30,000 barrels per year (plus or minus 2,000), which was very low compared to the pre-1924 era, but an improvement on the average of the 1920s (with the exception of 1928, when it reached almost 40,000). In May 1938 Beamish & Crawford and Murphy's announced a price rise of 12s per barrel of stout, which meant a rise in the price of a pint from 8d to 9d. They explained that the increase was necessitated by the 'advances in the costs of wages,

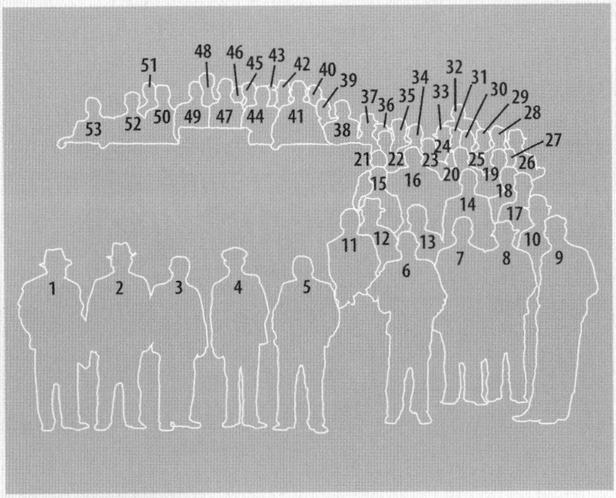

Brewery Workers Club outing to Tramore, July 1937.

1 Frank Creedon (cooper)
2 Wm. Rochford (cooper)
3 James Higgins (cooper)
4 ?;
5 Matt Higgins (cooper)
6 Thomas Ahern
7 Wm. Kidney (bottling store)
8 John O'Leary (bottling store foreman)
9 Jerry Kelleher (maintenance)
10 Thomas Kelleher
11 John Murphy
12 Eugene O'Sullivan (cooper)
13 David O'Connell (bottling store)
14 Dan Hurley
15 John Marratt (I.T.G.W.U. Rep.)
16 Daniel Carroll
17 ?; **18** ?;
19 John Barrett
20 'Boss' O'Connell (foreman cooper)
21 ?; **22** Fred Mulcahy
23 Phil O'Connell (aux. fireman)
24 E. Stevens
25 ?; **26** ?;
27 Con Kelly
28 James O'Connell
29 Jerh. O'Donovan
30 Dan O'Sullivan (mashing loft)
31 ?
32 Ned Kent (washing quay); **33** ?;
34 John O'Sullivan (foreman, mashing loft)
35 John Russell; **36** ?
37 Thomas O'Rourke
38 Patrick Kelleher
39 Christy Barrett (foreman cooper)
40 Richard Duff (stores)
41 Wm. O'Brien; **42** ?
43 James Murphy (office)
44 Patrick Curtin
45 Patrick Blake
46 ?; **47** Walter Buckley
48 John Connors (carpenter)
49 Frank Halnon (office)
50 John Hurley; **51** ?; **52** ?
53 Billy Hayes (vat room foreman)

rates, coal, brewing materials and, in fact, everything used in the breweries'. There had also been a rise in city rates.[33]

This unpopular price rise was followed immediately – with timing, according to the Murphy's board, that 'looked to be too opportune for a mere coincidence' – by the arrival in the city's public houses of a new cider from Bulmers of Clonmel that developed a name that was immortalised in the Cork ballad 'Johnny Jump Up' ('Oh never, oh never, oh never again / If I live to a hundred or a hundred and ten / For I fell to the ground and I couldn't get up / After drinking a quart of the Johnny Jump Up'). The drink became a 'craze' in the spring and summer of 1938 before its popularity waned considerably in the winter. Its key attractions were strength and price. It had an alcohol content that was almost twice that of stout, but it was taxed at mineral water rates of 12s per barrel compared to 100s for stout, and so was sold much cheaper. 'The local topers took to it like ducks to water,' according to the local brewers, 'none the less readily because it possessed a "kick" that no mere stout could possibly hope to rival.'[34]

Photograph (*c.* 1941) taken to mark seventy-five years' service of Con O'Shea (centre, front row). Standing (l–r): Jack Good (coopers' shop); David Kidney (washing quay); Tom Ashman (miller); Michael Kenneally (mashing loft); Jack O'Sullivan (mashing loft foreman); Paddy Deasy (mashing loft); Jack Marrett (cooper); Billy Kidney (mashing loft); Harry Jeffries (brewery foreman); Jack Duggan (mashing loft); Dan O'Sullivan (mashing loft); Doc Connell (washing quay foreman); Paddy Lynch (mashing loft); Seán MacSweeney (painter). Front row (l–r): Donie O'Sullivan (laboratory); Eugene O'Callaghan (mashing loft); Con O'Shea (mashing loft); 'Boss' O'Connell (foreman cooper); Finbarr Punch (mashing loft). (Courtesy Ed Hinchy)

Emergency

In 1939 the expansionist aggression of Hitler's Germany had reached a point that made war inevitable. In that same year, Beamish & Crawford engaged in some expansionism of its own when it purchased Woodhead's (Canonbury) Brewery in Islington, London. Towards the end of the war in 1944, Beamish/Woodhead's acquired the South London Brewery (formerly Jenner's), which had a number of tied houses in London and had been damaged during the Blitz. The South London Brewery was modernised and modern bottling plants were installed in both breweries; they worked to full capacity in strained circumstances (especially bottle, malt and hops shortages) to supply British soldiers abroad after D-Day and position themselves for the post-war market, reintroducing the famous Jenner's Golden Ale, which had been discontinued at the outbreak of war. J.J. Cummins was chairman and Richard P. Beamish sat on the board of the amalgamated company. Brian Glover, in his *Lost Beers and Breweries of Britain*, describes the South London Brewery as 'an unusual act. Controlled by Irish brewer Beamish of Cork and theatrical impresario Prince Littler, it did stout trade in theatre bars.'[35]

The southern Irish state, which declared its neutrality in the war, escaped the

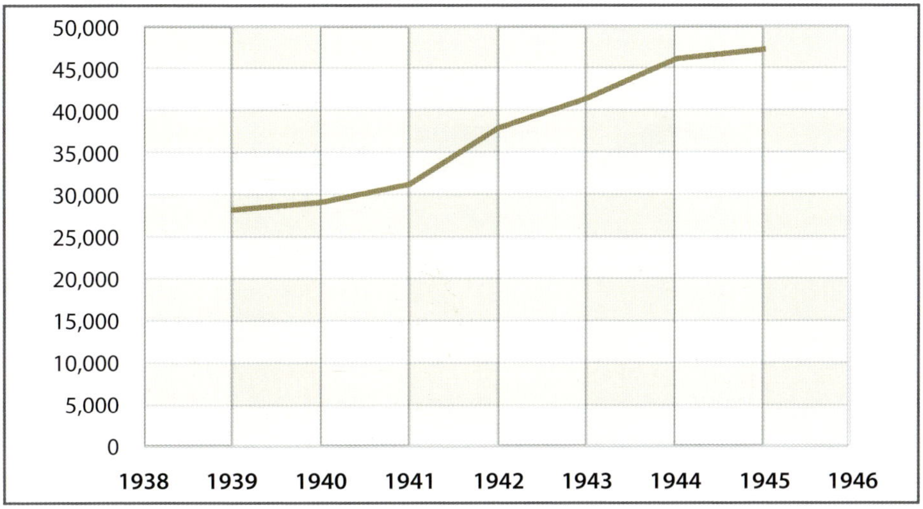

Beamish & Crawford, sales (in barrels), 1939–45.

bombings that devastated many parts of the UK and Europe, but the war, or 'The Emergency', as it was known, had a heavy impact on economic and social life, particularly from 1941 as the British imposed a de facto blockade that resulted in severe shortages and the closure of many businesses. The brewing industry was able to continue, but with difficulty. Despite the problems thrown up by wartime circumstances, trade increased for Beamish & Crawford, with sales rising steadily throughout the war years, although this was not matched by profits, which were eaten into by rising costs.

On the outbreak of war, the government immediately looked to soft targets in order to maximise revenue and build up reserves. An extra 12s per barrel (or a halfpenny per pint) was imposed, and the breweries had to decide whether to pass on the increase to a public still smarting from the 1938 rise. Following discussions between Beamish & Crawford and Murphy's, they decided not to pass the cost on to the customer, but rather divide it between the brewers and the publicans. A further rise at the same rate was similarly absorbed in 1940, as the price of barley and imported coal began to rise sharply.[36]

Shortages began in earnest in 1941 with the beginning of silent economic sanctions by the British on the stubbornly neutral Irish state. Imported petrol, coal and hops became scarce, and barley became less available and more expensive as the maintenance of essential supplies was prioritised by the government. Limits were put on the amount of malt that breweries could use, and at the beginning of the 1941 season the government, armed with emergency powers, ordered a halt to malting altogether. This decision was reversed, much to the relief of the breweries, which would have been forced to close.[37] The brewers at Beamish & Crawford made a failed attempt to

The Counting House, c. 1930. (Courtesy Ed Hinchy)

malt wheat at one stage and also used oats in the mash tun. In general, the brewery maintained production mainly through the utilisation of poorer-quality barleys.[38]

In early 1942 the Irish government proposed an exchange of beer for wheat to the British, which was initially refused, prompting a temporary halting of stout exports. The British Ministry for Food feared the 'serious' effect of this on output, especially in Belfast, and a deal was struck whereby exports were resumed in return for 20,000 tons of wheat. The US representative in Dublin complained to his British counterpart about this exchange of 'a vital necessity for what Americans regard at best as a luxury and at worst a poison'.[39] Coal imports from Britain dwindled to a trickle, and what came in was of increasingly poor quality – so called 'brussy coal'. Ireland underwent a 'turf drive', and in September 1941 *The Irish Press* reported that Beamish & Crawford had purchased 150 tons of turf and intended to take 1,000 tons more. A representative told the paper that they had been experimenting with using turf in their boilers. Dry turf was found to work 'surprisingly' well, and most of the coal available was so bad that it would only burn when mixed with the Irish fuel.[40] This was supplemented with timber.[41] A shortage of staves and other cooperage requisites forced the company to buy 300 kilderkins and fifty barrels from outside sources in 1943, reassuring its coopers as it did so that this was an exceptional move in exceptional times and normal service would resume with restored supplies.[42]

Despite the difficulties with maintaining production – and the necessity to improvise with turf, oats, old bottles and wood that would not normally have met the requirements of coopers – trade, as mentioned earlier, increased year on year between 1939 and 1945. Disruption to rail and road transport curtailed Guinness supplies in the city as the war progressed, to the advantage of the local breweries. Tens of thousands of Irish men and women emigrated to work in the British war economy; they returned on breaks with money to spend and also sent significant amounts home, which was spent by their grateful families. The mobilisation of the population for the 'national effort' included the aforementioned turf drive and mass enlistment into the Local Defence Force (LDF) and Local Security Force (LSF), together with the mobilisation of the regular army, creating a context for beer drinking as well as additional money. In 1943 Beamish & Crawford sponsored a performance in the Cork Opera House at which attendance was free and restricted to Cork members of the Irish army, navy and LDF.[43] Thousands of Irish people also joined the British forces, as did London-born Beamish & Crawford sales director Joseph Baillon, who had also fought in the First World War.

Director and former joint managing director A.F. Sharman Crawford died in 1943, and the following year another stalwart of the company, director and long-time secretary F.W. Le Flufy, also passed away.

The post-war boom peaked for Beamish & Crawford in 1948, when sales figures of 58,141 barrels were the highest since 1922. This was heavily influenced by the appalling winter of 1947–8, which severely curtailed supplies of Guinness. That severe weather also led to the worst harvest in living memory, and the brewing industry was only saved from disaster by the emergency import of Chilean and Australian barley. In January 1948 the government announced a 45 per cent cut in the allocation of barley for brewing due to the shortages. While Guinness and Murphy's announced an immediate cut in supplies, Beamish had sufficient reserves of barley to maintain supplies to existing customers, but would not take any additional orders until the barley situation had been restored to normal. The annual seasonal fall in the consumption of beer from January to March made the situation less critical.[44] The good returns for 1943–8 allowed the company to pay out arrears of preference dividends, which had not been paid out in many years.

In the final three months of 1948, trade was hit by another government measure, however – a 3d per pint increase in duty in October. This, among a myriad of factors, led to the fall of the Fianna Fáil government and its replacement with a coalition that reversed the increase, only for it to be reimposed by a returned Fianna Fáil in 1952; at least that duty increase was accompanied by a price rise of 1p per pint to the brewers, which helped offset the losses from sales, which dropped from 45,726 in 1951 to 33,998 in 1953. This rapid decline continued, with sales dropping below 20,000 barrels in 1959, the brewery's lowest ever output.

From top: Strongman Butty Sugrue shows his strength, 1959. (*Irish Examiner*)

Ireland's most famous wrestler, Danno O'Mahony of Ballydehob, County Cork, from a 1936 sports programme. (Courtesy Barry Cassidy)

Drums, dollars and harps

Guinness began experimenting with metal for barrels, tanks and tankers after the Second World War, and in 1947 began introducing the first metal 'drums' – initially known as 'iron lungs' – into the trade. They began arriving in Cork in 1948. The draught pint was traditionally produced by a combination of stout from two wooden barrels – one with highly conditioned brew and the other with flatter beer. Guinness had replaced the 'high' wooden barrel with a metal drum, which, according to Beamish & Crawford's brewers, improved the pint significantly, making the head creamier and longer lasting and generally providing a 'superior' drinking experience. Regular meetings were held in the brewery in 1949 and 1950 to find a way to respond. The coopers naturally argued against its development and set out to hold the line against this existential threat to their trade. The Dublin coopers had not managed to stop the tide and warned their Cork counterparts that Guinness was aiming to put all draught supplies in metal casks, replace wooden vats with aluminium and supply large bottlers in metal road tankers rather than in wooden barrels. They indicated that Guinness draught sales were rocketing and both publicans and customers preferred the metal, as for the publican there was less leakage and it was easier to handle, while customers were more confident that their drink was not adulterated. As customers in Cork began to show the same preference (according to Richard P. Beamish, virtually an 'insistence') in 1949–50, the firm attempted to convince the coopers that improved sales with metal would mean few if any redundancies; the alternative was continuing lost trade and redundancies in any event. Having failed to convince the brewery that oak casks were 'technically superior', the coopers' next strategy was to warn the company that if even one metal container was used, 'we were determined to use the strike weapon'.

The resistance of the coopers combined with difficulties in replicating the Guinness success in conditioning (a variety of pumping and other techniques were unsuccessfully tested) kept metal at bay for the remainder of the 1950s. Eventually, two to three metal containers were used for 'experimental purposes' in 1960 with the agreement of the coopers, so long as they were kept within 'the confines of the brewery'. In 1963 the first metal container from Beamish & Crawford was sent out to the trade, again as an 'experiment'. The coopers objected, but their position was becoming more Canute-like, as Guinness had now gone over almost entirely to metal and Murphy's had decided in 1961 that while 'Murphy's From the Wood' was 'Good', in the words of its famous advertisement, Murphy's from the metal was even better.[45] By 1963 Beamish & Crawford was a fully owned subsidiary of Canadian Breweries, and a new era that would see the demise of the coopers had begun in earnest. They were told baldly that the brewery was converting totally to metal. The older coopers were given retirement packages and the younger ones were redeployed in the brewery at their existing rates of pay.[46]

By the end of the 1950s the era of wooden casks was coming to an end for all Irish brewers. (Heineken)

Exports to the USA are celebrated on this brewery lorry, 1953. (Courtesy Mike Hannon)

In 1950 Beamish & Crawford's gaze turned again across the Atlantic. Guinness had been exporting to the US from Ireland consistently since 1934, following the lifting of Prohibition, and Beamish also had a small number of exports there in the 1930s. In 1949 Guinness decided to establish a brewery in Long Island and replaced the Irish-brewed stout with a New York brew. A market developed for 'genuine' Irish-brewed stout and Beamish stepped in.[47] In July 1950 a reception was held aboard the Irish Shipping vessel the *Irish Oak* in Cork to mark the occasion of the first shipment of fifty barrels of Beamish to the US. The chairman of Irish Shipping, Stephen McKenzie, and the Minister for Defence, Thomas F. O'Higgins, both praised Beamish & Crawford for its enterprise. Many had been 'preaching about the necessity for dollar trade,' said O'Higgins, 'but no preaching was as powerful as example and practice'.[48]

Beamish & Crawford bottling plant, 1953. (*Irish Examiner*)

Guinness was unhappy with the competition and instructed its distributors, Dublin Distributors, to cease handling Beamish or it would pull its contract for Guinness. They refused and Guinness pulled out, leading Dublin Distributors to sue the American wing of the company for $1 million in 1952. The action failed, and in 1954 Guinness shut down its American brewery and began exports from Ireland again, to the obvious detriment of Beamish.[49]

Richard P. Beamish spent three weeks in the US in August and September 1954 attempting to consolidate the American market and expand it beyond New York and the east coast. On his return to Cobh aboard the *Britannic*, which was the liner that had brought the first post-Prohibition shipment of Beamish to the US in 1934, Beamish declared himself happy that the brand had established itself in the US and, using the buzzword of the era, said it was a 'regular dollar-earner for Ireland'. He then had to field questions about a remark he had reportedly made to an American journalist to the effect that he was going to popularise vodka in Ireland. He denied it, saying that when he was asked by a journalist his opinion of US-manufactured vodka, 'I replied having tried it mixed with stout, that it was a very palatable drink. Beyond that I made no comment.'[50]

The lure of the dollar was a major factor behind the annual An Tóstal festival launched by the government in 1953. In what was essentially a tourism drive, the idea was to attract the Irish diaspora, particularly Americans, to Ireland by putting on a series of large-scale events and festivals. Although mired in controversy and ridiculed by many, the festival, which lasted until 1958, left some lasting cultural legacies, such as the Wexford Opera Festival, the Dublin Theatre Festival and the Cork Film and Choral Festivals. Richard P. Beamish was on the executive council of An Tóstal in Cork and also on the reception committee. Beamish & Crawford produced a special Tóstal Stout for the festival in late 1952, but it soon ran into trouble with its old adversary, Uncle Arthur. The problem was that the Irish tourist board, Bord Fáilte, had officially sanctioned a harp as the Tóstal symbol; Beamish duly put it on the label, only to provoke an objection from Guinness, whose famous trademark was, of course, a harp. A compromise was reached in February 1953 whereby the Tóstal harp was moved to the neck label to be replaced by the Beamish & Crawford shamrock on the body label.[51]

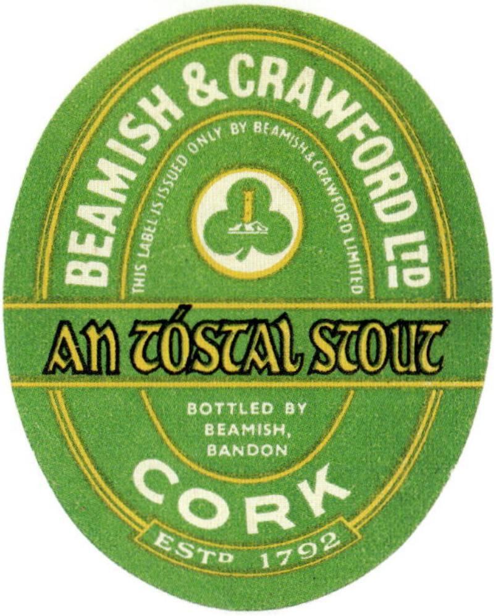

From top: An Tóstal Stout labels, 1953. (Courtesy Ed Hinchy); newspaper advertisement from 1953. (Courtesy Ronnie Herlihy)

Presentation to retiring employees (1957). Back row (l–r): Michael Kenneally; Tommy Ashman; Con O'Regan; Jack O'Sullivan. Front row (l–r): H.J. Larmour; Bill Collins; Jack Marrett; Dan O'Sullivan; J.J. O'Leary, R.B. Walsh. (Courtesy Ed Hinchy)

In late 1956 it was announced that Richard P. Beamish was to leave Cork and his post as managing director to take up the chairmanship and managing directorship of Beamish & Crawford's UK interests, which at this stage included a brewery in Devonshire, a mineral water company in the south of England as well as the merged London breweries (Woodhead's and South London) and several catering establishments in the English capital.[52] He was replaced as managing director jointly by Dick Walsh, manager in Bandon, and director H.J. Larmour. Beamish remained as chairman and returned several times a year to Cork, despite having sold the old family home in Glounthane.

Dick Walsh, whose grandfather, John Walsh, was a nationalist MP and had started the bottling firm that was absorbed by Beamish & Crawford Bottling on its foundation in 1914, had followed his father, R.S. Walsh, as manager of the thriving Bandon concern. Business was going so well, especially the popular Little Norah range of mineral waters, that the plant had to be expanded in 1945 and again in 1956, when its capacity was doubled. In the same year a state-of-the-art Redox Tank Conditioning System, 'the most modern chilling, filtering, bottling and pasteurising equipment available', was installed to produce the increasingly popular processed and pasteurised bottled beers. The new plant could perform in a fortnight what would have taken six weeks using the old, natural methods of maturation. It could process 200 dozen bottles an hour and was used for ale and lager, including Becks German beer, for which it had recently acquired the agency. The plant also continued to produce naturally conditioned beer, replete with sediment, for its diehard devotees.[53] The Bandon outpost of Beamish & Crawford lasted until 1967, when its operations were transferred to Cork. At that stage the brewery was under the management of United Breweries of Ireland, a Bass-Charrington/Canadian Breweries company.

Despite its many successes – the Bandon operation, headline US exports, its English companies and Dublin outlets, its fine Cork pubs and its continued high profile locally in Cork and Munster – Beamish & Crawford's sales continue to decline throughout the 1950s. While there were particular local factors at play – such as the increasing preference for Guinness in metal casks amongst the public and Beamish's slowness to adapt, plus having to share a small local market with a city rival – the fundamental underlying problem was the disastrous state of the Irish economy since the war. Ireland had the slowest economic growth in western Europe, unemployment reached record levels in 1957 and almost half a million people, mainly young, left the country in search of work throughout the 1950s – this represented 16 per cent of the population. In 1959 Seán Lemass became Taoiseach and launched a new direction in Irish economic policy. Planning was introduced and the Irish economy was opened to international investment, heralding the age of the multinationals. Beamish & Crawford would become one of the first major Irish firms to be taken over by a large transnational corporation, and a new era in its long history was about to begin.

14

'Behind the old "Tudor" façade': 1960–1969

The brewing industry underwent more changes in the 1960s than at any period since the First World War. This was an era of consolidation and 'merger mania', with the number of breweries in the UK and Ireland decreasing significantly and the size of the remaining ones expanding massively. Competition was ramped up, with the new giants introducing new products and developing and applying new technologies, and clashing in the expanding battlefield of advertising and branding. These developments coincided with the opening up and internationalisation of the Irish economy after decades of protectionism – the advent of the era of the multinationals and of foreign competition. Seán Lemass was the Taoiseach (1959–66) who drove this shift and he would also play a direct role in the story of Beamish & Crawford's experience of this transformative decade.

Beamish and J.J. Murphy & Co. both came under outside control for the first time in the 1960s, while Guinness absorbed the remainder of the independent breweries, coming within a whisker of taking over Beamish & Crawford in 1962. Guinness maintained its position as the dominant force in the Irish market and one of the world's leading brewing companies, presenting a huge obstacle to the market expansion plans of the Cork breweries despite their multinational backing. The overwhelming dominance of stout on the Irish beer market began to weaken in the face of the rising popularity of ale and lager in a changing socioeconomic environment. A growing population, a new urban middle class, modernised public houses, the growth of the off-licence trade and more female and young drinkers combined with the intensive marketing and branding of the competitive marketplace to transform drinking habits and, in turn, change the face of Irish brewing. By the end of the decade, furthermore, the writing was on the wall for the old tied-house system that had sustained the brewery over the previous century.

Cork city skyline from the roof of the Counting House. (John Sheehan)

(Courtesy Ed Hinchy)

The Battle for Beamish, 1962

Beamish & Crawford's profits were at such a low ebb in the decades following independence that no dividend on ordinary shares had been paid since 1924 and the last payment of a preference dividend had been in 1952. In early 1962 a spokesman declared that there was little prospect under the existing capital structure of the company of reaching a situation where preference dividends could be kept up to date and 'no prospect' of ordinary shareholders ever receiving a dividend. With this in mind, the company had passed a special resolution in October 1961 reducing its capital of £480,000 by £330,000 and applied to the High Court, as it was legally required to do, in January 1962 for confirmation of this reduction. Beamish & Crawford had been incorporated in 1901 with a capital of £480,000, divided into 56,000 5 per cent cumulative preference shares of £5 each and 40,000 ordinary shares of £5 each. With the new reduced capital of £150,000, preference and ordinary shares were replaced with 600,000 ordinary shares of 5s each. The shareholders now had shares, the company said, 'capable of being sold on the market'.[1]

The 'market' took the bait, and in late August 1962 an offer of 7s 6d per share was made through the Mostyn finance house in London on behalf of an undisclosed party. When a representative of Mostyn arrived in Cork on 7 September, he found, to his surprise, the Beamish & Crawford board in conference with representatives of the British brewers Charrington United, who had arrived through the newly opened Cork Airport on a private plane, accompanied by Beamish board member Lt. Col. Cotten. Chairman Richard P. Beamish had returned from England, where he had been based for the previous five years with the Beamish-owned Woodhead Brewery, to oversee the negotiations. Beamish & Crawford had an existing relationship with Charrington United, as they had recently become the distributor for Carling Black Label in bottles in the south of Ireland. No statement was issued following the meeting, and the Mostyn representative said he would remain in Cork to 'await developments'. A week later, Mostyn announced that the take-up on their offer of 7/6 per 5s share had reached an 'acceptable percentage', but within twenty-four hours Beamish shareholders saw their holdings soar in value and their company make headlines in three countries as two of the giants of world brewing began a takeover battle.

The Charrington United representatives who had held meetings with the board were acting on behalf of E.P. (Eddie) Taylor (see below), head of Canadian Breweries, who had a substantial stake in Charrington United.[2] Canadian Breweries now made an offer of 12s 6d per share. Its bid was supported by the Beamish board, who urged shareholders to accept the offer and reject the Mostyn bid. The directors, combined with a number of other large shareholders who supported them, controlled 44 per cent of the company. Taylor said he planned to build a new plant in Cork to brew Carling Black Label and to increase the shares in Beamish by at least 400,000 and offer them to the public, with preference given to existing Beamish shareholders.[3] The existing board would remain, with the addition of two Canadian Breweries directors. The following day Guinness dropped a bombshell into this carefully choreographed takeover when it made a conditional offer of 20s (or £1) per 5s Beamish & Crawford share. In its circular letter to shareholders, Guinness stated that 'the efficient conduct of the brewing industry in Ireland would be greatly helped by linking the future of Beamish & Crawford with that of their own organisation'. Guinness had been gradually taking over most small Irish breweries, and the acquisition of Beamish was a logical development. Guinness led the exploding Irish lager market with Harp, which it had introduced onto the British market the previous year, so it was anxious to scupper this attempt by the expansionist Taylor to muscle in on the Irish lager market. The Guinness move was also seen as part of the developing British 'lager war'; according to the *Financial Times*, Taylor hoped to 'start a skirmish' in his enemy's rear with a Cork-brewed Carling lager. There were also suggestions that Guinness feared a future challenge to its domination in the British stout market from a Canadian-controlled Beamish, which could utilise the extensive Charrington United tied-house system to export a competing Irish stout at the expense of Guinness.[4]

The brewery buildings from French's Quay, *c.* 1960. (Liam Kennedy)

The battle is joined

The initial Guinness bid was conditional on acceptance by 1 October 1962 by those holding at least 80 per cent of the shares in Beamish (the Canadian offer would close on 8 October). On 17 September Guinness made its offer unconditional; in other words, it would pay out no matter how many took up the offer. The reported speculation in London stock market circles was that the Guinness takeover bid would probably fail, but it hoped to secure enough shares to 'prove an embarrassment' to Canadian Breweries should the latter be victorious.[5] The Beamish & Crawford directors again urged shareholders to accept the Canadian Breweries offer, with its guarantee of management continuity, an attractive preferential share offer and assured extra employment in Cork in the future; Richard (Dickie) P. Beamish also intimated that Guinness might not be committed to maintaining brewing operations in Cork. Guinness countered with a stated commitment to keep the brewery open and to exploit Cork's position as a natural export centre in every possible way. The company outlined its track record in Ireland, such as the investment it had poured into the Great Northern Brewery in Dundalk, which it had acquired for the production of Harp, and Cherry's in Waterford, which brewed Phoenix Ale; it had maintained the small Perry's Brewery in Rathdowney, County Laois; and it had advanced significant funds to Smithwick's to modernise its plant in Kilkenny. Financial journalists urged shareholders to accept the higher offer; it was believed that the 56 per cent of shares that were being fought over were owned by approximately 200 individuals. Many were owned in trust, and trustees were warned about possible future legal action if they accepted a lower offer than one that was available.[6]

The 'battle for Beamish' garnered front-page headlines in Ireland and extensive coverage in the financial pages in Britain and Canada. London's *Investors' Chronicle* reported that in terms of investment, 'it matters little who gains control of a comparatively tiny Irish company'. The amounts involved – £600,000 in the case of Guinness, which had assets of over £50 million – were relatively small. The real questions concerned the motivations of both parties and the broader implications for the struggle to dominate the beer market in both Britain and Ireland.[7] Canadian Breweries executives flew in and out of Cork Airport and held closed-door meetings at the South Main Street brewery, while Guinness representatives hurried back and forth between Cork and Dublin.

Victory for Canadian Breweries

Finally, on 25 September 1962, Canadian Breweries effectively claimed victory via a dramatic announcement that appeared in the press in the form of an advertisement from the merchant bankers that had been operating on its behalf.[8] The statement claimed that the holders of more than half the shares in Beamish & Crawford had agreed to accept the Canadian Breweries offer. It had been increased to match the Guinness offer of £1 a share, and those who had already agreed to accept the earlier offer would receive this amount, as well as preferential treatment in the proposed offer of new shares when the Beamish share capital was increased. The latter, however, was dependent on Guinness and Mostyn releasing those who had accepted their offers, because if there were minority holdings outstanding when the Canadian Breweries offer expired, it might prevent the passing of an extraordinary resolution to increase Beamish & Crawford's share capital. Guinness directors met on the day the announcement appeared and in a subsequent statement to the press effectively conceded defeat. They noted the improved Canadian Breweries offer and said they would not increase their own bid. Furthermore, and crucially, they were willing to release from any obligation those who had accepted their offer so that they were free to accept the equivalent offer from Taylor. Mostyn also returned the forms of acceptance to those who had accepted their original offer, thus effectively completing the Canadian Breweries takeover of Beamish & Crawford.[9]

Eddie Taylor and 'merger mania'

E.P. (Eddie) Taylor, the head of Canadian Breweries and effectively the new boss of Beamish & Crawford, was a dynamic character who had been shaking up the British brewing scene for the previous several years. One of Canada's best-known and successful capitalists, in 1930 Taylor had taken over the Carling brewery in Ontario, which had been brewing Black Label since 1927. The brewery formed part of his brewing group that would become Canadian Breweries later in the 1930s. Taylor

Pictured at the brewery in July 1967, (l–r): Richard P. (Dickie) Beamish, Chairman, Beamish & Crawford; J.J. O'Leary, Head Brewer/Production Director, Beamish & Crawford; John Charrington, President-elect, Bass Charrington; Ken Richards, Managing Director, United Breweries Ireland and Beamish & Crawford. (Note the four principal Beamish & Crawford brands – Tower Stout, Bass, Carling Black Label and Celebration). (Roy Hammond)

had first introduced Carling Black Label in bottles to Britain in 1953 through a deal with the Hope & Anchor Brewery in Sheffield. In 1959 Taylor acquired control of Hope & Anchor, followed by a string of other small concerns, mainly in Scotland. In 1960 he established Northern Breweries (soon renamed United Breweries), which precipitated the consolidation of Scottish Brewers and Newcastle Breweries into the Scottish & Newcastle group. (In 1995 this group would take over Beamish & Crawford; in 2008 its own takeover by Heineken and Carlsberg led to the closure of the Beamish brewery the following year.) By the end of 1960, Northern/United Breweries controlled over 2,800 tied houses in Yorkshire, Scotland and the south of England. In 1961 Taylor made a hostile bid for Bristol Brewery Georges, only to lose out to Courage, Barclay & Simonds, which had itself been formed to escape a takeover by Taylor.

This frantic period of consolidation, or 'merger mania', in 1960–1, partly sparked by Taylor's expansionism, continued with the formation of Allied Breweries (by Ind Coope, Tetley Walker and Ansell's, incorporating fourteen breweries in all). This was followed by the merger of Bass, Ratcliff & Gretton with Mitchells & Butlers. In 1962 Taylor's United Breweries merged with Charrington to form Charrington United in an £80 million deal, creating the third-largest brewing group in the UK in the process, with over 5,000 tied houses. In the meantime, Watney Mann, which had acquired control of Cork's other brewery, J.J. Murphy & Co. in 1967, had swallowed up a half-dozen other British breweries.[10]

This period of consolidation would reach a high point with the merger of Taylor's Charrington United with Bass to create Bass Charrington in July 1967. This became the UK's largest brewery, with 19 per cent of the British trade and over 11,000 outlets. British brewing was now controlled by the 'Big Six': Bass Charrington, Allied, Courage, Scottish & Newcastle, Watney Mann & Truman, and Whitbread, along with Guinness. Their tentacles spread to Ireland through the Canadian Breweries/ Bass Charrington control of Beamish and Watney Mann's takeover of Murphy's, while Guinness had hoovered up what remained of the independent breweries in the rest of Ireland. The arrival of Taylor's empire into Ireland was primarily an extension of his expansion in the British market, with the development of Carling Black Label as the initial key. However, as mentioned above, there may have been a secondary consideration: the possibility of challenging Guinness's virtual stout monopoly, with an initial eye on the lucrative UK market, followed by the rest of the world. If this was in Taylor's mind (and he dropped a strong hint in that direction in June 1963), it was for the future; in the meantime, Canadian Breweries set about upgrading and modernising the old Cork plant to begin production of Carling Black Label.

The Carling era begins

Carling had been available in bottles in Britain since 1953. It went on draught there in 1965, by which time it had established itself as the quintessential 'British' lager. It was introduced to the southern Irish market in the summer of 1961. By now the world's largest-selling lager, Carling's initial introduction in Ireland was ostensibly to cater for the American and British tourist market. In the summer of 1960 the Ulster Brewery Co. of Belfast had been appointed bottler and distributor for Carling in Northern Ireland. By the end of that year, United Breweries had acquired its share capital and began the first exports south of the border in June 1961. Growing sales north and south led to a gradual expansion of the Belfast brewery, which 'reopened' as the New Mountain Brewery in November 1962. By this stage United had effectively taken control of Beamish, and until the old Cork brewery was modernised and rebuilt, Carling continued to be supplied in the Republic from Belfast.[11]

In March 1963, 400,000 5s ordinary shares in Beamish & Crawford were offered to the public, with Beamish shareholders who had been on the register on 17 September 1962 receiving preferential treatment. The issuing of additional shares promised by Taylor at the time of takeover never materialised. Meanwhile, Canadian Breweries proceeded with their acquisition of the remaining 0.2 per cent of shares it did not yet control, making Beamish & Crawford a wholly owned subsidiary.

The demolition of large parts of the old brewery was carried out between March and June 1963 to make way for the construction of a new lager brewing plant and, it was suggested in the press, increased capacity for the brewing of stout with an eye to taking on Guinness. 'In the rumbling destruction of centuries-old masonry,' wrote Michael Viney in *The Irish Times*, 'the Beamish & Crawford brewery takes the impact of control by Canadian Breweries. Behind the old "Tudor" façade and the old family names, £750,000 will be spent on reconstruction for the brewing of stout and lager and an export battle with Guinness for the world's stout market.'[12]

Charrington United itself had over 5,000 tied houses in Britain which could immediately take Beamish stout; it was being speculated in Britain that other large breweries with tied-house estates might be inclined to negotiate a deal and stock Beamish, especially in view of Guinness's link-up with Courage Barclay, Bass and Scottish & Newcastle in the promotion of its Harp lager. Canadian Breweries, however, continued to insist that it had no plans to launch a major challenge to Guinness on the international stout market.

(John Sheehan)

The old brewery, in the main part dating from the mid-1860s, was gradually demolished by the contractors P.J. Hegarty & Sons, with the exception of the mock Tudor-fronted Counting House (dating from the end of the First World War), malt storage bins, malt mills, the brewhouse mash tuns, kettle and hop backs. Production of Beamish stout continued during construction and Carling Black Label began to be brewed in Cork in June 1964. Canadian Breweries invested approximately £1 million on the first phase of the creation of the new brewery as part of a £2 million investment plan. The new brewery had hugely increased capacity and was designed for further expansion. The new state-of-the-art facility at South Main Street was blessed by Rev. R. Harris of St Fin Barre's Cathedral on 21 September 1964. Three days later, Taoiseach Seán Lemass officially opened the new brewery; speaking afterwards at a reception in Cork city hall, he hailed the involvement of Canadian Breweries in Irish industry, hoping it would attract the attention of other multinationals to the opportunities available in Ireland. He pointed to the knock-on advantages of expanded brewing operations in Cork for the barley growers and highlighted the 'double value to our national economy' of agriculturally connected industries like brewing.[13]

Dickie Beamish said that while Cork had been the principal market for the brewery in recent years, bottled and draught stout would now be launched on a much wider market. 'We are traditionally a Cork firm,' he declared, 'but we see the whole of Ireland as our field of endeavour' – and beyond, as exports would be central to development in the longer term, according to the chairman.[14]

The installation of huge fermenting and conditioning vessels that sat visibly on their foundations in the open air was a first in the brewing industry. The brewery claimed that the new facilities allowed it to produce stout of a more consistent quality. Beamish Extra Stout was pasteurised and closer to a 'sweet' rather than 'dry' stout, and a new dispenser had been developed that guaranteed the 'creamy head' so beloved in Ireland. Unfortunately, these dispensers were manufactured in England in a convoluted process involving up to sixty contractors, and bottlenecks, no less, delayed installation of the new Beamish stout dispensers by up to eighteen months, holding up the exploitation of the national trend towards draught. Even when they were installed, the dispensers were over-complicated and were identified as a major put-off for publicans. While Guinness sales in the mid-1960s were roughly 50/50 bottle and draught, Beamish sold three-quarters of its output through dispensers. The failure of the attempt to promote Beamish stout nationwide was an embarrassment for the brewery and it returned to the drawing board, working on a new stout product that would be launched in early 1968 and confined initially to the tried-and-tested Cork and Munster heartland.

'Mabel! Black Label!'

Carling was initially advertised in Ireland and Britain in the early 1960s using the slogan 'Hey Mabel! Black Label!', imported from America, which was soon modified to 'Mabel! Black Label!', the slogan reflecting the advertising imagery of 'laddish' beer drinkers 'ordering' from the eponymous barmaid. It was part of a successful strategy that aimed not only at establishing brand recognition, but the presentation of lager as a man's drink in the face of its residual effeminate image. It was also part of the project to make lager a mass-market drink, and not a niche product for middle-class types with 'continental' tastes. The crude masculinisation of Carling's image developed through the slogan 'Nothing comes between a man and his Carling', reaching its apogée with the famous 'I bet he drinks Carling Black Label' campaign in the 1980s as well as its sponsorship emphasis on male-dominated sports. This successful branding would backfire somewhat in subsequent decades, when the 'macho' image associated with Carling was difficult to shake off in a market with increasing numbers of female drinkers.[15]

In June 1963 the new era in marketing at Beamish & Crawford

began with the appointment of John Pickard as marketing manager. From the Isle of Man, he had originally joined Canadian Breweries in 1951 and had helped launch Carling Black Label on the English market in the early 1950s. For two years he was in charge of the lucrative Carling sales to the US forces in Europe, North Africa and the Middle East. Carling's first major deal in the Republic was its sponsorship of the feature race at the Festival of Kerry in Tralee in August 1963, which now became the £1,000 Carling Black Label Stakes. This was followed by sponsorship of numerous other horse racing and show jumping events throughout the island. In September 1963 Beamish & Crawford sponsored the six trophies for the all-Ireland speedboat championships which were held in Cork, and in November it became the first Irish firm to sponsor a major hare coursing event when Dick Walsh, joint managing director, presented the Cork Cup and a cheque for £500 to the Cork Coursing Club. The following November, Walsh said coursing was 'on the threshold of a big advance' and his firm was 'happy to contribute their own little portion to the success of the sport'.[16] In December 1964 Beamish sponsored the feature event at the three-day annual Kerry coursing meeting at Tralee, the Kingdom Cup.

In a crowded market, with Guinness and its lager, Harp, having made the early running, Carling had to get in where it could, sponsoring any sport it could, no matter how obscure, whether it was skydiving in Dungarvan or squash and darts tournaments in Dublin, as well as continuing the traditional Beamish & Crawford association with sports such as horse racing and coursing. In January 1964 Carling sponsored the new stand at the Cork soccer stadium, Turners Cross, home of Cork Celtic, presaging the brand's strong association with that sport in the 1990s. The emphasis of sponsorship was heavily on sport, though culture occasionally featured, such as Beamish's donation in 1965 of two 35mm projectors worth £600 to the Cork International Film Festival.

In June 1964 Beamish made the single biggest donation to the Irish Society for the Prevention of Cruelty to Children (ISPCC). A penny on every bottle of Carling sold between 6 May and 6 June was pledged to the ISPCC and in mid-June the cheque for £5,000 was presented to its president, Lord Killanin, the well-known Irish peer, who spearheaded an advertising campaign urging people to buy Carling. Dickie Beamish said 1.25 million bottles had been sold in the Republic in the month, and the brewery had rounded to figure to £5,000. Newspapers featured a large advertisement of a picture of Killanin along with the Carling Black Label logo and the heading 'Lord Killanin announces: Carling Black Label to help ISPCC', followed by details of the scheme. There had been some criticism of Killanin within the ISPCC for agreeing to such a blatant commercial tie-in (coincidentally or not, a decade later he joined the board of Beamish & Crawford). As well as securing a large cheque for the Society, the episode also earned Killanin a new nickname: 'Mabel'.[17]

'It's hard to beat Uncle Arthur'

Eddie Taylor had made inroads in the British market far more easily than in Ireland, not least because of the long-standing dominance of one of the world's leading breweries on its own patch; as one business journalist put it, '"It's hard to beat Uncle Arthur" is a truism of Irish brewing.'[18] In the face of increased competition from abroad, Guinness upped its game, advertising extensively in Ireland for the first time (it had not needed to previously), expanding its sponsorship portfolio, developing its export network and establishing breweries abroad, and taking over the majority of the remaining independent breweries in Ireland. While this was clearly in its own self-interest, it also had the positive effect of preserving and improving the small Irish ale industry, which would otherwise have folded under foreign competition in the newly open Irish economy.

Guinness began taking control of smaller Irish breweries from the early 1950s, beginning in 1952 with the struggling Cherry Bros brewery in New Ross, producers of Cherry's Ale. Production was moved to Waterford in 1955, where Davis, Strangman & Co., a brewery established in 1792, the same year as the Cork Porter Brewery, was acquired and a new chilled and filtered ale called Phoenix was developed. The malt for the production of the much-heralded 'bright young brother of Guinness' ('bright beers' was the term used to distinguish light ales and lager from stout) was supplied by Beamish. This was Ireland's first pasteurised ale and within a year it had secured 20 per cent of the ale market, mainly at the expense of Smithwick's No. 1. The newly named Cherry's Breweries absorbed Robert Perry & Son, Rathdowney, brewers of Perry's Ale, and Cairnes Brewery, Drogheda, in 1959. Guinness also acquired an interest in Macardle, Moore & Co. of Dundalk, brewers of Double Diamond and Macardle's No. 1 ales, in which British brewers Ind Coope also had an involvement. These breweries were organised by Guinness under the umbrella of Irish Ale Breweries (IAB), mainly for sales and marketing purposes, in 1962 (Guinness controlled two-thirds of IAB, with Ind Coope controlling one-third).

Guinness had bought the Great Northern Brewery in Dundalk from Smithwick's in 1960 for the production of Harp lager, and in 1962 advanced money to Smithwick's for the modernisation of its brewery in Kilkenny. Smithwick's developed a pasteurised ale called Time, and in turn pasteurised Smithwick's No. 1. Guinness secured a share in Smithwick's, which also brewed Idea lager, in 1963 and a controlling interest in 1964. Guinness completed its takeover in 1965, thus consolidating the Irish ale market under its umbrella, just as Watney Mann was preparing to begin brewing Red Barrel for the Irish market at Murphy's brewery in Cork and Beamish was planning its Celebration Ale, to be launched in 1966. Guinness countered with a new Smithwick's Draught in 1966, which drew level in sales with Celebration within a year and by 1968 passed out Phoenix to become the market leader.

From top:
A United Breweries Ireland Ltd truck leaving the brewery.
A float, St Patrick's Day parade, Cork, 1969.
(Roy Hammond)

Idea lager had been abandoned by Smithwick's just before the Guinness takeover, leaving the field clear for Harp, Carling and Carlsberg to fight it out in the growing Irish lager market. Carlsberg had been on sale in Ireland since 1955, when Bannow Bottlers of Dublin began bottling and distributing the Danish lager.

'Leader of the opposition'

Lager sales increased by 30 per cent in 1962–4, reaching a still modest 50,000 barrels annually (the total industry output was 900,000). The market was shared roughly equally by Carling, Harp and Carlsberg. A year later Carlsberg dropped behind, affected by strikes in Denmark and Ireland, import levy increases and a 'Buy Irish' campaign, leaving Carling and Harp neck and neck nationally, with the former leading the market in Cork and Harp remaining brand leader in the Dublin region. Beamish supplied Carling countrywide as far as a line running from Dundalk to Galway; customers north of this line were still supplied by Ulster Breweries.

In March 1966 Beamish announced its entry to the Irish ale market, initially in Cork city and county. Celebration Ale, named to mark the fiftieth anniversary of the 1916 Rising, was a strong ale sold in half-pint and pint bottles and on draught. It was the first Irish ale to be sold in pint bottles, which was made possible by the 'flash' or high-temperature/short-duration pasteurisation techniques employed at the Cork brewery.

At the end of 1966, Charrington United and Canadian Breweries announced the creation of a new marketing and management company called United Breweries Ireland (UBI), with the recently resigned Taoiseach, Seán Lemass, as chairman. The company, which began officially on 1 January 1967, was established to manage the business of Beamish & Crawford and the sales of Charrington's Northern Ireland subsidiary, Charrington Kinahan. Ken Richards of Charrington United was appointed managing director of both UBI and Beamish & Crawford. Richard P. Beamish, who remained as chairman of Beamish & Crawford in a non-executive capacity, and Robin Kinahan, chairman of Charrington Kinahan of Belfast, also joined the board of UBI.

Since leaving the office of Taoiseach in November 1966, Lemass had taken up a range of well-paid directorships, including Waterford Glass, Ryans' Tourist Holdings and Electrical Industries of Ireland. Lemass's rapid transition from Taoiseach to private sector multiple director (within two months of leaving office he held nine directorships) raised eyebrows in some political and journalistic circles. Commentator Proinsias Mac Aonghusa regarded Lemass as a Taoiseach who had operated in the interests of 'financiers' and was unsurprised that once he left the post, 'he grabbed

Below, from left: Ken Richards, Managing Director, United Breweries Ireland and Beamish & Crawford; Richard P. (Dickie) Beamish, Chairman, Beamish & Crawford; Alan Walker, Chairman, Bass Charrington; J.J. O'Leary, Head Brewer/Production Director, Beamish & Crawford; unknown. (Roy Hammond)
Inset, right: Seán Lemass. (Cork Airport)

all around him and brought the office of the head of Government into the market place'.[19] Notwithstanding such understandable discomfort about the direction Irish political life was taking in this new capitalist era, from a commercial point of view, securing the business-friendly and popular Lemass, who remained a Fianna Fáil TD until 1969, as chairman was something of a coup for Beamish's latest controllers.

Ale and lager had quickly come to dominate production at the Cork plant. By 1968 the 'bright beers' – Celebration, Bass, Gold Keg (a light ale launched in June 1967) and Carling – accounted for over 80 per cent of the brewery's output, with ale alone representing half of all the beer produced at the former stout brewery. The ale market was booming, having more than doubled since 1963. Celebration continued to increase its share of that expanding market, and following the merger of Bass and Charrington United to create Bass Charrington in 1967, UBI distributed bottled Bass ale in Ireland and began production of Bass on draught in Cork in late 1968. It was sold in a limited number of outlets in Cork and Dublin initially and was rolled out nationally in the spring 1969. Bass was similar to Smithwick's, but was darker and had a more 'male image'. It quickly became the main challenger to Smithwick's and won a 40 per cent market share in Munster. Another ale, Worthington's, began production in Beamish & Crawford at the end of 1969, and small quantities of the Canadian ale Piper were also distributed. Carling had become available on draught in 1966. Draught lager sales in Ireland leapt from zero in 1964 to 30 per cent of total lager sales in 1969. In the same period, the proportion of ale sold on draught went from 40 to 67 per cent, and stout from 60 to 70 per cent.

Beyond beer, other changes were afoot. In April 1967 UBI announced the imminent closure of the Beamish & Crawford Bottling Co.'s mineral water plant in Bandon, with the transfer of operations, and a significant proportion of the staff, to Cork. Also in April, UBI launched a new agency company called Wine and Spirit Traders to acquire new agencies for wines and spirits. The expansion into this area developed from the Charrington United acquisition of the Old Bushmills Distillery, Antrim, in July 1964 and the fact that UBI director Robin Kinahan's wine and spirits company had also been absorbed. Wine and spirit sales were up in 1967, especially UBI's whiskey range, Old Bushmills, Vat 69 and Cream o' the Barley.

As mentioned earlier, the failed Beamish stout foray into the national market had forced a retreat to Cork in early 1967. Throughout 1967 the brewery experimented and test-marketed a new stout for its local market. The new overall boss, John Charrington, who became president of Bass Charrington following the merger of Charrington United and Bass in July 1967, declared that until stout brewed at Beamish & Crawford succeeded outside of Cork and Munster, it would not be sold in the Bass Charrington tied houses in Britain. He clearly believed that the future lay

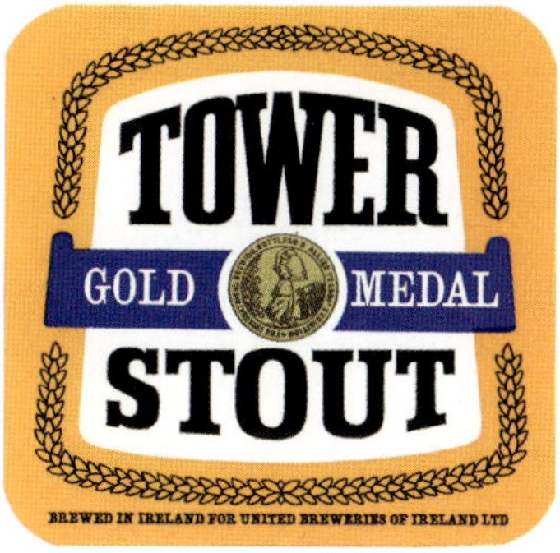

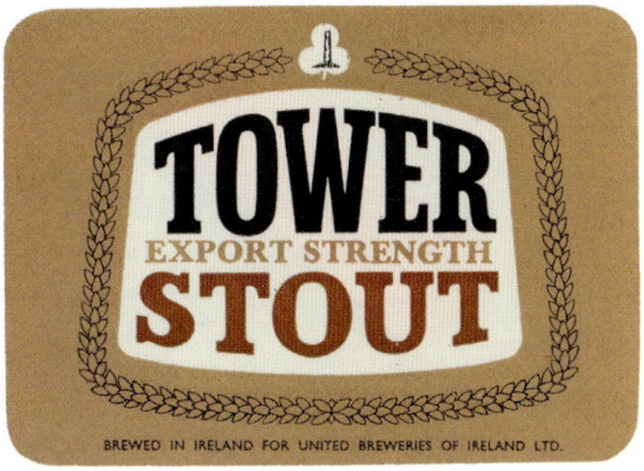

Top: (Beamish & Crawford Brewery Collection/Dori O'Connell)
Bottom: (Courtesy Ed Hinchy)

in ale and lager rather than stout, pointing out that he had seen porter and brown ale drop from 80 per cent of the British market to almost nothing. However, his approach was to 'keep Beamish going. In fifteen years' time, it might be top of the table.' The brewery's new stout, called Tower (Export Strength), was launched on draught and in bottle on the Cork market in January 1968. Tower – named after the round tower of the Beamish logo – had a 'dry' taste close to Guinness, but was pasteurised and artificially carbonated. In 1968 a test run in a number of British cities went down like a lead balloon and Tower returned, licking its wounds, to the local market. It was followed home a year later by Murphy's stout, which Watney had attempted to launch in a much more ambitious way on the British market under the title Colonel Murphy's, only for the initiative to end equally abysmally.

At the launch of Tower, UBI chairman Seán Lemass said that as UBI was describing itself as the 'opposition' to Guinness on the Irish market in trade press advertising, he as chairman could now describe himself as 'leader of the opposition'.[20] However, if the political analogy were to be developed, UBI more resembled a niche, sectional party rather than a serious electoral challenger to the all-powerful 'Uncle Arthur'. Although Beamish was undergoing a period of transition and development, its losses in the second half of the 1960s were a concern. The accounts for 1964–5 showed a net loss of £151,242, and continuing losses in 1966 probably prompted the formation of UBI. However, losses continued: £147,000 in 1966–7 and £208,462 for the seventeen months to September 1968. Despite improved sales, losses continued in 1969 due to increased operating expenditure and the high cost of a maintenance workers' strike that halted production for five weeks from late January to early March.

The South Gate Inn on the corner of Sullivan's Quay and Drinan Street, Cork, 1969. (Roy Hammond)

Tied-house troubles

By the end of the 1960s, the tied-house system that had been the mainstay of both Cork breweries' local business for almost a century was beginning to unravel. In the late 1960s Beamish & Crawford still had 195 tied houses – 68 in the city and 127 in Cork county – through which 70 per cent of draught Beamish output was sold. There were twelve different types of tie in all (in some cases, for example, a pub was only tied for porter and stout and not ale, in others for draught only, and so on), but in the large majority of cases, the tie specified that the publican 'shall deal exclusively with the lessor [Beamish & Crawford], its assignees or nominees for all Porter, Stout, Ale beer or other malt liquors, wines, spirits and mineral waters'.[21]

The problems began with declining demand for Beamish stout in the 1960s, due to its perceived poor quality. The Beamish Extra Stout experiment had failed (see above) and the new Tower Stout, launched in January 1968, fared little better; there were soon vociferous complaints about its inconsistency, sweetness and, more ominously, its 'laxative effects'. Sales of Beamish stout fell by over 20 per cent in the brewery's west Cork heartland between 1966 and 1967, and increasing numbers of Beamish houses, there and in the city, began to serve Guinness in response to consumer demand – some openly, others surreptitiously.[22] A number of injunctions were successfully sought by the brewery in the late 1960s restraining tied publicans from selling others' products – six in County Cork in one action alone in June 1967 – but the trend proved irreversible. A meeting was held in Bandon in June 1967 between representatives of the brewery and of its tenants. It was agreed that while a solution was being sought, the Beamish tenants could sell Guinness but would not advertise the fact and would keep the Guinness dispensers hidden. They agreed to provide Beamish with figures for the sales of Guinness and to promote Beamish stout and its other products. In July 1968 a Tied Tenants' Protection Agency was formed to campaign for freedom from the strictures of the ties, especially in relation to stout.[23] From late January 1969 until early March there was a countrywide strike of general maintenance workers, including those at Beamish & Crawford, which halted production at the brewery for almost five weeks, though the distribution of existing stocks was allowed. This strike also closed Murphy's brewery, and its effect on the two Cork breweries mirrored that of the Cork brewery workers' strike in 1920. As with the earlier occasion, Guinness was strike-free (in this case, it reached a private agreement with its workers) and its production was unaffected, giving it an even stronger foothold in Cork: at this stage, Guinness controlled over 95 per cent of the stout market in Cork, leaving slim pickings for Tower and Murphy's stouts.

In a curious aside, several of the Beamish workers who refused to pass the maintenance men's picket on the brewery decided to do some picketing of their own at three Beamish tied houses in the Cork suburbs in early February, claiming they were selling Guinness; they carried placards reading 'Trade Diverted – Support Cork Brewery Workers'. One publican in the Turners Cross area went to the High Court to secure an injunction to prevent the pickets. There was an ongoing disagreement in the city between owners of 'free' houses and tied houses, with the former claiming that the selling of Guinness in tied houses was affecting their trade. Four months later an agreement was signed between Beamish and Murphy's allowing the sale of each other's products in their respective houses. An injunction was successfully won by Beamish to stop a Bantry publican selling products other than those of UBI in November 1969, but a week later the Beamish tied-house director Dick Walsh wrote to the brewery's tenants informing them that Guinness could be sold in Beamish houses. The beginning of the end of the tied-house system had begun.

15

'A brewery in a back street in Cork' 1970–1986

Following the announcement that Beamish & Crawford had secured close to 30 per cent of the Irish lager market in July 1983, managing director Tony Halpin declared, 'it isn't bad for a brewery in a back street in Cork'.[1] But behind the parochial boastfulness lay a blunt reality: Beamish & Crawford really was the plucky underdog rather than a serious contender – it would never be in a position to challenge Guinness and at best would land the occasional punch as it slugged it out with its local neighbour for a slice of the 10 to 20 per cent of the Irish beer market that could be wrenched from the heavyweight champion.

The company had navigated some very heavy waters throughout the turbulent 1970s, but it emerged at the end of the decade in relatively healthy state. By 1983 it had shown a profit for the fourth year in a row, but the possibility of Beamish & Crawford consolidating its base for further national expansion by taking over Murphy's brewery, and especially its popular stout, passed in that year when its main competitor was taken over by Dutch brewing giant Heineken. Beamish & Crawford chairman Clayton Love had stated clearly in late 1982 that the company had 'no interest' in competing with Guinness, which had close to 90 per cent of the overall Irish drink market at that stage, but as long as Beamish could remain profitable, 'it would be there'.[2] The promised floating of half the company's shares on the Irish stock market remained on the long finger, but the brewery did return to profitability in the late 1970s and was holding its own when it came under the control of Elders IXL of Australia in early 1987 due to the latter's takeover of Carling O'Keefe. Stout remained the poorest of poor relations in the 1970s and early 1980s as first Bass and subsequently Carling and Carlsberg made the running. In the meantime, in another break with the past, the winding-down of the once emblematic tied-house estate was completed.

Demolition, December 1971, in advance of the brewery refurbishment the following year. (*Irish Examiner*)

The ties unbind

Sales through Beamish & Crawford's tied houses showed a dramatic increase following the agreements to sell Guinness (and to a lesser extent, Murphy's) products at the end of the 1960s. By February 1970, Guinness stout accounted for 75 per cent of sales in Beamish houses, with Tower holding 20 per cent and Murphy's stout 5 per cent. Although this resulted in 'happier' relations with the tenants, it highlighted the fact that the tied houses had outlived their usefulness, and a process of selling them off, mainly to the tenants, had already begun and continued throughout the 1970s. Between 1967 and 1970 the estate had been reduced by forty-two houses, all but four of those in the county; this left 153 houses in September 1970. Those that were shed in this period were mainly premises over which doubts existed about the legality of the trading contracts or those where trade was poor due to their location, the bad state of the structure or those with a particularly poor tenant. Tied houses were still returning a trading profit in 1970 of £98,600. Profits on sales and rent yielded £143,200, while expenditure on rates, repairs and so on cost £44,600. The net book value of the 153 houses still tied to the brewery in September 1970 was £180,000.[3]

In 1973 the divestment began in earnest when thirty-one houses were sold to tenants, thirteen in Bandon alone. In the same period the company purchased the tenants' interest in three large premises and proceeded to operate them as managed houses. A further twenty-eight tied houses were sold in 1974 and twenty more in 1975. By mid-1976, seventeen more had been shed plus a further nineteen by March

1977. A year later, 150 in total had been sold for a cash return of £774,000. Some £372,000 of this had been spent on the acquisition and updating of the brewery's three managed bars bought in 1973: the Silver Key in Ballinlough, the South County in Douglas and the Templeacre Tavern in Gurranabraher. All three were successful operations, and in 1974 a pitch-and-putt course was opened adjacent to the Silver Key premises. In the early 1980s the Templeacre Tavern and the South County were sold, leaving the Silver Key as the only Beamish-managed house.

Management changes

The United Breweries of Ireland (UBI) management model under which the brewery had operated since January 1967 came to an end in October 1970. It was announced in August 1970 that Ken Richards of Bass Charrington, who had been managing director of both UBI and Beamish & Crawford since the establishment of the former, was to stand down in October, to be replaced by Peter Zacharay of Canadian Breweries, signalling the latter's return to direct management of the brewery. It appears that Bass Charrington had an option to buy Beamish & Crawford outright, but the asking price was too high. The Canadian-controlled brewery continued to brew Bass and, briefly, Worthington ales under licence from Bass Charrington. Zacharay was due to oversee the 'second launch' of the Canadian era over the next two years, after which the intention was to install an Irish managing director and management team. Other elements of the management shake-up in 1970 included appointing former chairman of UBI, Seán Lemass (who had not stood for re-election to the Dáil in 1969), as a director of Beamish & Crawford. He also replaced Richard P. Beamish as chairman; the latter was appointed honorary president and remained on the board. Prominent Cork businessman Clayton Love, who would become long-time chairman the following year, also became a director for the first time.

In 1968 the Canadian tobacco giant Rothmans had taken a controlling interest in Canadian Breweries. Rothmans had a professed policy of 'nationalising' its newly affiliated companies as quickly as possible by installing 'native' management and floating 50 per cent of the relevant company on its national stock market. The new management at Beamish publicly maintained that it would follow this path when it was 'practicable' to do so.[4] Zacharay's first report as managing director in November 1970 stressed the need to re-establish Beamish's image as a 'master brewer', which had become tarnished in recent years. The hope was that Zacharay would kick-start a revival in fortunes over the following two years with management, marketing and research backing from the new owners, who committed themselves to the loss-making Cork operation for the long haul. A return to profitability would pave the way for floating half the shares in the company. But this was easier said than done, especially in the volatile economic circumstances of the early 1970s. In 1973, meanwhile,

Canadian Breweries itself was restructured and renamed Carling O'Keefe, after two of the major constituent brewing groups in the conglomerate.[5]

Profit, loss and investment in the early 1970s

The company had announced losses of £184,000 in 1969 and £225,000 in the seventeen months before that. However, 1970 brought improvements in the outlook. Operating losses were reduced and sales were up over 50 per cent – mainly due to Bass, which was selling over three times the quantity of Carling and completely dwarfing Celebration. The company's annual report for 1970 showed a trading profit of £57,855, but overall losses of £133,790. It had a loan of £2,449,005 from its parent company and a bank overdraft of £900,000. Even if sales continued to improve at the existing rate, it would be many years before the company would be profitable. It was estimated that to get an adequate return on resources, Beamish would need to be recording a before-tax profit of approximately £400,000. Zacharay would not be around to oversee this Herculean task, as he returned to Canada in August 1971 to take up a position as a vice-president of Canadian Breweries. He was succeeded in early September by David Broome. Company chairman Seán Lemass died in May 1971 and was replaced in the chair by Clayton Love.

Kegging line, 1970. Jerry Murphy, dressed in white, with Derry Desmond. (Courtesy Ed Hinchy)

Broome inherited an improving situation. In September the company announced that increased sales of Bass and Carling and a substantial reduction in its wine, spirits and soft drinks activities had buoyed profits. (Beamish effectively pulled out of the soft drinks market at the beginning of 1972 following the breakdown of its attempted takeover of John Daly & Co., the Cork-based Coca-Cola bottling group. The fall-back was a deal with Daly for the sale of its products through Beamish tied houses.) The company's liquidity was substantially improved in 1971 through a £1.71 million capital injection from Canadian Breweries, which was achieved through the purchase of 400,000 ordinary shares in Beamish & Crawford. There was also a sharp reduction in bank borrowings, from £689,500 in 1969–70 to £66,250 at 30 June 1971. This increased net current assets by £644,400 to £853,200. The utilisation of this capital for the extension and modernisation of the brewery was held up by planning permission delays. In April 1972 it was announced that Canadian Breweries had agreed to pump a further £509,000 into the Cork plant. The chairman's statement for 1972 (published in June) pointed to a modest profit for the previous nine months of £30,021. Net earnings in the first six months of 1972 were £140,256 as a result of an increase in turnover of 42 per cent. This allowed the company to absorb rising costs and also to part-finance a new capital programme, which was mainly financed through short-term local bank loans. By June 1973 net profits had more than doubled to £302,078, the result of a turnover increase of 25 per cent and the sale of tied houses.

A total of £513,000 was spent on plant and equipment in 1973, including a new brewhouse, twelve conical fermenting vessels and six conical storage vessels as well as new washing and refrigeration equipment. A further £424,000 was spent on two new depots in Dublin and Limerick and the upgrading of existing depots. By the end of 1974, approximately £2 million had been spent in three years in an intensive capital investment programme designed to meet the need for increased capacity. At peak periods in 1972 the brewery had been in operation twenty-four hours a day, seven days a week trying to keep pace with demand. Employment rose by twenty people during 1972, bringing the workforce to approximately 350.

All this good news was tempered, however, by a darkening economic landscape, especially galloping inflation. The consumer price index had risen by 11.7 per cent between May 1972 and May 1973, and the cost of brewing materials and wages was not far behind. Chairman Clayton Love's statement for 1973 pointed out that 'the return on capital employed ... falls far short of an acceptable level' and there was 'a long way to go to provide a return that would be adequate to investors'.

An interesting investment was considered in early 1974. The old enemy, Murphy's brewery, had been fully taken over by British brewers Watney Mann in 1967, but its various efforts at reviving the fortunes of Cork's second brewery had failed and in

Left to right: Aerial view of the Beamish & Crawford brewery during refurbishment, 1972. (*Irish Examiner*)
Fermenting tanks being installed, 1972. (Courtesy Mike Hannon)

early 1971 James J. Murphy & Co. was on the brink of liquidation. It was rescued by a state agency, Fóir Teoranta, a lender of last resort to troubled Irish companies, and saw a modest revival in its fortunes, especially its stout sales, which reached almost 15,000 barrels in sales in 1973 – almost five times the output of Beamish stout. Despite increased sales the company continued to lose money and in early 1974 Pembroke Investments made a bid for the brewery. Beamish & Crawford engaged in discussions with Fóir Teoranta about a possible takeover. A cash offer of £150,000 and a commitment to pay £350,000 within five years would have been necessary to improve on the Pembroke bid. Beamish did not make an offer, hoping that a new owner would find brewing stout at such small volumes commercially unviable and that Beamish could then offer to brew Murphy's stout under licence.[6] It is interesting to speculate on what might have happened in the event of a Beamish takeover of Murphy's in 1974; the likely scenario was a reversal of the roles in the Heineken/ Murphy's takeover of Beamish in 2008: the consolidation of brewing in one of the city's breweries and the closure of the other. A similar scenario would emerge in 1981–2, when Beamish was on the verge of a merger/takeover of its local rival once again. In the event, a consortium of publicans called the Licensed Vintners Co-operative Society made a successful bid for the Lady's Well Brewery in April 1974 and oversaw a brief revival in Murphy's fortunes.

'There is little confidence in Beamish as a stout Brewery'

The Murphy's revival was driven by increased sales of its stout, which quickly came to dominate the small segment of the market not controlled by Guinness – a segment that expanded to all of 10 per cent by 1976, due solely to the so-called 'Murphy Movement'. This was given lift-off by the fortuitous timing of a strike at Guinness in May–June 1974, which Murphy's took full advantage of, filling the void for stout drinkers across the country and highlighting the abject position to which the once-proud Beamish stout brand had fallen. It was now drunk almost exclusively by a small number of faithful customers in Cork.

When Zacharay's appointment as managing director was announced in August 1970, he was asked if he was tempted to withdraw completely from the stout market; his reply was ominously ambiguous: 'ask me again in six months'.[7] Tower was so unloved that it was the only product from both breweries that was not stocked by the other's houses under the agreement with Murphy's made in 1969. By the end of December testing had begun of a new stout (with a working title of '1792') to replace the detested Tower; this was born as a product in November 1971 as Beamish Cream Stout. The decision to relaunch into the stout market rather than abandon it altogether was informed by two main factors: the fact that Murphy's stout was also failing at that stage and no proper alternative to Guinness existed in the biggest sector of the market; and there was also the issue that stout was more of a winter drink, and by having no presence, Beamish was losing out on a potentially lucrative source of income. While there was no expectation of dislodging Guinness, the hope was that Murphy's would begin to feel the heat in a year or two. However, optimism was not all-pervasive amongst management, with the managing director, David Broome, declaring that 'if we're to look for sales we've to look in the growth segments of the market – ale and lager – not in the dying sector – stout'.[8]

On 4 November 1971 the latest incarnation of the company's stout was rolled out in Beamish tied houses on draught and in pint bottles. Beamish Cream Stout claimed a consistency that was achieved through pasteurisation. It made a positive start, but sales, which failed to grow beyond the tied-house and city trade, became static and were confined to what the company called an 'exclusive and intensely loyal group of Cork supporters' by late 1973. Its niche appeal and poor prospects were confirmed in 1974 during the three-week strike that shut Guinness in Dublin in late May to early June. Murphy's, which had recently been taken over by a vintners' consortium, upped production to meet demand, even striking a deal with Guinness to allow Murphy's to be poured through Guinness dispensers in the capital.[9] Beamish's Cork rival sold 7,000 barrels in June alone, while sales of Beamish only rose marginally and remained in the hundreds of barrels, with the board noting ruefully that its stout 'is not a viable alternative to Guinness' and that there was 'little confidence in Beamish as a stout Brewery'.[10] Sales of the brewery's other products rose, however, with Guinness drinkers turning to Carling lager in large numbers for some reason. Sales of all the brewery's products rose by 39 per cent as a result of the Guinness shutdown and supplies to pubs had to be rationed due to an inability to keep up with demand.

To add to the brewery's woes with regard to stout, the economic situation, especially a series of rapid price rises for drink in 1974–5, signalled a revival of the stout trade nationally as people abandoned the more expensive lagers and ales for the cheaper dark beer. Having dropped to 65 per cent of the national beer market at the beginning of 1974, by early 1975 stout was heading for 70 per cent, mainly at the expense of ale, Beamish's best seller, which fell from 27.7 per cent to 23.7 per cent of the national market in the same period. Between September 1974 and February 1975, the price of an average pint had risen by 6p; stout usually sold for 1p less than ale and 4p less than lager. By March 1975, stout was selling for 6p less than lager and 2p less than ale in the country's lounge bars. In September of that year, only 119 barrels of Beamish Cream Stout were sold in Cork; six were sold in Dublin, two in Limerick, two in Thomastown and three elsewhere. The starkness of the situation is highlighted when the sales of the three stouts on the market in the three pubs managed by Beamish is contrasted (see Table 15.1).

Table 15.1 **Stout sales (in barrels) in Beamish & Crawford managed houses, September 1975**

	SOUTH COUNTY	SILVER KEY	TEMPLEACRE TAVERN
Beamish	2	2	6
Murphy's	75	80	265
Guinness	36	74	144

The trend towards stout continued into 1976. In January of that year it was estimated that the old reliable accounted for close to 80 per cent of all beer sold in Cork as a result of the popularity of Murphy's and the continuing shift away from lager and ale in the straitened circumstances. 'Unfortunately our own stout is not presently in a sufficient number of outlets to take advantage of the situation,' the Beamish board noted, a situation exacerbated by its continuing sale of tied houses.[11] Reports of the death of stout appeared to have been exaggerated, and Beamish & Crawford belatedly attempted to hitch a ride on the bandwagon driven by Murphy's by launching a new stout with an old name, Beamish XXX, in April 1976. The move also reflected a belated feeling that Beamish & Crawford needed to 'fly its own flag' with its own brew, rather than being seen as purely a local supplier of international brands. Asked by a journalist if it wasn't a bad time for a launch given the recent 5p increase on the price of a pint in the budget, Richard P. Beamish replied mordantly, 'In these days, any time is a bad time.'[12]

The product was launched on 8 April at the brewery, where the local Barrack Street (brass) Band played, and later toured the city on a Beamish lorry. Some £100,000 was

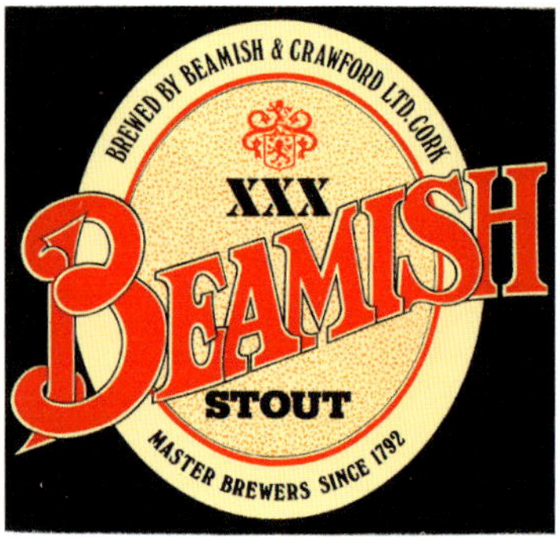

invested in dispensers, coolers, kegs, taps and advertising for XXX, which was to sell at the same price as Guinness; Murphy's was 2p per pint cheaper. Consumer research had resulted in a stout described as mild, clear and easy to drink, which maintained its creamy white head and did not turn brown.

Beamish XXX was sold for the first three months in Cork only, after which it was introduced in Kerry, Limerick and Dublin. It sold reasonably well on the south side of Cork city but less well on the north side, which was dominated by Murphy's. Sales were much improved on those of Beamish Cream, but they peaked in mid-1977 and declined thereafter (see Table 15.2). By March 1978 taps were being withdrawn in some areas and the board stated baldly about XXX in May: 'We do not at present have the time to devote to promotion of this product since our efforts are concentrated on retaining our lager market.'[13] It was, however, launched in the UK in mid-1978, where it was aimed at the 'real ale' market, and did reasonably well, while three containers of Beamish stout had been exported to Canada by the end of 1978.

Table 15.2

Sales (in barrels) of Beamish stout, 1974–8

YEAR ENDING	JUNE 1974	JUNE 1975	MARCH 1976	MARCH 1977	MARCH 1978
Barrels sold	2,949	2,342	1,740	6,042	5,513

'Ah, that's Bass!'

From the time of the Canadian takeover in late 1962/early 1963, Beamish & Crawford's days as a stout brewery seemed over and ale and lager became the primary products. While its neglected stout (in its various manifestations) struggled to rise above 1 per cent of the market, Beamish & Crawford had secured a very credible 16 per cent of the ale market by 1970 and close to a quarter of the lager market. Celebration, launched to mark the anniversary of the 1916 Rising in 1966, had been an initial success (climbing to around 15 per cent), but it was waning by 1970. The light ale Gold Keg had been discontinued, but Worthington's and a small quantity of the Canadian ale Piper's were being brewed at the beginning of the 1970s. The ale that dwarfed them all, however, was Bass, which continued to be brewed in Cork following the withdrawal of Bass Charrington from the brewery's management in 1970. Production of Bass on draught began in Cork in late 1968 and it had been rolled out nationally in the spring of 1969. It quickly became the brewery's leading brand, as can be seen from the sales figures in Table 15.3, which shows it accounting for 70 per cent of all sales in the primary brands.

Table 15.3 **Sales (in barrels) of Beamish & Crawford beers, June 1970 to June 1971**

Bass ale	60,660
Carling Black Label lager	19,600
Celebration ale	3,400
Tower stout	2,300

In April 1970 Celebration taps were withdrawn in Dublin and in the northern counties of the Republic and half-pint bottles were discontinued as a prelude to phasing out the product in 1971. (It was briefly revived in a small number of outlets in 1977.) Bass continued to grow spectacularly in 1972–3 and dominated the expanding ale market along with Smithwick's. In 1972 it had 20 per cent of the ale market and 40 per cent of that in Munster. The discrepancy revealed a key weakness: the failure to penetrate the crucial Dublin market and other areas outside Munster. Bass also developed the image most feared by all young marketing executives – that of an older person's drink, in contrast to the more youthful appeal of Smithwick's. In an attempt to address both of these issues, in April 1972 Beamish launched a new product, Crawford's Golden Ale, sold in Dublin only and aimed at under-35s. Though initial sales were encouraging, Crawford's failed to capture more than 3 per cent of the Dublin ale market and was phased out in less than a year.

While Bass sales were up 6 per cent in 1974, the ale market as a whole had increased by more, prompting worry at Beamish that its leading brand was on the wane. A sponsorship drive was launched in that year with the announcement in February of Bass sponsorship of the FAI Cup Final, and in August the company announced a £20,000 sponsorship deal of the country's premier soccer league, to be renamed the Bass League of Ireland. Bass remained synonymous with Irish soccer until 1979, when it pulled out of the sponsorship deals that had failed to revive the flagging brand.

The swing to stout, especially the resurgent and cheaper Murphy's, continued to hit sales of Bass as ale's share of the overall market dropped from 27.7 to 23.7 per cent across 1974. In addition, Smithwick's was beginning to make inroads in its Munster heartland and in 1975 a new competitor emerged when Murphy's began to brew its own Schooner ale, which was launched with much fanfare in December 1975. Schooner proved to be much less of a threat than feared, as did its successor, Younger's, while Smithwick's continued to expand. In the year ending June 1974, 108,652 barrels of Bass were sold; this had almost halved to 57,618 in the year ending March 1977. At this stage Bass had fallen to 12.3 per cent nationally and 27 per cent of the ale market in Cork, where it had peaked at 50 per cent in 1973. The decline continued, and by the end of 1978 its national share had dropped to below 8 per cent, with Smithwick's at over 90 per cent.

'Lager is a thing called Harp'

The decline in ale was partly offset by a growth in sales of the company's expanded lager portfolio. Carling had set the pace in the Irish lager market in the 1960s, but by the early 1970s had been well beaten into second place by its Guinness rival, Harp, which seemed to have cornered the mass-appeal lager market. Beamish & Crawford began looking for new angles, and in May 1970 started bottling, distributing and marketing the Danish lager Tuborg, which had just been acquired by the other major Danish brewer, Carlsberg. In March 1971 this 'continentalisation' process continued when Carling was relaunched in a new form and rebranded as Carling International Lager. This 'international strength' Carling had a gravity of 1044° (4.8 per cent ABV), the same as Carlsberg and Tuborg, so it was stronger than Harp or the previous Carling Black Label. It was a calculated risk, as Irish excise duties were based on gravity, so the new lager would cost more to produce but was being sold at the same price. By October 1971 it seemed as if the risk had paid off, with Carling increasing its share by 2 per cent (from 20 to 22 per cent), which more than covered the cost of the rise in strength.

In April 1972 Beamish & Crawford took over the agency for Carlsberg in Ireland from Bannow Bottlers in Dublin and began brewing, bottling and marketing it along with Tuborg. The latter was a niche product which sold mainly in the Republic's northern counties. Carlsberg, on the other hand, had been Ireland's first lager and had strong brand recognition. Over the next two years, however, it was Carling rather than Carlsberg that steadily increased its sales when the lager market was showing a definite trend towards draught over bottle. Carling sales were boosted in 1974 and over the following several years by an arrangement with Bass Charrington to export it to the UK due to increased demand that the British breweries could not fully meet. These exports were worth the equivalent of over £400,000 annually on the Irish market in retail terms.

Beamish began to sell Carlsberg in draught too, but its long-standing reputation as a bottled beer held back sales. Carlsberg Special Brew was introduced in bottles, but was a niche product and the Cork company could only reflect ruefully in the mid-1970s that the advertising slogan 'Lager is a thing called Harp' was uncomfortably 'close to becoming a reality'.[14] Harp was less dominant than Guinness stout or Smithwick's ale, both of which had around 90 per cent

Sales of Beamish & Crawford products (in barrels)

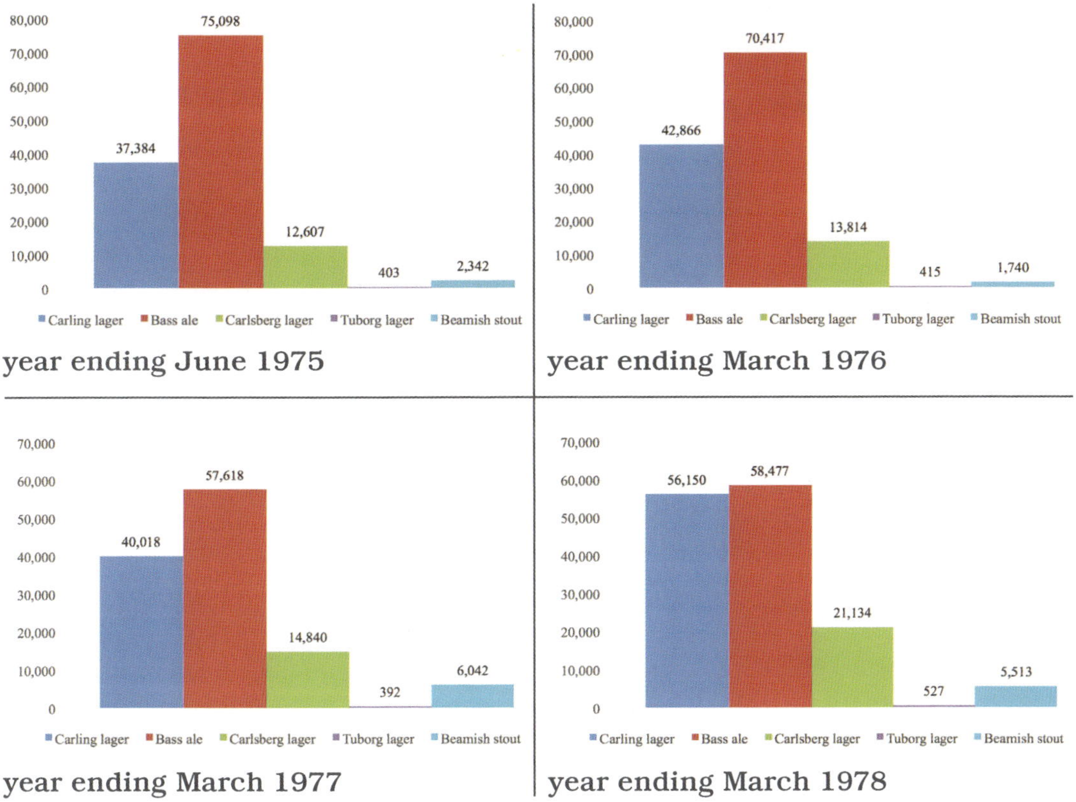

(plus) in their respective sectors by the late 1970s. However, the Guinness lager was expanding its share in a growing sector, climbing to over 70 per cent in 1978, just as Heineken was launched on the Irish market by Murphy's. Between them, Carling and Carlsberg still had approximately 25 per cent at this stage, but Heineken posed a dangerous new threat.

From loss to profit in the late 1970s and early 1980s

In 1974 Dickie Beamish retired as president of the company but remained on the board until 1979; in 1977 he assumed the honorary mantle of 'president for life'. David Broome was replaced by another Carling O'Keefe senior executive, Tony Gauntley, as managing director in July 1974. He lasted three years before returning to Canada as an executive vice-president at Carling O'Keefe in Toronto. In October 1977 Tony Halpin, the first Irish managing director since the Canadian takeover, was appointed. Halpin had been managing director of Seagram Ireland, a Canadian drinks group that controlled 20 per cent of Irish Distillers. In March 1978 Beamish began the

St Patrick's Day parade float, 1977. (Courtesy Ed Hinchy)

distribution of the Seagram range of spirits in Munster, including Bushmills whiskey. Gauntley's reign coincided with some of the toughest conditions the company had had to endure for many years. Rising unemployment, relentless VAT increases on drink and rising costs saw Beamish & Crawford's operating profits drop by 62 per cent in 1974–5 and pre-tax profits fell by over 50 per cent, despite the continuing sale of tied houses. The extra 10p on the pint in the 1976 budget led to an estimated 40 per cent drop-off in the pub trade in its aftermath. A pint of stout rose from 28p to 38p, ale to 39p and lager to 44p on average.[15] A loss of £88,600 was announced for the year ending March 1976, and relief was palpable when Minister for Finance Richie Ryan gave the drinks trade a 'break' in his last budget of January 1977 by not increasing duty for the first time in his tenure (1973–7).

This marked the beginning of a period of improved sales and profits, which were further helped following the January 1978 budget when the new Fianna Fáil government announced measures to compensate small breweries through a system of excise rebates. The brewers had been granted a price increase that kicked in in September 1977 and turnover in 1977–8 was up by £1.9 million to £12.9 million, while trading profits were £486,990 compared to losses of £53,893 in 1976–7. Profits retained after taxation were up from £120,177 to £460,283. Trading profit only rose marginally to £525,000 in the following twelve months, hit by bad weather and an oil strike, but pre-tax profits soared by 66 per cent to £778,000 due to the sale of tied houses and a rebate of over £100,000 under the government's scheme for small brewers. The first major capital expenditure since the construction of the new brewhouse in 1972 saw the opening of a new kegging line in late 1979 at the cost of half a million pounds.

The new kegging facility was credited with increasing efficiency and the stability of product quality, and a six-acre site in Little Island, County Cork, had been purchased with an eye to further development. Pre-tax profits for the year to 31 March 1980 were up 25 per cent on the previous year to £905,928 and turnover was up 16.5 per cent to £16.7 million. Trading profit soared by 52 per cent to £715,000 and net profit was up 26 per cent to £886,479. The excise duty rebate of £98,802 was less than the previous year, plus a lower return on tied-house sales saw exceptional items amount to the lower figure of £112,125. The next twelve months brought continued positive news with pre-tax profits of just under £1 million (as with the previous years, this equated to after-tax profit because of the substantial losses still being brought forward). Trading profit showed only a marginal increase to £719,390, however, and the key to the good returns was the exceptional items: £195,515 in a refund of rates paid over previous years (following a High Court decision in May 1978 that the company had been wrongfully charged rates for the fermentation and conditioning tanks at the brewery), £65,958 from the disposal of fixed assets, including seven tied houses (£28,932), and an excise duty rebate of £100,625. Nevertheless, Tony Halpin expressed satisfaction at the performance given increased costs and a general depression in the drinks trade. He claimed a 30 per cent share of the lager market with Carling, Carlsberg and Tuborg and said the new American-style 'malt liquor', Colt 45, which had been launched in late 1980, was performing well.[16]

Beamish Irish Stout exported to USA for St Patrick's Day, 1980.
(Beamish & Crawford Brewery Collection /Dori O'Connell)

'Merger' with Murphy's?

The central issue of 1981, however, was the possibility of a merger with Murphy's Brewery Ltd, as Cork's other brewery was now called since becoming a public company in 1976. As mentioned earlier, the latter had surfed a wave of initial success following its takeover by a vintners' consortium in 1974. However, by the turn of the decade losses on its troubled bottling plant that had opened in 1978, the costs incurred in improving brewing facilities and

Clockwise from top left: Malt screen in the mill loft. Malt screens and weighing apparatus. The three nineteenth-century malt mills in the mill loft were in use until the brewery modernisation of 1972. (John Sheehan)

high interest rates on its borrowings made the overall financial picture bleak, despite continuing healthy sales. During 1980 its financial position deteriorated further, and in January 1981 the company began protracted negotiations with Beamish & Crawford about a possible merger; these talks continued on and off for the rest of the year.[17]

Beamish was less than impressed with the Murphy's balance sheet, which showed losses of £660,000 in 1980 and borrowings of £4.22 million against net tangible assets of just £2.3 million. Its proposal involved a recapitalisation programme involving Beamish, the state's Industrial Development Authority and Murphy's own lenders. It was calculated that a £7 million investment was needed: £3 million immediately and a further £4 million over the following five years. During that period Beamish & Crawford would take over management of the company, and if the arrangement worked and the company returned to profit, it would acquire or merge with Murphy's, writing off its remaining debts and giving the Murphy's shareholders a 20 per cent equity stake. However, if Murphy's continued to lose money and its prospects did not improve, Beamish would withdraw.

Heineken was happy to support the 'merger' and provide technical and marketing support on the understanding that its lager was brewed in a different brewing facility to its Beamish competitors, Carling and Carlsberg. The majority of Murphy's shareholders were determined to maintain independence and believed the deal unduly favoured Beamish; amidst rumours that Beamish would close down Lady's Well Brewery, they duly rejected the proposed merger at an AGM in December 1981. In response, Clayton Love described the idea that his company would close down a brewery it was intending to invest heavily in as 'ridiculous'. He pointed out that the first merger proposals between the two breweries dated back to 1904, and that Beamish would leave its door open.[18] In late 1981 and early 1982 the Murphy's management tried desperately to raise the necessary £3 million, including the lay-off of 130 workers and the sale of the bottling plant. Other fundraising efforts floundered and debts continue to rise, and eventually in July 1982 a receiver was appointed. Beamish reiterated that it remained interested, though it had no immediate plans to make an offer for Murphy's: 'If and when the receiver comes along,' stated Clayton Love, 'we will be in the marketplace.'[19]

A month later, following a meeting with the receiver, Beamish announced that it was considering making an offer for Murphy's. Its main interest was in Murphy's stout, which had been far more successful than Beamish's own product, but Love did not rule out a link with Heineken too. 'It would be logical,' the Beamish chairman stated, 'for Beamish & Crawford to get together with Murphy's to streamline operations and establish one strong Munster brewery.' In response to journalists' questions regarding competition with Guinness, Love made the position clear: the company had no interest in competing with Guinness, who had almost 90 per cent of the market, but as long as Beamish could remain profitable, 'it would be there'.[20] In the meantime, Heineken stepped up its interest, and in early 1983 made a firm offer that was accepted by the receiver. On 1 April 1983 Murphy Brewery Ireland Ltd was established as a wholly owned subsidiary of Heineken International.

Market trends, 1982–6

With the distraction of the Murphy's merger now firmly behind it, the company concentrated on growing its market share, with some success – the Beamish & Crawford share of the national drinks market rose from 5.7 per cent in 1982 to 7.8 per cent in 1985. Beamish stout continued to languish in the shadow of Guinness's national domination and the local supremacy of Murphy's, and as a consequence was

Main image: J.J. (Seán) O'Leary began his career with Beamish & Crawford in the laboratory under Head Brewer J.L. Shimwell in 1935. He retired in 1984, having become Head Brewer in 1953 in succession to Phil Baylis. (Courtesy Ed Hinchy)
Inset: O'Leary's Celebration Stout was brewed in 1984 to mark the retirement of J.J. (Seán) O'Leary, Head Brewer/Production Director. (Courtesy Ed Hinchy)

given little or no attention in marketing or promotional terms. The decline of Bass that had begun in the mid-1970s continued in the context of a shrinking ale market. In 1982 it stood at 6.4 per cent of the national ale market, with Smithwick's at just under 90 per cent. By 1986 the Bass share had dropped to close to 3 per cent.

It was lager that was the dynamic sector, and Beamish was well placed to take advantage with Carling and Carlsberg, especially as the new lager drinkers showed an increasing preference for 'continental' styles and began to turn away from the sharper-tasting Harp. The latter lost 10 per cent market share in the early 1980s. In late 1984 the Harp brewery was hit by a strike, which hit sales further and allowed competitors, especially Heineken, to capture more of its regular drinkers. Guinness responded to the 'continental shift' by launching the German premium lager Fürstenberg on the Irish market in 1986. Meanwhile, another player entered the field in 1985 in the shape of the Scottish lager Tennent's, which was brewed in Belfast. It was slightly weaker and cheaper than the other lagers and quickly gained 5 per cent of a market sector that had expanded from 15 to 21 per cent between 1983 and 1985, mainly at the expense of ale. Guinness introduced Hoffmann's and Steiger in 1985 to meet the Tennent's challenge, but largely unsuccessfully. In the meantime, Heineken grew steadily to almost 15 per cent in late 1986.

From left: Rory Bevan; Jim D'Arcy; Ed Hinchy; Dave Twomey. Jim D'Arcy succeeded J.J. O'Leary as Head Brewer in 1984 and he, in turn, was succeeded by Rory Bevan, who was Head Brewer when the brewery ceased production in 2009. (Courtesy Ed Hinchy)

Beamish continued to brew tiny quantities of Tuborg and in late 1980 launched the American beer Colt 45. Following initial positive signs, it was phased out in late 1983 having failed to make a mark. In 1986 it secured the agency for Löwenbräu Pils, but the key to Beamish success in the lager sector was Carling and Carlsberg. The latter benefited from a concerted marketing drive ('Probably the best lager in the world') that gave it a foothold in the crucial Dublin and broader Leinster market. According to Nielsen market research, it grew from 8.9 per cent in 1982 to 10 per cent in 1985 and just over 12 per cent in 1986. Carling went from 15.3 per cent in 1982 to 19 per cent in 1985 before dropping back to 15.4 per cent the following year. Beamish & Crawford's overall share of the lager market at the end of 1986 was 27.6 per cent, though it had risen as high as 30 per cent in 1983. Harp had fallen to under 35 per cent by 1986, while Tennent's was close to 10 per cent.

The booming lager market, despite increased competition, was a key to the company's solid financial performance in the early to mid-1980s, and the aim of the 1981 strategic plan to increase overall market share to above 7 per cent was achieved. Economic recession and continuing price rises hit volume sales in 1982–3, but operating profits were up 36 per cent and margins were up by 4 per cent. Financial control was tightened with the reduction of working capital by 15 per cent, and according to one business commentator, the Beamish & Crawford balance sheet 'has

(Beamish & Crawford Brewery Collection /Dori O'Connell)

Beamish & Crawford brewed this Celebration XXX Stout to mark Cork 800 in 1985. (Courtesy Ed Hinchy)

all the signs of a company which is battening down the hatches in anticipation of a fairly difficult trading climate ahead'.[21] Turnover increased by 10 per cent in 1983–4 to £31 million and net profits rose by 6 per cent to just under £1.3 million. The continuing rise in lager sales saw pre-tax profits almost double to £2.4 million the following financial year, with turnover up £9 million to over £40 million. Carling maintained its Cork and Munster dominance and kept a high profile with sponsorship of a country music festival in Cork, followed by a series of rock concert promotions in the city. In 1986–7, Carling accounted for 47.2 per cent of the brewery's sales.

In the meantime, Beamish stout emerged tentatively from the shadows and some marketing weight was thrown behind it for the first time in many years in 1986 in the context of an unexpected turnaround in the steady decline of the stout market (a modest but significant increase from 55 to 56 per cent in 1985–6). While an increase in local market share from its position of 5 per cent was the initial priority, exports in bottle to the US began in 1984 and an export drive to the UK commenced in 1985, where Beamish stout was being promoted in bottles and kegs and distributed by Young & Co. brewers. Britain soon became the main market for Beamish stout, where sales would outstrip those in the Irish market.

In early 1987 a new kid on the world brewing block, the aggressively expansive Australian company Elders IXL, bought Carling O'Keefe and took over its subsidiary, Beamish & Crawford. As we will see, this would have serious knock-on effects that brought the company to the edge of extinction. It survived to fight another day, but the final chapter in the long history of brewing on Cork's South Main Street was about to begin.

The Final Chapter

1987–2009

From the moment Canadian Breweries took over Beamish & Crawford in late 1962, the company lost control of its own destiny. Its future fortunes were bound up with the dynamics of a consolidating global brewing industry; boardroom decisions in distant lands could make or break it, as shown in 2009, when the final such decision was terminal for the brewery. Beamish's vulnerability had been laid bare in 1987 when the expansionist Australian brewer of Foster's lager, Elders IXL, took over the brewery as part of its acquisition of Carling O'Keefe. This led directly to Carlsberg pulling its product from Cork and transferring it to Guinness, depriving Beamish of 40 per cent of its output at a stroke. Its replacement by Foster's failed to plug the gap, and a significant number of workers were gradually let go as part of a rationalisation plan. The unexpected revival of Beamish stout, and especially its creation of a healthy market in Britain, helped to reduce immediate job losses and revived something of the company's diluted Cork and Irish identity. However, a long-term strategy of downsizing was initiated, leading to a gradual halving of the workforce and industrial unrest in the early 1990s.

In 1995 Elders (which had been renamed Foster's Brewing Group in 1990) sold Beamish & Crawford, along with its British brewing interests, to the Scottish & Newcastle group. The latter was in turn bought out in a joint Heineken/Carlsberg deal in 2008. This global deal was played out locally in Cork because Heineken Ireland was located in the city, as was Scottish & Newcastle's Irish subsidiary. The two breweries co-existed until May 2009, when Heineken closed the South Main Street operation and centralised all brewing at its own production facility in Cork, bringing the 217-year history of the Beamish & Crawford brewery to an end.

Beamish & Crawford celebrated its bicentenary in 1992. (Beamish & Crawford Brewery Collection/Dori O'Connell)

'The victims of big-business dealings'

In February–March 1987 Elders IXL acquired Carling O'Keefe, thus placing its Irish subsidiary under new international ownership. The initial reaction in Beamish & Crawford was positive: 'In one particular respect – that of Beamish stout – it could be a very good thing,' said managing director Tony Halpin, and he was right. However, his broader optimism that the takeover 'could bring nothing but good' for the brewery was misplaced, as the vagaries of international capitalism wreaked havoc with its fortunes, neither for the first time nor the last.[1]

Elders IXL (not an erroneous Roman numeral, but a phonetic representation of 'I excel') was Australia's largest conglomerate, whose interests included farm services, food, oil and finance. It moved into brewing in 1983 in the largest corporate takeover in Australian history with its acquisition of Carlton & United Breweries, makers of Foster's lager. Elders set out to make Foster's a truly international brand and to make the company a global player in brewing. In September 1986 it acquired Courage Brewing, Britain's sixth largest brewery with a tied estate of 5,000 houses, before its expansion into North America with the takeover of Carling O'Keefe in early 1987 made Elders the sixth largest brewing concern in the world.[2] Carling O'Keefe had the franchise for Carlsberg in Canada, and the Danish brewers were anxious about

Above: The brewery buildings viewed from Clarke's Bridge, 2008. (John Sheehan)
Facing page: The Counting House, Christmas 2008. (John Sheehan)

Elders' intentions, given its global ambitions for Foster's. Chief executive of United Breweries/Carlsberg, Michael Iuul, flew to Toronto to seek guarantees that Elders would not 'cannibalise' Carlsberg, but he did not get them and pulled out of the relationship. In relation to Ireland, United Breweries had already made an offer to buy Beamish & Crawford from Carling O'Keefe but was rebuffed, and was rejected again by Elders. Carlsberg then demanded that Foster's be kept out of the Irish market for seven years; Elders promised three, which Carlsberg rejected, deciding it would be commercial 'suicide' to leave Carlsberg with Beamish given the brewery's new ownership. Elders, said Iuul, had made its intentions clear, meaning Carlsberg would be operating in a 'hostile environment' if it stayed in Cork.[3]

This was a nightmare scenario for Beamish, which had grown Carlsberg to a 12 per cent share of the Irish lager market since it acquired the franchise in 1972. In 1987 it represented 40 per cent of the brewery's output and close to half of the workforce of 400 was involved in the production and distribution of about 160,000 barrels annually; its transfer would mean a hit of £3 million per year and the possibility of significant job losses at best, closure at worst. Tony Halpin flew to Copenhagen to try to convince the Carlsberg managers to change their minds. He

(Beamish & Crawford Brewery Collection/Dori O'Connell)

(Courtesy Ed Hinchy)

gave assurances that Carlsberg would be treated 'properly' and its interests protected, but to no avail. He condemned the Danes' demand for a seven-year moratorium on Foster's as 'ridiculous' and tried in vain to convince them of the 'human devastation' that would result from their withdrawal, with the potential loss of up to half the brewery's workforce. In early September 1987 it was announced that Guinness would take over the Carlsberg franchise in Ireland from June 1988. 'In the end,' said Carlsberg boss Iuul, 'Beamish & Crawford were the victims of big-business dealings between Canada and Australia. They got big new masters who want to Fosterise the world.'[4]

For the next eight months the brewery and its 'big new masters' were in the curious position of handling a product that would soon be a competitor. An early victim of this anomaly was the Carlsberg Challenge, a major televised invitation snooker tournament held in Dublin. In the wake of the Carlsberg announcement in early September, the title and associated advertising was hastily rearranged and the event went ahead as the Carling Challenge. The following year, Foster's became the name-sponsor for Irish snooker. Beamish's newest lager was launched in Ireland in November 1987 by television personality Mike Murphy, whose *Murphy's Australia* travel programme had recently aired on RTÉ television. Australian actor and comedian Paul Hogan, who played the eponymous hero of the popular *Crocodile Dundee* films, was the poster boy for the 'amber nectar', which was imported at first and then began to be brewed in Cork in early 1988. Murphy pointed out that Foster's was what the Australian 'yuppies' drank, prompting Halpin to show why he was being considered as a possible Fianna Fáil election candidate: he said they were not targeting yuppies in Ireland – the real target was job security for Beamish & Crawford workers.[5]

Hopes were high for Foster's, primarily because the vintners' associations had indicated that they were opposed to the strengthening of Guinness's dominant position by the acquisition of Carlsberg and they pledged to boycott the product when Guinness took it over. The ambition for

Richard P. (Dickie) Beamish (1909–93), the great-great-grandson of William Beamish and the last member of the family to serve the company, celebrates his 80th birthday at a function in the brewery, 14 June 1989.
(Beamish & Crawford Brewery Collection)

Foster's was to reach a target of 25 per cent of the Irish lager market within seven years. The boycott failed to materialise, however, and Foster's failed to take off (it peaked at 5 per cent); neither did another new product, Miller Lite. In June 1988 Guinness took over the Carlsberg franchise and the job losses that were threatened a year earlier looked inevitable, with numbers of 100 and 150 being mentioned in press reports. 'It is appalling,' said Halpin, 'that purely because of a decision by a multi-national corporation thousands of miles away, people must lose their jobs.' Carlsberg boss Michael Iuul felt the need to defend his company's decision and to accuse Halpin, who had described the Carlsberg decision as 'immoral and unnecessary', of taking the issue 'personally'. He asserted that Carlsberg felt it had no choice given the Elders attitude, and that they had at least maintained Irish jobs, if not in Cork: 'We were prepared to buy Beamish & Crawford and invest heavily and secure the future of the brewery, but we were rejected. We can do no more and we have to protect our own interests.' Had Carlsberg taken over Beamish, the situation would have been much different – or would it? Iuul revealed that his company had examined the books and found Beamish to be an excellent prospect for investment and expansion. However, staffing levels did not match those at other breweries. For example, Carlsberg in Northampton produced 2 million barrels a year with 280 workers, while Beamish produced one-tenth of that with 400 workers. 'You can draw your own conclusions,' said Iuul.[6]

Rationalisation

If we do draw our own conclusions, they can only be that whoever gained control of Beamish would have instigated rationalisation and lay-offs. In the light of cold-eyed capitalist calculations, the brewery had an excess of staff, overly restrictive work practices, surplus capacity and unsustainable overhead levels. Halpin oversaw the initial phase of rationalisation when sixty workers aged sixty and over accepted early retirement packages in late 1988. Sites at Little Island in County Cork and Crosse's Green near the brewery were sold in early 1989, and the company's long-standing share of the Malting Company of Ireland was sold for close to £1 million later that year. In May 1989 Tony Halpin resigned as managing director and was replaced temporarily by Peter Ward, who had been director of the Yorkshire brewery John Smith's in Tadcaster, also owned by Elders. Ward was the carrier of the parent company's blunt message: unless a survival plan involving more redundancies, mainly in depots in Dublin, Limerick, Longford, Bantry and Cork, was accepted by the staff at the loss-making company, he had the authority to close the brewery down. Ward moved back to Britain and was replaced in September 1989 by another 'trouble-shooter' with the same brief, the Irish-American Rick Scully.[7]

By mid-1990 the company's workforce had been reduced from 400 to 305 and a number of changes in work practices had been negotiated with the trade unions representing the remaining workers. Scully claimed in May 1990 that the brewery was producing 50 per cent more with 25 per cent less staff. By the end of 1991 total sales and output were up 65 per cent; as discussed below, an export drive to the UK was a key element, but domestic sales were also up by 20 per cent.

Carling was still the brewery's number one lager. Despite its 'out-of-date' image and parochial appeal, it still sold more than double the amount of Foster's and in 1990 £3 million was invested in a big push to revive its appeal on the notoriously fickle lager market, where Heineken was now the leader with one-third of the sector, followed by Harp with 20 per cent and Carlsberg with 16 per cent. Carling was still king in Cork, with close to half the lager market, and over one-third in Munster, but it only had a tiny 3 per cent share of the lucrative Dublin market. The new promotional push yielded some dividends, with Carling's overall market share increasing from around 10 per cent to over 12 per cent by 1992. Foster's was effectively relaunched in 1991, with £1 million spent on advertising, promotions, new mountings and packaging, but it failed to push beyond a 5 per cent share. Other brands – Hofmeister, Kronenbourg, Carlton, Holsten – came and went, but the key to the brewery's improved sales was a product whose obituary had been written many times since the 1960s: Beamish stout.

'Diamond in the mine': The rebirth of Beamish stout

Exports of Beamish stout to Britain had commenced on a small scale in 1985, but they took off in earnest in 1987–8 as the new owners discovered that the brewery's original product was a 'diamond in the mine' that had been overlooked.[8] This dawning realisation was driven by necessity, given the crippling loss of Carlsberg, the long-term decline of Carling and the imminent disappearance of Bass, plus the failure of Foster's to become a serious alternative in the lager market. It was announced in July 1988 that the success of Beamish stout in Britain might save 100 jobs in Cork. Beamish's sister company, Courage, had an extensive tied estate, while a trading deal was also secured with Bass Charrington. By mid-1990 Beamish stout was on sale in 6,000 British pubs, up from just 400 two years previously. It was also popular in canned form. The popularity of Beamish was mainly amongst young British drinkers who were switching from lager, rather than the Irish community in Britain. In the year to May 1990, output of stout increased almost threefold and just under 50,000 barrels were exported in the same period as the newly branded Beamish Genuine Irish Stout secured close to a 5 per cent market share in Britain. Murphy's stout was increasing its market share even quicker; brewed under licence in Wales by Whitbread, it was available in 12,000 pubs in the UK and by 1995 had captured 13 per cent of the British market, with Beamish up to 8 per cent, others at 4 per cent and Guinness at 75 per cent, down from 90 per cent in the 1980s.

The new energy that success in Britain brought to the Beamish stout brand was applied to its revival in Ireland. In November 1988 a 20p per pint (about 12 per cent) discount compared to its rivals was launched, advertised initially as Beamish 'at London prices'. Conceived as a short-term measure to carve out market share before gradually raising prices, this 'discount' (or 'promotional pricing', as the company preferred to call it) became a permanent feature and remained in place even after the takeover by Heineken in 2008. This represented a dual strategy, as Beamish sold at the same 'premium' price as its rivals in the UK, including Northern Ireland, where it was launched in 1991.

By mid-1991 one-third of the brewery's output was for export, and the Beamish revival was such that the company felt ready to engage in one of its sporadic offensives against Guinness in Ireland by targeting the behemoth in its own backyard. It had a willing partner in this endeavour in Dublin's vintners, organised in the Licensed Vintners' Association, who harboured an ongoing resentment at Guinness domination of the beer market. In November 1991 a combined investment and trading joint initiative between Beamish & Crawford and the Dublin vintners, the awkwardly named Brewing and Dublin Vintners Investment Company (BDVI), was established with the aim of increasing the market share of Beamish products, especially stout, in the capital. Vintners were invited to buy shares for a guaranteed 8 per cent per annum return and an additional 5 per cent if they sold 250 kegs of Beamish products. The minimum investment per outlet was £2,500 and the maximum was £15,000. The scheme was oversubscribed by 100 per cent as one-quarter of Dublin publicans signed up, immediately doubling Beamish's expected return to £500,000. By April 1992, in the brewery's bicentenary year, Beamish stout was available in half of Dublin's 800 pubs as well as almost all houses in Cork city and county and many other parts of the country too. By now it had passed out Murphy's as Ireland's second best-selling stout, with a market share of almost 3 per cent. In Cork it had grown to over 21 per cent, while the continuing success of the BDVI venture gave it 7 per cent in Dublin by the late 1990s.[9] From brewing 4,000 barrels of Beamish stout a year in 1988, the brewery was turning out 80,000 barrels in 1994.[10]

Meanwhile, in the export market, particularly Britain, Beamish tried to land a blow on its rivals by promoting the fact that it was the only draught stout on the market outside of Ireland that was actually brewed in Ireland. In September 1994 the company took 1,800 poster sites in England and Wales to stress its 'genuine' Irishness, as opposed to the Welsh-brewed Murphy's and London-brewed Guinness. The campaign played on the notion that stout tasted better in Ireland; Guinness declared this to be untrue, citing 'psychosomatic' reasons, no less, for this common condition.[11]

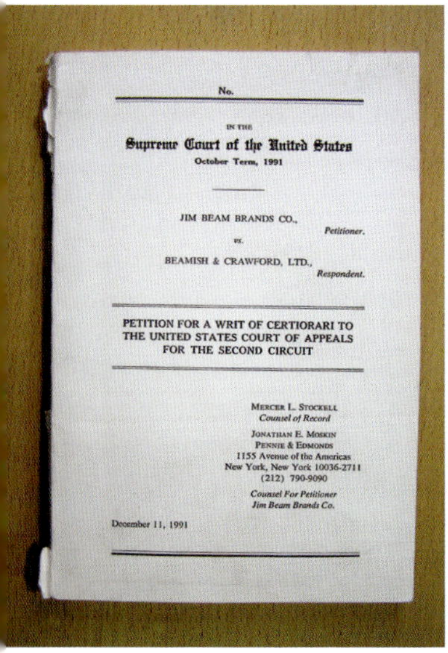
No.

IN THE

Supreme Court of the United States

October Term, 1991

JIM BEAM BRANDS CO.,
Petitioner,

vs.

BEAMISH & CRAWFORD, LTD.,
Respondent.

PETITION FOR A WRIT OF CERTIORARI TO THE UNITED STATES COURT OF APPEALS FOR THE SECOND CIRCUIT

MERCER L. STOCKELL
Counsel of Record
JONATHAN E. MOSKIN
PENNIE & EDMONDS
1155 Avenue of the Americas
New York, New York 10036-2711
(212) 790-9090
Counsel For Petitioner
Jim Beam Brands Co.

December 11, 1991

The curious case of 'Jim Beam-ish'

While the battle for Britain raged on, the company set its sights on Europe and beyond, registering its stout trademark in the key potential markets in the continent with an eye to the future. By 1995, Beamish stout was available in fifteen countries. The US was an obvious target, and Beamish had already exported there in the 1950s. In 1983, however, when the company registered the Beamish stout trademark in the US, the drinks company Jim Beam, makers of bourbon whisky and other spirits, who did not produce any beers, brought proceedings before the Trademark Trial and Appeal Board to cancel the registration, contending that there was a likelihood of confusion between the 'Beamish' and 'Beam' trademarks. The company argued that the '-ish' portion of the trademark implied 'of or belonging to' and that purchasers would assume that the Irish drink was really a 'Jim Beam-ish' stout.[12] The petition was denied on the rather obvious basis that the marks were sufficiently dissimilar and that stout and whisky were 'distinctly different products'. Jim Beam appealed and in 1989 the US Court of Appeals for the Federal Circuit reversed the decision, ruling that since the word 'beam' was 'at the heart of two alcoholic beverages, confusion was likely'. Jim Beam then attempted to secure an injunction against the use of the Beamish mark in the US on the basis of trademark infringement. In 1990 this was temporarily granted, but lifted again in late 1991. Beamish stout was launched in Boston, New York, Philadelphia and Atlanta on St Patrick's Day 1992, but a full roll-out was hobbled by ongoing legal wranglings. Eventually, in May 1994 the District Court in New York resolved the issue in Beamish's favour, finally dismissing the action and denying the injunction. The final judgement was an exemplar of common sense:

> I see no reason to believe that any consumer would think that BEAMISH is a Jim Beam product. ... The BEAMISH label not only looks different in arrangement and color, but it clearly identifies the products as an Irish stout, brewed in County Cork, Ireland ... 'imported' is emblazoned on every side of the case. The product's Irish heritage is its most salient marketing point. Jim Beam products contrariwise base their appeal on the heritage of the American South.

The judge pointed out that if a bar patron asked for a Jim Beam and received a Beamish stout instead, or vice versa, there would presumably be no confusion in their minds and they would no doubt shout, 'Take it back!'

The court ruling finally cleared the way for a proper roll-out on the lucrative US market from late 1994 in a distribution deal with Molson, which was also owned by Foster's. Promoted as the only Irish-brewed stout available in the US, it established a solid niche market, especially on the east coast, particularly in Philadelphia, and was exporting 120,000 cases, or 1 million litres, a year to the US when Beamish's then owners, Scottish & Newcastle, announced in early 2006 that exports there were to be terminated. However, by the end of 2006 the Cork brewery's old nemesis, Carlsberg, announced that its US wing had taken over the distribution of Beamish stout, where it would be pushed in particular through the expanding network of 'Irish' and 'English' pubs in the major cities.

Rationalisation once again

The initial phase of lay-offs and sell-offs, together with improved sales, especially of Beamish stout, had turned the loss-making brewery into a modestly profitable enterprise again by 1992. Towards the end of that year a young Cork accountant, Alf Smiddy, who had joined Beamish as a financial controller in 1988 and became financial director and company secretary in 1990, was appointed general manager. In

Alf Smiddy joined Beamish & Crawford in 1988 as financial controller and was appointed financial director in 1990. He later became general manager and in 1995 was appointed managing director of the company. He resigned in 2008 after the Heineken takeover. (Beamish & Crawford Brewery Collection)

1995, after he became managing director, Smiddy described the company as he saw it before the changes he was deeply involved in making:

> a very sleepy, inward-looking operation, which was highly bureaucratic. There was a lot of inertia and it was a stifling place to work for talented people, particularly those at middle management level. The company had no clear view of the future, no urgency for success, little or no focus and no marketing and sales strategies which had the commitment of management.[13]

From the company's perspective, restrictive practices and overstaffing were still blockages to efficiency. Management undertook the next phase of 'revamping' by introducing new information, measurement and planning systems. It also began moves to replace full-time employees with contractors. This latest and more radical phase of rationalisation put the company on a collision course with the trade unions at a time of high unemployment in Cork and huge uncertainty surrounding the future of other major industries in the area, such as Irish Steel and the computer support systems company Liebert.

In late 1993 the company announced that it was seeking 105 redundancies from among the remaining workforce of 305, amongst other changes. As talks proceeded with unions in early 1994, Foster's upped the ante in late February by announcing that if the redundancies could not be agreed by the end of March, the brewery would be closed and production moved to the UK. The Labour Court became involved in early March and declared that the company's approach had been 'purely finance-driven' and did not take account of the implications of their decision-making for the staff. It recommended that the scale of the changes sought – including voluntary redundancies, early retirements and widespread redeployments – called for full consultation with the trade unions at the brewery. The SIPTU branch secretary, Paddy O'Donnell, said that if the company engaged fully in dialogue, it should be possible to 'address the financial problems at least human cost', but insisted there should be no compulsory redundancies. Talks began the day before the initial Foster's deadline of 31 March, and a week later SIPTU members, about half the workforce, rejected the package on offer for the lay-off of 105 workers in maintenance, technical services and distribution areas, mainly in Cork, but also at depots in Limerick and Dublin.[14]

The company responded by issuing protective notice to the entire workforce of 305 people and said it would proceed with restructuring and compulsory redundancies. The unions threatened all-out strike and expressed the workers' anger that a profitable company was prepared to put secure jobs out to contract. The company denied being profitable and said the required changes, including the contracting-out of a number of services and the re-employment of a percentage of the laid-off workers in a new capacity as contractors, were needed to make it so. The contractors were in place and as Beamish prepared to bring them in, the unions prepared for an all-out strike. Last-ditch talks were held, and when the company offered improved redundancy payments, the SIPTU members voted to accept the restructuring package on 15 April 1994. In the meantime, Courage in the UK had been trial-brewing Beamish products and when production in Cork was halted the following month in a strike over contract workers and other lingering issues from the previous month's settlement, the company claimed it was ready to move production across the Irish Sea. Emergency talks at the Labour Relations Commission produced a solution that ended the week-long strike and averted the threatened closure of the brewery.

Trouble flared again in September over work practices when SIPTU members on the kegging line voted to strike following the suspension of six workers. The company reissued its warning that it would close the plant, and the Labour Relations Commission again intervened as work at the kegging and packaging plants was suspended for a week. The Commission's compromise was eventually accepted by both sides, with the details to be ironed out at the Labour Court, and the three-week dispute ended with full production resuming. The full-time workforce at Beamish & Crawford was down to 180 at this stage, having been at 400 only six years before.

Scottish & Newcastle: another new era

Meanwhile, the parent company, Foster's, was in trouble, having overextended itself in a number of international deals, and there were rumours in late 1994 of a possible sale of its British and Irish interests to either the US brewers Miller or the British group Scottish & Newcastle. In early 1995 a deal was made with the latter, but the takeover of the Foster's-owned Courage in Britain together with Beamish & Crawford was delayed while UK competition authorities looked into the possibility of brand conflict because the expanded company would have the franchise for six of the major lager brands on the British market. In May 1995 the *c.* £500 million deal finally went through. The Foster's man at Beamish, Rick Scully, moved on, to be replaced as managing director by the existing general manger, Alf Smiddy, in December 1995. The brewery kept its Carling and Foster's contracts and added Scrumpy Jack cider (made by Symonds in the UK and kegged and bottled at Cork) to its portfolio in August. The new owners declared a particular optimism for the prospects of Beamish stout, which were improved with the launch of a new canned Beamish Draught in July 1995, developed after a £300,000 investment. This was set to compete with the existing products by Guinness and Murphy's on the growing export and domestic canned draught stout markets; that market was worth £7.3 million in Ireland alone in 1995.

The company was in relatively rude health at this stage, with an annual turnover of about £50 million and about 8.5 per cent of the total Irish beer market. It claimed to have doubled production and halved overheads over the previous four years. With over 8 per cent of the domestic stout market and about the same in the UK (where the 5 per cent stout sector was much bigger in volume terms than the 50 per cent stout sector in Ireland), Beamish stout had, in Smiddy's words, 'come a long way since it was only available in a few pubs in Cork city'.[15] The company expected to turn a profit of £600,000 in 1995, despite a huge increase in its sales and marketing budget and the fact that Beamish stout on the Irish market was sold at such a discount that its margins were very low. A six-month review at the end of that year by its new parent company was very positive about its prospects and an investment of £2 million was announced in early 1996 in order to expand capacity to meet the increased demand for Beamish stout at home and abroad, which was expected to grow, especially in the UK, with Scottish & Newcastle's 'muscle' behind it.

A new ale, Beamish Red, was launched in May 1996, but even more significantly, in September of that year Beamish won the Irish contract for Miller beer from Showerings of

Clonmel, which had distributed this American beer, the pioneer in the 'longneck' bottle market in Ireland, since 1991. Bottled Miller Genuine Draft had 10 per cent of the premium bottled beer market and estimated sales of £18 million per year. While it had previously been imported, Beamish had the advantage of being able to brew Miller in Cork. Meanwhile, the six-year-old deal with Tennent's, whereby both firms distributed each other's products in their respective northern and southern strongholds, was terminated because of the number of brands they now had in direct competition. (In 2002, however, Beamish was given the distribution rights for all Scottish & Newcastle products in Northern Ireland.)

In August 1997 a £4 million marketing drive aimed at increasing Beamish & Crawford's share of the stout and ale markets in Britain was launched. Beamish stout was altered to make it less bitter and more appealing to younger drinkers. From a situation in the late 1980s when just 5 per cent of the brewery's output was exported, that figure now stood at close to 50 per cent. In Ireland there was a new TV and radio advertising campaign aimed at the 18–35 age market, new bar mounts and a canal barge named *Pride of Cork* visited eight cities to promote Beamish stout.

Miller was the fastest-growing beer brand on the market, where it was the second best-selling bottled beer after Heineken. Its share of the overall market was expanded with the introduction of canned Miller and Miller on draught (or draft) in 1997, and £2.4 million was thrown at a campaign to increase its market share in Dublin

In 2002 £7 million was spent on a new bottling plant where Miller Genuine Draft, the brewery's bestseller, and other products were bottled. (John Sheehan)

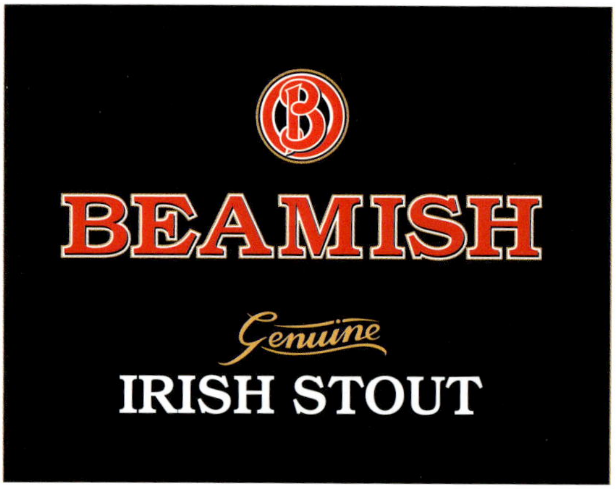

(Heineken)

in 1999, which grew to 5 per cent over the following year. The unique selling point of Miller on draught was based on a suggestion from a staff member, a result of Smiddy's 'staff suggestions' scheme that formed a part of his 'hands-on', 'all-in-it-together' approach that he saw as one way of motivating the workforce. A worker had suggested making Miller the coldest beer on draught and the technology was developed so that it was poured at 3 °C to 4 °C rather than the normal 6 °C to 10 °C.[16]

In late 2002 a new £7 million bottling facility was opened to replace the existing one dating from 1963; the latter had a capacity of 180 bottles per minute compared to 500 with the new technology. Beamish & Crawford was now the only brewery in Ireland with its own bottling facility, where Beamish stout, Miller, Foster's, Carling, Holsten, Tennent's and Bass were bottled. With the help of generous marketing budgets, the company sponsored local events like the Beamish Cork Folk Festival and national deals like the Miller sponsorship of *The Sopranos* on RTÉ television. Heavy advertising and sponsorship helped to maintain healthy sales throughout the 2000s. In 2002 the Beamish-brewed-and-bottled Miller Draft won a gold medal at the Brewing Industry International Awards. By then it had 4 per cent of the national lager market and 6 per cent in Dublin.

In October 2003 disagreements with production workers over shift-work on the new bottling facility reached crisis point, unofficial industrial action followed and the company issued protective notice to the 150 staff. SIPTU intervened, and following emergency talks the protective notice was lifted, new procedures were agreed and yet another threatened closure of Beamish & Crawford was averted. In 2004

Beamish escaped damage in a cost-cutting drive by its parent company that saw the closure of its 150-year-old Edinburgh brewery with a loss of 170 jobs. In that same year the Irish government introduced a smoking ban that hit the pub trade hard. Combined with other factors, such as a declining beer market, it led to a 10 per cent drop in on-licence sales between 2004 and 2005.[17]

Despite the declining beer market, in 2007 the company announced a 10 per cent rise in revenue from its three main brands: Beamish stout, Miller and Foster's; the latter had received a boost in the late twentieth century with Foster's Ice and in the early twenty-first century with the super-hyped, 'super chilled' beer-cooling technology for Foster's draught. In 2005 Foster's off-licence sales were boosted by widening its range of packaging sizes, while the price of Foster's draught was discounted to boost on-licence sales. Beamish was the only stout on the market to increase sales in 2006, though it was still neck and neck with Murphy's, at about 6 per cent each. The expansion of the Beamish & Crawford marketing budget was achieved by the continuing outsourcing of non-core activities, with the most recent

Time runs out for Beamish & Crawford. Tom Hickey behind the face of the Counting House clock. (John Sheehan)

Beamish & Crawford staff gather in the foyer of the Counting House for their last Christmas at the brewery, December 2008. The brewery closed in May 2009 after 217 years in business. (John Sheehan)

lay-offs, numbering twelve, occurring in 2001 following a switch to a national distribution centre. Layoffs were 'inevitable', said Smiddy, in a consolidating brewing industry.[18] His own job would fall victim to the same process before the decade was out.

Closing time

Behind the silver lining of positive news on the sales front in 2007, black clouds were developing. Scottish & Newcastle announced in February that despite increased profits, it was launching a cost-saving strategy designed to save £50 million over the following three years across all of its subsidiaries, including Beamish.[19] But before the impact could be felt in Cork, in October 2007 Heineken and Carlsberg teamed up to make a hostile bid for Scottish & Newcastle. Baltic Beverages Holding (BBH), which owned Russia's largest breweries, was a joint venture between Carlsberg and

(Heineken)

Scottish & Newcastle. The objective was for Carlsberg to gain full control of this joint venture and give it a greater foothold in the growing Eastern European market. Heineken, meanwhile, would gain Scottish & Newcastle's many UK brands as well as a number of international beer products and their breweries. Following further rejected offers, Scottish & Newcastle eventually agreed to sell in early 2008 and the acquisition, worth in the region of £7.8 billion, was completed in April. As part of the deal Heineken gained a multiplicity of UK brands as well as breweries in Portugal, Finland, India, Belgium and, of course, Ireland. The Irish dimension was a classic case of the global made local because, by a quirk of history, both Heineken and Scottish & Newcastle happened to be based in Cork city. This ensured an awkward and emotional outcome, and one that would signal the end for Beamish & Crawford, although not for Beamish stout.

Pride. Ed Hinchy, who worked at Beamish & Crawford for almost forty years, with Pat Rowe, left, and Tony Tynan. (John Sheehan)

The takeover was delayed for several months as the European Commission referred the question of a possible duopoly on the Irish market between Heineken and Diageo, owners of Guinness, to the Irish Competition Authority. On 3 October 2008 the authority ruled that the takeover would not substantially lessen competition in Ireland or result in price-fixing in the stout market.[20] Heineken announced a 'review of operations' and Alf Smiddy resigned as managing director, to be replaced by the Heineken Ireland managing director, Gerrit van Loo. There was press speculation that perhaps Heineken would close its Lady's Well Brewery and move production to the Beamish facility, but on 4 December the news that many feared was delivered to the Beamish & Crawford workforce by Heineken: the brewery on South Main Street was to close. Van Loo stated that 'retaining two breweries [in Cork] is not sustainable' and that the closure of Beamish & Crawford was 'a sad but unavoidable outcome'.[21] Forty Beamish & Crawford employees transferred to Heineken Ireland and the remaining 120 were made redundant. Head brewer Rory Bevan and other key personnel moved to Heineken and oversaw continuity in the brewing of Beamish, which became a stablemate of its long-time rival, Murphy's.

On 29 May 2009 the oft-threatened closure of the Beamish & Crawford brewery became a reality. Beer had been brewed continuously on that South Main Street site for at least 350 years and by Beamish & Crawford for 217 years. It had been an integral part of the fabric of Cork, and generations of the philanthropic and civic-minded Beamish and Crawford families had also left their mark on the city in myriad

Declan Farmer, Corporate Affairs Manager, Heineken, and Rory Bevan, last Head Brewer at Beamish & Crawford, close the brewery's gates following closure, 29 May 2009. (Dan Linehan, *Irish Examiner*)

ways. Its loss was felt keenly across the city, especially by its workers and former employees, many of whom had family connections to the brewery going back several generations.

In 2009 Mike Hannon made an awarding-winning, elegiac documentary, *My Beamish Boy*, which captures in pictures, music and words the affection felt for Beamish & Crawford.[22] Photographer Dave Creedon and musician Johnny McCarthy, who had been third- and fourth-generation workers at the brewery, contributed images and music, and local singer-songwriter John Spillane penned an original song, 'My Lovely Smiling Beamish Boy': '… And now a cloud hangs over town / The Beamish brewery has closed down.' Beamish workers reminisced, recalling the family atmosphere, the sense of camaraderie, the tradition and history that made it more than just a brewery, something beyond a mere workplace or business. Beamish & Crawford, said one, 'was the heart of Cork'.

Brewery workers, child and dog, 1913. (Courtesy Ed Hinchy)

Appendices

APPENDIX A
Beamish & Crawford sales (in barrels), 1793–1960

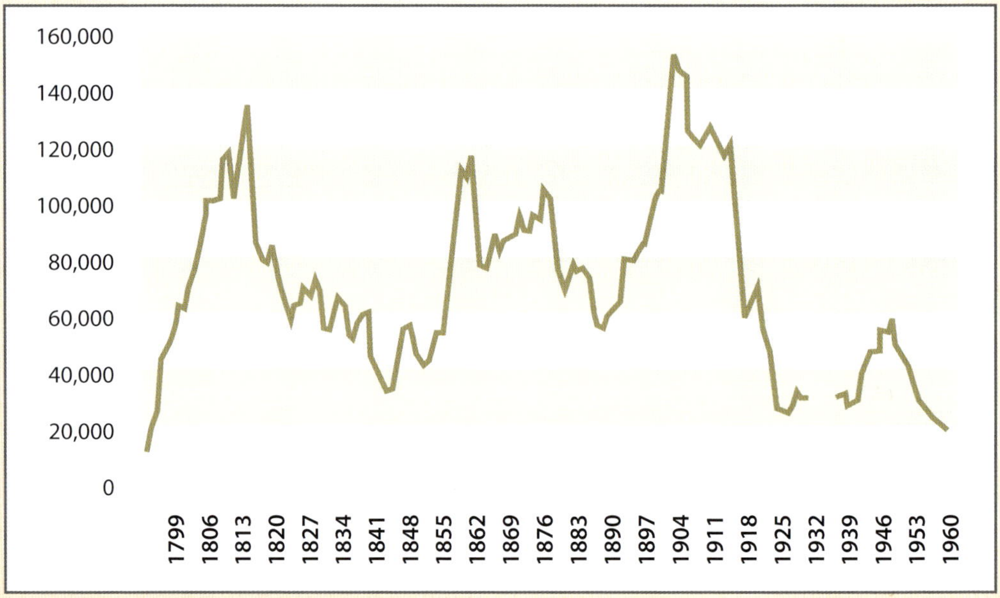

APPENDIX B

Beamish & Crawford sales (in barrels), 1793–1962

YEAR	BARRELS	YEAR	BARRELS	YEAR	BARRELS	YEAR	BARRELS	YEAR	BARRELS
1792		1827	66,778	1862	94,704	1897	86,558	1932	
1793	12,003	1828	72,399	1863	77,825	1898	94,357	1933	28,851
1794	21,688	1829	68,318	1864	76,983	1899	102,033	1934	
1795	26,412	1830	55,316	1865	82,889	1900	104,457	1935	
1796	43,911	1831	54,972	1866	87,750	1901	120,073	1936	
1797	46,778	1832	60,048	1867	82,563	1902	141,290	1937	30,538
1798	50,549	1833	65,585	1868	85,824	1903	151,734	1938	31,415
1799	55,103	1834	63,394	1869	87,626	1904	145,741	1939	28,151
1800	63,230	1835	53,388	1870	88,793	1905	144,926	1940	29,096
1801	61,950	1836	52,213	1871	94,142	1906	125,897	1941	31,204
1802	69,239	1837	58,429	1872	90,865	1907	122,181	1942	38,014
1803	74,074	1838	61,143	1873	90,910	1908	121,126	1943	41,509
1804	81,645	1839	63,031	1874	94,861	1909	123,992	1944	46,198
1805	94,142	1840	45,417	1875	94,252	1910	126,857	1945	47,319
1806	100,137	1841	41,925	1876	104,223	1911	126,987	1946	53,785
1807	99,889	1842	36,865	1877	101,658	1912	121,331	1947	54,611
1808	101,305	1843	32,848	1878	89,265	1913	117,378	1948	58,141
1809	115,496	1844	33,945	1879	74,783	1914	122,088	1949	50,975
1810	117,139	1845	38,339	1880	69,798	1915	122,281	1950	49,104
1811	102,473	1846	46,887	1881	74,281	1916	110,951	1951	45,726
1812	112,403	1847	54,584	1882	77,194	1917	82,887	1952	40,629
1813	123,054	1848	56,233	1883	76,015	1918	59,326	1953	33,998
1814	134,039	1849	46,738	1884	76419	1919	68,803	1954	29,704
1815	118,689	1850	43,070	1885	73,588	1920	74,977	1955	25,873
1816	86,689	1851	43,316	1886	61,645	1921	69,164	1956	24,457
1817	80,884	1852	44,221	1887	56,322	1922	52,880	1957	21,526
1818	78,928	1853	47,875	1888	55,851	1923	47,401	1958	20,383
1819	83,875	1854	53,487	1889	59,035	1924	33,169	1959	19,916
1820	77,971	1855	52,929	1890	61,527	1925	26,393	1960	
1821	69,517	1856	68,041	1891	63,878	1926	25,917	1961	
1822	65,682	1857	93,278	1892	69,738	1927	28,902	1962	29,629
1823	58,646	1858	103,826	1893	79,333	1928	39,090	1963	
1824	63,085	1859	111,113	1894	78,024	1929	31,741	1964	
1825	63,890	1860	108,998	1895	83,036	1930	31,726	1965	
1826	69,695	1861	116,076	1896	85,490	1931			

Appendix C
Customers supplied by Beamish & Crawford May–July 1804 and January–March 1805 (excluding non-city agents/wholesalers, exports)

Location	No.	Names
George's St	15	Nicholas Brown, John Daly, Cath. Corbett, Mary Mahony, Ml. Cogan, Sir Eyre Coote, Thos. Mahony, Maurice Daly, Peter Fagan, T. McCarthy, John O'Mullane, Wm. Cowen, Jos. Conroy, John Calanan, John Conway
Blackpool	12	M. Daly, Pat Murphy, John Hennessy, Thos. Parkes, Philip Walsh, Arth. Hyland, Dan Mahoney, M. Corkran, Con Curtin, T. Neill, D. McCarthy, Jas. Murphy
South Main St	11	Roger Cleary, F. Conway, J. Lane, Con McAuliff, T. Purcell, Ed. Russell, G. Sullivan, A. Wall, Dan McCarthy, John Franklin, David Hayes
Blarney Lane	9	James Daly, James Walsh, Wm. Quinn, Denis Horgan, Pat Coakely, John Murphy, Thos. Lane, Kane Mahony, Ed. Bodwin
Mallow Lane	9	John O'Mullane, Ed. Allen, J. Piggott, Luke Stritch, D. Leary, Henry Toher, Pat Keller, Pat Hennessy, G. Bromfield
North Main St	7	Geo. Carr, P. Armstrong, Wm. McDonnell, Wm. Maultby, Tim Mahon, Cath. Grainger, Wm. Ryan
Passage	7	Francis Boland, David Barry, Thomas Woods, James Cronen, Danl. Moriarty, John White, Thos. White
Bandon Rd	6	J. Barry, Wm. Haines, M. Murphy, Tim Leary, Tim Keefe, Tim Sullivan
Barrack St	6	John Lynch, F. McNamara, Mg. & Richd. Archer, Denis Lane, James Walsh, Dan Foley
Coal Quay	6	Ed. Fitzgerald, Maurice Lane, J. Knight, Ed. Fitzgibbon, Ml. Shinnick, Ml. McCarthy
Leitrim	6	J. McCarthy, J. Honan, Ml. Morrogh, J. Mahony, Ml. Sheehan, Jere. O'Brien
Old Market Place	6	Cremen/Tanner, John Mahony, Danl. Curtin, T. Sullivan, James Sullivan, Chas. Vaughan
Cove St	5	Cath. Kane, John Lane, Ellen & D. Twoomey, Anthony Donovan, J. Barry
Grand Parade	5	Batt Purcell, John Sullivan, Sir James Chatterton, Sir Eyre Coote, Daly's Club
Patrick's St	5	Thos. Atkins, Jos. Atkins, Geo. Gould, John Franklin, Daniel Meagher
Shandon St	5	Thos. Dixon, Humphrey Flinn, John Harrington, John Harrison, Thos. Woods
Carrigeens	4	John Topp, John Thomas, John Logan, Widow of John Byrne
Corn Market	4	Thos. Sullivan, James Flynn, Geo. Langley, ?
Duncan St	4	Thos. McCarthy, Mr. de L'Estang, Arth. O'Leary, Florence McCarthy
Fairlane	4	A. Moriarty, Ed. Hubbert, D. Lyon, John O'Brien
Fish St	4	M. Reidy, Ed. Marks, Robt. Hollis, R. O'Driscoll
Merchants' Quay	4	Wm. Crawford, Wm. Brady, Church & Co., George Galwey

Location	No.	Names
Potato Quay	4	Tim Kent, Geo. Smith, J. Mahon, Eliz. Fitzgerald
Princess [*sic*] St	4	Garret Smith, E. Cahill, Thos. Brosnan, Francis Power
South Gate Bridge	4	Pat Sexton, J. Regan, James Hayes, John ?
South Mall	4	Rev. Boyle Davis, John Martin, Jos. King, Richd. Foot
Ballintemple	3	John Fitzpatrick, John Leahy, D. Cullnane
Castle St	3	T. Curtis, Arth. Edwards, H. Smith
Cook St	3	Farrely & Roche, Robt. Rogers, James Roche
Exchange	3	Thos. Sheehan, Con. McAuliff, H.V. Larrymore
Fishamble Lane	3	Con Reeves, Wm. Thomas, Cath. Connor
Glanmire	3	David Kenealy, David Drady, Wm. Reeves
Lavitt's Quay	3	J.J. & P. Besnard, Peter Maziere, Ed. Parker
Maypole Rd	3	Mary Belcher, J. Haly, Tim Cremin
Parliament Bridge	3	Thos. Harvey, J. Lewis, Owen Cronin
Rathcormack	3	O. Daly, Denis Heffernan, Ann Honan
Ballincannan	2	Ellen Corkery, Wm. Blake
Ballinhassig	2	James Donegan, Mary Glascott
Camden Place	2	Samuel McCall, Rev. Hinks
Dominick St	2	Mary Gonnell, Denis Neill
Doneraile	2	Ed. Fethersten, Denis Duane
Evergreen	2	Wm. Agar, Gawen Emery
Knapp's Square	2	James Woods, Pat Sheehan
Lapp's Island	2	J.H. Hall, Alexander Deane
Mannix St	2	Mary O'Sullivan, Mary Scollard
Marlboro St	2	Daniel Connell, Jos. Spearing
Morgan St	2	D. Collins, T.B. Johnson
Nile St	2	W. Walsh, Wm. McDonell
North Abbey	2	S. Newsom, Ed. Quinn
North Gate	2	Wm. Murphy, Walter Murphy
Passage Rd	2	John Sheehan, John Shanahan
St Barry's	2	Chas. McDonnell, Wm. Cantillon
Academy St	1	T. Spearing.
Ann Mount	1	Joseph Linehan
Beaumont	1	Wm. Beamish
Blackrock	1	David Fitzgerald
Blarney	1	M. Buckley
Bottle Hill	1	Rob. Conway
Brickfields	1	John Cantlan
Broad Lane	1	Daniel O'Keeffe
Brown St	1	James Kelly

Appendix C continued
Customers supplied by Beamish & Crawford May–July 1804 and January–March 1805 (excluding non-city agents/wholesalers, exports)

Location	No.	Names	Location	No.	Names
Butlerstown	1	Samuel Martin	N.W.H. [?]	1	T. McCarthy
Castletownsend	1	J. Jones	Patrick's Place	1	Chas. Cole
Charlotte Quay	1	Thos. Dunscombe	Paul St	1	Ann Meade
Chiplee	1	Reuben Harvey	Pembroke St	1	Edw. Cotter
Clothier's Lane	1	J. Hendrick	Pope's Quay	1	Luke Stritch
Cockpit Lane	1	John Condon	Pump Lane	1	Denis Flinn
Crosshaven	1	? Keefe	Ranogue's Well	1	John Leahy & Danl. Murphy
Crown Tavern	1	J. Dennison			
Drawbridge St	1	Thos. Clarke	Riverstown	1	J. Freyne
Dunbar St	1	Tim Falvey	Rutland St	1	James Bell
Fair Place	1	Denis Sweeny	Skibbereen	1	Pat McCarthy
Garrycloyne	1	Wm. Hanlon	Square	1	John Crowley
Glandore	1	Richard Hungerford	Summerhill	1	Geo. Newenham
Glountane	1	D. Mahony	Sunday's Well	1	Pat Regan
Grafton's Alley	1	John Riordan	Sunville	1	Wm. Martin
Hanover St	1	Wm. Gove	Temple Hill	1	Ben. Parvin
Henry St	1	John Harding	Watercourse	1	Jane Barry
Kemp St	1	Pat Byrne	Whitegate	1	Ml. Cadogan
Lakelands	1	Benj. Bousefield	Youghal Hill	1	John Dill
Maylor St	1	Thos. Jones		1	Earl of Cork
Millboro	1	Mary Gonnell		1	Sir Richard Kellett
New Market Lane	1	Rich. Fitzgerald		1	15th Regiment

Advertisement, 1932. (Courtesy Michael Lenihan)

Appendix D
Agents and wholesalers supplied by Beamish & Crawford, 1804–13

IN COUNTY CORK

Charles Haines, Mallow
Thomas John, Youghal
S.W. Coppinger, Midleton
Christopher Owens, Cove
Bartholomew Symmonds (sometimes Simmons), Kilworth
John Sweete, Bandon;
William Newman, Kinsale (replaced in 1806 by John Spiller Newman)
George V. Dunn, Kinsale
William Orr Jun., Inishannon
Robert McCarthy, Macroom (replaced in 1808 by David Barry)
M. Fitzgerald, Crosshaven
John Young Robert, Bantry
Bart. Barry, Bantry
James Jones, Castletownsend
Edward Puxley, Berehaven
Morty O'Sullivan, Berehaven
William Brown Jun., Skibbereen
Richard Hungerford, Glandore;
James Moloney, Clonakilty
Thomas Ellis, Millstreet
Spike Island (no named wholesaler, but likely to have been military)

ELSEWHERE IN IRELAND

Lawrence Towke, Capoquin, County Waterford
John Flinn, Capoquin, County Waterford
Roger Robinett, Tallow, County Waterford;
Robert Barry, Lisnabrin, Tallow, County Waterford
William Galwey, Dungarvan, County Waterford
Jeremy Biggs, Waterford
John Carroll, Waterford
Hyland, Wexford
John Donovan, Tralee, County Kerry
Richard Teffcott Sen., Tralee, County Kerry
Daniel Sullivan & John Daly, Kenmare, County Kerry
Coe & Carpenter, Limerick
M. O'Brien, Limerick
Thomas McGrath, Limerick
Peter Nevill, Limerick
James Kennedy, Limerick
J.N. Russell, Limerick
S.J. Moriarty & Co., Dublin
Parke Telfair & Co., Belfast
Robert Stuart & Co., Belfast
Sam. & And. McClean, Belfast
J. Thraile, Kennedy & Co., Belfast
John Lavens, Londonderry; Coleraine, County Londonderry (no named wholesaler)
County Galway (no named wholesaler)

Appendix E
Cost of hops, 1864–1900[39]

YEAR	TOTAL COST OF HOPS	QUANTITY (IN CWT)	COST RANGE PER CWT TO 1880–1 Average cost per cwt from 1890–1
1864	£8,782	?	£5.9.10 to £6.4.0
1865	£11,158	?	£5.13.9 to £6.1.3
1866	£13,525	?	£3.18.0 to £6.3.8
1867	£8,944	?	£4.6.4 to £5.19.1
1868	£8,972	?	£4.6.10 to £6.4.10
1869	£6,738	?	£3.13.8 to £5.8.2
1870	£7,563	?	£2.18.4 to £3.11.11
1871	£5,125	?	£2.11.3 to £4.2.1
1872	£7,485	?	£2.4.9 to £4.14.1
1873	£6,214	?	£2.14.3 to £5.3.3
1874	£5,338	?	£3.4.6 to £4.1.8
1875	£7,561	?	£2.8.9 to £6.13.7
1876	£4,302	?	£2.9.10 to £6.16.6
1877	£9,593	?	£2.15.4 to £4.4.9
1878	£2,310	?	£2.10.6 to £5.11.9
1879	£6,289	?	£2.15.6 to £3.11.8
1880	£8,942	?	£2.17.9 to £6.18.6
1881	£3,783	?	£2.11.9 to £7.6.0
1882	£7,073	?	?
1883	£15,514	?	?
1884	£10,042	?	?
1885	£9,056	?	?
1886	£3,502	?	?
1887	£3,521	?	?
1888	£3,306	?	?
1889	£8,323	?	?
1890	£5,304	?	?
1891	£9,484	1,498 cwt	£6.6.7
1892	£9,111	1,490 cwt	£6.2.2
1893	£9,766	1,612 cwt	£6.1.2
1894	£9,347	1,544 cwt	£6.1.0
1895	£8,070	1,780 cwt	£4.10.7
1896	£6,412	1,876 cwt	£3.8.2
1897	£6,908	1,900 cwt	£3.12.10
1898	£8,162	2,017 cwt	£4.1.0
1899	£11,325	2,160 cwt	£5.4.10
1900	£11,040	2,107 cwt	£5.4.10

Appendix F Beamish & Crawford sales and sales income (1864–1900), net profit (1864–78), gross profit (1879–1900) and net profit per barrel (1864–78)

YEAR	SALES (barrels)	SALES INCOME	NET PROFIT (allocated to partners)	NET PROFIT (per barrel) (to nearest penny)
1864	76,983	£124,313	£20,261	5s 3d
1865	82,889	£133,169	£28,101	6s 9d
1866	87,750	£140,745	£29,554	6s 9d
1867	82,563	£132,546	£21,585	5s 3d
1868	85,824	£137,133	£25,525	5s 11d
1869	87,626	£139,875	£28,640	6s 6d
1870	88,793	£141,328	£33,413	7s 6d
1871	94,142	£150,153	£40,498	8s 7d
1872	90,865	£147,473	£38,332	8s 5d
1873	90,910	£147,988	£37,771	8s 4d
1874	94,861	£154,573	£41,270	8s 8d
1875	94,252	£154,045	£46,701	9s 11d
1876	104,223	£169,363	£43,628	8s 4d
1877	101,658	£165,386	£44,858	8s 10d
1878	89,265	£145,616	£30,488	6s 10d
1879	74,783	£139,875	£20,499	?
1880	69,798	£141,328	£17,330	?
1881	74,281	£121,562	£21,639	?
1882	77,194	£126,664	£26,305	?
1883	76,015	£126,234	£20,638	?
1884	76,419	£128,028	?	?
1885	73,588	£123,235	?	?
1886	61,645	£103,872	?	?
1887	56,322	£96,134	?	?
1888	55,851	£94,347	?	?
1889	59,035	£98,985	?	?
1890	61,527	£102,855	?	?
1891	63,878	£107,142	£15,657	?
1892	69,738	£116,575	£18,202	?
1893	79,333	£132,779	£21,434	?
1894	78,024	£130,414	£20,102	?
1895	83,036	£138,627	£26,580	?
1896	85,490	£142,868	£28,770	?
1897	86,558	£144,944	£29,179	?
1898	94,357	£158,328	£29,890	?
1899	102,033	£171,631	£32,848	?
1900	104,457	£175,774	£34,205	?

Appendix G Beamish & Crawford sales, sales income, barley spend, malt spend, malt duty and gross profit, 1864–1900

YEAR	SALES (in barrels)	SALES INCOME	BARLEY SPEND	MALT SPEND	MALT DUTY (beer duty from 1880)	GROSS PROFIT
1864	76,983	£124,313	£23,720	£6,091	£17,794	£22,530
1865	82,889	£133,169	£29,442	£5,784	£21,084	£29,043
1866	87,750	£140,745	£20,184	£30,938	£15,074	£29,456
1867	82,563	£132,546	£14,741	£32,344	£8,918	£22,472
1868	85,824	£137,133	£28,773	£10,152	£15,137	£27,126
1869	87,626	£139,875	£30,760	£8,680	£17,040	£30,181
1870	88,793	£141,328	£29,971	£13,265	£16,869	£35,469
1871	94,142	£150,153	£25,020	£12,381	£15,994	£43,074
1872	90,865	£147,473	£17,442	£19,772	£10,093	£39,587
1873	90,910	£147,988	£7,044	£47,405	£3,206	£39,646
1874	94,861	£154,573	£10,287	£12,913	£13,879	£43,196
1875	94,252	£154,045	£13,950	£10,696	£13,865	£41,398
1876	104,223	£169,363	£20,649	£33,554	£4,046	£46,302
1877	101,658	£165,386	£22,198	£15,137	£11,129	£47,538
1878	89,265	£145,616	£13,113	£13,802	£5,833	£33,833
1879	74,783	£139,875	£18,049	£33,147	£9,748	£20,499
1880	69,798	£141,328	£5,389	£51,235	£2,342	£17,330
1881	74,281	£121,562	£22,184	£15,368	£17,119	£21,639
1882	77,194	£126,664	£22,721	£11,486	£19,546	£26,305
1883	76,015	£126,234	£14,638	£7,683	£18,688	£20,638
1884	76,419	£128,028	£17,736	£14,415	£19,489	?
1885	73,588	£123,235	£20,640	£11,914	£19,748	?
1886	61,645	£103,872	£9,609	£12,224	£16,535	?
1887	56,322	£96,134	£9,197	£17,296	£15,760	?
1888	55,851	£94,347	£8,880	£11,185	£14,878	?
1889	59,035	£98,985	£10,028	£15,757	£16,001	?
1890	61,527	£102,855	£13,934	£13,141	£16,850	?
1891	63,878	£107,142	£15,246	£13,853	£17,758	£15,657
1892	69,738	£116,575	£13,952	£16,204	£22,363	£18,202
1893	79,333	£132,779	£14,156	£21,155	£22,646	£21,434
1894	78,024	£130,414	£13,923	£18,747	£24,914	£20,102
1895	83,036	£138,627	£13,130	£19,352	£25,558	£26,580
1896	85,490	£142,868	£13,371	£22,408	£25,764	£28,770
1897	86,558	£144,944	£13,770	£21,361	£29,300	£29,179
1898	94,357	£158,328	£14,456	£28,484	£32,790	£29,890
1899	102,033	£171,631	£10,028	?	£35,289	£32,848
1900	104,457	£175,774	£13,934	?	£37,345	£34,205

Appendix H
List of public houses in Cork City, 1900

including address and name of sitting tenant.
They are colour-coded according to the brewery to which they were tied or, in the case of Guinness, with which they traded:

☐ Beamish & Crawford ☐ James J. Murphy & Co. ☐ Arnott & Co. ☐ Lane & Co. ☐ Guinness

ADDRESS	NAME
23 Abbey Street	Margaret O'Leary
1 Academy Street	James J. Barry
1 Albert Street	Bridget Sexton
1 Anderson's Quay	Anne Reid
1 Anglesea Street	Edward Fitzgerald
9 Anglesea Street	Ellen Riordan
11 Anglesea Street	William Bateman
7 Anne Street	Margaret O'Hanlon
82 Ballyhooly Road	Ellen Tangney
83 Ballyhooly Road	Benjamin Wright
154 Ballyhooly Road	Matthew Barry
140 Ballyhooly New Road	John Cosgrave
1 Bandon Road	Patrick J. Healy
31 Bandon Road	Kate Murphy
37 Bandon Road	William Phair
38 Bandon Road	Ellen O'Callaghan
80 Bandon Road	Kate Egan
115 Bandon Road	Daniel Crowley
133 Bandon Road	Patrick McSwiney
141 Bandon Road	Jane McIntosh
152 Bandon Road	Jeremiah Spillane
160 Bandon Road	Catherine Roche
1 Barrack Street	John Kelleher
2 Barrack Street	Ellen Meade
4/5 Barrack Street	John Rahily
13 Barrack Street	Mary Anne Barry
16 Barrack Street	Ellen Jeffers
26 Barrack Street	Patrick Larrymore
32 Barrack Street	Kate Horgan
35 Barrack Street	Mary Crowley
47 Barrack Street	Daniel Noonan
48 Barrack Street	Thomas Kennefick
49 Barrack Street	Denis Crowley
52 Barrack Street	Ellen Ahern
56/57 Barrack Street	John Thomas Noonan
70 Barrack Street	John Murphy
80 Barrack Street	Ellen Linehan
94 Barrack Street	Charles Vaughan
111 Barrack Street	William F. O'Callaghan
113 Barrack Street	Margaret Buckley
122 Barrack Street	Margaret Buckley
125 Barrack Street	M.D. O'Brien
131 Barrack Street	Mary Leahy
137 Barrack Street	Vacant
138 Barrack Street	Ellen O'Connell
145 Barrack Street	Ellen Ryan
15 Blackrock Road	Anne Murphy
9 Blarney Street	Thomas Maher
14 Blarney Street	Kate McDonnell
16 Blarney Street	Michael Hogan
26 Blarney Street	John Cremen
40 Blarney Street	John O'Keeffe
56 Blarney Street	John J. Forde
70 Blarney Street	Timothy Healy
76 Blarney Street	Matthew O'Regan
110 Blarney Street	Michael Twomey
262 Blarney Street	Margaret O'Regan
326 Blarney Street	John O'Keeffe
354 Blarney Street	John Lennox
370 Blarney Street	Mary Anne Burke
379 Blarney Street	Nora Murphy
394 Blarney Street	Hannah O'Connor
1 Boyce's Street	Julia Sweeney
1 Bridge Street	Christopher Hemsworth

Appendix H List of public houses in Cork City, 1900 continued

ADDRESS	NAME
6 Bridge Street	Margaret Buckley
1 Buckingham Place	James Deasy
1 Castle Street	William O'Callaghan
15/16 Castle Street	Michael J. O'Connor
26 Castle Street	Margaret Dooly
10 Cattle Market Street	Mary O'Callaghan
15 Cattle Lane	Timothy O'Sullivan
15 Cattle Market Street	Catherine Healy
5 Chapel Hill	Patrick McNamara
5 Church Street	Cornelius Buckley
26 Church Street	Denis Ryan
27 Church Street	Maurice Murphy
29 Church Street	William Dean Swift
1 Clarence Street (Gerald Griffin Street)	Jeremiah O'Callaghan
19 Clarence Street (Gerald Griffin Street)	James Long
22 Clarence Street (Gerald Griffin Street)	Catherine Roche
38 Clarence Street (Gerald Griffin Street)	John Creedon
43 Clarence Street (Gerald Griffin Street)	Richard Barry
44 Clarence Street (Gerald Griffin Street)	Margaret O'Neill
53 Clarence Street (Gerald Griffin Street)	Elizabeth Lyons
56 Clarence Street (Gerald Griffin Street)	William Kelly
62 Clarence Street (Gerald Griffin Street)	William Hennessy
64 Clarence Street (Gerald Griffin Street)	Lizzie Creagh
82 Clarence Street (Gerald Griffin Street)	Mary Morrogh
84 Clarence Street (Gerald Griffin Street)	John C. Hemsworth
106 Clarence Street (Gerald Griffin Street)	Daniel Duggan
1 Coal Quay	John W. O'Mahony

ADDRESS	NAME
7 Coburg Street	Ellen Morrissey
8 Coburg Street	James Ring
9 Coburg Street	James O'Sullivan
10 Coburg Street	William Walsh
19 Coburg Street	Mary Twomey
21 Coburg Street	John Buckley
22 Commons Road	Denis Donovan
26 Commons Road	John Richardson
49 Commons Road	William Lynch
70 Commons Road	Timothy Sullivan
1/2 Cook Street	Nora Ryng
3 Cook Street	Edward Woods
29 Cook Street	Catherine Ryan
2 Corbett's Lane	Daniel O'Mahony
11 Cornmarket Street	Thomas Roche
17 Cornmarket Street	Patrick Riordan
31 Cornmarket Street	Mary Clifford
32 Cornmarket Street	Margaret Kelleher
33 Cornmarket Street	Hannah McCarthy
34 Cornmarket Street	John McCarthy
35 Cornmarket Street	Anna Buckley
39 Cornmarket Street	Anne O'Donnell
41 Cornmarket Street	Hannah Hennessy
43 Cornmarket Stereet	Michael McCarthy
46 Cornmarket Street	Hannah Riordan
56 Cornmarket Street	Patrick Foley
1 Court House Street	Ellen Murphy
2 Court House Street	Patrick Casey
3 Cross Street	Hannah Walsh
6 Cross Street	Kate McCarthy
8 Cross Street	John Sheehan
10 Curragh Road	John Butler
27 Dean Roche's Cross	Ellen Crowley
11 Devonshire Street	Mary Murphy
17 Devonshire Street	Ellen O'Connor
17 Dominick Street	David Rumm
19 Dominick Street	James Geelan
21 Dominick Street	Thomas Mulcahy

☐ Beamish & Crawford ☐ James J. Murphy & Co. ☐ Arnott & Co. ☐ Lane & Co. ☐ Guinness

ADDRESS	NAME
22 Dominick Street	John Buckley
45 Dominick Street	Jeremiah Ryan
65 Dominick Street	Hannah Riordan
1 Douglas Street	Denis Aherne
3 Douglas Street	Hannah Crean
7 Douglas Street	Harriet Coughlan
12 Douglas Street	Catherine Cogan
18 Douglas Street	Patrick McNamara
24 Douglas Street	James Arthurs
26 Douglas Street	Mary Connolly
32 Douglas Street	Margaret Collins
44 Douglas Street	Elizabeth Suttle
63 Douglas Street	Florence O'Brien
73 Douglas Street	Margaret Roche
97 Douglas Street	Catherine Mahony
94 Douglas Street	Kate Murphy
101 Douglas Street	Mary Keller
7 Drawbridge Street	Anne Conway
12 Drawbridge Street	Joseph Stanton
14 Drawbridge Street	Matthew Buckley
8 Dublin Hill	John Browne
2 Dublin Street	Mary O'Callaghan
5 Dublin Street	Mary Dorgan
7 Dublin Street	Patrick Dennehy
15 Dublin Street	Ellen Golden
16 Dublin Street	George G. Grant
29 Dublin Street	Ellen O'Sullivan
31 Dunbar Street	Michael O'Keeffe
12 Eason's Hill	Anne Harrington
1 Evergreen Road	Hanora Daly
12 Evergreen Road	Mary Murphy
24 Evergreen Road	Mary Anne Heelan
25 Evergreen Road	Bridget Hayes
34 Evergreen Road	Kate Neville
59 Evergreen Street	James O'Connell
91 Evergreen Street	Mary Creedon
15 Fair Lane	Eliza Leahy
17 Fair Lane	John Whelan

ADDRESS	NAME
37 Fair Lane	Daniel Murphy
1 Faulkener's Lane	Edward O'Halloran
2 Faulkener's Lane	Thomas Green
6 Fish Street	John McNamara
25 Fish Street	Edward Slynan
6 Fitton Street E.	Agnes O'Riordan
10 Friars Walk	David Murphy
113 Gardiner's Hill	Ellen Kelleher
3 George's Quay	Margaret Canty
12 George's Quay	Eliza Keatinge
22 George's Quay	Margaret Burke
21 George's Quay	David Canty
24 George's Quay	Ellen O'Sullivan
1 George's Street (Oliver Plunkett Street)	Michael Buckley
3 George's Street (Oliver Plunkett Street)	Abina Cashman
5 George's Street (Oliver Plunkett Street)	Denis Ralleigh
17 George's Street (Oliver Plunkett Street)	Hannah Noble
19 George's Street (Oliver Plunkett Street)	Daniel Duggan
37 George's Street (Oliver Plunkett Street)	Ellen O'Callaghan
41 George's Street (Oliver Plunkett Street)	Ellen Mangan
42 George's Street (Oliver Plunkett Street)	Thomas Browne
48 George's Street (Oliver Plunkett Street)	Denis Travers
61 George's Street (Oliver Plunkett Street)	Daniel Finn
62 George's Street (Oliver Plunkett Street)	Denis Wallace
70 George's Street (Oliver Plunkett Street)	John Timothy Nunan
72 George's Street (Oliver Plunkett Street)	John Fitzgerald

Appendix H List of public houses in Cork City, 1900 continued

ADDRESS	NAME
74 George's Street (Oliver Plunkett Street)	Daniel Joseph Horgan
88 George's Street (Oliver Plunkett Street)	John O'Neill
96a George's Street (Oliver Plunkett Street)	David O'Keeffe
98 George's Street (Oliver Plunkett Street)	Margaret Murphy
103 George's Street (Oliver Plunkett Street)	William Forrest
108 George's Street (Oliver Plunkett Street)	Patrick J. Kennedy
111 George's Street (Oliver Plunkett Street)	Thomas Lee
112 George's Street (Oliver Plunkett Street)	Anastasia Roche
113 George's Street (Oliver Plunkett Street)	William Scollard
126 George's Street (Oliver Plunkett Street)	Michael Kirwan
4 Gill Abbey Street	J.T. Nunan
9 Gill Abbey Street	Mary O'Connell
14 Gill Abbey Street	John Canty
21 Gill Abbey Street	Helena Flannery
30 Gill Abbey Street	Timothy J. Murphy
54 Gill Abbey Street	Bridget Barrett
35 Gould Street	Johanna O'Callaghan
13 Grafton Street	James Arthurs
1 Grand Parade	Margaret Haden
2 Grand Parade	Mary Carey
4 Grand Parade	Nora Forbes
64 Grand Parade	Bridget Madden
77 Grand Parade	Denis J. Murphy
93 Grand Parade	Denis O'Leary
17 Grattan Street	Edmond Twohig
26 Grattan Street	Margaret Aherne
46 Grattan Street	James Barry
60 Grattan Street	James Coleman
61 Grattan Street	Ellen Cox

ADDRESS	NAME
10 Great Britain Street (Great William O'Brien St)	James Long
58 Great Britain Street (Great William O'Brien St)	Kate Daly
60 Great Britain Street (Great William O'Brien St)	Norah McNamara
66/67 Great Britain St (Great William O'Brien St)	Hanora Cleary
87 Great Britain Street (Great William O'Brien St)	Michael Sheehan
88 Great Britain Street (Great William O'Brien St)	James Walsh
95 Great Britain Street (Great William O'Brien St)	J. O'Callaghan
20 Great George's Street E. (Washington Street)	David Bourke
21 Great George's Street E. (Washington Street)	William Kelleher
30 Great George's Street E. (Washington Street)	Patrick Casey
1 Great George's Street W. (Washington Street)	Ellen Thompson
9 Great George's Street W. (Washington Street)	James O'Sullivan
11 Great George's Street W. (Washington Street)	John Dunlea
22 Great George's Street W. (Washington Street)	Kate Riordan
26 Great George's Street W. (Washington Street)	William Kelleher
34 Great George's Street W. (Washington Street)	Annie Keane
1 Hanover Place	Francis O'Shaughnessy
3 Hanover Street	Daniel Murphy

☐ Beamish & Crawford ☐ James J. Murphy & Co. ☐ Arnott & Co. ☐ Lane & Co. ☐ Guinness

ADDRESS	NAME	ADDRESS	NAME
15 Hanover Street	Daniel O'Connell	87 Lower Glanmire Rd	John Hartnett
33 Henry Street	Margaret Heapes	95 Lower Glanmire Rd	Hannah Lyhane
34 John Street	Patrick Fogarty	98 Lower Glanmire Rd	Helena O.Sullivan
Kilbarry	Ellen Twohig	103 Lower Glanmire Rd	Kate McGrath
13 King Street (MacCurtain Street)	Mary Brennan	112 Lower Glanmire Rd	Hannah O'Mahony
14 King Street (MacCurtain Street)	Patrick Cotter	129 Lower Glanmire Rd	Margaret Walsh
16 King Street (MacCurtain Street)	Ellen Tagney	141 Lower Glanmire Rd	Ellen O'Keeffe
17 King Street (MacCurtain Street)	Bridget Sheehan	159 Lower Glanmire Rd	Charlotte Flynn
23 King Street (MacCurtain Street)	Mary Ellen Riordan	168 Lower Glanmire Rd	Ellen Buckley
27 King Street (MacCurtain Street)	Hannah Kelleher	179 Lr Glanmire Road	Michael Walsh
30 King Street (MacCurtain Street)	Timothy Murphy	3 Mannix Street	Daniel O'Connell
34 King Street (MacCurtain Street)	Daniel McCarthy	2 Marlboro Street	Richard J. Barry
38 King Street (MacCurtain Street)	Patrick J. McMahon	32 Marlboro Street	D.J. O'Callaghan
1 Kyle Street (MacCurtain Street)	Michael Stapleton	21 Mary Street	Mary Flaherty
30 Kyrl's Quay	Ellen O'Leary	39 Mary Street	Mary O'Donovan
4 Kyrl's Street	Norah Bowdren	23 Maylor Street	Daniel Horgan
17 Lancaster Quay	Cornelius Desmond	1 Meat Marlet Lane	Catherine Lyons
7 Lavitt's Quay	James Cahill	2 Meat Market Lane	William Wren
15 Lavitt's Quay	John Canty	4 Meat Market Lane	Albert McClenahan
24 Lavitt's Quay	Mary Jane Hoare	1 Merchants' Quay	Mary Anne Goggin
25 Lavitt's Quay	Mary Anne Mayne	2 Merchants' Quay	Mary O'Sullivan
15 Leitrim Street	Ellen Roche	19 Merchants' Quay	Henry Barry
31 Leitrim Street	Matthew Horgan	26 Merchants' Quay	William Lynch
42 Leitrim Street	Patrick Fogarty	27 Merchants' Quay	Mary Ashley
7 Little Hanover Street	Patrick Cotter & Co.	29 Merchants' Quay	John Daly
1 Little Market Street	Margaret O'Connell	8 Military Road	James Harrington
1 Lower Glanmire Rd	Julia Sheehan	9 Military Road	Alicia McCarthy
82 Lower Glanmire Rd	Wm Henry O.Sullivan	18 Military Road	Martin J. Maguire
84 Lower Glanmire Rd	Cornelius Mullany	19 Military Road	Joseph Michael Duff
86 Lower Glanmire Rd	Mary Ellen Tagney	9 Moore Street	Timothy Barrett
		10 Moore Street	Patrick Hayes
		12 Mulgrave Street	James Murphy
		14 Mulgrave Street	Julia Geary
		1 Mutton Lane	Norah O'Leary
		13 Nile Street (Sheare's Street)	Mary Murphy
		24 Nile Street (Sheare's Street)	John F. O'Mahony
		1 North Main Street	Hannah O'Connell

Appendix H List of public houses in Cork City, 1900 continued

ADDRESS	NAME
19 North Main Street	Hanora Hayes
25 North Main Street	Thomas Heffernan
26 North Main Street	Denis Dunlea
29 North Main Street	John T. Crowley
37 North Main Street	Margaret O Connell
39 North Main Street	Thomas Vesey
43 North Main Street	Patrick Conry
44 North Main Street	Margaret Cronin
48/9 North Main Street	Maurice Spillane
52 North Main Street	Mary O. Leary
71 North Main Street	Jeremiah O'Callaghan
76 North Main Street	Kate Kelleher
81 North Main Street	Bridget O'Sullivan
85 North Main Street	Annie O'Sullivan
98 North Main Street	Bridget O'Riordan
100 North Main Street	Maurice Carroll
112 North Main Street	Kate Harding
1 O'Connell Street	James Ryng
6 Old Market Place	Julia O'Connor
50 Old Market Place	Patrick Haren
13 Old Youghal Road	Kate O'Sullivan
16 Old Youghal Road	Humphrey J. Lynch
98 Old Youghal Road	Mary Murphy
111 Old Youghal Road	Hannah Mulcahy
173 Old Youghal Road	Andrew Desmond
175 Old Youghal Road	Helena Willis
179 Old Youghal Road	Dominick J. Daly
180 Old Youghal Road	Mary O'Callaghan
182 Old Youghal Road	Mary Anne Barton
184 Old Youghal Road	Kate Sexton
190 Old Youghal Road	Michael Prendergast
204 Old Youghal Road	Jane Rohan
290 Old Youghal Road	Thomas Egan
3 Parliament Street	Jeremiah Burke
5 Parliament Street	Margaret Dunlea
7 Parliament Street	Mary Cullen
8 Parliament Street	Patrick Horan
1 Paul Street	Mary Walsh
9 Paul Street	Charles Callanan

ADDRESS	NAME
10 Paul Street	William F. Hayes
20 Paul Street	Maurice McCarthy
24 Paul Street	Patrick Maher
3 Pembroke Street	Marie O'Brien
6 Pembroke Street	David Canty
6 Penrose Quay	Mary Lucey
16 Peter Street	Michael J. O'Connor
18 Pine Street	P.A. Hoskins
2 Pope's Quay	Timothy Hennessy
21 Pope's Quay	Denis Barry
2 Princes Street	Bartholomew Conroy
3 Princes Street	N. Bowdren
13 Princes Street	Patrick N. Fitzgerald
28 Princes Street	Ellen Kelleher
29 Princes Street	Julia O'Connell
35 Princes Street	John Canty
38 Princes Street	Mary Browne
45 Princes Street	Minnie Carey
1/2 Pump Lane	Ellen O'Connell
31 Quaker Road	Nora Millerd
3 Quarry Road	Timothy Flynn
15 Quarry Road	Timothy Keller
1 Roche's Road	Louisa M. Sheehy
2 Shandon Street	Cornelius O'Flaherty
7 Shandon Street	Mary J. Holland
9 Shandon Street	Patrick O'Mahony
17 Shandon Street	Jeremiah J. McCarthy
20 Shandon Street	Margaret Sheehan
28 Shandon Street	Denis Twomey
32 Shandon Street	Mary Lucey
33 Shandon Street	William O'Keeffe
36 Shandon Street	Lawrence O'Brien
40 Shandon Street	James Quinlan
41 Shandon Street	Margaret Herbstreit
42 Shandon Street	Framcis O'Sullivan
46 Shandon Street	Vacant
56 Shandon Street	Mary O'Riordan
58 Shandon Street	John F. Curry
60 Shandon Street	John Downey

☐ Beamish & Crawford ☐ James J. Murphy & Co. ☐ Arnott & Co. ☐ Lane & Co. ☐ Guinness

ADDRESS	NAME
62 Shandon Street	Patrick Casey
64 Shandon Street	Julia O'Connell
67 Shandon Street	Jeremiah J Murphy
88 Shandon Street	Kate O Callaghan
91 Shandon Street	James O'Regan
104 Shandon Street	Denis J. Murphy
117 Shandon Street	Richard O'Brien
9 Southern Road	Ellen Buckley
7 South Main Street	Patrick Casey
12 South Main Street	Deborah O'Driscoll
14 South Main Street	Timothy Hennessy
19 South Main Street	Thomas McCarthy
25 South Main Street	Anne Reidy
26 South Main Street	John Brady
29 South Main Street	Margaret Enright
34/5 South Main Street	John Purcell
49 South Main Street	Margaret O'Sullivan
50 South Main Street	William Landers
53 South Main Street	James McCarry
67 South Main Street	Daniel O'Leary
93 South Main Street	Michael Kennedy
99 South Main Street	Mary Hegarty
100 South Main Street	Ellen Corrigan
9 St Luke's	Caroline Heron
1 St Nicholas Square	Thomas Conway
17 St Patrick's Quay	James Quinlan
27 St Patrick's Quay	Julia Sheehan
28 St Patrick's Quay	Nellie Glynn
30 St Patrick's Quay	Walter Clifford
34 St Patrick's Quay	Catherine Mahony
35 St Patrick's Quay	Daniel McCarthy
37 St Patrick's Quay	Margaret Agnes Cotter
1 St Patrick's Street	John Canty
2 St Patrick's Street	Michael C. Daly
125 St Patrick's Street	John Canty
1 Sullivan's Quay	Eliza Barrett
3/4 Sullivan's Quay	Denis Corcoran
6 Sullivan's Quay	Timothy Courtney
10 Sullivan's Quay	David Francis Donovan

ADDRESS	NAME
2 Sunday's Well Road	Norah Wiseman
89 Sunday's Well Road	Patrick Casey
145 Sunday's Well Road	John Rooney
88 Sunday's Well Road	James Hayes
163 Sunday's Well Road	Cornelius Morley
37 Tower Street	Paul Higgins
38 Tower Street	Nora O'Leary
83 Tower Street	John Lee
1 Travers Street	Michael O'Driscoll
1 Union Quay	Edmond Heaphy
2 Union Quay	Mary Fleming
3 Union Quay	John O'Connor
4 Union Quay	William Drinan
17 Union Quay	Michael Madden
1 Victoria Road	Catherine Grogan
2 Victoria Road	Michael Moroney
4 Victoria Road	Thomas Coughlan
19 Warren's Place	William O'Shea
20 Warren's Place	Teresa Corkery
21 Warren's Place	Kate Desmond
22 Warren's Place	Catherine O'Mahony
23 Warren's Place	John Murphy
24 Warren's Place	Anne Donnellan
25 Warren's Place	Margaret Kelleher
26 Warren's Place	Ellen Harrington
28 Warren's Place	Eugene O'Sullivan
30 Warren's Place	David O'Brien
45 Warren's Place	Julia Anne Murphy
7 Watercourse Road	M. McCarthy
15 Watercourse Road	Peter Joyce
18 Watercourse Road	Daniel Barrett
24 Watercourse Road	Michael Collins
40 Watercourse Road	James Murphy
60 Watercourse Road	Eugene J. O'Callaghan
68 Watercourse Road	David Moran
39 Wellington Road	Patrick Hennessy
40/1 Wellington Road	John Henchy
18 White Street	Norah Lamb
7 Winthrop Street	Patrick Sullivan

Appendix H List of public houses in Cork City, 1900 continued

ADDRESS	NAME
16 Winthrop Street	Hannah J. Crowley
7 Woods Street	Margaret Ambrose
3 York Row	Patrick Corbett
1 York Street	Jeremiah Howe
19 York Street	Denis McCarthy
36 York Street	Kate Fitzmaurice
39 York Street	Daniel J. Cronin
41 York Street	Cornelius Coghlan
45 York Street	Edmund Culinane
54 York Street	James O'Callaghan
55 York Street	Michael Cahill
58 York Street	Jeremiah Looney
61 York Street	Hannah Cronin
79 York Street	Margaret Sullivan

☐ Beamish & Crawford ☐ James J. Murphy & Co. ☐ Arnott & Co. ☐ Lane & Co. ☐ Guinness

Beamish & Crawford tied public house on the corner of St Patrick's Street and Lavitt's Quay, Cork, 1890s. (Courtesy Michael Lenihan)

Notes & References

Note:

The Beamish & Crawford Collection at the Cork City and County Archives is available for consultation by the public, but is not yet fully listed or catalogued. As a finalised archival reference number is not yet available, the title or description of the document used is all that is provided here. The Archives have a full listing of the references used in this book with an indication of their current location so that researchers can follow up on any of the items referred to.

The data for all tables and graphs in the book (unless otherwise indicated) is derived from a range of sources in the Beamish & Crawford Collection at the Cork City and County Archives.

Frequently used abbreviations:

BC, CCCA: Beamish & Crawford Collection, Cork City and County Archives
BL/BC/MB: Murphy's Brewery Collection, Boole Library Archives Service, University College Cork
BL/EP/BC: Beamish and Crawford Estate Collection, Boole Library Archives Service, University College Cork
BLAS, UCC: Boole Library Archives Service, University College Cork

CE: The Cork Examiner *II: Irish Independent*
IP: The Irish Press *IT: The Irish Times*
SS: Southern Star

CHAPTER 1

1 K. Meyer (ed. and trans.), *Aislinge Meic Conglinne: The Vision of Meic Conglinne: A Middle-Irish Wonder Tale* (London, 1892).

2 Appendix E, *The City of Cork. Survey & Valuation (circa A.D. 1663–64)* in *The Civil Survey A.D. 1654–1656: County of Waterford, Vol. VI*, p. 402, lists the King's Arms, the Three Tunns, Droops Mill, the Friers House, Brock's House, the King's Old Castle, the Clothworkers Arms, the Golden Anchor, the Three Marieners, the Redd Leyon, the King's Head, the Star, Waters Mill, Shandon Castle, Redd Abbey, the Angell, the George, the Royal Oak, the Crown, the White Horse, Ye 3 Flower de Luces, the Swan and the Beare.

3 W.H. Welply, 'The Art and Mystery of Brewing (in Cork)', *Journal of the Cork Historical & Archeological Society* (*JCHAS*), Vol. 62 (1957), p. 105.

4 Transfer, 25 August 1682; Deed, 1682; 'Copy of Conveyance of Premises in the County and City of Corke: John Gamble to Onesiph. Gamble', dated 30 July 1719, Beamish & Crawford Collection (BC), Cork City and County Archives (CCCA); see also A.E. O'Brien, 'Early Brewing Activity in Cork City: Some Leasehold Evidence', *JCHAS*, Vol. 105 (2000), pp. 199–206.

5 Welply, 'Art and Mystery', pp. 107–8.

6 R. Caulfield (ed.), *The Council Book of the Corporation of the City of Cork, from 1609 to 1643 and from 1690 to 1800* (Guildford, 1876), entries for 28 March and 22 December 1743.

7 O. MacDonagh, 'The Origins of Porter', *Economic History Review*, new series, Vol. 16, No. 3 (1964), pp. 530–5.

8 R.W. Unger, *Beer in the Middle Ages and Renaissance* (Philadelphia, 2004), p. 23.

9 Anon., 'History of the London Brewery from the Beginning of King William's Reign to the Present Time', *The Gentleman's Magazine and Historical Chronicle*, Vol. XXX (London, 1760), pp. 527–8.

10 Madame Van Muyden (ed. and trans.), *A Foreign View of England in the Reigns of George I & George II: The Letters of Monsieur César de Saussure to His Family* (London, 1902), p. 158.

11 Unger, *Beer in the Middle Ages*, p. 185.

12 J. Feltham, *The Picture of London for 1802* (London, 1802), p. 249.

13 *Gentleman's Magazine and Historical Chronicle*, Vol. LXXIX (London, 1819), p. 394.

14 Anon., *The London and Country Brewer*, 2nd edition (London, 1736), pp. 36–42; Anon., 'History of the London Brewery from the Beginning of King William's Reign to the Present Time', *The Gentleman's Magazine and Historical Chronicle*, Vol. XXX (London, 1760), pp. 527–8; G. Watkins, *The Complete English Brewer or The Whole Art and Mystery of Brewing in All its Various Branches* (London, 1760). Pages 122–31 of the 1773 edition of this work are referred to here.

15 Mathias, *Brewing Industry*, pp. 22–3.

16 *Ibid.*, p. 12.

17 *Ibid.*, p. 10.

18 Works consulted for this section include: A. Bielenberg, *Cork's Industrial Revolution 1780–1800: Development or Decline?* (Cork, 1991); J. Carr, *The Stranger in Ireland or, A Tour of the Southern and Western Parts of that Country, in the Year 1805* (New York, 1805); D. Dickson, *Old World Colony: Cork and South Munster 1630–1830* (Cork, 2005); P. Lynch and J. Vaizey, *Guinness's Brewery in the Irish Economy 1759–1876* (Cambridge, 1960); P. Mathias, *The Brewing Industry in England 1700–1830* (Cambridge, 1959); T. Newenham, *A View of the Natural, Political and Commercial Circumstances of Ireland* (London, 1809); G. O'Brien, *The Economic History of Ireland in the Eighteenth Century* (Philadelphia, 1918); C. Rynne, *The Industrial Archaeology of Cork City and Its Environs* (Dublin, 1999); E. Wakefield, *An Account of Ireland, Statistical and Political*, Vol. 1 (London, 1812).

19 Dickson, *Old World Colony*, p. 386.

20 The original meaning of *síbín* or *séibín* was a mug or measure, and later ale or bad ale, whence the association with drinking houses, usually illicit. See entries for *síbín* and *séibín* in P.S. Dinneen, *Foclóir Gaedhilge agus Béarla, an Irish–English Dictionary* (Dublin, 1927).

21 Dickson, *Old World Colony*, p. 387; O'Brien, *Economic History*, p. 281.

22 In 1752 Irish brewers paid duty on just under 604,000 barrels of ale or beer, in 1761 on 588,000, in 1772 on 477,000, in 1789 on 455,000 and in 1792 on 456,000 (Lynch and Vaizey, *Guinness's Brewery*, p. 52, and O'Brien, *Economic History of Ireland*, pp. 211 and 279).

23 Dickson, *Old World Colony*, p. 386.

24 Wakefield, *An Account of Ireland, Statistical and Political*, Vol. 1, p. 746.

25 Lynch and Vaizey, *Guinness's Brewery*, pp. 50–2; Mathias, *Brewing Industry*, pp. 152–5; O'Brien, *Economic History*, pp. 210–12 and 279–82.

26 Lynch and Vaizey, *Guinness's Brewery*, p. 50.

27 Dickson, *Old World Colony*, p. 338.

28 Lynch and Vaizey, *Guinness's Brewery*, p. 66.

29 Mathias, *Brewing Industry*, p. 160.

30 *Hibernian Chronicle*, 19 July and 20 September 1756.

31 O'Brien, 'Early Brewing Activity', p. 202.

32 *Hibernian Chronicle*, 3 September 1772 and 19 December 1782.

33 *Ibid.*, 26 July 1787 and 9 April 1792.

34 *Ibid.*, 1, 6, 17 and 31 January, 7 and 21 March, 2 May and 12 September 1791.

35 R. Lucas, 'The Cork Directory for the Year 1787', *JCHAS*, Vol. 72 (1967), pp. 135–58; 'List of Freemen of Cork City 1710–1841', Cork City and County Archives (2007).

36 The details of partnerships and changes of ownership come from the following documents relating to Lane's Southgate Brewery in the Beamish & Crawford Collection, Cork City and County Archives: Lease: John Harding

to Thomas Fuller and Charles McCarthy, 22 October 1782; Lease, Thomas Fuller to Walter Fitzsimmons, Jerh. O Reilly & Geo. Fuller, 17 October 1796; 'Tracing from a Map on Deed dated 2 July 1798. Charles McCarthy and Walter Fitzsimmons Jeremiah O Reilly and George Fuller – traced 3/6/1919'; Memorial, 31 December 1799; 'Agreement respecting Brewery Premises between D. Lane Esq. & Messrs. O Reilly & Hadigan, dated 5 June 1809'; Deed, Jeremiah O'Reilly & Thomas Hadigan and Daniel Lane, 27 June 1809; 'Statement of Title of Lane & Co. Ltd. to the Southgate Brewery etc.', undated; Assignment: Michael Gould to Daniel Lane & Co., 13 January 1831; 'A Map of a small Brewhouse yards & a small House the property of Charles McCarthy of Ballin Lough Esq.', undated; 'Statement of the Title of Daniel Lane & Co. to the Brewery Concerns and Premises situate in the South Main Street in the City of Cork', undated; Memorial, 12 April 1842; an untitled and undated handwritten document noting title to fifteen numbered plots making up the Southgate Brewery site.

CHAPTER 2

1 Genealogical information on the Beamish and Crawford families comes from numerous documents, legal and otherwise, in the Beamish & Crawford Collection (BC) held at the Cork City and County Archives (CCCA), including leases, partnership agreements, wills, assignments of property, releases, deeds, settlements on marriage, etc., and from the following published works: C.T.M. Beamish, *Beamish: A Genealogical Study of a Family in Co. Cork and Elsewhere* (London & Bradford, 1950); G. Bennett, *The History of Bandon and the Principal Towns in the West Riding of County Cork* (Cork, 1869); Sir B. Burke, *A Genealogical and Heraldic History of the Landed Gentry of Ireland* (London, 1912); J.T.C., review of C.T.M. Beamish, *Beamish: A Genealogical Study of a Family in Co. Cork and Elsewhere* (London & Bradford, 1950) in the *Journal of the Cork Historical & Archaeological Society* (*JCHAS*), Vol. 56, 1951, pp. 129–31; P. Murray, 'A Narrative History of the Building and of the Crawford Family' in P. Murray (compiler), *Illustrated Summary Catalogue of the Crawford Municipal Art Gallery* (Cork, 1991), pp. 1–11; T.U. Sadleir, *Georgian Mansions in Ireland, with Some Account of the Evolution of Georgian Architecture and Decoration* (Dublin, 1915), pp. 33–5.

2 See D. Dickson, *Old World Colony: Cork and South Munster 1630–1830* (Cork, 2005), pp. 159–62 and 366–77.

3 Letters, 1779, BC, CCCA.

4 William Crawford to James Alexander, 21 March 1779 – draft/copy, BC, CCCA. 'Mr Bonwell' is probably James Bonwell, who was made a Freeman of Cork in February 1788 ('List of Freemen of Cork City 1710–1841', CCCA (2007), p. 19). As well as merchanting, he also ran a bank on Patrick's Street with Sir Thomas Roberts and John Leslie. He died in 1810.

5 Alexander to Crawford, 8 April 1779; Crawford to Alexander, 18 September 1779; William Crawford to John Crawford (brother), 7 October 1779, BC, CCCA.

6 Accounts of Church & Crawford for years ending 1 May 1780, June 1781, June 1782 and June 1784, BC, CCCA.

7 Alexander to Crawford, 7 August 1784, BC, CCCA.

8 Beamish & Crawford Charges Book 11 July 1785–17 July 1830, BC, CCCA. The starting date of 11 July 1785 indicates that the new partnership was in place from at least that date.

9 Material relating to merchanting in the Beamish & Crawford Collection at the CCCA: Copy Book: 26 May 1787–1 May 1788; Beamish & Crawford Charges Book, 11 July 1785–17 July 1830; The Balance Sheet of Messrs. Beamish & Crawford's Books from 30 April 1797–30 April 1798; Release – Executors & Residuary

Legatees of William Beamish Esq. (Deceased) to William Crawford Esq., 10 December 1831; Assignment of Premises in Merchants Quay and Merchants Street in the City of Cork [Draft. No date, but probably 1900–1910]; Indenture 1866 relating to Merchants Quay premises; letter and accompanying document relating to Merchants Quay premises [No date but probably 1905 or 1906]; Bills of Lading 1785–1816.

10 'The Cork Directory for the Year 1787' by R. Lucas, *Journal of the Cork Historical and Archaeological Society*, Vol. 72, 1967, pp. 135–58.

11 On Hare, see J. O'Shea, *Letterbook of Richard Hare, Cork Merchant 1771–1772* (Dublin, 2013); on Shea, see J. O'Shea, 'Henry Shea: Cork's First Mercantile Tycoon', *JCHAS*, Vol. 116, 2011, pp. 120–30.

12 'Assignment of Premises in Merchants Quay and Merchants Street in the City of Cork' [Draft. No date, but probably 1900–1910], BC, CCCA.

13 The most detailed information on the workings of the firm of Beamish, Crawford & Keating comes from the 'Copy Book: 26 May 1787–1 May 1788' in the Beamish & Crawford Collection held at the CCCA. This book runs to a little over 300 pages and contains handwritten copies of hundreds of letters written mostly by James Keating Junior from London to the firm's headquarters in Cork.

14 Each tierce of beef was to be bound by at least two iron hoops and contain 315 lb weight of meat. The tierces of pork were to be similarly bound and have 312 lb weight of meat. The butter was to be packed 'in full bound Firkins' containing 112 lb (1 cwt), and the oatmeal was to be packed in 'casks'.

15 Copy of 'Articles of Agreement 14 September 1787 between Thomas Everett, London, Merchant, 1st part, and James Keating Junior of Great St Helens, merchant, 2nd part', BC, CCCA.

16 Letters, 10 and 19 November and 17 Dececember 1787, in 'Copy Book: 26 May 1787–1 May 1788', BC, CCCA.

17 The Beamish & Crawford Collection at the CCCA holds 187 bills of lading from 1785–86, 1813–14 and one from 1816.

18 T.M. Truxes, *Irish American Trade 1660–1783* (Cambridge, 1988), p. 152.

19 Being a 'charges book', this book does not detail contracts, prices of exported or imported goods or commissions, but rather the day-to-day costs associated with running the business.

20 Charles Manners, the 4th Duke of Rutland, 1754–1787.

21 The Balance Sheet of Messrs. Beamish & Crawford's Books from 30 April 1797 to the 30 April 1798, BC, CCCA. See also C.T.M. Beamish, *Beamish: A Genealogical Study*, p. 22.

CHAPTER 3

1 'List of Freemen of Cork City 1710–1841' (CCCA, 2007).

2 Copy Book: 26 May 1787 – 1 May 1788, BC, CCCA. The firm is also listed in R. Lucas, 'The Cork Directory for the Year 1787', *JCHAS*, Vol. 72 (1967), pp. 135–58.

3 *Hibernian Chronicle* (*HC*), 15 September 1791.

4 'Deed between Richard Barrett and Wm. Beamish and Wm. Crawford Esquires', 31 January 1800, BC, CCCA.

5 *HC*, 3 September 1772.

6 *Ibid.*, 5 May 1771.

7 In the accounts of the Cork Porter Brewery, the brewery year begins on the first Monday of August each year. This remained the case until 1963.

8 'Mr. Edw. Allen's Agreement to accept a Surrender from Messrs. Beamish, Crawford, O Brien and Barrett', 13 January 1792, BC, CCCA.

9 These and all other details of the partnership arrangements are set out in 'Articles of Agreement of partnership between Messrs. Beamish, Crawford, O Brien & Barrett', 13 January 1792, BC, CCCA.

10 'A Map of the Cork Porter Brewery now in the Tenancy of Willm. Beamish Esqr., Willm. Crawford Esqr., Digby O'Brien Esqr. & Richd. Barrett Esqr. Surveyed in January 1792 – Barth. [?] Horgan', BC, CCCA.
11 Cash Book, September 1791–December 1798, BC, U18, Bay 1016, and Cash Book 1792–1797, BC, CCCA.
12 Private Ledger A, 1792–1801, BC, CCCA.
13 'Beamish & Crawford: Book containing their title to the premises belonging to the Cork Porter Brewery Establishment 1837', pp. 24–5, BC, CCCA. For further discussion on the lanes in this part of the city, see G. Johnson, *The Laneways of Medieval Cork* (Cork, 2002).
14 Untitled map, c.1887, showing the boundaries of the different lots of brewery property, BC, CCCA.
15 Details of maltings, malthouses used, malt duties paid, etc., as well as many other details of the workings of the firm in its first years, can be gleaned from Cash Book September 1791–December 1798, Cash Book 1792–1797 and Private Ledger A, 1792–1801, BC, CCCA.
16 'Book containing their title', 1837, pp. 1–6.
17 The Princes Street and Lapp's Quay malthouses were rented from Roberts & Co. and O'Brien & Barrett were paid £68.5.0 per year for the Hanover Street premises. Alexander Deane was paid a total of £755 during 1797 for work on the Fenn's Quay malthouse and a further £151.12.11 in 1798 for materials (Cash Book, September 1791–December 1798, and Cash Book, 1792–1797, BC, CCCA).
18 Ledger 1810–1818, BC, CCCA.
19 *HC*, 19 January 1792.
20 'Memorandum for Sleeping Partners', February 18th, 1879, BC, CCCA.
21 Cash Book, September 1791–December 1798, and Ledger 1798–1801, BC, CCCA.
22 Details of employees and payments to them are taken from Cash Book 1792–1797, Private Ledger A 1792–1801, Ledger B 1801–1822, Ledger 1810–1818, Private Ledger C 1822–1836, Private Ledger D 1836–1859, Ledger E 1860–1878, BC, CCCA.
23 Journal 1798–1801, BC, CCCA
24 *HC*, 19 July 1792.
25 *Ibid.*, 29 October 1792.
26 Ledger, 1798–1801.
27 *HC*, 17 September 1794.
28 'Articles of Agreement', 1792; 'Mr. Edw. Allen's Agreement', 1792; 'Deed giving proven surrender of sevl. premises at the end of Seven years ended upon the 29th day of Sept. 1798', BC, CCCA.
29 'Deed between Richard Barrett and Wm. Beamish and Wm. Crawford Esquires', dated 31 January 1800, BC, CCCA.

CHAPTER 4

1 R. Wells, 'The Irish Famine of 1799–1801: Market Culture, Moral Economies and Social Protest' in A. Randall and A. Charlesworth (eds.), *Markets, Market Culture and Popular Protest in Eighteenth-Century Britain and Ireland* (Liverpool, 1996), pp. 163–94.
2 C. Ó Gráda, *Ireland: A New Economic History 1780–1939* (Oxford, 1994), pp. 158–62.
3 *Ibid.*, p. 74.
4 1801 Deed of Co-partnership between William Beamish and William Crawford as Porter Brewers, dated 5 November 1801, BC, CCCA.
5 'Account of Capital for Years 1800–1862 incl.', BC, CCCA.
6 'Acting Partners Statement relative to Capital Stocks from 1792 to present date, October 1863', BC, CCCA.
7 'Beamish & Crawford: Book Containing their title to the premises belonging to the Cork Porter Brewery Establishment 1837', BC, CCCA. Further detail is accessible from annotations on an untitled plan, probably drawn in 1887 (BC, CCCA).
8 'A Map of The Cork Porter Brewery Surveyed for Willm. Beamish & Wm. Crawford Esqrs. By P. Aher Jany. 1802' (BC, CCCA). CCCA has another copy of this plan with added

annotations regarding leases, etc.

9 'Ground Plan of Messrs. Beamish & Crawford's Brewery', dated 19/12/99 (untitled folder of drawings, BC, CCCA), names the laneways crossing the brewery site as, starting from the south: Webber's (also Morgan's), Gosse's, Lavitt's (also Woodward's), Cramer's, Allen's, Franklin's, Lamley's, Bridge's (also Roache's) and Simmon's (also Cooke's). See also the outline tracing of the brewery area with all laneways named, dated 24 March 1870, in the same untitled folder.

10 Journal 1804–1805, BC, CCCA.

11 See C. Rynne, *The Industrial Archaeology of Cork City and Its Evvirons* (Dublin, 1999), p. 49, and Chapter 3, footnotes 28, 29 and 30; A. Bielenberg, *Cork's Industrial Revolution 1780–1880: Development or Decline* (Cork, 1991), p. 57.

12 Private Ledger C 1822–1836, BC, CCCA.

13 Information on the River Lee Porter Brewery is taken from the following documents in the Beamish & Crawford Collection: deed, dated 1 February 1813; 'Beamish & Crawford Title to Lee Mills & Middle Island & River Lee Porter Brewery'; undated and untitled document regarding Beamish & Crawford's acquisition of River Lee Porter Brewery; 'Statement of the title of the River Lee Porter Brewery concerns, and the other concerns in and near the city of Cork', undated; 'Statement of Title of B&C to land of Lee Mills & River Lee Porter Brewery'.

14 Bielenberg, *Cork's Industrial Revolution*, pp. 51–2; D. Dickson, *Old World Colony: Cork and South Munster 1630–1830* (Cork, 2005), p. 388.

15 Undated and untitled document regarding Beamish & Crawford's acquisition of River Lee Porter Brewery, BC, CCCA.

16 Lease of 1 May 1792, BC, CCCA.

17 Ledger B 1801–1822; Journal 1804–1805; Journal F October 1805–February 1808; Journal September 1810–1813; Ledger 1810–1818; Private Ledger C 1822–1836, BC, CCCA.

18 'Continuation of the Names of Customers to whom Advances for Licence has been given for the year commencing 29th September 1799 and for which cash was paid by the brewery', BC, CCCA.

19 Journal 1804–1805.

20 Journal F October 1805–February 1808.

21 E. Wakefield, *An Account of Ireland, Statistical and Political*, Vol. 1 (London, 1812), p. 744, fn.

22 Untitled document, dated 30 September 1814, BC, CCCA.

23 P. Lynch and J. Vaizey, *Guinness's Brewery in the Irish Economy 1759–1876* (Cambridge, 1960), p. 101.

24 For example, entry for 23 March 1805 detailing damage to empty barrels returned by sea from Youghal, Bandon, Kinsale, Cove and Bantry, Journal 1804–1805, BC, CCCA; see also entries for 6 June and 6 July 1805, *ibid.*

25 The development of roads and road transport in the late eighteenth and early nineteenth centuries, with particular reference to County Cork, is discussed in Ó Gráda, *New Economic History*, pp. 132–4; Dickson, *Old World Colony*, pp. 427–33; Rynne, *Industrial Archaeology*, pp. 176–85.

26 Ledger 1798–1801, BC, CCCA.

27 *Ibid.* and Cash Book September 1791 – December 1798, BC, CCCA.

28 Journal 1804–1805.

29 J. Carr, *The Stranger in Ireland: A Tour of the Southern and Western Parts of that Country, in the Year 1805* (New York, 1807), p. 212.

30 Balance Sheet: Cork Porter Brewery 28 July 1798; Balance Sheet: Cork Porter Brewery 3 August 1799, BC, CCCA.

31 Lynch and Vaizey, *Guinness's Brewery*, pp. 130–2; 'Beamish & Crawford Bristol Agency: Bond', dated 2 March 1842, BC, CCCA.

32 J. Coppinger, *The American Practical Brewer and Tanner* (New York, 1815), p. 230.

33 Journal 1804–1805.

34 Journal F October 1805 – February 1808.

35 Circular 1808, BC, CCCA.

36 Ibid.

37 Private Ledger C 1822–1836, BC, CCCA.

38 Ledger B 1801–1822; Private Ledger C 1822–1836, BC, CCCA.

39 *The Sixth Report of the Commissioners appointed to enquire into the Fees, gratuities, Perquisites, and Emoluments ... and Accounting for Public Money in Ireland* (House of Commons, 1808); *Eighth Report of the Commissioners of Inquiry into the Collection and Management of the Revenue arising in Ireland, Scotland etc.* (House of Commons, 1824).

40 Beamish & Crawford: book containing their title to the premises belonging to the Cork Porter Brewery Establishment 1837; Beamish & Crawford Title to Lee Mills & Middle Island & Lee Porter Brewery, BC, CCCA.

41 John S. Haines's valuation of Lee Mills and Stores, 17 December 1862, BC, CCCA.

42 Acting Partners' Statement relative to Capital Stocks from 1792 to present date, October 1863, BC, CCCA.

43 'Particulars of machinery in Lee Mills on the 3rd day of September 1842

No.1 East Mill –
Six pair of French Stones
Two pair of English Shellers
4 Barrel Screens
1 Seperator
5 Sets of Elevators
6 Sets of Fans

No. 2 –
3 Pair French Stones
2 Flour Machines
1 Spare Machine
1 Set Elevators
1 Screw Conductor

No. 3 –
6 Pair French stones
1 Pair English Shellers
2 Flour Machines
3 Separators
3 Barrel Screens
6 Sets Elevators
5 Sets of Fans
2 Screw Conductors

with all the nesessary appendages for the Mills in complete working order'.
(Rental agreement, dated 2 September 1842, BC, CCCA.)

44 Ledger B 1801–1822; Private Ledger C 1822–1836.

45 Figures taken from Private Ledger A 1792–1801, Ledger B 1801–1822, Private Ledger C 1822–1836.

CHAPTER 5

1 'Memorandum for Sleeping Partners, February 18th, 1879', BC, CCCA (hereafter, 1879 Memorandum).

2 'Staff of CPB. Date of commencement & various salaries of each individual Dec. 1863', a loose page within 'Staff Cork Porter Brewery: Date of Engagement & Various Salaries of each Individual June 1868', BC, CCCA.

3 This section on the temperance campaign of the 1839–45 period is based on readings of C. Kerrigan, *Father Mathew and the Irish Temperance Movement 1838–1848* (Cork, 1992); E. Malcolm, *Ireland Sober, Ireland Free: Drink and Temperance in Nineteenth-century Ireland* (Dublin, 1986); A. O'Callaghan, *The Statue: Cork's Monument to Father Mathew, The Apostle of Temperance* (Cork, 2014).

4 P. Lynch and J. Vaizey, *Guinness's Brewery in the Irish Economy 1759–1876*, (Cambridge, 1960), p. 80.

5 J.J. Lee, 'Money and Beer in Ireland, 1790–1875', *Economic History Review*, new series, Vol. 19, No. 1 (1966), pp. 183–94, p. 185.

6 1879 Memorandum.

7 'Memorandum for Sleeping Partners', undated, but covering the brewery years 1845–6 and 1846–7, BC, CCCA.

8 *Ibid.*

9 Lee, 'Money and Beer, pp. 183–94.

10 Lynch and Vaizey, *Guinness's* Brewery, p. 211, and Porter Account entries in 'Ledger E 1860–1878', BC, CCCA.
11 Based on Table 2, Lynch and Vaizey, *Guinness's Brewery*, p. 185, with the addition of Beamish & Crawford figures.
12 *Tenth Report of the Commissioners of Inquiry into the Excise Establishment, and into the Management and Collection of the Excise Revenue throughout the United Kingdom* (London, 1834), p. 6.
13 *Fifteenth Report of the Commissioners of Inquiry into the Excise Establishment, and into the Management and Collection of the Excise Revenue throughout the United Kingdom* (London, 1835), p. 194.
14 *Ibid.*, p. 62.
15 1879 Memorandum.
16 *Ibid.*
17 *Ibid.*
18 From a memo of North Ludlow Beamish, 1857, quoted in *Ibid.*
19 *Ibid.*
20 D. Ó Drisceoil and D. Ó Drisceoil, *The Murphy's Story: The History of Lady's Well Brewery, Cork* (Cork, 1997 and 2006), p. 45.
21 1879 Memorandum.
22 *Ibid.*
23 *Ibid.*
24 *Ibid.*
25 Lynch and Vaizey, *Guinness's Brewery*, p. 210.
26 *Ibid.*, pp. 209–10.
27 1879 Memorandum.
28 *Ibid.*
29 *Ibid.*
30 '21 February 1855: Copy Memorandum of Acting Partner of Beamish family to Sleeping Partners of same Family', BC, CCCA.
31 'John S. Haines valuation of Lee Mills and Stores, 17 Dec. 1862', BC, CCCA.
32 'A Map of The Cork Porter Brewery Surveyed for Willm. Beamish & Wm. Crawford Esqrs. By P. Aher Jany. 1802', BC, CCCA. Map Folder, BC, CCCA, has another copy of this plan, with added annotations regarding leases, etc. A number of plans in BC, CCCA, though undated, were, on the evidence of their content, drawn in the 1820s. The following two plans date to 1839: 'Ground Plan of Messrs. Beamish & Crawford's Brewery 1839' (CCCA) and 'Plan of Messrs. Beamish & Crawford's Brewery, Upper Storey 1839'. Two plans dated December 1863 were drawn by engineer O.C. Edwards, who was employed by the acting partners from 1863 to plan and oversee renovation works at the brewery: 'Ground-Plan of Messrs. Beamish & Crawford's Brewery'.
33 1879 Memorandum.
34 'Sketch of a Coal Wagon', BC, CCCA.
35 'Heads of proposed partnership agreement', undated, but drawn up soon after the death of William Beamish in April 1828, BC, CCCA.
36 Details of the 1831 agreement are set out in '1836 Copartnership Agreement', BC, CCCA.
37 '1836 Copartnership Agreement', essentially a summary, and '1836 Copartnership Agreement', the full text of the agreement, BC, CCCA.
38 'Acting Partners' Statement Relative to the Restoration in 1853 of Certain Sums Written off in 1841 & 1842', n.d. (1862–3), BC, CCCA.
39 M. B. Cosgrave, 'A History of Beamish & Crawford' (unpublished MA thesis, UCC, 1989), pp. 47–51.
40 'Deed Extending the Term of the Copartnership of Beamish & Crawford, 6 August 1849', BC, CCCA.
41 'Acting Partners' Statement', 1862–3; 'Memorandum of Acting Partner of Beamish family to Sleeping Partners of same Family', 21 February 1855, BC, CCCA.
42 Statement by R.P. Beamish, 15 December 1869, BL/EP/BC, 8/24, Boole Library Archives Service, UCC (BLAS, UCC).
43 'CB's [Charles Beamish] Notice of 27 Aug. 1853' to North Ludlow Beamish, BC, CCAI.
44 Appendix to statement by R.P. Beamish, 15 December 1869, BL/EP/BC, 8/24, BLAS, UCC.
45 Assorted correspondence, 1853–4 and 1866,

R.P. Beamish Letter Books, BL/EP/BC, 7/24, BLAS, UCC; 'Acting Partners' Statement', 1862–3.

46 Assorted correspondence, 1856, R.P. Beamish Letter Books, BL/EP/BC, 7/24, BLAS, UCC.

47 *Ibid.*, 1857–60.

48 The detail on this agency comes from a collection of letters, memos, notes, cuttings, etc. in BC, CCCA.

49 *Commercial Daily List*, 2 October 1862.

50 'Where do you get your Cooper?' in BC, CCCA.

CHAPTER 6

1 'Memorandum for Sleeping partners, February 18th, 1879', BC, CCCA (hereafter, 1879 Memorandum).

2 'Deed of Co-partnership 1863'; 'Extract from Partnership Deed of 3 August 1863', BC, CCCA.

3 '1879 Co-partnership Agreement, dated 4 August 1879'; 'Deed of Co-partnership between Messrs. Beamish & Crawford 8 July 1879', BC, CCCA; *The Freeman's Journal*, 3 August 1868 and 26 April 1870.

4 A. Barnard, *Noted Breweries of Great Britain and Ireland*, Vol. 2 (London, 1889), p. 357.

5 *Ibid.*, p. 358

6 *Ibid.*, pp. 359–60.

7 *Ibid.*, p. 361.

8 Proof copy of 'The Southern Porter Trade: Messrs. Beamish & Crawford, Cork', dated 14 March 1889, for publication in *The Wine Merchant & Grocers' Review*, BC, CCCA.

9 1879 Memorandum.

10 *Ibid.*

11 *Ibid.*

12 *Ibid.*

13 Two letters from 1890 show that Richard McNamara's career ended somewhat sadly. On 6 October of that year he wrote to Richard Pigott Beamish to confirm his intention to resign as he was not willing to suffer 'a repetition of the abuse and indignity which have been heaped upon me from time to time by one of the firm [probably acting partner William H. Sharman Crawford]'. He claimed he had been called 'a fool-idiot and a deceiver' and that 'on many occasions I have left your room more fitted for bedlam than for business and now I am compelled to decide upon either holding my situation or my sanity. It will not be surprising if I choose in favour of the latter.' In a letter of 20 October he wrote: 'I was told amongst other things that I am and have been an obstruction to all changes and improvements and the sooner I give place to others less dogged and antiquated the better for the establishment.' He concluded: 'This to me is a sad severance to a long connection and one which may entail serious consequences on my family whose sole dependence (under Providence) is upon the labor [*sic*] of my head and hands...' (BC, CCCA). McNamara had worked at the brewery since 1858.

14 *Ibid.*

15 'Workings of Brewing Dept.', *c.* 1865. Detail as to wages and salaries comes from 'Staff Cork Porter Brewery: Date of Engagement & Various Salaries of each Individual June 1868' and 'Staff Details 1863', BC, CCCA.

16 'Abstract of Barley Report' and 'Barley', both *c.* 1865, BC, CCCA.

17 Agreement with Telephone Company of Ireland Ltd., 6 November 1888, BC, CCCA.

18 A.J. Litton, 'The Growth and Development of the Irish Telephone System', *Journal of the Statistical and Social Inquiry Society of Ireland*, Session 115 (1961–2), pp. 79–115.

19 'Production Details etc. Porter & Ale 1864–1890', BC, CCCA.

20 Untitled notebook held in BC, CCCA.

21 No breakdown of production for brewery year 1892–3 appears in the surviving records. Head brewer William Gray retired in 1892, later replaced by Frank Thurston. It is possible that the change in management of the brewing department had an impact on recordkeeping.

22 'B&C Sales 1883 & 1884', BC, CCCA

23 Document in BC, CCCA.
24 Document headed 'Sales Year (53 Weeks) ending 5 August 1899' inserted in notebook of detail on rackings, sample tastings, sales, etc., day-to-day and cumulative, for the year ending 5 August 1899, BC, CCCA.
25 Five-page list of number of casks with customers, dating to 1862–3, BC, CCCA.
26 'Prices Charged to Customers & Agents, and Net Profits in each District for Year end 3 August 1895' and 'Prices Charged to Customers & Agents, and Net Profits in each District for Year end 30 July 1898'; diaries for the years 1892 and 1895; diaries for the years 1896, 1897 and 1898; 'Weekly Statement of Sales 1900–1904', BC, CCCA.
27 Untitled, undated notebook in BC, CCCA. The evidence of the notes suggests a date 1898–1900.
28 1879 Memorandum.
29 *Ibid.*
30 Journal August 1798–January 1801, BC, CCCA.
31 Journal 1804–5, BC, CCCA.
32 'Acting Partners' Statement relative to Capital Stocks from 1792 to present date, October 1863', BC, CCCA.
33 Barrel Account in Ledger E 1860–1878, BC, CCCA.
34 1879 Memorandum.
35 This feature on William Gray is based on a file of letters and memos dating from 1863 to 1880 and 'Staff Cork Porter Brewery: Date of Engagement & Various Salaries of each Individual June 1868', BC, CCCA. The biographical information and the photograph come from information supplied by Nicholas Pertwee, a great-grandson of William Gray, to Ed Hinchy, formerly of Beamish & Crawford, in a letter of 27 August 2000. We are grateful to Ed Hinchy for giving access to this material.
36 1879 Memorandum.
37 *Ibid.*
38 The detail of Thurston's dispute with the Cork Coopers' Society comes from a collection of letters and memos labelled 'Cork Coopers' Society re gauge of Porter Casks. November 1895–April 1897', BC, CCCA.
39 The figures in this table were computed from entries in Private Ledger 1858–1903, General Quarterly Abstracts 1869–1883 and Approximate Profits 1890–1900, BC, CCCA.

CHAPTER 7

1 Notes on plan titled 'A Map of a small Brew house and yards & a small House the property of Charles McCarthy of Ballin Lough Esq.', BC, CCCA.
2 Tracing, dated 14 June 1921, of a map attached to lease, dated 2 July 1798, Charles McCarthy to Walter Fitzsimmons, Jeremiah O'Leary [O'Reilly] and George Fuller, Brewers, BC, CCCA.
3 Lease, dated 17 October 1796, Thomas Fuller to Walter Fitzsimmons, Jerh. O'Reilly and George Fuller, in 'Statement of Title of Daniel Lane & Co. to the Brewery Concerns and Premises situate in South Main Street in the City of Cork', BC, CCCA.
4 Lease, dated 14 November 1800, described in Memorial, dated 12 April 1842, BC, CCCA.
5 Lease, dated 17 October 1796, Thomas Fuller to Walter Fitzsimmons, Jerh. O'Reilly and George Fuller, in 'Statement of Title of Daniel Lane & Co. to the Brewery Concerns and Premises situate in South Main Street in the City of Cork', BC, CCCA.
6 Lease, dated 2 July 1798, Charles McCarthy to Walter Fitzsimmons, Jerh. O'Reilly and George Fuller in 'Statement of Title of Daniel Lane & Co. to the Brewery Concerns and Premises situate in South Main Street in the City of Cork', BC, CCCA.
7 Note, dated 16 February 1801, BC, CCCA.
8 J. Carr, *The Stranger in Ireland or, A Tour of the Southern and Western Parts of That Country, in the Year 1805* (New York, 1807), p. 211.
9 'Agreement respecting Brewery Premises

between D. Lane Esq. & Messrs. O'Reilly & Hadigan, dated 5 June 1809; Deed, dated 27 June 1809, Jeremiah O'Reilly & Thomas Hadigan and Daniel Lane', BC, CCCA.

10 'Statement of Title of Daniel Lane & Co. to the Brewery Concerns and Premises situate in South Main Street in the City of Cork'; 'Statement of Title of Lane & Co. Ltd. to the Southgate Brewery etc.', BC, CCCA.

11 Indenture, dated 11 August 1821, BC, CCCA.

12 Letter, dated 25 August 1856, William Lane to William Andrew Drinan, BC, CCCA.

13 A. Barnard, *The Noted Breweries of Great Britain and Ireland,* Vol. IV (London, 1891), pp. 321–5.

14 *The Freeman's Journal,* 5 July 1838.

15 *The Cork Examiner* (*CE*), 26 May 1847.

16 Articles of Agreement, dated 22 October 1867, William Lane, William Lane Jr. and William Shaw, BC, CCCA.

17 Assignment, dated 31 December 1870, BC, CCCA.

18 'Memorandum & Articles of Association of Lane & Co. Ltd., Cork, 1877', BC, CCCA.

19 C. Ó Gráda, 'The Last Major Irish Bank Failure: Lessons for Today?', UCD Centre for Economic Research Working Paper Series (Dublin, 2010); Statement of Title of Lane & Co. to the South Gate Brewery etc.; entries for 17 August 1886 and 16 August 1889 in Lane & Co. Ltd.: Directors' Minute Book 22 October 1877 to 25 September 1899, BC, CCCA.

20 'Lane & Co.: Invoice Book November 1888–April 1901', BC, CCCA.

21 Barnard, *Noted Breweries*, p. 325.

22 Entry for 12 January 1897 in 'Lane & Co. Ltd.: Directors' Minute Book 22 October 1877 to 25 September 1899', BC, CCCA.

23 Minutes of AGM held 9 January 1901, 'Lane & Co. Ltd.: Directors' Minute Book 2/10/1899–20/9/1902', BC, CCCA.

24 The figures in this table are taken from entries in 'Lane & Co. Ltd.: Directors' Minute Book 22 October 1877 to 25 September 1899', 'Lane & Co. Ltd.: Directors' Minute Book 2/10/1899–20/9/1902' and 'Lane & Co. Ltd. Annual report & Balance Sheet for AGM of Shareholders' 6 February 1888 and 16 August 1889, BC, CCCA.

25 Entry for 14 March 1901, 'Beamish & Crawford Ltd.: Board Meetings', BC, CCCA.

26 See the entry for 20 September 1902 in 'Lane & Co. Ltd.: Directors' Minute Book 2/10/1899–20/9/1902' for valuation of the assets of Lane & Co. Ltd; 'Indenture made 29 January 1902 between Lane & Co. Ltd., incorporated 1877, in liquidation, and Beamish & Crawford Ltd., incorporated 1901' for a detailed list of all properties etc. owned by Lane & Co. Ltd; 'Lane & Co. Tied Houses' for a list all Lane tied houses, with a description of each property, its tenure, etc.; box labelled 'Purchase of Lane & Co. Ltd.' for a schedule of all assets, properties, etc. of Lane & Co. Ltd, BC, CCCA.

27 See 'Estimated Profits accruing from the amalgamation of Lane & Co. Ltd. with B & C Ltd.' and 'Estimated Savings on Amalgamation', BC, CCCA, for calculations and projections.

28 'Weekly Statement of Sales 1900–1904' and 'Diary 1901', BC, CCCA.

29 Document re: rental of Nos. 40, 40a, 41 and 41a, BC, CCCA.

30 Letter, dated 21 February 1936, re: Lane site being offered for sale, BC, CCCA. Various documents and letters re: sale of the Lane site in 1957, BC, CCCA. See also Goad fire insurance plans of Cork City 1906, 1909, 1938, 1941, 1944, 1957 and 1961 for changes in layout of the former Southgate Brewery site (Cork City Library, Cork Room and online at www.corkpastandpresent.ie).

31 Except where otherwise stated, this section on Murphy's brewery is adapted from the authors' book *The Murphy's Story: The History of Lady's Well Brewery Cork* (Cork, 1997, 2006).

32 See Chapter 5, pp. 90–91.

33 J. Johns, *The Celebrated Brewery of Sir John Arnott & Co Cork* (1873), p. 5.

34 *CE*, 21 January 1862; P.J. Dempsey and S. Boylan, 'Sir John Arnott', *Dictionary of Irish*

Biography, available online at http://dib.cambridge.org (accessed on 5 January 2015).

35 *CE*, 29 March 1898.

36 Ibid., 24 September 1862; , 'Memorandum for Sleeping Partners', 18 February 1879, BC, CCCA.

37 Johns, *Celebrated Brewery*, pp. 5–11, and Barnard, 'Sir J. Arnott & Co., Limited, Cork' in *Noted Breweries*, pp. 327–9.

38 *CE*, 14 and 23 March 1874; William Ladd to Beamish & Crawford, Report on Bottled Stout and Ale, 3 March 1883, BC, CCCA.

39 Johns, *Celebrated Brewery*, pp. 2 and 10–11; Articles of Agreement, Sir John Arnott & Co. with Sir John Arnott & Co. of Cork Brewers, Limited, 1 April 1876, Murphy's Brewery Collection, BL/BC/MB/94/2, BLAS, UCC; Public Houses in Cork City folders, 1886–1901, BC, CCCA.

40 *CE*, 27 April 1876, 30 April 1877 and 11 May 1878.

41 Ibid., 10 July 1883.

42 Cosgrave, 'Beamish and Crawford', p. 104.

43 'Valuation' in documents relating to the takeover of Arnott's by Murphy's, 1901, Murphy's Brewery Collection, BL/BC/MB/94/14(1), BLAS, UCC.

44 Documents relating to the takeover of Arnott's by Murphy's, 1901, Murphy's Brewery Collection, BL/BC/MB/94/14, BLAS, UCC.

45 *CE*, 17 October 1911.

CHAPTER 8

1 E. Malcolm, *'Ireland Sober, Ireland Free': Drink and Temperance in Nineteenth-Century Ireland* (Dublin, 1986), pp. 204–5.

2 *Ibid.*, p. 321.

3 *Minutes of Evidence taken before Royal Commission on Liquor Licensing Laws*, Vol. VII (Ireland) (London, 1898). Testimonies referred to Father Patrick O'Leary, pp. 196–205; Father Maurice Ahern, pp. 245–57; Richard Pigott Beamish, pp. 307–15; Denis Donovan, pp. 315–23; and Joseph O'Brien, pp. 345–8.

4 The Fr O'Leary Total Abstinence Hall on Bandon Road in Cork was named in his honour.

5 W. Lawson, 'Licensing and Publichouse Reform in Ireland', *Statistical and Social Inquiry Society of Ireland*, Vol. XI (1902), p. 109.

6 This number includes six spirit grocers with a beer retail licence (*Minutes of Evidence taken before Royal Commission on Liquor Licensing Laws*, Vol. VII (Ireland) (London, 1898), Table I, p. 350). See also Royal Commission on Liquor Licensing Laws, *Statistics relating to the Number of Licensed Premises, etc., in Great Britain and Ireland*, Vol. V (London, 1897), pp. 231–77 for further statistical tables relating to Cork and the rest of Ireland.

7 'Reports on Traders' runs to over 500 pages and in addition to providing detail on individual pubs and their trade, it also includes information on local economies, the way of life of the people and so on.

8 'Allman, Dowden & Co., 'Brewers, Bandon: Balance Sheets, Profit & Loss 1887–1911', BC, CCCA.

9 A series of 14 booklets, titled variously 'Licensed Publicans and their Localities and the Brewers with whom they deal for Porter in the City of Cork', 'City Publicans dealing with B&C and other Brewers' and 'City Publicans dealing with other Brewers than B&C' lists all the tied pubs in the city, the name of the publican and the brewery to which the pub is tied for the years 1886 to 1901, BC, CCCA.

CHAPTER 9

1 Letter dated 31 March 1826 from Charles Beamish, Paris, to William Beamish, BC, CCCA.

2 Letter dated 5 April 1828 from Charles Beamish, Paris, to William Beamish, BC, CCCA.

3 Letter dated 12 April 1828 from Charles Beamish, Paris, to William Beamish, BC, CCCA.

4 *Minutes of Proceedings of the Institution of Civil Engineers,* 40 (1874–75, Pt. II), p. 246.

5 R. Beamish, *Memoir of the Life of Sir Marc Isambard Brunel* (London, 1862).

6 Letter dated 30 October 1828 from Charles Beamish, Paris, to Robert Delacour Beamish, BC, CCCA.

7 J.A. Murphy, *The College: A History of Queen's/University College Cork* (Cork, 1995), p. 41.

8 F. Lane, *In Search of Thomas Sheehan: Radical Politics in Cork, 1824–36* (Dublin, 2001), pp. 48–9.

9 *Ibid.*, p. 23.

10 Appendix to statement by R.P. Beamish, 15 December 1869, BL/EP/BC, 8/24, BLAS, UCC.

11 Letter, Richard Pigott Beamish to North Ludlow Beamish, 16 December 1853, BL/EP/BC, 7/24, BLAS, UCC.

12 Letter, Richard Pigott Beamish to Fitzsimons (solicitor), 8 January 1859, BL/EP/BC, 7/24, BLAS, UCC.

13 *The Cork Examiner* (*CE*), 21 April 1976; P. Poland, 'When Cork's Ale Chief Met Nazi Germany's Air Chief', *Ireland's Own*, June 2013, pp. 22–4.

14 *Irish Independent*, 7 March 1908.

15 'Oberon', 'Reminiscences of Cork Thirty Years Ago', *CE*, 17 June 1933.

16 *Southern Star*, 4 February 1911.

17 *CE*, 20 January 1912.

18 A. O'Callaghan, *The Lord Mayors of Cork 1900–2000* (Cork, 2000), pp. 31–3.

19 *CE*, 21 February 1914.

20 *Ibid.*, 28 April 1913.

21 *Weekly Irish Times*, 13 June 1914.

22 Letter, Richard Pigott Beamish to North Ludlow Axel Beamish, 16 April 1863, BL/ EP/ BC, 7/24, BLAS, UCC.

23 Letters, Richard Pigott Beamish to North Ludlow Axel Beamish, 21 April 1863 and n.d. May 1863, BL/ EP/ BC, 7/24, BLAS, UCC.

24 A number of published sources name Elizabeth Cooke as William Crawford's first wife, but a document in the Public Record Office of Northern Ireland in the hand of his son William states that his father's first wife was Mary Bordman, who died in 1797, after which he married Mary Uniacke, probably in 1798. The document lists 26 children of the two unions, most of whom died. In addition to the names and dates of birth of each of the children, the time of birth is also given. The authors are grateful to Ed Hinchy, formerly of Beamish & Crawford Ltd, for giving access to a copy of this document.

25 Will of William Crawford, dated 30 August 1819, with codicil of 21 June 1828, BC, CCCA.

26 Leather-bound diary of accounts with 'William Crawford Jun. 16 May 1809' on the flyleaf, BC, CCCA.

27 *Cork Constitution*, 14 April 1840.

28 'The Fortunes of Misses Thomazin & Janett Crawford since 1842', BC, CCCA.

29 Estate of Arthur Crawford, son of William Crawford II, BC, CCCA.

30 'Opinion of Thomas Forsayeth to Beamish & Crawford partners re certain queries', 14 March 1863, BC, CCCA.

31 K. Lamb and P. Bowe, *A History of Gardening in Ireland* (Dublin, 1995), pp. 147–8.

32 *Cork Constitution*, 20 October 1888.

33 *Ibid.*

34 *Ibid.*, 26 October 1888.

35 *The Lakelands Library: Catalogue of the Rare and Valuable Books, Manuscripts and Engravings of the Late W.H. Crawford Esq., Lakelands, Co. Cork* (London, 1891). The price made by each individual item is written in the catalogue in the hand of Arthur Frederick Sharman Crawford, BC, CCCA.

CHAPTER 10

1 The figures in this table come from comparative trading accounts for the years 1902 to 1908, prepared by Cash, Stone & Co., London, Private Journal 1901–1909, Journal 1910–1926, BC, CCCA.

2 A. Barnard, *The Noted Breweries of Great Britain and Ireland*, Vol. 2 (London, 1889), p. 362.

3 A number of documents relating to this site, its purchase, various leases attached to portions of it, plans, etc. in BC, CCCA.

4 D. Breen and T. Spalding, *The Cork International Exhibition 1902–1903: A Snapshot of Edwardian Cork* (Kildare, 2014), p. 176; J. Wales (ed.), *An Introduction to the Architectural Heritage of Cork City* (Dublin, 2012), pp. 81–2.

5 Agreement between Beamish & Crawford Ltd and F. Cade & Sons Ltd of King Street, Cork, dated 24 December 1904, and a number of other documents relating to the agreement and subsequent legal action in BC, CCCA.

6 Bottling Store Diary 1911–2, BC, CCCA. This diary notes details of all bottling on a day-by-day basis for the year. Products bottled were Double and XXX Stout and Non-deposit Ale (called NDA).

7 Journal 1906–1912, BC, CCCA.

8 'Watergate Brewery: List of Annual Balances', covering the period June 1901 to August 1914, BC, CCCA.

9 Allman, Dowden & Co., Brewers, Bandon: Balance Sheets, Profit & Loss 1887–1911, BC, CCCA. Figures for 1912 and 1913 are also given.

10 Richard Henrik Beamish to William de Courcy Beamish, 3 October 1913, BC, CCCA.

11 Conveyance and Assignment 14 January 1914 (i.e. purchase of Allman, Dowden & Co.). This document lists all the tied houses, other properties and assets being acquired. See also 'Purchase of Allman & Co. £30,000', handwritten document, BC, CCCA.

12 *Cork County Eagle*, 27 September 1913.

13 *The Cork Examiner*, 10 October 1913.

14 *Cork Constitution*, 7 November 1913.

15 *Intoxicating Liquor Commission, Minutes of Evidence* (Dublin, 1925), 8 June 1925, p. 1.

16 Memorandum and Articles of Association of Beamish & Crawford Bottling Co. Ltd 1914, BC, CCCA. See also Beamish & Crawford Bottling Co. Ltd 'Private Journal' covering the period 1914 to 1921 and 'Private Journal' 1924, BC, CCCA.

17 *Minutes*, 1925, p. 1.

18 *The Freeman's Journal*, 15–16 November 1907.

19 *Ibid.*, 31 October 1905.

20 F. Devine and J.B. Smethurst, 'Historical Directory of Trade Unions in Ireland', MS copy, p. 131 (thanks to Francy Devine).

CHAPTER 11

1 D.W. Gutzke, 'Gender, Class and Public Drinking in Britain during the First World War', *Social History*, Vol. 27, No. 54 (1994), p. 372.

2 *House of Commons Debates* (*HC*), 17 November 1914, Vol. 68, Col. 363; *The Times*, 30 March 1915.

3 See, for example, J. Turner, 'State Purchase of the Liquor Trade in the First World War', *The Historical Journal*, Vol. 23, No. 3 (September 1980), pp. 596–7; and T.R. Gourvish and R.G. Wilson, *The British Brewing Industry, 1830–1980* (Cambridge, 1994), p. 318.

4 H. Carter, *The Control of the Drink Trade: A Contribution to National Efficiency, 1915–1917* (London, 1918), pp. 63–4. Breweries and pubs were nationalised in four small areas of Britain with high concentrations of military personnel, munitions factories and other military-related industry.

5 *The Cork Examiner* (*CE*), 11 April 1916 and 4 April 1917.

6 Carter, *Control of the Drink Trade*, p. 65; *HC*, 4 May 1915, Vol. 71, Cols. 1039–42; *Irish Times* (*IT*), 3 May 1915.

7 *HC*, 29 April 1915, Cols. 901–2. Such scare-mongering was politically understandable, but an example of how it could have tragic consequences emerged in April 1917 when Edward Barrett, a labourer at Beamish & Crawford, committed suicide. According to evidence presented at the coroner's court, he had 'got delusions that he was disemployed as a

consequence of the rumours that owing to the liquor restrictions, numbers of the employees of the local breweries were to be disemployed' (*IT*, 13 April 1917).

8 *Irish Independent* (*II*), 3 May 1915.

9 Companies Diary entry, 24 April 1916, BC, CCCA.

10 Assorted correspondence, 1916–17, BC, CCCA.

11 Gourvish and Wilson, *British Brewing*, pp. 320–1.

12 Letter to Food Controller, 17 July 1917, Letters Book, 16 February 1911 – 9 April 1925, BC, CCCA.

13 Guinness was by far the largest Irish brewery, with capital shares of £7 million quoted on the London Stock Exchange. Its closest Irish competitor was Beamish & Crawford, quoted at £730,000 (*II*, 30 April 1915).

14 Letter to Food Controller, 17 July 1917 and letter (no addressee indicated), 4 March 1918, Letters Book, 16 February 1911 – 9 April 1925, BC, CCCA.

15 Letter to Irish Recruiting Council, 11 July 1918, *ibid.*; Secretary's Diaries, 18 November 1914, BC, CCCA.

16 *CE*, 20 January 1916 and 26 April 1918.

17 Minutes of Directors' Meetings, 4 April 1918, Murphy's Brewery Collection, BL/BC/MB/206, BLAS, UCC.

18 *CE*, 8, 12, 15 and 19 July 1918.

19 Correspondence, 11, 12 and 13 July, Letters Book, 16 February 1911–9 April 1925, BC, CCCA.

20 'Ale Sales 14 May 1915 to 22 June 1918', and B&C to Army Canteen Committee, 7 April 1917, BC, CCCA.

21 Minutes of Directors' Meetings, 6 and 17 October 1914, October 1915, February 1915 and 14 March 1916, Murphy's Brewery Collection, BL/BC/MB/199-202, BLAS, UCC.

22 *CE*, 21 and 29 October 1914, 26 October 1915 and 27 September 1916.

23 *Ibid.*, 3, 6 and 16 November 1914, 16 and 18 December 1914 and 7 February 1916.

24 Quoted in J. Borgonovo, *The Dynamics of War and Revolution: Cork City, 1916–1918* (Cork, 2013), p. 155.

25 The sources for this paragraph and the next are the Beamish & Crawford Companies Diary, 1916 and 'Letters Book', 16 February 1911–9 April 1925, BC, CCCA; and LWB Minute Book No. 4 and Minutes of Directors' Meetings, 1914–18, Murphy's Brewery Collection, BL/BC/MB/198-207, BLAS, UCC.

26 Borgonovo, *Dynamics of War and Revolution*, p. 191.

27 *CE*, 31 January 1920.

28 *Ibid.*

29 Beamish & Crawford Letters Book, January 1919 – January 1920, assorted correspondence, BC, CCCA; D. Ó Drisceoil and D. Ó Drisceoil, *The Murphy's Story: The History of Lady's Well Brewery, Cork* (Cork, 1997, 2006), p. 83.

30 *CE*, 12 February 1920.

31 *Ibid.*, 17 February and 6 March 1920; Letters Book, 16 and 22 February 1922, BC, CCCA.

32 *Ibid.*, 14 February and 10 March 1920.

33 *Cork Constitution* (*CC*), 4 March 1920.

34 Letters Book, 15 March 1920, BC, CCCA.

35 *CE*, 9 March 1920.

36 Fears of Guinness encroachment, along with the overall detrimental impact of the war on the industry, had led Beamish & Crawford and James J. Murphy & Co. to hold discussions in 1918/19 about the possibility of an amalgamation. The talks broke down on the issue of management structures (undated [1918/19] handwritten document on proposed amalgamation, BC, CCCA).

37 *II*, 9 November 1923.

38 Borgonovo, *Dynamics of War and Revolution*, pp. 15–16.

39 *CE*, 3, 5 and 16 August 1920; *CC*, 4 August 1920.

40 *CE*, 5 August 1920.

41 *IT*, 21–22 January 1921; *II*, 21 January and 16 March 1921; *CC*, 21, 22, 25 and 27 January 1921.

42 *II*, 31 March 1921; *Southern Star* (*SS*), 1 April

1922; Ó Drisceoil and Ó Drisceoil, *Murphy's Story*, p. 84.

43 *SS*, 5 May 1923.

44 *CE*, 8 October 1921; *SS*, 17 June 1922.

45 *II*, 22 September 1921, and *SS*, 17 June 1922.

46 L. Harrington, *Chillingworth & Levie: 20th Century Architecture in Cork* (Cork, 1913). This brochure was prepared by Louise Harrington to accompany an exhibition of architectural drawings by the firm held at the Cork City and County Archives 2013–14.

47 J. Wales (ed.), *An Introduction to the Architectural Heritage of Cork City* (Dublin, 2012), pp. 95–9.

48 Harrington, *Chillingworth & Levie*.

CHAPTER 12

1 E. Wakefield, *An Account of Ireland, Statistical and Political*, Vol. 1 (London, 1812), p. 744, fn.

2 Untitled document, dated 30 September 1814, BC, CCCA.

3 'Publicans' Holdings & Mortgages'. This ledger gives the address of the premises, the nature of the lease, to whom it was let, tenancy terms, rent, etc. See also an untitled ledger detailing licences of between 131 and 151 named public houses, mostly in Cork city, for the years 1883 to 1889, BC, CCCA.

4 'Memorandum for Sleeping Partners, February 18th, 1879', BC, CCCA.

5 *Ibid.*

6 Letter, dated 28 May 1924, from John Linehan to Beamish & Crawford, BC, CCCA.

7 *Minutes of Evidence taken before Royal Commission on Liquor Licensing Laws*, Vol. VII (Ireland) (London, 1898), pp. 307–15.

8 *Intoxicating Liquor Commission, Minutes of Evidence* (Dublin, 1925), 8 June 1925, p. 8.

9 *Interim Study on the Liquor Licensing Laws and Other Barriers to Entry and their Impact on Competition in the Retail Drinks Market* (Competition Authority, 23 September 1998), p. 4.

10 'Heads of Agreement between Beamish & Crawford Ltd. and J.J. Murphy & Co. Ltd.', undated, but early 1900s, BC, CCCA.

11 *Intoxicating Liquor Commission, Minutes*, 7 April 1925, pp. 2–8.

12 Numerous documents relating to ongoing trouble with tied tenants wishing to sell Guinness, BC, CCCA.

13 High Court of Justice in Ireland, 1904, *Beamish & Crawford V Denis J. Murphy*: Statement of Claim, BC, CCCA.

14 Documents pertaining to the case in BC, CCCA.

15 Legal opinion of Hon. Cecil Atkinson B.L. re: 'Control Houses' 1907, BC, CCCA.

16 93/4 Parnell Street, Dublin; 111 Townsend Street, Dublin; 31 Wexford Street, Dublin; 30 Broad Street, Limerick; 48 Patrick Street, Fermoy; 4 Bridge Street, Cork; 125 Patrick Street, Cork; Albert Street, Cork; 25 South Main Street, Cork (the Oval); 12 Evergreen Road, Cork (the Beer Garden); Elm Tree, Cobh Junction, County Cork.

17 *Southern Star*, 4 March 1922.

18 Undated document, probably 1925, setting out Beamish & Crawford's rationale for introducing a new trading agreement. This is one of a number of letters and documents dating to the mid-1920s relating to the issues arising from the attempted introduction of a new trading agreement, BC, CCCA.

19 Trading Agreement with Mrs Bridget Rochford, 25 Evergreen Street, Cork, dated 27 June 1925, BC, CCCA.

20 A number of documents and letters from the early 1930s detailing legal opinions on the various issues connected with the brewery's right to offer different terms to different customers in BC, CCCA.

21 *Irish Times*, 22 May 1952.

22 'Sundry Concerns & Licences 31 July 1948' and 'Sundry Concerns & Licences 30 July 1949', BC, CCCA.

23 Letting agreement for 14 Drawbridge Street, Cork, BC, CCCA.

24 'Plan of proposed alterations to house – corner

of Drawbridge and Bowling Green Streets, occupied by Mr. Lindsay', dated 11 May 1877, BC, CCCA.

25 In the late 1930s Edwin Stevens was manager of the Oval Bar on South Main Street.

CHAPTER 13

1 *The Cork Examiner* (*CE*), 13 January, 2 June and 20 October 1922.

2 Quoted in M. Martin, *Freedom to Choose: Cork and Party Politics in Ireland 1918–1932* (Cork, 2009), pp. 68–9.

3 *CE*, 12 June 1922.

4 *Ibid.*, 17 Augusut 1922.

5 L. Dineen, 'The Search for the Workers' Republic: the Labour Movement in Cork City, 1922–23', unpublished MA dissertation (UCC, 2013), pp. 50–60.

6 *CE*, 26 October 1923; D. Ó Drisceoil and D. Ó Drisceoil, *The Murphy's Story: The History of Lady's Well Brewery Cork* (Cork, 1997, 2006), p. 85.

7 J. Regan, *The Irish Counter-Revolution, 1921–1936* (Dublin, 1999), p. 223.

8 *Dáil Debates* (*DD*), Vol. 9, Cols. 2319–20 and 2340, 10 December 1924.

9 Letter from Kevin O'Higgins to Intoxicating Liquor Commission (ILC), 23 March 1925, *Intoxicating Liquor Commission, Minutes of Evidence* (Dublin, 1925), 23 March 1925, p. 1.

10 *Minutes of Evidence*, 7 April 1925, pp. 2–8; 21 April 1925, pp. 1–6.

11 *Ibid.*, 4 May 1925, p. 1.

12 *Ibid.*, 8 June 1925, pp. 2 and 8.

13 *Interim Study on the Liquor Licensing Laws and Other Barriers to Entry and Their Impact on Competition in the Retail Drinks Market* (Competition Authority, 23 September 1998), p. 4.

14 *DD*, Vol. 18, Cols. 534 and 538, 8 February 1927; Myles na Gopaleen, 'The Trade' (1940), in J. Horgan (ed.), *Great Irish Reportage* (Dublin, 2013), p. 44.

15 *Irish Independent* (*II*), 4 February 1931.

16 Undated document [1925] setting out Beamish & Crawford's rationale for introducing a new trading agreement; Trading Agreement with Mrs Bridget Rochford, 25 Evergreen Street, Cork, dated 27 June 1925; 'Comparative Statement of Sales' [1930], BC, CCCA.

17 *Southern Star* (*SS*), 3 July 1935; see Ó Drisceoil and Ó Drisceoil, *Murphy's Story*, pp. 100–3.

18 *II*, 4 May 1928; Guinness Archives, Guinness Hop Store, Dublin, GOB/C005.02/02.0010.07 contains the reports from around the country: report to Guinness from Naas, 19 August 1927.

19 Ó Drisceoil and Ó Drisceoil, *Murphy's Story*, p. 99.

20 'Statement from Lt Col James Stafford Cummins, MD of Beamish & Crawford (made in relation to a legal case pertaining to shares)', n.d. [early 1930s], BC, CCCA.

21 *CE*, 21 May 1931.

22 'Comparative Statement of Sales' [1930].

23 *II*, 29 October 1930 and 29 September 1931.

24 *SS*, 2 December 1932.

25 *Ibid.*, 20 August 1932.

26 *II*, 11 July 1933; *SS*, 8 December 1933.

27 *CE*, 1 November 1934.

28 Letter Book, 1936–8, BC, CCCA.

29 *CE*, 19 December 1939.

30 'Irishman's Diary', *The Irish Times* (*IT*), 22 May 1952.

31 *CE*, 28 June 1934.

32 *II*, 24 December 1937; *Nature*, No. 140 (25 December 1937), p. 1110.

33 *II* and *IT*, 2 May 1938.

34 Ó Drisceoil and Ó Drisceoil, *Murphy's Story*, p. 100.

35 *II* and *CE*, 30 May 1945; *CE*, 29 April 1946; B. Glover, *The Lost Beers and Breweries of Britain* (Gloucestshire, 2013), p. 49.

36 Ó Drisceoil and Ó Drisceoil, *Murphy's Story*, p. 109.

37 *Ibid.*, p. 110.

38 J.J. O'Leary, 'Memoirs of Beamish & Crawford Brewery', recorded and transcribed by Ed Hinchy, 1995–6 (copy kindly supplied by Ed

Hinchy).

39 J.T. Carroll, *Ireland in the War Years, 1939–45* (Newton Abbot, 1975), p. 92.

40 *The Irish Press*, 11 September 1941.

41 *Ibid*, 11 September 1941; J.J. O'Leary, 'Memoirs of Beamish & Crawford Brewery'.

42 Cummins to Cork Coopers' Society, 30 June 1943, Cork Coopers' Society correspondence, U218/C, CCCA.

43 *CE*, 26 June 1943.

44 *II*, 3 January 1948.

45 'Metal Containers 1949/50' folder, BC, CCCA; Cork Coopers' Society correspondence re: metal casks, 1949–63, U218/5, CCCA; J.J. O'Leary, 'Memoirs of Beamish & Crawford Brewery', Ó Drisceoil and Ó Drisceoil, *Murphy's Story*, p. 116.

46 J.J. O'Leary, 'Memoirs of Beamish & Crawford Brewery'.

47 *Dublin Distributors v. Edward & John Burke, Limited*, 29 December 1954, available online at http://law.justia.com/cases/federal/district-courts/FSupp/109/125/1756197/ (accessed 1 May 2015).

48 *IP*, 3 July 1950.

49 *IT*, 9 August 1954.

50 *CE*, 16 October 1954.

51 *IT*, 28 February 1953.

52 *CE*, 24 October 1956.

53 *Ibid.*, 8 December 1956.

CHAPTER 14

1 Raymond O'Neill, senior counsel for Beamish & Crawford, *The Cork Examiner*, 20 February 1962.

2 Canadian Breweries was the holding controlling company for Carling Brewers Ltd (seven plants in Canada), Carling Brewing Co. (seven plants in the US), Dow Brewery (three plants in Canada), O'Keefe Brewery (five plants in Canada) and Western Canada Brewers (holding company for the seven western Canadian plants of Carling and O'Keefe).

3 *The Cork Examiner* (*CE*), 8 September 1962, and *Sunday Independent*, 16 September 1962.

4 *Financial Times*, 18 September 1962; financial commentator 'Magpie' quoted in *The Irish Press* (*IP*), 24 September 1962.

5 *IP*, 20 September 1962.

6 *CE*, 19 and 20 September 1962; *IP*, 19 and 21 September 1962; *Sunday Telegraph*, 23 September 1962.

7 *Investors' Chronicle*, 21 September 1962.

8 Philip Hill, Higginson, Erlangers Ltd statement, *IP*, 25 September 1962.

9 *Irish Independent* (*II*), 26 September 1962.

10 T.R. Gourvish and R.G. Wilson, *The British Brewing Industry, 1830–1980* (Cambridge, 1994), pp. 447–50; J. Spicer, J. Walters and S. Ward, *Intervention in the Modern UK Brewing Industry* (Basingstoke, 2012), pp. 2–3; P. Brown, *Man Walks into a Pub: A Sociable History of Beer* (London, 2011), pp. 241–2.

11 *The Irish Times* (*IT*), 8 June 1961; *IP*, 15 November 1962; *II*, 4 September 1963. Hereafter in this chapter, due to the sheer number of newspaper and trade paper sources drawn upon, specific references are only given where direct quotes are used.

12 *IT*, 14 May 1962.

13 *CE*, 25 September 1964.

14 *Ibid.* and *IT*, 25 September 1964.

15 For a discussion on Carling's image-making, see 'Theme for all seasons', *Management*, May 1983.

16 *II*, 11 November 1964.

17 *IT*, 18 June 1964.

18 *Ibid.*, 12 November 1965.

19 *Munster Express*, 6 January 1967.

20 *Southern Star*, 20 January 1968.

21 Beamish & Crawford, Annual Report for 1967, BC, CCCA.

22 *Ibid.* and marketing report, May 1968, BC, CCCA.

23 *Ibid.* and 'Tied Tenants' Protection Agency' file, BC, CCCA.

CHAPTER 15

1 *Sunday Tribune*, 21 August 1983.

2 *The Irish Press*, 19 August 1982.

3 Unless otherwise stated, statistics and financial information in this chapter are taken from the company's own monthly board reports and its annual reports and accounts (BC, CCCA) for the months and years referred to. Further details are derived from financial and business reports in *The Cork Examiner* (*CE*), *The Irish Times* (*IT*), *The Irish Press* (*IP*) and *Irish Independent* (*II*), unless otherwise stated. In general, specific citations are given from these sources only where direct quotes are used; the number of endnotes would otherwise be unwieldly.

4 *II*, 14 August 1970.

5 Coincidentally, the founder of the O'Keefe's Brewing Company of Toronto, Eugene O'Keefe (1827–1913), was a Corkman. He was born in Bandon and moved to Canada as a child.

6 D. Ó Drisceoil and D. Ó Drisceoil, *The Murphy's Story: The History of Lady's Well Brewery, Cork* (Cork, 1997, 2006), pp. 127–31; BC Board Report, 19 March 1974, BC, CCCA.

7 *IT*, 20 August 1970.

8 *Ibid.*, 26 October 1971.

9 *Ibid.*, 15 June 1974.

10 BC board report, 23 July 1974, BC, CCCA.

11 BC board report, 27 January 1976, BC, CCCA.

12 *IT*, 8 April 1976.

13 BC board report, 23 May 1978, BC, CCCA.

14 Beamish & Crawford Ltd: 1978–83 – Five-Year Plan, BC, CCCA.

15 *Dáil Debates*, Vol. 290, No. 2, Col. 447, 29 April 1976.

16 *Sunday Tribune*, 21 August 1983.

17 Besides contemporary newspaper reports, the key sources on the possible Murphy's merger are a folder entitled 'J.J. Murphy', a memo on merger discussions dated 21 September 1981, BC, CCCA, and Ó Drisceoil and Ó Drisceoil, *Murphy's Story*, pp. 135–9.

18 *IP*, 3 December 1981.

19 *II*, 28 July 1982.

20 *IP*, 19 August 1982.

21 *II*, 29 June 1983.

CHAPTER 16

1 *Evening Echo* (*EE*), 25 February 1987.

2 *International Directory of Company Histories*, Vol. 1 Michigan, 1988, available online at www.company-histories.com/ELDERS-IXL-LTD-Company-History.html (accessed 2 April 2015); D.M. Blocker, M. Fahey and I.R. Tyrrell (eds.), *Alcohol and Temperance in Modern History: An Encyclopedia* (Santa Barbara, 2003), pp. 247–8.

3 *The Cork Examiner* (*CE*), *Irish Independent* (*II*) and *The Irish Press* (*IP*), 3 June 1988.

4 *The Irish Times* (*IT*), 8 September 1987; *IP*, 10 February 1988.

5 *CE*, 27 November 1987.

6 *II*, 6 May and 3 June 1988; *EE*, 3 June 1988.

7 *IT*, 27 May 1988; Beamish & Crawford Operations Committee minutes, 16 February and 19 September 1989, BC, CCCA; *Business and Finance*, 14 June 1990.

8 Rick Scully, quoted in *IP*, 7 June 1990.

9 *IP*, 11 February 1992; *Business and Finance*, 12 November 1992; *IT*, 4 December 1997.

10 *CE*, 9 April 1994.

11 Quoted in *IT*, 31 August 1994.

12 The details and quotes are taken from the case details: '*James B. Beam Distilling Co. v. Beamish & Crawford Limited*, 868 F.2d 1277 (Fed. Cir. 1989)', available online at www.courtlistener.com/opinion/519122/james-b-beam-distilling-co-v-beamish-crawford-limi/ (accessed 5 May 2015); *Jim Beam Brands Co. v. Beamish & Crawford Ltd.*, US Court of Appeals, Second Circuit, Decided June 19, 1991, available online at http://openjurist.org/937/f2d/729 (accessed 4 May 2015); *Jim Beam Brands Co. v. Beamish & Crawford Ltd*, No. 89 Civ. 5835 (RO), United States District Court, S.D. New York, May 4, 1994, available online at http://law.justia.com/cases/federal/

district-courts/FSupp/852/196/1736184/ (accessed 4 May 2015).

13 'New Broom at Beamish', *Business and Finance*, 9 November 1995.

14 This account is based on the extensive newspaper reportage (*The Cork Examiner*, *Evening Echo*, *Irish Independent*, *The Irish Times*) of industrial relations at Beamish & Crawford in 1993–4. The O'Donnell quote is from *II*, 17 March 1994.

15 'New Broom at Beamish', *Business and Finance*, 9 November 1995.

16 *IT*, 7 November 1997.

17 *Irish Examiner*, 8 October 2003 and 24 February 2004; *Sunday Tribune*, 20 March 2005.

18 *Ibid.*

19 *IT*, 21 February 2007.

20 Report of the Competition Authority ruling, *Irish Examiner*, 1 November 2008.

21 *EE*, 5 December 2008.

22 *My Beamish Boy* (director Mike Hannon, 2009) can be viewed online at www.mikehannonmedia.com/mybeamishboy. It won the 'Made in Cork' award for Best Short Film at the 2009 Cork Film Festival and was screened on RTÉ television in 2010. Filmed soon after the closure, and featuring fifteen Beamish workers, it captures the Beamish 'spirit', from the perspective of those who worked there, better than any words on a page. Beamish workers also feature in Abú Media's overview of the brewery and its history in the *Croí an Cheantair* series for TG4, 2013. See also *The Counting House: Beamish Brewery in the '60s and '70s,* a ten-minute audio-visual documentary about the experience of working at Beamish & Crawford Brewery in the 1960s and 1970s, using rare images of the brewery taken by the late photojournalist Roy Hammond. It was produced by Mark Wilkins and Tom Doig for the Cork Folklore Project and can be viewed online at https://www.youtube.com/watch?v=8o28aWtm-3M.

Bibliography

Archives, official reports, and unpublished documents and theses

Archives

Beamish & Crawford Collection, Cork City and County Archives
Beamish and Crawford Estate Collection, Boole Library Archives Service, University College Cork
Beamish & Crawford brewery collection, Heineken Ireland, Cork
Cork Coopers' Society, minutes and correspondence, Cork City and County Archives
Guinness Archives, Guinness Hop Store, Dublin
Murphy's Brewery Collection, Boole Library Archives Service, University College Cork

Official Reports

Dáil Éireann Debates
Fifteenth Report of the Commissioners of Inquiry into the Excise Establishment, and into the Management and Collection of the Excise Revenue throughout the United Kingdom (London, 1835)
Interim Study on the Liquor Licensing Laws and other Barriers to Entry and their Impact on Competition in the Retail Drinks Market (Competition Authority, 23 September 1998)
Intoxicating Liquor Commission, Minutes of Evidence (Dublin, 1925)
Minutes of Evidence taken before Royal Commission on Liquor Licensing Laws, Vol. VII (Ireland) (London, 1898)
Report of the Intoxicating Liquor Commission (Dublin, 1925)
Royal Commission on Liquor Licensing Laws, *Statistics relating to the Number of Licensed Premises, etc., in Great Britain and Ireland, Vol. V* (London, 1897)
Seanad Éireann Debates
Tenth Report of the Commissioners of Inquiry into the Excise Establishment, and into the Management and Collection of the Excise Revenue throughout the United Kingdom (London, 1834)
The Sixth Report of the Commissioners appointed to enquire into the Fees, gratuities, Perquisites, and Emoluments … and Accounting for Public Money in Ireland (House of Commons, 1808); Eighth Report of the Commissioners of Inquiry into the Collection and Management of the Revenue arising in Ireland, Scotland, etc. (House of Commons, 1824)
UK House of Commons Debates

Theses

Bowman, M., 'The Brewing Industry in the Republic of Ireland', M.Econ.Soc. thesis (UCC, 1983)
Cosgrave, M.B., 'A History of Beamish & Crawford', MA thesis (UCC, 1989)
Lahiff, E., 'Industry and Labour in Cork, 1890-1921', MA thesis (UCC, 1988)
Mackey Dineen, L., 'The Search for the Workers' Republic: the Labour Movement in Cork City, 1921–1923', MA dissertation (UCC, 2013)

Unpublished Documents

'List of Freemen of Cork City 1710–1841', Cork City and County Archives (2007)

Devine, F. & J.B. Smethurst, 'Historical Directory of Trade Unions in Ireland' (MS copy kindly supplied by Francy Devine)

J.J. O'Leary, 'Memoirs of Beamish & Crawford Brewery', recorded and transcribed by Ed Hinchy, 1995/6 (copy kindly supplied by Ed Hinchy)

Letter from Nicholas Pertwee to Ed Hinchy, 27 August 2000 (copy kindly supplied by Ed Hinchy)

Newspapers and periodicals

Beamish News
Brewing and Distilling International
Business and Finance
Carling O'Keefe Quarterly Newsletter
Commercial Daily List
Cork Constitution
Cork County Eagle
The Cork Examiner/Irish Examiner
Evening Echo
Financial Times
Food Ireland
The Freeman's Journal
Hibernian Chronicle
Investors' Chronicle
Irish Independent
The Irish Press
The Irish Times
Management
Munster Express
Nature
The Sunday Business Post
Sunday Independent
Sunday Telegraph
Sunday Tribune
United News
Weekly Irish Times

Books and articles

Anon., 'History of the London Brewery from the Beginning of King William's reign to the Present Time', *The Gentleman's Magazine, and Historical Chronicle*, Vol. XXX (London, 1760)

Anon., 'Mr. Richard Beamish', *Minutes of Proceedings of the Institution of Civil Engineers*, 40 (1874–75, Pt. II)

Anon., *The London and Country Brewer* (2nd edn., London, 1736)

Barnard, A., *The Noted Breweries of Great Britain and Ireland*, Vols. I–IV (London, 1889–1891)

Beamish, C.T.M., *Beamish: A Genealogical Study of a Family in Co. Cork and Elsewhere* (London & Bradford, 1950)

Beamish, R., *Memoir of the Life of Sir Marc Isambard Brunel* (London, 1862)

Bennett, G., *The History of Bandon and the Principal Towns in the west Riding of County Cork* (Cork, 1869)

Bielenberg, A., 'The Irish Brewing Industry and the Rise of Guinness, 1790–1914' in R.G. Wilson & T.R. Gourvish (eds.), *The Dynamics of the international brewing industry since 1800* (New York, 1998)

Bielenberg, A., *Cork's Industrial Revolution 1780–1800: Development or Decline?* (Cork, 1991)

Bielenberg, A. & R. Ryan, *An Economic History of Ireland Since Independence* (London 2012)

Blocker, D.M., M. Fahey and I.R. Tyrrell (eds.), *Alcohol and Temperance in Modern History: An Encyclopedia* (Santa Barbara, 2003)

Borgonovo, J., *The Dynamics of War and Revolution: Cork City, 1916–1918* (Cork, 2013)

Breen, D. and T. Spalding, *The Cork International Exhibition 1902–1903: A Snapshot of Edwardian Cork* (Kildare, 2014)

Brown, P., *Man Walks into a Pub: A Sociable History of Beer* (London, 2011)

Burke, Sir B., *A Genealogical and Heraldic History of the Landed Gentry of Ireland* (London, 1912)

Cadogan, T. & J. Falvey, *A Biographical Dictionary of Cork* (Dublin, 2006)

Carr, J., *The Stranger in Ireland or, A Tour of the Southern and Western parts of that country, in the year 1805* (New York, 1807)

Carroll, J.T., *Ireland in the War Years, 1939–45* (Newton Abbot, 1975)

Carter, H., *The Control of the Drink Trade: A Contribution to National Efficiency, 1915–1917* (London, 1918)

Caulfield, R. (ed.), *The Council Book of the Corporation of the City of Cork, from 1609 to 1643 and from 1690 to 1800* (Guildford, 1876)

Cleary, R. M., 'Medieval Town Wall off Lambley's Lane, Cork City', *Journal of the Cork Historical & Archaeological Society*, Vol. 93, 1988

Coakley, D.J. (ed.), *Cork: Its Trade and Commerce* (Cork, 1919)

Coleman, J.C., 'The Craft of Coopering', *Journal of the Cork Historical & Archaeological Society*, Vol. 49, 1944

Coppinger, J., *The American Practical Brewer and Tanner* (New York, 1815)

Cork Chamber of Commerce, *Cork Commercial Handbook* (Cork, 1919)

Coyne, J.S., *The Scenery and Antiquities of Ireland, Vol. II* (London, 1842)

Coyne, W.P., *Ireland: Industrial and Agricultural* (Dublin, 1902)

Crowley, J., R. Devoy, D. Linehan and P. O'Flanagan (eds.), *The Atlas of Cork City* (Cork, 2005)

Dennison, S. R. & O. MacDonagh, *Guinness 1886–1939: From Incorporation to the Second World War* (Cork, 1998)

Devine, F., *Organising History: A Centenary of SIPTU, 1909–2009* (Dublin, 2009)

Dickson, D., *Old World Colony: Cork and South Munster 1630–1830* (Cork, 2005)

Dinneen, P.S., *Foclóir Gaedhilge agus Béarla, an Irish–English Dictionary* (Dublin, 1927)

Feltham, J., *The Picture of London for 1802* (London, 1802)

Glover, B., *The Lost Beers and Breweries of Britain* (Gloucestshire, 2013)

Gourvish, T.R. & R.G. Wilson, *The British Brewing Industry, 1830–1980* (Cambridge, 1994)

Gutzke, D.W., 'Gender, Class and Public Drinking in Britain during the First World War', *Social History*, Vol. 27, No. 54 (1994)

Guy's Directory, Cork (various)

Harrington, L., *Chillingworth & Levie: 20th Century Architecture in Cork* (Cork, 2013)

Herlihy, R., *Tales from Victorian Cork, 1837–1859* (Cork, 2012)

Horne, J. (ed.), *Our War: Ireland and the Great War* (Dublin, 2008)

J.T.C., review of C.T.M. Beamish, *Beamish: A Genealogical Study of a Family in Co. Cork and Elsewhere* (London & Bradford, 1950), *Journal of the Cork Historical & Archaeological Society*, Vol. 56, 1951

Jeffries, H.A., *Cork: Historical Perspectives* (Dublin, 2004)

Johns, J., *The Celebrated Brewery of Sir John Arnott & Co Cork* (1873)

Johnson, D., *The Inter-war Economy in Ireland* (Dublin, 1985)

Johnson, G., *The Laneways of Medieval Cork* (Cork, 2002)

Kerrigan, C., *Father Mathew and the Irish Temperance Movement, 1838–1848* (Cork, 1992)

Lamb, K. & P. Bowe, *A History of Gardening in Ireland* (Dublin, 1995)

Lane, F., *In Search of Thomas Sheehan: Radical Politics in Cork, 1824–36* (Dublin, 2001)

Lawson, W., 'Licensing and Public-house Reform in Ireland', *Statistical and Social Inquiry Society of Ireland,* Vol. XI, 1902

Lee, J.J., 'Money and Beer in Ireland, 1790–1875', *Economic History Review*, new series, Vol. 19, No. 1 (1966)

Lenihan, M., *Pure Cork* (Cork, 2011)

Litton, A.J., 'The Growth and Development of the Irish Telephone System', *Journal of the Statistical and Social Inquiry Society of Ireland*, Session 115, 1961–2

Lucas, R., 'The Cork Directory for the year 1787', *Journal of the Cork Historical & Archaeological Society*, Vol. 72, 1967

Lynch, P. and J. Vaizey, *Guinness's Brewery in the Irish Economy 1759–1876* (Cambridge 1960)

MacDonagh, O., 'The Origins of Porter', *Economic History Review*, new series, Vol. 16, No. 3, 1964

Malcolm, E., *Ireland Sober, Ireland Free: Drink and Temperance in Nineteenth-century Ireland* (Dublin, 1986)

Martin, M., *Freedom to Choose: Cork and Party Politics in Ireland 1918–1932* (Cork, 2009)

Mathias, P., *The Brewing Industry in England 1700–1830* (Cambridge, 1959)

Measom, G. S., *Official Guide to the Great Southern & Western Railway* (London, 1866)

Meyer, K. (ed. & trans.), *Aislinge Meic Conglinne: The Vision of Meic Conglinne: A Middle-Irish Wonder Tale* (London, 1892)

Murphy, J.A., *The College: A History of Queen's/University College Cork* (Cork, 1995)

Murray, P., 'A Narrative History of the Building and of the Crawford Family', in P. Murray (compiler), *Illustrated Summary Catalogue of The Crawford Municipal Art Gallery* (Cork, 1991

Newenham, T., *A View of the Natural, Political and Commercial Circumstances of Ireland* (London, 1809)

O'Brien, A. E., 'Early Brewing Activity in Cork City: Some Leasehold Evidence', *Journal of the Cork Historical & Archaeological Society*, Vol. 105, 2000

O'Brien, G., *The Economic History of Ireland in the Eighteenth Century* (Philadelphia, 1918)

O'Brien, J.B., 'Merchants in Cork before the Famine', in P. Butel & L.M. Cullen (eds.), *Cities and*

Merchants: French and Irish Perspectives on Urban Development, 1500–1900 (Dublin, 1986)

O'Callaghan, A., *The Lord Mayors of Cork, 1900–2000* (Cork, 2000)

— *The Statue: Cork's Monument to Father Mathew, The Apostle of Temperance* (Cork, 2014)

O'Connor, E., *A Labour History of Ireland, 1824–2000* (Dublin, 2011)

Ó Drisceoil, D. & D. Ó Drisceoil, *Serving a City: The Story of Cork's English Market*, (Cork, 2005 and 2011)

— *The Murphy's Story: The History of Lady's Well Brewery, Cork* (Cork, 1997 and 2006)

O'Flanagan, P. & C.B. Buttimer (eds.), *Cork: History & Society* (Dublin, 1993)

Ó Gráda, C., *A Rocky Road: The Irish economy since the 1920s* (Manchester 1997)

— *Ireland: A New Economic History, 1780–1939* (Oxford, 1994)

— 'The Last Major Irish Bank Failure: Lessons for Today?', UCD Centre for Economic Research Working Paper Series (Dublin, 2010)

O'Leary, J.J., 'Developments in the Brewing Industry', *Technology Ireland*, November 1972

O'Mahony, C., *Cork's Poor Law Palace: Workhouse Life, 1838–1890* (Cork, 2005)

O'Nolan, B. (Myles na Gopaleen), 'The Trade' (1940), in J. Horgan (ed.), *Great Irish Reportage* (Dublin, 2013)

O'Shea, J., 'Henry Shea: Cork's First Mercantile Tycoon', *Journal of the Cork Historical & Archaeological Society*, Vol. 116, 2011

O'Shea, J., *Letterbook of Richard Hare, Cork Merchant, 1771–1772* (Dublin, 2013)

O'Sullivan, W., *The Economic History of Cork City from the Earliest Times to the Act of Union* (Cork, 1937)

Pike, W.T., *Contemporary Biographies* (Brighton, 1911)

Poland, P., 'When Cork's Ale Chief met Nazi Germany's Air Chief', *Ireland's Own*, June 2013

Regan, J.M., *The Irish Counter-Revolution, 1921–1936: treatyite politics and settlement in independent Ireland* (Dublin, 2001)

Rynne, C., *The Industrial Archaeology of Cork City and its Environs* (Dublin, 1999)

— 'Two Centuries of Cork Porter', *Technology Ireland*, September 1992

Sadleir, T.U., *Georgian Mansions in Ireland, with Some Account of the Evolution of Georgian Architecture and Decoration* (Dublin, 1915)

Shepherd, E., *Cork Bandon & South Coast Railway* (Leicester, 2005)

Spicer, J., J. Walters and S. Ward, *Intervention in the Modern UK Brewing Industry* (Basingstoke, 2012)

Stratten & Stratten, *Dublin, Cork and Southern Ireland* (London, 1892)

The City of Cork. Survey & Valuation (circa A.D. 1663–64) in *The Civil Survey A.D. 1654–1656: County of Waterford, Vol. VI*

The Lakelands Library: Catalogue of the Rare and Valuable Books, Manuscripts and Engravings of the late W.H. Crawford Esq., Lakelands, Co. Cork (London, 1891)

Truxes, T.M., *Irish American Trade 1660–1783* (Cambridge, 1988)

Turner, J., 'State Purchase of the Liquor Trade in the First World War', *The Historical Journal*, Vol. 23, No. 3, September 1980

Unger, R.W., *Beer in the Middle Ages and Renaissance* (Philadelphia, 2004)

Van Muyden, Madame (transl. and ed.), *A Foreign View of England in the Reigns of George I & George II: the Letters of Monsieur César de Saussure to his Family* (London, 1902)

Wakefield, E., *An Account of Ireland, Statistical and Political*, Vol. 1 (London, 1812)

Wales, J. (ed.), *An Introduction to the Architectural Heritage of Cork City* (Dublin, 2012)

Watkins, G., *The Complete English Brewer or The Whole Art and Mystery of Brewing in all its various Branches* (London, 1760)

Wells, R., 'The Irish Famine of 1799–1801: Market Culture, Moral Economies and Social Protest' in A. Randall & A. Charlesworth (eds.) *Markets, Market Culture and Popular Protest in Eighteenth Century Britain and Ireland* (Liverpool, 1996)

Welply, W.H., 'The Art and Mystery of Brewing (in Cork)', *Journal of the Cork Historical & Archaeological Society*, Vol. 62, 1957

White, G. & B. O'Shea (eds.), *A Great Sacrifice: Cork Servicemen who died in the Great War* (Cork, 2010)

Wright, G.N., *Ireland Illustrated, from original drawings, by G. Petrie RHA, W.H. Bartlett, & T.M. Baynes* (London, 1831).

Online

Cork City Libraries, 'Cork Past and Present' (www.corkpastandpresent.ie)

Dublin Distributors v. Edward & John Burke, Limited, 29 December 1954 (http://law.justia.com/cases/federal/district-courts/FSupp/109/125/1756197)

International Directory of Company Histories, Vol. 1 Michigan, 1988 (www.company-histories.com/ELDERS-IXL-LTD-Company-History.html)

'James B. Beam Distilling Co. v. Beamish & Crawford Limited, 868 F.2d 1277 (Fed. Cir. 1989)' (www.courtlistener.com/opinion/519122/james-b-beam-distilling-co-v-beamish-crawford-limi)

Jim Beam Brands Co. v. Beamish & Crawford Ltd , No. 89 Civ. 5835 (RO), United States District Court, S.D. New York, May 4, 1994 (law.justia.com/cases/federal/district-courts/FSupp/852/196/1736184)

Jim Beam Brands Co. v. Beamish & Crawford Ltd., US Court of Appeals, Second Circuit, Decided June 19, 1991 (openjurist.org/937/f2d/729)

My Beamish Boy (Dir. Mike Hannon, 2009) (www.mikehannonmedia.com/mybeamishboy)

Royal Irish Academy/Cambridge University Press, *Dictionary of Irish Biography* (http://dib.cambridge.org)

The Counting House: Beamish Brewery in the '60s and '70s (www.youtube.com/watch?v=8o28aWtm-3M)

The Peerage (www.thepeerage.com)

Television

Abú Media, *Croí an Cheantair*, TG4, 2013

Index

Illustrations are indicated by page numbers in **bold**.